ALSO BY JILL ABRAMSON

The Puppy Diaries

Strange Justice: The Selling of Clarence Thomas
(coauthored with Jane Mayer)

Where They Are Now

MERCHANTS OF TRUTH

THE BUSINESS *of* NEWS *and* THE FIGHT *for* FACTS

JILL ABRAMSON

Simon & Schuster
NEW YORK · LONDON · TORONTO · SYDNEY · NEW DELHI

Simon & Schuster
1230 Avenue of the Americas
New York, NY 10020

First Simon & Schuster hardcover edition February 2019

SIMON & SCHUSTER and colophon are registered trademarks
of Simon & Schuster, Inc.

For information about special discounts for bulk purchases,
please contact Simon & Schuster Special Sales at 1-866-506-1949
or business@simonandschuster.com.

The Simon & Schuster Speakers Bureau can bring authors to your
live event. For more information or to book an event, contact
the Simon & Schuster Speakers Bureau at 1-866-248-3049
or visit our website at www.simonspeakers.com.

Manufactured in the United States of America

1 3 5 7 9 10 8 6 4 2

Library of Congress Cataloging-in-Publication Data is available.

ISBN 978-1-5011-2320-7
ISBN 978-1-5011-2322-1 (ebook)

*In memory of my friend Danny Pearl,
and the other great reporters who lost
their lives digging for the truth.*

CONTENTS

PROLOGUE

The party had a distinct fin-de-siècle air. On a wintry night in early 2016, the battered lions of journalism gathered at the Newseum in Washington, D.C., for a party to toast the 100th anniversary of the Pulitzer Prizes. These editors and reporters had spent their careers at newspapers such as the *New York Times*, which had won 117 of the coveted awards, the most of any news organization. Scattered throughout the room were representatives of the *Washington Post*, which had won 47, the second-most. Their stories over the years had chronicled Watergate, the Pentagon Papers, war zones, terrorism, financial scandal, poverty, political corruption, civil rights, China, Russia, and on and on. The "first rough draft of history," popularized by Phil Graham, scion of the family that owned the *Post*, had become a self-congratulatory cliché, but for this body of journalism's most honored work, it was true.

Arthur Ochs Sulzberger Jr., the *Times*'s publisher since 1992, took immense pride in the announcement of the Pulitzers each spring, just as his father had. The *Times* almost always had someone on the Pulitzer board that picked the winners. For nearly a decade, the paper's emissary was Tom Friedman, the *Times*'s influential foreign affairs columnist and a three-time prizewinner. After the board made its decisions, Friedman would call the publisher to leak the results the Friday before they were announced. Seldom did he have anything but good news. Almost every year the boyish-faced Sulzberger added at least one framed picture of a winner to the corridor below his office. Most of the other guests knew that Sulzberger, 64, hoped to hand over the reins to his son, Arthur Gregg, as Arthur's father, "Punch" Sulzberger, had done for him.

Absent from the crowd of luminaries was the *Washington Post*'s Donald Graham, the self-effacing, beloved company chairman who had executed a changing of the guard three years before. Despairing that the paper's quality couldn't survive deep staff cuts and vanishing advertising revenue, he sold the newspaper his family had owned since 1933 to a tech billion-aire, Amazon's Jeff Bezos. The *Post*'s sleek new offices were no longer fes-tooned with the famous front page "Nixon Resigns" from Watergate days. They were dominated by flat-screens displaying real-time traffic statistics on how many readers were looking at each story. Prominent was a Bezos mantra, in blue and white: "What's dangerous is not to evolve."

Also missing was the younger guard, the founders of the digital media companies that had used Facebook and Google to build giant audiences of younger readers and viewers. Though very few had won Pulitzers for their news coverage, companies such as BuzzFeed and Vice Media were giving the old guard serious competition—and heartburn.

The party celebrated journalism's golden age, but the celebrants were living through journalism's Age of Anxiety. All of them knew a colleague who had taken a buyout or been laid off. The newspaper industry had shed $1.3 billion worth of editors' and reporters' jobs in the past decade, some 60 percent of its workforce since 2000. Some of the newspapers that won the prizes had gone out of business—more than 300 altogether—or were shadows of what they'd been. There had been repeated assurances that more could be done with less. Even the newcomers, despite their bloated valuations, were hard-pressed to show profits.

Global news-gathering, meanwhile, remained monstrously expensive. The kind of investigative stories that won Pulitzers took months to report, took still more time to edit and make legally bullet-proof, and were ever more costly. Editors had to safeguard accuracy and fairness: if a big story broke and they needed to scramble helicopters or flood the zone with report-ers, they couldn't agonize over budgets. What was being threatened were the very qualities these prizes were meant to recognize. What was at risk was far bigger than just one industry—it was truth and freedom in a demo-cratic society, an informed citizenry, and news sources that were above pol-itics in their reporting.

All the editors there were mustering their troops to cover the presi-dential election, never suspecting that voters would bring to power a man who cast them as agents of evil, the "fake news media." At Donald Trump's rallies, his supporters jeered the campaign reporters behind their ropes. Trump's penchant for serial lying would challenge all the old rules of so-called objectivity and force journalists into the uncomfortable role of seem-ing to be, at least in the eyes of many conservative Americans, combatants against a sitting president.

Everything these journalists cared about was under attack. As they sipped wine in a cavernous museum devoted to their profession's glorious past, the laurels that mattered were now quantitative: clicks and likes and tweets and page views and time of engagement.

Beyond the political climate, the traditional news media itself had played a role in the public's eroding trust. Self-inflicted scandals had damaged their credibility, including those involving Janet Cooke at the *Post* and Jayson Blair at the *Times*, the run-up to the Iraq War, and, soon, controversies over coverage of Hillary Clinton's emails, hacked messages from the computers of Democratic Party officials, as well as the failure to recognize Trump's electability. Most Americans now got their news on their smartphones, on social media, from a jumble of sources, such as family members they trusted far more, or from alt-right websites, increasingly polarized cable TV news shows, Russian bots, and branded content from corporations.

I surveyed the room with the eyes of an outsider, nervously glomming on to old friends and former colleagues from the *Times*, the author Anna Quindlen, and Isabel Wilkerson, resplendent in a red dress. She had been the first black journalist to win a Pulitzer for feature writing, for a wrenching portrait of a fourth-grader from Chicago's South Side. In 2014 I had been fired as executive editor of the *Times*, but Arthur Sulzberger Jr., the man who pink-slipped me, had generously invited me to be part of the *Times* family celebrating our Pulitzer heritage. During my time as managing editor and then executive editor, and as the first and only woman to hold those jobs, the *Times* had hauled in 24 Pulitzers.

I'd become a reporter during Watergate. As a college-age woman, my odds of joining the ranks of Woodward and Bernstein were slim, but their groundbreaking investigations of turpitude in the Nixon White House had inspired me to try. From a starting job at *Time* magazine, I'd climbed to journalism's highest rung and then fallen. I was well-versed in the new landscape of news, with its native advertising for brands, clickbait headlines, and 24/7 rhythms, but it wasn't the world I'd grown up in. As the newspapers tried to keep up with technology, executive editors were expected to be digital gurus and let business imperatives guide their editorial judgment.

One particular post-Watergate book that inspired me to become a journalist was *The Powers That Be*, published in 1979. The author was David Halberstam, who won a Pulitzer as a *Times* reporter covering the Vietnam War. The book examines the histories and paths of four influential news companies: the *Post*, the *Los Angeles Times*, CBS News, and Time Inc. Halberstam was writing at the moment of journalism's zenith, after the *Post* had broken stories that led to the first resignation in history of a U.S. president and CBS had played a central role in opening the country's eyes to the futility of the Vietnam War. This was long before online publishing proliferated in the 1990s; it was a time when newspapers were printing money, stuffed with want ads and department store ads and enjoying profitable monopolies in more and more cities. Smaller papers such as the *Baltimore Sun* could afford to deploy foreign correspondents to postings in faraway capitals like Tokyo and Berlin.

Halberstam chronicled how those four institutions achieved not only financial success but journalistic excellence in the postwar era. As the longtime *New Yorker* political commentator Richard Rovere wrote at the time, the big political issues of the period—McCarthyism, civil rights, Vietnam, Watergate—were primarily moral issues. Halberstam's four news organizations played an admirable role in getting the country through these crises. Rovere also warned that trouble was looming, as family-run papers became increasingly tethered to Wall Street and various bean counters.

Surveying the scene, I had the overwhelming sense at the Pulitzer party that, just as it was when Halberstam wrote his book, a power shift was taking place under our noses. News had become ubiquitous in the digital age, but it was harder than ever to find trustworthy information or a financial model that would support it. Newsrooms had made drastic cuts and were still at it. The *Boston Globe* had closed its foreign news bureaus in 2007; the *Post*, too, closed its domestic bureaus in New York, Los Angeles, and Chicago two years later. Newcomers, notably BuzzFeed and Vice, were opening international offices, taking advantage of the internet's capacity to give anyone a global audience but not coming close to replacing the reporting muscles lost.

We had moral crises of our own, some of which the press fumbled: the flawed coverage of the lead-up to the Iraq War, troubling surveillance of citizens by U.S. intelligence agencies, and blindness to the forces that led to the Trump election. The trust and authority lauded by Halberstam, along with the business model, seemed to be crumbling.

Shane Smith, Vice's founder and one-time hard-partying lads-mag editor, had recently bragged of being "the Time Warner of the streets" and talked of elbowing aside CNN. Jonah Peretti of BuzzFeed had won the hearts of the hard-to-reach millennial audience with photo links of adorable puppies, then parlayed that into an investigative reporting staff that was the size of the *Times*'s investigative unit. Meanwhile, the *Times* and *Post* were trying to teach digital users to pay for the content they consumed, a lesson that went directly against the internet mantra that "information wants to be free." Each had begun charging subscribers for their digital news reports, not knowing if that would be enough to save them.

The *Times* had already and unsuccessfully challenged the free-news orthodoxy a decade earlier, by charging readers for its opinion section and columns, but had quickly thrown up its hands after reaping a scant $20 million from its readers on the web. There had been dark talk inside the paper of bankruptcy, until a Mexican billionaire rode to the rescue with a huge loan. Now things had stabilized, and a more flexible digital subscription plan was bringing in sizable revenue. But the *Times* was still heavily dependent on its print circulation base for survival, and these print subscribers were aging and their numbers decreasing.

The partygoers around me, like print newspaper readers, were relics of Halberstam's golden age. But their essential gift—nosing out the truth in a city that thrives on greed and lies—had never been more vital to the health of our democracy. The *Times* was still in a fight for survival in the digital age, trying to attract enough paying subscribers to support its $200 million annual news budget and remain in the hands of the family that had owned it since a Tennessee newspaper baron, Adolph Ochs, Sulzberger Jr.'s great-grandfather, bought it in 1896. The *Post*, seemingly rescued by Bezos, was trying to restore its reputation, hurt by years of cost-cutting and staff reductions that the Graham family couldn't prevent.

As for the new digital competitors, the question was whether they were ready to step up to be our guardians of truth. They considered themselves disruptors, hammering the power structure as if it were the Big Brother screen in Apple's legendary "1984" TV commercial. Some of them didn't even believe that editors needed to be gatekeepers. They were sometimes hasty in putting news "out there" and letting readers decide whether something was true. Their headlines were hyped, although recently their desire to be serious news providers had improved quality. BuzzFeed and Vice depended on social media sharing, a broad metric called "engagement," which included time spent reading, the number of likes, shares, and comments on social media, and a host of other factors. The wisdom of crowds, with commenters rather than professional journalists setting the terms, drove coverage. The breathless news cycle left little time for formal training of the young, aspiring journalists who mostly sat behind computers scraping previously published content off the internet and rewriting it or spinning it in new directions.

By understanding the power of social media and video, BuzzFeed and Vice had won millions of devoted readers and viewers, largely using the giant tech platforms of Facebook and Google to amass followings among the young, the demographic most prized by advertisers. Their financial success was rooted in so-called native advertising, ads that were virtual carbon copies of stories created by journalists. Facebook, which supplied the life-blood to new digital media sites, was all about deriving ad revenue from the fast-paced social sharing of their 2.2 billion global users. Eschewing its responsibilities as mankind's biggest publisher, Facebook would be badly tarnished after the 2016 election for sharing users' data with a Trump-tied outfit, Cambridge Analytica, and for failing to police its platform, enabling fake-news creators in Russia to disrupt the election.

All in all, it felt like a singular moment. The fate of the republic seemed to depend more than ever on access to honest, reliable information, and people were consuming more news than ever, but every news company was turning itself upside down to produce and pay for it in the digital age. I determined to capture this moment of wrenching transition—and to do it as a reporter, my first calling.

Copying Halberstam's template, I would chart the struggles of four companies to keep honest news alive. But my narrative would be less triumphal and more personal. I'd lived through the fight to keep facts alive in a new economic climate. I'd lost my way when I became executive editor of the *Times*, trying to fight for what I viewed as the necessary balance between safeguarding the independence of the news and the urgent need to find new sources of revenue. Halberstam's four companies were pillars of a rising news establishment, and he told their fascinating origin stories. The two newspapers I chose to chronicle, the *New York Times* and the *Washington Post*, were both struggling through an extremely disruptive technological transition and fighting to retain their importance and essential values. The two newcomers I chose, BuzzFeed and Vice, were improbable players in the news arena but were claiming the upper hand at a time when huge social media platforms rather than individual publishers drove audiences to news.

In the Trump era, the news wars were no longer the stuff of lofty discussion on public TV and in journalism classrooms. They were center stage every day. The man who vilified the media as "enemies of the people" was in fact a creature of the media. His rise to fame in New York City was fueled by tabloid newspapers like the *New York Post* and the *New York Daily News*. He sold papers and he worked these outlets, all the while stewing that the *Times* and other mainstream media organizations scorned him. Later he built a national profile as a master of reality television. The paradox of Trump's view of the media only deepened after his election. As he tried to delegitimize traditional news organizations, sometimes successfully, he wound up energizing them and helping drive new subscriptions. Journalists wringing their hands about technological pressure were suddenly forced to focus on the importance of their mission—and were less concerned about being marginalized. Courtesy of Trump, they were more threatened than ever, but also more vital.

The threats to trust and authority were evident at the time of the Pulitzer party, and by the time Trump assumed power the remains of any true common source of news and information for a broad swath of the American public were gone.

"There is a risk that one third of the electorate will be isolated in an information loop of its own, where Trump becomes the major source of information about Trump, because independent sources are rejected on principle," wrote media critic and New York University professor Jay Rosen in April 2018. "That has already happened. An authoritarian system is up and running for a portion of the polity."

Although the panic about the business model had retreated a bit in some newsrooms, especially after the *Times* and *Post* both witnessed a "Trump bump" in new subscriptions following the election, the old guard and the young had a common, persistent problem: the advertising that supported newspapers throughout the 20th century was rapidly disappearing. In terms of ad revenue, print dollars had become digital dimes. The ads that cluttered readers' screens were cheap and plentiful, while a full page in the *Times* still cost north of $100,000. Mobile phones were driving the prices of ads even lower. Though digital audiences, well into the millions for all four companies, were far bigger than any newspaper reader base, most readers and viewers were paying little or nothing for the content they read or watched online. Facebook and Google, with their automated ad systems that pinpointed specific audiences, were hoovering up 73 percent of whatever U.S. digital ad revenue there was.

At the same time, a basic tenet of quality journalism was under attack: the wall between church and state. Part of what slowed the *Times* and the *Post* from adapting to the digital age was a concern about separating the business side of the papers from the editorial side. The *Post*'s former editor Leonard Downie was known to walk out of meetings where business issues were being discussed because he believed so fervently in that separation.

Joe Lelyveld, a former *Times* executive editor, protested when the head of advertising once walked through the newsroom to find him.

The dam held for a while, but mounting financial pressures broke through practically overnight. At the *Times*, journalists were asked to appear at conferences with advertisers where some questions were vetted by the marketing department; the paper's ombudsman complained about the too-cozy appearance of reporters and sources at these events. The *Washington Post* had been hit far worse. Its advertising base in D.C. had been decimated, as was the case with many local newspapers, and it would be left to grasp for creative new ways to bend professional ethics in order to shore up some more revenue.

The pain was most acute at local, smaller papers. The *Charleston Gazette-Mail* in West Virginia would win the Pulitzer for investigative reporting but was forced into bankruptcy soon after the Champagne was uncorked.

During the years after 2008, when global financial calamity was intensifying, the need for quality journalism increased. The forces of nationalism were massing across the Western world. There was record income inequality even with a record low unemployment rate. The financial crisis of 2008 cost the U.S. economy some $10 trillion, according to the Government Accountability Office. Economic dislocation and technological change were upending life everywhere. Climate change was wrecking the environment; catastrophic events, such as the British Petroleum oil spill in the Gulf of Mexico, were becoming more commonplace. Terrorism was on the rise. The U.S. was involved in two wars, in Iraq and Afghanistan. There had to be reputable news organizations digging into all of these cataclysmic stories. If not, who would tell the people? It's easy to forget how desperately afraid of centralized power the Founders of America were. The First Amendment protecting freedom of the press was first for a reason.

It seemed to me that a good place to start my book was 2007, when it seemed almost everything changed. That year saw the introduction of the iPhone and the news apps that have become the dominant reading device for many of us. Facebook had just introduced its News Feed, which would become the news distribution channel for many Americans. It was when Vice decided to use digital video on YouTube to create immersive documentaries in far-flung locales that it drew new audiences to news. Jonah Peretti, a wonkish visionary, was beginning to experiment with how news could go viral and tinkering with a new website he called BuzzFeed.

For the *Times* and the *Post*, still the country's dominant general-interest papers, 2007 was the year everything began to fall apart. With the financial

crisis looming, and heavily burdened by the costs of a new skyscraper they moved into that year, the *Times* would soon go hat in hand to mogul Carlos Slim for a $250 million loan. This forced the company to rent out most of the floors of its new headquarters, which Sulzberger Jr. had envisioned as the home for a powerful new multimedia empire. At the *Post*, Katharine Weymouth, very much her grandmother's girl—she even sometimes wore Katharine Graham's signature pearls to work—became publisher and CEO, only to be slammed by financial woes. Newspeople started asking if these two pillars of journalism's establishment, the papers that still broke by far the most important stories, could survive the transition to digital.

The climate for creating the kind of journalism the First Amendment was intended to protect, the stories that held powerful people and institutions to account, had grown noticeably chillier. During President Barack Obama's administration there were more criminal leak investigations, far more of these chilling probes than in previous administrations. Though the *Times* and *Post* each had exposed classified operations eavesdropping on citizens and secret overseas prisons where terror suspects were tortured, sources and whistleblowers inside the government clammed up, fearful of prosecution. Reporters, forced to testify and reveal their secret sources, were threatened with jail time for refusing to comply with coercive subpoenas. Some of these investigations touched *Times* reporters, and I had publicly attacked the leak investigations, observing that the Obama White House was rivaling Nixon's for secrecy, much to the chagrin of the White House press secretary. I agreed with a former *Post* editor who said that if a war on terror was being waged in the name of the people, the American public needed the press to tell them about it. That was what "consent of the governed" required.

In the age of Trump, these questions heightened. Could the weakened traditional news organizations still carry out the mission the Founders intended for a free press? Had the shiny rewards for entertaining the public eclipsed their duty to inform? Would a business model, other than the whims of certain billionaire owners, emerge to support quality news-gathering? Could trust in the news media be restored when the president, almost daily, called it fake news? These seemed to me the vital issues.

Trying to answer them would take time, but working on this book, a narrative history told through four different news companies, would give me a passport into the newsrooms on the front lines. After two years of hanging out with their leaders, their technologists, their reporters and editors, I might have some sense of whether there was a future for quality news.

What do I mean by "quality news"? News that isn't commoditized, merely chronicling what happened and where, like the stories doled out by public relations firms or announced at staged events. Such stories were published every day.

Quality news involves original reporting, digging to find the real story behind the story. Investigative reporting on the murky nexus of money and politics and corporate behavior. International reporting from hard-to-reach places and dangerous conflict zones. Stories that require the skills of professional journalists using state-of-the-art reporting tools, such as databases and crowdsourcing, and age-old shoe-leather techniques to fill in gaps in the backstory. Stories that are thoughtfully presented, taking advantage of digital technology to provide on-the-scene accounts and visuals that further explain how events transpired. Stories that are edited so as to honor the intelligence of readers rather than exploit their emotions.

There are not that many places left that do quality news well or even aim to do it at all. But these four can and sometimes do: BuzzFeed, Vice, the *New York Times*, and the *Washington Post*. BuzzFeed because its success exemplifies Facebook's impact on how information spreads online. Vice because digital video and streaming services are rapidly replacing conventional TV broadcasters and cable stations and earning the loyalty of younger audiences who would rather watch than read. The *Times* because it covers more subjects and places more deeply than any other news organization. The *Post* because of its inspired quest to reclaim its lost glory as the most important digest of American politics and the government. These four are among the leaders in producing the big stories—I can't always bring myself to call it "content"—that we discuss every day. And all four are endangered.

PART ONE

BUZZFEED I

Jonah Peretti, who would upend the news business by injecting the data science of virality into it, was born into a world in which people still knew how to fold a newspaper, and grew up just a short distance from the garage where two guys named Steve were tinkering with what became the first Apple computer. His mother and father, a schoolteacher and lawyer in Oakland, California, were perplexed by a child who loved to talk to the life-size monsters he molded out of clay. His creations were so fantastical and compelling that a local art gallery put them on display. But he couldn't make sense of books.

His younger sister, Chelsea, who went on to establish herself as a successful actress and stand-up comic, remembers her rail-thin brother as relentlessly chatty and precocious. Their parents divorced when he was six. As they grew up, the siblings had their own private world. But for Jonah each day of elementary school was what he later described as seven hours of punishment that left him feeling "invisible and insignificant." He spent class time confounded, "alone in a room full of strange children who pass the time transfixed by incomprehensible symbols," he once wrote. He shrank from his teachers and spent recess hiding in a bathroom stall, crying. When he entered third grade and still couldn't read, his mother took him to a psychologist and received the verdict she had long suspected: her son was dyslexic.

Peretti's stepmother and father took consolation in the possibility that their son's brain was no less capable, just wired differently. In art class, while the other kids produced banal little pots, teachers marveled at the anatomical complexity of the sculptures the practically illiterate boy had concocted. "The goal of cognition was not to be right, but to make something interesting, provocative, and original," he wrote. "When I played the game of right and wrong at school, I always lost. But when I built something evocative in the studio, adults would stare in wonder and admiration."

Eventually he did learn to read, and at that point he gave up clay but never lost his interest in the connection between art and technology. In high school he became fascinated by philosophy and economics. Computing came to him intuitively. His mother's friend let him play around on an early-model Macintosh, and Peretti became transfixed. "I loved it because you could create with it," he recalled. He struck a deal with his parents to do extra yard work for a modest stipend and used the money to buy a Mac of his own from a secondhand store.

During his high school summers, he taught at day camps and fixed computers to earn some money. He supplemented screen time with a self-guided tour of the philosophical canon, rode his bike, and established a small community garden near home. His sister recalls these years as his "crunchy period."

Peretti finished high school in 1992 and matriculated at the University of California at Santa Cruz, where he balanced his major in environmental studies with Foucault, Barthes, Marx, JavaScript, and HTML. His senior thesis, published in the British quarterly *Environmental Values,* was on an emerging environmental doctrine called mixoecology.

He graduated Phi Beta Kappa with little clue of what he wanted to do next. He looked at a couple of tech start-ups in the area but found cubicle culture off-putting. For the time being, he decided to follow in his mother's footsteps and become a teacher. He filled out an application form and took it to the teacher placement service, telling them, "I'll go anywhere." They sent him to the Isidore Newman School, an exclusive private institution in uptown New Orleans dually distinguished by its brainy student body and storied football program, whose alumni included the writers Walter Isaacson and Michael Lewis, and the football legends Peyton and Eli Manning.

He taught four different classes, from kindergarteners to seniors, in addition to directing the computer department, where he had 15 teachers working under him, none of whom were too pleased to be answering to a man half their age, and who looked it. His rangy frame still hadn't filled out. (It never would.) He decided to wear a tie.

As an entry-level teacher, he was earning just $24,000 a year, but the challenge of making the abstrusely technical field of computer science accessible to children proved satisfying. He taught students what probability was and how to gauge it, what constituted randomness as opposed to order. His students designed their own websites, learned to write programs that generated petitions to politicians, and supplemented their study of history with virtual role-playing. His classroom became a sort of R&D lab for him to test how these young minds grappled with high-flying concepts and processes and how to adapt them to real life. Sometimes he tailored his lessons to the special needs of a dyslexic sixth-grader, whom the principal had written off as a problem child. After a year with Mr. Peretti, the child might have developed an original version of Myst, the famous computer game.

Louisiana culture was a far cry from the liberal enclave he had grown up in. The funky pair of John Fluevog wingtips he wore and the indie songwriters he listened to stuck out against the backdrop of New Orleans jazz and pickup trucks. Peretti's quirks attracted the brainier students, who signed up for the electives he taught on communist philosophers and postmodernism. He led one such class on a field trip to New York City, where three particularly admiring students went to Greenwich Village to buy Fluevogs to match his. One of them, Peggy Wang, would stay in touch with her teacher and become one of his first employees at BuzzFeed.

At night Peretti would reconvene with the philosophers he'd read in college and write erudite papers for little-known academic journals. One from his first year in New Orleans, titled "Capitalism and Schizophrenia," lamented the disorienting effects wrought by the torrent of commercial images on the internet and TV, a trend that in 1996 was in its mere adolescence. Much later the topic was fodder for myriad books and studies about how the web was shortening people's attention span.

"The increasingly rapid rate at which images are distributed and consumed in late capitalism necessitates a corresponding increase in the rate that individuals assume and shed identities," he wrote. "The viewing subject, 'glued' to the screen, mistakes himself or herself for an ideologically laden 'image-repertoire' " in which "the images must have some content to create the possibility for a mirror stage identification." The essay read like the last gasp of an idealist in the jaws of the capitalist machine. Ironic, then, that within a decade the author would build a billion-dollar company catering to the world's largest brands by preying on these very same vulnerabilities in consumers' collective subconscious. Years later, when a reporter found the paper and asked Peretti whether BuzzFeed subverted or capitalized upon the phenomena he once critiqued, he replied "lol."

On the weekends he would travel to academic symposia to discuss the digital future. At one conference on social networking, held around the turn of the millennium, he met a Cornell graduate student named Duncan Watts, who was working out the math behind the six degrees of separation and investigating how chirps spread from cricket to cricket. The result was the Watts-Strogatz theorem, which describes the traits that characterize a "small world" network, one where, through a few short hops, you can get from one node to any other node. In college Peretti had been fascinated by the question of how things could catch on and spread from person to person, but until now he had not dared to believe there could be a scientific principle that explained it, let alone a means of replicating contagious phenomena in the lab.

In 2001, after five years in New Orleans, Peretti applied to study at the MIT Media Lab, where he could dedicate himself full time to his obsession with tech-powered creativity. The lab was founded and headed by Nicholas Negroponte, a digital optimist whose book *Being Digital* forecast a better, interconnected world. Peretti's time at the Media Lab felt like the recess he had never been able to enjoy as a child. He described MIT as his playground, where "my goal is the same as everyone else's: to build something interesting." There he met Cameron Marlow, who became the head of data science at Facebook, then a Ph.D. candidate doing dissertation research on "media contagion." Marlow's conclusion contradicted Watts's theory. He argued that viral content was impossible to engineer, replicate, or predict. But Peretti would soon prove him wrong.

In a sense, BuzzFeed was born as a prank. For an online promotion, Nike launched a website where shoppers could personalize their shoes by selecting the color patterns and appending a nickname or chosen phrase. The 27-year-old Peretti submitted his design for a pair of shoes emblazoned with the word "sweatshop," an obvious reference to Nike's reputation for manufacturing its products overseas with cheap labor. An email came from Nike informing him this constituted "inappropriate slang." The real reason for the rejection, Peretti knew, was that Nike was defensive about its sweatshops.

"After consulting Webster's Dictionary," Peretti emailed back, "I discovered that 'sweatshop' is in fact part of standard English, and not slang. . . . Your web site advertises that the NIKEiD program is 'about freedom to choose and freedom to express who you are.' I share Nike's love of freedom and personal expression. The site also says that 'If you want it done right . . . build it yourself.' I was thrilled to be able to build my own shoes, and my personal iD was offered as a small token of appreciation for the sweatshop workers poised to help me realize my vision." The exchange continued, with the Nike representative standing staunchly behind the rejection, and Peretti increasing his sarcasm. "I would like to make one small request. Could you please send me a color snapshot of the 10-year-old Vietnamese girl who makes my shoes?" He got no response.

He forwarded the email chain to a group of friends, who found it amusing enough to forward to some friends of their own, and before he knew it, a large online community was buzzing about the Nike Sweatshop Emails. Peretti had started a chain reaction organically and had seen it grow to reach millions of people, on all seven continents. He was getting calls from reporters morning, noon, and night. Katie Couric invited him onto the *Today* show to debate labor rights with Nike's head of PR. Sitting in front of the cameras, Peretti wondered, "Why am I here instead of people who've dedicated their lives fighting for human rights?"

He described how what had started as a laugh among a circle of friends "began racing around the world like a virus." As he watched all this play out, it struck him that the email chain behaved according to a framework he recognized from his college biology courses. "Without really trying," he wrote, "I had released what biologist Richard Dawkins calls a meme. Dawkins describes the meme as a 'unit of cultural transmission,' such as 'tunes, ideas, catch-phrases, fashions,'" that caught on with the public. "The most important thing about memes," Peretti added, "is that they replicate themselves, 'spreading from brain to brain.'" Peretti's meme exhibited the very same phenomenon as the cricket chirps that had so captivated him about Watts's work.

Back in the Media Lab, he pondered the circumstances of his celebrity ascent with his friend Marlow, who still thought it was impossible to do twice. He challenged Peretti to go viral again, and, with hardly a lull, he did. With his sister, Peretti dreamed up something he called "the rejection line," a phone number for people to give out to unwanted suitors. When the number was called, an answering machine played the following message: "The person who gave you this number does not want to talk to you or see you again. We would like to take this opportunity to officially reject you." The hotline quickly became inundated with callers taking up all eight of its lines while overflow callers waited to get on, day after day. The project earned Peretti more acclaim. One write-up heralded him as "the poster boy of guerrilla media."

Within a year he would strike a third time, teaming up with his sister to create a parody website called Blackpeopleloveus.com that poked fun at white people's affected claims of racial sensitivity. He had all but officially disproved Marlow's theories. The buzz from the Nike emails had died off after six months, Rejection Line after three, Blackpeopleloveus after one month. Although his viral triumphs now had shorter lifespans, he was figuring out virality and, to Peretti, this signaled something about the direction online media was going. "The networks and the ability to share kept getting more and more tightly connected so that media would spread faster," he observed. As the metabolism of internet audiences quickened, its appetite for content was growing. Peretti would adapt.

He created a new term for his experiments: "contagious media." In a 23-point manifesto, he described its theses. "For the contagious media designer, all that matters is how other people see the work," he wrote. "The audience is the network and the critic." To be successful, "a contagious media project should represent the simplest form of an idea" and "must be explainable in one sentence or less." For example, "a phone line for rejecting unwanted suitors" or "a technique to make bonsai kittens."

Simplifying the content and ceding control of the distribution to the audience were the touchstones of Peretti's contagious discovery. This line of work, he realized, did not require particular brilliance or originality. Rather it demanded above all a receptiveness to the whims and weaknesses of the masses. The internet was a burgeoning lifeline for people who otherwise lacked sufficient distractions from their daily toil. It was the perfect moment, Peretti determined, to introduce the opiate they longed for.

That contagious media appeared trivial and innocuous made it all the more catchy; like the ice-cream-truck melody, it worked by worming its way into your head. But Peretti knew full well that this was more than just a passing fad. Long before others were willing to admit it, he grasped the political dimension of this new form. When asked by the host of a CNN talk show whether his viral hits made him any money, he told her, "It is just sort of an experiment in democratic media."

He knew his projects relied on an audience he characterized as the Bored at Work Network, which had arisen as "a by-product of alienated labor" and had already become, by his estimation, "the largest alternative to the corporate media," with enough manpower for "building world class encyclopedias . . . vanquishing political leaders . . . finding life on other planets and curing cancer." Their influence was vast—he appreciated this as much as anyone—but their ranks were decentralized and the network as a whole lacked discernible leadership. None of the mainstream outlets appeared to serve their interests or even grasp them, as far as Peretti could tell. And that vacuum provided opportunity.

During graduate school at the Media Lab, Peretti began working for Eyebeam, a tech lab, and moved in 2001 to New York City. He was thrilled to be working with a team of forward-thinking web developers and network scientists who tinkered away at futuristic-seeming inventions. The consortium was founded by John Johnson, whose great-grandfather had founded Johnson & Johnson and whose father, a bronze sculptor, had established an atelier where sculptors could study and produce works far bigger than most personal studios would have allowed. Eyebeam was the younger Johnson's atelier, dedicated to the tools and technologies that would enable a new era of artistic production.

The team of creators were idealists who made their experiments open-sourced and free for other coders. "We were sort of activists, artists, hackers," Peretti recalled. At Eyebeam, Johnson saw promise in the young techno-whiz. He invited Peretti to his gadget-filled Soho penthouse, where they had rousing brainstorm sessions while tinkering with Johnson's high-tech gadgets and taking in the view of downtown Manhattan. The Eyebeam job came with a small stipend, which Peretti spent on treating his comrades to cheap meals. He called his clique of like-minded digital wonks the Pizza, Beer and Innovation Consortium. One member was Ze Frank, who early on saw the potential for connecting with digital audiences and would later take charge of BuzzFeed's video and movie arm in Hollywood.

The online networks then in existence—MySpace, Friendster, and other now-extinct domains—would, within a few years, be glorified guinea pigs for the giants yet to launch. In 2003 Johnson hosted the Social Network Soiree, a glamorous evening that began with a panel featuring Peretti and Malcolm Gladwell, followed by a party sponsored by Moët Champagne. Guests were affixed with "meme tags," bugging devices that collected and analyzed the content of their small talk. Piggybacking on this, Johnson rolled out a series of events called Contagious Media Showdowns, where he and other experts held court on the viral potential of videos, websites, and other comedy projects that attendees submitted for appraisal. The Wild West theme of the first event was appropriate, considering the unexplored frontiers of social networking.

With his sister, Chelsea, Peretti put on a Contagious Media show at the cutting-edge New Museum of Contemporary Art in downtown New York, highlighting standout projects by others alongside their own viral creations: the Nike emails, the Rejection Line, and Blackpeopleloveus. Hired models dressed as museum attendants were instructed to give out the Rejection Line number to anyone who hit on them. Black actors roved the gallery striking up uncomfortable conversations about race with white attendees. "Digerati Vogues, Caught Midcraze" was the headline of the *New York Times*'s review of the show, which blasted the work as "adolescent" and "sad and shabby."

Peretti took the pan as evidence that the *Times*'s critic was out of touch with the sardonic humor that defined the digital world and its younger audience. This came with the territory of being what his friend Watts called a "cultural hacker." "The same way that a hacker looks to exploit vulnerabilities in software to make a point," Watts said, "Jonah does the same to make a cultural point." But it was a point apparently lost on the *Times*'s critic.

While Peretti continued to consolidate his influence over the underground world of technologists, he met the man who would become his godfather in the business world, Kenneth Lerer, a public-relations mogul who had made a fortune representing NBC, AOL, Microsoft, and other corporate clients, and who now, for some reason, wanted to pick Peretti's brain. At first Peretti wasn't interested in a meeting, but after Lerer offered to have a chauffeur drive him and a friend around New York, he accepted. As it turned out, Lerer was not the tycoon he had imagined. He was animated by political issues like gun control, and in 2003 the issue on his mind was renewing President Bill Clinton's ban on assault weapons. He was organizing a petition drive and thought Peretti's knowledge of what made content go viral could help. The antigun campaign the two men devised did not succeed, but it mustered an impressive 150,000 signatures in a short time.

A few weeks later Lerer was invited to dinner by a friend, Tom Freston, a Viacom executive who had helped invent MTV. They met at an Italian spot on the Upper East Side, where Freston had also invited Arianna Huffington, a tall and imposing woman with red hair and a thick Greek accent. Huffington was by then a well-known global socialite based in Los Angeles. After dating the British cultural critic Bernard Levin, she married the Texan oil heir Michael Huffington. She had played a crucial part in her husband's election to Congress as a Republican from California in 1992 and had carved out a role for herself in Washington as a political pundit, palling around with Newt Gingrich to promote an agenda they called "compassionate conservatism." She divorced her husband after he lost a Senate bid in 1994 and announced her rebirth as a liberal Democrat. When Lerer met her, she was fresh off the campaign trail, having run for governor of California before pulling out of the race after polling at less than 2 percent of the vote. The conversation at dinner revolved around John Kerry's loss to Bush in the 2004 presidential contest and the need for a more muscular liberal media. Huffington asked to meet Lerer again.

In the meantime Lerer approached Peretti about working with Huffington. "You know the web," Peretti recalls Lerer saying, "and I know business. Let's do something together." Peretti's response was tepid at first. "I was never interested in business or making money, that wasn't the point," he told me years later. "Business wasn't cool." His experience was in the classroom and the research laboratory, where as a rule anything he created was offered, free of charge, to any technologist who had a use for it. But as he listened to what Lerer was proposing, he began to come around to the idea.

Lerer had been monitoring the conservative blogosphere, which arose alongside right-wing talk radio, and was dismayed by the havoc he saw them wreaking for liberal candidates and causes. He identified the command center of the right's digital battlefront, Matt Drudge, who had launched the Drudge Report in 1995 and turned it into a high-traffic powerhouse. It was Drudge who had broken the story of Monica Lewinsky back in 1998, as it was Drudge again in 2004 who trumpeted the right-wing's false allegations about John Kerry's record in the navy. With Peretti and Huffington and a former Drudge assistant and Huffington researcher, Andrew Breitbart, Lerer wanted to strike back.

Before Peretti's first meeting with Huffington at her home in California, he googled her to find out who she was. His search results painted an eccentric portrait: born Arianna Stasinopoúlou in Athens, she had gone to Cambridge University and become the first foreign student elected president of its prestigious debating society. She already had 10 books to her name, on topics ranging from conservative feminism to Maria Callas, Pablo Picasso, Greek mythology, and New Age spiritualism.

The Oakland-raised son of a schoolteacher could hardly have known what he was getting into when his red-eye flight touched down at LAX and a chauffeur whisked him off to the Huffington mansion in the elite Brentwood Hills neighborhood. The next morning he came downstairs at 7:00 to find his host at the kitchen table, juggling three BlackBerry smartphones and welcoming him to her second breakfast meeting of the day. (She usually had more than three.) As she was pressed for time, they had a brief exchange on a possible collaboration. Huffington envisioned some kind of blog that would curate and link to other content, like Drudge but for the left. Then Laurie David, wife of *Seinfeld* creator Larry, arrived at the door and Peretti learned he would be joining them on a private jet to Sacramento to campaign for Huffington's friend, her fellow Greek American politician Phil Angelides, a Democrat who was running an ultimately unsuccessful campaign for governor.

This was Peretti's first glimpse at the satellite system orbiting Huffington everywhere she went. She was, in her own words, a "gatherer" who made adroit and unapologetic use of her bulging list of contacts. On that list were many key ingredients for the media company she would build: contacts culled from the upper strata of London, Los Angeles, D.C., and New York. Their value to Huffington resided less in their money and power—although there was plenty of that—than in what they represented as personalities. She had at her disposal the likes of George Clooney, Madonna, Alec Baldwin, Bill Maher, Nora Ephron, Deepak Chopra, Diane Ravitch, David Geffen, and many other A-listers, all willing to write on her blog for free.

Peretti, recalled Lerer, still looked like a little boy, and Arianna, as everyone called her, made his eyes go wide. "I learned from Arianna," Peretti told me, "seeing the limits and opportunities of celebrity, the importance of social networks."

The final member of the founding quartet, Andrew Breitbart, bore certain similarities to Huffington. He too had changed his political stripes, having grown up a Brentwood liberal before turning sharply to the right. He was proud to call himself "Matt Drudge's bitch." But at the Huffington Post he was expected to play for the other team, and this did not come naturally. He barely survived the launch of the new site. Although he was brilliant at writing catchy headlines that drew traffic, Lerer fought with him and forced him out. Breitbart went on to start his right-wing site, Breitbart News, and was best known for breaking the Anthony Weiner scandal. Breitbart News in 2016 became Donald Trump's *Pravda*. By then Breitbart himself was gone—he had died suddenly in 2012 at 43—but Breitbart News lived on under the leadership of Steve Bannon.

A clear division of labor sprang up among the team's remaining members. Huffington served as their public face, working mostly out of her L.A. home, where she maintained a stable of six assistants upstairs. Lerer, Peretti recalled, "was a master at understanding the press" and was in charge of luring investors. Peretti was to shape the technological architecture of the site and was responsible for the broad category they labeled "innovation," the word that would become contagious in every newsroom.

This was the golden age of blogs, the shorthand term for weblogs, when new, easy-to-use programs like Blogger enabled anyone to establish a home for their commentary and coverage. Soon there were tens of thousands of blogs, some with a readership of one. What distinguished them was their more personal, often opinionated perspectives and loose, conversational style. Respected journalists like Andrew Sullivan, a former editor of the venerable *New Republic* magazine, broke off on their own to reinvent themselves as bloggers and built sizable followings. Gawker, a blog that published gossipy items about journalists and celebrities, arose during this period. The blog format was perfect for Huffington, who was already a celebrity and liked to jump from subject to subject.

Meanwhile the *New York Times* and the *Washington Post* were turning some of their own writers into bloggers on subjects in which they had expertise and a following among readers. In the mid-2000s, the *Times* had 47 blogs, including one devoted to tennis, another to chess, and others to pet interests observed in the readership. For the Huffington Post to beat conventional publishers, Peretti determined, it would have to be not only contagious but also "sticky," his term for the quality that kept readers coming back for more.

When launch day arrived in May 2005, Peretti and the technologists had been working frantically for 24 hours straight to gussy up the site's appearance and root out any catastrophes in the lines of code that composed its infrastructure. They weren't quite finished and pleaded for more time, but Huffington had managed to get booked on NBC's *Today* show and refused to squander the opportunity to promote the launch. So, with the click of a button, the site appeared out of thin air on May 9, 2005, with the musings of celebrities Larry David, John Cusack, Ellen DeGeneres, and Laurie David, then the wife of Larry.

Initial reviews in the mainstream media were mainly negative, and indigenous bloggers ridiculed Huffington's sanctimonious invasion of their little world. Even so, Peretti knew that "they wouldn't be able not to look. Even the haters would come every day." Stickiness was achieved, with celebrities and left-leaning politics. It took only six months for the Huffington Post to surpass the web traffic of the *Wall Street Journal*, the *New York Times*, and the *Washington Post*.

After the VIPs lent their stardust to prime the pump of Huffington's superblog, she opened the site to anyone, regardless of fame, and offered to publish their submissions alongside the big names. The only catch, of course, was that they'd have to write for free. It was a clever ploy on Huffington's part, reminiscent of Tom Sawyer convincing the neighborhood boys how fun it was to whitewash his fence. It meant she and her partners could escape the financial burden of investing in a large number of editors and reporters. All she had to do was provide space, a commodity with infinite reserves on the internet.

The strategy hit traditional publishers where it hurt most. Ever since the earliest incarnation of internet publishing, readers had been treated to a feast of content—more than you could read in a thousand lifetimes—for which they would never be expected to pay a dime. Deprived of any revenue from visitors, accountants for news publishers struggled to balance the paltry sums they made selling ad space on news sites with the costly enterprise of employing journalists. By paring down the cost of personnel to almost nothing, the Huffington Post could balance the budget much more quickly without having to sacrifice its output. There were so many contributors that it became known as a "content farm."

It was an experiment in making a little go a long way. As the official innovator, Peretti tinkered with the mechanics of the website to optimize its offerings around what most appealed to its visitors. A "click-o-meter" measured the traffic on the website's headlines, and Peretti pored over the data it collected to see which stories were gaining momentum and which were dying off; he could adjust the homepage accordingly. An A/B testing system was installed that allowed writers to publish the same story under two different headlines and see which proved more enticing. When big news broke, Peretti, who had no training in journalism, deferred to Lerer on what belonged on the homepage. "When Kenny weighed in, the click-o-meter didn't matter," Peretti recalled. "He had a good sense of what powerful people would be interested in."

To get a sense of what interested everyone else, the small paid staff had only to look to Google's constantly updated log of the most popular searches. When February rolled around, for example, Google identified a surge of the query "What time is the Super Bowl?" The Huffington Post's search-traffic analyst alerted the newsroom staff, who nimbly whipped up a post that answered the question on everyone's mind. That post, in turn, appeared atop the list of results Google fetched, giving Huffington's site a windfall of visitors, who represented advertising revenue in crude form. It was brilliant, and with time and diligent testing, it became only more so.

Peretti's pod of analysts noticed, for example, that people tended to google nouns instead of verbs—as in "Michael Jackson death," not "Michael Jackson dies"—and advised the site's editors to style their headlines accordingly. When the actor Heath Ledger died of an overdose, they saw a profusion of Google searches for "Keith Ledger" and cleverly tagged their coverage of his passing with the misheard name.

The Huffington Post held itself accountable not to journalistic rules but to readers' enthusiasm. It did not purport to dictate the terms of the national conversation but rather to reflect it. It aimed not to change hearts and minds but to resonate with them. Company leadership was notably void of anyone with editing experience. "Digital is painting in oil," Lerer told me. "You can always paint over it." A story that was wrong on first publication could be corrected right away. Accuracy, in any event, was not going to bring as many readers as the sheer amount of output. The challenge was to feed the beast.

Even as the business became profitable, it would be crucial to keep overhead costs at an absolute minimum, no matter the toll it took on the workforce. From inception, the Huffington Post determined that paying its bloggers was "not in our financial model," according to Lerer, no matter how profitable the business became. The company began staffing its newsroom with writers recruited right out of college, catching them at their most desperate, and paying them barely enough to qualify as lower middle-class. To get by, many full-time staffers moonlighted as tutors, babysitters, or waiters. The work was strenuous and tedious. Some staffers almost never left the long plastic tables where they sat at computer screens finding stories already published elsewhere on the web, lifting and quickly repackaging them as Huffington Post originals, and siphoning off advertising that might otherwise have gone to the actual creators. Employees quit in droves. One former staffer described the work environment as "so brutal and toxic it would meet with approval from committed sociopaths."

Just four years after Peretti had been catapulted to stardom as an opponent of sweatshop labor, he was responsible for what the *Los Angeles Times* decried as the sweatshop of publishing, characterized by "speedup and piecework; huge profits for the owners; desperation, drudgery and exploitation for the workers."

In the five years between the new millennium and the founding of HuffPost, the worldwide population of internet users quadrupled in size to one billion. The volume of information being trafficked online grew 28-fold.

Old newspapers tried to learn the new tricks of the digital sphere. They were reaching audiences there that dwarfed what they had known in even the golden days of hard-copy circulation, when newspapers held local monopolies in many regions. But the economics didn't add up. Online readers weren't paying anything for newspapers' reporting on the web, while a weekly, year-round home-delivery subscription could cost more than $700. As readers grew accustomed to reading on the web, both print circulation and print advertising began an irreversible downturn.

Shortly after the Huffington Post's grand opening in 2005, the Times Company announced a plan to lay off 500 employees, one of the deepest cuts in its history. Two years later it announced it was shaving the paper's width by an inch and a half and also shutting down one of its printing plants. Still, it was much worse elsewhere. The once highly profitable publishing conglomerate Knight Ridder sold all of its 32 newspapers and disappeared. The *Washington Post* spent millions to compensate employees who agreed to retire early. Smaller local papers suffered the most and retreated in the greatest numbers, leaving town councils and some state capitals without full-time coverage.

With the advent of sites like Craigslist, classified advertising for jobs, apartments, and cars—once the lifeblood of local newspapers—began rapidly migrating to the web, where the ads were free to place. At the *Post*, Weymouth recalled the horror of seeing her paper's special section for classified job ads, which usually netted $100-plus million, go from the size of a small phone book to barely a wisp. As more and more renegade news organizations arose, journalists and readers alike sensed the paradox: they were entering a world with seemingly unlimited possibilities, yet discovering that their time-honored ways of producing and consuming the news were no longer viable. One such outlet was Yahoo! News, a billboard of news items from other sources picked and placed by machine. Because Yahoo was a popular email portal, many Yahoo users found it convenient to scan the news on its site rather than sitting down to read a newspaper. Veteran institutions watched how easily readers seemed to shift their time and loyalty to this free content. Newspapers, still digital innocents, operated in the mistaken belief that all they had to do was remake versions of their daily publications for display on computer screens.

The information explosion was staggering in speed and scale. The amount of digital data produced worldwide in 2006 alone was three million times the material of all the books ever written. A 2008 study commissioned by the Associated Press diagnosed "news fatigue" in young-adult readers. "That is, they appeared debilitated by information overload," the authors observed. "The irony in news fatigue is that these consumers felt helpless to change their news consumption at a time when they have more control and choice than ever before." A Pew study conducted in 2007 found that the share of Americans who could name the vice president had dropped 5 percent from 1989.

The true bête noire of the news industry, however, was not Yahoo but Google, its successor in the search-engine business and a product of Stanford technologists. Founded in 1998, the most disruptive element of Google's business model hardly seemed threatening: that Google did not want to compete with the wider web for your time or attention; it simply wanted to organize the web and help you find what you were looking for. In providing that service, the Google machine effectively "learned" two crucial pieces of information: what you were seeking and where you found it. This formed the foundation of the most brilliant and hypertargeted advertising platform that had ever existed, one that has since attracted the lion's share of ad revenues, along with Facebook, and continues to dominate the market year after year.

Once it had stockpiled enough intelligence to flesh out a satisfactory map of the internet, Google began to sell the rights to advertise on the page of search results it presented when queried. Beginning in 2000 an advertiser could pay Google to feature its page among the top results displayed to people who searched, for example, for "sneakers," so that shoe-shoppers would be more likely to visit their web store. The balance of objectivity and sponsored messaging the company served up was "not very different from what you'd see say in a newspaper," Google explained in a memo to the Securities and Exchange Commission, "but now it's much more targeted."

"Google users trust our systems to help them with important decisions," the memo continued. That much was true too: the algorithm that powered its search engine delivered answers faster and more reliably than any other tool out there. It was only a matter of time before the machine began encroaching on the work of the mortal journalists once entrusted to go out into the world, dig out answers to timely questions, and relate them to curious readers.

When airplanes crashed into the Twin Towers on the morning of September 11, 2001, the online news sphere faced the most significant trial of its young life. The newspapers delivered that Tuesday morning went stale as soon as the first plane crashed, leaving the entire population of the nation to rely on TV broadcasts and online news. More people consulted the web than ever had before, and under the pressure of unprecedented traffic, many websites buckled. From 60 blocks north of ground zero, the *New York Times* marshaled its team of reporters, newly trimmed by two rounds of buyouts after the bursting of the dot-com bubble earlier that year, to cover the story of a lifetime. As the scope of the disaster unfolded, and the U.S. declared a war on terror and deployed troops to the Middle East, *Times* journalists proved their mettle and earned seven Pulitzer Prizes, a single-year record. And though its fortunes were diminishing, the publisher added a daily section, "A Nation Challenged," to accommodate the crush of post-9/11 news, which contained, in a dignified tribute to the calamity, not a speck of advertising.

But the biggest winner was Google. While the *Times*'s journalists took testimony from firefighters and grieving families, embedded with battalions in Afghanistan and Pakistan, and conducted comprehensive assessments of the terrorist threat worldwide, Krishna Bharat, a 31-year-old research scientist at Google's headquarters in Mountain View, California, pored over millions of queries that flooded Google's portal that morning.

"People came to us and said, 'Give us information about what just happened now,'" he observed, "and we didn't have a good answer." The challenge was to deliver the freshest material, incorporating as many sources as possible, and to display the package coherently and without the help of human oversight. Within six weeks Bharat had developed a functioning prototype of a tool called Google News. The service kept constant tabs on 150 news sources from across the web, detected new stories as they broke, and updated its front page every 15 minutes. Within a year it had harnessed the reporting power of 4,500 sources worldwide, aggregating their top stories and serving them up on the Google News page virtually as soon as they were published. By 2015 its funnel would widen to include 50,000 news sources, digested and displayed in 70 different regional editions.

That a chunk of code written by one person in six weeks could summarize the state of the world was revolutionary. To Google, it was another step toward its stated goal of making the company "an institution that makes the world a better place." But others in the news business begged to differ. "There are those who think they have a right to take our news content and use it for their own purposes without contributing a penny to its production," said then News Corp. chairman and CEO Rupert Murdoch. "Their almost wholesale misappropriation of our stories is not fair use. To be impolite, it's theft."

Both the Huffington Post and Google relied on aggregation to power their new operations, but they did so by different means and for different ends. Google's virtual newspaper used an algorithm to pull from thousands of outlets worldwide and display their stories on its page in the form of headlines (plus a sentence or two) that linked to the original source. By collating a broad base of reports and arranging them all in one place, it presented the paragon of convenience for news consumers—hence the animosity from outlets whose readers it won away. But Google made no secret of the fact that these were not its stories. Huffington Post's aggregators, by contrast, were humans who lifted as much of the original report as copyright law permitted. They then republished it on their site with only oblique reference or link to the original article.

For the Huffington Post, it was crucial to game Google's search system. Peretti helped optimize the site's presence so that its own knockoffs would appear in Google's search results above the original versions and thus attract more clicks. More clicks meant more advertising revenue, although internet ads cost a fraction of what full-page newspaper ads did. (A full-page ad in the *Times* fetched $100,000, compared to the tiny amount an advertiser would pay for a banner on the young Huffington Post.) The ability to target specific audiences rather than reach the undifferentiated mass of *Times* print subscribers or broadcast network viewers became, for many marketers, not only the cheaper but also the more effective targeted ad buy.

To editors who were brought up on journalistic ethics and knew all too well how costly it was to fund original reporting, the ascendance of bootleggers was beyond galling. I remember my own horror in 2010 after the *Times* published an exclusive story based on mountains of leaked, classified data from Wikileaks, which had taken us months to report. The Huffington Post's version of the story, with the same headline, appeared almost simultaneously, with no original reporting—and ranked above the *Times* on Google.

As the *Times* and other publishers prepared cease-and-desist letters and considered suing for copyright infringement, the old guard's leading lights came forward to denounce Huffington's heist. Chief among them was my boss, Bill Keller, who had served as executive editor from 2003 to mid-2011. A razor-sharp writer who had won a Pulitzer Prize as a young foreign correspondent in Moscow, Keller enjoyed using his wit and pen to go to war. He blamed Arianna Huffington, "the queen of aggregation," for what he diagnosed as "the 'American Idol'-ization of news," and lamented the kleptocratic regime she threatened to impose once she vanquished the industry's incumbents. "In Somalia this would be called piracy," Keller wrote. "In the mediasphere, it is a respected business model." He called attention to the moment of reckoning this model would inevitably produce. "If everybody is an aggregator, nobody will be left to make real stuff to aggregate," he wrote, adding that Huffington's half-hearted foray into employing actual reporters was "like hiring a top chef to fancy up the menu at Hooters." Soon similar analogies would be applied to Peretti's next venture.

Huffington struck back with a retort that borrowed a page from Donald Trump. She dismissed Keller's charges as "lame" and "laughable," accused him of stealing her work, and attributed his frustration to the fact that her site, including traffic that went to its owner, AOL, had nearly double the page views as his. "Winning" was all that mattered.

The traffic scoreboard was, undeniably, a source of ire for the institutions that were committed to the brutally expensive high road of original reporting. More infuriating was what it signified: that readers didn't seem to distinguish between the original and the imitator. At a moment when conventional journalism appeared in freefall, public opinion seemed to be coalescing in support of the very people whose disruptive new strategies further undermined it. Twelve months after the Huffington Post was born, *Time* ranked Arianna one of the 100 most influential people in America, right up there with her nemesis, Matt Drudge. From opposite ends of the ideological spectrum, the king and queen of aggregation had elbowed their way into the top tier of the media world, without regard for the consequences of their success. Now they were being toasted as revolutionaries, their triumphs exalted as underdog stories. "It took just two fingers, a modem and guts," Drudge was quoted as saying in his *Time* profile. "And not giving a shit."

A year into the life of his new site, Peretti grew restless. Gaming Google had been fun for a little while, but winning the game was no longer a challenge. It hadn't been hard to master the dynamics of search engine optimization, SEO. The Huffington Post's entrepreneurial spirit rewarded him for each incremental breakthrough by funneling more resources toward his next project. "I was just always interested in how you get from A to A plus one," he explained. His contributions to HuffPo endowed the site with machine intelligence it would continue to profit from a decade hence. It was time to crack a new code.

By now Peretti knew what people searched for online and how Google's algorithm decided to deliver it. He also knew what kind of content people clicked on: a funny blog post by Larry David, for example, or a newsy story with an eye-popping headline. The Huffington Post had become contagious and sticky, but the main system it relied upon to reach readers was Google, and that limited its potential. It meant readers had to wonder, first, then search before they would land on his site. They had to seek out HuffPo content rather than searching out readers. Taking a step back, he glimpsed a window of opportunity for a new type of publisher: one that would serve content that readers neither sought out nor found particularly vital to know. Rather than taking cues from the psychology of individuals in isolation, it would be grounded in insights about social dynamics.

Once again Peretti's timing was preternatural. This was the very moment that the now-internet-fluent audience was becoming socialized. On the web, people were constituting new communities. Their online interactions were more than mere approximations of their in-person interactions—they were the majority of their personal communications. Life on the web and "real life" were merging. People were spending more time on what they chose to read, although anything longer than 10 seconds per click was considered on the long side. Readers were spending several hours a week on the web. The *Times* reported that its online readership spent 25 minutes per month reading its online offerings. (For the print newspaper, the average was 25 minutes per day.)

Peretti had a theory: content would become a form of conversation on the internet. He approached Huffington about setting up a skunkworks team that would run experiments on how and what people shared with each other online. She gave him the go-ahead, provided that he would export his best findings to the Huffington Post. With her blessing, he set out to fill the new power vacuum he had identified. Years later Lerer would recall this pivotal moment. "Arianna caught the SEO wave," he told me. "Then the world started to change and Jonah caught the social wave." Peretti extended the metaphor: "It's like we happened to start surfing a few minutes before a great wave rolled in."

That wave had been rippling for a couple of years, but now, just a few hours up the northeast corridor in Cambridge, Massachusetts, a sophomore named Mark Zuckerberg was amplifying it into a full-blown tempest. When he launched TheFacebook.com in February 2004, membership was restricted to his fellow students at Harvard. By submitting their university email addresses, users could enter the virtual world Zuckerberg had created and build a personal profile for their peers to find—and perhaps judge them by. Within 24 hours some 1,200 students had joined, and the cascade of interest would only ratchet up from there. Facebook expanded to other elite schools, and Zuckerberg dropped out of Harvard and moved to Palo Alto.

To join Facebook, internet users had to be willing to drop their anonymity, something taken for granted in blogging and chat rooms, to join a genuinely useful service. Facebook opened the network to all U.S. college students, launched internationally, and welcomed high school students. In September 2006 it took a leap of faith, allowing anyone with an email address—regardless of institutional affiliation—to join the party. It exploded.

That same month Facebook introduced the core feature of its platform, the News Feed, described as a "living newspaper" by Zuckerberg. "Living" referred to the fact that when users logged on and looked at this feed, they saw content shared by friends rather than stories selected by some monolithic publisher or algorithmic robot. "You had the underpinnings of a circulatory system that could be a publishing platform," said Chris Cox, the engineer behind News Feed. "Each person was receiving updates from the set of people that interested them." Cox would become a key person in Peretti's life.

Six months before Facebook reorganized its site around the News Feed framework, Twitter had launched with a similar premise. If Facebook was the living newspaper, Twitter's 140-character limit made its platform more like a hyperspeed news wire. From the start, the network attracted journalists and political junkies—not only to plug their own work but also to find and follow sources and track newsworthy events and cultural conversations in real time.

The device that forever changed how those events and conversations unfolded was introduced soon after Peretti broke off on his own. On January 9, 2007, a scruffy, owl-eyed man in a turtleneck whose lab had produced the Mac, the mouse, the laptop, iTunes, and the iPod strode onto a stage in San Francisco to announce his most innovative and disruptive invention yet. "iPhone is a revolutionary and magical product that is literally five years ahead of any other mobile phone," Apple CEO Steve Jobs announced. The release date was set for June—expectant techies marked their calendars for "iDay"—and as the day approached, thousands took their spot in lines outside Apple stores across the country for the privilege of spending $499, or $599 for the deluxe model, on what early testers had already dubbed the "Jesus Phone."

For journalism, the iPhone meant that readers would never again be more than a few swipes away from the latest story. Their new pocket computers quickly begot insatiable appetites for information and diversion at even the slightest lull in activity—the panacea for Peretti's Bored at Work Network. It encouraged the public's expectation that news be relayed in real time, upending the traditional newspaper schedule that for over a century had served as the de facto circadian rhythm of the profession. As important, it meant journalists would be armed with the power tools of the newsroom—word processors, internet hookups, cameras and video equipment—no matter where they were when news broke. The old, diurnal news cycle gave way to the 24/7 news cycle in a world in which people got updates constantly (and, to a degree, passively) from their smartphones, as if staying informed via an IV drip.

Now that a growing share of the population was connected through online social networks and their connections could travel with them wherever they went, Peretti decided to break away from Huffington entirely and devote himself full time to his skunkworks. With seed funding from Lerer and John Johnson, he was able to hire a few engineers and lease an office in Chinatown, on the third floor of a shabby walkup on Canal Street above a Mahjong bar once home to Chiang Kai-shek's Kuomintang Party. For now, he was calling his new company Contagious Media LLC.

As a cofounder of Huffington Post, Peretti could one day expect a behemoth payday, though he'd have to wait another five years until AOL bought the company for $315 million. For now, he had already done enough to earn the confidence of deep-pocketed tech investors, who saw in him their best shot at capturing the burgeoning mediasphere. If the funding ran dry, it would be replenished. This meant he had the luxury of what he called his company's "lab phase," when it was insulated from the pressure to make money that often ruined promising start-ups.

It was time to start his own site. In the early going, his compass was the massive stockpile of data he had accrued and analyzed at the Huffington Post. This would bolster his intuition; without having to guess, he could grasp what types of content would succeed and could therefore avoid the duds. He purchased a few servers to get the new site up and running and tucked them into the office's kitchen pantry. On the other side of the office he set up a long table where his first young hires could play video games when business was slow. The facilities were a far cry from the glassy palace where HuffPo lived, but there was a certain charm to the dilapidation. When the upstairs tenants moved out, their cockroaches descended en masse upon the Contagious Media office and built colonies in the backs of the colorful iMac G3s Peretti had bought.

Peretti by now understood that media, by any other name, was simply another mode of communication. It had been a one-way line during the print and broadcast eras, but as millions logged on to the internet, they entered a connective framework where media content, whether interoffice memoranda, vacation photos, or wartime reports, could move not just in one or two directions but ubiquitously and faster than the speed of light.

His idea, at first, was to create a computer system that would send out content along the same channels used for communication. Its function would be twofold: to monitor the public conversations of blogs and forums to glean what people cared about, then to cull the best material on those topics and serve it up in the form of an online "chat" message. Function No. 1 would be handled by a software program he devised called the Trend-Detector, and Function No. 2 would, for now, assume the form of BuzzBot. Anyone who signed up for the service would receive regular dispatches from BuzzBot, informing them of the Trend-Detector's latest catch. It was an imaginative model for the future of publishing, one that was easily a decade ahead of its time. But the public wasn't ready for the brave new world of BuzzBot, and automating the process by which a trend was spotted and converted into an intelligible piece of content proved unwieldy.

Peretti disbanded the bot but would keep the Trend-Detector and simplify the process by publishing the buzz it collected on a plain old website. It was time to name this protean beast he was raising, so he scoured the listings of for-sale domain names, looking for "something that sounded cool but was broad enough that we could experiment and do lots of different things." By 2006 most of the good names were taken. He scrolled and scrolled until he came across one that fit the bill: BuzzFeed. He liked the futuristic ring of the portmanteau. The guy who owned the domain seemed to have no use for it and was happy to sell it to Peretti for a few hundred dollars.

Now Peretti knew what to call it, but he had only a vague notion of what the *it* would be. He relished the ambiguity, knowing as he did that open-endedness meant versatility, and versatility was crucial to success in a changing landscape. As late as 2008 BuzzFeed described itself mysteriously as a "platform" that "offers publishing tools and trend detection for a select group of trendspotters and buzz-makers." Though it had been up and running publicly for two years, it played up the mystique by suggesting, "We are currently in private beta."

The mumbo-jumbo notwithstanding, BuzzFeed's site offered visitors something fairly straightforward: a daily crop of five or six posts covering cultural trends or rising gossip, each consisting of a sentence or two, followed by a roundup of links to other outlets' articles, blog posts, or pictures on the topic. The posts were selected not for their newsworthiness or any higher purpose but for their entertainment value and shareability. Behind the simple edifice, however, was a complex and finely tuned algorithmic contraption that did most of the legwork to select which topics were catching fire. It was a marvel of "machine learning," Peretti boasted, the process by which computers analyze patterns in order to develop, over time, un-canny intelligence, perception, and judgment. If it seemed like something out of a science fiction novel, BuzzFeed hoped it sounded more utopian than dystopian. In an overview of how the process worked, the company emphasized the role of its "network of human taste-makers" (i.e., a couple of staffers) who manned a "special terminal interface" to look out for "sub-tle trends our robots might miss."

Humans would analyze the data, supervise the detector robots, and re-view and repackage the trending stories dredged up, but they would not be performing journalism. "The original editors were content test-pilots," Per-etti told me. "We created content almost as R&D." As publishing models went, this one was especially supple in bringing man and machine together in cooperation. It was a bionic marvel that purported to cater to readers' tastes better than their closest human friends could do. Its slogan: "Find Your New Favorite Thing."

The earliest BuzzFeed blog posts included a compilation of the seven best links about gay penguins, four clips on Snoop Dogg's new clothing line for pets, 20 celebrity nipple slips, and 15 links to animal pornography. As long as readers liked the stuff enough to pass it along to friends, Peretti was happy.

Most of these posts were about entertainment and fun, and he was ag-nostic about their content. The few items in those days that touched on hard news and serious subjects were presented no differently than the penguins and nipple slips, and weren't intended to be. The web was a great leveler—foreign wars shared a room with the funny pages.

They were effective means to the end Peretti had in mind: the "social reproduction" of content. To get himself oriented, he roped in his old friend Duncan Watts and signed him to a contract that obliged him, every so often, to talk shop with Peretti over a beer. He dubbed it "the beer clause." To-gether they devised a sort of litmus test that would be used to determine how well BuzzFeed's content reproduced across the social web, expressed in the form of a quotient called Viral Rank—essentially the distillation of how likely a reader was to share the post with friends. If the post on "Inter-species Friends" mustered a higher Viral Rank than the post on a novelty line of lingerie made out of bacon, that was a hint to pivot toward animals and away from edible XXX nightclothes.

Shareability was the beginning and end of BuzzFeed's model, as well as its organizing logic. "Buzzfeed wasn't a content site," Lerer told me, re-calling the company's early days. "It was to see how to make content travel virally." Content wasn't sorted by categories like business, the arts, or politics. "We organized the site around the emotions that lead to sharing," Peretti said. For example, "if a football player does a funny touchdown dance, you share the video because it is funny, not because it is sports." Touchdown dances and the like would be filed under the heading "LOL," while posts that evoked awe, disgust, indignation, and Schadenfreude were filed, respectively, under "OMG," "Trashy," "WTF," and "Fail."

This methodology reflected BuzzFeed's core innovation: its foremost concern was with readers' *subliminal* predilections, not with the topics they consciously followed. This marked a departure from the search-based publishing model that Peretti devised for the Huffington Post, where editors looked to Google's most-queried topics for their cues on what stories to pursue. Instead of tracking down information readers sought out, BuzzFeed's algorithms and editors plumbed the innate inclinations of its audience—items most people shared some fondness for but would never cite as an interest. Things like "basset hounds running," to use an example from BuzzFeed's former chief revenue officer Andy Wiedlin. "No one searches it. But everyone clicks when they see it." And, of course, anything to do with cats.

BuzzFeed didn't need any high-tech trend-detectors to seize on the fact that the web loved cats. That much was too obvious to ignore. "We started with cute kittens and internet memes and humor, because that's where the social web was when the company started," Peretti said. "Cats on the web aren't about the cats," he added. "It's about being human." For BuzzFeed's purposes, cats went viral because they so profoundly resonated with the emotional disposition of the online community.

As BuzzFeed grew, its understanding of what people liked—and, more to the point, what they liked to share with friends—became increasingly fine-tuned. "We start[ed] to get a sense," Peretti would later explain, "of where's the beating heart of the internet." For most of its existence, the web was hailed as the ultimate information repository, a reservoir that contained and catalogued the sum total of human knowledge. Peretti, by contrast, saw it as the aggregate of human emotion, a living and breathing thing more sentimental than rational.

He considered his new venture a technology company, not a news site. This distinction was fundamental to other new digital media sites too. Technological tools for discovering existing content, rather than gathering new information or news, were powering BuzzFeed's pioneering foray.

The young people Peretti hired were a motley crew, but in each he saw a prowess that served his purposes, even if they wouldn't fly in a more conventional workplace. They straddled two identities—geek and tastemaker—and like little Perettis, they had their fingers on the pulse of the Bored at Work Network. These were decidedly not the people applying to journalism school.

One was Peggy Wang, Peretti's admiring former student who had bought shoes like his on the field trip to New York. She had gotten her college degree and moved to Brooklyn and was bouncing around from job to job—developing software for a real estate company until they fired her after two weeks for never showing up on time, managing the website of a hipster nightclub after seeing the opening on Craigslist, and playing gigs with her indie-rock band, The Pains of Being Pure at Heart. She was working as a programmer at MTV and subsisting in a $200-a-month apartment in her friend's basement when Peretti found her profile on Friendster, the social network. He got in touch to lure her to his lofty but ill-defined new venture. It would mean taking a substantial pay cut (she was earning $75,000 at MTV with health benefits, while Peretti offered her only $40,000). She discussed the options with her parents, Chinese immigrants who ran a combination video-rental and flower shop in New Orleans. Because Peretti had been her teacher, they said, she could go with him if that was what she wanted. Taking a leap of faith, she told Peretti she was in. "What's the game plan after six months?" she asked him. "If we hate it," he said, "we just won't do it anymore."

Wang became the site's trend editor, the human counterpart to BuzzFeed's algorithmic culture-combers, responsible for selecting which trends would make for shareable posts, then dressing them up with simple but intriguing headlines and one-line subtitles that Peretti told her should sound like "something you'd say if you were at a cocktail party." While Peretti and his engineers tinkered with the algorithm, Wang drafted five posts for BuzzFeed to publish each day—the sum of its original content. One day, when all she could muster was three, Peretti marched up to her desk and requested she pick up the pace. She'd gotten food poisoning, she explained politely.

To help Wang handle the growing workload, Peretti hired a shaggy-haired, jean-shorts-wearing NYU student, Matt Stopera, as BuzzFeed's first summer intern. If there was ever an archetypal Bored at Work member, Stopera was it. He came to BuzzFeed from a "nightmare" internship at a relative's insurance company, where he was supposed to be digitizing files, but, he said, "I just kind of gave up because the people there had no idea what I was doing anyway." He spent most of his daily eight-hour shifts scouring YouTube for hidden gems with fewer than a thousand views, which he would post to his website, Underonethousand.com. Stopera was an avid Britney Spears fan, so devout that MTV aired a segment on him. His childhood bedroom was festooned with Britney paraphernalia, and he zealously defended her reputation in online chatrooms under the screen name BIGHUGEspearsfan. The year he finally got to meet her, his family's Christmas card showed the young Stopera posing with his idol.

As a high schooler he had taken pride in finding ways to turn his essays—whether they were supposed to be about ancient myths or *The Odyssey*—into ruminations on Britney's greatness. In college he decided to major in communications after learning it would allow him to earn credits for classes on pop culture. "I originally wanted to go to school for journalism because I thought it was cool or something," he later said. "I took the intro class and hated it." Besides the insurance internship, his only professional credential was as a dishwasher at an Italian restaurant that somehow failed to notice the tonnage of cheese he embezzled every day when his shift ended. For Stopera, working at BuzzFeed was the best job imaginable. He was getting paid for doing what he loved. His marching orders from Peretti were "Just keep scouring the Internet," looking for offbeat material he found funny or cool.

Rounding out the original team was Jack Shepherd, who came from PETA, the animal rights group, where he worked in the marketing department. His expertise was in composing promotional materials chock-full of images of tenderhearted animals to tug at donors' hearts and purse strings. Shepherd approached his job with the rigor of a scholar. He appreciated that critter pictures possessed a tremendous degree of nuance, and he understood that, when done right, they could be enormously evocative. Shepherd realized that by serving up the right visuals, he had the power to recast the grim issue of species extinction in a new and infectiously uplifting light. He created a website that rebranded fish as "sea kittens." The idea was funny enough to spark a few conversations, and before he knew it, a few became a few million, and from newspapers to radio to TV to the web the media world buzzed about sea kittens. At BuzzFeed he'd perform a similar function, though without the activist bent. He was given the title "Beastmaster."

Stopera, the baby of the group, relied on BuzzFeed's Trend-Detector as well as publicly available tools like Google Trends, which displayed the most popular queries of its search engine. With these tools, he would know whenever some new controversy or personality seized hold of the pop culture conversation. The inspiration for his very first BuzzFeed post, for example, was an uptick of popular interest in Jill Biden, specifically her appearance, during the lead-up to the 2008 presidential election. His write-up was simple: seven links to pictures and fawning comments about the surprising beauty of Joe Biden's wife, a grandmother. Stopera's come-on: "Dare I say GILF?"

"It was like going through a lot of crap and making a punchline," Stopera recalled of the early days. "It was just a traffic game." The spirit of gamesmanship infused the Canal Street office with a footloose energy and was further stoked by the shared understanding that nothing they published would be taken too seriously. Every so often, Peretti would announce an office-wide "sprint," for which the staff would divide into two teams and race to publish as many posts as possible on a single topic—funny babies, say, or conspiracy theories. Each time a new post went up, the author banged a gong. It was one of the many madcap methods Peretti came up with to spur his staff to be maximally productive. On Fridays he would organize "game battles," another competitive post-writing contrivance, all the wilder for the fact that it involved a steady intake of alcohol throughout the day.

When the buzz du jour was especially vulgar—like celebrities with "cameltoe"—some younger staffers were reluctant to author the post for fear that their mothers would see. Peretti adapted by giving them permission to publish under pseudonyms. (Stopera's was Crumpetz.) Writing under aliases, Peretti recognized, had the added benefit of making Buzz-Feed's staff seem larger than it actually was. Falsifying a byline is grounds for firing at most news organizations, but BuzzFeed wasn't yet trying to be a news company.

Still, most of the early team members seemed utterly unbothered by the off-color aspects of their job. When a nude photo of Kate Moss hit the internet, Wang didn't think twice before posting it on BuzzFeed, entirely uncensored. To lure the especially depraved web surfers, she tagged the post "Kate Moss orgy video," though no such video existed. Peretti too joined in the vulgar fun, publishing posts like "Penis Size Chart" and "YouTube Porn Hacks." Looking back, he told me with a note of nostalgia in his voice, "Everything was disposable."

Publishing serious news ran completely counter to BuzzFeed's founding model. But Peretti was becoming a more sober person. His wife had given birth to twins. He was the head of a company with employees who depended on him. He was about to meet with executives and potential investors from Silicon Valley, like Marc Andreessen, to begin a new round of fundraising. He'd become a businessman who now cared about money. Peretti and BuzzFeed were beginning to grow up.

As more people discovered BuzzFeed's mysterious mechanical acuity and infectiously wacky sense of humor, word of its success started generating interest in venture-capital circles, and before long, potential big-ticket investors started visiting the cramped and roach-ridden digs. One early believer was Andreessen, whose venture capital firm, Andreessen Horowitz, was probably the most important funder in Silicon Valley. "BuzzFeed was set up as a virtuous feedback loop," he told me, where tech, content, and advertising all blended. This struck him as a new model, and his firm eventually made a first investment of $50 million. Andreessen loved newspapers. He had started reading them when he was four, he said, beginning with comics, then the sports pages, then the stock tables. He had no trouble with the notion that newspapers were a blend of the entertaining and the serious.

Peretti's PowerPoint pitch to venture capital scouts emphasized that the BuzzFeed machine required little human input. It would increase traffic without hiring editors. "Raw buzz is automatically published the moment it is detected by our algorithm," the document pronounced. This would streamline the process of making content for BuzzFeed's audience, but as Peretti's presentation made clear, the audience was merely a means to attract marketers. Brands and their spokespeople were the intended beneficiaries of Peretti's trend-gauging and hit-making machine. The presentation invited them to "use BuzzFeed's tools to promote the buzz you want to."

"The future of the industry is advertising as content," he proclaimed. BuzzFeed would be not the website or outlet but rather "the agency of the future." It was first and foremost a tech company, the pitch stressed, which distinguished it from media companies that mostly made content, and from ad agencies that produced persuasion. BuzzFeed occupied the middle ground, which made the venture capitalists salivate, even as other publishers denounced it as a paramount conflict of interest that made a mockery of the fundamental separation of news from commercial storytelling.

Peretti's biggest breakthrough was seeing that technology and creativity could be offered directly to advertisers in the form of what would be called "native advertising." BuzzFeed would pursue business with advertising clients, but it wouldn't accept their spots because Peretti didn't want that clutter to distract visitors to his site. Instead it would sell them a more tailored service: BuzzFeed would have its staff create ads for the clients, in the form of signature BuzzFeed content, doing it all in-house. Native ads would be BuzzFeed's only ads until 2017, when new economic winds forced Peretti to change models again. Creating viral content and viral ads was BuzzFeed's core.

Could a site driven by the values of advertising and technology for the purpose of spreading buzzy tidbits like social viruses ever be a source of serious news? Peretti was, as always, restless for a new frontier, a new ground to test more of his hypotheses.

CHAPTER TWO

VICE I

The notion that news, especially when delivered by the aging, all-knowing anchors of broadcast news, had become a stodgy turn-off to anyone below the age of 35 had also animated the rise of another new media mogul, Shane Smith. Having beaten his path to the cutting edge not through the laboratory, like Peretti, but via the underground cultural scene, Smith never tired of telling the story of his rags-to-riches odyssey, which he often embroidered.

In 1994 Smith graduated from Canada's Carleton University in his hometown of Ottawa with little notion of what he would do next. He knocked around Europe for a while and dreamed of becoming a novelist.

One of his best friends from home was Gavin McInnes, a tree planter who drew cartoons in his spare time. At Carleton they had played together in a band called Leatherassbuttfuk. This much was true.

While the old media barons like Henry Luce incubated their creations at elite universities like Yale, Smith's origin story was hard to pin down. Wearing long dark hair, an earring, and a beard, he loved portraying his rebellious early years. "When I was young I was in kind of a quasi-gang," he said. "And then by the time I was eighteen, you know, nine had died. So I would just get wasted and get into fights and screw and smash things. I didn't care." He described his family as "dirt poor." McInnes, who had a falling-out with Smith in the mid-2000s, said all of this was an exaggeration. Smith also told *Playboy* that after college he was a war correspondent in Bosnia and the *Financial Times* that he was a currency hedger in Hungary, but a friend from those days said he spent the time loafing in Budapest.

Smith returned to Canada and at a bar met Suroosh Alvi, whose family was Pakistani. Alvi was a recovering heroin addict, newly released from rehab, and a music lover who shared his new friend's gritty love for underground culture. Through a friend in his Narcotics Anonymous group, he had just gotten a job as the editor of a local alternative monthly newspaper focused on hipster culture, and he had hired McInnes after seeing the comic book he was working on, called *Pervert*, and taking a particular liking to a strip about heroin. Finally sober after a nearly decade-long period he called his "dark years," Alvi was finding a viable substitute for his addiction in an obscure corner of publishing known as hate literature, magazines that trafficked in antifeminism, spotlighted human deformities, and glorified rape and violence. The stash of titles he pored over in his parents' basement offered a veritable encyclopedia of taboo takes: magazines like *Sewer Cunt*, *Fuck Magazine*, and *Murder Can Be Fun*. "Everything else was so boring to read," he later said, "and this stuff actually felt alive because it was seething with hate."

Having displayed in Europe a bit of a knack for sales, Smith thought he could run the business with Alvi. Drunk at the bar, slurring his speech, Smith was enthusiastic, if not altogether coherent, in describing his vision for the trio to "take over the world." McInnes said he could write the copy. He fancied himself the wordsmith of the three.

Almost on a whim, the trio applied for funding from a nonprofit agency in Haiti, of all places, called Images Interculturelles. To qualify, they had to be on welfare, which took little finessing, since they were already living on a steady rice-and-beans diet and sleeping on friends' floors. When the Haiti funding dried up, they each asked their parents to kick in $5,000.

They worked in the loft where they lived, in spartan fashion, sleeping on futons and eating canned food. At night they indulged in their vices: drugs, drink, and women. Smith told one of his girlfriends that he was dying of a mystery illness, maintaining the lie for over a year. "They were feral," said one woman who knew them. Though Smith would come to court respectability, his company never shook the misogyny at its roots.

Voice of Montreal, their free counterculture newspaper, debuted in October 1994 with an interview with Johnny Rotten of the Sex Pistols, an impressive get for a brand-new publication. During the early years, McInnes said, he wrote 80 percent of the copy and made up fake bylines so it looked like they had a real staff. "You need more blacks, you need more women writing," people would tell him. "In order to meet those demands, I eventually decided to become those blacks and women." Since McInnes would later become the far-right founder of an antifeminist fraternal order, the role-playing was quite a stretch. At the time the paper launched, he and his partners hated anything that smacked of political correctness, especially feminism.

They ran an issue with advertisements featuring pubic hair on the back cover and left a bunch of copies around the gay and lesbian center at Carleton, their alma mater, knowing it would stir a reaction. And sure enough, the administration banned the publication, touching off a campus debate about censorship and earning *Voice of Montreal* some welcome publicity.

One early story, headlined "Was Jesus a Fag?," landed McInnes a spot on *Politically Incorrect* with Bill Maher. He came out of the green room stammering drunk and drooled all over one of the women guests. Almost all the magazine's cover stories were equally provocative: "Retards and Hip Hop," "Pregnant Lesbians," "80s Coke Sluts." After one of the countless times its editors were accused of sexism, this time for featuring nude porn stars, they responded to critics by posing nude for the next issue.

Needless to say, none of this was journalism. They were producing an entertaining, purposely offensive lad mag at a time when *Maxim* and others were in vogue. Smith and McInnes would ingest a bunch of uppers to produce each month's magazine, then, once the issue hit the stands, they'd need to unwind with their relaxant of choice, mescaline. They eschewed the notion of objectivity and just-the-facts reportage and maintained that position for years, even after they began employing a robust newsroom. "If you're looking at Vice for being news and the truth," Smith would tell the camera for a 2012 three-part day-in-the-life feature on himself that he was paying his friend to make, "then you're in trouble."

Smith, whom McInnes called "the Bullshitter," was good at selling the space in their magazine to advertisers, often by using the tactics of a scam artist. He told one potential advertiser that their publication was distributed across North America and then mailed a few hundred copies to a skate shop in Miami and another batch to a clothing store in San Francisco. He developed a perversely fraternal rapport with the men in advertising departments and to win their business would send them "cool" goodies in the mail. (Some, unsurprisingly, were illicit.) His strategy for sealing deals with the women clients, he bragged, was to take them to bed.

Smith pursued the growth of his business like a man possessed. When he went to Ottawa to get the magazine established there, he called McInnes and Alvi at 4 a.m. and shouted, at the top of his lungs, "We're going to be huge!"

When the local Montreal paper came by their office to do an interview, the partners lied, claiming that they were courting investors, including Larry Flynt, the strip-club and skin-magazine magnate, and Richard Szalwinski, one of the richest men in Montreal, whose pockets were flush from the dot-com boom. As they would later tell it, when Szalwinski read the article, he called them. "Who are you fucking guys?" he demanded. He ended up inviting them to lunch at a restaurant he owned. When they got there, one of Smith's partners confessed up front, "Shane's hungover." Szalwinski looked at Smith, sizing him up. "Oh, you drink?" he asked. Smith didn't miss a beat: "Oh, I can drink." Szalwinski then presented a full bottle of Jack Daniels and challenged him to finish it before the meeting ended. Smith made it halfway, then sat through lunch trying his best to clinch an investment.

A few days later they went back to Szalwinski with a formal contract that, between the doodles, proffered a valuation of their company at a preposterous $4 million. Szalwinski was dubious. "That's a lot of money," he said. But he signed it and had his minions whisk them off, promising an up-front $50,000 for each founder, to hold them over. Smith kept his cool till they were safely out of earshot, then took off running in circles, baying joyfully. They flaunted their big break by throwing a blowout bash at which they wore rented mascot costumes without their accompanying character masks, inflated cartoon figures with tiny heads. But Smith and McInnes did too much cocaine and found it impossible to have a good time in the ridiculous costumes.

Shane Smith certainly was a bullshitter, but he had the moxie to make his exaggerated boasts come true, and as they did, his new boasts got bigger. In his gambit with Szalwinski he saw a blueprint for his future: over the decade that followed, his home-cooked valuation of the company would inflate so steadily and determinedly that the market eventually bought it, making him a billionaire.

As the founders of *Voice* told the story, Szalwinski's cash injection, which made him the majority owner, financed the magazine's relocation to New York. (Szalwinski later told *Wired* magazine that he doesn't remember reading the article and that his investment was a few hundred thousand dollars.) Smith, McInnes, and Alvi could scarcely believe their luck. They found a loft in Chelsea and, lest their work-life balance be upended, splurged on a mountaintop getaway in Costa Rica. With the move to New York, they would have to rename the magazine or risk getting sued by the *Village Voice*. They dropped the "o" from *Voice* and decided they liked the name better in all caps: *VICE*. After a strike at their printing plant, they abandoned newsprint for glossy paper. "When we got it back," Smith remembered, "it was like the coming of the Holy Grail."

"When we initially moved to the U.S. we were faced with a choice,"

Smith told an interviewer: "Go mainstream or only print enough copies for cool kids." Going mainstream would mean competing with the likes of *Rolling Stone* and *Spin*, magazines that already had a lock on the mass market of music and pop culture.

"We realized if we were going to try to go mass," Smith said, "and try to go for a million copies, we were going to have to dilute how we wrote and how we did everything." Instead they doubled down on catering to the cool kids and consciously kept their circulation number lower than market demand. They printed 150,000 issues to distribute across the U.S. and similarly small batches overseas, in Japan, then the U.K., then Germany. "We got to a million copies that way," Smith said. Each of those cool kids would pass their issue on to six or eight friends, expanding the magazine's circulation by word of mouth.

McInnes was always pushing the limits of bad taste. In 1999 *Vice* published "The Racist Issue." He had previously thought up a popular monthly feature called "Fashion Dos and Don'ts," and "The Racist Issue" featured four different models with exaggerated features that were obvious racial stereotypes. A young Chinese man with fake buck teeth appeared in a coolie hat as he made a kung fu pose; an African Canadian was dressed as a "mammy." The spread featured a bald woman giving the Nazi salute with a KKK doll. A few advertisers pulled out, costing the company $10,000.

While they focused on expanding the magazine, they diversified the brand. The Montreal magnate's investment gave *Vice* leeway to branch into retail, and they opened stores in Manhattan—on Lafayette and Prince—and in Toronto, Montreal, and Los Angeles, selling streetwear labels like Stüssy. At one point they owned two warehouses full of skater clothes. There was also a Vice record label.

"It paid to be perceived as edgy," Smith wrote. "We were literally buying up the phenomenon that was streetwear . . . stores, magazines, clothing companies, the works. We actually had letters of intent to buy companies that were fucking 10 times our size." McInnes asserted, "This is the first time young people have had a revolution that involves them getting paid." Szalwinski's investment encouraged Smith to think bigger, given the infinite potential of the internet, which had a low investment entry barrier. They envisaged a "multichannel brand" with a state-of-the-art website.

The brand, however, was elusive. Smith's formula was for Vice to be a bad-boy brand, but its laddie magazine was also a kind of bible for hipsters. And he didn't want to scare away advertisers and investors. When he moved into news, he applied the same formula. There would be serious, worthy work, but it would be subsidized by plenty of sex, drugs, and rock 'n' roll.

This momentum would come to a halt, as Smith would relate it, when Szalwinski fell victim to the dot-com bust. Vice appears to have been one of his few holdings to survive, but he couldn't keep funding it, and they were nowhere close to being profitable. Smith, Alvi, and McInnes struck an agreement to buy the company back from Szalwinski and moved to Brooklyn, where they got back to being poor and punk, without even an internet connection. But before Szalwinski could sell them back his stake, he went missing. The three hunted him down in Nantucket, where he showed up in a Mercedes with its power steering shot, appropriately symbolic. "What the fuck is going on?" they demanded. Szalwinski confessed he couldn't fund them anymore. Alvi recalled the absurdity of Szalwinski's hosting them for a steak dinner before sending them off the island.

Determined to save their little company, Smith and Alvi threw themselves into the business of selling ads while McInnes stuck to editorial. "Those guys had a real struggle, trying to get people to buy ads and market the Vice brand," McInnes recalled. "I was still writing the Vice 'Guide to Eating Pussy' and having a great time."

Vice's edginess could still be a liability. Despite expanding circulation, many mainstream brands still refused to advertise. Beer companies had signed on, but getting fashion ads from good labels was beyond reach. The trio had not yet found the right balance between underground rebellion and entrepreneurship. It was harder than they thought to pull off what Alvi called "punk-rock capitalism."

If advertisers remained wary of the magazine, the hipsters loved it. It was much edgier than BuzzFeed, with its cuddly "No Haters" ethos. It was a shameless assertion of masculine id, the epitome of a new brand of North American lad culture. Vice was shocking, transgressive, seductive; the devil opposite BuzzFeed's angel on readers' shoulders. An undeniable undercurrent of hatred ran through its pages, with half-baked reportage on depraved situations "and other manifestations of the societal underbelly from the perspective of their perpetrators," as Casper Hoedemækers has written. Early issues featured writing by a friend of the founders, Robbie Dillon, whom McInnes described as a "loan shark ex-con," on what life in prison is like. Once, Dillon brought them a story that would have been Vice's first true blockbuster scoop: in Canada's biggest drug bust ever, 35 tons of hash had been seized but only 27 tons disclosed, as dirty cops had secretly funneled the remaining eight tons to their informant as a payoff. The issue had already been sent to the printer when Dillon reappeared to demand they kill the cover story. They were reluctant at first, but Dillon produced a shoebox of cash, and that settled it. "So he gave it to us and we divided it up, spent it, and ran 'Interview with a Potato' or something like that instead," Smith later said. "No big deal."

As its readership grew internationally, its coverage broadened to include gonzo-style tale-telling and other absurd, often bacchanalian stories from foreign destinations. There were also kernels of what could be seen as journalism, reports from exotic locales and profiles of various subcultures.

By the spring of 2001 *Vice* was more popular with readers in their 20s than were famous "trendsetting" monthlies with more than 10 times the circulation, according to the Cassandra Report, a marketing survey. Within two years *Vice* was no longer in financial straits.

Still, its notorious reputation could make life hard for writers. Music writer Amy Kellner described her attempt to profile an all-female band called Bratmobile in an article titled "Rebel Girls: The Time Bratmobile Hurt My Feelings." In the article, Kellner explained how she was refused an interview because of *Vice*'s sexist reputation, despite the fact that she was friends with the band.

Kellner tried to explain to Bratmobile that *Vice* was "operating in an ideal fantasy world where you can poke fun at every kind of stereotypical 'identity' group and it's just all in good fun." The explanation fell flat. "The girls each began to list the various affronts they'd either read firsthand or just heard about. Advertisements for skater clothes featuring porn models were mentioned, as well as an article where girls tell of their experiences of being raped. I could come up with defenses or explanations for those things but I wasn't sure how much I wanted to stand behind them." The band told Kellner she couldn't be a real feminist as long as she stayed at *Vice*, and she silently agreed. "I hate me," she confessed.

When Alvi was interviewed about the Bratmobile contretemps by Toronto's *Globe and Mail*, he lashed out at the band. "Their non-approval is emblematic of everything we despise about the last decade—uptight PC counterproductive thought, a form of liberal fascism that promotes censorship rather than freedom of expression at the end of the day." *Vice* fashioned itself a rebuke to political correctness. While traditional news companies mostly leaned left and were careful not to insult any reader constituencies, *Vice* flaunted its offensiveness. To the founders, staying punk was a business principle, though McInnes's insistence on championing the posture in its logical extreme—telling the *New York Times* in 2003, for example,

" 'No means no' is puritanism"—would ultimately become an obstacle to his partners' ambitions.

Vice had already sent its issue to the printers when Osama bin Laden struck the United States. In a letter to the editor right after the 9/11 attack, one reader pleaded, "I hope and I pray that you don't do some asinine piss take on the World Trade Center tragedy that took place on Sept. 11th. This is not a time for your irreverent and cruel take on things. You can't make fun of this. In a sense your magazine is over now."

Vice responded in typical form in its next edition: "This issue was on the way to the printers when the attack happened. It was, coincidentally, our most vapid issue in six years. . . . Some of the staff here was concerned with the juxtaposition of wasted partying and this monumental tragedy but fuck it—life goes on."

Alvi had once said, "*Vice* had to be a well-balanced combination of smart and stupid content—stupid done in a smart way and smart done in a stupid way." The response to 9/11 was clearly stupid done stupid.

They were taking in $350,000 in ads per issue and had a circulation of 150,000—decent but hardly breathtaking. A full-page color ad cost $6,500, which was peanuts by the standards of the *New York Times* or *Time* magazine, where a single page could fetch $100,000. Despite Smith's best efforts, he was still struggling to get big-name advertisers. A letter from a *Time* executive, responding to a pitch from a *Vice* ad sales person, summed up the stigma it was working against.

Dear Suroosh,

   Ann Moore passed along your package on Vice Magazine. While I am a fan (knew about Vice via one of my kids), it won't work for Time Inc.: too edgy for our mainstream advertisers, too likely to get chucked out of Walmart (where we make one-third of our newsstand sales). Many thanks for sending along, best of luck.

   Yours Sincerely,

   Isolde Motley

   Corporate Editor, Time Inc.

Vice published the letter in the next issue. It was a clever pose, dissing the corporate mainstream while attempting to sell to it. But the delicate dance would end in a tight embrace that required *Vice* to shed part of its radical identity and cede a measure of creative independence to multinational marketers. As Smith sought to shore up control over the magazine's editorial operations, a struggle broke out between him and McInnes. Smith and Alvi already had concluded that McInnes's overt racism, Nazi imagery, and misogyny were too risky at a time they were trying to rebuild the business. The relationship was nearing the breaking point.

Outside of *Vice*, McInnes's politics were increasingly toxic. He wrote a column in *The American Conservative*, a magazine run by Pat Buchanan, calling young people a bunch of knee-jerk liberals (a phrase McInnes and his ilk often used) who would believe anyone with dark skin over anyone with light skin. He lamented the liberal views of his magazine's readers, saying they were "brainwashed by communist propaganda." In an interview with the *Times* in 2003, he said, "I love being white and I think it's something to be very proud of," adding, "I don't want our culture diluted. We need to close the borders now and let everyone assimilate to a western, white, English-speaking way of life." Such utterings were unlikely to open doors for Smith to land new business, and he was beginning to have a bigger vision for his company.

Although *Vice* was still a street brand, its focus was shifting and so was its platform. In 2006 Spike Jonze, the award-winning filmmaker and avid skateboarder, picked up a copy of the magazine on the floor of a sandwich shop. He liked what he read and decided to cold-call the main office in Brooklyn. An early recruit, Eddy Moretti, answered the call, and soon he, Smith, and Jonze were lunching together at a Williamsburg diner nearby. Impressed by Smith's vividly told stories of exotic locales, Jonze offered some advice. "You guys are going around the world doing these insane stories, buying dirty bombs in Bulgaria or wherever," he said. "I hope you're bringing a video camera." Of course they were, Smith bullshitted, then got the check, ran back to his office, and ordered a bunch of equipment.

At 36, Jonze already boasted a dazzling curriculum vitae as a filmmaker, directing critically acclaimed movies such as *Being John Malkovich* and *Adaptation*. For the small screen he made commercials, music videos, and shows on MTV. He had a knack for the visual realm, a cinematic cognition. He could see in his mind's eye that Smith's vision for *Vice* was meant to be visual. He wasn't sure where or how it would be best to broadcast its unique point of view, but he knew it had to be seen.

Jonze's past projects blurred the line between home video and professional production. His work was distinguished by the raw, often grainy texture of his shots and editing that lent it the pulse of punk authenticity. Blond and bespectacled, Jonze was Central Casting's hipster, the physical opposite of his new alter ego. While Smith was dark-haired and portly with a goatee,

Jonze had perpetual bedhead and was rail-thin. While Smith had grown up relatively poor, Jonze was the heir to the multibillion-dollar Spiegel Catalog fortune, raised in Bethesda, Maryland, where as a teen he worked in a dirt-bike shop. His mohawk earned him the moniker Spike, bestowed on him by his bike-shop coworkers in what Jonze took to be a reference to his street cred. He much preferred that to the legacy-laden family name.

In 1999, the same year Jonze made *Being John Malkovich*, he married Sofia Coppola, the talented director and daughter of the legendary Francis Ford Coppola. They wed at her father's vineyard, with Tom Waits providing the soundtrack. Their nuptials were the "it" wedding of the year, certified by a spread in *Vogue*, but Jonze, holding fast to his air of mystique, some-how managed not to appear in any of the photos.

His family wealth and his own ambivalence toward fame notwithstand-ing, there was much about Jonze's hipster persona that put him on com-mon ground with Smith. He had skipped college and moved to California to start working for a BMX magazine, *Freestylin'*. When the BMX fad faded, he found his place in the equally tattooed and scabby skateboard-ing community. He founded a magazine for boarders and another more general-interest publication called *Dirt*, for young men like himself. As a skilled skateboarder, he was well-suited to making videos, and unlike most other videographers he could keep pace with pros on a skateboard, even while manning the camera. His early skate videos became cult classics, and as he gained stature, he linked up with other tastemakers like Jeff Tremaine, whose *Big Brother* magazine was pushing the envelope of underground youth culture. Tremaine also dabbled in skateboarding videos, and intro-duced Jonze to a group of maniac misfits and masochists whose stunts were more dangerous than artful: the lovable deadbeat Bam, a former clown with a cocaine addiction named Steve-O, a dwarf they called Wee Man, and their fearless frontman Johnny Knoxville.

With Tremaine, Knoxville, and characters like them, Jonze created the hit MTV show *Jackass*. Over the three seasons the show aired, it was a touchstone of youth culture, laddie entertainment in its purest form. The on-screen participants flung themselves into pits of slithering anacondas, snorted wads of wasabi, got tattoos in the back of fast-moving off-road ve-hicles, and locked themselves into brimming Porta Potties rigged to bungee cords that launched them 80 feet into the air. The content was deemed so injurious that each segment began and ended with a warning not to try this at home. Many viewers couldn't help themselves, however, and several died in the process, causing Senator Joseph Lieberman to call for Congress to censure MTV for its complicity in the recklessness. Nevertheless the show continued to air, and the audience flocked to it like rubberneckers at a 10-car pileup. By 2007 *Jackass* had spawned six different spinoff shows, four feature-length films, and a video game.

In format, *Jackass* marked a departure from the tidy half-hour reality shows that predominated among the televised programming of its day. Each episode strung together a dozen or so shakily filmed stunts—one-offs that trafficked in slapstick shock and awe, one after another in a sequence unbound by narrative trajectory. The show was a mélange of gut-wrenching clips that did not necessarily relate to one another but rather felt like compiled footage. Each clip could take on a life of its own, beyond the airtime it got on the network. And with the advent of websites that hosted online video, the moment was fast approaching when such clips would be able to find vast audiences without ever needing to be aired on TV in the first place.

There was another area in which Jonze had injected hipness and edge for profit: advertising. Although he was becoming a film auteur, earning big bucks to create TV spots for selected brands was a great way to get rich and extend his own brand. In 2002 he created a commercial for the Swedish dorm-room DIY furniture chain, Ikea, that became an instant cult classic. Silly as it was, the Ikea ad, created by Crispin Porter + Bogusky and directed by Jonze, illustrated the power of basic storytelling, and brands loved it. Like Peretti at BuzzFeed, Jonze was on the frontier of a new form of "native advertising" that mimicked narrative journalism and movies. *Vice* too was soon signing clients to six-figure contracts.

The dawn of web publishing brought with it the unbundling of the newspaper package. Readers who had once been forced to purchase the entire paper to access any of its contents no longer faced that all-or-nothing choice. Each individual article now lived on its own web page, where it had a unique URL and could be shared, and spread virally. This put stories, rather than papers, in competition with one another. And just as news organizations were getting used to digital publishing, there arose a new disruptive force. YouTube would lead a revolution in the realm of video content.

A clip from an episode of *Jackass* or one of Jonze's skateboarding videos or quirky ads might air on television and be seen by a live audience of a few hundred thousand viewers, but then it either faded from memory or cost the network hefty sums to re-air. The same clip, uploaded for free to YouTube, would live on the site indefinitely and could rack up millions and millions of views through the years, reaching audiences who did not have a cable hookup. Like Twitter, which launched the next year, YouTube had immediacy and authenticity, both often missing from local and national TV news. And unlike cable, YouTube was a free and open platform.

Like Facebook, YouTube moved swiftly from garage experiment in San Bruno, California, in 2005 to worldwide sensation. With the slogan "Tune In, Hook Up," YouTube was basically a video dating service. The idea was that strangers would film themselves and send in the footage for the chance to be judged by a community of people they had never met and might never see in person. When this turned out to be a tough sell, the founders, Chad Hurley, Steve Chen, and Jawed Karim, veterans of the online bill-paying service PayPal, broadened their approach.

They knew the world of online video was wide open. When they searched the web for video clips of two highly publicized events, they found nothing. One was the tsunami that ravaged coastal communities along the Indian Ocean in 2004; the other was Janet Jackson's infamous "wardrobe malfunction" during the Super Bowl halftime show earlier that year. Both were indelibly imprinted on the collective memory of anyone with a cable hookup, but online there was hardly a trace of either besides written accounts and some still photography.

That spring the site opened itself to video uploading, this time without the stipulation that videos be romantic. They hoped it would catch on better than the dating site, but they were apprehensive as to whether anyone would take the bait. But the uploads came streaming in to the renovated site faster than its servers could accept them. They scrambled to buy more servers, taking care to stretch the seed money they'd solicited as far as possible.

The volume of untapped demand was staggering; or was it untapped supply? It was as if people had been saving up entire lives' worth of home-video footage, waiting for the chance to screen it for the wider world. In three months the site celebrated the first viral YouTube hit. Unlike most of the site's videos, this one wasn't homemade: it was a brand ad produced by Nike, in which the Brazilian soccer superstar Ronaldinho tried on a new pair of cleats and performed seemingly impossible feats of skill. But which videos became sensations was not always so predictable. Alongside Ronaldinho's showcase was another viral video called "Bus Uncle," of a Hong Kong man exploding in anger at a fellow passenger who asked him to keep his voice down on his cell phone.

For the most part, the uploads were in keeping with the site's new slogan, "Broadcast Yourself"—hortatory spiels and tangential rants shot and (lightly) edited by amateurs on fuzzy, low-resolution webcams in the depths of their basements. But it didn't take long for users to discover the loopholes this new service exposed and begin exploiting them before the authorities could get wise. YouTube's open call for submissions made it easier than ever for any average Joe with a camcorder to tape shows on network television and upload their bootleg version to the site, undermining the revenue models of the networks and violating their copyright.

After YouTube was up and running for a few months, people at the networks began poring through its endless listings and found, to their horror, segments they had paid to produce. This was piracy! Or was it aggregation? One clip in particular, a music video spoof from *Saturday Night Live* called "Lazy Sunday," starring Andy Samberg, who just so happened to have been Jonah Peretti's elementary-school carpool buddy, had been posted to YouTube and was spreading virally. Considering whether to clamp down on the content theft or negotiate a deal with the website hosting it, the networks wisely chose the latter. They set a precedent: the disruptive new online broadcaster would become a vital distribution outlet for the TV networks, and professional content would live side by side with no-budget frivolity.

The rapid flattening of the broadcasting landscape affected more than just the entertainment sector. It drastically changed the way breaking news was disseminated. Anyone could play. The middlemen and gatekeepers, the professional news editors, were being cut out.

Developments of this scope caught the attention of Google, whose scouts were always looking for acquisitions to bolster the company's portfolio. In October 2006, just after Jonze and Smith found each other, Google announced it was acquiring YouTube for $1.65 billion in stock—a windfall for the founders of the year-old site, and a pittance for Google, which already had triple the market capitalization of the next-biggest media company. "This is the next step in the evolution of the internet," declared Google's CEO, Eric Schmidt. The site was attracting a daily average of 100 million video views, and some 65,000 new videos a day were uploaded by virtual nobodies. Schmidt called them "the broadcasters of tomorrow."

YouTube made a frictionless connection between content creators and their audience. It had immediacy and authenticity. It provided news and information unmediated by anchors or news editors who still reigned at CNN and decided which footage was worth viewers' time. In August 2006 an engineer at Lockheed Martin discovered major defects in the ships his employer was manufacturing for the Coast Guard, and after his bosses, government investigators, congressmen, and mainstream media outlets ignored his whistleblowing, he sat down at his computer and delivered his testimony to YouTube, where it could no more be smothered than could wild-fire. Four years later his whistleblower lawsuit was settled by Lockheed for an undisclosed sum. The next year footage recorded on a cell phone camera of Saddam Hussein's execution found its way onto the website.

Since its founding by Ted Turner in 1980, CNN had seen its audience balloon during the first Gulf War and then again after 9/11. Its website, launched in 1995, had become the third biggest global source of news by 2009. But its cable audience was aging, the expense of running a 24-hour news channel was exploding, and CNN's reputation had been tarnished by controversies, including the retraction in 1998 of a special investigation into the use of sarin gas during the Vietnam War era.

Unlike CNN, YouTube ranged wisely and news was a small portion of the videos found on the platform. A proud mother from Ontario began uploading videos of her 12-year-old son's talent-show performances and found an audience that grew to include talent scouts and music executives, who signed the young boy, Justin Bieber, to a label. When the race for the presidency rolled around, seven of the 16 candidates announced their 2008 campaigns on YouTube. The site collaborated with CNN to host two de-bates, with questions submitted by everyday citizens in the form of You-Tube videos. They called it "The World's Largest Town Halls." YouTube was becoming a major news platform.

Like the other emergent social media platforms, YouTube could also be a dark place. It hosted recruiting videos of an al-Qaeda militant, Anwar al-Awlaki, inciting his followers to violent acts. YouTube did make efforts to take down terrorist propaganda, but like Facebook it did not want to assume the role that journalists play in editing or take responsibility for the material that was posted. Nor did it make content itself. It made instant stars out of tod-dlers ("Charlie Bit My Finger") and academics speaking at TED conferences.

In 2005, when bombs exploded in the London Underground, tradi-tional broadcasters couldn't cover the destruction quickly enough. The BBC deputized citizens as stringers and received thousands of images and text-message reports from YouTube. When protests erupted in Burma later that year and the government barred journalists from entering the country, a legion of local bloggers exposed the military's campaign against its peo-ple. A true endorsement from the media establishment came in 2008, when YouTube won a Peabody, broadcasting's most prestigious award, for "pro-moting a free exchange of ideas" in a way that "both embodies and pro-motes democracy."

The earthquake in Nepal, the *Charlie Hebdo* shootings in Paris, and popular uprisings like the Green Revolution, the Arab Spring, and the protests in Ferguson, Missouri, could be seen on YouTube almost as they unfolded, from the unprocessed point of view of those present. Cell phone videos of police violence, uploaded to YouTube, were transforming the criminal justice system. And there wasn't just news content: by mid-2010 the site was attracting a viewership nearly double the combined primetime audience of America's three biggest TV networks. (To be sure, broadcasters have long argued that online video numbers are inflated by including more casual viewers.)

YouTube became the world's living archive, a democratically populated database of citizen-level perspectives on the globe at large. *Vice*, holding fast to its fight-the-power cachet and unfettered rebel spirit, found common cause with the upstart social platform, as both sought to upend the top-down elitism that the news networks tacitly enforced. By 2008, *Vice*'s cool-kids-only growth strategy was paying off, as the magazine's circulation had almost reached Smith's goal of one million copies and reached 22 countries. He bragged that within three hours of issues hitting newsstands, they all disappeared from the face of the earth. His magazine was the toast of global hipsterdom and his record label was signing hot bands. He was bringing the brand to new markets where crowds greeted him with adoration.

Smith knew he could sell more magazines, but *Vice*, as a print product, was never meant for a mass audience. From inception it had stuck to its young, city-dwelling demographic: "urban hipsters that are well-educated, rich and all that comes with it," as Smith put it. But the ground was shifting, and he saw the opportunity to go well beyond that small subset. The new readers, Smith said, "spend a lot of time online finding out cool shit, you know, the suburban or secondary market, little-city kind of kids, wanna-be cool kids that don't know much about anything . . . the huge disenfranchised group of young people from say Oklahoma or Kansas City who don't know and aren't really interested in politics beyond 'I don't like this thing happening to me.'"

Few news companies had figured out video's place in their offerings, and none had yet figured out YouTube, even forward-leaning sites such as BuzzFeed. At the *New York Times*, video accompanied more print stories, but it was watched by few readers. For *Vice*'s online version, Jonze envisioned video content that would be a cross between hard news and entertainment—video documentaries that took audiences to places in new ways. "Let's go to places and learn and be more humanistic than journalistic," he told Smith. To sound like a real channel, he and Smith named their endeavor Vice Broadcasting System, or VBS.tv, as they would call it. Jonze also wanted to bring aboard his friend Knoxville. Soon they found themselves in the slums of Rio, shooting material for what they called *The Vice Guide to Travel*. With characteristic bravado, they sold VBS as the antithesis of everything corporate media stood for, a menace to the powers that be and a force of liberation for fed-up youth. "Rescuing you from television's deathlike grip," they promised.

Engagement—staying on a website or reading an article to the end—was becoming harder. The author David Foster Wallace had called the information environment "total noise," and it was getting harder to pierce it to command a loyal audience. *Vice* had proven it could win engagement in text and video. Now, with YouTube opening new vistas, Smith could take his company to the next level. Brands were hungry for ads that young people would watch till the end. Jonze and Smith knew how to make them. Jonze was installed as creative director of *Vice*. He was becoming the understudy for the role McInnes used to play in Smith's buddy movie.

Now it was cool to market Vice as a video brand. Its content, like most everything else on the Web, was free on Vice.com and its YouTube channels on music and other cultural topics. They hoped fans would subscribe, and as they did in greater and greater numbers, the company was able to get a concrete sense of its audience. Without YouTube, Vice would have little distribution for its new videos. But Smith knew that YouTube was hungry for web-only original content like his, and he managed to get the video service to pay for some of it.

Jonze wanted bigger production budgets for VBS and suggested working with MTV, with whom he had a track record. The network's parent company, Viacom, coughed up a big enough investment to get them going. "They gave me a pitch of '60 Minutes' meets 'Jackass,'" recalls the MTV executive who green-lighted the idea. From the beginning, Vice's video unit was determined to subvert the dry and prepackaged programming that dominated network television and be raw. So before they could overthink it, they set off on a mission to find the precipice of civilized society.

The Vice Guide to Travel, for which the site's correspondents visited destinations that were anything but vacation-friendly, was the first big project. They sent Derrick Beckles to embed with Nazi descendants in the Paraguayan redoubt of Nueva Germania. Trace Crutchfield went to the drug lord–run slums of Rio de Janeiro, David Choe to the Congo to hunt for dinosaurs and peep at pygmy pornography. McInnes and comedian David Cross were dispatched to China, where they donned Uncle Sam costumes and holed up in a sports bar to watch the Super Bowl while eating dog meat. Smith visited Chernobyl, where he measured the radiation with a Geiger counter and fired machine-gun rounds at buildings overrun by mutant boars. Alvi went to Pakistan for a tour of the world's largest illegal gun markets, where locals described the desire of terrorists to drink the blood of Americans; Jonze pronounced the story "gnarly."

At the time, Freston, the CEO of Viacom who had co-created MTV, became a mentor. Though he didn't have a drop of journalism blood, he soon had time on his hands: in September 2006 Viacom forced him out with a $59 million golden parachute. Smith made him Vice's first outside board member.

In 2008 the breaking point with McInnes finally arrived. He too would be given a parachute, albeit a far more modest one. He went on to land a contract with Fox News and wrote some books, including a memoir, *How to Piss in Public,* with a few chapters devoted to *Vice.* His hurt and anger were palpable.

Smith had outgrown his roots in Canada. He'd written a movie with Jonze that was going into production. His company had outposts in New York, Montreal, London, Australia, Scandinavia, Italy, Germany, and Japan. He had proven that hipster culture was a viable international export. Now, if Vice could attract the global brands that were also marketing to the youth audience, the company could grow more aggressively.

Smith spent the year globetrotting with a small camera crew, blazing an itinerary that put him in contention for the mantle of World's Most Interesting Man. He consorted with gun-waving dancehall mobs in the slums of Kingston, Jamaica, for the annual Passa Passa party and went to Pyongyang, North Korea, where his government-issued tour guides took exception to his antics. The rest of the delegation, the Koreans could tell, were journalists. But Smith, not so much.

"Their default position for something they don't understand is 'Oh, they're spies,'" he later told an interviewer. "So, they took our cameras, went through them, took them apart and wouldn't let us go anywhere. We finally got drunk with them one night and they asked, 'What're you doing here?' And I'm like, 'Oh, I'm trying to be a movie star.' And then they go, 'Oh, OK, fine.' And then I could do whatever I wanted after that."

Though a movie star he was not, Smith *was* aspiring to a certain brand of video stardom, and already he was seeing the payoff. From North Korea he went to Beijing, where locals kept approaching him in bars. "Hey, I know you," they would say. "You're from VBS!"

By the middle of 2007 Vice's videos were reaching more people than its magazine. Smith was on the cusp of becoming a new media baron. He had lived 30 years as a wild man, sometimes calling himself "the poor man's Hemingway." But he was constantly hungover. Recalling this period, he said, "There's a quote from Napoleon, which is, 'Conquest has made me, and conquest will sustain me.' And so I used to say, 'Alcohol has made me, and alcohol must sustain me.' Because everything I did—my hilarity, my lunacy, all the stories, all the crazy things I did—was all just booze-fueled." One day he woke up and recognized, "I was just sort of overweight and tired."

Beyond McInnes's extremism, other aspects of the young company's culture offended some establishment partners. One was the absence of women employees. Some were repelled by McInnes and Smith, who openly recruited women to work for the magazine with the intention of pursuing them at the office, others by freelancers like photographer Terry Richardson, who had been tainted by at least seven sexual harassment allegations since 2001. Another issue was the presence of drugs, especially cocaine, in the office. As the staff grew and its name spread, young people, men and women, were flooding the place with résumés, often volunteering to work for free. Everyone headed to the same bars after work. That was part of the appeal. Smith himself became involved with a young producer, Tamyka, whom he married in 2009. Sexual relationships within Vice were commonplace. But until the Harvey Weinstein scandal 10 years later, Smith was not held to account for his company's rampant misconduct. Sexism infused both Vice's content and culture, but in the early days no one seemed to see this as a big problem.

One female intern recalled coming back from lunch to discover the three founders in diapers sucking on baby bottles for some kind of prank. She felt uncomfortable, found them offensive, but was certainly not surprised. "This was just the culture of the place," she sighed. And since they were the bosses, there was no one to complain to.

There was always an inherent tension between maintaining an authentic voice to attract the loyalty of the millennial audience and making Vice corporate enough to build a real business. Smith always believed he could bridge the divide and pick the perfect moment to take on the ossified old media giants, especially the broadcast and cable networks.

Before most media executives, he saw that young people were not only *not* watching television news each night, but they were watching less and less TV, period. The high point for television news audiences came in the

1960s. In 1985 almost 50 million Americans watched a nightly network news program, but by 2008, when VBS was attempting to invent a new kind of documentary news, the number had declined sharply, to 29 million. The combined viewership of NBC, ABC, and CBS was about what Walter Cronkite's was when he sat in the anchor's chair and was the most trusted man in America. CNN, though it built a big audience for cable news after it started in 1980, was not stemming the tide.

The audience had splintered. There were 120 channels in 2008, whereas there had been 15 in the early 1980s. Trust was way down after a series of scandals, including CNN's retracted coverage of Operation Tailwind, leading to the downfall of its most famous correspondent, Peter Arnett, and CBS's apology for a story based on forged documents about George W. Bush's draft record, which precipitated the exit of anchor Dan Rather. A bland conformity had set into television news. To goose their ratings, all the network nightly news programs were larding themselves with celebrity gossip and other subjects deemed more entertaining than edifying. Local TV news, still the way most Americans got their news, was filled with sensationalist crime stories. "If it bleeds, it leads," was the cliché. Audience members who remained loyal were getting older and grayer.

Young people age 18 to 29 were the least likely to watch network news regularly; nearly half said they never watched the news. Almost no one in this age group could even name a network anchor. This was the same buying demographic that advertisers were desperate to reach, and it was Vice's sweet spot. Fox News, meanwhile, which Murdoch and Roger Ailes launched in 1996, was winning the hearts and minds of older, conservative viewers.

Teens and young adults were spending more and more time watching their computer screens, playing video games, and looking for snackable content. They'd been raised on television, and many preferred watching to reading. YouTube was their grand bazaar.

Vice had the right content; it only needed to crack the code of making money on YouTube. The company would need to become a content factory, for ads as well as news and entertainment. It was about to devise a digital magic formula. Or, at least, Shane Smith was good at convincing people so.

In late 2007 the august *New York Times* profiled the success of this "guerrilla video site," proclaiming, "Vice magazine has built a small media empire out of a raw, ironic sensibility, risque photographs and a willingness to deal in taboo subjects." While most of the subjects, like dope and sex, were cultural, the *Times* pointed to "a surprising number of ambitious news reports, like an interview with Hezbollah's self-proclaimed 'mayor of Beirut,' investigations of environmental abuse, and a story about a Colombian date-rape drug."

Vice's site actually had only about 200,000 unique visitors a day, plus the nascent audience on YouTube. McInnes had to laugh. His former best friend had bullshitted his way into the *Times*.

But in the ensuing five years, Smith, like Peretti, would transform his little company, building Vice on the back of the ascendancy of YouTube. The video site was overflowing with amateur uploads and bootlegged clips, and Smith saw an opportunity to mimic aspects of its alluring, uncut aesthetic while outclassing the citizen journalists with higher quality videos and stories told "from the edge." To bring along a young audience, the stories would be told from street level, often in rarely shown sites in the Third World, by people with absolutely no training in the news. Could this be the transformational vision that advertisers had been seeking to reach the bullshit-detecting young audiences they so yearned to win over? Bullshitter Shane certainly thought so.

CHAPTER THREE

NEW YORK TIMES I

I n 2007 Arthur Sulzberger Jr. was having grand visions of the *New York Times* becoming a multimedia empire. Although he had led ultimately fruitless and expensive forays into broadcast television, he fervently believed the internet opened new vistas for his family's crown jewel. The newspaper could be an information hub that fed all kinds of related endeavors, he thought, including entertainment. Quality information, in which the *Times* surpassed the abilities of other media companies, was more valuable than ever in an era of commodity news.

But the business model on which the *Times*'s future expansion hinged was badly broken. The internet had decimated newspaper advertising, and the mantra that the news should be free damaged the newspaper's other source of revenue, paid circulation. The "secular problem," as his colleagues called the digital disruption, was about to be compounded by the worst financial crisis since the Great Depression. During that earlier trauma, his great-grandfather had doubled down on news content in the paper and lowered its price to a penny. Circulation ballooned and the paper survived and prospered. During the bleak period of the 1970s, when New York's economy soured, his father had added feature sections to the *Times* that became magnets for new advertising. His son needed a similar transformational idea to secure the family patrimony and keep the *Times* alive while other family-owned chains sold or went out of business altogether.

His partner for such a bold gamble was not an industry visionary but the former general manager and head of the paper's advertising department, who, like most of her colleagues, had a purely print background. Janet Robinson, the *Times*'s CEO, was a native of Fall River, Massachusetts, an ailing coastal town; she was a former schoolteacher. Her biggest success was transforming the paper into a national force and from running the magazine division she rose through the ad department and kept climbing until being named CEO. On occasion, she spoke in an impatient tone to

Sulzberger, as if she were the teacher and he an unruly fourth grader. But if she was the teacher, she had little to teach him about the digital world crashing down on them.

The period in the mid-2000s that had been so dynamic and full of promise for technology and digital start-ups had been the most financially miserable in the *Times*'s modern history. Though Sulzberger had the support of "the Trust," the secretive eight-member order through which the Sulzberger family owned and controlled the *Times*, the unthinkable was happening: outsider shareholders were mounting a rebellion. Unhappy with Sulzberger, Robinson, and the *Times*'s sagging stock price, they represented the first real management threat to the Sulzberger-Ochs dynasty in its five generations of ownership. A dissident investor from a Morgan Stanley Investment Fund based in London had launched a proxy fight, campaigning to get other *Times* shareholders to join him in challenging the dual stock structure of the company, a strategy used by some media proprietors but less common in the wider world. There were A shares sold on the public market, and B shares, owned by the family, that were not. The B shares had voting control over 70 percent of the total shares. The dissidents also wanted to reduce Sulzberger's power—he was both chairman and publisher—by taking away one of his titles. If the dissidents won, the *Times* would cease to be the *Times*.

In only five years the *Times*'s stock had sunk from a high of $40 to $15, but the dual stock structure gave the Sulzbergers an iron hold. It would take a vote of 6–2 of the family's Trust to change it. The *Times* board of directors hired one of the priciest lawyers in New York, the mergers-and-acquisitions legend Martin Lipton of Wachtell, Lipton, Rosen & Katz, to evaluate its dual-share form of corporate governance. Lipton pronounced it healthy.

This burst of shareholder activism was a distraction at a time when the challenge to the *Times* had never been greater. Sulzberger and Robinson were trying to hold on to their 800,000-plus loyal print subscribers when newspapers were losing readership, in large part because people preferred to do their reading on computers. The print advertising base, which then accounted for the most money made by the *Times* by far, was nosediving. The growing popularity of blogs and the sudden appearance of young competitors like the Huffington Post, BuzzFeed, and Vice were a reminder that there were new stars in online publishing attracting a large audience among the prized 18–35 demographic. (The median age of the print *Times* reader in 2015 was 60.)

Sulzberger had preserved his boyish looks by staying trim through exercise, yoga, and rock-climbing. Some found his manner awkward, as if uncomfortable with what was expected of him. He was plenty smart but felt compelled to talk about the number of books he read. It got to him that people called him "Pinch" behind his back (a diminished version of his father's nickname, Punch), and because of the recent setbacks, the *New York Post* had resumed running a caricature of him with a black eye. There were also unflattering stories in *New York* magazine, the *New Yorker, Vanity Fair,* and the *Wall Street Journal.* The *Journal,* whose proprietors loved to tweak Sulzberger, also ran a weekend cover story on how some women preferred feminine-looking men, featuring an unmistakable photo of the bottom half of his face along with others. The *Journal* denied it was deliberately mocking him.

The climate was crueler than in the days of his father, the courtly and charming Punch Sulzberger, a pillar of New York society who served as board chairman of such venerable institutions as the Metropolitan Museum and Columbia University School of Journalism. The older Sulzberger was remembered as the hero who published the Pentagon Papers in the face of possible prosecution by the Nixon administration that could have ruined him and his newspaper. The son, who replaced him as publisher in 1992, didn't enjoy the same level of affection within the newsroom. But his staff recognized that times were much tougher and saw him as the protector who stood between them and dire measures, the massive job cuts that were decimating the newspaper industry. They trusted him to put the quality of the news report above anything else, a trust he had earned.

It was rare for Sulzberger to be seen on the third floor of the stately, mansard-roofed *Times* building on West 43rd Street, where the most senior editors worked. He worked in the elegant, wood-paneled 11th-floor office his father and grandfather once occupied. The corporate floor was carpeted in brown and evoked an earlier, more refined age, with a golden ashtray by the elevators labeled "Cigar Ends." In that boisterous age, presses roared in the basement of the Times Building (the namesake of Times Square), typewriters clacked, and bookies ran in and out of the newsroom.

Next to Sulzberger's office was the imposing boardroom dominated by a huge mahogany table and walls that were covered with signed portraits of dignitaries who had visited the offices, including several American presidents, Charlie Chaplin, Charles Lindbergh, and an array of foreign leaders. There were so many that there was a special book in the room to identify them. President Hamid Karzai of Afghanistan and Secretary of State Condoleezza Rice had been recent guests at sessions where Sulzberger introduced them, then handed them over for questioning by the journalists on his editorial board.

Sulzberger would occasionally attend the front-page meeting, but only rarely and without ever commenting on the stories editors pitched for the six precious spots on A1 of the next day's paper. Unaccountably he almost always left immediately after the lede of the paper, the one in "column right," was chosen. He sometimes took groups of reporters out to dinner to check the pulse of the newsroom. At the annual announcement of the Pulitzer Prizes he stood proudly in the third-floor newsroom with the editors, but never spoke. He didn't need to, because each winner paid homage to him and his family.

During this period he and Robinson were at business dinners together most nights of the workweek, reassuring investors of the long-term survival of the *Times*. Sulzberger dressed in suits from Bloomingdale's, stylish without being ostentatiously bespoke, and wore suspenders before they went out of fashion. In his early years as publisher, he walked around in his socks. At the break of dawn most mornings he met his friend, Wall Street investor Steven Rattner, at a high-end gym near his Central Park West apartment. On the weekends he would sometimes burn off stress by riding his motorcycle around New Paltz, New York, where he had a second home. He had married his wife, Gail Gregg, out of college; their son, Arthur Gregg, had graduated from Brown University, and their daughter, Annie, lived in England after she finished college. He eventually placed his hopes for a successor on Arthur Gregg, who had come to the *Times* in 2009 as a reporter after working at the *Providence Journal* in Rhode Island and the *Portland Oregonian*.

Robinson, one year his senior, was a formidable figure. The people who worked on the business side were afraid of her, as Sulzberger sometimes seemed to be. Her job was difficult, wedged as she was between Sulzberger and his cousin Michael Golden, the *Times*'s vice chairman, a nebulous role that seemed to change with the seasons. Golden oversaw the regional newspapers owned by the *Times* before being sent to Paris to take charge of the business affairs of the struggling *International Herald Tribune*. For a little while, he and Robinson watched over the financially troubled *Boston Globe*, which Punch Sulzberger had acquired for the wildly inflated price of $1 billion at the end of his tenure and that was now badly foundering. Then Golden was asked to turn his attention to human resources at the *Times*. None of these jobs had any real power, but the genial cousin, who had worked for Ochs's original newspaper, the *Chattanooga Times* (where his mother, one of Ochs's granddaughters, was chair), was tasked with something vital: he was the liaison between the New York Times Company and his extended family. Robinson and even Sulzberger could be dismissive of him, but his importance was his bloodline, which made crossing him perilous, especially for her. Sulzberger once told me that Golden was the only person at the company in whom he fully confided.

Some recent business blunders had made the structural damage inflicted by the internet even more painful. The worst was the purchase of the *Boston Globe* at precisely the moment the glory days of newspaper franchises were ending. Another ill-timed move was buying from the *Washington Post* the 50 percent stake the *Times* didn't already own in the *International Herald Tribune*. The English-language paper, which had provided travelers and expats the best of both newspapers, was based in Paris, where labor costs were astronomical and headcount almost impossible to trim. The *Globe* blunder wasn't Sulzberger Jr.'s bad call, but the *IHT* was his doing. Besides draining revenue, the breakup of the partnership irked the *Post*'s Donald Graham. He felt strong-armed, that the *Post* had been pushed out, damaging a relationship between the two newspaper men that traced back to their parents.

Sulzberger had another important relationship that was souring, with his executive editor, Bill Keller. Keller was a brilliant journalist who had come up as a correspondent in Russia and South Africa and later served as foreign editor during a period when the *Times*'s international coverage reached a new level of excellence; as executive editor he had strengthened the news report. His predecessors had largely been insulated from business issues because of a traditional wall between news and advertising, but the severity of the internet's disruption had embroiled him in the paper's business turmoil.

Keller was a handsome man with piercing blue eyes who at 57 had few gray hairs and was happiest writing at his desk, plugged into his iPod with his headphones on. He read poetry on the subway on the way to work. Sulzberger and some journalists found him distant but recognized that he had flawless news judgment and ethics. Keller was not a fan of the *Times*'s business side in general, and he stubbornly opposed some moneymaking initiatives Sulzberger had been pushing for, such as sponsored conferences and a *Times* wine club. Keller thought such ventures cheapened the *Times* name and trespassed the boundary between news and advertising.

Keller had a sardonic sense of humor and was known to send biting emails, later regretting them. Although the *Times* was constantly attacked for leaning left, he was a stickler for fairness and combed through news stories to excise anything that sounded reflexively liberal. He once threatened to kill a long article based on Justice Harry Blackmun's papers because he thought the writer, the respected Supreme Court reporter Linda Greenhouse, had been too soft on the liberal justice. Keller had also insisted that the paper apologize for overly prosecutorial coverage of an Asian American scientist who was wrongly jailed for passing on nuclear secrets. Keller's distant predecessor, the long-serving and tyrannical Abe Rosenthal, had famously vowed always to "keep the paper straight," and Keller too lived up to the pledge. Sulzberger had passed him over for executive editor in 2000, but had to reconsider three years later, when his first choice, Howell Raines, imploded under the scandal caused by Jayson Blair's fictive news stories. Once Keller was in the job and had calmed a roiling newsroom, he no longer needed to fear or curry favor with Sulzberger, and his irritation with some of the publisher's ideas was apparent. To calm himself, Keller would frequently say that as a Sulzberger, Arthur Jr. was the *Times*'s best hope for surviving as the publishing world made the transition to the web. The Sulzberger family had always been faithful stewards of good journalism and Keller knew he had the publisher's backing when it came to protecting the paper's quality. Sulzberger had furnished Keller with sufficient room in the budget to expand culture coverage, add bureaus around the country, and lure expensive talent, like Anthony Shadid of the *Washington Post*, a star Middle East correspondent; Joe Nocera of *Fortune* magazine, a distinguished business journalist; and James B. Stewart, a best-selling author and a former top editor at the *Wall Street Journal*. When Keller was forced to cut the newsroom staff for the first time, he protected all the international coverage and took a pay cut along with his masthead editors (the top-ranking deputies) in order to save some positions.

Meanwhile other newspaper families were calling it quits and cashing in, including the owners of Times Mirror, Knight Ridder, and Dow Jones. In 2007 the Bancrofts sold their family jewel, the *Wall Street Journal*, to Rupert Murdoch for an astonishing $5 billion. The previous year the Ridder family had sold its entire chain of papers, Knight Ridder, for a bit more than that. There were reports from the New York tabloids that Mayor Michael Bloomberg wanted to buy the *Times* after he left office, which the billionaire denied. "I don't want to be in your business," he told me one day at lunch.

Keller had weekly lunches with Sulzberger in the formal dining rooms the *Times* still maintained, with waiters, china, and printed menus. Sweetened iced tea, Sulzberger's favorite, was always served unless a guest requested something else. The opulence jarred with the forecasts Sulzberger faced, which seemed to have darkened overnight: classified ads, which formerly accounted for millions of dollars in ad revenue, had been wiped out by Craigslist, a free internet bulletin board that lured away the "for sale" ads, and Monster.com and other sites, which grabbed the "help wanted" and "job wanted" ads. Once-strong advertising categories like travel and autos were also getting hammered by digital competitors such as Expedia and AutoTrader. Movie companies and even Broadway theater owners had new digital methods of reaching ticket-buyers that made them less dependent on advertising in the *Times*—and on its critics' reviews.

In 2005, following the *Wall Street Journal*'s lead, the *Times* decided to put a paid gate on the website to block free access to popular columnists such as Tom Friedman and Maureen Dowd. By requiring readers to pay, Sulzberger expected to begin to compensate for other losses on the web. The reasoning was that, unlike hard news, these opinion pieces were tougher for digital competitors to match. Although her top digital people opposed it, Robinson pushed it through, and Sulzberger approved the online subscription program. To conjure the air of sophistication, it was branded "Times Select."

The program was an embarrassing flop. By 2007, two years after the gate went up, it would be dismantled, having mustered a meager 247,000 paying subscribers. The web's tenet that content had to be free seemed insurmountable. Meanwhile Friedman and the other columnists—the stars with high salaries, big travel and entertainment budgets, and relaxed ethics rules that allowed them to accept some big speaking fees—complained to Sulzberger about their diminished readership, especially among young people, who, Friedman argued, desperately needed to understand the post-9/11 world. Digital revenues accounted for less than 10 percent of the company's earnings. The print edition of the *Times* was still the breadwinner, though how much longer that would last was anyone's guess.

In the swirling uncertainty, Sulzberger became increasingly comfortable bringing in outside advisors to help. He spent a rumored $1 million to hire McKinsey & Company, hoping they would be able to answer the two most pressing questions for the future of the newspaper: How much longer would the print edition endure, and when would the digital operation make up for the paper's rapidly depleting ad revenue? The fate of the institution lay at the intersection of two countervailing curves: the upswing of digital ads and paid subscriptions and the downward spiral of print advertising, which still accounted for 68 percent of the company's revenues, as well as slower leakage of print home delivery subscriptions.

Robinson convened the top editors and businesspeople to hear the consultants' findings in words straight from Dante. *Paradiso* for the *Times* would be the wildly unlikely scenario in which revenues from print advertising recovered and the losses endured by the newspaper industry as a whole turned out to be a cyclical blip. The *Inferno* scenario, on the other hand, would take the form of print revenue declining inexorably and precipitously, while digital revenue plateaued. *Purgatorio* was the newspaper's current home. Robinson explained to Keller and his masthead that the *Times* was in a state of limbo that McKinsey labeled "Altered Print"—a slow bleed that might become fatal if the paper didn't make changes fast. These included introducing new products that readers would pay for, like trips, live events, and conferences, as well as more specialized news on money-making subjects such as business and luxury fashion.

To move more quickly, Sulzberger wanted the news and business sides to work much more closely together, something the editors who preceded Keller had been loath to do. There had always been an impenetrable wall between the business and news sides, and for good reason: it ensured that no journalism decisions would be seen as influenced by advertisers or motivated by commercial concerns. Sulzberger intended to lower that wall, even in the face of newsroom resistance. He convened a small committee of eight senior business executives and news editors, which he called the Mohonk Group for the historic Mohonk Mountain House hotel in the Sulzberger getaway of New Paltz. The committee's mission was to seek compromise; only in the case of a stalemate would the group go to Sulzberger to make the final decision. He hated conflict, so such logjams were to be avoided. As managing editor for news, I was the highest-ranking representative from the newsroom on the committee.

There was pressure on the group for revenue-producing ideas, such as a travel show that the newsroom opposed but that took place at the Javits Center anyway, though with none of the paper's travel writers participating. The ad department representatives pressed for an additional Styles section on Thursdays. The paper couldn't afford to turn away advertisers, and Sunday Styles had been one of the few sections that was overbooked with luxury ads. However, many *Times* journalists turned up their noses at the notion of a Thursday section filled with features on fashion and a column by a shopping critic. (One outside critic blasted the section as "luxury porn" and claimed the Gray Lady was suddenly wearing Prada.) Another new addition, a luxury magazine called *T*, would run on certain Sundays, with ads for bejeweled purses and watches that cost more than $100,000. But by this point even Keller was saying, "If luxury porn is what saves the Baghdad bureau, so be it."

At stake was the wall between church and state, a bulwark that had been sacrosanct at serious news organizations. It was what separated journalists from PR flacks. It was the cause taken up in the 1950s by the *Wall Street Journal* when it published two articles that offended General Motors, its biggest advertiser, to which GM responded by pulling all its ads. The *Journal* had stood its ground in an editorial titled "A Difference of Opinion." "In the end the truth about what is happening is the only thing that is of value to anybody," the editorial declared. "And when a newspaper begins to suppress news, whether at the behest of its advertisers or on pleas from special segments of business, it will soon cease to be of any service either to its advertisers or to business because it will soon cease to have readers."

Neither Sulzberger nor his team would dream of asking editors to kill an article rather than offend an advertiser, but the fact that the idea for "Thursday Styles" came from the ad department was a leap over the wall. It was the first of many ventures that blurred the traditional lines, not because "the business side," as Sulzberger and his corporate team were called, wanted to transgress but because survival depended on filling the void created by the advertising crash.

Keller and the paper's art director began to field requests from the business side for ads that previously would have violated *Times* standards, including strip ads across the section fronts. Though Sulzberger once pledged never to spoil the paper's elegant look with a front-page ad, they too soon began appearing. These were small compromises that did not affect the quality of the paper's journalism but did clutter the design.

It seemed almost nothing was sacrosanct anymore. Even the Ochs motto, "All The News That's Fit To Print," was threatened. Its daily spot in the upper left of the front page was precious real estate that the ad department wanted to sell, much to the chagrin of the art director. Sulzberger decided to keep the motto off limits to advertisers, but the decision was a hard one for him.

Sulzberger and Robinson never asked for the kind of deep cuts that would truly harm the quality of the overall news coverage. Instead they cut almost half of the business-side staff and took other cost-saving measures. As noticeable gaps in coverage became evident at the *Washington Post*, which had made a series of staff reductions, the *Times* stood apart. Sulzberger was certain his paper could be "the last man standing," as long as he was careful not to damage the quality of the news. Making this hope into a strategy meant investing in the core journalism and not cutting his way to profitability. But the "last man" strategy also put him in a bind. To keep his

$200 million-plus newsroom fully budgeted, he couldn't afford to spend on other vital parts of the company. If he had to, as ultimately he did, he would sell off the *Boston Globe* and starve other parts of the media conglomerate he had once dreamed of leading. Even so, the McKinsey team reminded him, the *Times* might not survive, especially as the financial crisis of 2008 loomed and the flames of Inferno threatened.

Desperation had taken hold elsewhere and gravely damaged one-time competitors. At the *L.A. Times*, where parent-company Times Mirror's CEO Mark Willes was known as the "Cereal Killer" (he had come from General Mills), the wall was bulldozed when, in 1999, the paper forged a revenue-sharing agreement with Staples, the office supply company, to publish a 168-page magazine devoted to the opening of the Staples Center, a vast new convention center and sports arena. Although it was produced by *L.A. Times* editors as part of regular coverage, these staffers didn't know their employer was splitting the revenue from the issue with the owner of the arena. They were outraged when they found out: it undermined their coverage, made it look like they were engaged in ad puffery. The newspaper's publisher and editor were forced out of their jobs, and the paper was sold to the Tribune Company not long after. A decade later, that scandal seemed quaint next to the industry's new digital Frankenstein, so-called native ads that so closely resembled news stories they fooled readers and quickly became the new pillar of advertising revenue at digital upstarts like BuzzFeed and Vice. Native advertising, more carefully labeled, would also come to the *New York Times* and *Washington Post*. By that time, however, there was far less indignation about the chinks carved in the wall.

Though nervous about the tense quarterly calls with Wall Street analysts, which he left to Robinson, Sulzberger's "last man standing" strategy meant lowering profit margins and seeing the *Times*'s stock price go even lower. (The stock fell below $5 in January 2009.) Competitors like Tribune still insisted on hitting a 20 percent profit margin and cut so ruthlessly that in no time their new editor and publisher left.

John S. Carroll, the *L.A. Times* editor who swept away the Staples mess and then walked out rather than strip down his newsroom, used the time after his exit to survey the capsized world of newspapers. This was the only world he had ever known; the news was in his blood. His father, Wallace Carroll, had been the beloved Washington editor of the *New York Times* and later the editor and publisher of the newspaper in Winston-Salem, North Carolina. His son too had never wanted to be anything other than a newspaper editor. As John mulled over the problems facing his beloved industry, he concluded the obvious: the business model for newspapers had been irreparably broken by the internet.

Central Casting's idea of an editor, with his white hair and glasses, Carroll was a revered journalist and the right person to survey the wasteland. But he was the wrong person to guide his profession into the future. He shared his findings at the annual meeting of the American Society of Newspaper Editors, a formerly raucous affair for swaggering types like Abe Rosenthal and Ben Bradlee. "Our corporate superiors are sometimes genuinely perplexed to find people in their midst who do not feel beholden, first and foremost, to the shareholder," he began his 2006 speech, entitled "Last Call at the ASNE Saloon." Carroll was correct in pointing out that newspapers were responsible for breaking almost all of the most important news, from the Watergate break-in to the secret CIA prisons and illegal domestic eavesdropping carried out by the Bush administration. But their managers had become prisoners of Wall Street and were deaf to his rallying cry: "Our mission is more daunting than that of our predecessors. It is not merely to produce good stories. It is not merely to save our newspapers. It is—and this may sound grandiose—to save journalism itself. It is to ensure the existence, long into the future, of a large, independent, principled, questioning, deep-digging cadre of journalists in America."

But like his audience of newspaper editors, Carroll had no feel or foresight about how the internet would provide journalists with immediacy, a much closer relationship with readers, and better reporting tools, or how it would open the field to far more diverse voices once printing presses were no longer needed to publish. For Carroll and his ASNE compadres, the internet seemed an assassin that threatened the fabric of democracy itself by choking the profession that had produced the Pentagon Papers and Woodward and Bernstein.

Although Sulzberger had pronounced himself "platform-agnostic," his company's culture and work rhythms were set by the clock of printing presses, which started rolling nightly at 9:45. He and Robinson could call for fast changes, as the McKinseyites urged them to, but a combination of arrogance and tradition was embedded in the historic Times Building. The *Times* had been setting the news agenda for so long that its primacy was taken for granted, especially by its journalists, who never dreamed the authority of their institution could be challenged by the new digital competitors, or by bloggers (Keller called them "bloggers in bathrobes"), or by so-called citizen journalists who were witnessing international events like the tsunami in Indonesia and writing about them in real time, or, ultimately, by readers using the new platforms of Google and Facebook. Insulated as it was, the *Times* convinced itself that although the mechanics of the industry were changing, the fact remained that "it wasn't a story until it was in the *Times*." Most *Times* editors barely noticed when competitors had a scoop, unless it was the *Washington Post* or the *Wall Street Journal*. But as the internet became a more adaptable and vital place to search for and consume information, that insularity turned into true myopia.

News and opinion sites like the Huffington Post were robbing the *Times* blind, siphoning off for free the cream of its news report, its digital advertising, and its readers. Gawker, a gossip site, was feeding readers the internet equivalent of crack. Blogs like Josh Marshall's Talking Points Memo were covering national security more skeptically and with more edge than the *Times*. And then there was Matt Drudge, whose Report readers depended on like their morning coffee. The immense traffic Drudge generated for any story his blog promoted became a source of leverage for him.

Newspapers were attracting digital audiences that dwarfed the readership of their pre-internet days. If the same number of people had been buying the hard-copy newspaper, the *Times* would have been bathing in profits. The problem was that because the websites were free, the traffic they brought in was less valuable, making advertising on them very cheap. And the web was swimming in free alternatives and new all-digital news sites, most of which did almost none of the expensive, original reporting that made the survival of quality, legacy newspapers so crucial.

The person most frustrated by the *Times*'s print-focused culture was Martin Nisenholtz, a forward-looking, genuine internet pioneer, who was, at least in title, head of all things digital at the *Times*. He and Robinson wasted time and energy fighting each other or vying for Sulzberger's favor. Because Robinson had once been head of print advertising at the *Times*, she zealously guarded that precious but diminishing revenue and resisted Nisenholtz's pleas for more resources to hire web designers and technicians. Nisenholtz was relegated to overseeing About.com, an internet site for answers to diurnal problems that the *Times* purchased in 2005 for $410 million, a price that Rattner, Sulzberger's financier pal, thought was way too steep. For a while it was a cash cow for the Times Company, but not for long. It was a casualty of Google, which once gave high rankings to its simple, explanatory articles. But when Google changed its algorithm to reward more in-depth, original journalism, About's content sank along with its advertising. Nisenholtz believed the internet offered the company a vastly expanded readership and profits as soon as the advertising world caught on to the digital boom. But while he was well known in Silicon Valley, Nisenholtz was a virtual unknown in the *Times* newsroom. It was telling that when NYTimes.com first launched, a septuagenarian former foreign editor known for falling asleep in meetings was tapped to run it and the website staff worked in a separate building blocks away.

The journalists grudgingly created some blogs (in *Times*ian fashion, there was eventually one devoted to bridge), but their eyes glazed over when Nisenholtz explained crucial tools such as search engine optimization. SEO was what Peretti and the tech team at Huffington Post were using to make sure their articles ranked first when people searched for topics on Google. The items and stories at the top of Google's results always got the most eyeballs, and eyeballs produced ad dollars. By crafting snappy or intriguing headlines, one could game the system, a phenomenon later known as clickbait. But at the *Times*, editors clung to their notion that the website would be a simulacrum of the print paper. They insisted on sticking to sober headlines that fit the "*Times* standards" and were not naked appeals for clicks.

Everything seemed to be crashing at once: ad revenues, the stock price, and the newspaper industry at large. With the failure of Times Select, there seemed little hope of generating digital revenue besides selling ad space. In 2008 Sulzberger survived a proxy vote that sought to split his job in half, separating the CEO and publisher titles he had won from his father. He did not come away unscathed, however: more than 30 percent of the class A shareholders had turned against him, and the dissidents won two seats on the board. But the Sulzbergers still occupied four board seats, and their hold was made firmer by the fact that it would take a 6–2 vote of the family to declassify the B shares, which were not publicly traded. Not beholden to the family, the dissident board members could still keep pressure on the company for improved results. To mollify them, Sulzberger and his cousin Golden decided they would forgo any stock compensation in 2006 and 2007.

The *Times* also went on a selling spree: the nine television stations it owned went for $575 million, while the company's stake in the Times-Discovery cable channel (another unsuccessful foray into television that cost $100 million for a 50 percent stake) was sold at a loss. The company shuttered one of its two printing plants in the New York area and laid off 200 pressmen. When that was still not enough to even the keel, Sulzberger's team announced another cut, this time to the broadsheet itself, which would shrink by a few inches to save on newsprint costs.

That brought more unflattering press for Sulzberger. In one article, the ex-*Times*man and author Gay Talese was quoted saying, "Every once in awhile you get a bad king," a cutting remark Sulzberger never forgave. Murdoch's *New York Post*, meanwhile, kept trotting out the cartoon of Sulzberger with a shiner.

Up until this point the *Times* had shed journalists by offering voluntary buyouts to anyone who had worked there a long time. But considering the remarkably low turnover rate, the list of in-house veterans was long. The average age in the newsroom was nearly 50, and many reporters were well into their 60s and even 70s. Some of those forced to retire tried to cling to their desks by writing occasional freelance articles; others, for whom the hallowed phrase "of the *Times*" had become such an essential part of their identity, begged to keep their position. Following his father's custom, Sulzberger let former senior editors, like Arthur Gelb, who had remade the *Times* with Abe Rosenthal, have ceremonial jobs. Gelb was still a Pied Piper for many of the best talents at the paper, including Maureen Dowd and Frank Rich, and during this period of crippling uncertainty he became the house shrink, welcoming a stream of former colleagues into his cozy den of an office. Gelb represented many of the things people cherished most about the *Times* of old, when the editors wore black tie to opening nights on Broadway and the opera. The tall, lanky, silver-haired Gelb had been close to the elder Sulzberger, but he sometimes rolled his eyes when the son was mentioned.

The biggest personal sacrifices came from the Sulzberger family itself, whose members were soon living without the dividends from their stock, having pledged to let that money (upwards of $20 million in some years) go back into the company while the forecast was so bleak. Although the family was wealthy, much of that wealth was depleted by its fourth generation. They took immense pride in the paper's journalism; if there was any restiveness among them over the sinking stock price or the missing dividends, there were no outward signs.

Meanwhile those who eagerly dove into the digital world grew tired of the hand-wringing over the plight of newspapers. Clay Shirky, a journalism professor at New York University, wrote an influential article called "Newspapers and Thinking the Unthinkable." The unthinkable was the total disappearance of the printed product, but Shirky had a decidedly different point of view on that. He argued that as long as journalism itself survived, the eventual death of newspapers would not be a tragedy. He saw the birth of the internet as a profound and exciting revolution that, akin to Gutenberg's introduction of the printing press in the 15th century, democratized the flow of information. He chastised newspaper publishers for refusing to see the futility of their old business model and urged them to innovate digitally instead of singing the same old song of "You'll miss us when we're gone."

"The problem newspapers face isn't that they didn't see the internet coming," Shirky scolded. "They not only saw it miles off, they figured out early on that they needed a plan to deal with it, and during the early '90s they came up with not just one plan but several." But all their plans were either desperate or ineffective, such as building websites to be replicas of their print editions rather than designing them to be distinctly digital or technologically advanced. Shirky advocated the social sharing of articles, linking to a story and sending it on to friends to create communities of interest. At this point, the *Times* knew nothing of Peretti's discoveries about virality. Shirky, who did, was part of a group of journalism school professors who were called "the Future of News Group." Its members included Jay Rosen, another NYU professor, and Jeff Jarvis, who taught at the City University of New York. Rosen and Jarvis shared their ruminations about journalism on their blogs, which were beginning to get attention.

The *Times* invited Jarvis to speak to its senior leadership team at a restaurant in Manhattan. Jarvis was bombastic, declaring that the *Times* was "the canary in the coal mine," as newspapers stumbled their way into the digital world. Dessert sat untouched as he described a dystopian future for newsprint.

Characteristically, Sulzberger faced the *Times*'s problem by creating committees, of which the Mohonk Group was just one. A joint business-news group began looking at new ways to generate revenue and decided to try offering a *New York Times* "membership" program, offering special benefits. In came yet another group of pricey consultants, the Dog House, which had done work for American Express, a company known for its pioneering membership program. The consultants dreamed up a package of extra benefits to accompany the subscriptions, like early peeks at certain stories or the chance to attend the New York Auto Show with the *Times*'s car writer. The new slogan they unveiled captured the thrust of their vision: "Don't read The New York Times, Experience It." The catchphrase was ridiculed by some editors as counterproductive: Why on earth urge people *not* to read the paper? The consultants presented the idea to a focus group of readers, who roundly rejected not only the slogan but also the slate of add-on benefits they were proposing. The *Times* was a plenty rich course as is, said the readers; they had no desire for dessert. (But in less than a decade, the *Times* would be offering experiences, like around-the-world trips with its journalists on chartered 757s, with seats going for $135,000.)

Around this time another publishing model was on the rise, as online newsrooms such as ProPublica were formed as nonprofits to help fill the void left by the failing newspapers. National Public Radio, also donor-based, was expanding. But Sulzberger was loath to "look as if we're shaking a tin cup," he announced. He was not going to ask readers to become donors to keep the paper afloat.

In the end, the only real product the *Times* had to sell was the quality of its journalism. Its highly educated and affluent readership had an extremely personal relationship with the paper, trusting it to guide its decisions on everything from whom to vote for to what movie to see. When the Gray Lady dared to make changes in her looks, such as printing in color to showcase photographs, there were howls of protest at first. When, to save money, the *Times* stopped printing weekly TV listings—on the assumption that most of its New York readers had this information on their cable boxes—letters of polite protest, mainly from aging readers with lovely penmanship, arrived for years afterward. When I gave speeches, I could spot the TV list protesters, usually gray-haired subscribers who would come barreling toward me, arms crossed, the second I stepped from the podium.

More than anything, the special relationship between the paper and its readers rested on the depth of the *Times*'s reporting and the elegance of its editing, which honored the intelligence of its readers. Many newspapers and magazines enjoyed such loyalty, but connection of the *Times*'s audience to its paper was part of their identity, a manual for living in a complicated and chaotic world. Editors acted accordingly, punctilious to the point that a misplaced comma was cause for a correction. Readers trusted them for pointing out a fabulous new Vietnamese restaurant, or the discovery of a new manuscript by J. D. Salinger. The editors also knew what to stay away from: the paper never had a true gossip column, though it covered society parties and the doings of hip, downtown trendsetters. Though the internet and the pressure to attract ever-larger audiences would change this, the *Times* generally eschewed celebrity news, the coverage that had begun blurring the line between news and entertainment, especially at the networks. Though other papers once made a fortune on the comics, the *Times* never ran them because Adolph Ochs thought they would offend the seriousness of his readership. In their place there was a chess column and the crossword puzzle, which advanced in difficulty each day so that by the end of the week even Ph.D.s had difficulty filling in all the squares. Being a *Times* reader was a kind of status symbol, not only for New Yorkers but also for out-of-towners, on whose lawns the distinctive blue plastic bags that held the paper landed each morning. One devoted reader made a giant sculpture out of those blue bags and had it delivered to me, while a well-known conceptual artist, Nancy Chunn, drew her own daily interpretation of the front page each day, which a New York gallery sold for hundreds of dollars apiece. (Sulzberger bought an entire month of them to hang on the walls.)

The flip side of this was that some thought the paper smacked of liberal elitism. With the rise of Rush Limbaugh, then Fox News, powerful right-wing media sprouted on television, radio, Facebook, and other social media platforms. The *Times* became the poster child of all that was wrong with liberals. The editorial page, which Sulzberger directly controlled and which was the voice of the *Times* as an institution, grew more liberal under him, though his opinion editors sometimes held him back, as was the case when the publisher wanted an editorial calling for a withdrawal of troops from Afghanistan. This produced a rare, closed-door argument between Sulzberger and the opinion editors, led by Abe Rosenthal's son, Andrew.

The *Times* made errors, of course, but rarely ones that angered readers enough to provoke them to cancel their subscriptions. There were lapses. Abe Rosenthal's homophobia slowed coverage of the AIDS crisis. Some readers complained that the paper made the Whitewater real estate story that dogged the Clintons into more than it deserved to be. The paper was too prosecutorial in its coverage of a nuclear scientist accused of giving secrets to China, stories for which the editors later expressed regret. And in the early years of the new century, there was a series of full-blown scandals that rocked the foundation of trust between the institution and its readers. These controversies shook the leadership of the *Times* at precisely the moment that the digital transition was building steam and should have been the focus of both worry and change. Instead everybody's eyes were elsewhere.

Keller's appointment in 2003 as executive editor resulted from a scandal involving a young reporter, Jayson Blair, who invented some stories and plagiarized others. When his supposed scoops were unmasked, brewing resentment directed at the newsroom's leadership team of Howell Raines and Gerald Boyd erupted into the kind of media frenzy that Sulzberger hated and feared. He fired Raines and Boyd, and Keller was called back from his writing duties to be executive editor.

The more serious transgression was the paper's coverage of the lead-up to the war in Iraq. That coverage came under intense criticism in the summer of 2003, after no weapons of mass destruction were found in Saddam Hussein's kingdom. WMDs had been the casus belli used by the Bush administration, and the *Times* had run many poorly sourced front-page stories lending credence to administration officials who warned that Hussein was stocking a nuclear arsenal that could target the U.S. directly. National Security Advisor Condoleezza Rice called it a "mushroom cloud." The bad intelligence was peddled, circulated, and leaked to the press by a combination of government sources, unreliable Iraqi defectors, and other dubious sources. Judith Miller, a longtime Middle East correspondent and investigative reporter for the *Times*, used the specious intelligence from these sources for "scoops" that were blasted onto the front page. Though other reporters and publications also jumped at the same poisoned bait, Miller's prewar stories were especially egregious and justifiably assailed. Then came the drama of Miller's going to jail when she wouldn't reveal her sources in a subsequent leak investigation, followed by her exit under pressure from the *Times*.

Miller had been close to Sulzberger when they were younger and worked together in the paper's Washington bureau. Along with Rattner, they were journalism's version of the rat pack. Sulzberger staunchly defended Miller for not revealing her sources in service, he proclaimed, of the First Amendment protections given to reporters. He handed out "Free Judy" buttons while she was in jail. Her court case ended up hurting the news media's long-held position that reporters are entitled to be shielded from being forced to testify. When Miller eventually named her source, another media firestorm ensued. A long article in the *New Yorker* ridiculed Sulzberger for racing down to Washington to see her freed.

In the years after the Blair and Miller stories unfolded, Keller, who picked me to be managing editor for news, was under pressure to restore the paper's reputation for having the best quality coverage. At the Democratic National Convention in 2004, I was interviewed for a segment of Jon Stewart's satiric *Daily Show*, and one of the show's correspondents, Samantha Bee, asked me, "How does it feel to be the managing editor of the paper that makes stuff up?" The editors were bombarded by angry questions asking why the paper had relied on Miller and her dubious sources. Keller had been exiled to the opinion section during the Blair and Iraq War imbroglios, but he was handed the Miller mess to clean up, which he did, albeit by publishing a belated apology for some of the *Times*'s bad stories and, ultimately, getting rid of Miller. Keller clamped down on reporters' uses of anonymous sources, especially national security officials who sold "scoops" but wouldn't attach their names to the information they peddled. He was deeply skeptical about anonymous sources in Washington, D.C., where he had briefly worked at the beginning of his career.

Sulzberger used these ethical breaches to force a change he had long wanted: the appointment of a so-called ombudsman to police coverage on behalf of readers. The *Washington Post* and other papers had them, but the *Times* had held itself above such an outside critic.

With the new "public editor" watching for missteps, the Keller team worked assiduously to return to the traditional strengths of the *Times*, reconstituting its investigative reporting group, where Miller had been allowed to run free, adding resources, journalists, and a new editor. Soon the *Times* once again had important exclusives about abuses and overreaching by the Bush White House. Sound reporters from the Washington bureau like Eric Schmitt, David Sanger, and James Risen were again all over the front page. Keller was criticized for holding back a story about secret domestic government eavesdropping at the request of the White House, which argued that disclosure of the National Security Agency's secret monitoring would inhibit the government's counterterrorism abilities. When the *Times* finally did publish the story, it shocked the country and won a Pulitzer Prize. This story, in fact, was the prelude to the even bigger disclosures of Edward Snowden years later.

The *Times* was hardly the only quality news organization to misreport the lead-up to the Iraq War, but because of its stature its mistakes damaged the institution more deeply. There were a few organizations, like the McClatchy chain's Washington bureau, that reported skeptically about the prewar intelligence. But their voices were whispers in comparison, in part because the chain did not have a newspaper in D.C. and wasn't widely read. The loss of credibility coincided with Americans' growing lack of confidence in all of their institutions, according to polls that showed approval for almost everything, especially Congress, falling. Although the *Times* was still viewed as the supreme authority inside the mainstream news media, its reputation with the public was sinking along with the rest of the profession, in part because of constant hammering from the right. When I was managing editor, I began monitoring the number of times Bill O'Reilly demonized the *Times* on his nightly program on Fox. I protested periodically to Roger Ailes, an old Republican source of mine, when the critiques contained lies, but, unsurprisingly, they were never corrected.

The cynicism directed at establishment news opened the public to all kinds of new voices on the internet and made it vulnerable to the rise of so-called fake news. By 2006 the *Times* had recovered its journalistic reputation, and as competitors weakened, it was clearly the best general-interest newspaper. Its regained journalistic stature and life coincided, unfortunately, with the death of its business model. And maintaining the revenue to subsidize its quality news report was a problem far too taxing for the executives left in its downsized and ill-prepared business side.

Respite from the never-ending financial troubles arrived only when Golden walked into Sulzberger's office with updates on the new Times Building they were erecting a few blocks away on Eighth Avenue, designed by the master architect Renzo Piano. The new building was a vast undertaking and cost more than $850 million, but Sulzberger wanted a glitzy headquarters fit for the modern media conglomerate he had until recently hoped to build. The old, historic Times Building on 43rd Street could not be retrofitted or rewired without astronomical spending. As the project neared completion in 2007, the New York Times Company was stripped down to its newspaper core: the *Times*, the *Boston Globe*, which Sulzberger wanted to sell off, and the *International Herald Tribune* in Paris.

The Renzo Piano building, with its modern glass and steel exterior, would be filled with natural light, unlike the 43rd Street building, which had few windows and mice skittering around. Despite this, the 43rd Street building with the mansard roof sold for $175 million, a price that seemed to please Sulzberger. (In three years it sold again, for three times the price.) The third floor newsroom became a bowling alley.

When the new building was almost finished, Sulzberger took his father, who had Parkinson's disease and was confined to a wheelchair, to see it. They were taken to a temporary platform on the unfinished upper floors. With his father wrapped in a blanket, they stepped onto the exposed platform, the wind whipping around the steel girders of the top floors. Father and son looked out on the streets of New York as if they could see the future.

CHAPTER FOUR

WASHINGTON POST I

T he future of newspapers looked grim beyond repair to Donald E. Graham, who had diversified the Washington Post Company so that he now spent most of his time on issues wholly unrelated to the news or politics. He believed he had secured his company's future, at least for the short term, by expanding its for-profit education subsidiary, a holding that his famous mother, Katharine Graham, had purchased as an afterthought.

In the land of slick lobbyists and congressional dealmakers, he was an earnest, uncynical man. His defining feature was his love of the actual city of Washington, D.C. Unlike Capitol Hill barons who were abusive toward staffers, he showered his journalists with appreciation and complimentary notes they called "Donniegrams." His courtesy and modesty were unusual for someone who still held considerable power.

He was overshadowed by his regal mother, who, with the legendary editor Ben Bradlee, led the *Post* in the glory days of the Pentagon Papers and Watergate. Since then the paper had strengthened its news coverage to the point that many believed it had eclipsed the *New York Times* in the quality of its writing and national political reporting. The *Times* was known as an editors' paper; the *Post* was a reporters' paper, with stylists like David Maraniss and Anne Hull and investigative reporters like Bob Woodward and Dana Priest. Don Graham had tried to maintain that quality, and the *Post* won 25 Pulitzer Prizes during his time as publisher and chairman, second only to the *Times*. But the battered state of the newspaper industry had forced hard decisions; to keep his company profitable he'd been making deep cuts to his newsroom.

In some ways Don was a better businessman than his mother. Until the rocky period of the mid-2000s, the Washington Post Company was flawlessly managed. Its stock price remained high and its profits held steady at $120 million annually. Its pension fund flourished. It was more diversified than the *Times*, with a gold mine in its education business and rich television holdings. The education company, Stanley Kaplan, generated far more revenue than the newspaper; reflecting this reality, Graham had changed the Post Company's official description to "an education and media company."

Graham's mother had inherited the paper from her father, Eugene Meyer, who bought it out of bankruptcy in 1933. Her husband, Philip Graham, ran the company until 1963, when, suffering from manic depression, he committed suicide. Katharine and Donald had been tutored in how to run a business by the same mentor, investor Warren Buffett. Besides running the conglomerate Berkshire Hathaway, Buffett's loves included newspapers. He believed that local papers, besides being pillars of democracy, could be great businesses, and as local newspapers began shuttering with the arrival of the internet, Buffett bought more than a dozen of them. Berkshire Hathaway owned $12 billion worth—some 21 percent—of the *Post*'s stock. He played such an important advisory role at the Post Company, serving on its board for 26 years, that Don Graham referred to him as "the Supreme Court."

Buffett viewed the *Post* as first and foremost a local newspaper, quite distinct from the *Times* or the *Wall Street Journal,* which had national and international reach. Priced for a long time at 25 cents a copy, the *Post* had nearly saturated its local market, finding a deeper and broader market in D.C. than any of its rivals did in New York. Washington was growing bigger and more prosperous, and Buffett was convinced that the *Post* would be printing money along with the paper for a very long time. When it acquired the *Washington Times-Herald* in 1954 and then saw its lone rival, the *Washington Star*, fold in 1981, it was the only quality daily publication in a city that generated the most important national news—a monopoly in the seat of power. Local supermarkets and department stores generated so much advertising that extra pages were added to accommodate them. Local classified ads, with a bustling Help Wanted section, were as much as 40 percent of the paper's revenues. The *Post*'s affinity for local coverage was once so strong that even more writerly hires for other sections were encouraged to do a stint covering news in Prince Georges County.

When Graham succeeded his mother as publisher in 1979 and as chairman in 1993, there was no reason for him to question the *Post*'s local strategy. His ties to the local, black-majority city of Washington were far stronger and more personal than his mother's. Following a year of service in Vietnam after graduating from Harvard in 1966, Graham joined the city's police department as a patrolman in the Ninth Precinct of Northeast Washington, a tough and mostly poor part of the city, which was still recovering from the riots following Martin Luther King's murder the year before. He was a good cop and enjoyed the job, according to friends who saw him for the year and a half he was on the force. He once talked a burglar out of shooting him by saying, "You really don't want to kill a cop." Tall, dark-haired, with red cheeks, he even looked the part of a man in blue. He saw being on the police force as a way of getting to know the "real city" rather than the government bureaucracy or Georgetown elite of his mother's set. His career choice, along with volunteering in the army, left him out of step with his Harvard friends, who were surprised to see him on the police line during one of the Vietnam Moratorium protests on the Washington Mall. His early choices would later be seen as steps in becoming a thoroughly honorable man.

When he joined the *Post* in 1971 as a Metro reporter, Graham began a dutiful apprenticeship, much as Arthur Sulzberger Jr. had, serving in just about every department of the newspaper, from news to sales. At Harvard he'd been the hardest-working journalist at the *Crimson*, writing more news stories than anyone and mastering every facet of publishing, even the linotype machine. His favorite reporting assignment at the *Post* was his time on the sports desk, but from there his work mostly related to the skills needed in the job everyone knew he would inherit: the publisher's chair. Instead of having salon society neighbors in Georgetown, Graham and his wife, Mary, whom he met at college and remained married to for 40 years, lived in a fairly modest house on Newark Street in Northwest D.C. When he didn't take the metro he drove his Buick.

It was typical that rather than someone like the swashbuckling Bradlee, who retired as executive editor in 1991, Graham picked as his editorial partner an unflashy, steady, and conservative man, Leonard Downie. Downie was such a straight arrow and stickler for objectivity that he did not vote. He was never happier than when he was running the paper by himself. Just as Graham had learned to fix the *Crimson*'s linotype machine, Downie mastered every aspect of the printing process and could have stepped in to run the presses if he had to. Graham and Downie made a congenial duo, but neither was a visionary. And it was vision that was most needed at a time when the presses looked ready to be silenced once and for all by the new digital platforms.

It wasn't that Graham was unaware of the changes transforming his profession. It was a short-sightedness about how the *Post* could make money from them. Before investing in new technologies or digital endeavors, he wanted to be shown a definite path to profits. In meetings he'd often say, "I am willing to invest in the future if you can show me the future." And when decisions had to be made about whether to change both the business and the editorial models, Graham chose to keep the focus of the *Post* local, on the D.C. region.

An early alarm that a new world was dawning came in 1992, a year into Downie's editorship, when his second in command, Robert Kaiser, fired his flare gun. A bow-tied editor with keen intelligence, Kaiser had been invited to attend a media conference hosted by Apple at a resort in Japan. There he heard presentations about the "collisions of technologies" that were about to revolutionize the news business. Kaiser was astounded. As he settled into his first-class seat on the Nippon Airways flight back to Washington, he began to compose a long-hand memo for Graham and his closest associates, who called themselves the Tuesday Group. "None of this is science fiction—it's just around the corner," he wrote. Knowing the memo's readers would be quick to dismiss visions of a future they could not fathom, he related an analogy that Alan Kay, a famous computer scientist who had worked in Apple's Advanced Technology Group, had imparted to conference attendees.

"You can put a frog in a pot of water and slowly raise the temperature under the pot until it boils, but the frog will never jump. Its nervous system cannot detect slight changes in temperature," Kaiser began. "The Post is not in a pot of water, and we're smarter than the average frog. But we do find ourselves swimming in an electronic sea where we could eventually be devoured—or ignored as an unnecessary anachronism. Our goal, obviously, is to avoid getting boiled as the electronic revolution continues."

Prescient though it was, Kaiser's report harbored some doubt as to the full extent of the impending revolution and expressed skepticism that may have seemed healthy at the time but appears nostalgic in hindsight. He disagreed with the prevailing attitude among conferees "that the public will love the idea of playing editor—of organizing the information stream around personal needs and preferences to create individualized 'newspapers.'" Instead, he professed, "most of us are still like the members of the circle around the fire, listening to the elder tell the ancient stories of our tribe." Unwilling to believe that the integrity of the full-length newspaper would one day be chopped up and offered online in piecemeal form, Kaiser argued that readers "like the package much more than any of its elements." Newspapers are valuable because "they are the products of talented reporters and, above all, editors who make informed choices for their readers and viewers."

Those qualifications notwithstanding, Kaiser's counsel for the *Post*'s business operations was insightful. He envisioned that absorbing news on computers rather than newsprint could one day become publishing gold "without using an ounce of ink or a roll of newsprint—all gravy at the bottom line."

"No one in our business has yet launched a really impressive or successful electronic product, but someone surely will," the editor prophesied urgently. "The Post ought to be in the forefront of this—not for the adventure, but for important defensive purposes. We'll only defeat electronic competitors by playing their game better than they can play it. And we can." He proposed two ventures to initiate with haste, before others cornered the markets. The first was to build a digital version of classified advertising. (That would be preempted by Craigslist.) The second: "Design the world's first electronic newspaper." Four years later, an eternity in digital innovation, that became WashingtonPost.com.

Graham considered Kaiser's proposals, but he wasn't convinced. It would cost a bundle to build a new electronic classified platform, and the task of convincing skeptical journalists that they would soon be reading news on their computers seemed daft. Kaiser's memo did not light the fire under the Tuesday Group that he had hoped for. It received cursory consideration and was shelved among other white papers to revisit someday.

The next missed opportunity for a course correction came a decade later, in 2003, following Sulzberger's surprise decision to end the *International Herald Tribune* publishing partnership. For both newspapers, the *IHT* was the one platform through which their readership reached beyond the U.S. Distributed primarily in Europe and later also in Asia, the newspaper gave both partners global reach. In the 1990s the *Times* had eclipsed the *Post* by becoming a national newspaper, with printing plants across the country, making the paper widely available. Janet Robinson was pursuing a successful national advertising strategy, while the *Post* hewed to its local base. The *Times*'s foreign coverage now outclassed the *Post*'s.

Steve Coll, a Pulitzer-winning reporter who succeeded Kaiser as Downie's second in command, saw a possible opportunity in the loss of the *IHT*. The *Post*'s website was attracting a large audience, six million readers a month, mainly from outside of D.C. It had a million readers outside the country. Coll believed the *Post* could attract a much bigger national and international audience online, in part because much of the world was affected by decisions made in Washington, where the *Post*'s coverage was strongest. In a digitally connected world, Coll reasoned, why not make the *Post* a global brand, as the *New York Times* was beginning to do. Building truly national and international audiences would open up more areas for the *Post* to stretch its journalism and be a true equal of the *Times* and *Wall Street Journal*, perhaps even surpass them. Coll's youthful looks masked a fiercely competitive and determined journalist. He looked like a tech guy from Silicon Valley, and he was one of the few editors at the *Post* who knew a lot about the internet and was enthusiastic about new ways of telling stories on it.

A generation younger than Graham, Coll joined the paper in 1985 and won his first of two Pulitzers just five years later. Hoping one day to succeed Downie, he had immersed himself in the economics of the internet. Graham and Downie asked him to set up a task force to come up with different business models that could secure the *Post*'s future. Coll worked with a small team for six months. He was struck by the *Post*'s ability to build such a large online audience without spending a dime on marketing. He studied how Graham had cultivated the newspaper's dominance in the local market and appreciated the reliable profits that strategy had long produced, but he could see that expanding into the online sphere would require a drastically different approach.

The *Post* would have to look far beyond D.C. and its surrounding suburbs, where Graham wanted to invest in more coverage. Coll was ready to present a proposal at the annual off-site gathering hosted by Graham that included the Tuesday Group and all the most senior people. In 2005 the meeting was held on Maryland's Eastern Shore, at the luxurious Inn at Perry Cabin. He had prepared a PowerPoint illustrating how the *Post* could succeed in creating a completely new and much wider audience digitally. He had the attention and focus of the entire senior ranks. "Let's ride the wave," he implored.

Graham dismissed Coll's plan for global digital expansion on the spot, calling it dangerously elitist. Some of the other editors in the room were surprised that the genial Graham was so dismissive. "I care less about The New York Times than the cop in Prince William County," he responded, making it clear the plan was doomed. In near despair and feeling as if he'd been shot in the head, Coll argued that Graham was managing decline with a local strategy that wasn't going to work. He described how the decline of other quality regional newspapers, like the *Philadelphia Inquirer, Baltimore Sun*, and *Charlotte Observer*, was not going to be reversed and that the *Post* would not be immune to the structural problems bedeviling its onetime competitors, almost all of whom had shuttered their domestic and foreign bureaus and begun relying on the wires for international news.

Graham's dispute with Coll was part of an identity crisis at the *Post*. Coll's strength was long investigative pieces that Graham viewed as better suited to magazines like the *New Yorker* or the elite readership of the *Times*. Graham believed the *Post*'s readership was much broader, from the most powerful policy-makers to teachers to office cleaners. The local identity was what connected everyone and couldn't be lost. "To focus on a totally elite readership was to forego one of the *Post*'s greatest strengths," he told me. "In any event, I should have and believe I would have welcomed the idea of a national edition—if it were done right, and if it didn't reflect an abrupt turn away from our broad readership and local base."

Coll spent the spring of 2005 making plans to leave. He was tempted by an offer from David Remnick, the editor of the *New Yorker*, who had once covered Russia for the *Post*. Remnick too had won a Pulitzer, for his book about Russia, *Lenin's Tomb*. (Coll's *Ghost Wars* was about Afghanistan.) Hoping to mend the relationship, Graham invited Coll for lunch at a local Ethiopian restaurant. On the walk back, Graham explained that Buffett did not think there was room on the web for a second digital American global newspaper and thought the *Times* would always be number one there. The "Supreme Court" had handed down its ruling.

Coll's exit in August 2005 began a period of gloomy staff morale and quickening departures. That same year saw the first in a series of five staff reductions that would decimate the paper over the next decade. Typical of Graham, the buyout offers were unusually generous: a year's salary for most employees, two years for those who had been at the paper for 30 years. The newsroom was downcast over the departures of respected veterans, and Graham was heartsick over the number of farewell parties he attended. But his advisors insisted the staff cuts were necessary. Wall Street expected healthy profits from the *Post*, the *New York Times*, the *Los Angeles Times*, and the *Chicago Tribune*, margins of at least 20 percent. Analysts were slow to change expectations despite the fact that the newspaper industry was cratering.

A sinking stock price was something all publishers of public newspaper companies feared, and many owners, especially the Tribune Company, were still aiming for tight margins. Graham was known as someone who took Buffett's longer-term view of the stock market and resisted quarterly Wall Street pressure, but even he was not immune. The only way to sustain profits seemed to be to cut personnel. Each journalist cost nearly half a million dollars when you added in healthcare costs and other coverage fees. The old-timers cost even more. Thinning the herd was the only way to achieve significant savings. So the newsroom shrank from almost 1,000 journalists to 640 over the next seven years. The buyouts tied up funds that

Graham might have better invested in technology, design, and other areas that would prepare his company for the digital future. But they were necessary, as Graham's president and general manager, Steve Hills, never ceased to remind him. Hills was reviled as a "slasher" by most of the top editors, but his hold on the purse strings gave him power. The cuts eventually robbed the *Post* of its domestic bureaus and constricted foreign coverage. But by any measure, its news report was strong, especially compared to smaller cities where papers were closing. With Kaiser, Downie had written a book, *The News about the News*, lamenting the cuts and expressing fear of the press losing its raison d'être of holding power accountable, whether in the form of local police departments or state legislatures.

Downie's Cassandra warning was on target: the most devastating cuts at smaller, local newspapers almost wiped out local accountability coverage, a bigger crisis for many readers than the decline of the national chains and papers. In a 2011 report the Federal Communications Commission concluded, "The independent watchdog function that the Founding Fathers envisioned for journalism . . . is in some cases at risk at the local level."

Like Coll, there were forward-looking journalists in the newsroom who were excited about the potential of the web, but many newspaper veterans felt little kinship with the younger and less experienced staff being hired to work at WashingtonPost.com and were quick to dismiss their ideas as lame. Graham had decided to keep the two staffs separate, which he later conceded was a mistake. While the print journalists worked at the paper's headquarters near the White House, which was made famous in the movie *All the President's Men*, "the web people" worked a good distance away, across the Potomac River, in Virginia. The print team didn't trust the people working on the web to have the same values that Bradlee and Downie had inculcated in the newsroom on 15th Street. Graham thought the culture of the main newsroom would suffocate its digital twin. He also liked that Virginia was a nonunion state.

Its storied history and strong local ties did little to save the *Post* from the inexorable decade of decline that began in 2002. The internet had changed people's reading habits, and circulation of the printed paper fell by nearly half. Ad revenue plummeted too, as local department stores and businesses of all kinds closed. In a period of national chain consolidation, local department stores like the venerable Woodward & Lothrop, an anchor advertiser, disappeared. Classified ads made up 40 percent of the *Post*'s revenue—far more than for the *Times*—and were wiped out virtually overnight by the advent of Craigslist, Monster.com, and other online services. It seemed no amount of cutting could forestall the nosedive of the company's stock price, from nearly $1,000 a share to under $400.

A year after he left, Coll ran into a longtime member of the *Post*'s business staff, who told him, "You got out just in time."

For a while, at least, the *Post* had a golden goose in Kaplan, its subsidiary company that marketed student test preparation and was beginning to enter the for-profit education sector. Though it had nothing to do with the newspaper business, the company provided a source of steadily increasing profits. So when the *Post*'s board advised Kay Graham in 1984 to acquire it, her response was "I don't give a shit about it, but if you think it will be profitable, let's do it." Only later, when Kaplan had become the company's lifeline, would her avowed apathy appear so acutely ironic.

Stanley H. Kaplan had started a test-prep and tutoring firm back in 1938, at the ripe age of 19. As a generation of prosperous Gen-X parents became obsessed with sending their kids to the best college or law school, Kaplan was always there for SAT and LSAT help. Buffett, the Oracle of Omaha, reviewed Kaplan's books in preparation for the 1984 investment and found the business financially sound.

Graham appointed Don to oversee the business, and he installed a new CEO with an MBA, a young spark plug named Jonathan Grayer, who approached Kaplan with the analytical rigor of a researcher doing a case study. In 1998 Kaplan debuted its first online-only program, offering juris doctor degrees to a group of 33 budding lawyers who enrolled in the new virtual school. Two years later 600 students were enrolled and on their way into the legal profession, one click at a time. There was clearly a market for online academics.

Next Grayer found Quest Education Corporation, an Atlanta-based consortium of 30 schools, mostly for healthcare and information technology, located in different states. The company did not come cheap: at $165 million, the price tag represented the entirety of the profits generated that year by the newspaper and *Newsweek*, the declining weekly magazine the *Post* owned. The move kicked off a spree of education acquisitions by the *Post*; by 2010 its holdings would include 75 small colleges, as well as its massive online arm, Kaplan University. All of them were part of the burgeoning field of for-profit education.

The year after the Quest acquisition, revenues from the *Post*'s newspaper division declined for the first time in more than a decade, but the company's new education operation brought in enough to cover the shortfall and then some. The Clinton administration had regulated the sector, requiring schools to hold at least half of their classes on campus in order to qualify for federal funding and making it illegal for schools to pay their recruiters based on the number of students they enrolled. But George W. Bush packed the Department of Education with former executives at for-profit schools and lifted the ban against compensating employees on what the industry dubbed an "asses in classes" basis.

The floodgates were open; may the best salesman win. As Kaplan mounted an even larger and less restrained marketing and recruitment effort, its student population swelled dramatically, and by 2004 the education division was generating more income than the newspaper. Two years later another statutory change took effect: Title IV student loans, offered by the federal government, could now be used to cover tuition for online-only schools. Many of Kaplan's programs existed on the internet and had therefore been catering only to students who could pay their way without the help of federal financial aid. The $101 million in Title IV funds Kaplan collected in 2001 became, by 2010, a whopping $1.46 billion.

The subsidiary had eclipsed the flagship. In 2006 the Post Company employed three times as many people at Kaplan as it did at the newspaper, propelling Graham to change the moniker of the company to lead with education the next year. Sulzberger was openly jealous of the Kaplan investment, which turned out the way he had once hoped About.com would. And yet inside the *Post* it was looked upon as the corporate stepchild, just like the website. One former executive at Kaplan said that the journalists apparently thought, "What we do is important, and what you do is merely test prep."

About rebranding the company, Graham explained to Wall Street analysts, "It is likely that the Washington Post Co. of the future will be more an education company and a little less a media company every year." Grayer suggested the makeover was overdue. "It has been amazing to me that, despite our size and our impact on the company, because of the fame of the Washington Post name and brand, the company is still described in the media as a newspaper publisher," he said. His comments were unwelcome in the newsroom.

While Graham lived fairly modestly, Grayer and his underlings took home tens of millions of dollars every year, leaving little to bootstrap the struggling newspaper. Eventually, after taking another apparent swipe at Graham and the newspaper in a 2008 interview, Grayer resigned. His severance package would cost the *Post* dearly: it was his base salary, plus incentives, plus a bonus of $76 million to be paid out in installments until 2011.

The final installment, $20 million, amounted to more than Kaplan University's entire operating income for that fiscal quarter. The paper, meanwhile, posted a $6 million loss, closed most of its regional bureaus, and resumed the painstaking cuts.

Shortly thereafter the Washington Post Guild accused the company of "unjustly laying off employees and targeting employees of color." There had been racial tensions inside the *Post* for many years, and the sour economy worsened the problem.

On the editorial side, the *Post* was criticized for credulous coverage of the Bush administration's bad intelligence leading up to the Iraq War, although its transgressions weren't as bad as the *Times*'s. The *Times* published "From the Editors: The Times and Iraq" in May 2004, expressing regret for some of its coverage, and in August the *Post* apologized for being overly credulous. The *Post* also published a 3,000-word article by its media reporter, Howard Kurtz, called "The Post and WMDs: An Inside Story," which exposed lapses in both reporting and editing.

While Judy Miller was the public face of the *Times*'s mistakes, the man whom Ben Bradlee called the greatest investigative reporter of his time, Bob Woodward, was the *Post*'s most visible spokesman on the WMD issue. On the eve of the war, Woodward went on CNN's *Larry King Live*, where a viewer called in with a question for him: What happens if we go to war against Iraq, knock them out, and then find they had no weapons of mass destruction in the first place? Woodward's response would haunt him for years: "I think the chance of that happening is about zero."

Graham and the *Post*'s opinion editor, Fred Hiatt, were both in favor of the U.S. invasion of Iraq. The paper's editorial page, which reflected Graham's views, had grown noticeably more conservative during the Bush years. And while that should not have influenced the news pages, the owner's imprimatur was part of a general pro-war fervor sweeping over Washington at the time and inevitably coloring the reportage. As the *Times* had Jim Risen and Eric Schmitt reporting on doubts about the administration's intelligence, the *Post* carried skeptical stories by Walter Pincus, its curmudgeonly CIA reporter, and Joby Warrick, a young investigative star who focused on national security. But they were drowned out by more than 140 stories that ran on the *Post*'s front page, littered with quotes from anonymous government sources who echoed the Bush line that Saddam's WMD program necessitated war.

Around the time of his appearance on *Larry King*, Woodward was approached by Pincus, who told him about a story he'd written exposing some of the WMD intelligence as doubtful. He said he feared his editor was going to bury the story. He appealed to Woodward to intervene, but Woodward told him there was nothing he could do. Thomas Ricks, who covered the Pentagon, earlier had turned in a piece titled "Doubts" that shed light on the reluctance of senior intelligence officials to proceed with the invasion of Iraq. The editors killed Ricks's piece; they hid Pincus's story on A-17.

Though Woodward enjoyed greater access to the White House than just about any other reporter in recent history—his material was ample enough for four books on Bush and Iraq and much later a blockbuster on the early days of chaos inside the Trump White House—he could not shake his belief that the WMDs were there. Once that had been debunked and the *Post* began to walk back its narrative, Woodward confessed his regrets, which Kurtz quoted in his "inside story" on how the paper got things wrong. "We did our job but we didn't do enough, and I blame myself mightily for not pushing harder," Woodward said. "We should have warned readers we had information that the basis for this was shakier" than widely believed. "Those are exactly the kind of statements that should be published on the front page." He stopped short of saying the administration willfully lied about the WMD intelligence.

Downie too, who had worked with Woodward on the *Post*'s coverage of Watergate, admitted failures. "We were so focused on trying to figure out what the administration was doing that we were not giving the same play to people who said it wouldn't be a good idea to go to war and were questioning the administration's rationale," the editor told Kurtz. "Not enough of those stories were put on the front page. That was a mistake on my part."

Woodward continued to cover the Bush administration, relying heavily on Secretary of State Colin Powell and his deputy for sourcing, and his stories continued to bring controversy to the *Post*'s doorstep. In 2005 Lewis "Scooter" Libby, one of the most prominent Iraq hawks in the White House, was to stand trial for his role in revealing the identity of an undercover CIA agent, Valerie Plame. Woodward had learned her identity from Powell's deputy during an interview for his book, but he hadn't published the information or shared it with Downie. Libby's trial soon became the hottest drama in D.C., and everyone inside the Beltway became consumed by the guessing game of who had unmasked Plame. It was a crucial issue in the criminal case against Libby, but Woodward had decided to sit on his secret. When it was later revealed that Woodward was the first reporter who was told her name, Downie called his silence "a mistake."

Because Libby was suspected of being Judy Miller's source, his lawyers called me to testify, hoping I would damage her credibility. My lawyer had figured out that as a reluctant witness my testimony would be minimal, which it was. It consisted of two questions, neither important to the trial's outcome, and lasted all of three minutes. Libby was convicted in 2007 for lying to the FBI.

Critics on the left continued loudly to condemn the establishment press for becoming a mouthpiece for the Bush administration. McClatchy's Washington bureau, lesser known and read, got the story right, while the *New York Times* and *Washington Post*, the pillars of the establishment, fumbled it.

Television networks, as well as cable and local stations, were cutting their staffs, leaving the two papers to play a more influential role in setting the agenda for news coverage. Since 2000, however, blogs had been eating away at the authority and audience of the *Post* and the *Times*. Left-leaning blogs, especially Talking Points Memo, launched by a former graduate student in history, Josh Marshall, grew exponentially in influence and credibility during the political battles over the Iraq War. Marshall's opposition to the war was supported by the investigative reporting he had done online, dredging up findings that no amount of shoe-leather reporting could ever have unearthed. He built a network of devoted readers, including lawyers, activists, and intelligence and policy experts who helped him do his digging. When there were government document dumps, he called upon his readers to help him comb them for newsworthy nuggets. Collaboration instead of competition was his model, and with the financial support of his readers, he could tunnel into specific stories and ignore other news that the *Times* and *Post* were obliged to cover. When those two papers found themselves chasing the same story as Marshall, they would assign teams of reporters to sift through buckets of documents, all to contend with the blogger and his larger team of no-names.

Along with Marshall, journalists Andrew Sullivan and Mickey Kaus wrote political blogs that quickly gained followings (including many of the *Times*'s and *Post*'s leading lights) due in part to their looser style, which made virtually no distinction between opinion and news reporting, and their narrower scope. Soon the *Post* entered the mix with its own political blog, The Fix, which gained traction among those disaffected by the so-called mainstream media. Writing with "voice," once considered a mark of dubious objectivity, now came to be viewed as a sign of authenticity. The *Post* and the *Times* could coerce their staffs to do more blogging and inject more of their own voices, but the fact remained that their institutions were inescapably "mainstream," a term that intensified in derisiveness with each successive scandal. Although the causal relationship between the flawed coverage and public mistrust of the press can't be proven, polls taken by the Poynter Institute show journalism's stature plummeting after 2003. The phrase "fake news" would not become widely used until the 2016 election, when the extreme (or alt-right) media distributed made-up stories on topics such as the pedophilia ring Hillary Clinton allegedly conducted out of a Washington pizza parlor. Though neither the *Times* nor the *Post* set out to mislead readers about weapons in Iraq, their coverage damaged the press's credibility and helped to create a rush to war.

To this day it's hard to pin down exactly why two generally liberal papers, the *Post* and the *Times*, were so credulous in their coverage of the Bush administration's flawed intelligence. Three reasons seem likely candidates. Both papers were influenced by the wave of patriotism that swept the nation after 9/11. Their reporters were better sourced at the upper echelons of the intelligence agencies, where officials spouted the White House line. Graham, a former cop, had hired more conservative writers for the paper's opinion pages. It was a damaging case of groupthink and a failure of imagination that the Bush administration would not lie about WMDs.

By 2006 the country and the *Post*'s editorial page had soured on President Bush, and Graham had become obsessed by figuring out a business model that would sustain the family jewel. The internet was killing off newspapers, and because of his stature—he was a member of the Pulitzer board and a regular at the invitation-only Allen & Co. media mogul conclave in Sun Valley—the rest of the industry looked to him for answers. Graham was a genuine internet enthusiast, and though his tastes remained old school, observing his four children, he could tell that younger people read practically everything on computers and then, when Steve Jobs rolled out the iPhone, on smartphones.

During the dawn of digital media, he also had the benefit of a few smart, forward-looking business advisors working under him, like Christopher Ma, who in 1996 became both the editor and the developer of the *Post*'s website and later took charge of all digital business development. Ma's daughter, Olivia, had made a friend at Harvard named Chris Hughes, who happened to be Mark Zuckerberg's roommate. Zuckerberg was already on leave from the college, working on a venture that was then called The Facebook. Ma was hunting for digital acquisitions for the *Post* when his daughter suggested he take a look at The Facebook, which was already wildly popular at Harvard and a few other colleges. Ma liked what he saw, and the next time he was in Palo Alto he got in touch with the college drop-out whose brainchild this was. Over lunch at the very end of 2004, Zucker-berg explained the site to Ma, who did his best to restrain his delight at the promising investment prospect; he suggested that Zuckerberg give him a call if he was interested in having the *Post* as an investor.

Two weeks later, in early 2005, Zuckerberg arrived in D.C. and found his way to the fifth floor of the 15th Street building, where he was surprised to see that he and Ma would be joined in the conference room by Don Graham. Graham remembered receiving a hard-copy directory of freshmen at Harvard, long before Zuckerberg came along, and thumbing through the pages of his classmates' headshots. He could tell that this, The Facebook, was an entirely different beast. The Facebook was actually connecting people, an idea that captivated Graham. He was stunned to hear how many hours students were spending on the site. He was impressed by the 20-year-old computer whiz and told him on the spot that the *Post* would be interested in making an investment. Graham later told me he told Zuckerberg that he thought Facebook might well be the best business idea he'd ever heard. Zuckerberg, according to a history of Facebook written by former *Fortune* tech journalist David Kirkpatrick, told Graham he thought he was "cool." Graham said he thought Zuckerberg was unusually thoughtful but, "by a mile, the shyest, most awkward 20-year-old I had ever met." He also seemed remarkably untutored in business fundamentals, Graham remembered. "The future tech titan did not then know the difference between revenues and profits." Talks continued for the next two months.

Eventually Graham offered $6 million for a 10 percent stake in Facebook. Zuckerberg had all but given a final commitment to the *Post*; he had an affinity for the *Post* brand, and it appealed to him that Graham, like his mentor Buffett, had a long-term and relatively hands-off view of investing. But Zuckerberg's partners wanted to test interest among venture capital firms whose approach would be the opposite of Graham's, with expectations of a quick return on their investment and an inclination to take the company public sooner rather than later.

According to an account in Kirkpatrick's book, *The Facebook Effect*, Graham was feeling secure in the handshake deal he had made with Zuckerberg for the $6 million, when a venture capital firm, Accel, approached The Facebook with a $12 million offer for a 15 percent stake. Accel could also bring the fledgling company Silicon Valley experience, Zuckerberg's partners argued. They and Zuckerberg went to a fancy dinner with the men from Accel, but Zuckerberg became so consumed by guilt over having given Graham his word that he excused himself and went to the men's room. When he didn't return to the table, one of his partners went to the restroom and found him on the floor crying. The man persuaded Zuckerberg to call Graham the next day and come clean.

When Graham heard the news about Accel he was disappointed, but he refused to put pressure on the young, emotionally vulnerable Zuckerberg. He also feared that if he upped his offer, so too would Accel, and he had no interest in starting a bidding war. He kindly counseled Zuckerberg to trust his instincts to lead him out of this moral dilemma, and bid him adieu. Zuckerberg notified him soon after that he was going with the bigger offer. Graham's forgiveness notwithstanding, the *Post*'s 10 percent stake in Facebook would today be worth $12 billion, more than enough to have solved whatever problems the company had. (Graham was not the only executive to miss an early internet investment that turned out to be a gold mine; Sulzberger and his business team had passed up an early chance to invest in Google.)

In any event, the generous-hearted Graham had made a friend for life. Zuckerberg came to idolize Graham, even coming to Washington to shadow him for a few days to see what a CEO really did. He also copied the dual stock structure that the Sulzberger and Graham families had created to keep family control of their companies. Graham joined the small Facebook board in 2009, one of the few outsiders invited in. The relationship he forged with Zuckerberg was not unlike the one his mother had with Buffett. And their friendship did make Don Graham cool.

The connection with Facebook also gave him a perch from which to observe the transformation of his own industry. He understood how important the *Post*'s push onto the internet was, which is why he made one of his biggest mistakes, keeping the Post Company's digital operations separate from its journalism core. He had the best of intentions, trying to protect the fledgling web operation from being crushed by the old guard. But what was needed was for the core, the newspaper, to embrace innovation, and that wasn't happening. While he was fascinated by it, Graham did not see how the social web or most digital news could make money for the *Post*.

That lack of vision, shared by almost every newspaper owner, led to another bad call in late 2006 when Graham missed out on another breakout experiment in digital publishing. Two of his best political journalists, John Harris, the paper's political editor and one of the *Post*'s biggest talents, and reporter Jim VandeHei were itchy to start an all-politics digital news operation that would have a much faster metabolism than either the newspaper or the website. They submitted a proposal to Graham, asking for funding for a separate staff of journalists to go deep inside campaigns to produce news with a narcotic appeal for political junkies. With the raucous 2008 election looming, and a wide open field in both parties, they argued there was tremendous opportunity for the *Post* to completely dominate the campaign with a new kind of fast-paced coverage that captured the drama and gyrations of politics. Harris and VandeHei saw traditional campaign reporting as lacking in sauce and spark. The digital news site they were proposing would provide multiple doses of campaign gossip and political intrigue throughout the daily news cycle, beginning at dawn.

Around Thanksgiving, they made their pitch at a meeting attended by Graham, Downie, and other editors. The pair also talked about their idea for an all-politics site with Robert Allbritton, another scion of a Washington, D.C., newspaper family. The Allbrittons had owned *Washington Star*, once the *Post*'s main daily rival, and now had TV holdings, including the local Washington, D.C., ABC affiliate. With Fred Ryan, a well-connected Republican who once worked for the Reagans, Allbritton wanted to launch a newspaper focused on Capitol Hill that would be published several times a week, although there were already two similar papers. Ryan talked to Harris and VandeHei about combining Allbritton's newspaper proposal with the online operation the two *Post* journalists were proposing.

Harris, who had joined the *Post* in 1985 as an intern, was torn and hoped Graham would come through. But after the pitch meeting, the *Post*'s offer was skimpy: Harris would remain at the newspaper as political editor, VandeHei would become political editor of WashingtonPost.com and together they'd be given three reporters. Harris and VandeHei were looking for at least a dozen new reporters and enough of an editing staff to launch a real news start-up. The project would need at least $2 million to get off the ground. But Graham and Downie didn't see the money-making potential of an all-politics site, and housing a separate operation that competed with the *Post*'s regular campaign coverage seemed unwieldy.

So Harris and VandeHei left and accepted Allbritton's offer to launch the Politico, as their news operation was christened. The gamble paid off and soon Politico's scoops, especially a morning column called Playbook, dominated the political conversation in Washington. Mike Allen, Playbook's author, was soon being hailed as "The Man the White House Wakes Up To."

The Politico founders also heavily promoted their stories on cable. Politico's reporting style, covering campaigns like exciting sports events,

CHAPTER FIVE

BUZZFEED II

On most summer afternoons, Jonah Peretti raced up the stairs past the Mahjong betting parlor to the experimental lab he had set up in a stuffy, roach-infested workspace in Chinatown. There, with nine others, he pilot-tested humans' responses to various digital content. He called on some of Ken Lerer's contacts for his first foray into fundraising and walked away with $3.5 million of venture capital from Softbank, where his friend Eric Hippeau was a managing partner, and Hearst.

Peretti now could see search-based publishing waning as the era of social media dawned. "Media and content are human businesses," he said. At HuffPo he had focused too narrowly on "making content that the robots like." Moving into position to catch what Lerer would later call "the social wave," Peretti, for his part, would call on his inexhaustible reserve of analogies to describe the birth of BuzzFeed. He wrote to his staff "We built a locomotive and a few days later the train tracks got built."

The bet Peretti made with BuzzFeed was that eventually computers wouldn't primarily serve content to people who requested it. Instead people were exchanging content organically, with the crucial assistance of computers increasingly going unnoticed. He would explain this watershed moment as a pivot from the "Google World View" ("Connect people with the information they need") to the "Facebook World View" ("Connect people with their friends, and give them the means to communicate and express themselves"). BuzzFeed would rely on Facebook and other social networks over Google and other search engines. It was an insight that inexorably shaped the nature of the content BuzzFeed would produce. The search engine platform had trafficked in information. The social network, by contrast, was a marketplace for emotional experiences.

Peretti's new worldview was informed in part by firsthand experience on Facebook, communicating with and expressing himself to friends by sharing status updates such as "at work," "likes to party," "should be sleeping." When he and his wife, Andrea, decided it was finally time to leave their apartment in Chinatown—Andrea had never acclimated to its odor of rotting trash—he shared photos of the shag-carpeted one-bedroom on Facebook and implored his friends to consider leasing. And when they moved into a Brooklyn brownstone with enough room to move the fish tank off the kitchen counter and shelve the books they'd kept stacked on the radiator, he offered his network a glimpse into his picturesque new home life.

Classified advertising and relocation notices were just two of the ways people were leveraging their social connections on Facebook. Four years old, the site was already a well-established forum in which real people's voices could be heard, where the unthinkably vast and anonymous nature of the web at large was presented in fathomable, personalized scale. This was a welcome departure from what Zuckerberg maligned as the "top-down way" that Google organized the internet, which made the user feel like a casual reader alone in the Library of Congress. Facebook, by contrast, felt like a Friday night house party. The top-down way was also how editors molded news at the *New York Times* and the *Washington Post*.

Peretti agreed with the direction Zuckerberg was taking Facebook, and he took the opportunity to post boosterish messages to his Facebook account whenever Zuckerberg made news. When the site updated its homepage layout, he wrote that it was "awesome!" He was "excited" to attend the annual conference where Zuckerberg would dramatically unveil the latest updates to tech insiders and entrepreneurs. When Zuckerberg shared a photo of himself giving out full-size candy bars for Halloween, Peretti made known that he "liked" it and shared a link to BuzzFeed's coverage of a trick-or-treat stunt, led by Matt Stopera's fawning confession, "I personally really admire him for this."

He kept in touch with Cameron Marlow, his grad-school friend who had since become Facebook's chief data scientist, by posting public messages back and forth on each other's "walls." He made "Facebook-official" friendships with the company's heads of product, media partnerships, and global creative strategy, one of its cofounders, and a board member.

Facebook was growing fast. By 2008 the number of monthly users had nearly tripled, and over the next two years it would more than quadruple to over 600 million. For BuzzFeed's purposes, there was no alliance more important.

Peretti's experience observing viral trends offered him some perspective for monitoring the growth of this new community, but even he and his consortium of brainiac network theorists were somewhat mystified by what they were seeing. "If I had to guess why sites like Facebook are so popular, I would say it doesn't have anything to do with networking at all," his friend Duncan Watts told the *New Yorker* in 2006. "It's voyeurism and exhibitionism." This skepticism was coming from the sociologist and scientist widely regarded as the preeminent expert on social networks.

But it soon became apparent that Facebook's motto—"Move fast and break things"—was more than just bluster with a ring to it. Facebook wasn't just breaking the rule of six degrees but shattering it. Five years after its public launch, researchers at Cornell University and in Milan analyzed connections among Facebook's 700 million active users and calculated that each person was separated from every other by an average of merely 3.74 degrees. When Facebook replicated the study five years later, once its virtual population had swelled to 1.59 billion, the number had dropped to 3.57.

A remarkable thing was happening. Facebook's expanding headcount corresponded to the tightening of its social fabric; as the network grew more crowded, and users grew more accustomed to its social dynamics, it was becoming a smaller world. From its origins as a platform for reviewing last night's frat party, Facebook was becoming the type of forum Peretti would use to announce the birth of his twin sons, Artie and Yoshi, by sharing a photo of the newborns in matching onesies emblazoned with BuzzFeed's signature yellow stickers—one labeled "Cute," the other "LOL."

Never before had "catching up" been so painless. If your old college roommate got engaged, you could expect to be apprised within hours, without ever having to interact with her. When a former colleague celebrated his sister's birthday, or a distant in-law enjoyed a particularly photogenic meal, you received the update as if it were breaking news. Indeed breaking news would soon start to appear on this ecosystem of personal posts, and to compete it would have to be camouflaged as such.

Though the Facebook forum seemed organically social—early reviews likened it to the water cooler of old—its easy interface masked the complex considerations that were hardwired into the network's code. Users were in control of one input: they chose whom to declare a Friend. After that, Facebook's invisible hand took over. Its unseen algorithm, operated by 26-year-old Greg Marra, decided which of your friends' posts to show you, and in which order. The calculus was mysterious but had an uncanny knack for serving up the photos, messages, and links you wanted to see, whether you knew it or not. It determined the priority level of the items based on whose post it was, how popular it was among other users, what type of medium it was, and how recently it was posted, along with other micro factors indexed and assessed by the Facebook machine. Some reports cited this number as 100,000.

Facebook was the arbiter of importance and was unabashedly social. Its prescriptions were based on the preference for personally relevant material over material with global relevance. News organizations were in the business of deciding what mattered to you (or ought to matter) as a citizen of your city, country, and world. Facebook did them one better: it decided what mattered to you as a friend.

News Feed addressed the problem, as phrased by one of Zuckerberg's cofounders: "How do we get people the information they most care about?" The feed didn't purport to keep you informed, at least not in any higher sense of the word. Its function was to keep you in the loop. The network succeeded when it gave users the sense that theirs was a small world. To achieve this, it trafficked in what might be called small news. Zuckerberg summarized it for his staff this way: "A squirrel dying in front of your house may be more relevant to your interests right now than people dying in Africa."

On Facebook, online friends showed an insatiable appetite for new and lighthearted fodder they could share to spark conversations. To the news organizations who made it their business to report on genocide, this was an afterthought. The way they saw it, Facebook was nothing more than the kids' table wrought virtually, and they had little interest in ducking out of the grown-ups' conversation. To their thinking, it had nothing to do with distributing real news.

But for some youth-oriented publishers, Facebook's ascendance was an opportunity. By 2006 two-thirds of Facebook users visited the site daily, spending an average of 20 minutes browsing its pages. In short order it became the number-one website among American college students: 85 percent of them had profiles by 2009. That year the average time spent on the site by American users tripled; they spent more time on Facebook than on any other site. By the following year it had absorbed more of users' time than the next four most popular sites combined. Well more than half of U.S. users were between 18 and 34 years old, the demographic prized by advertisers.

In other words, Facebook gathered in one place a cross section of America that was younger and better educated and possessed of more disposable income than any assembly in history. They weren't just passively spending time on the network, either. They were clicking on the content their friends shared, discussing it in the comment threads, and, if they found it especially worthwhile, sharing it for all their friends to see. For businesses Facebook represented an unimaginably fertile tract in which to sell products by word of mouth.

Peretti realized the potential advertising value of an audience whose preferences could be mathematically determined. He understood the unspoken social rules that governed the game. He could read the subtext when, for example, one of his friends took to Facebook to share an article from the *New York Times* about the elections in Egypt. By sharing that story, the friend was communicating things about himself: that he cared about being informed, leaned left, took himself seriously, and might want to talk about the Arab Spring. (He might also want merely to be seen as wanting to talk about the Arab Spring.) Peretti also realized that serious geopolitical concerns represented a tiny sliver of the overall conversations. Observing the distance between what traditional news outlets offered and what people wanted to share, he imagined a type of publication whose tone and interests matched that of the Facebook demographic. If well executed, such an outlet could slip into social conversations so naturally that over time it might be indistinguishable from the rest of readers' friends.

As he got more comfortable on Facebook, Peretti started to share some of BuzzFeed's patently shareable posts, videos like "Tooth Extraction by Rocket" and "Penguin Being Tickled," and a quiz, "Which Political Figure Are You?," to which he self-deprecatingly appended his own result: "OMG I am Hitler."

He registered the feedback he got from friends, especially his sister, Chelsea, who would leave comments on his posts, remarking on how funny or weird or sad the items were. These were not quantitative data, but for the time being, they were what Peretti had to work with.

On February 9, 2009, Facebook introduced the Like button, a gleaming thumbs-up icon that hovered below each and every item in your News Feed so that you could, in Facebook's words, "give positive feedback and connect with things you care about." Over one billion likes were registered within the first 24 hours, and from then on, the impact of a simple, universal feedback button only proliferated.

"The Like button changed BuzzFeed forever," the site's viral hitmaker Matt Stopera declared. It reduced the palate of available responses one could have, from the binary of up or down to a single, Panglossian thumbs-up. You could still comment, but it was no longer necessary. If you wanted to give your friend affirmations for his or her post, all you had to do

now was click the little icon. Even though it wasn't cumbersome or inconvenient to interact with your friends online anymore, the act was streamlined.

Likes became the currency for web publishers who played to the social
network. For people too: their profile pictures, marriage updates, birth announcements, and the rest were now all quantifiable according to popularity. Each item competed in the democratic arena that was News Feed, not
only with other personal dispatches but also with publishers' news updates
and stories.

This development was in perfect harmony with the exceedingly likable slogan BuzzFeed had championed in its early years: "Find Your New
Favorite Thing." Even before Facebook had become the dominant social
platform, BuzzFeed's raison d'être had been to serve up things that people
liked. And now that everyone had a simple button at their fingertips, people
could like things with unprecedented quickness and ease. They could like
things prolifically, recklessly. The only factor limiting their liking was the
shortage of likable content. His pockets flush from the fresh venture-capital
injection, Peretti knew that his company was in a perfect position to take
advantage of that shortage.

The emerging mania to get a Like on Facebook, of course, was antithet-
ical to news. Complicated information about the financial crisis or acts of
terrorism wouldn't inspire anyone to hit the thumbs-up. But neither Facebook nor BuzzFeed was yet in the news business.

BuzzFeed still relished its flexibility to experiment freely, but as it
grew into the media market, Peretti gained a clearer notion of his company's identity. He picked a corporate motto inspired by internet culture: "No
Haters." It was a sentiment that would infuse every aspect of the business,
a stipulation that would appear on all of the company's job listings, accompanied by the requirement that the candidate possess "a positive, curious,
playful disposition" and self-identify as an "internet-savvy badass." (Signing bonus: No work on your birthday!) Peretti could fill the ranks with people who would represent the healthy aspects of the social web and supply
what it demanded.

"People are looking for things to enjoy and to celebrate," Peretti said.
In praise of Zuckerberg's management decisions, he'd say, "Lots of people have asked for a 'dislike' button, but there isn't one." No hater himself,
Stopera was even more forthcoming about the rationale behind BuzzFeed's
rose-colored worldview. "We just found out that being positive is the best
way to create Buzz," he said. "It just shares the best." It was a business strat-

egy, not a higher ideal. Born out of audience analysis and data-crunching, "No Haters" was a breakthrough for the BuzzFeed brand, but it was no nobler a posture than McDonald's marketers naming the Happy Meal.

Later, when BuzzFeed finally got around to hiring a book editor, he told the Poynter Institute that he would not be publishing negative book reviews. "Why waste breath talking smack about something?" he demanded, adding that he intended to follow the "Bambi rule": "If you can't say something nice, don't say nothing at all." It would have been unthinkable to ask book critics at the *Times* or *Post* to steer clear of frank, unfawning criticism. Both papers had Pulitzer Prize–winning critics and arts editors who saw themselves as the most serious and important arbiters of cultural worth. The *Times* existed to discomfit the affluent and highly educated in order to get them engaged in global issues.

This wasn't how BuzzFeed thought. It aimed to occupy a different position, as the arbiter of likability. This was a significantly easier metric to judge, especially now that the Like button was hardwired into Facebook. With such a cut-and-dried goal, Peretti's company could churn out content with a singleness of purpose. They would publish posts and observe how they performed, then tweak their approach accordingly, and repeat, until they achieved consistent likability. The editorial strategy was unprecedentedly hitched to popular opinion. Market insights would be at the very heart of BuzzFeed's operation. The success of the venture, as Peretti conceived of it, rested on three pillars: data, learning, and dollars. BuzzFeed would publish content in order to harvest data about it, then scour the data to learn how to improve for the next post, and once its staff and machines had sorted out the preferences of its readers, the company would be in a place to convert that body of intelligence into dollars.

Step I was under way, as BuzzFeed released its content into the cybersphere and registered data points each time it bounced off something new. The early editors were test pilots, Peretti liked to say, and each post was a guinea pig. Once you published it, you could monitor its performance to glean general principles about what traits thrived in the social environment.

The content was useless without a yardstick to measure how it resonated with the audience. BuzzFeed had invented its own yardstick in-house, along with the entire suite of data-mining tools its scientists used, and these implements were widely regarded as the finest in the industry. It had taken nearly all of the small fortune that had supported BuzzFeed so far to develop these gadgets. Peretti wagered that with superior intelligence about his readers—who they were, what they liked, how they thought of themselves—he could create the world's first publishing operation that was guided entirely by empiricism.

In the beginning they could learn only from their own posts. The small sample size capped the pace at which they could discover effective mutations in their content. So while Peretti studied the time readers spent on his pages and tallied the number of people who shared a particular story with their friends, his business partner John Johnson conducted experiments at an offshoot lab called the Harmony Institute. He brought in volunteers and showed them various media, measuring their fidgets, fluctuations in skin temperature, and EEG activity to unlock shortcuts to engaging the average web surfer.

Peretti understood that data were the fuel that would keep his furnace blazing, and he began to consider how he might score more data without BuzzFeed having to publish more posts, which was costly. What he wanted was a window into the psychological factors that determine readers' habits: what caught their eye, which topics they followed, how they arrived at a given article, and where they navigated immediately upon finishing the read. At the time, most other publishers were too anxious about their digital transitions to care about safeguarding their data, besides the usual contact information newspapers kept on their subscribers. Few realized what a precious resource it was, and even fewer possessed the quantitative capacity to glean anything worthwhile. As they cast about frantically for someone fluent in the language of this kind of data, Peretti came knocking to offer them a deal that just might solve their problems.

He invited the publishers to join a coalition he was assembling, called the BuzzFeed Partner Network. Joining meant the publishers agreed to let Peretti survey the reader traffic on their sites. In return for these jewels, they would be privy to the coveted Social Intelligence Report that BuzzFeed compiled. This, the publishers figured, would entitle them to the benefits of Peretti's industry-leading aptitude at virtually no cost. They enthusiastically signed on the dotted line and welcomed the wizard of BuzzFeed to step behind their curtains and observe. Unaware of the precious intelligence they were forking over, or too charmed by Peretti's acumen to resist, the publishers consented in staggering numbers. By 2013 the network boasted more than 200 partner sites whose diversity reflected that of the wider web: the *New York Times* and the *Guardian* were publishers who became partners, as were CollegeHumor and FunnyOrDie.com.

To keep them happy, Peretti periodically issued reports on the general trends he was seeing: readers tended to log on to Facebook around 5 p.m., for example, but because Mondays were typically busier, the peak on those days occurred a tad later; people were more likely to share posts that projected happy rather than sad emotions, and as ever they loved content about celebrities. Publishers should do their best, BuzzFeed counseled, to accentuate the "emotional" elements of stories and to showcase controversy and scandal whenever possible.

News stories often had this kind of emotional charge. As an example, BuzzFeed pointed to the killing of Trayvon Martin in 2012, one of the early cases that fueled the rise of the Black Lives Matter movement among young people. In the aftermath of the tragedy, BuzzFeed flooded the zone with posts like "10 Reasons Everyone Should Be Furious about Trayvon Martin's Murder" (sub-headline: "Get Angry") by Stopera. Another Stopera post spotlighted a Florida state representative's "emotional speech about Trayvon Martin's shooting." Additional headlines hawked, "Court Case Takes Emotional Turn as Photo of Trayvon Martin's Body Shown to Jury" and "Closing Arguments . . . Appeal to Emotion, Justice" and coverage of celebrity tie-ins: the actor-singer Jamie Foxx serenading Martin's parents at a vigil, basketball superstar Dwyane Wade inking an homage to Martin on his sneakers, Bruce Springsteen calling for justice. BuzzFeed did almost no original reporting on the story. It simply lifted what it needed from reports published elsewhere, repackaged the information, and presented it in a way that emphasized sentiment and celebrity.

The tone and scope of BuzzFeed's content aimed unsubtly to incite its readers' outrage, elicit their laughter, or engender a sort of sanguine conviction in the essential goodness of the human spirit. It aimed to provoke. Peretti had discovered the potency of provocation when his Nike email chain had gone viral. He knew that in order to be successful, content had to resonate with readers enough that they felt compelled to share the item with their friends. Getting them to share was the central challenge for publishers who catered to social media users.

Understanding this, Peretti determined that BuzzFeed would tailor its content to readers who demonstrated their extroversion online, a bloc he identified as "super-sharers." This was a strategy he proselytized vehemently, grounded in the insight that the old model of publishing—wherein editors determined the day's top stories and blasted them out to the masses—was dead. Nowadays, Peretti would explain, there were too many outlets competing with each other for any one of them to possess the agenda-setting authority that Walter Cronkite or the *New York Times* had once enjoyed. On the web, the audience established its own priorities.

Readers themselves held the power to disseminate a given story among their entire social network, and they would do so only if it suited them.

If the challenge was to make things that suited people online, Peretti had the advantage of knowing who these people were. "The web is ruled by maniacs," he told an audience in 2010. "Content is more viral if it helps people fully express their personality disorders." The specific personality types he deemed most worth catering to were those who promised him the highest yield: the super-sharers. An overwhelming majority of them belonged to a category Peretti labeled "histrionic/narcissistic."

The point wasn't that they were influential, just that they were profuse. Histrionic narcissists lived for the attention of their online audience and kept up near-constant "conversations." Providing stories for them to forward would be an essentially populist line of business. He would be playing to the masses. If he could succeed this way, it would be in defiance of the popularly accepted Law of the Few, at the time being argued by Malcolm Gladwell, which held that influence online was something wrought by an influencer elite, not something that came up organically from the ground floor. Peretti decided to make this play in part because he knew Duncan Watts was knee-deep in research that he was convinced would empirically debunk Gladwell's so-called law once and for all. If Peretti could capture the loyalty of the web's everyday fanatics, he could deputize them for the purpose of further disseminating BuzzFeed's content.

"The lesson here," BuzzFeed's Beastmaster Jack Shepherd explained to the *Guardian*, "is that on today's internet, your readers are your publishers." The main idea, as BuzzFeed's viral-content experts repeated again and again, was to "appeal to their vanity."

BuzzFeed's tool kit to accomplish this objective was anything but pedestrian. When it came to posting photos on social media, their data showed that "texture-heavy" or "blue-dominant" images garnered more likes. Tweets should be terse, and Facebook posts even terser. Human-interest stories attracted more attention when their headlines began with definite articles, as in "*This* Mother Found a Huge Snake in Her Son's Bed." (They had a more conversational ring that way.) They knew that, for whatever reason, more people tended to click on a post when it was accompanied by an image of a circular food item, like a pizza or pancakes. And that people who read stories about Jennifer Lawrence also demonstrated a predilection for penguin-related content.

They charted the migratory patterns of readers as they navigated from Google's search engine to NYTimes.com to Twitter to BuzzFeed to Facebook, and they didn't stop surveilling when the readers logged off. They reckoned that 92 percent of Americans used their smartphones to browse the web or chat with friends while on the toilet, and found that 95 percent kept their phones within reach while they slept.

When he felt he'd extracted all the intel his data analytics team could find, Peretti wanted more still. He hired Dao Nguyen, a young technologist and internet entrepreneur who had launched a start-up just before the new millennium. When the dot-com bubble burst, she'd gone through the painful experience of having to fire all her friends. She decided to escape to Paris, where she intended to use her money to drink wine and eat cheese. Instead she was hired to create the website for one of France's premier publishers, *Le Monde*, which she named Le Post. Its slogan: "Info, buzz, débat." The site hosted snappy news updates and guilty pleasures like celebrity coverage, which ultimately ruffled *Le Monde*'s decorous self-image and led to her firing. She returned to New York and was snatched up by Peretti, who instructed her to do what she did best: optimize.

By the time Nguyen came aboard, BuzzFeed had a pretty good idea of what people on the social web liked. Their analysts could see which topics attracted the most eyeballs, and their writers were content to cater to readers' demonstrated appetites. The challenge for Nguyen was to solve the abiding mysteries of why something went viral, and how.

Nguyen got to work developing a digital dashboard that arrayed dozens of dials to illustrate how a given BuzzFeed post was performing. Her team created the software internally, a feat of computer science that was beyond most of their competitors. Nguyen's dashboard tabulated the total number of people who viewed a post and visualized the various paths that had led them to it—whether they happened upon the item while browsing Buzz-Feed's website, or querying Google's search engine, or scrolling their Face-book News Feed, or visiting some other source.

Most important, it would calculate the ratio of people who'd found the post themselves to those who'd landed there by clicking on a link their friend had shared. This was called Social Lift, and while the engineers acknowledged there was no such thing as "one metric to rule them all," and some debunked the phenomenon, Social Lift mattered at BuzzFeed.

The dashboard offered more than just retrospective, performance-review feedback. It was meant to be deployed before a post was published. When a writer was ready to release a post, he or she was encouraged to come up with as many as eight different potential headlines and several options for the accompanying photo. Nguyen's software would then publish each permutation of these inputs, so that for a few minutes a dozen or more versions of the post would bounce around the internet, each appearing to different readers. Once her machine collected a sufficient data sample on the relative popularity of each rendition, the computer would select the best-performing one and eliminate the others.

Nguyen's work was based in the conviction that the time-honored conventions of publishing were not to be taken for granted. Each piece of content was infinitely manipulable and recyclable. Every facet of every post—from the copy and artwork to the length and layout—represented a decision, and every decision was worth tinkering with and rethinking. For instance, when she noticed a preponderance of smartphone readers sharing articles over email, she enlarged the email icon on BuzzFeed's mobile displays. In the span of a week, the number of shares via mobile email doubled.

The technology Nguyen had designed for BuzzFeed's data collection and analysis was proprietary. In her first two years at BuzzFeed, the site's audience quintupled. With the possible exception of Facebook, no other site had a better system for decoding their readers' habits and anticipating their needs.

Peretti was careful not to appear too data-obsessed and robotic. "There's the misconception that we are crass data monkeys who only care about what's popular," he observed. "People will come up to me and say, 'What's the algorithm?' And it's like, enhhh . . ."

He was speaking out of both sides of his mouth. "The viral distribution strategy is as important as the idea itself!" he announced at a 2013 *Guardian* conference. While other publishers spent 95 percent of their time on content and just 5 percent on strategic distribution, BuzzFeed's creative director Philip Byrne estimated that BuzzFeed was splitting its focus 50–50. This drastic reordering of priorities was at the heart of what made Buzz-Feed successful. To Peretti, it was obvious where the rest of the industry was going wrong, and he showed no bashfulness in calling this to their attention. He told a Gainesville, Florida, audience at an explanatory presentation that the biggest misconception among publishers was that "quality is all that matters."

Peretti's goal was to win the numbers game. The surest way to achieve that was not by improving his writers' craftsmanship but by optimizing the business strategy. If BuzzFeed could outsmart its competitors in the game of distribution, it could leapfrog the incumbents regardless of the fact that much of its content was derivative. Peretti was by no means the first person to realize this, but he was the first to champion this strategy so audaciously.

"Which is better: Judaism or Mormonism?" he'd ask. Then he'd point to a graph displaying the "performance metrics" of the two religions: for most of recorded history, Jews vastly outnumbered Mormons, but over the 20th century the Mormons narrowed the gap, and in 2007 their ranks equalized. "Learn from the Mormons!" Peretti implored audiences. "Quality is not enough, build evangelism into your ideas."

Some topics, like environmental conservation, were inherently evangelistic. They bespoke a higher cause that supporters promoted in order to change hearts and minds. But for Peretti, evangelism was rarely about saving the world. It was most potent when it operated subliminally. The easiest way to pull off this effect was to compose posts that gave readers the illusion that it was for them, personally—or even better, *about* them. When people encountered what they thought was good press for their personal brand, they publicized it almost without fail.

Peretti preached, "Content is about identity." It was an entrepreneurial philosophy rooted in the same ideas as the capitalism critique he'd published a decade prior—that "the viewer 'narcissistically identifies' with an image-repertoire that defines the ideological content of a period in history." BuzzFeed's thesis was that the most successful content would replicate Narcissus's mirror. Hence the deluge of posts testifying in the second person to some kernel of the reader's character which began to predominate in social spaces throughout the internet: "Weird Thoughts You Have in the Shower," "Why You Should Run a 5K," "40 Things That Will Make You Feel Old," "20 Ways to Tell Someone Secretly Hates You," "31 Thoughts You Have When Your Mom Doesn't Answer Your Phone Calls."

Items that weren't explicitly *about* you often seemed to be composed with "you" in mind. These posts were "relatable" content, and BuzzFeed's staff doubled down on them. They created more than 275 categories of posts for one demographic or another, including Hypochondriacs, Virgos, Picky Eaters, Australians Who Sunburn Easily, and Literally Everyone. Each identity post was a bank shot; posts about Virgos weren't going to perform well among Leos. The idea was that by narrowing the scope of the piece, the writer guaranteed it would resonate with one particular subgroup whose members would feel flattered and more likely to evangelize the post.

Relatability was the watchword, and BuzzFeed's most talented staffers excelled at it. To them, relatability was a principle that applied not only to the post's subject matter but to its formal considerations as well. In this, Stopera was king. For one, his own taste profile equipped him for maximum relatability: he described himself as "a normal person" with "normal opinions"—a sort of lowest common denominator. "I tell people, when you work at BuzzFeed, write like you talk," he told me. "I talk wrong"—here he caught himself—"incorrect." He added, "I write like a 9-year-old." If nothing else, this style of prose ensures that people who land on a Stopera story will never find it over their head.

"I've always been good at pleasing," Stopera confessed to me with a boyish grin. It's a talent that comes in handy when he's forced to pick a restaurant for two friends with different cravings. Or, he said, when he's "targeting urban 25- to 35-year-olds."

After nearly a decade on the job, Stopera had an intimate familiarity with the archetypal reader. He dubbed it "the default human being," whose interests include "pizza, Netflix, and Beyoncé." Pleasing these people wasn't the most arduous task, but in the era of relatable internet, Stopera found it was wiser to aim low than high. One might suspect aiming low gets old after a while, but 7,500 posts later Stopera still seemed genuinely to enjoy creating posts like "24 Pictures That Prove Teenage Girls Are the Future" and "19 Pictures That Show the Difference between Your Life and Mariah Carey's." Without a trace of ennui, he told me, "Getting the viral hit is fun no matter what."

BuzzFeed's young hitmakers had an arsenal of secret weapons for winning the internet's attention. Most of them, even the low-key and unexcitable Nguyen, felt the adrenaline and endorphins of going viral. Very few of the longtime BuzzFeeders showed any aspiration to take on more serious reporting projects if it meant stepping away from the hit parade.

This was BuzzFeed's culture, from its first incarnation as a self-described "internet popularity contest." Management insisted on quantifying the popularity of its employees' work using Nguyen's dashboard. Every afternoon they sent out a company-wide "scorecard" and awarded virtual badges to the day's winners. A running tally ranked the top-performing post-writers in terms of the eyeballs they won. Notching 10 posts with at least a million views each qualified you for induction into the Players' Club, a distinction commemorated by a dinky plastic trophy and a handwritten letter of congratulations from Beastmaster Shepherd, in crayon. A few ascended to the Silver and Gold Players Clubs. Upon authoring his 100th million-view post, Matt Stopera was admitted to the Crystal Players Club. The only one on a higher rung was his younger brother, Dave, sole member of the Platinum Players Club.

BuzzFeed had a glossary of slang terms for different types of viral growth curves. The biggest hits were designated "mega-vi" and could be detected as such in the early stages if one was attuned to the right signs. One sign of a mega-vi post, for example, was the "tweetslam," which occurred when a post on Twitter appeared and circulated so rapidly that the network's servers couldn't keep up.

The quest for ever-bigger blockbusters kept BuzzFeeders glued to their computer screens. Someone would publish a post that went mega-vi and receive invitations to appear on a television talk show, but the staff joked that it was only worth doing so their parents could watch them on air. The pace of BuzzFeed's growth meant employees faced consequences if they weren't meeting traffic goals. One former staff writer, Arabelle Sicardi, whose essays on womanhood and self-image packed more substance than most content on the site, was reassigned when her numbers lulled. "They had me stop writing essays and only concentrate on viral," she said. Posts like "This Piglet Dressed as a Unicorn Is Making Everyone Cry Rainbows" and "13 Emotions Everyone Experiences in Sephora" then took the place of her expositions on feminism. "That's when I decided to leave."

BuzzFeed's tireless aspirations had the effect of disincentivizing originality. Faced with an unbudging bottom line—go viral or get out—the staff reverted to ground they knew was lower risk: topics with track records of going mega-vi and familiar formats that followed established templates.

The most tried and true was the list, a BuzzFeed standby. There were three types of list: the listicle, which assembled some number of entries conforming to a theme ("11 Reasons Why You Should NEVER Eat a Horse"); the definitive list, which enumerated the superlative items in a given category ("The 30 Most Important Cats of 2010"); and the framework list, which employed bullet points to guide the reader through a loosely defined narrative ("Scenes from the 2011 Florida Corgi Picnic"). Having selected a list template to use, the writer chose from Stopera's index of "frames"—A Ways to B, N Reasons You Q, X Facts about Y, and so on.

They then consulted an accompanying catalogue of emotions for a suitable match. Over the years Stopera and his fellow pioneers of the viral list had taxonomized the palette of human emotion into subflavors, as Baskin-Robbins had done for ice cream. Now producing them was as easy as dipping for a scoop. Joy, arousal, awe, *awwwww*, indignation, good humor—each emotional category already boasted myriad BuzzFeed posts. One of the most effective emotions was one for which there existed no English word: the feeling of having one's faith in humanity restored. By studying its data, BuzzFeed distilled this sensation and resolved to play to it doggedly. The past few years alone had seen several dozen mega-vi posts about how such-and-such "will restore your faith in humanity." Among the subjects it claimed had restorative powers were pugs, kids, pizza, a hospital for bats, pictures of Jon Hamm's penis, so-called "Aussie Moments," and "this man eating a muffin in the background of a Labour MP's interview."

One emotion on which BuzzFeed went all in was nostalgia. As Stopera put it, "There's no better feeling than being nostalgic. It's like a chemical. It makes your body warm." He had observed readers' surprising affinity for the posts he would write in reminiscence of '80s culture and become convinced that BuzzFeed could capitalize on people's soft spot for things past. It worked so well that Stopera promptly pivoted to nostalgia production, taking a step back from the trendspotting responsibilities he'd been given at first.

By enumerating the human emotions of online behavior and boiling down the options for framing each, Stopera had his job down to a science: "You combine a frame with an emotion, and you have a BuzzFeed post." He kept a bulging book of frames that were akin to golden oldies.

It became standard for BuzzFeed writers to recycle posts wholesale, adding or removing a few words or examples to avoid obvious self-plagiarism. "Like, '10 ways to improve your day,'" Stopera offered. "You can frame it a different way in a month and you have a whole new piece of content." "That's why I love my job," he added. "It's like remixing things, basically. A constant remixing of content." The hype surrounding Buzz-Feed's ascension portrayed a radically innovative force with its sights set on reinventing the publishing industry. It really was nothing more than adapting familiar content to the age of digital reproduction.

Having itemized and indexed internet users' fears and desires, their self-image, aspirations, and guilty pleasures, BuzzFeed now had to feed that material back to them. The packaging was shiny, if unsubtle. In a frenetic social environment, the list appealed for its brevity. It achieved the ends the culture wanted, according to a famous quote by the novelist Umberto Eco: "To make infinity comprehensible . . . [and] create order." The form allowed any topic to be rendered as an entirely visual experience— a vertically arranged slideshow—that was all the more conveniently digestible for being postliterate.

Social media users were getting used to scrolling briskly through their friends' posts. The sheer volume of photos, stories, updates, and opinions shared made it impossible to do otherwise. Settling into a substantive read carried an increasingly steep opportunity cost. BuzzFeed's lists appealed to overwhelmed readers for the same reason that Cliff's Notes was enticing to overworked college students. "If we take the same point and make it not a list, people don't like it as much," Peretti told the *Independent*. That was the data talking, and the data were telling the truth. Of BuzzFeed's 30 most-liked posts in 2011, 24 were lists.

When Peretti got flak for relying so heavily on this dumbed-down form of publishing, he zealously defended the practice. "Lists are an amazing way to consume media," he wrote in a public memo. "They work for content as varied as the 10 Commandments [and] the Bill of Rights." Another BuzzFeed editor claimed that lists worked for Homer. "You could call that [book, *The Odyssey*,] 24 Chapters about Odysseus. That's, like, a really great list. Really top notch. Really, really viral. Super viral."

Their arguments may not have convinced the rest of the publishing industry to rethink the contributions of Homer or Moses or the architects of American democracy, but they didn't need to. What mattered wasn't whether BuzzFeed's lists were high-minded but that they were irresistible. They proved so effective that soon even the most esteemed publishers were mimicking the form.

The *New York Times* hopped on the trend, and by 2014 three of its six most popular pieces were lists. (Another two were celebrity coverage, and the third was an interactive quiz that purported to pinpoint the taker's regional dialect.) New websites such as Listverse.com appeared, with the sole purpose of publishing snackable servings. The *Onion*, a satirical newspaper, launched an entire website to parody the BuzzFeed form. Called Click Hole.com, its slogan was "Because all content deserves to go viral."

The other mainstay of BuzzFeed's content was the quiz, a digital adaptation of the classic flowcharts from the pages of *Cosmo* and other magazines that proffered answers to questions like "Is he into you?" They were pitch-perfect for luring the egomaniacs and navel-gazers who Peretti was convinced dominated the web. Summer Anne Burton, BuzzFeed's managing editorial director, sat down with Harvard's Nieman Journalism Lab to explain why her organization had invested so heavily in quiz production. "When people share things, it's partially because of what it says about them," she said. "Quizzes are like the literal version of all that." Each Buzz-Feed quiz contained a nugget of potentially revelatory data about each and every reader. Like the Evil Queen's talking mirror in *Snow White*, it presented an opportunity to get someone's opinion of you, even if that someone was an algorithm. "For me, it's almost impossible to not take a quiz," Burton added. "You're like: I must know what Muppet I am." After a while BuzzFeed's readers knew not only that but also what kind of cookie, which Greek god, and what percentage Kardashian they were.

There was something oracular about the ability of BuzzFeed's machines to deduce personal insights based on the seemingly random information the quiz-taker fed it. Enter your go-to salad fixings and it would take a crack at your age and dream job. By answering the eight simple questions (favorite vacation destination, color, hobby, and so on) that composed the "Which Billionaire Tycoon Are You?" quiz, Rupert Murdoch got himself. Even critical feedback about oneself was considered worth publicizing, if not to testify to the quiz's accuracy then to lodge a complaint with its verdict. BuzzFeed's quiz-makers recognized this, which is why they rigged the one about political figures so that everyone, including Peretti, got the Führer.

BuzzFeed's technologists knew how to use mind tricks and pressure points, how to twist arms, dangle carrots, and use reverse psychology. They had it down to a science: blend one part tough love into two parts obsequious flattery, filter that through nostalgia, and glaze it with scot-free optimism. This was what they called "making a thing a thing." As tastemakers, it was their remit to do so from their seat of power, aided by BuzzFeed's suite of custom digital tools for amplifying their influence. It was as if BuzzFeed had developed a special sauce that when applied to a piece of content—no matter how trivial or unfounded—made that piece irresistible, even if it was nothing more than an advertisement.

The dynamics of social sharing could be applied and extended to both advertising and news. In 2008 Peretti laid out how BuzzFeed would parlay its formula for popularity into profitability. His pitch to investors had prophesied that the direction of the digital publishing industry was "ads as content." Having all but mastered the science of successful content, the task was now to apply those clickable trappings to messages from their sponsors.

In January 2010 BuzzFeed signed Comedy Central as its first client. In May, with its native advertising operation beginning to bring in revenue, the company landed another $8 million injection of venture capital and hired a new president, Jon Steinberg, who had managed part of Google's business. The pitch he made to advertisers was somewhat counterintuitive: Be bashful about what you are selling. Peretti used some of the same employees who created BuzzFeed's listicles to make native ad content that appealed to BuzzFeed visitors and wasn't too heavy-handed with the branding. To promote the idea of shareability to the ad agencies, BuzzFeed hired ad copywriters and formed a "creative" division. They would incubate under veteran buzz-writers and conform to BuzzFeed's signature.

The most profitable relation between the organic, or editorial, posts and the advertisements would be one of verisimilitude. It was better to have BuzzFeed itself create the ads, Peretti told agencies. That way they would look as authentic as possible. He estimated that when it came to making content tailored to the social web, a BuzzFeed employee was 10 times as effective as someone from an outside agency.

Some of his business advisors thought it was daft that Peretti wanted to confine advertising on BuzzFeed to so-called native ads that told stories with the same emotional triggers as the rest of BuzzFeed, but he seemed to have no doubts. He detested the ubiquitous cheap click ads that had ruined the design of other websites. He believed native advertising would allow BuzzFeed to sell not merely the space to place an ad but also the ad itself. Profits would pour in as the ads pinballed around the web, registering a long tail of impressions. He pointed to data showing that when an ad was properly dressed up, readers didn't seem to care whether it was a sales pitch. They cared only that it spoke to them, as BuzzFeed did with native fluency. The ads attracted clicks and shares in numbers that astounded advertisers, who leaped at the opportunity to watch their brand campaigns light up Nguyen's data dashboard.

Most people who visited BuzzFeed and shared its content were not journalistic purists. They noticed no difference between the ads and the rest of the site's content. In the beginning "there was no church, there was no state," recalled one of Peretti's first hires, his former student Peggy Wang. That BuzzFeed's content produced a conflict between editorial integrity and commercial interests hardly affected whether or not it made them laugh. When it came to evaluating the content his company produced, Peretti followed the same standard, insisting that pieces should be judged on their enjoyability, not their objectivity. "Some editorial content sucks, some ads are awesome," he said, "and for many readers this line is even more important to them than church and state."

Whether it came in the form of an ad or an impartial post, readers wanted to read about themselves. They wanted content that flattered them and offered the advice they needed to thrive. Taking a partner out this weekend? Try "10 Date Ideas That'll Take Your Game to the Next Level," courtesy of Bud Light. Feeling middle-aged and alone? Here are "20 Tactics to Help You Find a Husband," brought to you by Bravo. Worried about what to feed the in-laws this Christmas? Consider this recipe for a holiday ham ring, and share it with your friends! That it was an ad for Walmart was an afterthought. It was a recipe for a ham ring, which when shared with one's

Facebook friends gave the impression of quaint neighborliness and pre-cious family time.

Peretti hadn't invented native advertising. Advertorials had for de-cades been used to get attention. The *Times* sometimes ran pages that were sponsored by foreign countries to attract visitors or investors, but carefully labeled them as advertisements. What was novel about these first-wave na-tive advertisements was their packaging, which allowed the brand to im-part more information to readers before they realized they'd been had and flipped the page. The effect was to increase brand recognition—a prior-ity for advertisers. But more than recognition, advertisers aspired to es-tablish brand affinity, and if they were particularly ambitious, to cement brand identification. What Peretti had invented was viral advertising—a new form that accomplished all of the above. It got the consumer to iden-tify not only with the brand but through it, on its own terms. Moreover this identification wasn't just personal but public. Sharers happily amplified their brand's message by sharing it. As BuzzFeed's current president, Greg Coleman, told me, "If I share an ad or sponsored story, it's like sending a selfie."

Peretti was untroubled by any sleight-of-hand, but readers could be confused over which material was native ads and which was original sto-ries. The main point was that the audience, turned off by traditional ad pitches, found these sponsored ads interesting and worthy of sharing. In the early days, those who worried about native ads mostly resided in news-rooms. "I enjoy working in morally ambiguous spaces," Peretti said in 2013, "I find that is where the most interesting stuff happens." Distinctions between news, opinion, entertainment, and native ads continued to blur. Everyone seemed to be a storyteller. As BuzzFeed began to build its news operation in 2012, the lines between the business and editorial sides be-came more complex.

Meanwhile, a native ad for Purina produced by BuzzFeed, "Dear Kit-ten," was an unambiguous viral hit, viewed more than 30 million times on YouTube, translated into six languages, and followed up by six spin-off spots, including one that aired during the Super Bowl. "Dear Kitten" was widely considered one of the most successful marketing campaigns in the era of the social web. Narrated by BuzzFeed's creative director, Ze Frank, playing the role of a wise, older cat taking the household's new kitten under its wing, it told a funny, heartwarming story, noteworthy for its lack of overt salesmanship. Its brilliance was its authenticity, he said. The sage elder cat's advice was entirely "based in cat truths" and "grounded in cat ownership." (Both Frank and Robertson are cat owners.) It didn't hurt that Frank possessed the vocal nuance and sonorousness of Morgan Freeman.

In 2008 Peretti posted a new Facebook status: "Thinking about the economics of the news business."

Until this point he had managed BuzzFeed's growth organically, investing in areas where he could build on proven success. That's how he had decided to categorize BuzzFeed's content according to which emotions it activated: LOL, Cute, Fail, WTF. Lists and quizzes had become the site's pillars only when Peretti's data analysis justified the move. Gradually BuzzFeed organized its content into verticals according to topic, again proceeding only when the topic had proven its efficacy: celebrities, animals, food, nostalgia.

By this point Lerer and Peretti were wealthy beyond imagination. When AOL acquired Huffington Post for $315 million, Lerer maintained a role in the merged company, but Peretti had already freed himself to devote all of his energies to BuzzFeed. With new funding and his own wealth, he could take risks and expand BuzzFeed in new directions.

"We had this huge hole," Peretti recalled of the latter half of 2011. "It was particularly obvious to Kenny [Lerer], who never loved the fun, playful Internet comedy."

The hole in the company was news, but it certainly wasn't hindering growth. By 2011 revenues were over $4 million—still a tiny operation when compared to the incumbent publishers, but growing exponentially.

But even the king of the listicle, Stopera, was telling Peretti, "We have one arm tied behind our back because we're missing news and reporting which should be part of the mix of the stuff that matters."

By 2011 Stopera was a true student of trend dynamics. He had seen success with celebrity posts pegged to timely issues (like the Kardashian divorce, or the decision of *People* magazine to name Bradley Cooper the "Sexiest Man Alive" instead of the crowd favorite Ryan Gosling). As popular as BuzzFeed's LOL, Trashy, Cute, WTF, and other stories were, he understood that amusing readers was short-lasting, low-impact work. At the end of 2011 he unwittingly tapped into a new corner of the brain that was undeniably promising. Stopera published "The 45 Most Powerful Photos of 2011," a collection that included shots of Japan's earthquake, London's riots, and the White House Situation Room at the moment Osama bin Laden was killed. Emotionally it operated along similar lines as the posts that claimed to "restore your faith in humanity." Combined with that was the element of nostalgia and a measure of empathy. The post marked a departure from BuzzFeed convention by accessing these emotions through universally important stories rather than hyperlocal tidbits about the relatable heroics of everyday people, such as "this single mom." The post was widely shared on Facebook, and the traffic it generated made for the biggest day in BuzzFeed's history. More important, it signaled a way forward for the young company.

Peretti told Nieman Lab, "I think the future is going to be about combining informational content with social and emotional content," as that post had shown. "In the past, sites like Facebook have been about cute cats and what your friends are up to. I think, increasingly, we're going to see the content in Facebook's feed come more into balance and include more informational content—news content."

Cute pandas and backflips gone awry, by contrast, were information-free. They were also evergreen: a cute panda photo was no more or less appealing today than it would be next year. But when content related to the news, its timing affected its popularity. News stories showed peaks, and where there were peaks there was business for BuzzFeed.

"Okay," Peretti thought, "the web is growing up. The social web is growing up. We need to grow up. And we need to add capacity to do all kinds of stuff that we're not doing now."

This watershed moment was inspired by a shift in the site's audience. "The reason people are coming [to BuzzFeed's website] is changing," Peretti told Politico in December 2011. In the past "they [came] to see what's the Zeitgeist." That had given way to a new trend: "Increasingly they're coming for something to share." This required a shift in BuzzFeed's focus, away from hopping on the bandwagon of popular trends and toward steering the conversation itself. It was a pivot from aggregation to original reportage, from an essentially diagnostic function to a prescriptive one. If BuzzFeed was going to remain essential to its readers, it would have to fulfill their desire for new and interesting material. "Beyond just telling people 'this is what's hot,' " Peretti insisted. "We've been finding that it's a lot more exciting and a lot more fun, and better for business as well, to show people new things that . . . inspire them to share."

"The reason to have an editorial or a reporting team," he continued, "is that right now the biggest piece we're missing is telling people things they didn't know before because we are the ones finding it out." The way to add that capacity was to hire people who specialized in finding things out and telling people: reporters.

BuzzFeed's traffic had been growing exponentially, but Peretti wondered whether it might hit a ceiling if it subsisted primarily on fodder for distraction. News coverage would give BuzzFeed a means of grabbing and holding a reader's attention not just during the doldrums of their workday but also when they were curious or concerned. Not only when they looked to tune out the world around them, but also when they looked to tune it in. Peretti pointed to Ted Turner, the founder of CNN and TBS, whose two-pronged approach enabled him to compete for people's attention with double the efficacy. "When it was a slow news day, people could watch baseball games and old movies on TBS," Peretti said. "When a war was starting they would watch CNN."

Entering the news industry would also burnish BuzzFeed in the eyes of advertisers. Ad execs "respect companies that do news, even if they don't want to advertise on the news content itself," Peretti told an interviewer with The Verge. "The fact that you're doing news is a reason they want to meet with you, and a reason the company is seen as being legitimate, substantial."

Peretti had a mental picture of the person he wanted to hire as the site's founding editor in chief: a bona fide journalist with a proven capacity for tastemaking, someone who brought rigor to traditional shoe-leather reporting as well as an eagerness to innovate. He or she would possess an outsider's audacity with an insider's connections, a sense of gravitas commensurate with a sense of humor.

Surveying the news blogging vanguard, Peretti spotted an eligible candidate in Ben Smith, a 35-year-old journalist whose political coverage had earned him a robust following on Twitter. His background displayed the skill set BuzzFeed was seeking. Smith had been born on Manhattan's Upper West Side; his father was an attorney who became a judge on the New York Court of Appeals, and his mother was the author of domestic primers like *My New Baby and Me* and *Parents' Guide to Raising Kids in a Changing World.*

At Yale he'd interned at the *Jewish Daily Forward*, a bilingual English-Yiddish newspaper whose circulation, the staff often joked, was "two old Jews—but the *right* two Jews." After graduating, Smith ran the gauntlet of print journalism in the waning years of its solvency. He covered cops for the *Indianapolis Star* before shipping out to Latvia, where he reported for the *Baltic Times* and the *Wall Street Journal*'s European edition. Back in the States he joined the *New York Sun*, whose founder and editor, Seth Lipsky, expected him to file five stories a day. He then jumped to the

New York Observer, where he established a blog on state politics called The Politicker, which quickly gained a following of wonks and decision-makers and eventually spawned spin-off blogs devoted to local coverage in the other 49 states. From there he went to the tabloid *New York Daily News*, where his reports—on politicians angling for Mayor Bloomberg's endorsement, for example—ran under house-style headlines such as "Parties' Pols Vie to Catch Bloomy Aye." Smith filed stories for page 17 and occasionally landed scoops that won front-cover treatment. He established a Politicker-esque blog on the paper's website that he hawked as "a running conversation about New York's political scene."

He then became a star at Politico, where he landed with another blog of his own. Politico's posture as "a running conversation about politics" was reminiscent of the one he'd left behind, but national instead of local. He worked remotely, at a desk he rented for $350 a month in a Victorian mansion that had been converted into a communal office for freelancers, a precursor to WeWork. Operating as a one-man news bureau, Smith broke stories that got people talking, such as the $400 haircuts John Edwards's campaign footed, and the fact that Mayor Rudy Giuliani had tapped taxpayer funds to cover visits to his mistress. He thrived on the speedy, digital-first pace at Politico and he took pride in winning the daily sprint races. He and his colleagues saw themselves as scrappy upstarts who stood out from the rest of the press pack covering the 2008 presidential race, he later recalled. "I could sit at a press conference, type what a politician said in my blog, and it'd be online 20 minutes before anyone else because they had editorial processes that weren't fast enough for the Internet."

Smith began to earn a reputation as an agile, tech-savvy purveyor of breaking "scooplets," as I called them, which helped him attract the right kind of readers, more legislative aides than armchair quarterbacks. Government officials who avidly followed his coverage entrusted him with hot tips. Sensitive information was best transmitted using Google Chat, AOL Instant Messenger, or old-fashioned email. He advertised his contact information far and wide to be as reachable as possible. Increasingly the running political conversation lived on Twitter, and so too did Smith.

When Peretti got in touch with him in December 2011, Smith had almost 60,000 followers on Twitter—nearly the sum total of technologically proficient members of the American political sector—and they were true followers in the sense that he was their go-to guy. Twitter had become the essential provider of their news diet, and though it was a vast, decentralized, and babbling domain, they could trust @benpolitico to tell them everything they needed to know. He was like their Cronkite, except that rather than half an hour a day, he was at his audience's disposal nearly all of his waking hours, dispatching 40 or 50 tweets a day.

When Smith learned that Peretti wanted to sit down and discuss things with him, he was confused. Peretti wasn't a known name in politics, nor was he a fellow journalist, and those two camps accounted for nearly all of the inquiries that landed in Smith's inbox. Peretti, Smith knew, was an innovator. As a journalist, Smith fancied himself as at least innovative. After all, he was a leading light of the Twitterati. But he didn't see where he would fit in at BuzzFeed.

Smith agreed to meet Peretti and Lerer at the Lure Fishbar in downtown Manhattan. He found Peretti to be headier than he'd expected. For a man whose business was cheap laughs, he was strikingly cerebral in conversation. "There was a lot of very abstract stuff about six degrees of separation and the Social Web," he recalled. "I didn't really understand what he was talking about."

Smith was conditioned to believe that the news was about the story and how it unfolded. The product was information. Peretti posed it differently: if newsmakers focused instead on the audience, what they offered would be an *experience*. Peretti described the first ever truly social news organization. He offered the job to Smith, who turned it down, despite pot-sweetening benefits like stock. "I could never do anything like this," he thought. They shook hands and parted ways, leaving Smith to ponder what he had left on the table as he traipsed back to his desk.

Smith liked Peretti but thought of him as a clever strategist rather than a newsman; he was too fixated on the hacks and tricks you could pull to hotwire the human brain, too preoccupied with scoring easy popularity to do justice to what Smith considered the main event. But as Smith kept mulling over this "social news" concept, the opportunity to lead this bold exploratory venture began to seem more appealing. He took a couple days to think about it, then spoke with his former boss at the *Observer*, Peter Kaplan, who was friendly with Peretti. Kaplan reassured him that Peretti's intentions were serious, not just passing: he wanted to compete with the real news outlets, such as the *Times* and CNN, at what they did best. Smith took another two days thinking it over, then sent Peretti and Lerer a seven-page email with his thoughts.

"I hope I didn't convince Jonah Tuesday that he and I just don't speak the same language," he wrote, "though I can't blame you if I did." He clarified his misgivings. "BuzzFeed has the structure and the tone of a website that could be central to people's lives. But it's built on sharing everything BUT the big stuff—each item at its core is a bank shot off the culture, a running joke or a joke on a joke. It feeds off and drives the Internet's undercurrents, but it doesn't ripple on the surface. . . . Being visible on the surface means covering the big news, and covering it head on. And it means devoting space on the site to something that may not always drive as much traffic as the guy masturbating at Starbucks." The big news Smith had in mind was the 2012 presidential election, and before he went any further he needed Peretti's assurance that he wasn't thinking any smaller.

Unlike the vaguely newsy odds and ends that sometimes got written up on BuzzFeed—heartwarming homecomings of embattled soldiers and their reunions with their long-lost dogs—this was big-boy news, straight up and high stakes. Smith wrote, "The idea that BuzzFeed has some formula to make content 'viral' would have an incredibly powerful appeal to the political class, which would only hazily understand what that meant, but be eager to buy into the magic."

To staff the enterprise, Smith had in mind a few journalists he knew, and he urged that BuzzFeed spend money for some big names to turn heads out of the gate. "I'd like to be a kind of player-coach," he wrote. The job was his, effective New Year's Day 2012.

With 10 months and six days until the polls opened, Smith had no time to waste. On his first day he showed up in Des Moines, Iowa, sporting the new press pass emblazoned with BuzzFeed's dizzying red and white spiral logo, which he told a fellow reporter "looks like we're from the future and we're here to check your radiation levels."

With the other pool reporters in the lobby bar in the downtown Des Moines Marriott, he couldn't help but notice them looking at him differently. He acknowledged that his move may have been startling to the traditionalists among the group: "It was a mind fuck," he called it. But he didn't see anything contradictory about what he was doing.

"I like cat pictures, and I like great reporting," he said around the time of his hiring. He realized these two prongs were hard to reconcile, but they were not mutually exclusive. In fact he was coming around to the view that they could exist symbiotically. He was happy to play the outsider but took exception to the notion that he was some abject underdog. "We're not starting from scratch," he said in one interview. "We're sort of starting with the beating heart of the Internet."

On the trail with him in Iowa, Smith had two of his new staffers, representing both poles of BuzzFeed's sensibility. Stopera, the reliable laugh-getter, and Zeke Miller, a straitlaced fellow graduate of Yale whom Smith had just hired from Business Insider. Miller and Stopera had spent New Year's Eve in the hotel room they were sharing, a test-run of how company culture would take shape and they could blend. While Stopera composed "29 Things I Learned from Spending Two Days with Rick Santorum" ("#1. Rick Santorum always has a 'muffin top' ") and collected supporters' descriptions of the senator in five words or less, Miller reported on Romney as he stumped in Sioux Falls.

Meanwhile, a few desks over, one of the newly hired members of Smith's newsroom, 22-year-old Andrew Kaczynski, practiced his area of expertise, dredging the internet's sprawling archives to find long-buried video clips of politicians embarrassing themselves. That day he released a snippet from 2006 of Rick Santorum campaigning awkwardly at a polka night for senior citizens.

Kaczynski, a history student at St. John's University, had been living in the basement of a Russian family's studio apartment in Briarwood, Queens, and spending his evenings scouring footage of campaigns and congressional proceedings that had not seen light in years. His excavations laid bare the flops and flip-flops from the past lives of politicians who were now contending for the presidency and other high offices. When he landed something juicy, he would publish it to his YouTube profile and let the swarm of news professionals have at it. By the time Smith got in touch about openings at BuzzFeed, Kaczynski's contributions as an amateur already had the political web buzzing. A profile in *New York* magazine headlined "Playing with Mud" warned that for campaign operatives, "Kaczynski's hobby can ruin your news cycle, or worse." Josh Marshall's Talking Points Memo quoted him: "I think it's kind of cool it can influence the presidential election from my couch." Occasionally he flipped an email to Smith with a discovery he thought might be newsworthy.

Kaczynski was looking at one more semester as an undergrad when Smith approached him with an offer of $1,000 a month. That was all it took to get him to drop out. "I told Ben I was taking online classes, which was like a total lie," he later confessed. He showed up for work in a suit and was surprised to find the rest of the office clad in T-shirts and hoodies, except Smith, who wore an editor in chief's sport coat. Kaczynski dressed down thereafter.

About a week into 2012, Peretti landed his second round of venture capital, this time a $15.5 million lode courtesy of a few of the same firms that had ponied up back in 2008. The money was needed for a "Ben Smith makeover," said *New York* magazine. "It's so expensive competing against major media organizations," Peretti said. "And now we can do it."

First they relocated to an office with enough space to house the site's lofty aspirations, at least for the time being. The new digs, a multifloor space around the corner from the Flatiron building, would accommodate three times the staff of the old office. Within 15 months they'd relocate again, to an office twice again as spacious.

Smith got down to assembling his dream team. Instead of angling for reporters in their mid- to late 20s, he recruited "people who were killing it at their first jobs," as he put it. It was a headhunting strategy born of necessity, but Smith executed it with swagger. "I don't like hiring stars," he told me. "It's better to make them." He was a great talent-spotter and became a mentor for young, inexperienced reporters.

One hire was Rosie Gray, who had been covering the Occupy movement for the *Village Voice*. Smith reckoned that her success covering one radical camp qualified her for another; he assigned her to Ron Paul's libertarian campaign in the Republican primaries. Other hires belonged to the crowd of regulars with whom Smith spent his days conversing on Twitter.

Another was McKay Coppins, who after graduating from Brigham Young University had reported on the election for *Newsweek* and habitually sent the scoops he published to Smith in hopes of mentions on the Politico blog. Another was Michael Hastings, already a star in his early 30s who had written several books. He was best known for a blockbuster profile in *Rolling Stone*, in which General Stanley McChrystal conceded that the war he was prosecuting in Afghanistan was destined to fail. McChrystal was forced to resign. Hastings, Smith said, was attracted to BuzzFeed for its "cyber-punk vibe."

Hastings brought along his young researcher, Ruby Cramer, fresh out of Vassar. She was the daughter of the late Richard Ben Cramer, a political writer Smith worshipped. His masterwork, *What It Takes*, about the 1988 presidential campaign, was a mammoth, deeply reported character study. It didn't sell well when it was first published in 1992, but it became a classic of the campaign book genre. Ruby Cramer wanted to follow her father's example.

Not all the newcomers had backgrounds in the news business. Their ranks included Katie Notopoulos, whom BuzzFeed hired away from her sales job at Warner Bros. because of an off-hours hobby: she liked to troll the far-flung corners of the internet for people who felt free to express their strange predilections openly: diaper fetishists, grown men obsessed with

My Little Pony (aka "Bronies"), and so on. She had a knack for spotting these strange affinity groups. After starting her job at BuzzFeed, Notopoulos said, it took her a while to adjust to a work environment that paid her for her social-media obsessions rather than discouraged them.

Notopoulos and her colleagues were assigned to computers on long assembly-line tables and instructed to get to work chasing scoops, the approach Smith had mastered at Politico. He understood his readership: "They don't really care who you are and where it's coming from. Credibility is sort of won and lost day to day."

He focused on tallying as many wins as he could get, setting a scoop-a-day goal for his reporters. Smith wanted his team to do old-school reporting on the fly, using Twitter and other social platforms to break news before they had posted a fully written story on BuzzFeed, just as he had done at Politico. A scoop headlined on Twitter could make news go viral. He was only 38 himself, but he had been transformed from a tabloid print reporter at the *Daily News*, where his only desire was to get "the wood," having his story appear in huge letters on the front page ("Ford to City: Drop Dead"), into an editor using social media to drive political news. He liked to think he would make his own mentor proud: Peter Kaplan had schooled his young team at the *New York Observer* to chase scoops, even if the internet remained a mystery to him. Sadly, Kaplan died of cancer just a year after Smith joined BuzzFeed.

Smith knew that establishing BuzzFeed's reputation as a vital part of the political conversation would be an uphill battle, especially with a team as green as his. "They were undercredentialed and working for a ridiculously named place," he recalled. Rosie Gray remembered the doors to sources being closed to her at first. "I'd call people on the phone and they'd be like, 'What's BuzzFeed?'" Politico, only five years old, was already occupying the digital space for instant political news. Few thought there was room for another.

To gain momentum, Smith immediately made good on his promise to Peretti and Lerer to be a player-coach. On the third day of 2012, he broke the news that Senator John McCain would endorse Mitt Romney. It caught other outlets off guard. The *Observer* ran a story on the story itself, headlined "BuzzFeed Scooped CNN Last Night." Gray remembers how preposterous it seemed at the time. "That was like 'Man Bites Dog,'" she said.

Kaczynski too was breaking news. Within a month he had discovered the McCain campaign's 200-page book of opposition research on Romney, which the Massachusetts governor's campaign had carelessly left unsecured on its servers. He also tracked down and published a video of Newt Gingrich beside Hillary Clinton, offering support for a health insurance mandate in 2005. Another video was of Romney going door to door in his 1994 senate campaign. When greeting one woman, he said, "I know you haven't got your makeup on yet, right?," only to be contradicted. "Ha ha. You do!"

Coppins, meanwhile, chased down a story about Romney's choice for a potential running mate. When Senator Marco Rubio's name came up, Smith urged Coppins, a member of the Church of Latter-day Saints, to tap into the "Mormon grapevine." Coppins did as he was told and discovered that Rubio had been baptized a Mormon—a fact that all but disqualified him in the interest of a "balanced ticket." These were respectable notches in BuzzFeed's belt, but from the get-go it was clear that the news coverage would operate in a different universe than its less serious siblings. Smith's story about the McCain endorsement, for example, garnered 200 likes—a blip on the radar next to the post about a 70-year-old box turtle named Willie.

The point wasn't for the different verticals to compete. "We don't expect a politics story to compete with a cat story," BuzzFeed's president Jon Steinberg said. They just had to coexist. Peretti saw nothing contradictory about offering web surfers a balanced diet. The recipe was precisely what Facebook served up via its News Feed, and Facebook was already an essential source of traffic for BuzzFeed, accounting for 35 percent of its referrals. The diversity of conversation topics on Facebook presented an opportunity. As Peretti told the *Atlantic*, "Next to people getting drunk at a party is a story about the Arab Spring next to a celebrity next to all these things you and your friends are interested in." BuzzFeed, unlike almost any of its competitors, possessed the range and occupied the perfect position from which to insert itself into all of the above story lines.

The notion that silliness could coexist with substance was neither new nor particularly objectionable. It was when BuzzFeed began to mix those two silos that problems arose. Smith unleashed Hastings on the campaign trail knowing that his inclusion in the press pool would be incendiary, but he could hardly have imagined the antics of his new hire. Lucky enough to be invited aboard Obama's plane, Hastings quickly ran afoul of journalistic etiquette, and not by mistake. During one leg of the journey, the president gathered the pool of reporters who'd been following him, and over drinks the group held an off-the-record conversation, which Hastings was bold enough to cover. It nearly got him thrown off the plane for good. Things had barely cooled off when he was upbraided by the Clinton campaign for a similar breach of ground rules. The tense back-and-forth between Hastings and Philippe Reines, Clinton's aide, ended with Reines calling him an "unmitigated asshole" and telling him to "have a good day. . . . And by good day, I mean Fuck Off."

"They didn't even know what rules they were breaking," Smith told me, and he liked it better that way. As an editor, Smith preferred letting readers, not politicians or editors, decide what interested them. He would err on the side of airing matters out.

Hastings, who had covered the Iraq War for *Newsweek*, won the George Polk Award for his McChrystal investigation, and published two books, was an iconoclast. The 2012 campaign was for him a year-long bender, and he was anything but shy about sharing the incriminating details of it. He came by the habits honestly: drugs had gotten him suspended from college and landed him in a rehab clinic. But after 10 years sober, stalking the beat for BuzzFeed seemed to send him over the edge.

"I was caught in the full destructive force of a campaign-induced relapse," Hastings confessed. He wrote that during one stretch of the journey, he managed to down the full contents of five mini-bars in five states. These and other exploits filled the pages of *Panic 2012*, his book on the campaign, which reads like a reprise of Hunter S. Thompson's 1972 *Rolling Stone* stories which became *Fear and Loathing on the Campaign Trail*, down to the deliberate overuse of ellipses and painstaking narration of his substance abuse. Recounting the damage he'd done in just the distance between Las Vegas and Los Angeles, Hastings described a "path of unexplained credit card charges through the state of Nevada, cabana fees, a lesbian bar with a dungeon in Los Angeles, and one unfortunate drunken incident in Vegas . . . where I insulted the *Wall Street Journal* reporter in the most graphic and offensive terms possible, bringing shame to my family and requiring me to apologize to her."

Most of BuzzFeed's output, however, was well short of book-length. The challenge Smith issued to his newsroom was to distill their stories down to the snappiest possible kernel. They would avoid doing hackneyed, straight-ahead news. Their election coverage was run-and-gun, anything goes. Just like BuzzFeed itself, the new unit's reportage evinced the dangerous mentality, often associated with start-up culture, of being willing to try anything once.

Rather than producing a steady stream of accountability journalism, the enterprise and investigative stories that sometimes turned an election, Smith's team specialized in inside-baseball campaign news breaks that created buzz in one news cycle and were largely forgotten by the next. Smith had a tabloid metabolism and had learned how to dominate a news cycle at the *Daily News*. At Politico reporters were trained to "win the morning" with bite-size scoops. One political hand called these stories "the Chinese food of journalism," referencing the hoary joke about a tasty meal leaving you hungry soon after.

Inspired by Peretti's outlook, Smith treated his new role as an opportunity to rethink conventions that had long governed news reportage. The challenge was to do news in a way that departed from the authoritative, disembodied voice that readers, especially young ones, now found stale and mirthless. He approached the problem the way Peretti might, from an angle that valued readers' enjoyment over all considerations. This way of thinking was a defining trait of Silicon Valley companies, where it was referred to as "User Experience" or "UX." It was the digital cousin of the old theory of salesmanship, "The customer is always right."

Even in 2011 the digital operations at most of the major news outlets amounted to a website that was only marginally sleeker than it had been more than a decade prior. News websites were still designed to be digital twins of newspapers. For Smith, this presented an enormous business opportunity. "I feel in general the 800–1,200 word form of the news article is broken," he said in a Nieman Lab interview. The basis for that conclusion: "You don't see people sharing those kinds of stories."

BuzzFeed's stated goal was "reinventing the wire story for the social web." Within a week of naming an internal candidate to run the effort, Smith was crowing about a BuzzFeed post on North Korea's supreme leader Kim Jong-un assuming command over the country's military. Headlined "Kim Jong Un Gets a Promotion," the post excerpted the first four sentences of an AP wire story under a photograph of the dictator lifted from Reuters. Under the text were six old pictures of Kim, followed by nine GIFs of people and animals applauding. The basic philosophy was spelled out in a sign outside one of the newsroom's bathrooms: "STOP TWEETING BORING SHIT."

When a story involved everyday people, as it did when a gunman opened fire on a crowded movie theater in Aurora, Colorado, in July 2012, BuzzFeed was uniquely well-positioned. Its strong suit was its hold over the social channels most users turned to when tragedy (or good fortune) struck. From her gyroscopic desk chair, BuzzFeed's reporter nimbly navigated to the tweets and other online accounts of the shooting by those who had witnessed it firsthand. A few copy-and-pastes later, BuzzFeed had a grippingly personal report ready to be published. It even featured selfies taken by one of the moviegoers who'd suffered a gunshot in the torso. The best part: it took all of 45 seconds to read. This method of sourcing was descended from one Smith had pioneered at the *Observer*. He conducted brief exchanges with political operatives and aides over online instant messages, or IMs, and published the transcripts to his blog. The shortcut made for speedier reporting, but Smith caught some criticism for short-circuiting the reportorial process. Marc Tracy, a staff writer at the *New Republic*, wrote that the format of Smith's "IMterview" ultimately did little beyond offer spin doctors "a platform to spew pure, unedited talking points."

Six months in, Peretti was pleased with the new mission. In a July 2012 memo he sent to the whole staff, titled "The Top 7 Reasons BuzzFeed Is Killing It," he asserted that BuzzFeed's politics team had "already become THE defining outlet of the 2012 presidential campaign." It was a stretch, but one Peretti made in the interest of company morale.

BuzzFeed's business was also enjoying the boom Peretti had predicted the news effort would bring. Revenue was on track to triple the prior year's; full-time employee rolls had nearly quintupled since the start of 2011, to 117; and political coverage was attracting several million visitors a month. In a financially challenged news industry, BuzzFeed was a shining success.

Eight months into the job, Smith won a stamp of approval from the *New York Times* when the paper announced it would team up with Smith's group to livestream news reports at the Republican and Democratic national conventions. A surprise to some at the *Times*, the collaboration was proposed by the paper's assistant managing editor, Jim Roberts, who had just celebrated a quarter-century at the Gray Lady. "The lessons we can learn from BuzzFeed are going to be valuable," he said. BuzzFeed had done more live video on its website than the *Times*, which had experimented with it only once, during the Oscars.

"We have indeed come a long way!" posted Steinberg when Stopera, unshaven and wearing a T-shirt, appeared on the homepage of the *Times*'s website for a live report on the GOP's fashion at the convention. He graded attendees' cowboy getups, blinged-out brooches, and elephant-topped fascinators as either "Fab or Drab." Stopera's lighthearted contribution stood in contrast to reporting by Zeke Miller, who appeared alongside *Times* deputy news editor Megan Liberman to discuss drier topics such as weather forecasts and contingency plans for the convention. But by and large, the buzz BuzzFeed generated revolved around how much more *fun* they brought to the drudgery of campaign coverage.

In a vivid demonstration of the "true social news organization" that BuzzFeed aspired to become, the company spent months leading up to the convention planning a party for the political press that would announce its arrival on the main stage of American media. Slated for the night before Romney would take the stage to accept the GOP nomination, the event's theme was "Party Animals," an authentic reflection of BuzzFeed's brand identity. ("We're very pro-animal," Stopera explained.) It took place at Tampa's world-class aquarium, where attendees swapped gossip and pleasantries beside floor-to-ceiling tanks in which a troupe of young and attractive professional divers made up to look like mermaids and affixed with resplendent mechanical fishtails flipped and flitted elegantly among schools of fish and stingrays. Spirits flowed as some of journalism's biggest names—including Maureen Dowd, Chuck Todd, Craig Unger, and Ben Smith's former bosses at Politico—watched the women and tried to stay out of the way of the penguins that were being wheeled in a cart around the party. The coming-out party for the Washington media establishment was a success. It also cost a bundle.

As candidates Romney and Obama barreled into autumn with the polls showing them neck-and-neck, Obama, who'd won in 2008 on the strength of his online campaign, decided it was time to take BuzzFeed up on its offer to help the incumbent go mega-vi. In October his campaign became the first political entity to pay BuzzFeed for a native advertising campaign that would target the crucial bloc of first-time voters, with whom the site had undeniable credibility.

The native advertising team got to work on a package of six videos for Obama. One featured a stump speech by Jay-Z and juxtaposed concert footage of the rapper with clips from the president's rallies. Another lampooned Romney for his widely ridiculed debate comment about commissioning "binders full of women" to address workplace inequality as governor of Massachusetts. They had the look and tone of most of BuzzFeed's editorial content, which was crucial for them to be spread along the same viral growth curve as nonsponsored pieces.

The verisimilitude was what made BuzzFeed's native advertising such a powerful model, but as the site tried to establish itself as trustworthy for objective reportage, the fact that its business was supported by an internal ad agency became a liability. After the Obama videos rolled out, Romney's campaign decided to get in on the action, and BuzzFeed was happy to oblige. Political messaging was a natural point of collaboration for the bicameral publisher whose strengths lay in designing ads and lightening up political reportage.

The gray area BuzzFeed was exploiting was unfamiliar territory for the

Federal Trade Commission, which regulated corporate messaging. A year would pass before its chair issued an official warning to BuzzFeed and others. "By presenting ads that resemble editorial content," she charged, "an advertiser risks implying, deceptively, that the information comes from a nonbiased source." Citizen watchdogs were quicker to sniff out the distressing trend. Shortly after Obama was sworn in for a second term, the prominent political blogger and media critic Andrew Sullivan decided BuzzFeed's flackery had run afoul of journalistic ethics. "Once you slip into the advertorial vortex at Buzzfeed," he wrote on his widely read blog, The Dish, "everything that is advertising appears as non-advertising."

Smith challenged Sullivan to a public debate at New York's annual Social Media Week, where Sullivan charged, "You're *clearly* trying to trick people. Journalism has never done product placement before in its actual text." Smith vehemently denied the allegation. "Our trick," he protested, "the trick that the business side here is attempting to pull off is to produce great content for people." Sullivan replied that by "great content" Smith meant ads. "So what distinguishes that content from your content?" he asked. Smith's answer: "Only the label."

The label, however, was strategically camouflaged. Advertisements appeared on BuzzFeed's site in the same size and shape as editorial posts, marked by a faint text overlay noting it was "presented by" the brand, whose name appeared in the post's byline next to the words "featured partner." By 2013 BuzzFeed had partnerships with more than half of the biggest brands in America, including GE, Virgin, Pepsi, Google, Geico, and Intel. When readers seemed to be catching on, BuzzFeed adapted the verbiage and visuals of its labels.

Peretti insisted the distinction between ads and BuzzFeed's own content was obsolete and immaterial to the readers. When it was frivolity from Dunkin' Donuts or Pepsi, the stakes may have been low. But once BuzzFeed began accepting payment to run glowing coverage of the same politicians they purported to report on objectively, the ethics became decidedly murkier.

In 2013 BuzzFeed kicked off a series of live events called BuzzFeed Brews, held at its New York headquarters. National politicians visited for a beer or two and a chat with Ben Smith that focused as little as possible on policy. They hosted Senator Marco Rubio, New York City mayoral candidate Anthony Weiner, and Congresswoman Nancy Pelosi, but made sure to keep things fun by booking Hollywood actors and actresses in the alternate weeks. In September, Peretti was touting the series as "a leading venue for newsmakers to reach a young, web-savvy audience." Celebrities of all kinds started to visit the office to post photos of themselves on Facebook or Instagram. BuzzFeed was considered cool.

The editorial staff came up with another enticing product for politicians. In return for sitting down with BuzzFeed for a brief, semi-substantive interview, the company would collaborate with the candidate on a goofy, substance-free video designed to go viral. They debuted the two-part packages when the next election cycle dawned in 2016 and found plenty of politicians eager to participate. In came presidential candidate Ted Cruz with his favorite party trick: impressions of characters from *The Simpsons*. He was followed by Republican rival Carly Fiorina, for whom BuzzFeed's producers scripted a starring role in a millennial-friendly video called "What If Women Talked Like Men in the Workplace?" Then it was Governor Bobby Jindal of Louisiana, telling canned jokes and competing in a pushup contest (which, spoiler alert, "America won"). Hamilton Nolan of Gawker called the practice "access-whoring" and "image-laundering."

To the fun-loving team at BuzzFeed, ambiguities were unthreatening, even exciting. "It was anything goes, until Ben Smith started," Stopera told me. "And even then." Even then, Smith realized, it would not be easy to graft traditional virtues onto a brand-new, fast-and-loose company. Peretti stood by his vision for BuzzFeed to be different things to different people, and Smith had to accept that journalistic standards, whether made explicit or unspoken, might not always apply. But as he continued to add capacity to BuzzFeed's team of reporters, he undertook a herculean housekeeping project that would get the site closer to shipshape.

Evidence of Smith's cleanup job wouldn't surface for four months, and even then only thanks to the dogged digging of the rival bloggers at Gawker who disclosed a scandal: BuzzFeed had silently and slyly deleted more than 4,000 posts from its website. It was a redaction of unprecedented scale, pulled off without a peep from the site's editors. They had done it to erase some of the awkward and unseemly traces of the early days, but that was just one reason. The more damning motive behind the monumental disappearing act was that editors knew the site contained hundreds if not thousands of plagiarized posts—including, it appeared, by the Stopera brothers, Peggy Wang, and Jack Shepherd—and they were eager to sweep that under the rug. "It's stuff made at a time when people were really not thinking of themselves as doing journalism," Smith explained in an interview. "They saw themselves as working in a lab." Besides, there had been nothing stopping him from giving the old mullet a spiffy new haircut. Unlike other newsrooms, which typically held staff accountable to a set of internal rules, BuzzFeed wouldn't have an agreed-upon set of standards and ethics until January 2015.

Even then, the rules weren't always followed. Just four months after ratifying the company's code of ethics—the rulebook stated that "editorial posts should never be deleted for reasons related to their content, or because a subject or stakeholder has asked you to do so"—Smith hit delete again. Three posts had gone poof—again without acknowledgment from the editors—although this time for a different reason. The posts were critical of corporate brands whose advertising business BuzzFeed wanted to keep: one complained that Monopoly was too slow a game, another took issue with a new TV ad for Dove soap that shamed women with "average" bodies. The problem wasn't the veracity of the posts, it was that they offended advertisers. When Smith realized he'd been caught, he reinstated the posts and offered a sheepish apology over email. "I reacted impulsively," he admitted, "and I was wrong."

BuzzFeed's sacred guideline was not to strictly separate news from advertising, the cardinal rule of old, but to create shareable (as distinct from merely likable) content. Smith's news operation helped BuzzFeed distinguish itself from the shameless traffic factories that made money from eyeballs lured by clickbait. If your only goal was to play to people's desires, Smith suggested to the *New Republic*, "why would you do politics? Why not do porn? I mean, seriously?" At BuzzFeed, its boosters often explained, the business model demanded that content not just get you to click on a headline but to value and share what you found underneath it. Peretti and Smith believed this condition maintained quality control.

Smith was following through on the intention he'd announced in the first memo he sent Peretti: "The idea that BuzzFeed has some formula to make content 'viral' would have an incredibly powerful appeal to the political class." Now that appeal could be used for leverage.

BuzzFeed had attained industry leadership by being different things to different people. Pundits from other publishers—even those who found this trend abhorrent—pointed to the young company as a noteworthy force of disruption. It was enshrined as such in a case study by the venerable *Harvard Business Review*. Peretti had invented this protean machine of a company, and he welcomed comparisons of it to the media empires in their golden age. BuzzFeed now seemed less like "a lab that created content as R&D" and more like a breakthrough that might alter the course of history by preserving an informed public. "BuzzFeed has a major role to play in the coming years, to fill the hole left by the ongoing decline of print newspapers and magazines," he wrote to his staff in the early fall of 2013. "The world needs sustainable, profitable, vibrant content companies staffed by dedicated professionals; especially content for people that grew up on the web, whose entertainment and news interests are largely neglected by television and newspapers."

The problem was that BuzzFeed was reactive. Its central innovation was the speed and accuracy with which it discerned readers' desires and catered to them. The mechanism was so advanced that if it had gone further it would have become an echo chamber.

"Hard news" is so called because it challenges readers, broadens their knowledge, widens their perspective, presents them with information based not on their cravings but on what happens in the outside world. BuzzFeed knew that to challenge readers would be to risk losing their loyalty, so as it expanded its news coverage, the company was careful to invest in areas it already knew were stable commodities. Gender politics and LGBT issues were reliable traffic drivers, and based on this Peretti approved BuzzFeed's emphasis on those topics. He gave the green light to Smith, who hired Chris Geidner, a lawyer and prominent D.C.-based blogger.

Geidner came to Smith's attention at Politico, where Smith had enjoyed a veritable monopoly on the gay marriage beat, which he covered part time, until one day a new contender stepped onto the scene. Geidner "came along and stole all my sources and beat me on every story," Smith recalled. Other publishers treated the beat as a niche, whereas BuzzFeed knew that LGBT rights, and marriage equality in particular, was "something that our core 18–35 audience cares a lot about."

"We see it as an absolute front-burner area to go after with the same kind of intensity as politics," Smith told the Poynter Institute. "Maybe animals, even." It involved what Smith called "the mix of intelligence and emotion that is central to what we do." It was an issue on which, by taking a side and coming out slugging, BuzzFeed ingratiated itself with the younger generations. Smith said in an official announcement that BuzzFeed's coverage would ditch the outmoded pretensions of equivalency and objectivity. This was house policy, he announced. "There are not two sides." Stopera elaborated that other considerations may have entered the calculus. Well aware that posts on the LGBT topic consistently saw high numbers of shares among readers on one side of the debate, they saw an opportunity to solidify that interest group's trust. "I want all that sweet traffic," Stopera told his higher-ups.

Peretti threw more money into news, and Smith hired Lisa Tozzi, a 13-year veteran of the *Times*, to be his news director. It was a coup and seemed to suggest a turning point in the quest for respect from more established outlets. At the *Times*, Tozzi's path up the editing ladder was uncertain. With relatively little actual journalism experience, she was not considered qualified for many senior roles in the *Times* newsroom, but she was a whiz at digital audience-building. BuzzFeed provided an avenue for career growth. Smith told Tozzi on her first day that she should start by making 10 hires. He would forward her a sheaf of résumés.

Smith also commenced talks with another recruit from an old-line newspaper, Miriam Elder, Moscow bureau chief at the *Guardian*. He wanted her to lead BuzzFeed into foreign coverage. Elder received an email from him: "I want to start a foreign desk. Do you want to talk? I love cats." It was so bizarre that Elder was unsure how to react. She went with a friend to Costa Rica for a yoga retreat she hoped would grant her some clarity. "I spent the whole time torturing myself about my career," she said. She noticed that Smith had taken an interest in the photos she was posting on Instagram from the oceanfront oasis. She had a friend snap a photo of her wading into the pristine waters and published it to Instagram with the caption "New Horizons." She had made up her mind, she said. "It was a sign for Ben."

In a year Smith, using the revenues generated by native ads like "Dear Kitten," pictures of cute animals, and quizzes, had built what Politico, his old stomping grounds, described as "a massive reporting engine." He convinced Peretti to take the next big step, building an investigative reporting unit like the ones at the *New York Times*, the *Washington Post*, and the all-investigative digital newsroom ProPublica, which was launched in 2006 by veterans of the *Wall Street Journal* and the *Times*.

Investigative reporting would be a big step up. Reporters often spent many months reporting and digging dry holes before a story was publishable. But it could be the most high-impact journalism out there, in the tradition of Watergate. Peretti agreed to open his wallet again, even if BuzzFeed's young audience might not have the patience for long, complex investigations. To head up the unit, Smith hired Mark Schoofs, an editor at ProPublica who had won a Pulitzer at the *Village Voice* for an eight-part series he wrote about AIDS in Africa. He was not easily converted: it took three conversations for Peretti to convince him BuzzFeed was serious about the enterprise.

In an encouraging sign, 300,000 readers viewed one of their biggest early stories, on the state of Texas sending people to prison for not paying their parking tickets. The dashboard showed an impressive completion rate, users who read the whole thing. The day after it was published, the reporters' colleagues combed the article for its most eye-popping points and distilled them into a shorter, viral version that attracted one million readers.

Within a year Schoofs's unit had almost as many investigative reporters as did the investigative reporting group at the *Times*. His deputy, Ariel Kaminer, was herself a former *Times* editor. Within two years the team of green berets was 19 strong, and growing. One editor quipped, "It's like the debt clock: You look away for a second and when you turn back the number's jumped!" The growth was part of a comeback for investigative reporting with the advent of all-digital newsrooms like the nonprofit ProPublica. BuzzFeed's diggers also used technology to facilitate investigative reporting.

BuzzFeed was showing no signs its boom would dissipate. They had relocated to midtown just after Smith came aboard, and now, 15 months later, they were ready to double their footprint again and took a two-year lease for an entire floor in the Fifth Avenue building owned by Tiffany's.

To the web-nurtured millennials, the confines of the company's new headquarters looked like Xanadu. Assistants zipped around on Bluetooth-enabled hoverboards delivering packages and catered spreads. In case the internet should ever run dry of diversions, they had on hand an endless supply of toys and tchotchkes to keep them entertained: stuffed animals, Ruth Bader Ginsburg coloring books, a Donald Trump piñata, LOL and OMG stickers, bottles of Champagne. Like a start-up in Silicon Valley, there were free snacks everywhere. Catered Mexican lunches arrived on certain days. Everyone, even the serious investigative reporters, looked like they were having a ball. Shani Hilton, Smith's deputy, made sure the staff was diverse and that provided an immediate and stark contrast to the more established newsrooms with so few high-ranking minority or female journalists.

Decked out in red BuzzFeed hoodies, staffers sat glued to their double-monitor computers, wearing over-the-ear headphones and following the water-cooler conversation via online chat rooms. Every so often one group or another would feel their wrists vibrate and in unison they would lift their arms and inspect the latest update from their company-issued Apple Watches. The tone that prevailed throughout the office resembled the hushed whir of cognitive gears one might find at a hackathon. It may have been pictures of pets or party fouls that preoccupied them, but the staffers brought razor-sharp focus to their beats nevertheless.

Watching her staffers chase stories down the internet's back alleys, Elder realized they had a thing or two to teach her. She saw how much material could be gotten from the web alone. Her reporters stalked the Instagram profile of a Russian soldier and ascertained that the pictures he was taking were of Ukraine. "Does This Soldier's Instagram Account Prove Russia Is Covertly Operating in Ukraine?" read the headline. The evidence pointed to yes. "BuzzFeed understands that online life isn't secondary," Elder told me. "It is real life."

Upon joining BuzzFeed at the age of 43, Kate Aurthur, a veteran of the *L.A. Times* and Daily Beast, felt like a fish out of water. She referred to BuzzFeed's newsroom as the Army of Children, but said there was plenty she could learn from them.

Ken Bensinger, another *L.A. Times* veteran, was assigned a desk among the boisterous young staffers who would give him grief for the large-print font his computer was set to display. He took it with good humor because he realized the kids were all right. He especially liked his colleague Ellie Hall, whose tenacious tracking down of sources Bensinger found inspiring. In one case, Hall used the internet to sniff out the trail of a notorious pedophile in Belgium who'd fled Spain. She combined internet savvy with traditional reporting hardball. "She'll get on the phone with a source who's trying to avoid her and break him down: 'You're shaming your family, you need to talk.'" She didn't come up through a traditional journalist's background. As a child Hall would internet-stalk her crushes, such as Benedict Cumberbatch. "There's the temptation of, if you wanna be Picasso, you have to learn perspective and color theory and so on," said Ken. "But maybe for Ellie, that's not the right approach."

By February 2014, BuzzFeed had more than 150 journalists, an ever-growing investigative reporting unit, bureaus in Australia and the U.K., and foreign correspondents in far-flung places such as Nairobi and throughout the Middle East. They had transitioned into a company that published pieces that gave readers more than just a sugar high. It seemed as if Peretti had begun to factor the greater good into his decisions on where to steer his company.

What gave him doubts was that he still couldn't explain the actual value of the news unit other than in terms of lofty public interest. BuzzFeed's journalists "aren't just a hood ornament to lend the site prestige," he said back in 2012. Three years later he still found himself in the uncomfortable position of having to argue against the data in defense of his decision to enter the news industry. Politico reported in 2015 that while nearly half of BuzzFeed's 300 editorial staffers belonged to the news division, its output accounted for a much smaller part of its traffic. Trying to head off the story before it undermined the fragile egos of his young newsroom, Peretti issued another proclamation, entitled "Why BuzzFeed Does News." "News is the heart and soul of any great media company," he professed, but already his apologia seemed wishful. "News might not be as big a business as entertainment, but news is the best way to have a big impact on the world."

He disliked wishy-washy barometers like "impact," but for the time being the term would have to do. The practical value of journalism was too nebulous for his quantitatively inclined mind. Then he received a gift from Nguyen and her team of data scientists. It was a new tool built into the dashboard, which they called a Heat Map. The software noted how far down the page a reader scrolled, then collated those data in one simple visual with whether the story lost readers' attention and where. It was just what BuzzFeed needed to apply its analytical rigor to stories that were longer and larger in scope. By reading the Heat Map, BuzzFeed's reporters and editors could ascertain whether the lede was snappy enough or that the audience found one of the story's subjects underwhelming. Then Nguyen's team added another tool, one that would shed light on the impact a story had at a social level, a widget that scrutinized not just how many people shared a particular article but who shared them. If an exposé of racism in the American South was shared by the director of the Southern Poverty Law Center, this was a valuable data point.

For the vast majority of BuzzFeed's content, though, little regard was given to whether a piece resonated with political elites. It was a fickle game, playing to their high-brow tastes, and they were so few in number that even a smash hit with the VIPs registered as a pin-drop in the culture at large.

News, where Smith ruled, was fortified and supported by buzz, where Stopera was king. There was little sense of church and state. It was important to Peretti that the two shared a common culture. But his notion of happy coexistence would not endure. In the early days of doing news, a win for one unit was a win for the other, and while the newsroom's wins tended to be more modest in scope, the buzz team felt legitimized by the work of their peer reporters. Underlying both units was the swaggering confidence that together they could make anything, no matter how small, "a thing." BuzzFeed's online domination was such that both news and buzz teams could take just about anything that fell into their laps and give it household recognition. BuzzFeed's advantage was its omnipresence, not its authority. Readers didn't care which side of the office a story originated in. Besides, BuzzFeed presented buzz items with the same urgency as breaking news stories. They had the technological launchpad to blast out a buzz item to all corners of the social web, and once everyone was talking about it, it might as well have been breaking news.

So when BuzzFeed had its crowning achievement, in February 2015, the viral explosion was set off by a piece of buzz that the editors covered as if it were a terrorist attack. It was a photograph of a dress that ignited a web-wide conversation and created a craze fueled by BuzzFeed for fun and profit. The phenomenon began when a young Scottish bride-to-be posted a photo to Facebook of one of the dresses her mother was considering wearing to the wedding. She had shown the picture to her fiancé, who said it was black and blue. The bride saw it as white and gold. On Facebook, their friends were similarly divided. They had on their hands an optical illusion unlike anything they'd ever seen. One of the bride's Facebook friends posted the picture to Tumblr, where it touched off a lively conversation among her followers about whether the dress was blue and black or white and gold. It seemed that everyone who saw the photo had an opinion about its color scheme.

Before she took off for the weekend, BuzzFeed's Cates Holderness, whose job was to scour Tumblr and other networks for noteworthy content, found and posted the picture to BuzzFeed's Twitter with the question "What colors are this dress?" By the time she got out of the subway near a friend's apartment in Brooklyn, she saw her phone flooded with responses. Holderness was overwhelmed. Before she had come to New York to work for BuzzFeed, she'd been an unpaid contributor from her home in North Carolina, where she worked at a kennel and dog-grooming business. Now she had the internet in the palm of her hand.

Twitter was ablaze with debate over #dressgate, with the #blueandblack camp against the #whiteandgold camp, and BuzzFeed started to mobilize the full brawn of its viral-industrial complex. Noting that the dress was on a trajectory unlike anything they'd ever seen, the public relations department began pitching the story to morning talk shows, hoping to further stoke the craze. BuzzFeed's systems administrators—the people who ensured no traffic jams occurred on the website and everything loaded quickly and smoothly—found themselves flung into the greatest challenge of their young lives. The unprecedented influx of traffic totally outstripped the capacity of BuzzFeed's servers. They needed to add more—40 percent more—and quick. "I am throwing servers into the internet!" the company's server administrator was overheard yelling at the office. By 9 p.m. the dress had set a new record for BuzzFeed: 450,000 concurrent active visitors, all dialed in at the same time. An hour later it had peaked at 673,000.

BuzzFeed was built to thrive under these conditions. Their "sys admins" had run drills that replicated this very scenario. One of them, Jay Destro, quarterbacked the operation from the comfort of his living-room couch, his two pugs sitting on his lap "for moral support." BuzzFeed followed up its initial post with a flurry of dress-related supplements: a scientist's explanation of the illusion, a profile of the woman who first posted the photo, a roundup of celebrities weighing in, and a poll that received 2.7 million votes. The next morning it was featured in full segments on *Good Morning, America* and *Today*. Holderness's original post was viewed 28 million times as of the next morning.

And Smith was proudest of all. It didn't matter to him that the dress, which was actually blue and black, was not hard news. The phenomenon itself had become news and had generated a record audience for BuzzFeed. He presided over a celebration, with pink Champagne and strawberries, for the biggest story of the year.

CHAPTER SIX

VICE II

Vice jumped into the field of documentary news without much regard for or knowledge of long-established ethical standards that bound the broadcast and cable networks. The company spent no time pondering the differences between news and entertainment. It was a cool blend of the two, according to its founders. The operative word was "cool."

Vice's cool had been so associated with the provocations and antics of Gavin McInnes that young Thomas Morton, a recent college graduate who had just been welcomed aboard after surviving his internship, couldn't imagine the place without him. It was McInnes to whom Morton had originally written an application that read like a fan letter, gushing over his adoration of *Vice* magazine, whose pages teemed with his debauched fantasies of taboos that in many cases had never been committed to paper until *Vice* published them.

Morton, wiry and bespectacled, had grown up in the suburbs of Atlanta and fit the mold of *Vice*'s archetypal reader, a well-educated aspirant to a place in American counterculture. He listened to punk rock and southern gangsta rap, wore skinny pants and T-shirts with ironic slogans, and bought psychedelic drugs online, shipped in hollowed-out paperback books and CD covers to evade his parents' detection. He'd earned a scholarship to New York University, where he arrived for freshman year two days before 9/11. He studied English lit. Morton had always fancied himself a decent writer, and he took a few journalism classes before deciding it wasn't for him.

"I fucking hated those kids in the journalism school," he told one interviewer. "Nobody had a sense of humor at all." The atmosphere was too preprofessional, the other students too primped and polished. "The broadcast kids were worse than anything," he added, likening them to wannabe Anderson Coopers who lacked mental firepower. Those kids were missing the story. They were crippled by their fluency in journalese, too caught up in their ascent to power, speaking as if from a teleprompter. They mistook 10-dollar words for intellect, sobriety for seriousness. When it came to cool, they were clueless.

Morton was under no pretense that he was cool, but he did at least know it when he saw it. He had seen it at one of his favorite streetwear shops on Lafayette and Spring streets, where the new issue of *Vice* magazine was available in a fresh pile for free every month. "You could get it there—if you were quick," he said. Morton could see he was not the magazine's only devotee; there were other hipsters in New York who knew what was up. "*Vice* combined humor and writing sensibly," he said. "It was how smart funny people would speak at bars."

He had been so flattered that McInnes even bothered to respond to his fan mail, so excited by the offer of an internship at Vice, that he didn't waste time quibbling about the pay rate. Morton, 21, would happily work for free. When he showed up in Brooklyn for his first day, in the fall of 2004, he found a pile of boxes on the sidewalk out front—Vice's latest issue, "The Party Issue," had arrived. Morton flipped one open to an article called "The Vice Guide to Partying," accompanied by a boldly uncensored photographic spread that featured a topless transsexual manually stimulating a fully naked man while a young woman snorted a line of cocaine off his genitals.

"It was a really good article," he said.

From the second he arrived, Morton felt at home in the Brooklyn office, everyone crammed together, the bathroom walls decorated with Dash Snow Polaroids, and an organ discarded from an old recording studio placed randomly in the middle of the floor. Except for dark and sweaty basement venues he attended for concerts, he'd never been around such a concentrated population of tattooed hipsters. It was a far cry from his mirthless journalism seminars. These people were cool, funny, and unpredictable. In the context of civil society, they were hardly even presentable.

Civility was boring; it was to be subverted whenever possible. Vice had made its name as a tireless force of subversion. In the decade since its 1994 launch, it had managed to upend every norm and offend every person, place, or thing it could. Now it was time to celebrate, and do so in typical Vice style. They called their anniversary bash "THE WORST PARTY EVER." It was a raucous shebang that more or less replicated the experience of stepping inside Gavin McInnes's twisted mind. Hopped up on Sparks, an energy drink, guests raved and moshed to the booming lineup of punk bands. On the walls Vice projected videos of "Japanese puke porn," which proved contagious in several cases. "That was our peak," he later wrote in his memoir.

McInnes's fast-and-loose approach to editorial decision-making was what gave the magazine its air of recklessness. Pitches were judged not for prudence but for visceral effect. The dictum, Morton recalled, was "Sure, why not? What do you got? What's funny?"

For Morton, the environment was as liberating as it was bewildering. It felt as if he'd pledged into a fraternity. The guys at Vice could read this in the nervous twitching of his eyes and found themselves unable to keep from hazing him. He'd been there less than a week when the office went out for happy hour at a nearby patio bar, and as the group pounded drinks on Shane Smith and Suroosh Alvi's dime, the conversation escalated to daredevilry. One colleague bet Morton that he wouldn't smash the ketchup bottle over his head. He took the dare under consideration as the beer continued to flow, but by the time he'd made his mind up to do the deed, the offer was off the table. "Missed your chance, Baby Balls!" exclaimed one colleague. The nickname stuck. "It was like lightning had written it on my forehead," Morton said.

He understood the goading was meant to groom him for Vice, which is to say ungroom him. Taking note of the lumberjack look that was in vogue among his coworkers, Morton tried his best to grow a beard. But it came in patchily, leading to further mockery by McInnes et al., for whom Morton was the kid brother they'd never had. At five-feet-six and 120 pounds, he certainly looked the part. "I was very dandruffy and unkempt," he said. "If you look at me back then, I don't carry myself like someone who expects to be seen." But discomfort in the limelight was central to his charm: there was something intriguing about a man who admitted to having a face for radio appearing on-screen. Years later, after Morton had established himself as a star persona at Vice, a critic would write that he "channels Ira Glass." Better that than Anderson Cooper, he thought.

Smith was impressed by Morton's pledgeship. The first milestone was an assignment from the departed McInnes, who saw fit to entrust Baby Balls with his beloved invention from Vice's Montreal days, the Gross Jar. Over the course of nearly a decade, the glass receptacle had been stuffed with a monthly addition of the most repulsive ingredients he could get his hands on: used tampons, chicken blood, urine, and so on. When Morton was awarded custody of the Jar, he dialed up the grossness. In went a dead rat, a mouthful of spit from a colleague who'd come down with the flu, five scabs picked from the face of an editor who'd blacked out drinking, and the droppings of his cat, which the veterinarian had recently pumped full of radioactive medication.

As was the custom at Vice, Morton's first few columns were published under pseudonyms, one being Leroy Gumption. He and the rest of the team at Vice were under no illusions that this was serious journalism. "We were mostly writing for ourselves," he recalled. "It was a big deal when Gawker even noticed us." Morton was more concerned with getting a laugh out of his colleagues than with impressing the magazine's readership, which was showing unstoppable growth. In his first three years at Vice, circulation nearly tripled, and the company sprouted editions in a dozen different countries. There was also a Vice record label, a book-publishing branch, and a few retail shops selling cool stuff like skateboard gear. They had come a long way from a 16-page Canadian lad mag.

Morton began to realize the party couldn't continue forever. Fissures were appearing in the foundation. As McInnes's relationship with Smith and Alvi was increasingly strained, his duties were assumed little by little by Baby Balls, now heir apparent to his authorial role. This included "Dos and Don'ts," the snarky roundup of street-fashion looks that McInnes had established. To the editors, the irony of having Morton as the magazine's arbiter of style was too priceless to resist. They even designed an edition of Dos-and-Don'ts action figures, including one of Baby Balls in a light blue striped golf shirt and snug-fitting corduroys, with a bottle of beer that snapped into his plastic palm. "The expression on his face is the classic lost but determined look," read the description on the back of the package. His figurine was branded a "Do."

When Vice needed a website editor, Smith approached Morton's desk to congratulate him on the promotion. Morton had studied Chaucer, not computer technology. For the time being, his new role would consist primarily of taking articles from the magazine and copying and pasting them onto the site. He learned the necessary skills on the fly, and before long was redesigning Vice.com and carrying the brand into a bright new era. Smith assured him he could keep up the writing he was doing too.

Newly entered into its second decade, Vice had all but mastered its patented posture of irreverent mischief-making and was now prepared to broaden its scope. The magazine's remaining editors and writers appreciated the need for growing up. They knew that readers wouldn't stay forever young, and they understood that they would have to keep pace with their fan base.

Little by little, a semblance of actual journalism began to appear in the pages of Vice's magazine and website. The new still had the fun and games of the old, but increasingly the magazine had informational value about the outside world. A watershed moment in the magazine's evolution came in November 2005, when the month's theme was Immersionism. The neologism encapsulated the transition the editors sought: instead of applying drug-addled gonzo showmanship to their own perverse exploits and fantasies, they would turn it on the world at large.

The issue featured Morton's first byline under his own name and presaged the serious role he would play in Vice's coming-of-age. He had packed an overnight bag, ridden the subway to north of West Harlem, gotten off in Washington Heights, and gone door to door in search of a "Hispanic" family who would agree to host him for a couple of days. He found takers on 181st Street, a Dominican family generous enough to give him the childhood bedroom of their adult daughter. His piece revolved around his comic inability to fit in. This reflected no shortcoming on the Dominicans' part but rather an unavoidable fact of the correspondent's background. Still, he dove into the immersion headlong, and before the visit was over, Morton was fast friends with his host family, cooking meals, helping them host Bible study, and occupying the role of adopted son. His commentary made light of the cultural divide but stopped short of derisiveness. Nor was it politically correct. The article was headlined "Hispanic Panic" and contained Morton's observations about Latin Americans. "They're waaay into TV," he mused and focused on peculiar details like the fact that they soaked their junk mail in the sink before throwing it away. He admired their sense of community, which he summed up as "SU CASA ES THE WHOLE DAMN BUILDING'S CASA." It was tongue-in-cheek. More remarkable, thought Morton's editors, it was actually very good.

Baby Balls had survived his first "embed" as a reporter. He would keep managing the website, but his mind wandered to other immersions. The following year he joined three religious cults—Adidam, the Moonies, and Aleph—and reported at length on the experiences for the October issue.

Another year went by before he pitched his next immersion. He'd set his sights on a strange music festival for white rap bands in southern Illinois called "Gathering of the Juggalos." (At BuzzFeed, Matt Stopera did a story on the festival a bit later.) It opened with a bang: "With the possible exception of the Jews, no other group has eaten as big an amount of shit over the course of its existence as the Juggalos." His lede would never have gotten by the fly-specking copy editors at the New York Times, where the enforcer of the paper's punctilious stylebook was the man who wrote it, Al Siegal, a powerful, rotund, and feared editor. Joe Lelyveld, the former executive editor, once said that Siegal was the only truly irreplaceable journalist at the *Times*. A curse word never flew by him. If breasts were visible in a painting reproduced in the Arts section, out came his scalpel. The photo display accompanying Morton's story showed a fat, bearded, white guy wearing a T-shirt that said "Show Us Ur Tits."

"I saw us as being the biggest thing in the underground," said Morton. "I had little interest in what was going on in mainstream media. We had a nice little fiefdom."

It was precisely the sensibility that Spike Jonze hoped to infuse into "guerrilla video" for Vice. The stories would be a mix of news and travelogue documentary. All the correspondents, cameramen, and producers would be young. They would not stand apart from the stories they did as commentators; they would be participants in the action. That was the way to maintain authenticity. Morton agreed with Smith that the younger generation had been marketed "to death," and the only way to get past their bullshit detectors was not to bullshit.

CNN meanwhile was also diversifying its programming and showcasing new stars like the food writer Anthony Bourdain and letting him do immersive travelogues. But the cable network's programming had a produced gloss, unlike Vice's purposely raw look. The guerrilla videos would have no blow-dried, voice-of-God anchors or correspondents. The camera would take viewers close to the action in rarely shown places, Third World countries and war zones. That was the conceit for one of their first projects, *The Vice Guide to Travel*, with destinations in Africa and Poland; Smith pined to go to North Korea. Working only with a cameraman, Vice correspondents would aim to have their pieces up on the web within a day or so. They could use some of their existing staff on camera. On a whim, Smith decided that Baby Balls, the quintessential back-office factotum, would be in front of the camera.

But not everything could be DIY. They needed real money. Tom Freston was a bridge to the investment world. From his MTV days, he had a good gut for youth culture and had already done business with Jonze, when the two had brought *Jackass* to the network. Under Freston's leadership, MTV had grown from a music-video showcase into a destination for youth-oriented shows such as *The Real World*, one of the first reality shows, which followed a group of young people living together in a new city. MTV was also home to the animated *Beavis and Butt-Head*.

MTV and Vice shared an outsider's sensibility and attempted the same tightrope walk: the commercialization of underground culture. This involved projecting authenticity and packaging it for a mass audience without the audience noticing that it was another form of marketing. Both MTV and Vice relied on the appeal of asinine male humor. It was a universal language, funny to young people in Berlin or Los Angeles. And with video rather than print, language barriers didn't matter. It was easier to market a global brand that could be watched instead of read.

Smith had already pursued a global strategy with the magazine, and his video start-up would be more aggressively international. Vice's London office was growing, and Vice had recently bought its own pub, The Old Blue Last. The ceiling had collapsed three times, but with its footprint in music, Vice attracted big-name acts like the Arctic Monkeys and Amy Winehouse.

Having survived one near-death experience, Smith, the master marketer, was not about to see his company become a victim of what the Austrian economist Joseph Schumpeter called "creative destruction," the process by which an industry is revolutionized from within, its old economic model destroyed by the new. Over the previous 25 years, the overall audience for network news had been cut in half. The concerns of those who remained were reflected in the ads for dentures, adult diapers, and pharmaceuticals to treat erectile dysfunction. Cable news, Fox, CNN, and MSNBC weren't attracting many young viewers either. The median age of the Fox audience was nearly 70. In a craven search for younger viewers, the old nightly news shows began tarting themselves up with celebrity news and lifestyle fluff, but that only diminished quality and fueled distrust of the news media among the core audience, without producing a new generation of viewers.

In the spring of 2006, Jonze brought his burly, tattooed friend Smith to meet Freston in his corner office in Viacom's building on Broadway. Although he was "a suit," Freston was not the usual corporate type. He had once run a clothing company in Afghanistan, where he lived for a few years. He loved exotic places and hit it off with Smith immediately. Freston also loved the idea of using YouTube, which in its early days was little more than a visual bulletin board for amateurs.

When Google purchased YouTube in 2006, it had 50 million users and was quickly becoming a platform for sharing more professionally produced videos and TV clips. YouTube's relationship with Vice was similar to BuzzFeed's with Facebook. The separation of content providers and distributors was inherent to the web, unlike in the old days of newspapers, when the printing presses and journalists worked for the same owner, giving those owners profitable monopolies.

Facebook and Google were set up as neutral platforms for user-created content. They didn't employ editors or view themselves as publishers. This structure, which separated them from responsibility for the particular content on their platforms, would be tweaked over the years, in a mostly failed attempt to limit pornography, content that incited violence, and other blatantly offensive content. But with advertising and audience growth booming, there was little incentive to limit content. As internet bullying, trolling, and "fake news" spread on the web, Facebook and Google would face mounting criticism for not controlling the content on their platforms.

Smith wasn't focused on the platform business. He saw an opening for Vice on the content side of web publishing. "We saw that everyone was building a YouTube or a Hulu or a Facebook," he explained. "Everyone was spending all their money on platforms but none of it on what you put in the pipe. So we said, okay, eventually the market's going to catch up, and everyone's going to need content." A deal with MTV came together quickly. Vice Media created a subsidiary company, VBS, to create the video. Viacom took a 50 percent stake. Smith, Jonze, Alvi, and Eddy Moretti would make and supply the videos with Viacom's money. Almost overnight the magazine became a production company.

It was at this time, in what could have been a repeat of the sudden Szalwinski change of fortune, that Freston was fired by Viacom. The company's mercurial chairman, Sumner Redstone, fired him because he had let Rupert Murdoch outbid Viacom to acquire MySpace for $580 million, which had sent Viacom's stock plunging nearly 20 percent. Unlike Szalwinski, though, Freston had his multimillion-dollar parachute to cushion his exit, and with time on his hands he could open doors for Vice with other investors. A short time later, Freston jumped at Smith's invitation to become a full-time advisor to Vice and the first outsider to join its board. With Freston gone, Viacom unloaded what it thought was a worthless stake in Vice and sold its half back to Smith for $3 million. Smith now controlled the majority of the company. Vice would turn out to be a gold mine, while MySpace became one of the biggest internet dogs of all time, an embarrassment for Murdoch.

With a friend in private equity, Joe Ravitch of the Raine Group, formerly of Goldman Sachs, Freston quickly raised $30 million in new capital for Vice. It was like the early days in Canada, when Szalwinski had infused the magazine with enough cash to expand and move to New York. But Freston, with his MTV background, credibility in the business world, and personal fortune, was a solid benefactor. Freston saw that Smith was quite the impresario and marveled that he had dragged his little company out of a basement in Montreal to the edge of becoming, if their hopes were realized, the next MTV. (In just a decade Smith would have bigger ambitions: to be the next CNN.)

The videos they began to create were not news per se, but versions of immersive journalism shot on location and taking the audience to remote and dangerous places, like music and drug subcultures, where broadcast news correspondents seldom ventured. "Our aesthetic is raw," one of the VBS editors explained. This extended to the look of the anchors. "If it's raggedy, if they're hungover, it's part of the shoot." The producers on set would coach Vice's on-camera talent to let out their inner mavericks, proposing lines that could use another curse word, urging them to booze up, and pushing them to narrate the story in the most sensationalist terms. Created for the internet, the video had a different DNA—a raw, cinéma vérité feel. One clip featured Morton returning to his native Georgia for a meeting with Atlanta-based gangsta rapper Young Jeezy. Seated next to each other at a conference table, the pair offered a study in contrasts, which was precisely why Vice had picked Morton instead of a more seasoned interviewer. For two and a half minutes, Baby Balls fidgeted in his seat, trying to come up with something worth talking about. Finding nothing, he asked, "Do you ever eat boiled peanuts?" Even Jeezy could hardly bear it. When the segment went online, one media critic deemed it "the most awkward rap interview, EVER."

Of course, that alone was a convincing case for watching it. This was the central function of Morton's on-air persona. "Initially," Smith explained, "because Thomas was the most socially awkward person we have ever seen, we said, 'We should make Thomas the star of these documentaries because it seems so absurd.' We sort of realized that a host doesn't have to be Superman. It can be the quintessential, 98-pound weakling, know-it-all nerd. People resonate with him."

After his spectacular failure with Young Jeezy, Morton was determined to go bigger. He pitched a story about the Gullah people, a pidgin-speaking culture living on South Carolina's Sea Islands, whose sole deliverance from abject poverty was their famous moonshine recipe. Morton embarked on a search for the Gullah and their noxious nectar. And as if that alone wasn't on-brand enough for Vice, Morton threw in another sweetener: he would be joined on his quest by a punk rock band called the Black Lips, who had recently signed to Vice Records. "Great," he remembers his editors saying. "You go do it. Take a cameraman. You have a weekend."

What ensued was a weekend of hijinks and high drama. Morton arrived, city-slick and packed into the band's rickety van, for a sojourn into the backwater landscape, where he met "a million-year-old distiller," was "ferreted away to a terrifying compound in the middle of the woods where the black version of Buffalo Bill makes his own shine," before being "chased off a farm by a truck full of angry rednecks, and abandoned by our local guide." He somehow landed on his feet, struck up a rapport with a group of local skateboarders—who else?—and was shown to a secret source of moonshine. "We left the islands blind drunk on some of the roughest-tasting hooch any of us had ever gulleted." For Morton, the moral of the story was that he had no script; his lack of the trappings of professional journalism had been an advantage. Of his subjects he said, "A lot of them are a lot more comfortable with us than a dude with anchor hair and a microphone and a tie. It's much easier for them to relate."

It was clear to the folks at Vice that this new strategy was working. "Video was as much of a cash cow as we could have hoped for," Morton said. "And it was the saving grace of the magazine, because the landscape at the time was pretty fucked for print."

Morton, with a cameraman, immersed himself in survivalist culture. It took him days to find the couple he was assigned to profile in northern Alaska, where they lived in complete isolation, eating what they foraged or killed. At night Morton was frightened by the darkness and animal noises. When a large bear came too close, his host shouted to his wife, "Get the gun!" She did, and in an instant the bear was dead. Morton helped skin the animal for the benefit of the camera, and his hosts offered him the pelt as a souvenir. When Smith heard this, he jumped at the opportunity to have the bear stuffed and sent back to Brooklyn, where it became the company's mascot, situated ominously in a corner of the main conference room. They named it "Juicebox."

Morton was part of a broader revolution sweeping journalism. As circulation and ad revenue shrank, print newsrooms cut and cut. If you worked at a newspaper, your colleagues were suddenly out of work. Newspapers were only slowly adapting to the age of video, and reporters looked down on the videographers their papers hired as "not real journalists." Smith didn't care about such distinctions. If the same people could write articles and advertisements, they could do guerrilla documentaries for Vice.com.

Soon Morton's calendar was packed with immersions. He was sent to Ghana for a tour of a casket factory that specialized in fun and frivolous coffins designed to look like planes, pianos, coconuts, or wrenches, like the one Morton tried out and found to his liking. He went to El Alberto, Mexico, to try out the small town's main attraction, a park that simulates what it's like to illegally cross the border into the U.S. He shipped out to Mauritania to try out the local custom of force-feeding young brides to plump them up and in just two days gained 10 pounds on the fat-rich diet. In China he flung himself into the state-sponsored dating scene and toured a sex-doll-manufacturing plant.

He hosted a series of mini-episodes on a toxic garbage heap the size of Texas in the Pacific Ocean. Joining an expedition of conservationists, he set sail for the vast whirlpool where the trash collected. He helped catch and study jellyfish and other ocean life for adverse effects, then sliced and served them as sushi, testing the toxicity firsthand.

Gradually his assignments became more serious. He snuck onto a lifeboat in Laos to join a secret expedition of escapees from North Korea en route to safety in Thailand, and trekked to the far reaches of Kazakhstan, where the lingering effects of Russian nuclear tests were causing severe defects in newborns. In Bogota, Colombia, kids were living in the sewers trying to escape the roving death squads who were cleansing the city for an upcoming visit by President George W. Bush—by pouring gasoline down the tunnels and lighting them. Twenty-two had been burned alive. With a cameraman, Morton flew down to investigate, donning rubber waders and descending into the sewer tunnels to slog, "knee-deep in human shit," with a local activist. Living in the filth and stench, Morton met pregnant women, babies, guys doing drugs, and people cooking in the crawl spaces where they hid. The camera focused as much on Morton as his subjects. That was Vice's style, to put themselves in dangerous situations where they could show derring-do. "I'm fucking scared," Morton said directly into the camera, in the house style.

The line between sensationalism and journalism shifted from story to story. After the sewers, Morton was whisked across the country to the mountains outside Cartagena for a piece on a tribe with a tradition of having sex with donkeys, a subject guaranteed to be a hit with Vice's fan base. The travel and adventure were pure adrenaline for Morton. It didn't seem to matter that he lacked any real knowledge of the places he parachuted into. At the *Times*, such surface reporting—rushing in and out of places—was derisively called "toe-touching." For its foreign reporting the paper instead relied mainly on experienced foreign correspondents who lived in the locales and had studied the culture for years.

Morton's stories did what they were intended to do: attract the eyeballs of younger viewers who spent hours surfing YouTube. Vice was one of the first companies to pipe its stories into YouTube channels and ask its audience to sign up as subscribers. Though the channels were free, the sign-ups gave Vice and Google, which owned YouTube, valuable data about the young audience, and the data helped fetch advertising revenue. Soon the Vice content proved so valuable that YouTube was paying tens of millions to Vice for its immersive docs. There were channels for Vice segments on technology, music, and, eventually, food and weed. By 2009 the mini-docs were drawing 3.5 million monthly unique visitors, who spent an average of nearly 15 minutes on the site.

Vice's eye-popping antics and hip repudiation of media conventions had attracted attention but had not given it legitimacy as a news brand. Like Peretti with BuzzFeed, Smith wanted Vice to be taken seriously. The brand was widely viewed as a fount of coolness worth following by anyone who cared about what was cool. As the company entered its teenage years, Smith began parlaying the thrall in which it held millennials into a role for Vice as a purveyor of actual substance. It was a bait-and-switch. Vice's fans tuned in for their dose of heavy metal, say, and got a feature on heavy metal—in Baghdad. They kept coming back to watch Morton navigate his next caper and found him in increasingly newsworthy predicaments, such as embedded with the Kurdish militia as it waged war against Syrian jihadists, or covering environmental problems in the Pacific Ocean. This was the strategic equivalent of a parent pretending the spoonful of veggies is an airplane flying loop-the-loops into the baby's mouth.

As its readers matured, Vice needed to pay for all the nutritious content it had invested in their upbringing, since it turned out to be much costlier than the fodder they'd served up in their early days. Smith saw how well Vice's bad-boy tone worked as a conduit for topics with news value, and he wondered if it might work as well to sugarcoat topics with value that he could take to the bank. Vice had all but monopolized the market for mock-authentic cultural rebellion, first in the magazine world, then in the realm of online video. Now it was in a position to leverage this cachet by charging advertisers for the cool points they could confer. So inside the company's Brooklyn offices, Smith started his own advertising agency. It was dubbed Ad-Vice, but when this punny reference to depravity proved unnerving to would-be clients, they renamed it Virtue. The branded ads Virtue made would have the same look and feel as Vice stories, which was crucial to their guise of authenticity. This was similar to BuzzFeed's strategy, and the consonance was by design: Vice's journalists were encouraged to write copy for Virtue and the copywriters to try their hand at editorial work.

Since Vice didn't strictly define itself as a news provider, no one there worried about church-state issues, such as when advertisers influenced the content of stories. Vice would bring the relationship even closer, asking advertisers to work with them on shaping and sponsoring programming, something that was verboten at most news companies until they, too, under financial pressure began wooing sponsors. Eventually its advertising division grew to offer nearly every service a regular ad agency did, down to purchasing ad spots that appeared on other websites. The lapsed antiestablishmentarians now seemed to have no reservations about tightening their monopolistic control over the ad-packed media diet they were feeding cool, credulous young people.

"With each new territory that launches, our hold on the elusive and rare bird known as the 'tastemaker' grows," Vice boasted to advertisers in its media kit. "Together, we can grow drunk and bloated with power."

Smith's eyes were big, but then, at 230 pounds, so were his appetites. "Let's have 14 bottles of wine at dinner, roast suckling pig, and a story about chopping a dude's head off in the desert," was how he once described his approach to life. He was a self-identified "bon vivant, storyteller, drunk." Employees likened his presence around the office to Teddy Roosevelt's, though he preferred to think of himself as Vice's Stalin. Smith seemed to take delight in pitting himself against the old guard to consolidate the "media empire" he had always imagined Vice would become. Freston recalls that when Vice began its first video story, Smith gave him a tour of the modest office and said, "One day this is going to be a football field of edit suites." The new video venture had a tagline: "In ten years, we'll be the mainstream." Smith had kindled the company's impoverished beginnings; now it was time for Vice to feast at the expense of the powers that had been. "I go to war every day," he told the *Wall Street Journal*. "I go to war with the big guys because they're all throwing spears because I'm coming to eat their lunch."

"Readers are leaving newspapers, and people are having an even harder time getting to our demographic," Smith told the *New York Times* in 2009. The chief problem for advertisers was that young people had developed bullshit detectors as they grew up online. Vice, Smith said, was "the go-to solution for these brands." He gloated as if it were due to some pearl of insight that eluded his old-school competitors, but in reality the suggestion that they should bamboozle their readers by blurring editorial content and ads had mainly repulsed them. When as managing editor of the *Times* I asked our digital ad director about native advertising, she recoiled, saying, "The *Times* would never do that. It's so sleazy."

The digital era had enshrined a new business model as the industry standard: places like Vice and BuzzFeed would give away their journalistic content for free to win adherents to the publisher's brand identity, then use this leverage to present sales pitches for their sponsors' sales pitches, soft-pedaling them to the same unsuspecting readers whose loyalty they had won. Their unsponsored editorial work sold readers on how awesome and uncompromised they were. And the depth of that connection with readers was what they sold to advertisers, charging them for the opportunity to compromise it. "In particular," the company boldly divulged in legal filings, "Virtue Worldwide capitalizes on Vice's audience and Vice's knowledge of the market by selling advertisers, businesses and/or consumers expertise and other services on how to reach the consuming public."

Moretti, head of Vice's "creative" division, pointed to Virtue's foremost asset. "What we have is all about our voice," he told the *Wall Street Journal*. Tom Punch, another Vice creative officer, suggested the company's chief commodity could be distilled even further: every single request the company receives from advertisers, he said, "has the word 'authenticity' in it." It may have occurred to them that, like any precious natural resource, authenticity would inevitably be depleted. But the influx of cash made that eventuality easy to dismiss for the time being. The plan was to milk Vice's street credibility for all it was worth. If it dried up, they would find a new tack.

Rather than the cheap click ads that cluttered the web, Virtue made well-produced pre-roll ads that ran before the short immersion docs on Vice's site—and that could have been mistaken for them too. It already had in hand one of the early masters of the native advertising form in Spike Jonze, whose directorial reel included popular spots he'd made for such brands as Ikea, Adidas, and The Gap. His ads told intriguing stories. People wanted to watch them. Some became cult classics, just like his films.

The famous Ikea ad that regularly made the lists of greatest ads of all time tells the story of a red lamp that is abandoned by its owner and left on the street. As sad music plays, the lamp is bombarded by wind and pelted by rain while its old owner can be seen in the window, lit by the warm glow of a new lamp. At the end, a strange man with a Scandinavian accent appears out of nowhere and says, "Many of you feel bad for this lamp," as the rain also soaks him. "That is because you're crazy. It has no feelings! And the new one is much better." Cut to the yellow and blue Ikea logo.

Another, for Absolut, was slyer in its salesmanship: a 31-minute film Jonze wrote about robots falling in love in Los Angeles. Featuring music by the in-vogue indie act Sleigh Bells and costumes designed by the same guys who dressed Daft Punk, the film debuted at Sundance to positive reviews. It had nothing to do with vodka and included no reference to its sponsor aside from a brief "Absolut Presents" among the beginning credits.

Native advertising was a hidden sell. To be effective, the ads needed to harmonize stylistically with the content that surrounded it. The sales pitch was subtle and secondary to the story. Viewers and readers could easily confuse the real stories with the ads. That was the whole point. Many brand-sponsored segments carried little or no label. Some ran only with Vice's watermark.

In addition to the short-form video advertisements, Vice offered clients the opportunity to sponsor nominally journalistic segments packaged as a series. Brands would pay as much as $5 million for "custom co-branded content initiatives." For The North Face, Vice created a series of feature-length films called "Far Out" that "offered insights into the lives of individuals that truly live The North Face philosophy—'to Never Stop Exploring.'" For Harley-Davidson, which wanted to cement its appeal to younger bikers, Vice concocted six episodes in which a cast of skateboarders rode around Mexico, showcasing the Harley-Davidson product line. The Virtue PR team later claimed responsibility for a 23 percent jump in young people buying Harleys.

For Volvo the team created a more cosmopolitan play. Vice cooked up 30 short video profiles of successful young "creatives" hand-picked as a sampling of Volvo's target market: "sculptors, photographers, chemists, cake decorators." "Ecomagination," General Electric's series about energy, bore the same name as its long-running ad campaign, and aptly so. The *Times* and the *Post*, meanwhile, did not allow advertisers to sponsor particular content, since they regarded such arrangements as transgressive of the church-state boundary. When Vice started a health vertical called Tonic, it landed two giant healthcare companies to sponsor series that would pass off their advice on navigating the medical market as magically unbiased. The *Times* fretted over whether to permit a nonprofit healthcare foundation to pay for some of its health coverage, ultimately deciding not to, since the foundation had for-profit donors.

For sums in high eight figures, brands could buy whole verticals from

Vice for themselves. Marketing executives jumped at the opportunity to be seen as Vice's coequal collaborator. One of its most ambitious advertising collaborations—"campaign" doesn't do justice to the full-on ventures Vice undertook—was the Creators Project, a fully staffed website under the Vice umbrella, established in perpetuity for Intel in 2007. The idea had come out of a conversation between Smith and Jonze over dinner. What would you do, Jonze asked, if you could do anything, with no financial constraints? What could have passed for a hypothetical conversation-starter a few years earlier was now a pragmatic question. Smith's answer was uncharacteristically high-brow. He said he would establish an institution like the Parisian salons of the 1920s, breeding grounds for new ideas about art, music, theater, and literature, crucibles of cultural cross-pollination. Intel was a perfect deep-pocketed patron. Its chips were ubiquitous but invisible, which meant there was almost no brand identity. Being seen as a supporter of creativity could begin to create that identity.

Desperate for a chunk of Intel's $327 million marketing budget, Smith arranged to annex the offices of an architecture firm next door ahead of the first client meeting, thinking the glass walls would make the right impression. Employees were instructed to spiff up and bring their laptops, and a plumber arrived at the last minute to install a state-of-the-art Japanese toilet for the occasion. Smith wanted to exude the vibe of a smart tech start-up, not a rough pizza-box-strewn frat party. According to *New York* magazine, when he was wooing clients, Smith sometimes commanded his employees to show up at the bars where he'd be trying to finalize deals so the scene would look hip and lively. "Dance," he would whisper to them.

His spiel worked on Intel, scoring Smith a victory that would define the arc of Vice's future growth. The Vice-Intel coproduction would feature musicians and other artists performing and discussing their work at the nexus of culture and technology. The otherwise faceless chip maker paid $40 million for the privilege. What bought them was a way to plant positive, if subliminal, associations with their brand in the minds of young urbanites. Their logo would grace the stage at the series of music festivals Vice put on in New York, London, Seoul, and Beijing to hype the launch of the Creators Project, and it would loom above the articles and videos Vice staffers published on its site. But for Intel, the usefulness of such a partnership was not confined to the realm of the unconscious. By footing the bill for an entire team at Vice, Intel had purchased itself a say in the substance of what was displayed, as well as what wasn't; this was the "cultural cross-pollination" of Smith's dreams. To wit, writers and editors were assigned to write articles that would portray the chip maker glowingly. One story touted the ingenuity of the technologists at Intel who had created a hologram character to appear onstage in Shakespeare's *Tempest* at Stratford-upon-Avon. Another story, titled "Exploring Our Relationship to Our Computers," led with blunt promotions of Intel products, committing a cardinal "Don't" of branded content.

The vast majority of sponsored content was more subtle and indirect, which made it all the more insidious. So soft were the sells that a reader scrolling through articles on the Creators Project might stumble upon one titled "Are Brands the New Medicis?" and would have no way of knowing the extent to which Intel or any other brand influenced the thrust of the author's argument, which was this: "In the art world, branded projects can often be stigmatized as creatively and morally bankrupt, but as high-profile brand collaborations become increasingly common, it seems the cross-pollination between art and advertising is no longer quite as scandalizing."

Virtue was a scandal in the eyes of many traditional journalists. As the engine driving 90 percent of the company's revenue, native ads, or branded content, as it was also called, were impossible to ignore, but traditional news organizations such as the *Times* and the *Post* were still spooked by the ethical taint of blurring church and state. Later, as they watched Smith win over clients in Coca-Cola, Anheuser-Busch, Nike, Dell, AT&T, moneylenders, and consumer packaged-goods conglomerates, the newspapers too dropped their compunctions. In 2014 *AdWeek* named Smith a "Brand Genius."

The Creators Project, Smith said, was a "holy shit" breakthrough. "That program built the company." The template it offered was one of alignment between Vice content and client objectives, the exact opposite of editorial independence. "We don't have a disconnect between the creative and the business," he said unapologetically.

Starved for revenue, older magazines like the *Atlantic* and *Forbes* were quick to take note of Smith's "solution" to the industry's business problem and scrambled to establish agencies of their own within their walls. In just a few years' time, the *Times* and the *Post* also had in-house agencies to produce native ads. The *Times* stole *Forbes*'s chief revenue officer and ad director, one of the most aggressive users of native advertising, to launch theirs. But Vice's operation dwarfed the others, with clients paying millions for its hip, edgy campaigns, told in the same immersive style as its docs.

Smith insisted that Vice maintained "creative control" of these ad partnerships and that it had never edited any of its content for sponsors. But he also said, "All brands should think of themselves as media companies." He came out swinging to contest the perception that Vice was compromised. "We don't do branded content," he declared, only to admit, "We do content sponsored by brands." The distinction, he thought, preserved Vice's claim of authenticity, although it was a distinction without a real difference.

So even as he loudly maintained the falsehood that Vice's corporate clients "don't give notes," Smith continued in private to enshrine their say-so in the editorial process. When Gawker reporter and self-appointed ombudsman of Vice, Hamilton Nolan, heard that the site was killing stories that might offend its sponsors, he pounced. Nolan got in touch with Charles Davis, an editor Vice had fired after he'd blown the whistle on the company's censorship. Davis had edited a freelancer's article, headlined "It's Time to Start Boycotting the NFL," and okayed it for publication before his higher-ups could intervene on behalf of the League, a potential business client. What ensued was a series of chastisements and injunctions from a more senior editor, who clarified Vice protocol in an email to Davis: "Any 'brand' mention—basically any mention of a large entity that we might be making some kind of business deal with—should get run up the flagpole to Hosi [Simon]," Vice's global general manager. Davis noted, "In my experience, every single time—every single time—I had a story 'run up the flagpole' it was killed."

The controversy was similar to Ben Smith's erasure of some content that might offend BuzzFeed's advertisers. Both instances of overt bowing to ad clients would have caused major scandals at the *Times* and *Post*, which long ago created their walls. In failing to be scrupulous about fencing off advertisers, BuzzFeed and Vice showed they were still immature news brands.

Accounts from other whistleblowers from within Vice started to pour into Nolan's inbox. "They constantly edit to keep brands happy," said an editor who worked on the site's music vertical underwritten by Heineken, which Vice afforded "lengthy and irritating approvals processes before any video made it to the website." Another writer said stories that appeared on a vertical sponsored by the beverage giant Brisk were sanitized of mentions of certain places and names that brand representatives found objectionable. Another recounted how one editor got "hammered" for publishing an article that criticized Nike. Representatives at the sportswear company objected to Vice's three-part documentary on the Ku Klux Klan, which featured a subject wearing a Nike T-shirt. Vice obediently erased the image when Anheuser-Busch complained about the Klansman who appeared on-screen in a Budweiser cap, drinking a Bud Lite.

Smith learned not to offend advertisers from a bitter lesson from Vice's early days in Canada. He had tried and tried to get Time Warner to advertise in the magazine. When he finally succeeded, the company's ad ran next to a lewd article by McInnes about old men and sex. Time Warner never advertised with him again, although years later HBO, a subsidiary, would become a partner.

So when Bank of America forked over $5 million for a personal finance series, "The Business of Life," the company knew Vice wasn't going to feature stories about bank fraud. The sponsors would always see the show before it aired, and their requests for changes were heeded. Everyone working on the show was clear on this. So it did not come off as entirely genuine when the creators introduced it as "a new kind of talk show from VICE News . . . an eclectic panel of writers, thinkers, policy experts, and scholars to break down everything you need to make sense of the most complicated topics of our time." Topics such as how to get funding for that movie you've always wanted to make, and how your income level determines your access to healthy, organic foods. Not that the topics much mattered; the impeccably diverse cast of millennials being paid to attend a panel on "finance" in a warehouse would smile and nod thoughtfully regardless. In the top right corner of the screen, the Vice News logo loomed prominently, as if to throw the full weight of its journalistic reputation behind the impartiality of the report. It was a performance that managed the aesthetics of authenticity and factual accuracy without any of the substance those terms connoted.

Vice wanted to have it both ways, seeming to give the middle finger to the whole sold-out corporate media, while elsewhere in the building incubating a sponsored project that promised to abandon the "cynicism and negativity" that supposedly plagued mainstream news reportage in favor of a more sanguine, sunny-side approach. Virtue created and curated the stories for the project, named Collectively and underwritten by an armada of big companies, including Coca-Cola and Unilever. Absurdly the promotional materials for Collectively promised that Virtue, itself an ad agency, would enjoy "complete editorial independence" in creating the material for the site.

Vice's branded content was often a reverse image of its own content, which by 2010 was painting a darker picture of the world, as its documentaries began to focus more on war, environmental crimes, and prisons. Collectively remained relentlessly upbeat. "Today's media is obsessed with fear-mongering tactics, and a pervasive pessimism that would have us all believing that 'everything is f*cked, and it's all our fault,'" Collectively told its audience, promising to "help people learn how they can help. Take meaningful action. Choose to make a difference."

Smith joyously straddled the two worlds, schmoozing corporate clients and hosting documentaries about war and climate change while maintaining his bad-boy image. Inevitably the mix turned awkward. The clunkiest case occurred when Vice paired a documentary on violence in Chicago with selling a revenge-themed video game. The documentary, "Chicago Interrupted," was shown in two parts and was underwritten by the video game manufacturer Bethesda Softworks. It would be used to amp up interest in the game Dishonored, but viewers weren't told of the connection, and media critics pounced.

Critics were kinder to other pieces, especially parts of the travel guide and documentary made by Suroosh Alvi about a heavy metal band in Iraq. Alvi went to Baghdad after the bombs fell to try to find a band that he had followed since before the war. His documentary, "Heavy Metal in Baghdad," traced the band's fight to stay together in the rubble, and then their forced exile to Syria. For young American viewers with war fatigue, a story told from the perspective of a bunch of Iraqi Metalheads captured their interest.

Music was Alvi's lane at Vice; he launched its YouTube channel, Noisey, which had an array of corporate sponsors, including Budweiser. He looked like a young grad student or Silicon Valley geek, with glasses and a beard. He was as wiry and calm as Smith was bulky and explosive. For one of the travel guides, he returned to his parents' native country, Pakistan, to visit a gun market near the Khyber Pass, where his mother had taken him as a child. Dressed like a native and wearing sunglasses, he walked to where bullets were being made from the molten metal of rotting Soviet tanks, the camera following him, zooming in close as he fired a Kalashnikov. Gunfire and danger were often hallmarks of the Vice documentaries.

Smith and a very small crew snuck into North Korea from China for a subversive and revealing look at the Hermit Kingdom. The three-part series included a visit to the state library totally devoid of books and a sports arena where acrobatic military marches were performed in their honor. But there was no sighting of Kim Jong-il, the country's deified "Dear Leader." Smith and his cameraman repeatedly were warned that it was illegal to film, but they went ahead surreptitiously and came home with video that illuminated both the absurdity and the terror of life in North Korea. There was plenty of footage of Smith drinking and cavorting. But his camera presence also had a touch of charm, such as when he played pool and Ping-Pong with one of the female servers at a restaurant where, Smith claimed, she had not seen another customer for the past 10 months.

When Kim Jong-il's son took over, a Vice crew began plotting its return to Pyongyang, this time under the auspices of a delegation whose aims were friendly to the despotic regime. To win over Supreme Leader Kim Jong-un, Vice picked one of Kim's favorite American celebrities, the retired basketball superstar and reputed wild man Dennis Rodman, to be part of the shoot. Rodman's charm proved sufficient to earn Vice access to the sealed-off empire, and before they knew it Rodman and another member of the Vice crew were being treated to a 10-course meal with Kim Jong-un at the royal palace. They'd also brought three members of the Harlem Globetrotters, who entertained the dictator and a stadium filled with his subjects, whose obedient applause endured for much of the pickup game. Rodman watched from the stands, seated courtside next to Kim, and afterward summarized the spirit of the trip for Vice. "Guess what! I love him," he said. No acknowledgment of his crimes against humanity. "The guy's really awesome."

Vice's report ran under the headline "North Korea Has a Friend in Dennis Rodman and VICE," and touted the history-making geopolitical breakthrough Smith's fearless delegation had achieved. Two weeks passed before the real story emerged, and by that time the Vice crew was back in Brooklyn, safe and sound. This left the rest of the international press corps to report on North Korea's withdrawal from a 60-year armistice and its announcement that the "warmongering" U.S. could expect "merciless retaliation" in the form of a nuclear strike. Embarrassingly, Rodman seemed to apologize for the bad relations between the U.S. and North Korea. Though some media critics tut-tutted, no one much noticed them. The celebrity stunt garnered a massive audience, earning Vice its biggest mainstream breakthrough to date.

Vice was scoring cool points like its business depended upon it, which was true. Besides focusing on the weekly HBO show, Smith diversified Vice's offerings, establishing new topical sections or verticals on the website that he hoped would win the loyalty of the growing number of hipster phenotypes appearing on its radar. The verticals included music, technology, food, and health and were given hip names like Noisey, Motherboard, Munchies, and Tonic. They were driven by advertising and optimized for it too. Brands preferred to make their buys for targeted audiences rather than a single general audience, and Vice wanted to please its clients. In time the verticals became even more targeted: Noisey gave rise to Thump, specifically for fans of electronic music; Sports spun off a vertical called Fightland devoted to covering professional mixed martial arts and underwritten entirely by Ultimate Fighting Championship, the company that organized, hosted, and profited from the fights.

Traditional news organizations such as the *Times* and the *Post* had general-interest audiences and built sections on style and food to lure more specific advertising. But print ads were no longer effective, according to advertisers, who were suddenly mad for video. The *Times* and *Post* had to expand their video capabilities slowly, since they lacked the in-house expertise of an auteur like Jonze. Their expansion into video was mainly fueled not by a desire to deepen their journalism through visual storytelling but by economics. Advertisers paid higher premiums for the pre-roll ads that ran at the beginning of whichever video viewers had clicked on to watch. It was a window of opportunity to present a captive audience with a mini show before the main event, a far more valuable commodity than the mere screen real estate other sites filled with banner ads. The virtual billboards crowded and overwhelmed the internet, degrading the sites' appearance and drowning each other out until it all seemed to the visitor like the white noise David Foster Wallace had warned about. Apps that blocked ads were becoming popular.

Newspaper organizations were used to working within the constraints of the static page. To the extent that they employed visual thinkers, their expertise was in using photographs, maps, and charts to convey information that the text did not. Their design directors were not yet fluent in video and weren't able to muster the animation and motion graphics that were so eye-catching on BuzzFeed and Vice. The *Times* and *Post* hired a few videographers and assigned them to follow print reporters, posting video doppelgangers of their stories. But the print reporters always took the lead and didn't know how to enhance their journalism with the new digital tools. Behind their backs, the older reporters complained that the digital specialists in their newsrooms weren't "real journalists."

Imitating broadcast television, the newspapers built expensive studios and assigned their print journalists to start doubling as anchors and talking heads. But replicating a genre that was also in decline got them nowhere. Mainly their video news reports were dreadful and only cost money. In the space of a few years, the *Times* hired and dispensed with a half-dozen video directors. The ad department kept complaining that the newsroom was leaving revenue on the table by not producing more video inventory. But when Sulzberger let the digital ad director help choose the next head of video in the newsroom—a breach of the wall between church and state—she failed as well.

In order to keep attracting investments from venture capital and new corporate partners, Vice had to show expansive audience growth year after year. So new shows and more and more videos had to come through the assembly line, and cracks began to show. In a weak imitation of Martin Sheen in Coppola's *Apocalypse Now*, Smith trekked through a malaria-infested swamp in Liberia to profile a rebel leader with an irresistible name: General Butt Naked. The general supposedly cannibalized children before battle and drank their blood, although Vice offered no corroboration. The camera focused on a beach covered with human feces. Smith's dialogue on camera was simplistic, stereotypical, and filled with hyperbole. Liberia was "severely fucked up," he thundered. "It's civil war on steroids, a postapocalyptic Armageddon."

Some experienced foreign correspondents and international policy experts were critical of Smith's Liberian jaunt, and the blogosphere began to howl. "Your video stirred a lot of debate among people who care about Liberia," wrote one commenter. "The consensus, it seems, among people who know Liberia, is that your sensationalist, naive and utterly narrow take is misguided." Another accused the show of treating its subjects "like animals in a zoo." Less than a week after the piece appeared, the *Times* ran its own travel piece showing a placid Liberia that had become a great destination for surfing.

Smith routinely criticized the traditional news media for "not telling the full story," a charge he made in the Liberia video. He was inviting pushback, and eventually it came, during an interview of Vice's three founders by the *Times*'s media columnist David Carr, who had gone to Williamsburg with a video camera to meet the triumvirate. In a clip from the interview that went viral and was preserved on camera in "Page One," a documentary about the *Times*, Smith charges ahead on a characteristically far-out and impassioned monologue:

SMITH: Well, I've got to tell you one thing: I'm a regular guy and I go to these places and I go, "Okay, everyone talked to me about cannibalism, right? Everyone talked about cannibalism." Now I'm getting a lot of shit for talking about cannibalism. Whatever. Everyone talked to me about cannibalism! . . . That's fucking crazy! So the actual—our audience goes, "That's fucking insane, like, that's nuts!" And the *New York Times*, meanwhile, is writing about surfing, and I'm sitting there going like, "You know what? I'm not going to talk about surfing, I'm going to talk about cannibalism, because that fucks me up."

CARR: Just a sec—time out. Before you ever went there, we've had reporters there reporting on genocide after genocide. Just because you put on a fucking safari helmet and looked at some poop doesn't give you the right to insult what we do. So continue.

SMITH: I'm just saying, I'm not a journalist, I'm not there to report—

CARR: Obviously.

SMITH: I'm just talking about what I saw there.

Despite his bluster, Smith ultimately felt compelled to apologize in a posting on the Vice Website:

> Our recent *Vice Guide to Liberia* stirred a lot of controversy, and some misunderstanding about how we tell stories. We are not strangers to controversy, but this is different, and we would like to take this opportunity to apologize for any harm we may have caused to the image of Liberia. This was not our intent. Our "Vice Guide to Travel Series" is not a typical travel guide. The intention of the VGTL was to look at what happens to former child soldiers, former generals and other people left behind by the massive development effort in the society. Like all of our Travel series, we focused on going through areas of Monrovia facing serious challenges, and our final product reflected those experiences. As in any post-conflict country, we realize that development and recovery cannot be achieved immediately. Liberia has come a long way, but continues to face many challenges: this is what we wanted to show. While we accomplished this, reactions—especially from the Liberian community—have expressed disappointment that we could have focused on the more positive aspects of Liberia today. The Liberians we worked with and talked with were very friendly, welcoming and caring, despite all the violence and injustice they faced over 14 years of civil war that the international community did little to stop. To the people of Liberia, we would like to sincerely apologize for any harm this may have caused to the perception of your country and to all of those that were offended.
>   Sincerely, Vice

It wasn't the first time Vice took flak for the showy antics of its correspondents upstaging the actual story, and it certainly wouldn't be the last.

But it raised questions of what exactly was motivating Vice to shine a light on far-flung places. If it wasn't the substance of the story unfolding in that foreign land, perhaps it was just that the land was so—foreign. When members of the Russian punk band Pussy Riot were imprisoned on charges of anti-Putin "hooliganism," Vice responded with a story that described their correspondents sitting around the office, chatting about their shared dismay at the Russian government's ruling and the feeling that they were not "doing enough to show that we felt something about this. That we cared." Unable to go on feeling so guilty about Pussy Riot's incarceration, they resolved to take action. "Fuck it," they decided. "Let's get tattoos." The story "We, Too, Are Hooligans" documented its staffers' journey to a nearby tattoo parlor, where, once they were sufficiently inebriated, they got inked with the Russian word for "hooligan."

Part of the problem was that the news division had grown out of Smith's personal boredom. "I get a lot of shit because I used to like cocaine and supermodels and fuckin', and now we're gonna try to do news," he told countless journalists attempting to profile him. It was as if he felt the need to hedge against the possibility of seeming too serious. The origin story of news at Vice felt like a monologue that belonged in *The Hangover Part II*. As told by Smith to Wired, it went like this: "We started doing Vice and we got into fashion and music and lifestyle and all that crap. Suddenly, you're at a Chanel party and you're with some model, with coke running down your nostrils, and you kind of get lost in the vortex. But as we expanded internationally, we started to see a lot more of what was happening in the world. I started to get really pissed off about politics and economic disparity and the environment. I said, 'There's all this shit going on, and we aren't doing anything about it—although we have the ability to do so.'" To the *Guardian* he said, "There was a time in the Nineties when it was all about cocaine and asymmetrical zippers. We did a lot of drugs and went to a lot of parties and had sex with a lot of supermodels. But you realise there's a whole world out there."

But in making the rather abrupt transition to doing news, important work like developing standards, ethical guidelines, security and safety rules, a fact-checking system, and training for new reporters didn't happen. The networks and CNN each employed a high-ranking editor to enforce standards and in-house rule books that were given to every employee. And even this did not always prevent mistakes and ethical breaches.

Morton, meanwhile, was keeping his head down and continuing to immerse himself. When he was in Brooklyn, he served as the direly needed

conscience in Vice's offices. He was also the guy they went to for literature reviews, sit-downs with reputed film directors, and media criticism, as
when the mainstream outlets overdid the exploitative coverage of blighted
Detroit. Even so he was liable to commit the same errors in judgment as his
higher-ups, and without real training or the guidance of experienced news
editors, he too was soon caught making basic mistakes.

He had gone to Uganda in 2012 to do a documentary on the strong
homemade alcohol made from bananas, which he tasted. That wasn't the
problem. The problem was the entire thrust of the documentary: it revolved
around Morton's claim that Uganda, despite having "had a pretty good spell
the last 25 years," with "no major civil wars," was "the drunkest place on
earth." The assertion fell apart after it was fact-checked, but it wasn't fact-
checked until it was published, and even then the fact-checking was done
by an independent journalist who felt it necessary to hold Vice accountable. First, Uganda was in the throes of multiple conflicts that had claimed
some five million lives and displaced two million since fighting started in
1998. Second, as a blogger at MIT named Ethan Zuckerman pointed out,
there were more than 20 countries—spanning Africa, Asia, and Europe—
that boasted higher rates of per capita alcohol consumption.

This was a rookie mistake, both by Morton and at the institutional level.
Morton clearly lacked knowledge about some of the places and people he
covered, and most of the time this was the central conceit of his correspon-
dence. But when he did pass off his uninformed commentary as founded
fact, Vice had no standardized measures in place to check him, and even
less interest in doing so at the cost of a good story. It mattered less when the
topic was donkey sex or sex dolls, but when it came to international politics
there was more than frivolity at stake.

Foreign correspondents for the *Times* and the *Post* went through rigorous training. They were assigned to their countries and regions for tours
that usually lasted years. They were paid to study foreign languages so they
could report without the local door-openers, known as "fixers," who were
routinely used by Vice. Before he landed in Russia, Cliff Levy, who, at 40,
was young for the *Times*'s foreign desk, took six months off to learn the
language and steep himself in Russian history and literature. After 9/11 all
the correspondents received elaborate safety and security training for emer-
gencies like kidnapping. Vice saw fit to sidestep the cumbersome process
of contingency planning, confident its reporters could manage just as well
on guts alone.

Morton, for one, admitted that there was something being lost in the substitution of new outlets for old ones. "If we are the place people get news," he said, "it shows how much trouble news is in." He was sent to the front lines of the Syrian Civil War in the spring of 2014, and even given the context, Vice managed to find a comic angle for his story. Baby Balls was assigned to spend a night with a unit in the Kurdish militia composed of teenage girls. As he marches in formation with them and hits the ground for a simulated firefight, he tells the camera about one girl in the battalion who's wearing pink scrunchies. "I was a Cub Scout," he told me. But Vice wagered that his unsuitability for the role made the piece all the more compelling. He summoned his inner swashbuckling daredevil by following the example of his mentors at Vice and choosing not to wear body armor. "We're safe in a very smart and nimble way," he said, but admitted that he was maybe too comfortable. "A bullet passed by us when we were goofing off."

Before going to Afghanistan in 2011, I took a basic safety course that included training for dire situations, including kidnapping. Once I was there, a safety consultant who worked full-time in the Kabul bureau went through still more drills and gave me body armor, although I did not go into the battlefield and didn't end up wearing it. A bombing did occur near our compound while I was there.

Vice's reportorial excursions had always posed as "news from the edge," and its correspondents had always exhibited the showmanship of circus performers, going out of their way to demonstrate, since the Gross Jar, a healthy respect for masochism. They had made their name putting themselves in the line of effluvia, Ebola, terrorist fire—less in pursuit of the story than as the story themselves.

"This is risky, it's dangerous. People would say it's really fucking stupid for us to be doing this," Alvi had told the camera in the opening scene of Vice's first documentary. "But, um, you know . . . heavy metal rules." That was the actual first scene of "Heavy Metal in Baghdad." It came after the animated vignette at the very top of the film, introducing it as a Vice production, which depicted a devil-masked executioner decapitating a helpless captive and laughing as the head rolls away and blood spells out VBS.

In a story about an Ebola clinic in Africa, the correspondent wore no protective clothing. In contrast, *Times* correspondents followed the same protocol as doctors (one reporter was herself a doctor), covering every inch of their bodies with protective clothing. (Morton's nimbleness alone was sadly not enough to dodge leptospirosis, a fever-inducing disease transmitted via animal urine, which he caught on the job in Venezuela.)

Vice was generally not prepared to help when their reporters got in trouble, such as when one was imprisoned in Turkey. Because so many of the correspondents were freelancers, if they fell in harm's way Vice had no legal obligation to help them. But when one of their more experienced correspondents, Simon Ostrovsky, was kidnapped in Ukraine by pro-Russian separatists, Vice hired a consultant to help free him and began frantic efforts to get politicians in Washington to help. Ostrovsky was released after three days. Journalists at other institutions faulted Vice's cowboy style and reputation for unnecessary risk-taking, something its leaders denied. In order to be immersive, they said, the correspondents had to be seen in the middle of war zones.

Notwithstanding the risks, Vice had no trouble finding recruits. It was expanding its global reach just as more established names in news were cutting down or shutting down. Quality newspapers had once stationed their own correspondents in London, Paris, Russia, China, Jerusalem, and Cairo, but almost all of them were gone, including the television network correspondents who once had such lush expense accounts they could afford to feed everyone else. Even CNN was cutting back on stories from the field because it was so much cheaper to have so-called experts and partisan officials come into its studios to expound. At the beginning of the Iraq War, hundreds of American journalists flooded into Baghdad, but after two years, as the war raged on, the only news organizations that were left full time were the wire services, CNN, the BBC, the *Los Angeles Times*, the *Washington Post*, and, of course, the *New York Times*, which spent several million dollars a year to keep a bureau compound secure and fully staffed. It did not cut its foreign desk, but it was the exception.

The risks paid off when Vice assigned a filmmaker and former *Al Jazeera* correspondent, Medyan Dairieh, to investigate Isis in 2013. Although Syria was arguably the most dangerous place for journalists, Dairieh had done other stories there and had a network of trusted fixers and contacts. He got a message to one of the many media officers of Isis and was invited to film the rebel terror network in Raqqa, once one of the country's most Westernized cities.

Dairieh and his cameraman were embedded with various Isis leaders for two weeks, filming fighting and rallies and interviewing members, including many young children being trained to fight for the caliphate. In a chilling scene, he rode with the group's "morals police," capturing an encounter where a man in Raqqa is stopped and warned that his wife must change the fabric of her veil because it is too diaphanous and shows her facial features.

Atrocities such as the beheading of James Foley had not yet happened, but many correspondents stopped entering Syria because so many had died. When Dairieh's 42-minute almost-documentary, "The Islamic State," appeared on Vice, all the network news shows used footage from it, crediting Vice and giving it priceless props for journalism. "The Islamic State" was viewed by more than three million people.

Vice had succeeded so far by doing everything on the cheap and being selective about what it covered. Its payment structure, for Dairieh and other freelancers, was nowhere near network or cable salaries. Because digital journalism arose at a time when the labor movement was weak, the newsrooms of most digital start-ups, including BuzzFeed, Vice, and the Huffington Post, were nonunion. Smith called his workplace a "sweatshop for trustafarians." The low wages became a sore point when the gossip site Gawker published its salaries. They averaged little more than $28,000 for full-time editors and producers—hardly enough to support even a bare-bones hipster lifestyle in Brooklyn. One longtime Vice employee told Gawker about low-level staffers whose pay necessitated moonlighting but for whom "the appeal is street cred, lots of free parties/booze and the hope that one earns a coveted Vice ring," a piece of jewelry with the letters V-I-C-E plated in gold.

The meager paychecks were not a matter of financial necessity for Vice; the issue was how Smith and his executive cabinet allocated the funds. One producer told Gawker that after working at Vice for more than a year, he finally quit after being denied a raise to $30,000 and seeing funds earmarked for the buffet of drugs at the annual company party. The following year's party was more extravagant, as the company booked a lineup of even more spectacular musical acts, including Lil Wayne. Smith took the stage that night with a million dollars in cash and handed each full-time employee a $1,500 bonus. That performance only underscored the fact that Vice was far from strapped for cash.

Eventually some employees received stock, which would be worth something if Vice was sold or went public. The writers, 70 people out of a newsroom of 700, ultimately voted to unionize, and most received raises of almost 30 percent. But freelancers complained of late checks and no payment for their work. Vice would not match the average $75,000 salary of a journalist from an ailing national newspaper. By contrast, Smith, estimated to be worth a billion dollars, showed no misgivings about spending his fortune gaudily. On a trip to Vegas with Vice's board of directors, he dropped nearly half a million dollars on dinner at the Bellagio steakhouse. When media-industry gossips caught wind of this, Smith did not demur, even boasting, "I broke the Vegas tip record." As he plotted his relocation to Los Angeles, where he would be able to focus more on Vice's TV and video operations, Smith plunked down $23 million on a Spanish Colonial–style mansion in Santa Monica without setting foot inside. The home had appeared in Hollywood movies as the supervillain's lair and featured a hidden "drinking room" walled with onyx, which one entered via the trick bookcase. In the backyard a sprawling palm forest shrouded the 72-foot pool, with statues of Roman goddesses adorning the deck. *Variety* broke the news of Smith's purchase, reinvigorating Vice employees' lagging push to unionize and helping them shore up the necessary votes the next day.

Besides the indentured status of the workforce, there was the issue of institutionalized sexism that Vice couldn't shake. Young women, who made up less than a third of the staff, complained that their assignments were less interesting. One said she received a promotion and more work but no raise. Another was asked to go undercover as a hooker for a story, which she refused. Vice hired a famous photographer, Terry Richardson, who had been accused of sexually abusing a number of his female subjects.

When Ellis Jones, a soft-spoken woman who became the first female editor of the magazine, tried to bring up the problem with Smith, according to one of her colleagues, she got nowhere. Soon after, on the occasion of Vice landing its two-millionth subscriber on YouTube, Smith got naked and pranced around the office, backslapping his favorite male staffers and grossing out the women. The culture traced back to the earliest days, when practically the only women portrayed in *Vice* magazine were strippers or nude models. Until the serial sex abuse scandals revealed by the *Times* and the *Post* in 2017, Smith seemed satisfied with a company culture he once described as "like an incestuous family."

An experienced journalist who had worked for one of the network news divisions before joining Vice in 2013 burst into tears describing how her ideas were dismissed by Smith and other male producers. "It was always this trade-off," she said, "work at the coolest place in media and tolerate the sexism or leave." It was only after other female-oriented sites such as Refinery 29 began siphoning off ad dollars that Vice started a women's channel called Broadly, which aimed to be "fun and feminist" with features like "Ovary Action." Vice chose an unusually apt motto for Broadly: "For women who know their place."

Some employees were afraid to discuss publicly any of these issues because they had all signed nondisclosure agreements, unusual for a news organization. The "non-traditional workplace agreement" they were given warned, "Sexually provocative and other explicit images, videos and audio recordings are regularly present in VICE's offices." The *Baffler*, an intelligent magazine for political and cultural analysis, dubbed Vice "the vertically integrated rape joke."

The entrenched culture of misogyny was one major problem. Another was uncontrolled expansion. Smith kept adding and adding. "The growth became cancerous," said Morton. As NBC hired Tim Russert and ABC George Stephanopoulos, Vice hired some veterans of the Obama White House, including Reggie Love, the president's body man, and Alyssa Mastromonaco, his deputy chief of staff for operations who had worked for Obama since 2005. Mastromonaco was named to the senior position of chief operating officer and charged with creating a management structure, a job Smith described as "a nightmare for most status-quo managers." What qualified her for the role, he said, was that "the only thing in this world crazier and more freaky than Vice right now is the U.S. government." Despite her oversight, there was still chaos. With clients such as Facebook, Google, Dell, and other new-economy giants, Vice's ad revenue and licensing fees were soaring, but its expenses were out of control and media analysts doubted whether the company was profitable. Because it was privately held—Smith controlled 90 percent—it didn't have to file its finances publicly. Nonetheless investors kept coming to Brooklyn in their town cars.

Rupert Murdoch made the journey in 2013 to meet Smith, who took the octogenarian tycoon to one of his favorite neighborhood drinking spots. "Who's heard of Vice Media?" Murdoch tweeted afterward. "Wild, interesting effort to interest millennials, who don't read or watch established media. Global success." The tweet was followed by a $70 million investment from 21st Century Fox for a 5 percent stake in the company, which brought its valuation to $1.4 billion. On Murdoch's heels came $250 million from A&E, a partnership between Disney and Hearst, another $200 million from Disney, and $250 million from a venture capital firm. As it grew, the company's valuation skyrocketed to $2.5 billion, then $4.5 billion. Smith had ideas about selling the company one day or taking it public, but its valuation was putting it out of reach. It was becoming more like Time Warner than "the Time Warner of the Streets," as Smith had always preferred to think of his company. There was still a taint from Virtue, and Smith himself began to say he wanted to be less dependent on native advertising. "Can you believe these companies pay all this money for the shit we do?" he was overheard saying in a Brooklyn bar.

Smith's sense of timing in building the business had been uncanny. He had been at the forefront of distribution on every visual platform: first You-Tube, then Snapchat, which began as an app for sending promiscuous pictures that disappeared once seen. Vice was one of the first media companies given a privileged placement on Snapchat's platform. After that, it had colonized Pinterest, another social network platform, which was popular with women and where users posted pleasing images. On top of the advertising revenue, these deals gave licensing fees to Vice for its content, from all over the world.

Nonetheless Smith wanted to be known for journalism as much as business. In 2013 his dream of becoming a player in news arrived in a deal with HBO, the premium cable channel, brokered by superagent Ari Emanuel, one of the inspirations for HBO's show *Entourage*. He introduced HBO's chief, Richard Plepler, to Smith.

Like Freston, Plepler was in search of a younger cable audience, but HBO was subscription-based and an expensive sell for millennials. Under the stewardship of Sheila Nevins, HBO had a highly regarded documentary division. Why not try developing a show with Vice? Plepler was convinced Smith had serious ambitions.

That same year Vice established a separate news division, Vice News, meaning, at least in theory, that the company was doing some pure news and would no longer have a loose ethics policy whereby writers wouldn't do both advertising and news. It added investigative reporting, hiring Jason Leopold, known for using the Freedom of Information Act to break open scandals. It was Leopold's FOIA request that led to the scandal over Hillary Clinton's private email server.

At HBO there was a slot open late on Friday night, right after Bill Maher, whose left-wing politics appealed to the younger demographic. Vice's weekly segments would air then, and HBO would fund them generously, giving the half-hour show higher standards and production values than Vice's typical guerrilla content.

The concept was simple: "News from the edge." The stories would "expose the absurdity of the modern condition." If the show was too edgy or in bad taste, HBO risked tarnishing its brand. But there was an upside for the network, as summed up by Deborah Conrad, the Intel executive who had championed her company's collaboration with Vice: "There's a level of risk or thrill that comes with standing up next to Shane or Vice." HBO wanted to lower the risk factor and buff up Vice's journalism cred, so the well-connected Plepler asked Fareed Zakaria, the foreign affairs columnist and pundit who had his own Sunday public affairs show on CNN, to be an executive producer of the show. Zakaria was exactly the kind of stentorian television "authority" whom Morton had reviled when he was studying journalism at NYU. Now Morton was one of the stars of the HBO show Zakaria was helping to oversee. Soon, however, Zakaria, who was hired to lend Vice legitimacy, was tarred in a plagiarism scandal; HBO kept him on nonetheless.

For the first season, most of the producers of the show worked on a short leash in HBO's Manhattan offices. The debut, which aired in April 2013, followed Smith to Afghanistan for a story on boys recruited by the Taliban to be suicide bombers. The episode, called "Killer Kids," featured plenty of Smith bloviating in local costume and plenty of gore, including severed body parts. Morton was assigned a piece on North Korean women who had escaped the country but were then being sold into the sex trade in Laos. Critical reaction from the establishment media was mixed. The show was "plenty earnest but insufficiently skeptical, favoring outrage and shock over context and depth," wrote the *Post*'s reviewer. "It is journo-tourism for hipsters, with an attitude that sometimes makes it difficult to appreciate the value of the stories being told."

HBO was a premium subscription service, so there was no advertising and little need for ratings, a freedom Smith relished. In the first season the on-air correspondents were all white men, but the stories they told showed more brown, black, and Asian faces than did the broadcast networks. At the close of its first 10 episodes, the show was nominated for an Emmy for outstanding documentary series. Though it didn't win, Smith was exhilarated and wrote his staff, "*It makes all the dysentery worthwhile*, was my first thought when we found out that we had been nominated. My second was, *a bunch of dirtbags from Brooklyn finally make good*. We are insanely stoked and a little bit stunned to be nominated in our virgin season, and really have to thank HBO for giving us the creative freedom to make the show we wanted."

Plepler renewed the show, and the next year it won three Emmys, including one for Ostrovsky's coverage of Ukraine, and claimed two Peabodys. At the beginning of the third season, Smith interviewed President Obama. Morton got face time with Michelle Obama, who pronounced herself "a big fan" on camera. The big-name Democrats Vice had hired from the White House were already proving their worth.

Amid this newfound prestige, the pressure to grow never slackened, especially if Smith and Alvi were going to reap the big payday in an IPO or takeover. So while HBO was paying Vice a big licensing fee for the weekly show, Smith entered talks with A&E, another Disney property, about taking over one of its cable channels for Vice entertainment programs like *Fuck, That's Delicious*, which starred an overweight rap star as a hipster version of Anthony Bourdain. Other programs were *Gaycation*, a gay travel show, and *Weediquette*, about marijuana connoisseurship. Jonze took over the creative control of the new channel.

The ultimate symbol of Vice's mainstream acceptance came in 2015, when Smith won the prestigious Frank Stanton Award for Excellence in Communication and was rewarded by being subjected to a roast at the Pierre Hotel. A procession of media bigwigs took the stage to share their insults. Taking stock of how far Smith's company had come, Freston told the audience that Vice "has got a valuation now as bloated as Shane is." Plepler observed, "With the blink of an eye, our boy went from being a voice of the downtrodden to a member of the extraordinary up-trodden." Referring to Smith's recent interview with Obama, he added, "The president called Shane to thank him for the interview and the delightful contact high." Smith's less esteemed friends went even further. "Shane is to journalism," said the creator and star of *Jackass*, Johnny Knoxville, "what Jared from Subway is to Save the Children." For the last laugh, Smith wore a blue dress shirt, sedate dark suit, and tie.

Morton too carved out a measure of stardom. He was now recognized by fans in airports and New York supermarkets. He didn't let it go to his head much, though. He had come to Vice for the camaraderie and sense of brotherhood, in pursuit of the ring. He would do anything for the band of brothers he worked with, and by 2016 he in fact *had* subjected himself to just about everything he could think of. They had been there for him.

When a long-term romantic relationship Morton was in ended, he crashed on the sofa of his friend Hamilton Morris, another on-air personality at Vice, and had liked it so much he decided to move in for good. The son of the famous documentary filmmaker Errol Morris, Morton's new roommate was more trustafarian than self-made man, but he was neat, and cool enough. He loved psychedelic drugs. The two built little clapboard rooms, Jack & Jill style, in their shared loft, and as the *Times* noted in a profile that ran in the Sunday Styles section, they displayed the spoils from their globe-trotting exploits with Vice; Morris had cacti he'd been given by the widow of his personal idol, Dr. Alexander Shulgin, the earliest promoter of the drug Ecstasy in the science world. Photographs of psilocybin mushrooms hung on the walls. On the nightstand in Morton's bedroom he kept the skull of an Amazonian crocodile adorned with toucan feathers, the skull of a vole, and a rubber fetus. Morton was fighting the leptospirosis he'd picked up in Venezuela, but he happily regaled the *Times* reporter with stories about minding the Gross Jar.

Nearby in Brooklyn, where he still lived, Gavin McInnes, his bitter breakup with Alvi and Smith still a sore subject, was gagging.

CHAPTER SEVEN

NEW YORK TIMES II

Anxiety still radiated inside the *Times*'s new Eighth Avenue tower. It was breathtaking how quickly other newspapers were being swept away. After the financial crisis in 2008, more than 166 papers went out of business. Under new ownership from a Chicago real estate man named Sam Zell, the Tribune Company, the chain that owned the venerable *Los Angeles Times, Chicago Tribune, Baltimore Sun*, and other papers, was driven into bankruptcy after piling up $13 billion in debt. Ten thousand newspaper jobs were lost across the industry. Print ad sales fell 30 percent, and 23 of the top 25 newspapers reported circulation declines between 7 and 20 percent. The Gannett chain suffered a 31 percent profit decline in the fourth quarter.

The Pew Foundation, which published an influential annual assessment on the state of journalism, introduced its report this way: "The newspaper industry exited a harrowing 2008 and entered 2009 in something perilously close to free fall." Business Insider, a new digital start-up, proclaimed, perhaps with a note of glee, that 2009 was "the year newspapers died."

The next five years would bring turmoil and shakeups in the company's leadership. The crises were constant and there were many casualties, including me.

On top of the secular changes in the newspaper industry, the *Times* had a $450 million loan coming due. Banks weren't lending. One week a rumor swept the building that payroll couldn't be met. It proved untrue, but the atmosphere of doom permeated the gleaming tower the *Times* had spent so many millions erecting. It was supposed to show off a prosperous multimedia company built for the digital age. Had the winds shifted so much? The bedeviling question was when digital revenue would begin to offset print losses. There was still no answer. The paper was engaged in a daily fight for survival that distracted its leaders from making necessary innovations. People were reading news on their smartphones, but the *Times* did not yet have an app for the iPhone. Its storehouse of wonderful recipes could not be monetized because they weren't digitized. There were 50 projects stacked up undone on the business side's list of top priorities. Creative thinking about how to fix the broken business model came to a halt. What the *Times* needed urgently was money to pay off debt. Before the storm was over, the paper would teeter on the brink of insolvency, turn to a foreign investor, give him a large stake in the company's future, and make a risky decision to charge for its digital news report that every internet sage predicted would fail. In the course of all this its culture and leadership would profoundly change.

A third source of worry came from the *Times*'s longtime rival, the *Wall Street Journal*. After his acquisition of the *Journal* in 2007, Rupert Murdoch had transformed the newspaper, pushing it in a general-interest direction with more national and international news that was not strictly about business. He was determined to knock the *Times* off its throne as America's most influential and widely read daily newspaper and hated the *Times*'s facile liberalism. As the *Times* contemplated cuts, the *Journal* added a local New York news section, weekend feature sections, and a luxury magazine, *WSJ*, to appeal to women. The cover featured a young blond woman, casually dressed for work, lugging a briefcase. These additions were carbon copies of the *Times*'s sections, but they were smartly edited and Murdoch was picking off the talent being shed elsewhere. The *Times* worried he would steal its readers too.

Sulzberger took the assault seriously, and his business team followed each move by the *Journal*, which also had something the *Times* didn't: a pay gate on its website. Because of their business focus and news that traders and people in business needed to have to do their work, the *Journal* and the *Financial Times* could defy the "News is free" orthodoxy and get their readers to pay online. The *Journal* also came at the *Times*'s advertisers, as did the *New York Post*, where the recession had forced some *Times* advertisers to flee. The tabloid *Post*, also owned by Murdoch, featured gossip items about Sulzberger (replete with black eye), who separated from his wife of 33 years, Gail Gregg, in 2008, on its notorious Page Six.

The sharpest chronicler of the crisis was David Carr, whose column, "The Media Equation," usually ran on the front of the *Times*'s Monday business section. The skinny, stooped chain-smoker was the Pied Piper of a team of media reporters who often found themselves covering the travails of their employer. With a raspy Minnesota accent and somewhat unkempt, Carr came up from alternative weekly newspapers; his was not the pedigreed résumé of most of his *Times* colleagues. He wanted young tigers in the hunt with him and helped recruit and mentor Brian Stelter, a 20-something television blogger who scooped up insider items and quickly became a prominent *Times* byline.

Self-satisfaction had defined *Times* journalists of the pre-internet period. Most had enjoyed what they assumed would be lifelong job security. The *Times*'s hiring process was still protracted, but once a reporter or editor was hired, he or she joined an institution that was widely viewed as the best in journalism and, despite the rocky climate, one of the few places to do work of consistent value. When a new reporter's story got onto the front page, he or she was given the printing plate from that day's A-1. The paper had launched many legendary authors, among them David Halberstam and Anthony Lukas. Of course, from gonzo journalist Hunter S. Thompson to novelist David Foster Wallace, outsiders lampooned the air of superiority its reporters exuded.

It was still full of the old traditions, but there was a dwindling number of storied characters from the glory days. Editors had incentive to push out the older writers to save the jobs of younger, more productive rookies. Some of the elders begged to keep their desks after they retired and kept coming in each day because their lives were empty without the *Times*. Some went out with panache. The sports columnist Dave Anderson, the first sportswriter to win a Pulitzer, had been an institution, with 40 years of service. In late 2007 he donned a suit and tie for the day he said goodbye and assured Bill Keller he'd still be available anytime the paper needed the long view of the sports world. The average age of the newsroom was near 60 because few left so graciously.

Although the *Times* was occasionally put in its place, as when the *Washington Post* ate its lunch on Watergate, or shamed, as in its pre–Iraq War coverage, or rattled, as when Howell Raines and Gerald Boyd were fired during the Jayson Blair scandal, each time it reclaimed its crown as the prestige name in American journalism. Its print circulation had fallen, but it still had a stable base of 800,000 readers who had subscribed for two years or more, the point at which they were likely to be hooked for life. Circulation revenue would prove the cornerstone holding up the company.

The *Times* saw itself as the arbiter of the good, cultured life—the best books, the most important ideas, the best parties, and much more—for its readers. A bad review from Ben Brantley could still close a Broadway show, even as television and online reviewers and theater blogs were displacing the *Times* as the sole voice that mattered. Notice of a new boutique hotel in the travel section could fill a reservation book. Most important, its editors set the agenda of what news was important, although this was being challenged by online competition and a changing world. Some no longer trusted "the mainstream media" or the hierarchy of news selected by an unknown editor.

The *Times* was mainly the voice of the coastal elites and reflected their interests and values. The liberal opinion pages offended some nonurban readers. The news pages also leaned left and reflected cosmopolitan values, giving heavy coverage to subjects such as the movement for gay marriage. Its newsroom was filled with Ivy League graduates, with especially large contingents from Harvard, Yale, and Princeton. These ranks bore little resemblance to the men who came before, many of whom had not graduated from college or had gone to City College, the alma mater of the legendary editors Abe Rosenthal and Arthur Gelb. The once-raucous newsroom of Gelb's early years had been replaced by the sedate tapping of computers and free coffee wheeled in at 4 p.m. The 24/7 digital news cycle destroyed old customs such as repairing to nearby bars after the presses started to roll at 9 p.m.

This wealthier, better educated newsroom was full of anxious overachievers. Although the reporters had reached the pinnacle, it was an unhappy place even before the crash. Envy dripped from those whose stories were not considered the best that day. The crisis surrounding them was layered onto a newsroom that, even in its heyday, was filled with tension. During and after the financial crisis the jobs of the two most senior people making the biggest news decisions, the executive editor and the managing editor, also became focused on the paper's financial problems. Often, after the famous Page One meeting, where these editors picked the six stories for the next day's front page and selected the above-the-fold photograph, there would be meetings with nervous reporters to reassure them they would have jobs. Everyone seemed preoccupied with the possibility of layoffs and the reporters who often needed the most reassurance were, oddly, some of the biggest stars who joked that they were required to stay in a Motel 6 when they were on the road. In truth, the directives to cut expenses were not draconian, especially when compared to other newspapers, but the reporters groused nonetheless, especially about a new rule that they could no longer expect the company to pay when they took each other out to meals. Pricey midtown restaurants like nearby Esca were still canteens for the editors, even though the new double-height *Times* cafeteria offered sushi and a fully stocked salad bar.

Two events in early 2009 rocked the newsroom. On February 18 the *Times*'s stock price fell to $3.77, less than the $4.00 price of the Sunday paper. The *Atlantic* published an article claiming the *Times* might go bankrupt, and—only partly exaggerating for effect—predicting the end of the print newspaper by May. Digital revenue alone, it said, would support a newsroom only one-fifth its size, with almost 1,100 journalists relying on the shrinking stream of print revenue. Although a *Times* spokeswoman debunked the story, no one knew what to believe; Janet Robinson privately told me that the newsroom would have to be cut in half if we needed to live solely on digital dollars. At the Page One meeting each afternoon, colleagues read the expressions on the faces of masthead editors and rated them according to the degree of worry.

Sulzberger and Robinson were slashing the ranks of the business side in order to spare the newsroom the kind of deep cuts that were making quality newspapers a rare breed. No one on the business floor upstairs ever questioned how much it cost to cover a story. The newsroom's budget still supported squads of political reporters to be on the campaign planes of the presidential candidates full time. When the president traveled, the *Times* was always with him. When big news hit, the *Times* "flooded the zone," to use a favorite phrase of Howell Raines, sending as many reporters as needed. No foreign or national bureaus had been shuttered. American journalism's purview had narrowed to just a few newspapers, wire services, and international broadcasters such as CNN that could afford global correspondents. The *Times* still had three full-time bureau chiefs in different regions of Africa. It had the only stand-alone Sunday book review left. Though its homepage was cluttered with the same kind of junky click ads that propagated all over the internet and remnant ads that would never have been seen in the far more expensive pages of the print edition, its digital design maintained an air of elegance and refinement.

One *Times* reporter, Dennis Overbye, was devoted to physics and mathematics, and there were three physician-journalists in its science section. The paper reviewed most important books (there were three daily critics, besides the freelancers who filled the *Book Review*), every movie in general release, and almost every play of interest, on Broadway and off. There were few intellectual pursuits it did not cover. There was a reporter whose beat was the intelligentsia. One of its biggest attractions online, and a money-maker, was the daily crossword.

But some costs were proving unsustainable. Its monthly digital audience was the largest of any daily newspaper, but digital advertising did not generate enough revenue to support the operations of the website alone. And as the staff grew to include more web-first editors, producers, designers, and technologists, they were paid from the same print revenue. The print newspaper was still supplying more than 80 percent of revenue. The steep losses of print advertising were not nearly offset by growing digital revenue.

Sulzberger took increasingly strict measures to keep the paper afloat, but cut like a surgeon intent on preserving the quality of the news report. The *Times* had withheld the annual dividend, but after watching Dow Jones's Bancroft family tear itself apart, Sulzberger and Golden didn't take the Trust for granted and assiduously kept the family informed about the paper's finances. A 5 percent pay cut was levied across the company. Sulzberger announced the termination of another 100 business-side employees. He still delighted in showing guests around the new 52-story Renzo Piano building, but the building was no longer his. In a sale-leaseback deal finalized just before the *Atlantic* article was published, he brought in $225 million in emergency cash by selling the 20 floors of the building that the company used and owned. The *Times* became a renter in its own building.

Sulzberger was aware that *Times* reporters leaked as much as some of their sources did, and suspected the damaging stories published about him in *Vanity Fair* and *New York* magazine came with help from the newsroom. Sometimes he would stomp into Executive Editor Bill Keller's office, close the glass sliding door, and vent his frustration. Distrust between the news and business sides of the company turned into frosty embitterment. The heads of the advertising and circulation departments groused that the journalists were shielded from reality like spoiled children. The newsroom's art director was still rejecting print ads with unusual formations because they were "un*Times*ian," while the ad sales force was killing itself to make its targets. When these spats reached Sulzberger, he almost always decided the revenue was more important than the ugliness of the ads.

On the one hand, Sulzberger had the newsroom, which viewed the *Times* as a sacred mission, not as a business. The journalists rejected ideas for new initiatives, such as travel shows and paid conferences, based on ethical conflicts he thought trivial. On the other hand, he had his business colleagues, who were going to send-offs for their coworkers and seeing ghastly monthly reports. The company was carrying a $1.1 billion debt load, almost the same amount as its current valuation. The May deadline for repaying the $400 million line of credit loomed, the first of two. The sale leaseback of the building brought him part of the way there, but Sulzberger needed more.

He urgently needed a loan.

A few months earlier, the Mexican Carlos Slim, one of the richest men in the world but a relative unknown in the U.S., had bought a large chunk of *Times* A stock. His holdings quickly lost more than half their value as the stock price tumbled, but he might be interested in acquiring more. He was known for investing in brands he thought were undervalued. With its bonds near junk grade, the *Times* qualified. The idea of having a foreign magnate as the newspaper's largest creditor was risky; the *Times* could easily be used to gain influence in the U.S. But Slim's interest seemed benign.

Slim was involved in virtually every industry in Mexico. Much of his estimated $60 billion fortune came from his monopoly ownership of Mexico's main telecommunications company, but he also owned banks and department stores. He did not have other major media holdings. A plainspoken man with dark hair, a mustache, and a double chin, he eschewed press attention and usually drove himself to business meetings in a Ford SUV. A banker approached him on the *Times*'s behalf to ask if he would lend the company $200 million.

Robinson met with the Mexican magnate over an Italian meal at Bice in Manhattan. Slim demanded stiff terms for a loan of that size, and with the credit markets otherwise frozen, he was in a position to get them. In talks that went on until Thanksgiving, he offered his money, but at the enormous interest rate of 14 percent. He bargained for warrants to buy 16 million shares of *Times* stock in six years for $6.36 a share, which would give him a 17 percent stake in the company. This would make him one of the paper's largest shareholders and its largest creditor. For Slim, the warrants were the most important part of the deal. For the *Times*, facing the possibility of insolvency, six years seemed like an eternity. The warrants were approved.

Before a deal could be reached, in swooped Hollywood producer and philanthropist David Geffen. He approached Sulzberger's best friend, Steven Rattner, with a counteroffer to lend the money at the same interest rate. But Slim swore that he would never interfere in the paper's affairs and did not even want a seat on its board. Sulzberger did not trust a man with an ego as outsized as Geffen's, a big Democratic donor, to keep the same distance. So a deal was struck with Slim. When news of the lifeline broke, the *New York Post* reprinted the caricature of Sulzberger with a black eye, this time wearing a sombrero. While it was easy enough to dismiss a bit of bad press in the *Post*, the same was not true for the financial problems the emergency loan exposed.

Pressure for more revenue-producing ideas began cascading down to

Keller's office on the third floor from the executive floors above. Sulzberger wanted the newsroom to consider a proposal to have the Times Company take over a conference business Rattner operated as part of his investment firm, Quadrangle Group. Keller argued it would be ethically compromising to have *Times* journalists invite the bigwigs they covered for live, money-making events with extremely high attendance fees, and the proposal was tabled. Because the *Wall Street Journal*'s conference was raking it in, however, Sulzberger tried several times to resume the discussion, but never could do so fruitfully.

Keller also tried to veto a *Times* wine club, which would send members a case of selected wines each month. When Sulzberger insisted, Keller got him to agree to an ethical concession, that the club could in no way be tied to the wines that Eric Asimov, the wine critic, recommended in his column. That would be a breach of the church-state wall. But the rule inhibited the club's success: people wanted to join a *Times* wine club precisely for Asimov's considered choices.

The ancillary ventures the business side pushed were not news per se, but they would have to involve *Times* journalists to succeed financially. In the digital universe, commerce and news were not always separated, and technology and design were not clearly the province of either news or business. But the wall between news and business was a sacred part of *Times* culture; when anyone tried to take a brick out of it, the standards editor, Al Siegal, would be there to wedge it back in. Before these lines could be clearly remapped for the digital age, however, in 2006 Siegal retired.

The publisher grew more impatient with the newsroom's slow, deliberative attitude. Surely, he argued, there were ways to squeeze more revenue and greater value from the *Times*'s best-known journalists. He lobbied for a project he called "Biznico," modeled on the success of Politico, which was dominating coverage of politics as the *Post*'s coverage began to wither from cuts. Business news, he thought, would lend itself to the same fast pace and insider intrigue.

If the *Post* had not let go of Politico, it could have become a separate revenue-producing arm of the company, which was what Sulzberger planned for his new business site. Biznico, rechristened DealBook, would angle for a Wall Street audience that might be willing to pay extra for a premium product of scoops about deals. It would be the first of what Sulzberger envisioned as a group of premium products both in print and on the web.

The face of DealBook was Andrew Ross Sorkin, who at 30 was already an established star. He had been writing for the *Times* since high school, and later worked the mergers and acquisition beat, had a column, and wrote a best-selling book about the financial crisis, *Too Big to Fail*, which was made into an HBO movie. He was a frequent guest on business shows on cable TV. His new venture would carry up-to-the-minute news on Wall Street produced by a team he was assembling.

Few of the reporters he hired had much experience. The more seasoned business reporters, who mostly came from smaller papers and magazines and worked their way up to the *Times* over decades, resented the parallel operation. Gretchen Morgenson, a Pulitzer winner and business columnist, thought Sorkin was too cozy with sources such as J.P. Morgan Chase CEO Jamie Dimon. After the financial crisis, she argued, the last thing the *Times* needed was to go soft on Wall Street. But DealBook, replete with a conference headlined by Sorkin, launched with the publisher's keen support, despite the objections from Morgenson and others who saw the venture as driven more by financial than journalism goals.

Nate Silver, a popular political blogger who created FiveThirtyEight, licensed his site to the *Times*, and alongside Sorkin would come to represent a new breed of reporter, better known as individuals than belonging to the institution. Both stars negotiated special pay-for-performance packages under a new system that Sulzberger and Robinson had installed. With his job cohosting a CNBC morning cable show, *Squawk Box*, plus his *Times* column and DealBook, Sorkin was making a small fortune. All this too bred resentment.

Silver wasn't a journalist; he was a statistician and election odds-maker who had first honed his skills on predictive baseball statistics and then applied the same techniques to politics. He had never done any shoe-leather reporting or interviewed voters. He believed data were what mattered, not anecdotal evidence about humans. The scruffy savant did his work at home in New York, usually in the middle of the night. Although he regularly appeared as a television analyst, most of the *Times*'s political reporters had never met him and criticized his methods. He felt ostracized, and they felt the *Times* was bending its journalism standards to predict election outcomes. But he was an immediate draw for readers when he arrived in 2010 and correctly predicted the winners of 34 of the 37 contested Senate races, a pickup of Republican seats in the House, and 36 of 37 gubernatorial races.

While he selectively invested in additions to the newsroom, Sulzberger had to mandate the first sizable cut of journalists. In 2009 Keller was told to cut 100 positions. The company offered fairly generous buyouts, some with almost two years of accrued pay for long-serving journalists, and 80 people took the deal. Although only 20 people were actually fired, the newsroom was in deep despair.

The independence of the newsroom was something that I watched both Lelyveld and Keller fight zealously to guard. But we had reached a point where it seemed futile to fight back on everything.

Some cuts were unavoidable, but telling longtime reporters, especially those who had covered wars or had sacrificed their family life for the paper, that their job was being eliminated was the absolute worst. After the buyout lists were submitted, to meet the target number given to the newsroom by Sulzberger, additional layoffs were often necessary. In those cases, it fell to me and two other senior editors who focused on newsroom administration to deliver the bad news. (Keller dealt with special cases and appeals.) We had scripts supplied by the human resources department, and we delivered the bad news in unoccupied, glass-walled, warren-like offices in the upper business floors, where there was usually only a desk and a small table holding two bottles of water and a fresh box of Kleenex. It physically sickened me to have these conversations, which replayed in my head, over and over, like horror movies, for months and sometimes years after they took place. On the phone I had to push two women who had done stellar work in the Washington bureau to take buyouts and I felt like a traitor when I hung up. Sulzberger and Robinson, in slashing the business side, had had it even worse.

Besides personnel, there were other cuts, including to the physical paper. Along with shrinking the page size, the metropolitan and sports sections were combined most days of the week, and separate New York regional sections were eliminated. That meant cutting news coverage in New Jersey and some in Westchester and Long Island, but none of these cuts caused an exodus of subscribers. As the *Times* gave readers a bit less, it charged them progressively more. Sulzberger knew that, unlike his competitors, he could not cut his way to profitability. Quality was his core product, and though he got rid of more than two-thirds of the business staff, he continued to leave untouched his newsroom's most expensive endeavors, such as foreign and investigative reporting. As competitors buckled, he gave Keller the money to hire away their brightest stars, like Alissa Rubin and Ellen Barry of the *L.A. Times* and Anthony Shadid and Peter Baker of the *Washington Post*.

Although the recession began to lift, business did not recover. The only solution left had been tried—charging for the *Times* on the web—and failed. Times Select had been an embarrassing failure, fetching no more than $13 million. The *Wall Street Journal* and the *Financial Times* were still the only newspapers with a sizable number of paying digital readers. As she faced worsening forecasts, Robinson, who had been the proponent of Times Select, became convinced that they had to try turning to readers again. Yet the risk of a second failure was great, and she faced considerable internal opposition from her chief rival in the corporate hierarchy, Martin Nisenholtz.

Their backgrounds separated them. Nisenholtz adhered to the prevailing digital belief that news on the web should remain free. Even though the quality of the *Times* was much higher than that of any other news site, with so many free alternatives, from CNN to virtually all other newspapers, who would pay? Building scale, not a paywall, was the way the *Times* should grow, he argued. He also argued, often at loggerheads with the print-focused Robinson, for precious resources to be spent on the best digital design and technology. With that, people might eventually see more value and pay.

Sulzberger stewed. He hated being the decider when his minions were at war. So he appointed internal committees to study various proposals and hired outside consultants to advise him. In the imposing Eagle Room, the dining room where he hosted famous visitors, the publisher gathered his most senior executives from the news and business departments around his giant table. He went around the room, letting each person make their case. Robinson and Nisenholtz spoke briefly and let others make the central arguments. Keller, somewhat surprisingly, allied with Robinson, which pitted him against one of his favorites, Jon Landman, the editor in charge of the website, who made a fervent argument for remaining free so the paper's digital audience could continue to grow. The technology director, Marc Frons, supported Landman. I was with Keller and thought readers would pay for the one-of-a-kind stories that the newsroom produced.

Then a voice piped up from the corner, where a balding, mustachioed John Malkovich lookalike sat. It was the paper's solemn and soft-spoken president and general manager, Scott Heekin-Canedy. "In our history," he began, "we have always been sustained by two sources of revenue." His voice quavered a bit—he rarely held the floor at group meetings—but he continued, "When advertising hit headwinds, circulation revenue helped save the paper." He went on, eloquently, for 10 minutes. Then came Andy Rosenthal, the editor of the editorial page, who had dealt with columnists' anger at Times Select and its eventual curtailment but still favored giving paid digital subscriptions another try. His words carried force, in part because, like Sulzberger, he was *Times* royalty, the son of the legendary Abe Rosenthal. When the room turned to the publisher, he acknowledged the integrity of both arguments. Then he cast his lot with Robinson and Keller.

It took a year and $25 million for the *Times* to design its digital subscriptions, with different tiers for different devices in a pricing plan devised by McKinsey. On March 28, 2011, everyone held their breath as the pay meter began counting the articles people were reading and registering users. Most media pundits predicted another bomb. In his blog, BuzzMachine, Jeff Jarvis posited that the *Times* was suffering from amnesia and forgetting the lesson of Times Select's failure: "There is only one thing that can happen should The Times put a meter on us. It will shrink." Clay Shirky, an adherent of social media, argued that paywalls were self-defeating because they "locked the public out" of important conversations about the news.

Within the first weeks the gurus were proven wrong. Despite the internet ethos of free news, 324,000 readers signed up for digital subscriptions, far more than the *Times* had expected. Sulzberger threw a small Champagne reception for his team at a nearby hotel, encouraged by the early results that showed the online traffic was not declining because of the new metered paywall. They were not losing page views or ads. The unexpectedly strong results were a feather in the cap of David Perpich, Sulzberger's nephew, who was coleader of the team that developed the pay model. Perpich was one of three contenders inside the *Times* from the fifth generation of the family for the publisher's job when Sulzberger retired. The other two were Arthur Gregg Sulzberger and Sam Dolnick, an editor and member of the Golden branch of the family.

Why had Times Select failed so miserably and the new subscription plan succeeded? One reason was that the pay gate in its first iteration had been impervious. The second, more flexible metered model didn't charge casual readers, those who only occasionally followed the links to *Times* articles they found on other websites. This gave the *Times* a chance to earn their loyalty. After 20 free articles, more habitual readers were asked to subscribe. The real answer, however, may have been that the internet, with so much free content, had become a news sewer. Certain discerning customers were now willing to pay for news of immense quality from a trusted source.

For Sulzberger, it was a brave decision and public success precisely at the time he needed one. If his family had begun to doubt his leadership, this bold gambit helped secure their trust. The pay model produced a second digital revenue stream that could support future operations. Bankruptcy predictions suddenly looked foolish. While the business model was not yet fixed, the crisis had passed. Sulzberger had made a gutsy, save-the-company decision.

Success should have helped unite his leadership team, but the existing rivalries festered. Nisenholtz felt stuck in a dead end, managing the sinking fortunes of About.com, the *Times* subsidiary that had become a dead weight. He was certain that Robinson had pawned off the failing company on him, and decided it was time to retire. He became a professor at Columbia Journalism School and, later, Boston University. At his farewell party, Robinson made an elaborate toast and enveloped her vanquished rival in a hug. His absence, rather than cementing her power, would turn out to undermine it.

Sulzberger, Robinson, the financial problems, and the urgent transition to digital news had left Keller feeling depleted. Rather than focusing on journalism and projects that drew him to editing in the first place, much of his job dealt with business. The layoffs of 2010 were surely not the last. He saw less of his two school-age daughters and was dog-tired on weekends. The once boyish-looking editor had aged considerably over eight years in the job, much as a president does. In the summer he told his wife, Emma, that he planned to give up his job and return to the writing life sometime in the next year.

In August 2010 he asked me to have dinner at a restaurant in Greenwich Village. After a lot of wine he confided in me his plan to step down. I already felt a little dizzy but absorbed the surprising secret, realizing that it would soon put my own future in play. Although I had watched his mounting frustrations in the job, I thought it was too early for him to retire. According to *Times* tradition, masthead editors often served until the end of their 65th year, and Keller was only 61. When I couldn't repress the urge to ask him whether he thought I had a shot at succeeding him, he responded, "I think you'd be great." He planned to ask Sulzberger for an opinion column, as some of his predecessors had. So another important decision was placed before the publisher.

Any narrative, even one that is scrupulously factual and deserving of the omniscient third-person voice of the journalist-historian, is subjective by nature. The lens through which events are seen inevitably colors how they are interpreted and presented. The story I have presented is an attempt to be factual and historical, to be guided by reporting and the testimony of key participants.

Because I am inextricably connected to the *New York Times*, and during this time was managing editor, the second in command of the newsroom, the events that follow involved me in such a direct and personal way that the detachment necessary for distanced authority is impossible. A third-person accounting of my part in the story would be disingenuous. Just as there is no pure objectivity in journalism, a profession filled with human frailties, I cannot pretend to be objective about all of my experiences at the *Times*.

I could, of course, skip over them as lightly as possible. Although I too am attempting to chronicle a fundamental and technological transformation of society, I am no Henry Adams, who fast-forwarded his own life story by 20 years so that he could delete his marriage and the painful suicide of his wife. The period I am writing about brought a lot of challenges and acute pain to my life as well. But like Adams's education in a world of dramatic scientific and technical changes, my digital education was both revelatory and searing. I've checked my memory against documents I saved and with my colleagues and the people involved, and I've interviewed many of them for this book. The *Times* disputes parts of the account that follows and I have noted these cases.

Keller and I had become a close and complementary team. He gave me a lot of freedom to run the news report. His strong suit was foreign news; mine was long investigations of corruption. Reporters in the newsroom talked about "Bill and Jill," as if they were talking about "Mom and Dad." We were seen as a unit. We consulted each other and joked throughout the day. I was careful to brief him on anything of importance. He included me in sensitive internal matters, including his weekly meetings with Sulzberger. Often we could confide things only to each other. We got along well and had become closer over the eight years that we were a team.

We had not known each other well before he chose me to be managing editor for news in 2003. I hadn't been at the *Times* for very long, having joined its Washington bureau in 1997, right before the Monica Lewinsky scandal blew up. Keller was then managing editor. Dean Baquet, who would be one of my rivals for Keller's job, was the national editor. Marty Baron, the third likely candidate to succeed Keller, was the night editor when I came aboard.

For a *Times* career, which usually involved several tours of foreign or national reporting and editing on several of the main desks, such as business or national, my rise was fast. In a decade at the *Wall Street Journal*, also in Washington, I had won a reputation for my tough coverage of money and politics. Mentored by Al Hunt, who had assembled a strong political team, I became emboldened to expose the ethical breaches of those in power. Hunt once told a reporter profiling me that I "had balls like iron cantaloupes," a heartfelt compliment that nonetheless captured the gender disparities still pervasive in the media.

My work exposed personal loans to a congressman that were tied to legislative favors, costing him his job. I revealed illegal, offshore donations to the Democratic Party. I investigated the hidden ties between independent counsel Kenneth Starr and a cabal of conservative lawyers, nicknamed "the elves," who were out to destroy President Clinton. The work I was proudest of was a book I cowrote with Jane Mayer of the *New Yorker*, a close friend since our teens, about the Anita Hill–Clarence Thomas confirmation battle. After three years of digging, we proved that Hill's account of being sexually harassed by Thomas was truthful. The book was a best-seller and a finalist for the National Book Award. It was made into a movie by Showtime.

To become familiar with the digital news operation, I spent six months embedded in what was then still called "the web newsroom." It had a separate cast of editors and producers. They set their hierarchy of stories, completely apart from the newspaper. There was wasteful duplication of effort. Reporters frequently resisted assignments if they came from "web editors," who were seen as having little authority. Getting fresh stories when news happened was hard. But the most senior web editors enjoyed their autonomy and were suspicious of my presence.

I was hardly a digital native, and neither was Keller, who had already started writing a column in the Sunday magazine and trashed Twitter early on. The *Times*'s biorhythms were still attuned to the printing press, even as readers were migrating to their computers and phones. The monthly audience of unique users was the largest of any newspaper, and its homepage was the much bigger showcase for stories. Still, reporters pined for their stories to make Page One. Only the foreign correspondents, who rarely saw the print paper, seemed to fully appreciate the homepage's value.

I was a convert to the web's power to democratize information and make it more transparent. When Keller went to Iran in 2009 to cover the failed Green Revolution, the streets were so dangerous for Westerners that the photos and comments posted by protesting students on social media platforms like Twitter and Facebook were the best ways to follow what was happening. Crowdsourcing and citizen journalism were beginning to bear important fruit.

I was influenced by Clay Shirky, author of the book *Here Comes Everybody*, who warned against pointless nostalgia for print papers, which would inevitably die. The important thing was that quality journalism survive, and the greater engagement of audiences on the web was a very healthy development. I agreed with his directive to become "platform neutral," as did Sulzberger. But that was old hat. What we needed to be was a digital-first news organization, without letting the quality of the print paper or our news standards lapse.

It was striking how much multimedia technology could deepen narrative storytelling. I worked closely with the multimedia editors, Andrew DeVigal and Aron Pilhofer, who did data and social media and who both felt pushed to the side of the news operation. Now I was seeing firsthand how video and data brought journalism to life, especially in a series about a military unit returning from the Afghanistan war. At a narrative journalism conference at Boston University, after I showed a video clip of a soldier on leave taking his sons to a barber to get the same buzz cut he had, hard-bitten editors in the audience were crying. After the *Times* received the massive Wikileaks files, Pilhofer, an expert on storing and housing data, was the first editor I consulted in order to make the material searchable. During my immersion, I also became determined to unite the web newsroom with the print operation. It was ridiculous and costly to have separate news meetings and separate editing systems. While newsroom administration wasn't part of my portfolio, I worked with two editors on a plan to merge the operations, which was completed in my six-month tour. Somehow the two operations became one without crushing each other.

An additional motive for my going digital was to prepare in the event I succeeded Keller. He would be the last executive editor whose first thoughts were about the newspaper, not the website. When I finished my digital tour, the *Times* did not yet have an app for mobile, even as smartphones were becoming the favored devices of our readers. Because I also spent time in the newsrooms of BuzzFeed, Politico, and the Huffington Post, I knew we were laggards in some areas, especially social media. Digital life was moving from a search model to a social, sharing model as Facebook became a competitor to Google.

During the eight years I managed the news report, I tried to build a relationship with Sulzberger but was rarely sure of where I stood with him. He had a cool relationship with Keller and sometimes asked me how to talk to him. He entrusted me to help recruit his son, A.G., and then his nephew Sam Dolnick to become *Times* reporters. A.G. had taken down a local sheriff at the *Portland Oregonian*, and Dolnick had been based in India for the Associated Press. They were both first-rate journalists who easily fit on the Metro desk, where many reporters started out. But both were intensely worried about the appearance of nepotism.

Sulzberger could be kind and thoughtful, but sometimes said things that were baffling to me. One day during the Scooter Libby coverage I returned exhausted from Washington and joined in a meeting in progress when he made a joke referring to a gossipy item about the trial in which I'd been mentioned. Afterward I followed him into his office and told him he'd hurt my feelings. The next morning I found a contrite, handwritten note from him on my computer keyboard saying he saw me as a true friend. Waiting for an appointment, I later asked him if he thought I was doing a good job, as he had never said anything one way or another. "Oh you know," he said, "you're my go-to girl," a comment that sounded dismissive to me.

In 2007 I was hit by a delivery truck while crossing the street in Times Square. I was hospitalized for weeks, with dangerous internal bleeding and many broken bones. I was out of work for nearly two months and had to learn to walk all over again. Keller was already at Bellevue Hospital with my husband before the ambulance with me in it arrived. Sulzberger came the next day. I was on huge doses of painkillers awaiting surgery for a broken femur. The only thing I remember about seeing Sulzberger was that he had been going through *Times* memorabilia in preparation for the move to the new building, and he brought me a large, framed award to the *Times* from the Optimist Club of New York. The visit was awkward, but I knew he meant well. By the next year I was fully recovered.

When Keller's retirement was announced in 2011, it was clear that I was a leading contender. Robinson had promised me she would do what she could to tip the decision my way. She was a booster of mine and was clearly excited by the idea of my becoming the first woman executive editor. The other contenders were Baquet, who had done well as the Washington bureau chief, and Baron, by this time editor of the *Boston Globe*, where he'd spearheaded its investigation of pedophilia in the Catholic Church, work that won the Pulitzer for public service and inspired the Oscar-winning film *Spotlight*.

I was the devil Sulzberger knew best. I'd been a steady manager through layoffs and other setbacks. He trusted my judgment on journalism. My ethical hackles were easily raised, which annoyed him, and some of his colleagues on the business side found me gruff; the seeds of a broader conflict had been planted.

In the digital realm, where new products could be monetized, teams were necessary to develop them. Because each of these products, like a cooking app or a news app geared to younger readers, required technologists, designers, and journalists to be involved, the traditional news/business divide, the old wall, did not precisely apply. But I was wary of having the business side overly involved in decisions that touched on what we should cover. Resources were not merely additive; when a green light came for a digital project, something else went on the slow track or got tossed overboard. Just as Thursday Styles had not been my first choice for a new print section, I did not want audience data or popular subjects that would drive new subscriptions to be the main priorities for our journalism. Because I was so used to dealing with Robinson whenever I had concerns that the balance was tipping, this tension did not become acute until after she was gone. But I'm getting ahead of the story.

Although there was considerable excitement in the newsroom about seeing the first woman executive editor, I was well aware that I was not universally popular. I was seen as playing favorites and as being overconfident of my opinions. I had a bad habit of cutting people off and didn't listen enough. In short, I was seen as "pushy." This last perception is a familiar refrain about women in powerful jobs. In many studies, likability and success are negatively correlated for women. Qualities that are seen as leadership in men are seen negatively—as being overly ambitious—in women.

I had also never had any formal management training and should have asked for some. I had been the boss in only one job at the *Times*, as Washington bureau chief, and that lasted less than three years. In that time I had not built a new leadership team; instead editors in New York called most of the shots. Keller and Raines had been sent to Dartmouth and Wharton, respectively, for formal management courses. Such a training program was never offered or suggested to me.

Sulzberger saw downsides in Baquet and Baron as well. Baquet had left the *Times* in 2000. A great national editor and investigative reporter, he had been wooed by several newspapers for top jobs, including the *Miami Herald*. The *Los Angeles Times* was replacing its newsroom management after the Staples scandal, and John Carroll, the incoming editor, offered Baquet the number two post. I knew he was torn. But he told me in a phone call right after lunch with Sulzberger that the publisher had left him with the impression that Gerald Boyd might be promoted ahead of him. After he went to L.A., where he succeeded Carroll as editor, won numerous Pulitzers, and enjoyed tremendous loyalty from his staff, we stayed in touch. He was under constant pressure to cut the newsroom and in two visits there I pressed him to think about coming back. When he was fired by the publisher of the *L.A. Times* for resisting layoffs, I lobbied Keller to make Baquet Washington bureau chief, a job that traditionally had a lot of power and that he had done extremely well. He would, as the first black journalist to become executive editor, be an exciting choice too. Baron had also fought to protect the people in his Boston newsroom when Sulzberger ordered cuts prior to selling the *Globe*. He, too, was a superb editor.

The tough spines both editors exhibited made them heroes to reporters, but maybe less so to the publisher. He scheduled meetings with all three of us and asked us to write memos about what we might do if we got the job. Mine focused mainly on our digital challenges. Several editors with whom I'd had minor clashes went to Sulzberger and implored him not to choose me, though I learned of this only later. As he weighed his options, Sulzberger invited me to lunch at Le Bernardin, a pricey midtown restaurant where he had reserved a quiet table in the very back. I ordered a piece of fish I barely touched.

"Everyone knows there's a good Jill and a bad Jill," he began. "The big question for me is which one we'll see if you become executive editor." As he ticked off my faults, I tried to explain what I thought were some misperceptions. I copped to some of the complaints: I could be self-righteous when I felt unheard, I interrupted, I didn't listen enough. I told him I'd work hard to correct these shortcomings. I left the restaurant feeling a bit queasy and downcast. It struck me that little of the conversation had focused on the "Good Jill." Because I hadn't touched my food, I bought a hot dog on the street and crossed the intersection of Seventh Avenue and 44th Street, where the truck had hit me. I realized that having lived through that, I'd survive not being executive editor.

Dean Baquet was a more jovial personality, liked by almost everyone. He was the first editor to really make me feel at home at the *Times* after I joined. He and I had grown close and we both loved investigative stories and vivid narratives. When we first met we discovered we both had loved the same story, published back in 1981 by the *Post* about Strom Thurmond's execution of four men when he was a local judge in South Carolina. We were often reading the same novel. There had been the usual tension between us that often existed between the Washington bureau chief and the top editors in New York, but nothing I perceived as disturbing the basic bond of trust. As friendly as he was, I found him somewhat unknowable. And he sometimes sidestepped messy confrontations and decisions. He had grown up in New Orleans where his family owned a restaurant; Baquet mopped floors after school. He was a first-generation college student, but dropped out of Columbia University to begin life as a reporter back home.

Marty Baron was a first-rate newsman. As night editor he could be picky, and I sometimes fought with him about changes to stories late at night. He grew up in Tampa, went to Lehigh University, got a degree in journalism and business, and left the *Times* to become editor of the *Miami Herald*, where he had racked up Pulitzers. He was whip-smart and quiet, with a sardonic sense of humor. A straight shooter. We could talk openly about our frustrations with Robinson and Sulzberger.

May turned to June. Sulzberger left on a trip to London. I had no idea when he would make a decision but stopped myself from bugging the always discreet Keller. I made plans to meet Keller and his wife one morning at the Metropolitan Museum, where the *Times*'s art critic, Holland Carter, was going to give us a tour of the Alexander McQueen exhibit before the doors opened to the public.

As I was putting on my coat, the phone rang. "I'd like you to be the next executive editor," Sulzberger said. "It would be the honor of my life," I responded. I felt light-headed and thought the conversation was over. "Who are you thinking about for managing editor?" Sulzberger asked. I told him I worked extremely well with Rick Berke, who was an assistant managing editor and had been my deputy in Washington. His name was met with a long silence. "I'm not sure he's ready," was all Sulzberger said. It had not occurred to me to be ready with an instant answer, though I had told Berke that I wanted him right beside me if I got the job.

"What about Dean?" he continued. "I love Dean too," I stammered. I would be seeing him over the weekend at a conference of black student journalists. We'd arranged to have dinner. "Why don't you discuss it with him," Sulzberger suggested. Without expressly asking me to pick Baquet, he had all but done so.

This phone call was the only conversation Sulzberger and I had about my becoming executive editor. I didn't ask him about the salary. I assumed I'd be paid at parity with Keller. That was a critical mistake, one made, I later learned, by many women as they climbed the ladder. Study after study shows that, unlike women, men do not hesitate to negotiate their salaries or ask for bonuses and raises.

My husband, kids, and sister were with me as Sulzberger formally anointed me as executive editor. All the journalists gathered around to watch and celebrate, as they did on Pulitzer day. I only wished that my parents could have been there. In my remarks I talked about the women whose shoulders I stood on, including Nan Robertson, one of the reporters who sued the *Times* over sex discrimination in the 1970s and put pressure on the paper to hire and promote women.

The PR department had scheduled endless interviews. There was tremendous interest in "the first woman" angle, and I was more than happy to speak on the topic. I was deluged with speaking invitations. Robinson encouraged me to accept many of them. "This is good news for the *Times* for a change," she told me.

At the end of September, Sulzberger would celebrate his 60th birthday. The party was also the official coming-out of his relationship with Claudia Gonzalez, a Mexican woman with whom he had fallen in love after they met at a conference in Davos. She was in Switzerland with her two children and working for the World Health Organization, but planned to move into Sulzberger's apartment on the West Side. Sulzberger had already equipped the apartment with a playroom for her kids.

I had heard that his family did not approve, and Robinson complained that he was always traveling abroad to see Gonzalez and absent from the *Times*. Gonzalez complained that the reverse was true. The invitation for the soiree, to be held at a glitzy disco and supper club in Times Square, went out under her name.

Sulzberger's children, an elderly aunt, and other relatives looked stiff and uncomfortable inside the Copa. His father, Arthur Sr., who had entertained in such stately places as the Metropolitan Museum, was briefly wheeled in by an attendant. A year later his son would eulogize him at the museum during a solemn memorial service. Sulzberger and Gonzalez, who in spike heels was taller than he, danced the night away. Robinson left as soon as the toasts were over. Other guests began grabbing for their coats then too.

Although I was completely unaware of it at the time, these were Robinson's final days as CEO. By mid-December she was gone, abruptly dismissed by Sulzberger in a way that seemed needlessly hasty and mysterious. He had entered her office, handed her a folder with separation documents, and said, "We are prepared to be generous." The extent of his generosity would astound the newsroom: her package was close to $25 million. Sulzberger hadn't told the board of the firing beforehand, and some of its members were angry. Besides rumors that she had tried and failed to force out his cousin, Vice Chairman Michael Golden, no reason was given. And there was no one ready to take her place.

Sulzberger took me aside to tell me about the firing while Robinson was still in her office making calls. "This shouldn't affect your life," he tried to reassure me. But in truth, the person on the business side who had been my main advocate and mentor on office politics was now gone. And Keller, my advocate in the newsroom, was now many floors away in the opinion department.

In picking my masthead, the senior team of editors under me, I deferred to Baquet in a lot of the choices. He would be running the daily news report, which had been my job as managing editor, and I knew from watching Keller that I would have less time to devote to it. This meant many editors would work more closely with Baquet than me.

The existing masthead had some great people but was not the team I needed. Most crucially, it lacked someone to lead digital strategy under me. This was a void I never completely filled and one that I constantly worried about. It became an even more pressing issue after Sulzberger, who had stepped into the void left by Robinson's sudden departure finally, in late 2012, hired a new CEO, Mark Thompson from the BBC, who was much more aggressive about the need to generate new products and revenue. From that point on, I spent nearly all my time in business-related meetings without a real digital partner. And disputes over reporting lines and refashioning newsroom jobs so that they were jointly accountable to Thompson and me became extremely worrying and preoccupying.

Why was I so worried? I knew that Thompson, as head of news and business at the BBC, was used to being in charge of both. He had told someone that there was no job at the *Times* he believed he couldn't do, including mine. He clearly had the publisher's ear. I desperately wanted the *Times* to survive and make money, but I did not believe that the business side should influence news coverage or be jointly in charge of certain news positions. I never saw, either as managing or as executive editor, a bright line being crossed, but I was always on edge and felt that a trespass was looming. Arthur Gregg Sulzberger and the *Times* spokesperson, Eileen Murphy, both strongly disagree and say my concern was unwarranted.

To send a strong message to Thompson, Sulzberger, and the newsroom that I was pushing and prioritizing digital, I stopped going to the Page One meeting in the late afternoon and gave my input at an early-morning meeting that was focused on the day's news and video for the web. Baquet ran the Page One meeting, which gave him immediate clout. He would later review his choices of stories for the front page with me in my office.

Two young women, Lexi Mainland and Liz Herron, educated me in how to use social media to connect with readers. One of my early tweets went viral; it was an invitation to comedian Aziz Ansari, a known foodie, to apply for the *Times*'s restaurant critic's job when it was open. (My son had suggested him.) My Twitter following zoomed upward as soon as I posted. But in real time I had little awareness that social media, especially Facebook, was revolutionizing the way people got their news. I did work at Google on an experiment to develop new templates for breaking news stories and gained weight gorging on all the free snacks. I tried out Google glasses, but they made me dizzy; I had no desire to see my email while I was walking down the street.

The 200 different stories the *Times* published each day were available to readers as soon as they opened their paper and turned the pages. Those stories were harder to discover online, where there was minute-by-minute competition for readers' attention and no guarantee that once they clicked on a story, they would finish it and click on another. In fact, they were more likely to flit off to another site. Stickiness, which Peretti had mastered at BuzzFeed, was incredibly hard to achieve on the internet, with its infinite attractions. I did not yet understand that sharing *Times* articles on Facebook had become an essential part of the digital publishing process. Facebook promotion gave stories a big lift and attracted millions of readers. It created more traffic. And traffic lured advertisers.

What turned me into a true convert was watching digital changes improve journalism. I saw Steve Duenes, the *Times* graphics editor, transform his department from old-fashioned mapmakers into wizards of animation and motion graphics. Duenes, a taciturn and stubborn editor, became the innovator in chief of the newsroom. He was the driving force behind a big, multimedia project that came from the sports desk. The story, called "Snow Fall," chronicled a fatal avalanche near a ski resort in Washington State that killed three backcountry skiers. In some ways it was the type of disaster story commonly told in newspapers. What made "Snow Fall" dramatic was the way it made elaborate multimedia elements an organic part of the storytelling and reading experience. Three-dimensional graphics showed the routes the skiers took down the mountain as readers scrolled through the story. Video testimony from the characters popped up as the reader absorbed their parts of the story. Some of the skiers wore cameras on their helmets, so there was real-time footage of their descent. There was audio of their frantic calls for help. Its design and perfect synchronicity dazzled readers. Within a week, three million had viewed the story. It set a new standard for digital narrative. It also cost an arm and a leg and involved a team of more than a dozen people in the newsroom, the kind of all-out effort that very few news organizations can muster. "To Snow Fall" became the new terminology for digital stories with lots of bells and whistles, but few of the imitators on other sites were as good.

The two editors I was closest to from my time as managing editor, Matt Purdy, the investigative editor, and Larry Ingrassia, the business editor, were both directing investigations I was passionate about. Ingrassia had a team scrutinizing how and where Apple manufactured its products, which turned out to be mostly in China. While selling billions' worth of products in the U.S., the Cupertino-based company was not creating many jobs here. David Barboza, the paper's correspondent in Shanghai, had told me about the vast wealth secretly acquired by family members of China's rulers. That was right up my alley—money and politics—and when he told me about it I greenlighted his project. In Purdy's orbit, David Barstow had been given documents indicating that Wal-Mart had bribed its way into Mexico, which had become its second biggest market. In Metro, Sam Dolnick was poking around cronyism in Governor Chris Christie's circle in New Jersey. I made sure these reporters were protected from other assignments so they could dig as long as they needed to. I was determined to deepen the *Times*'s footprint in investigative journalism, which was disappearing in many newsrooms because the work is so time-consuming and expensive. Most of these projects take a year or more. The stories also invited controversy and lawsuits that cash-strapped publishers wanted to avoid.

Barboza's story about the Chinese princelings highlighted two crucial aspects of investigative reporting: that it could be practiced in the most repressive countries, and that it could disrupt the business interests of the newspaper. With the Chinese government's approval, the *Times* had recently launched a separate website in Mandarin to produce journalism for a giant potential audience, even with the country's strict censorship. The site included stories published in the *New York Times* and original reporting produced by a Chinese staff of about 30 journalists. It had been up for only a few months but was already generating healthy ad revenue from brands eager to break into the Chinese consumer market. The *Times* had sunk $20 million into the project, hoping it would be a template for expanding internationally with other sites in native languages. Brazil was up next.

Barboza, who grew up in working-class New Bedford, Massachusetts, had joined the *Times* as a young clerk after graduating from Boston University and going to graduate school at Yale. The skinny, bespectacled reporter had worked his way up the business desk to a foreign assignment in

Shanghai. I had met him there when I was managing editor and had been impressed by his contacts in the elite corners of China's booming economy. With his wife, Lynn, a Chinese woman with a U.S. business degree, he had painstakingly gathered documents from little provincial offices across the country to get to the bottom of who really owned and was profiting from its biggest companies. This led him to the family members of Wen Jiabao, China's premier, including his wife, who was known as "the Diamond Queen" because of the family's investment in precious jewels. Barboza quietly continued assembling his trail of damning documents that exposed shell companies, straw investors, and other tactics of disguise. When he contacted government officials for comment, they were angered at the prospect of a *Times* exposé just as the Communist Party was choosing its new leader, Xi Jinping. Worried that they might be endangered, we moved David and Lynn to Japan to finish their blockbuster.

Right before we were set to publish, the Chinese ambassador requested a meeting with Sulzberger to discredit Barboza's story and stop its publication. I joined the meeting, held in a small windowless office called the Churchill Room. The ambassador didn't offer evidence that Barboza's reporting was inaccurate, but he threatened that there would be "serious consequences" if we published. Sulzberger was wary that this meant Chinese censors would block our new website, but after reading a draft, he made the right decision, despite the financial stakes of being banned in China, to publish. He promised only to let the ambassador know before the story ran.

Then the story went up on our websites in China, including with a Mandarin translation. Within an hour the story was pulled off the internet in China. The Chinese censors had delivered on the ambassador's warning. Although publication of the Barboza story demonstrated new global reach for investigative journalism, the price the *Times* paid was steep. The Barboza story was the last time the *Times* would be publicly available in China in any form for years to come. Both the general website and the new China site were blocked and remained so. To access the *Times* in China readers need a VPN, a technical means to avoid the censors.

There were other consequences. No new visas would be issued to *Times* reporters, and I worried that the correspondents' existing visas might not be renewed. The Chinese staff was followed, and some were detained. The day I arrived at the Beijing office, Chinese authorities questioned Patrick Luo, a young clerk, for 10 hours, an ordeal from which he emerged amazingly unfazed. Like the other journalists in the Chinese bureau, he was proud to work for one of the few news organizations that refused to cave to the censors.

What the staff didn't know was that I had been instructed to trim the staff and stem the losses the *Times* had incurred by keeping the journalists employed while the websites were blocked. Golden wanted to close the Chinese site altogether; I argued that it would look like we were bowing to the censors. So instead I was ordered to cut the losses in half, which meant freeing up millions of dollars. But once there I could not bear to deliver bad news. The Chinese journalists were so idealistic about the *Times,* and their effort to continue publishing was so valiant. I would find the savings somewhere else in the news department's budget.

Bloomberg had also had its website blocked after publishing a story on the new president and his family's hidden wealth. But Bloomberg killed another political corruption story, bowing to Chinese pressure in hopes its website would be unbound. When I found out about Bloomberg's actions from one of its reporters, I put the story about the killed piece on the front page. I also hired the Bloomberg reporter who was under suspicion for divulging this shameful episode. Sulzberger had gone to China to lobby the government to reopen the site, unsuccessfully, but he didn't object to publishing more of Barboza's findings. Only then did I discover that our joint stance wasn't quite as valiant as I had thought. Without my knowledge, Sulzberger, with input from the Chinese embassy, was drafting a letter from the *Times* to the Chinese government all but apologizing for our original story. I found out when someone involved leaked me a draft because he was worried the *Times* was about to do something embarrassing. The draft I saw in my view was objectionable and said we were sorry for "the perception" the story created. My blood pressure rose as I read it. I showed it to Baquet, who agreed it was a disaster. He encouraged me to confront the publisher, which was my inclination too.

I told Sulzberger I needed to talk to him privately, and we repaired to a Starbucks. I reached into my bag and produced my copy of the letter. He seemed startled that I had it and he kept saying, "I didn't do anything wrong." He tried to slip the letter into his folder, but I snatched it back. He agreed not to send it until it could be reworded once again, this time with input from Baquet and me. In the end, in my view, the letter was still objectionable. The word "sorry" remained in the final draft of the letter that I saw, despite protests from Baquet and me. In any event, the site remained blocked. The episode strained the relationship.

The distrust would widen when disputes over word choice gave way to decisions where the stakes were life and death. Such was the nature of war reporting, and though I was well aware of the risks, I never fully appreciated

their gravity until I got the call about Anthony Shadid, the prize-winning reporter we'd hired away from the *Post*. Shadid had been sent to Syria, where
a number of reporters had become casualties. He was on assignment with
Tyler Hicks, a war photographer I admired greatly. I didn't know Shadid
very well, but I read and admired his reports from the front lines. He and
Hicks and two other *Times* journalists had once been kidnapped in Libya, a
hair-raising experience. Sadly I had gotten used to these horrible incidents.
Two other correspondents had been kidnapped a few years earlier in Libya;
another one had been held by the Taliban for seven months before escaping.
Danny Pearl, kidnapped and murdered in Pakistan in 2002, had been a good
friend from the *Journal*.

I didn't know it at the time he entered Syria, but Shadid was torn over
the assignment. Based in Beirut, Shadid agonized about the trip in discussions with his editors on the foreign desk in New York. He and Hicks had
a productive reporting trip and were heading home to the Turkish border
when Shadid had a fatal asthma attack, brought on by his acute allergy to
the horses of the guides accompanying the journalists. Hicks had to carry
his body into Turkey. In the dead of night, another reporter who had come
to help had to practically steal a coffin to get him back to Beirut, where he
lived with his wife and young son. Hicks had called the *Times* photo editor
screaming that Anthony had died. His wife was waiting to reunite with him
at a small hotel near the border, and I had to call her to tell her the devastating news that her husband was dead.

Within hours I was flying to Beirut with the new foreign editor, Joe
Kahn. We could tell there was tension over why Anthony had been sent to
Syria when we met with his family, especially a first cousin who fired angry
questions at Hicks the night we arrived. Hicks was exhausted and stammering. He'd done his best; he'd tried and failed to resuscitate him. I tried to
comfort Shadid's parents and other family, who had traveled from Oklahoma. I talked to Hicks about getting counseling and tried to calm the other
reporters in Beirut.

But it was clear a lawsuit was inevitable. The family had an attorney at
Williams & Connolly, the Washington firm, which tried to negotiate a settlement. There were protracted and tense negotiations over the monetary
terms.

A friend and longtime reporter at the *Washington Post* called me to say,
"The *Times* is looking really horrible in this. You are losing your reputa-
tion for taking care of your people. You have to do something." I asked the
Times lawyer to come with me to see Sulzberger, who called in Golden.

I told them what I was hearing. Soon the case was settled, but I felt that this tragic matter had tarnished the newspaper's reputation for caring for sick employees and taking care of personal catastrophes. From that point on, I allowed only the briefest reporting trips into Syria. More journalists died there, though none from the *Times*. With every death, I remembered the *Wall Street Journal*'s managing editor Paul Steiger telling me about the unspeakable beheading of Danny Pearl. When I thought about my call to Shadid's wife, I would lose my breath.

Many people have asked me how being a woman affected my work as executive editor. I am never sure how to answer. I knew that after I became executive editor I became even more of a worrier, about everything, from the safety of correspondents to the *Times*'s financial problems. I brooded, and this interfered with how I led. I hated being closeted in business meetings where everyone sat silently following PowerPoint presentations and holding thick decks of charts summarizing the identical information. I talked to Keller, who managed to seem so outwardly steady, even during kidnappings. "I compartmentalized," he told me. "You have to learn to do it. It's the only way you'll survive." This was something men were used to doing, apparently. I could not. I don't know whether or not taking everything so personally and agonizing over tempests that were sure to pass had to do with my gender.

One thing I was adamant about was that the newsroom leadership was going to be more diverse. There were never enough female bylines on Page One, though there were also fewer days when it was uniformly male, and compared with other publications, the *Times* had many more women who were star writers. (I nagged my pal David Remnick a few times when his magazine's table of contents was all-male.) There were ridiculously few women in the most senior editing jobs. By the end of my first year, also for the first time in history, the masthead was half female. Black, Asian, and Latino journalists won promotions, though there was not enough racial diversity at the *Times* or any other newsroom. I kept the pressure on. We weren't where we needed to be, but we were getting closer.

Our coverage also needed to be more diverse. The lives of women needed to be reflected in our pages. In Kabul I had covered my head and gone with the bureau chief and my old friend Alissa Rubin to a women's shelter. Though I could see only their faces, it was clear that many of the women, even those with babies, were in fact girls themselves. Through an interpreter I learned they were 17, 14, 12. One girl had been kept in a cage in the kitchen of her family's house. Another had been forced to marry her

60-year-old uncle. They had all run away, and if they had been captured the punishment would have been death. I asked Rubin to consider a series on women in Afghanistan. Freeing girls from the horrors of the Taliban had been a cause célèbre in the U.S. right after 9/11, but interest in the issue had waned. Rubin's fabulous series would run after I was gone and win a Pulitzer Prize.

I encouraged Jodi Kantor, a reporter whose work I admired, to spend a year on gender-related stories. She investigated Harvard Business School's failed efforts to make women feel welcome in its hypercompetitive culture. In another deep dive, she described how automated scheduling used by the big chain stores was wreaking havoc on employees' lives, especially those of mothers with children. They couldn't plan their day care without knowing what days and hours they were working. She focused on the daily struggle of one barista at a Starbucks. The day after the story ran, Starbucks changed its policies. Later Kantor would win a Pulitzer for her investigations of Harvey Weinstein's sexual abuse that helped ignite the #MeToo movement. When I first plucked her from the Culture Department to report on the 2008 campaign, the other political reporters resisted. Almost immediately she was a scoop machine, breaking the story, among others, about Barack Obama's controversial pastor, Jeremiah Wright.

A young reporter, Sarah Maslin Nir, visited a 24-hour nail salon near the office to get a late-night manicure. She asked her manicurist, "When do you sleep?," and uncovered an underworld of Asian women working more or less as indentured servants. The New York attorney general immediately opened an investigation. Such was the impact of a big, investigative series blasted across the homepage. Louise Story, a business and investigative reporter whom I had hired as a college intern, produced many high-impact stories on the wealthiest New Yorkers.

Starting when I was managing editor, I encouraged more gender coverage in the less serious parts of the paper too. The Styles editor had the idea of doing a column of freelancers on relationships. It became Modern Love. In 2006 the most-read story in the *Times* was not a news scoop but a Modern Love column called "What Shamu Taught Me about My Marriage." (The secret from the sea: stop nagging.) I attended shows with the fashion writers to demonstrate my interest in their work (my father was a garmento) and attended story conferences in the Styles department, a door no executive editor had darkened. I hired Deborah Needleman away from the *Journal* to revive *T*, the Sunday styles magazine; her efforts paid off as the title fattened with luxury ads.

I went to Paris to see Suzy Menkes, our international fashion critic, who thought her feature stories were not getting enough attention. Suzy was an old-school newspaper star whose upturned forelock was her trademark. I had a cartoon of her drawn to add visibility to her articles. She was extremely knowledgeable about many things, an eccentric treasure, the kind of older savant being tossed out by other news organizations. I accompanied her to a Chanel haute couture show at the Palais Royale in Paris, a display of gilded excess worthy of Marie Antoinette. Golden told me that Suzy was responsible for 25 percent of the revenue of the *International New York Times*, but no editor had paid homage. I called this aspect of the job "diva management," and I quickly learned that it would require tending to divas and gods of both genders.

But before I fully got the hang of it, Politico published an in-depth and strident criticism of my personality and my leadership style, asserting I was losing support among the troops. It recounted that after I had returned from traveling, I made Baquet furious by telling him the news report on his watch had been boring. The story described Baquet slamming his hand into a stairwell and leaving the building, which was accurate, and not exactly the image of a well-oiled journalism machine. The disparaging quotes about me were pieced from anonymous sources.

Sulzberger assured me, "It's not your fault, it's just your turn." He didn't seem concerned, and Baquet acted sheepish. But a number of women journalists, many of whom I did not know personally, protested the article as a sexist and stereotypical smear. Soon after the incident, I gave a speech in Washington, D.C., where two editors I had never met before came forward to give me flowers. I took it as a sign that women were behind me and had pinned their hopes on my success. It meant the world to me.

Pulitzer Prize day was around the corner, and as this was my first full year as executive editor, I knew the scorecard mattered. Before the official announcement, nearly everyone knew we had won four prizes, as leaks from the Pulitzer jury spread on the internet. But it had been a tradition at the *Times* since the old days, when the only timely news was first reported by the wire service, for all the journalists, including the publisher, to crowd around the main staircase in the newsroom as the Associated Press moved a story about each of the prizes. As the AP reported the good news (trophies for "Snow Fall" and Barboza's exposé of the Chinese princelings, as well as investigations of Wal-Mart and the Apple economy), Sulzberger held up four fingers in exultation.

In the middle of the celebration there was a news alert: there had been a bombing at the Boston Marathon. As the honorees made jubilant speeches, I ran to the national desk to make sure we had enough reporters in Boston. A bare-bones story was already up on NYTimes.com, but the only person we had on the scene was a freelancer who was running the race. I dispatched a battery of reporters and photographers, some of whom would also shoot video.

The story, which dominated the headlines for days, was one of my first encounters with "fake news." There were several completely wrong early reports, including one by CNN that arrests were about to be made. A wrong suspect was named on social media sites like Reddit, and reporters flooded to his parents' house. News came at warp speed, amplified by digital news sites that picked up stories without checking them independently. I stressed that we not post anything until it could be confirmed by our own journalists.

The Pulitzer celebration and the Boston bombing play back in my memory on a split screen. Technology was rending the way we did our work and also enabling the best of it, like "Snow Fall." That technology allowed us to bring readers the news almost the instant it happened, and we were expected to do so without sacrificing the story's accuracy and authority. My job, which sometimes felt impossible, was to ensure that no aspect of the reporting was compromised.

A credible report on the suspects' whereabouts didn't emerge until days later, at 1 a.m. When I got the news I literally ran back to the *Times* to make sure the crew on the graveyard shift didn't fall for unverified information and publish it. The astounding rate at which news stories now moved sometimes required playing agile defense. This was the dark side of a news operation struggling to maintain its values with a digital metabolism.

On another big story, the U.S. Supreme Court decision on Obamacare, I instructed every editor not to publish anything until David Leonhardt, the new Washington bureau chief I had chosen, called me with a fully checked report on the decision. My caution paid off. Fox and CNN raced onto the air with wrong reports, saying Obamacare had been overturned.

There was a new celebrant standing next to Sulzberger at the Pulitzer event, Mark Thompson, the new CEO. In a bold move to find his "digital visionary," the publisher had gone outside and across the ocean to hire the man who was known for pushing old Auntie Beeb into the digital age with new video technology. Though I barely knew him, there were already tensions between us.

Thompson was smart as an Oxford don and proud of it. With a

shadow of facial stubble and reddish hair, his casual dress concealed a command-and-control ferocity. Sulzberger was impressed and seemed to snap to attention every time Thompson's English accent was heard.

I was not quite a year into my job when the publisher and the new CEO mandated sizable cuts in the news budget, the equivalent of 100 employees, which was as deep as any we had had. Digital subscriptions had plateaued and print advertising had disappeared in a number of categories. Even real estate, a *Times* franchise in New York, had moved online. Figuring out how to slice with the least pain occupied nearly all my time. Union-protected reporters were already working with no contract, and there were rumors of a strike.

Thompson immediately made what I considered to be predatory moves. He made the art director, who had worked for me for years, a report jointly to me and him, a change that seemed to trouble the art director as much as me. Even before Thompson's arrival the job of the new head of video had been restructured to report jointly to me and a top executive on the business side, an unusual arrangement for someone in charge of making news content. (Previously video was directed by a news editor who reported to me. I had bitterly protested the new arrangement, lobbied Michael Golden, and lost.) In the digital realm, Thompson argued, design and technology were both part of user experience, which was core to the business. Video drew the most lucrative digital advertising, which the company dearly needed. Its director had to be responsible for revenue too.

Thompson's strategy involved developing what he called a "suite" of new paid products on top of the basic *Times* subscription for the main news report. These were to include a lineup of smartphone apps devoted to categories such as magazine-length stories, cooking, and opinion, or targeted toward sectors of our readership, for instance, millennials. Consultants from McKinsey picked out categories that promised the largest financial upsides. Thompson wanted the suite on a fast timetable. I scrambled to find the appropriate editors to work on these projects in teams often co-led with the business side.

I invited Thompson to accompany me on a trip to Silicon Valley. I had been invited to give a speech at San Francisco's Commonwealth Club, to be the guest at one of Sheryl Sandberg's monthly gatherings in her home for the most influential women in tech, and for lunch with Apple CEO Tim Cook, with whom I was trying to create better communication after he took umbrage over the *Times*'s series on his company. We chatted amiably through the three-day trip. He told me several times that he was developing a plan to restructure the leadership of the *Times*. I feared this didn't bode well for the independence of the newsroom.

Soon another issue strained our relationship, a big scandal at the BBC in which he became embroiled and I believed the *Times* had to cover aggressively. It involved the former host of several programs, Jimmy Savile, who had recently died and then been exposed as a pedophile. A key question became what Thompson knew and when. The scandal was attracting coverage in the U.S. and I assigned David Carr and others to begin hurling questions Thompson's way. He denied knowing anything about the crimes that had taken place inside the BBC, but damning articles kept raising new questions. Sulzberger wanted to see every story we published on the matter before it went up on the internet. He never once asked me to change anything, but this made me uncomfortable. The board was concerned. His choice of CEO seemed to be blowing up.

But Thompson was ultimately cleared and emerged from a Parliamentary investigation unscathed, and the scandal blew over. He returned his full focus to developing new products and generating new digital revenue. If he took umbrage at the *Times*'s coverage of his BBC problems, he said nothing. He decided we would have a robust program of paid conferences sponsored by big companies. He took me aside and asked me not to stand in the way of native advertising, although I was on record saying I thought it was awful. "I need this from you," he told me, as if any objection from me would be seen as a mutiny.

I felt lonely and depressed at work. Everything was about saving or generating money. In order to save the jobs of reporters, I pressured some of the most senior editors, including several on the masthead, to take buyouts and retire. This meant losing some old supporters. I cut new reporting clusters I had created as managing editor, such as an environment pod whose work on global warming was vital. That didn't mean we weren't covering the subject; it just meant we could no longer afford a whole team devoted to it. I hated making these announcements.

My most difficult year was 2013. The Obama administration initiated more criminal leak probes, and I became embroiled in fights with the White House over publishing intelligence stories it deemed irresponsible. When I was quoted saying the Obama administration was the most secretive of any I had covered, the president's press secretary, Jay Carney, accused me of abusing my position.

Then we were beaten by the *Washington Post* and the *Guardian* on a purloined document revealing widespread NSA eavesdropping. The disclosure of far more pervasive domestic spying came from Edward Snowden, a young contractor for the agency who had stolen massive numbers of files about the most sensitive programs run by the government and its British counterpart, the Government Communications Headquarters. Knowing we had held James Risen and Eric Lichtblau's story on NSA wiretapping eight years earlier, Snowden didn't trust the *Times*. Seeing the *Post* brandish its exclusives each day was deeply frustrating. Although we eventually got most of the documents, the *Post* and *Guardian* later would share the coveted Pulitzer for public service.

Also in 2013, a series of church-state conflicts were not resolved as I had hoped. The first occurred after I left the office for a couple of days when my son-in-law suddenly fell sick. Upon returning I learned that Baquet had agreed to Thompson's request to let the writers being hired to write native ads also write for the news report after a one-year cooling-off period. I believed our journalists shouldn't include people who had also once written ad copy and wanted an absolute ban on ad writers later appearing in the *Times*. After our morning news meeting, I told Baquet that I intended to overrule him. As I argued my point, probably too adamantly and self-righteously, he lashed out at me, saying, "You won't even listen to people who disagree with you," and left the room.

I felt very alone. I wanted to fight what I saw as the good fight with a managing editor with whom I could share everything, the way I had with Keller. I had not invested enough time in building a supportive team with the masthead, a group of whom had complained about me to Sulzberger. No one doubted my journalism chops or that I cared deeply about the reporters, but with no management training, I was not handling these multiple problems or clashes well.

The second clash took place at a lunch with the publisher. Around a table with a white linen tablecloth sat Rosenthal, the editorial page editor, Denise Warren, the head of digital operations, Thompson, and me. At one point, Thompson told me that he expected the ideas for new, revenue-producing products to come from the newsroom. The last thing the *Times* needed, I believed, was to have its best journalists distracted from their work by endless meetings with product managers who reported to Thompson. That had become the essence of my job, and I knew my having to spend time in unproductive meetings on tasks I mostly hated left the news report without some of the edge it had during my first year as executive editor. I had thrown my energies into the launch of a millennial news app because I worried it wouldn't measure up to *Times* quality. I found the development of the cooking app important because I was certain we could monetize the thousands of fabulous recipes the *Times* had published over the decades. But these endeavors tore me away from core news.

"If that's what you expect," I snapped at Thompson across the table, "you have the wrong executive editor." It was the kind of frank admission, uttered in an angry tone, that was never heard at the sedate publisher's lunches we had every Wednesday in one of the small executive dining rooms. The truth had flown out of my mouth before I could edit either its substance or its tone. As I spoke, the uniformed waiter serving us spilled the water he was pouring. No one said anything for several minutes.

The third incident should never have happened. The new ad director had invited the marketing directors of several car companies to the Page One meeting during the New York Auto Show. This might have been allowed at *Forbes*, the native ad factory where she came from, but it was shocking at the *Times*, and I wanted to make that clear.

Although we met privately once a week, Sulzberger didn't bring up any of these incidents. I mistakenly thought this meant I had his tacit support to push back. He knew I'd spent my life as a journalist exposing ethical lapses and conflicts of interest, so that the slightest hint of them set me off. And despite his "Good Jill, Bad Jill" warning, he had given me the job. So I was jolted when, in January 2014, he hand-delivered a very negative written evaluation. He remained in my office while I read it. In shockingly personal terms, the letter described my moodiness and statements from my closest colleagues that I was a difficult manager. It said nothing about the substance or quality of my work. If I had to boil it down to one sentence it would be "People think you're a bitch."

"Arthur," I asked, "do you want someone else in the job?"

"No," he responded, "but I want you to take these issues seriously."

Some of his criticisms were valid, such as the fact that I traveled a lot. I did so for two reasons: to get to know the paper's foreign correspondents and to get a personal feel for current world events. Keller too had gone on long trips; he said it was a way to keep his sanity. Although I too needed that outlet, I figured this criticism would be easy to fix.

Some criticisms I viewed as sexist. For instance, Sulzberger portrayed my forcefulness as high-handed rather than leaderly, and, as I was now accustomed to hearing, I was not "likable." It was clear to me that people had talked behind my back to him. I certainly suspected Baquet.

I still didn't understand how personally endangered I was. I told myself that after the Raines debacle, the publisher wouldn't fire another executive editor he had picked, especially the first woman to hold the job. As the first woman, I also took umbrage at each example of perceived gender imbalance and discrimination. Earlier I had asked one of the masthead editors to study the issue of pay equity in the newsroom. When she was finished, she walked into my office, plunked a spreadsheet on my desk, and said, "You are Exhibit A." The numbers showed that during my eight years as managing editor, my salary lagged behind one of the male masthead editors I outranked. The year I joined the masthead as managing editor, a special pension plan that paid the most senior executives and editors almost half their salaries for life had been frozen; I was part of a far less generous plan. My current salary was what Keller's starting salary had been in 2003, a full decade earlier. Idiotically I had not asked Sulzberger what Keller's salary and compensation had been when I took over his position. The *Times* later disputed that I was underpaid and said my full package, reflecting changes the company made in awarding stock and bonuses, was as good as my predecessors'.

So, with the evaluation letter in hand, I consulted a famous and feared gender discrimination law firm headed by Anne C. Vladeck, known for her work in "employment divorce" cases. A partner of hers thought both issues—the gendered criticisms and the unequal compensation—looked serious, but ultimately I had no desire to end my career in messy litigation against the institution I loved. Though I was not as good at it as Keller, I had learned to compartmentalize. I could separate my frustration with Sulzberger, Thompson, et al. from my love of the news and my devotion to the *Times* as an institution and an irreplaceable element of American democracy. It was still my religion.

The new head of video, Rebecca Howard, who came from the Huffington Post, confided in me that she was having similar problems. She reported jointly to Thompson and me and was under tremendous pressure to increase the volume of videos to attract ads. But I, as her second boss, insisted that the video be *Times* quality, which required the best production values and scripts. This meant slowing down. She and I were in the same "upstairs, downstairs" dilemma of pitting standards against speed and volume. She confided in me that the *Times* was paying for an executive coach who was greatly helping her cope. I asked Golden, who was now handling human resources for the company, to allow me to have the same coach and began seeing her once a week.

The coach, who had been an executive at CBS, agreed that both the evaluation from Sulzberger and the pay issue were sexist. She referred me to a contract lawyer who negotiated pay for many top CBS people. "You should not be negotiating yourself. A lawyer should do it," she instructed. Even though I knew Sulzberger and Thompson might be freaked out by receiving a lawyer's letter rather than coming to a gentleman's agreement with me, I asked the lawyer to represent me anyway and redress the pay issue. Looking back, perhaps I was being self-destructive. He did not get a response from Sulzberger or Thompson. (The *Times* disputes that I was underpaid.)

Then came the famous "Times Innovation Report," which announced to the world that we had fallen way behind our competitors on the internet. As if I needed another issue to drive me over the edge. For me, it was an epic defeat. I had been so determined and worked so hard to be the transitional editor who would succeed in making the newsroom digital-first without causing a cultural meltdown or letting the best traditions die, like protecting the news from being colored by crass commercialism. We would lead ourselves into the digital world without stooping to the tactics used by BuzzFeed. There would be no metric charts influencing editors to promote stories according to their traffic. We would not use clickbait headlines that seduced readers into clicking on stories that delivered little, if anything, the headlines promised. We would have a website worth paying for. Quality would be our successful business model. But my reading of the "Innovation Report" showed us to be laggards. It was a call to arms and also called for something Thompson wanted desperately: more collaboration between the news and business sides. The wall was getting in our way, the report concluded.

It wasn't meant to be personal but I couldn't help taking it that way. I felt betrayed by the innovation committee I had created six months earlier. Arthur Gregg Sulzberger needed a new assignment, and Thompson continued to press for more product ideas from the newsroom. Since he would likely be moving to the business side soon anyway as part of his grooming as a possible successor to his father, I thought leading a committee devoted to making news products would be the perfect job. I let him have the pick of the newsroom, and he plucked the best business reporters and multimedia editors. There were also two business-side advisors. All were relieved from their day jobs, and they were given a secret conference room.

About halfway through the project, A.G. came to see me in my office. He wanted to change the mission of his committee. "I don't think our focus should be new products," he said. "I think we need to focus on the core."

By that he meant the *New York Times* news report itself. This made sense to me, since I vividly recalled those consultant-led focus-group sessions that showed readers didn't want extras, just the main news bundle. "Growing from the core" had become a *Times* mantra. In a decade the company had gone from being a $6 billion empire with all kinds of subsidiaries to one valued at around $1 billion. With the recent sale of the *Boston Globe* for a pittance—$70 million—the company was indeed down to its core.

I didn't realize that young Sulzberger was opening a Pandora's box. He would be using his committee to dissect every part of the newsroom in a comprehensive autopsy of how we stacked up against new, digital rivals. He would be interviewing Peretti, Huffington, and others who had built their traffic, though hardly their quality, to be bigger than the *Times*'s. A.G. assured me that the report would be for the masthead's eyes only. I quickly and naively approved his course alteration, not fully realizing that whatever report he wrote would get outsized attention because he was the publisher's son and likely successor.

One member of the committee later told me A.G. was spending long periods upstairs on the business floors. On those days he wore a suit instead of jeans. Sometimes he would return to their conference area in the newsroom and reverse himself, or offer completely new ideas out of the blue. They thought this was surely coming from his father or Thompson. Then A.G. closeted himself to write his committee's report alone. He delivered a draft of the study to Baquet and me. It was more than 100 pages long. I quickly realized its findings and criticisms were devastating: the newsroom had not transformed far or fast enough. It criticized an ossified newspaper culture with too much focus on the front page. It called for far more collaboration with the business side and greater emphasis on "audience development," meaning social media self-promotion.

The report said digital innovators like BuzzFeed and the *Guardian*, which used social media aggressively and had built up a large digital audience in the U.S., were "closing in" on the *Times*. There was considerable ink on the lack of communication between the news and business sides, including anonymous comments from members of the business team who felt dissed and ignored by the editors in the newsroom and examples of rudeness and snobbishness in the way journalists talked to their business cohorts. "There is widespread concern that it is inappropriate to speak with colleagues on the business side payroll. This runs directly counter to best practices," the report stated. Another damning conclusion was that the newsroom often judged digital initiatives as "un-Timesian," which echoed some of the divisions that were already becoming evident at the *Washington Post*.

One of the senior news editors was quoted as saying, "The question of what is Timesian has been both the saving grace and artificial limiter of the newsroom." Moreover, the report stressed, digitally focused talent was fleeing the newsroom because *Times* journalists looked down on people working on the web as service personnel, not co-creators. The report said nothing about what I considered my biggest accomplishment: uniting the web and main newsrooms in 2012.

The publisher and Thompson were overjoyed with the "Innovation Report" and arranged for A.G. and one of his lieutenants on the committee to present its findings to small groups across the company. It might have been the tough love the newsroom needed to become more digitally focused, but it did not recognize the progress I believed we had made. I issued a somewhat disingenuous memo to the newsroom embracing its findings and promising informational sessions.

At this time I attended a farewell party for the *Guardian*'s Janine Gibson, who had won a promotion and been called back to London. I admired her guts and rigor in editing the Snowden stories, and she was well-regarded for expanding the *Guardian*'s huge American audience. She was known for her digital smarts. I'd heard she preferred to remain in New York with her children rather than move back to England, so I pulled her aside and asked if she'd be interested in the *Times*. She told me she was being moved back to be a contender for the top editing job, and I concluded that to interest her my offer would have to be big, with room to move up.

The idea of having a true partner, another woman who had made brave journalism decisions and was forging her way into the future, appealed to me immensely. The next day I had my weekly lunch with Sulzberger and Thompson. They pressed me on how I intended to implement the "Innovation Report" and reconfigure digital. I said I didn't have a strong digital partner, and knowing they would quickly offer to find someone, I mentioned Gibson. Thompson, who knew her from Britain, jumped at the idea. They pressed me to get her over to the *Times*.

There was, in fact, a senior position open. When Keller had become executive editor, he had created a new masthead job, managing editor for administration, and appointed John Geddes, a superb manager. I had kept him on, but in 2013 he took a buyout.

I knew Baquet liked the authority he had as the sole managing editor and would certainly not welcome someone from the outside coming in with that title. What I didn't know was that he'd clashed with Gibson during the editing of the Snowden material. I consulted Thompson for advice on how to handle Baquet.

"Tell him you both need a new digital leader," he said, "and don't tell him you want Gibson straight off. Tell him you are considering several people." More or less, I followed that script, knowing that it was wrong to mislead Baquet, but also wanting to avoid more angry confrontations. He took the news coolly but did not resist, at least at first.

I assumed Thompson, who has denied encouraging me to obfuscate, was briefing Sulzberger. I pressed ahead with Gibson and put together a plan to offer her a second managing editor title. I consulted Thompson throughout and had him call Gibson, whom he knew in Britain. I invited her to meet Sulzberger and have lunch with Baquet. I still left Baquet with the impression that I was looking at different people, and he grew justifiably furious when Gibson let the cat out of the bag and told him I had more or less offered her the job. A few hours later he came into my office and told me off. He said I wasn't treating him like my managing editor and I had not been transparent with him. This was true. I was following Thompson's advice to withhold my true objective. I should have been straight with Baquet. The angry words in my office were the last I saw of him. He stopped coming to the office and claimed he had jury duty. I left messages for him and heard nothing back.

I knew I had been clumsy. I went to see Sulzberger and asked him to take Baquet to dinner to assure him that he would probably one day get my job. I didn't explain that I had misled Baquet about who I was considering for the digital managing editor's job, assuming, wrongly, that he knew about the preliminaries. I asked Sulzberger to call me after his Wednesday night dinner.

When he called, his voice was ice cold. He said that it had been a "very tough" conversation. He hung up quickly, providing no details. Later someone told me Baquet had presented him with an "it's either her or me" ultimatum. On Friday morning I arrived to a message that Sulzberger wanted to see me in his office. When I got there, he said, "I've decided to make a change. Dean will be executive editor." Then he handed me a press release announcing that I had decided to leave the *Times*. I asked why I was being fired. "Because of the way you handled the Janine Gibson matter," he said. Then I looked him straight in the eye and said, "Arthur, I've devoted my entire career to telling the truth, and I won't agree to this press release. I'm going to say I've been fired."

"We are doing this for you," he said.

"Arthur, I think people are going to be very upset by this."

"No, I don't think so," he said. "I want to settle this soon. You'll know the terms over the weekend."

I rode the elevator down to the lobby and left the building. When I hit the street, I realized how oddly calm I felt.

I took a long walk in Central Park. I told my husband and children. Perhaps I was in shock, but I was not feeling upset. I was angry. I called Gibson and told her she should stay at the *Guardian*, which was her inclination anyway.

No terms came over the weekend. I came to work as usual on Monday and Tuesday because Baquet was still out and I wanted to be there to oversee the news for the last time. A lawyer hammered out my deal: nothing like the millions that had gone to Raines or Robinson, but enough to give me the freedom to figure out what I wanted to do over the next year or two.

An announcement was set for Wednesday in the newsroom. I had offered to be there because I wanted to thank all the journalists who had driven themselves so hard and made me look so good. They had supported me through life-and-death situations. On Tuesday night, Sulzberger called and said, "Don't bother to come in tomorrow." Even Raines was allowed a final goodbye speech.

On Wednesday morning a stunned newsroom heard the news. The *Times* immediately cut off my email. I lost all my contacts and messages. (Luckily I had thought to copy Thompson's emails and all the materials relating to my pay.) My assistant of 11 years was told to pack up my office and send everything to my apartment.

Flowers arrived, as did friends from the *Times* who wanted to make sure I was okay. A gaggle of paparazzi gathered outside my small loft building. A reporter and photographer followed me when I walked my dog. Every television host wanted an interview. Bloggers began debating whether I was a victim of sexism, since some of the men who had written about me called me pushy. Sulzberger said publicly that he had problems with my "management style." It was blowing up into a huge story. I asked friends and family to monitor the coverage because I couldn't bear to read it all.

My sister helped pull me back from despondency. She had been by my side when I became executive editor, and now she called to tell me, "Our parents would be just as proud of you today as they were the day you were named executive editor." I remembered that my father always told me that setbacks offered you an opportunity to "show what you are made of."

Usually on Thursdays I worked out with a trainer, Gene Schafer, at a gym near my apartment. When I arrived that Thursday, he was wearing boxing gloves and held out a pair of red ones for me. "You need these today," he said. I had taken one previous boxing lesson, but he was right. Smacking his gloves for an hour, my punches becoming harder each time, was therapeutic. Before we were done, I asked him to take a picture of us so I could show my kids that I was okay. My daughter, who appointed herself my PR agent, posted the photo on Instagram with the caption "Mom's badass new hobby" and added the hashtag #pushy. Two hours later she called and said, "My Instagram is going viral." On Friday there I was, boxing gloves and all, on the cover of the *New York Post*. My firing was an obvious opportunity for the *Post* to go after its favorite punching bag, Arthur Sulzberger Jr.

Suddenly I was the fight-back symbol for every woman who had been fired or told she was pushy. My friend Paul Steiger's wife, Wendy, a jewelry designer, produced a line of Pushy necklaces and sent me one. The former national editor of the *Washington Post*, Susan Glasser, wrote an essay, "Editing While Female," that revealed in scalding detail the same sexism she had encountered before she too had a forced exit in 2008.

The fact that I would openly say I was fired seemed to be liberating to other women. As more women took to social media over the weekend to express outrage over the way the *Times* had treated me, the paper itself didn't seem to have much of a counternarrative. BuzzFeed wrote, "Abramson was literally being seen as a fighter—and on the PR battlefield, she's unequivocally come out the winner." In an effort to turn the tables, Sulzberger gave an interview to *Vanity Fair* in which he criticized me, but his remarks only created more backlash.

I hadn't given any interviews and didn't want to be at war with the *Times*. But I was not in control of how this played out. I decided to honor the commitment I had made to be the commencement speaker at Wake Forest University and receive an honorary degree. More than 100 reporters flew down to the leafy North Carolina campus to report on me. Did they think I would try to inspire graduates by denouncing Sulzberger? Instead I reiterated my love for the *Times* and admitted to the students that I was probably as scared as a lot of them. I too had no idea what I would be doing next. Then the media calmed down and the attention abated.

I was a classic example of what masqueraded as news in the internet era: a meme. My firing was an event that could be important to only a small elite of journalism insiders and people who paid attention to the *New York Times*. But it had become a national story covered live by CNN.

There was no simple reason I was fired. I was a less than stellar manager, but I also had been judged by an unfair double standard applied to many women leaders. Most of all, I became the first woman editor at a very bad time in journalism, when a failed business model was bringing into question almost every principle of journalism that I had learned during more than 30 years in the profession. I was not willing to sacrifice my ethical moorings for business exigencies. My scruples were rooted in the golden age of newspapers, which had long since passed. But I didn't think technological change should sweep in moral change. I fought back. Perhaps my principles were too rigid; perhaps to save the *Times* the old strictures needed to be relaxed.

In the end, all the journalists who are my contemporaries were transitional figures playing blind man's bluff. Lena Dunham, the young feminist writer who created the hit HBO show *Girls*, wrote her friend David Carr, the *Times*'s media columnist, to ask him how she should think about my firing. Wise about the *Times*'s internal politics and protective of the institution, he gave an honest appraisal, perhaps the most perceptive commentary of anyone, on my firing: "You should feel bad about it and a little scared for our shop. We always manage to mangle success. Even if you accept Jill was a handful—not to me and a lot of the people I like at the paper—still doesn't scan. i.e. . . . business was good, journalism was good, culture was tough. All the editors of the paper . . . become monsters and she was an incredibly effective one. A great, forgive me, newsman. And regardless, did she deserve to be dragged out into the public square and be stoned to death for being a bitch? Hell no."

After a few weeks I accepted an offer to teach writing and journalism to undergraduates at Harvard. I couldn't bear to sit out the 2016 election, so I began writing an opinion column for the *Guardian*, mostly online. In the end, Janine Gibson was passed over to be the *Guardian*'s editor and joined Ben Smith at BuzzFeed to run its U.K. website. After Trump was elected, a column of mine ran on the op-ed page of the *Times*, about how Jared Kushner, Trump's son-in-law and White House advisor, was behaving like one of David Barboza's princelings.

Before his tragic and premature death in 2015, I kept in contact with David Carr. After I emailed to compliment one of his Monday columns, he pinged me back, writing, "Boss, I miss your balls."

CHAPTER EIGHT

WASHINGTON POST II

The financial crisis slammed the *Post* even harder. Its aftermath exposed fatal weaknesses in the paper's local business strategy and lack of vision. It put something previously unthinkable in question, whether the Grahams were the right stewards to lead the company.

Katharine Graham had fought valiantly to keep control and had almost lost the paper after her magnetic but manic-depressive husband, in whose hands her father had entrusted the paper, tried to wrest it away from her. Then he shot and killed himself. Her consigliere, Edward Bennett Williams, the famous Washington litigator, had gallantly protected her interests from other incursions over the years. Against the odds, she had gone on to become a courageous and legendary publisher, the woman who risked publishing the Pentagon Papers the same week her company went public and who then printed Woodward and Bernstein's stories on Watergate in the face of threats from the Nixon administration. She even won a Pulitzer Prize for a strikingly candid memoir that she wrote after her tenure as publisher. Her son Don knew that in taking over the *Post*, he would play an essential role in keeping society informed as well as maintaining his mother's sterling legacy. When he stepped into the publisher's chair he said, "My mother has given me everything but an easy act to follow."

For most of the 20th century, the most successful and influential newspapers were family-owned, and some of those families dominated political and cultural life in their cities, especially the Chandlers of Los Angeles and, to the extent that anyone other than the president dominated Washington, the Grahams. Newspapers then got used to profit margins that were 20 percent or better, and the industry came to expect fat profits as the norm. In theory and practice, however, family ownership protected papers from the vagaries of the economy and the stock market. In the economic downturn of the 1970s, for example, the Sulzbergers invested in the *New York Times* and added new sections on culture and food, improving both the quality and the finances of the paper. The Grahams were known for running an extremely well-managed company with a reliably healthy stock price, smartly diversified in television, education, and other new business lines. Because their newspapers were their crown jewels and the source of real influence, the first families of the newspaper industry had every incentive to protect quality, hire the best journalists, and take home the most Pulitzer Prizes.

But as a new century dawned, the era of the great, family-owned papers was ending. In 2000 the Chandlers sold the *L.A. Times* to the Tribune Company and the paper became part of a publicly owned chain. The Ridders sold their Knight Ridder papers to the McClatchy chain. The Bancrofts bailed on the *Wall Street Journal* and in 2007 sold to Rupert Murdoch for the stunning price of $5 billion. The digital transition that laid waste to advertising profits and circulation revenues took an immense toll on the quality of journalism, as newsrooms were slashed and the most expensive areas of journalism, investigative and foreign reporting, were downsized. The chains, still insisting on margins greater than 15 percent to impress Wall Street, cut most brutally. That left the Sulzbergers and the Grahams the last families standing and the most reliable stewards of accountability journalism. Their mettle had been tested by a previous president, Nixon, and soon would be by another.

For three decades Don Graham had done his best to continue his mother's mission, to run a company that was extremely profitable and a bulwark against corruption and overzealous power by the federal government as well as passionate in its devotion to the First Amendment. In 2008 it was time to pass the torch again. Graham was 63. Unfortunately none of his four children wanted to devote their lives to the paper. Although his niece, Katharine Weymouth, was not very well known in the *Post* newsroom and had never worked in it, Graham and the board deemed her ready. For eight years she'd been at the center of the storm as head of advertising, and had served in the legal department before that.

Like everyone in the *Post*'s building on 15th Street, Weymouth was greeted each morning by the oversized photograph of her grandmother with Ben Bradlee that hung in the lobby, a daily reminder of the paper's mission. Lately, because of buyouts and forced staff reductions, the *Post* had lost the stature it had in its glory days of the Pentagon Papers and Watergate. Its business model was broken. Weymouth, 41, was inheriting a weakened institution, a reality she knew just by looking at the devastating backslide of print advertising revenue.

This alone would have been a challenge for any publisher. But in a few months the economy of the entire country would crater during the worst financial crisis since the Great Depression. Later she would sardonically joke about her "perfect sense of timing." Yet neither she nor her uncle had any sense that they were facing the possible end of a nearly 80-year family dynasty.

Weymouth didn't have Don's earnest demeanor and had barely a trace of her grandmother's queenly bearing. She lived a down-to-earth lifestyle as a young single mother raising three children in a four-bedroom house in Chevy Chase. She drove a family SUV but also owned a BMW convertible. Rather than entertaining the kind of grandees that had gathered around her grandmother, Weymouth, a divorcee, mainly socialized with a group of very close women friends, her posse. Blond and fashionable, she was misjudged and dismissed from the start by some of the older, more powerful men in the newsroom who saw themselves as the proper keepers of the Watergate flame.

Although it was a generation after her grandmother had faced blatant sexism when she took over the paper, Weymouth was also underestimated because of her gender. At one early presentation, her shirt was not properly tucked in and as she moved around, her midriff was partially visible. After the meeting, her women friends heard some of their male colleagues talking about how "slutty" Weymouth's attire was.

Cory Haik, an admirer of Weymouth's and leader of the newsroom's digital efforts, could not believe how the men at the *Post* talked down to their new leader. "The condescension of the men who walked into her office to mansplain how she should do her job was unbelievable," Haik said. They seemed so tin-eared and unaware that their advice dripped with sexism, not the same open hostility that Katharine Graham had faced when she took over, but a definite echo. They had little regard for the fact that she was a Harvard and Stanford Law graduate who had faced the plight of the newspaper industry through the prism of the *Post*'s ad department and knew the future of journalism would be digital. For the time being she had to stem the losses and keep the paper alive. She had already decided the *Post* needed new editorial leadership for the digital age and that she had to quickly reverse her uncle's mistake of separating the newspaper from the website.

Her elevation coincided with the hinge moment in which readers, for the first time, got more of their news from the internet than from newspapers, a secular change that would kill hundreds of papers by the time it was done. The *Post* had already slipped behind the *Times* on the web, where its audience was smaller and its site lacked basic offerings like news alerts. Editors still waited until the newspaper's deadline at night to dump fresh stories onto WashingtonPost.com, at which time most of the news was stale. Reporters and editors viewed the website as a distant, much less worthy relative that published stories too quickly, before they were fully checked or polished, and covered "dancing bears," the clickbait more suited to Buzz-Feed or the Huffington Post that was intended to build audience. This was not what Ben Bradlee meant when he said he wanted "Holy Shit" stories.

The newspaper culture at the *Post* was even more inbred and suffocating than at the *Times*. For nearly 50 years there were only two editors: the dashing Ben Bradlee, followed by the stolid Len Downie. (During the same period the *Times* had five different executive editors.) Downie, who had already been executive editor for 17 years when Weymouth came on board and was not digitally conversant, said that he expected to remain several years more, until he hit 70, as Bradlee had. But to Weymouth he was too much a creature of the print world and a stickler about the wall separating news and advertising. Once, when she asked him to approve an unusual ad layout, he had chewed her out, accusing her, a member of the Graham family, of "sullying the brand."

Her grandmother had been blessed with Bradlee, a perfect match who called her "Mums." Her uncle Don had chosen Downie to be his utterly dependable and unflashy doppelganger. Dislodging Downie would be a delicate challenge. He was the soul of journalistic integrity and enjoyed the complete trust of his newsroom. But he was not the leader to fuse the print and digital wings of the *Post*, which Weymouth viewed as her most important mission. The survival of the newspaper depended on it.

Although no one had ever hired an executive editor from outside the *Post*, Weymouth had scoured her newsroom and not found a viable candidate. She began inviting a number of different editors from other papers to meet her, and quickly zeroed in on Marcus Brauchli, the outgoing editor of the *Wall Street Journal*. He had successfully merged print and digital there and had years of experience running a news operation that fed both sides. He was strong in finance, an area where the *Post* was weak, a great plus as the financial crisis took hold. He did not have experience in the *Post*'s two traditional areas of core coverage, national politics and metro news, but he was reportedly a fast learner. Weymouth had picked him up from the airport in her BMW, and on their drive to the offices downtown Brauchli had impressed her by unflinchingly disposing of a big spider. They seemed to have similar ideas about what needed to be done.

Brauchli was available because Murdoch, having shelled out billions to buy the *Journal* and its parent company, Dow Jones, wanted his own man, a fellow Australian, to be editor. About to be booted, Brauchli had retained the superagent Bob Barnett, also a lawyer at Williams & Connolly, to negotiate his separation agreement, and had received more than $5 million. Some of his colleagues took a dim view of the rich package, calling it "hush money" to muzzle him from criticizing the changes Murdoch would soon be making at the *Journal.*

Superb at managing up, he had become a favorite of the most powerful figures at Dow Jones but had no true champions at News Corp., the new owner. On his fast way up at the *Journal*, the slightly balding 50-year-old editor, who wore suits and looked like the investment bankers he covered, was quick to take credit for successes, distanced himself from failure, and left few footprints on the backs of the more senior editors he climbed over to reach the summit. He had been an excellent foreign correspondent in China, where he had invested in a hip Shanghai nightclub and seemed to know everyone in the hard-to-penetrate Chinese ruling and business elite. He had a lot of strengths, but being unfamiliar with the *Post*'s internal politics and prone to look out for himself, he was probably not the best person to watch the new publisher's back. In July, Downie sullenly vacated his office and headed to a desk upstairs, making his discontent over his fate known throughout the building, and Brauchli moved in. In choosing Brauchli, Weymouth passed over Phil Bennett, the managing editor, an excellent journalist who was widely trusted by the staff and he too ended up leaving. So a newsroom that was used to steady, homegrown leadership was plunged into uncertainty.

Weymouth wanted to immediately formulate a new business plan. No one, not even the best minds of Silicon Valley, whose technology was crushing newspapers, had yet devised a new model that would support large and expensive news-gathering operations like those of the *Post* and the *Times*. Weymouth began by wrangling an unwieldy committee of 40 problem-solvers from inside the company. She took some members of this strategy group to boot camp at Harvard Business School to comb for new ideas. Then the committee submitted their best ideas to her and Brauchli. There were countless skull sessions with a core group of 15.

The strategy group got bogged down in long meetings that left everyone's head hurting. The journalists, meanwhile, were awaiting a plan that would save their jobs. The newsroom was already down to 700 journalists from a high of nearly 1,000. The most recent cuts were deep: 100 heads. With so many taking buyouts, it would have been torture to have individual goodbye toasts—they'd be happening by the hour—so there would be just one big farewell party. The invite read, "They Took the Cash, Now Watch Them Get Smashed." Among those leaving were some big franchise players: national security expert Tom Ricks, whose book *Fiasco* was the definitive study of the disastrous Iraq War; David Broder, the aging dean of the political press corps; and Nora Boustany, an experienced foreign correspondent. The buyout offers had been tempting; longtime employees got two years of paid salary.

The shrunken staff reflected the pinched ambitions of a once glorious paper. The *Post* had folded its business pages into the front A-section, killed its book review, and would soon shutter all domestic bureaus. In a gesture to show that he too was sharing the pain, Bob Woodward took his salary down to $100 a month (his books had made him a multimillionaire) but remained on call for assignments and from time to time still brought in blockbusters.

The *Post*'s decline became a much discussed subject, at least among journalists. The *Times*'s Washington bureau regularly beat the *Post* and had snatched away some of its best political reporters, including White House veteran Peter Baker. The *Post* alums running Politico were upstaging the paper on campaign coverage. All of this sapped morale.

Murdoch's *Journal* had fewer ambitions for its political coverage and more or less left the crucial field of national security reporting to the *Post* and the *Times*. In the post-9/11 world and with the incursions of the Bush administration on civil liberties, investigations into secret counterintelligence programs and law enforcement were never more important. Even in its weakened state, the *Post*'s journalism was vital. Its reporting on secret black-site CIA prisons for terror suspects, torture, and government contractors was stellar and irreplaceable.

With buyouts and a new publisher and editor, everyone was on edge. Weymouth further spooked them by asking for a desk on the fifth floor, the main newsroom floor. Brauchli's answer was final: "No fucking way." But the very idea made the journalists frantic that the wall between news and business, which Downie had protected so fiercely, was eroding.

Finally, in December, the strategy memo arrived. It was called "The Road Forward" and was filled with so much media industry jargon and generalizations that it was ridiculed both inside and outside the paper. At a town hall–style meeting for the staff, Weymouth outlined three "pillars" that would guide the *Post* forward, relying on a chart that resembled the Lincoln Memorial.

First, the *Post* would remain local, "being for, and about Washington." This would involve the usual elements, like "strong news coverage, enterprise and investigative reporting," which Weymouth's staff thought they were already providing quite well. There would be more service journalism on weather, traffic, and entertainment and stories to guide readers on how to make a "purchase decision." Few reporters saw service journalism as their calling, but Weymouth's memo dismissed such snobbery. "We must focus better on what the consumer indicates they want, and be less quick to emphasize only what we think is important."

The second pillar, which would soon collapse on Weymouth's head, offered "new products" to generate revenue, especially in areas where "business and policy intersect." These new products would include paid conferences for "business decision makers with a stake in Washington policy-making," code words for lobbyists.

The third pillar involved "realigning our cost structure," code words for more cuts.

While the memo's title was meant to sound visionary and reassuring, an actual road map was entirely missing. Furthermore, "For and about Washington," which was to be a new slogan, sounded straight out of Don Graham's old playbook. If it was intended to lift morale, it did the opposite. One media critic described the mood in the newsroom as "suicidal" after the memo circulated. "I hated this strategy," said a veteran in the ad department who thought the *Post* needed national and international ambitions to survive. Instead of well-known global brands, Weymouth was obsessing about winning back local advertisers like car dealerships who had supported the *Post* in the print era.

For all of her tenure, print remained the *Post*'s biggest revenue driver, and that reality limited Weymouth's choices. The culture of the paper, as everyone called it, was still print-centric. There were almost no digital natives on her top leadership team, including her chief business advisor, the general manager Steve Hills. She was under enormous pressure to make certain the paper was profitable again, so new investment was out of the question. While her grandmother had Warren Buffett, and Don Graham had trusted business advisors like Alan Spoon and Chris Ma, Weymouth had Steve Hills. He became a despised figure in the newsroom because he was seen as a relentless cutter. He did not see a digital future and often cited a grim statistic: a daily print subscriber represented $500 in revenue, while a website reader fetched only $6. As smartphones became a favored platform for news, the comparison became worse. "Hills really got inside her head," said another business side manager. "He was constantly reminding her of the limits of what we could do."

Brauchli, meanwhile, set about fusing digital and print, a feat that was done in 2009 when the Virginia digital people came to work at the main *Post* building in Washington. But that involved costly renovations of the downtown building and uprooting journalists from their accustomed workspaces, changes that were not entirely welcome. He also faced an uprising from some change-resistant readers when, to save newsprint, he canceled five of the comics in the newspaper, including one that had a small but intense following, *Judge Parker*; after readers rebelled, it was saved.

The fusion of print and digital was far more complex on a psychological level. Katharine Zaleski, a bright light at WashingtonPost.com, said she and her digital colleagues were constantly being told by the veterans on 15th Street that they were "not real journalists." Effectively there was a caste system, and at the apex sat the men who had spent decades fighting for the Page One slots of the newspaper. For them, the website was, at best, an afterthought. The cultural divide made it difficult for Weymouth to recruit and keep digital talent. She designed a special pay package with stock to keep Cory Haik, the digital editor, on board.

Because of his experience advising Facebook, one area of digital experimentation that Don Graham had insisted on was social engagement. Even though he had passed up becoming an original investor he later joined its board. His daughter Molly went to work there. As a result, the *Post* was a bit ahead of other newspapers in having reporters communicate with readers and in publishing reader comments on all articles. The *Times*, by contrast, opened few articles to comments, and even then had editors review every comment before making it public to be sure that even readers were held to *Times* standards.

Mark Zuckerberg was certain that news would be shared by Facebook users on their news feeds. Facebook offered the *Post* a massive new audience that, in turn, would help WashingtonPost.com attract more advertisers who were looking for scale. Graham also saw partnering with Facebook as a way to excite and enlist a younger generation of readers. The *Post* had several social media experiments, the biggest being its Social Reader, an application tied to Facebook that allowed *Post* readers to share what they were reading with their Facebook friends. The stories on Social Reader ranked high in a reader's news feed. At its height, the app was a big success, with 17 million monthly users. But when Facebook tweaked its algorithm, the audience was cut nearly in half practically overnight. Eventually the *Post* moved Social Reader off Facebook and then dropped the experiment altogether. The failure demonstrated the power of computing algorithms to dictate success or failure for new journalistic endeavors.

Although the *Post*'s daily journalism was uneven, it was still doing episodic work of superlative quality. Some of its long enterprise stories, original investigations, and beautifully crafted features met the gold standard of Watergate. In 2008, a terrible year in terms of business, and Weymouth's first year on the job, the *Post* won six Pulitzers, its biggest one-year haul. There was Dana Priest and Anne Hull's investigation of poor conditions at Walter Reed, the military hospital where wounded veterans of the Iraq and Afghanistan wars languished for months and received inadequate medical care. Priest, one of the best investigative reporters in the profession, had worked her way inside the hospital and secretly interviewed patients. Another winner was an in-depth exploration of the outsized influence of Dick Cheney in the Bush administration, although one of its authors, investigative reporter Jo Becker, had left the *Post* for the *Times* by the time the prizes were conferred.

The *Post*'s hallmark was this kind of investigative reporting, and that made it a magnet for the best talent, especially after so many other newspapers virtually abandoned it, leaving the public with only a few reliable press watchdogs. Reporters in its investigative unit often spent months on a single story, sometimes digging dry holes. Jeff Leen, its editor, was the rare talent who could guide reporters to fruitful paths when they were lost. He covered the walls of his office with maps and elaborate outlines for stories. Many smaller newspapers had withdrawn entirely from investigative work, leaving few watchdogs over state and local corruption.

These investigations were what Marilyn Thompson, a veteran reporter and editor, called "slow journalism" and a reason she aspired to work at the *Post*. After cutting her teeth as a daily beat reporter, she had gone to work at the *Philadelphia Daily News*, a tabloid where she published exposés of the mob's grip on the East Coast casino industry; then to the *New York Daily News* to investigate political corruption and corporate wrongdoing. Her stories hit hard, in one case resulting in federal indictments of 20 white-collar criminals. So when she came to the *Post* in 1990, she saw it as the promised land for the specialized craft she practiced. She spent 14 years there, working her way up from local county coverage to citywide projects to investigations of national scope, and by 2004 she was overseeing an investigative unit that was routinely producing work that won the highest honors.

Petite and charming with an upcountry South Carolina accent, Thompson, a native of Greenville, had fallen in love with journalism at Clemson and become a true newshound. Though her background was southern, as a young reporter she'd become expert in big-city, urban corruption and, once she moved to Washington, political corruption. Through scandals like Wedtech during the Reagan years to the anthrax attacks following 9/11, she'd been involved in the coverage of many national controversies. But she was obsessed with a single story from back home that she had been trying to nail since 1984. It was the kind of story she adored, a secret buried in history and one that would define her career when she revealed it in the *Post*. She had continued to chase it through family crises and her own bout with cancer.

Working as a cub reporter at the *Columbia Record*, Thompson had heard that Strom Thurmond, the one-time segregationist presidential candidate and senior senator from South Carolina, had fathered a black daughter. The hypocrisy and bigotry of her home state and its leaders hurt her conscience and sense of morality. In 1984 Thompson found a trail that led to Essie Mae Williams, a schoolteacher in Los Angeles. "I knew Essie's secret," Thompson later wrote. "Her father was James Strom Thurmond, once one of the nation's most spiteful segregationists, a political opportunist who had seized the moment in 1948 to carry the banner of the Deep South's Dixiecrat revolt against civil rights." It was a situation "laced with Faulknerian irony," but not uncommon in the South; Thurmond had impregnated a 16-year-old black maid who worked for his family when he was 22. Ever since, he had been sending his daughter money and had even paid her tuition at an all-black college, all in secret.

For Thompson, this ghost from the past revealed something important about race, and not only in the old days, given that Thurmond had attempted to recast himself as a champion of blacks in his state. She eventually managed to find some yellowing letters that indicated that Thurmond had given Williams some financial support and had taken them to Los Angeles, where she arrived unannounced at Williams's office and presented the long buried documents. At first Williams denied that Thurmond was her father. Patience, even when it clashed with urgent obsession, was a vital part of investigative reporting, Thompson knew. She likened the process to a 500-piece jigsaw puzzle, its pieces scattered randomly on a table. "If the reporter lucks out," she wrote, "the search quickly yields a corner piece, giving logic and symmetry to the hunt." The hunt for that corner piece could sometimes take years, and cash-strapped papers did not have that kind of time anymore.

At the *Post* she worked on the story between other big assignments, and by 1992 she had gathered enough pieces for a long piece about the rumors of Thurmond's illegitimate black daughter. But even then she didn't feel what she had was definitive enough, so she kept going. Another decade passed as she managed her daily workload and searched for new clues to the Thurmond mystery when she could. In 2003 Thurmond died at age 100, and with Thompson's persistent encouragement, Williams was finally ready to confirm the true identity of her father. By this time Thompson was too sick from chemo to go back to Los Angeles, so she completed her reporting, interviewing Williams again, by phone.

No one admired Thompson's gritty pursuit of this story more than I did. Having lived in South Carolina a few years myself and having profiled Thurmond when I worked at the *Wall Street Journal*, I too had heard the rumors. I remember sitting on the creaky wooden porch of the former state secretary for the South Carolina NAACP, Modjeska Simkins, a 90-year-old civil rights legend and lifelong Thurmond adversary, as she told of the senator's secret daughter while treating me to a bowl of gumbo.

"The state police used to drive him to visit her when she was in college," Simkins told me. In the late 1980s I chased the story as far as Edgefield, Thurmond's birthplace, where the eccentric and ancient editor of the weekly newspaper dug out a fraying front page from the 1940s with a headline that screamed, "Strom Thurmond Has a Colored Daughter." But he had no concrete proof, and with a deadline back in Washington, I had dropped the tantalizing lead. I was jealous but also admiring when Thompson finally cracked the case.

Thompson left the *Post* in 2004 because she got an offer to be the top editor of the *Lexington Herald-Leader*, a quality regional newspaper in Kentucky. She wanted to nurture local and regional investigative reporting, and being able to run her own show was a challenge she couldn't pass up, especially considering there were almost no women newspaper editors at the time. The *Herald* was part of the Knight Ridder chain, which seemed to be solid and respected. So, painful as it was, she left the *Post*.

From this point, her career mirrored the roiling troubles bedeviling her industry. Soon she was dealing with the financial squeeze that was decimating reporting ranks at so many papers. Though she hadn't known it when she moved to Lexington, Knight Ridder, a once profitable, family-run, quality empire, was on the verge of collapse. As a vice president of the company, she was suddenly summoned to California, the chain's home base, to work on an emergency five-year plan. Before the plan was finished, the entire Knight Ridder chain was sold to another company, McClatchy.

With a new owner she thought was secure, Thompson decided to take on another Kentucky institution, its senior senator Mitch McConnell, whose record of raising funds by dangling legislative favors had to date gone unscrutinized and unchallenged. The *Herald*'s senior political correspondent had been dying to investigate McConnell, but to do it right would take months, and the paper didn't want to have to assign another reporter to fill in. Determined to move ahead, Thompson found herself in the unusual situation of soliciting a donation from a nonprofit as the vice president of a supposedly solvent for-profit corporation. The California-based Center for Investigative Reporting, which had partnered with newsrooms on similar projects in the past, agreed to pay the reporter's salary for six months, about $37,500, so he could complete the investigation. McClatchy applauded Thompson's resourcefulness.

Then, close to publication, a powerful voice chimed in to kill the story. McConnell's office claimed that the paper's investigation had been compromised: the foundation that funded it, they charged, was itself funded by liberal interest groups, including one that championed campaign finance reform, which the Kentucky Republican opposed. Thompson was spearheading a hit job financed by the left, McConnell claimed. And in the face of pushback from the senator, her publisher, McClatchy, bowed. They returned the Center's money and softened the series, unwilling to stand behind its journalists the way the *Post* always had. The fiasco sent Thompson looking for a new job where she could champion her signature slow journalism.

She went back to Washington, this time as the *Los Angeles Times*'s deputy bureau chief, then bounced to the *New York Times*'s bureau there before returning to the *Post* in 2008. While these once great newspapers were known for stable staffs with little turnover, print journalism had become a game of musical chairs. The *L.A. Times* was a shadow of its former self, and at the *New York Times*, where she had returned to investigative reporting, she clashed with her editors.

The *Post* came forward with an offer to bring her back, though it too was hurting. This was early in the Weymouth-Brauchli regime, when the financial outlook was darkening and the national desk, of which Thompson was soon named editor, was in tumult. After three years back at the *Post*, she left for Reuters, which was global but not the right home either. From

Reuters she took a job as deputy editor at Politico, where the pace of the journalism was anything but slow, and then to a digital news start-up funded by the Kaiser Foundation that focused on health. She had hoped that the new digital news platforms, without the expenses and cultural baggage of legacy newspapers, might be good breeding grounds for investigative journalism, but they were not exactly the right fit for her either.

An investigative editor and reporter as good as Thompson would probably have had a stable career at a single newspaper in the old days. Her journey from place to place to find the right home, from local newspapers to digital start-ups, was emblematic of the uncertain media business environment. It was hard to find a good fit for an editor and writer whose strength was long-form projects. There was ProPublica, an all-investigative nonprofit journalism group, which partnered with bigger news organizations and did Pulitzer-quality work. After he stepped down as executive editor of the *New York Times*, Bill Keller started an accountability journalism nonprofit called The Marshall Project, which focused on law enforcement abuses and related subjects. But they were still relatively small and openings were few. Ultimately Thompson accepted a fellowship at Harvard to research presidential campaign finance for a year and published her findings on the *Atlantic*'s website before retracing her steps back to Politico, briefly, and then coming full circle to land for the third time at the *Post*.

In announcing her return, the *Post* noted, "Among her many attributes, Marilyn is also perhaps the most peripatetic editor in America." She ran the national news report on Sundays, but during the week she tried to focus on deep political dives. But news seemed to break faster and more furiously than ever, and there were always so many spot news stories that she almost had to sneak in the investigative projects in between. Days off became a rarity. The news cycle was dictated by the speed of Twitter, which had become an insatiable marketplace for political news. In late 2018, she left the *Post* for a third time for ProPublica, where she was chosen to head a project focused on reviving investigative reporting at the state level, where it was so urgently needed and increasingly rare.

Thompson's career reflected the difficulties of keeping the most vital part of journalism—investigative reporting—alive during the digital disruption. The career trajectory of another talented woman at the *Post*, Melissa Bell, showed something different—the exciting new paths that opened for editors schooled in the new information ecosystem. Originally she thought, like Thompson, that she wanted to do deep dives, be a magazine writer. But if technology was a disrupter of Thompson's career, it became the guiding light for Bell, who began at the *Post* in 2012, writing for the famous Styles section. Soon she was tapped by Raju Narisetti, Brauchli's managing editor and someone who had worked closely with him at the *Journal*, to work on news blogs for the *Post*.

This was the era of blogs, web columns that focused on specialized subjects, like technology, or general ones, like the breaking news blog Bell was asked to anchor. They were usually written in a personal voice and did not follow the old pyramid structure of news stories that hewed to who, what, when, and where. Instead blogs were spontaneous and up to the minute, emphasizing the most recent happenings rather than the most important ones. Technically they could be published faster using a web template called WordPress, which was different from the *Post*'s regular digital publishing system. WordPress was free and open-source, available to anyone and any news organization for blogging. And it was fast. Rather than crawling through the *Post*'s layered editing system, blogs could go up almost the second they were written, with less editing and fact-checking.

"It was the ultimate in being up there with no net," recalled Bell, who found herself writing about everything from the Arab Spring to local murders. She soon forgot about wanting to write long magazine stories. Speed was a kind of narcotic. Luckily for the *Post*, Bell was a stickler for accuracy and found it could be achieved with speed, as long as she was willing to work punishing hours. But elsewhere, accuracy became a victim of speed.

What did bother her was the way her former colleagues on the newspaper changed the way they viewed and treated her once she became a blogger. "Suddenly," she recalled, "I wasn't a real journalist any more." But that didn't cause her to regret changing gears. "I was in love with the internet," she confessed. For most *Post* journalists, editorial and technology were utterly separate realms. For her, they existed in beautiful harmony.

Bell and a few digital colleagues, most of them also young, smart, and female, sat in a workspace near Brauchli and Narisetti, who encouraged the bloggers to expand. Soon Bell was leading a blogging empire. There were 131 blogs, including one about the Civil War. Few had any sizable revenue (ads) attached to them. (Oddly, the Civil War blog was an exception.)

"I was blogging the Egyptian elections," she recalled. "I was in heaven." It was 2012 and she was 33. But the respect from print colleagues never came. They seemed ignorant that Bell's blog posts were often the first stories on important topics *Post* readers saw. Only the fully edited versions of stories that ran in the print paper each morning rated as "real *Post* journalism," Bell recalled.

She was getting more responsibility, and two of the *Post*'s blogs, Ezra Klein's Wonkblog and Chris Cillizza's The Fix, which focused on policy and politics and tried to be competitive with Politico, were getting huge internet traffic. Bell was in charge of them all, but Brauchli and his deputy, Narisetti, would not give her the simple title she wanted: editor. She was told, she said, that if she was called editor, long-serving print reporters might think she was their boss. Unthinkable. Instead she was given the murky title director of platforms. Zaleski, too, had a murky title that was unfathomable to many of her colleagues: executive producer and head of Digital News Products.

Petty battles over titles had long beset American newsrooms, but the straining to find names for digital jobs represented something serious. It showed a failure of imagination, the inability to see that editorial and technology had to be of equal quality to win the loyalty of highly educated and affluent readers in the digital age. Editorial always took precedence at the *Post* and the *Times*. This was, needless to say, dispiriting for the technologists, who could have been making far more money working at tech companies but chose newspapers because they wanted to be included in the mission of journalism. Bell eventually joined a *Post* colleague, Ezra Klein, and launched a successful digital news start-up geared to younger audiences, Vox.

Meanwhile the internet's 24/7 news cycle created a hyperactive news biorhythm whereby journalists fought one another for the same crumbs. Scandalmongering, a reliable driver of clicks, seemed to overwhelm both journalists and readers, who were bombarded with news about corruption and scandal. But those were the subjects that drove clicks. There was little time for the long view of history that Thompson used in framing her probes in the rich writing style she loved. These were antitheses of web news-writing, with its overuse of stock words like "high stakes" and "unprecedented" that pumped air rather than facts into stories and sold them as "bombshells."

The Monica Lewinsky scandal had helped usher in the change of both the subjects and the standards of reporting. Tellingly, the story of President Clinton's illicit affair was broken by the Drudge Report, then chased by everyone in the traditional media. Though the *Post* and its sister publication, *Newsweek*, had the story, they were holding it for some final fact-checking and response from the White House. When Drudge, whose site leaned to the right, got the story, he posted it in an instant, and then so did the *Post*. Every night for months the story dominated cable news as well as the front pages of the *Post* and the *Times*.

Then came the Bush and Obama years, with even bigger stories to cover and a shorter and shorter digital clock.

Weymouth's goal was to fully heal the rift between print and digital, but her attention was always on the bottom line. That financial pressure soon drove her onto murky ethical ground, a plan to hold small policy salons in her home. Lobbyists would be asked to pay dearly to dine at Chez Weymouth with members of Congress and *Post* journalists. These gatherings were to be intimate and off the record. When Politico broke the story (the reporter was Mike Allen, an ex-*Post* man) it attracted attention and coverage in part because people, especially press insiders, loved to see the paper famous for uncovering Watergate hoisted on its own petard. Dubbed "Salongate," the painful episode showed cracks in the new leadership team of Weymouth and Brauchli and also how easily a newspaper could lose its institutional principles under unrelenting financial pressure.

Like Sulzberger, Weymouth thought conferences and live events could be moneymakers. Both publishers called them "live journalism." At the *Journal*, Brauchli had watched two technology journalists, Walt Mossberg and Kara Swisher, turn a single annual conference, "All Things Digital," into a money gusher that attracted just about every big name in Silicon Valley and a ton of paying sponsors. Weymouth was eager to begin her experiment.

The difference between Weymouth's salons and the scores of such dinners that happened in Washington each night was that the lobbyists would pay to sponsor these salons, at $25,000 per event. (Sponsorship for the first 11 events was discounted to $250,000.) The unsavory new twist was offering the lobbyists the chance to buy access to *Post* editors and reporters, who would be seated at the table engaging in the off-the-record discussions.

The appearance of impropriety was so glaring that it was hard to believe anyone at the *Post* would entertain such a notion. Yet while Weymouth was away on business, glossy flyers for the first salon, on health policy, went out from the *Post*'s marketing department. Some invitations went to lawmakers directly from Weymouth's email, failing to mention that the health salon was sponsored by lobbyists for the industry. It was a glaring omission.

The *Post* promised "intimate and exclusive gatherings" and conversations that would be "spirited" but not "confrontational." The guests would include Weymouth, Brauchli, and the reporters covering whatever topic was up for discussion. The lobbyists were promised they could "build crucial relationships with *Washington Post* news executives in a neutral and informational setting." The selling of access to the *Post*'s journalists wasn't subtle.

Allen got hold of an invitation, and when Politico published the story, Weymouth was plunged into a public relations fiasco. The first health salon was canceled. Brauchli, moving away from the spreading stain, sent a message to his newsroom saying, "We will not participate in events where promises are made that in exchange for money the Post will offer access to newsroom personnel or will refrain from confrontational questioning." He left the impression that the salons were in no way his idea. That left Weymouth holding the bag, sending a staff note the afternoon the Politico story ran meant to "reaffirm our commitment, first and foremost, to our journalism and our integrity. There is nothing more important and no amount of money that would cause us to jeopardize that." That she even had to say this was a bit pathetic.

She said neither she nor the newsroom had vetted the promotional flyer and that she would have stopped it if she had. Her memo laid the blame on the marketing department, but still she reiterated the need to "always [be] looking for new revenue streams" and insisted that new initiatives would "uphold our high standards of journalism." Reporters could not believe the idea of the salons had ever gotten off the drawing board. With all their talk of new ways of publishing and creating revenue, the new publisher and editor had managed to create a full-fledged scandal in almost no time. The trust of readers had been shaken.

The episode wounded Weymouth's reputation. But what struck her allies, including Bell, as most important was that it revealed an ugly truth about the *Post*: that many of the paper's leading journalists seemed positively titillated and thrilled that the new ways and new leaders were exposed as corrupt. "Suddenly," said Zaleski, an admirer of Weymouth who also worked closely with Bell, "it became obvious that some people inside the *Post* were actually rooting for it to fail. That was a tragic realization."

Weymouth never completely recovered from the black eye or the newsroom's rising distrust of her. Afterward, in the eyes of her newsroom, she could do no right. In late November, the *Washington Post Magazine*, part of the Sunday bundle, included a heart-tugging profile of a young teenager, born a dwarf, who was trying to lengthen her legs in order to be taller. The story detailed her painful surgery, putting pins in her legs that needed to be tightened with a wrench each day. The surgery helped her grow six inches, from her original height of four-feet-two. Weymouth then discovered another writer, a friend of hers, was working on a story about someone who had their arms and legs amputated. In what she meant as an offhand comment, she mentioned to him that advertisers might think the paper was running too many of these "downer" stories. The writer took this as an edict from the top. The Sunday *Magazine* ended up killing his story, and rumors spread that Weymouth was insisting on "happy news" and trying to meddle in news content. The minor episode over an ill-considered comment illustrated how much the newsroom, where morale was low because of layoffs, was thrown off kilter.

It also fed an anxiety in the newsroom that the *Post* was lowering its standards to make money, featuring stories about popular subjects like animals, the weather, and dating. There was actually a weather editor. Because additions viewed by the old guard as flighty were coming at the same time long-respected reporters were taking buyouts, they were especially unwelcome.

All of this added to the tension over the unification of print and digital, the highest priority for Weymouth and Brauchli. Narisetti became another flash point. He was a bright, creative man who had started his own newspaper, the *Mint*, in India. At the *Journal* he was on the leading edge of a trend that brought data into the editing process, one that was already established at websites like Gawker and the Huffington Post but was foreign to most legacy newspapers. At the *Post*, however, the journalists were up in arms over the fact that right outside his office he kept a traffic board, a screen with data on how many readers each story was attracting. Editorial judgment, not popular will, had governed where and when stories were published and how they were played. When asked why the *Times* avoided using reader data to make editorial decisions, Keller's response was simply "We're not *American Idol*." Editorial judgment was precisely what readers were paying for. Soon, of course, metrics became an accepted part of digital news everywhere, led by Peretti at BuzzFeed.

Narisetti, age 45, brought with him what he called "a culture of measurement," scrutinizing numbers of page views, visits, and time spent by readers on WashingtonPost.com. More than 100 editors and other journalists were soon receiving a daily report showing how the *Post* had performed in a variety of metrics, nearly 50 in all. If traffic lagged, Narisetti sent notices to editors to put new stories or photos or videos up on the website. He required reporters to identify Google keywords in their pieces so editors could play them up in headlines and at the top of stories in order to enhance their standing in Google searches. This was the same search engine optimization that Peretti had introduced at the Huffington Post years earlier, with no backlash. But the traditional newsrooms were unaccustomed to such feedback.

There were audible groans in the newsroom when a photo of a smiling Narisetti, standing next to his traffic board, accompanied an article about newspaper metrics in the *New York Times*. But eye-rolling turned into resistance when Narisetti began to make the next newsroom cuts partly based on reporters' traffic rankings. He was overheard bragging that he had squeezed 200 jobs from the newsroom without a noticeable decline in the paper's quality. (Regardless of what the data said, this simply wasn't true.) Traffic metrics were also used in performance reviews. By 2012 the newsroom headcount had slipped below 600, and those who remained had been taught the lesson that their contributions to the mission were valued only if they showed up in the stat sheets. The Defense Department budget, for example, was not likely to generate lots of clicks, but it was a vital subject for many *Post* readers who worked in the industry. Brauchli tried to reassure his newsroom that metrics were not the sole measure of what journalists covered, but he insisted the numbers were instructive and couldn't be ignored.

Also annoying, Narisetti spoke in the jargon-filled language of the tech world, declaring that the newsroom should be "in a perpetual state of Beta" and dispatching "innovation" editors to the major news desks, like sports and politics. He hired a team of other tech-savvy editors. To Weymouth and Brauchli, Narisetti was exactly the change agent the *Post* needed to push it into the future.

The metrics in which Narisetti was so conversant were available from a company called Chartbeat, which had established itself as a powerful force in America's data-focused newsrooms. As Nielsen measured TV ratings, Chartbeat measured internet traffic, and just as Nielsen ratings could raise the price of a show's advertising, Chartbeat's data were used to hook advertisers. In the newspaper era, ads were blasted out to the readership as a whole. On the web, advertising could be targeted to specific slices of the audience and placed near or in stories that would attract the brand's ideal consumer. In large part, this intelligence came from Chartbeat and a few other data collectors.

Chartbeat was soon being used by editors to decide which stories to assign and showcase based on traffic performance. Some reporters, who by and large were denied the data, became desperate to know how their stories were being rated. BuzzFeed, which used its own proprietary system to measure audience, actually published the numbers at the top of articles. Headlines were written to spur traffic to stories that sometimes bore little resemblance to these so-called "clickbait" teasers.

The little tech company that had invaded the news industry was improbably located above a mecca of the printed word, New York's Strand Bookstore, the famous redoubt of secondhand-book hoarders. It was the brainchild (some would say Frankenstein's monster) of a nonjournalist, Tony Haile, who launched the start-up after returning from an expedition to the North Pole. Haile's company had made a breakthrough discovery: its software could, in real time, provide objective answers to the age-old mystery of how to make an article "work," as in "get the reader to read it." Importance now lagged behind popularity.

Until Chartbeat the news media world had largely insulated itself from the changes it feared might be based on cold, hard numbers. Haile saw an opportunity to create a company that would challenge journalists' narrow-minded but deep-seated view that the scientific method had no place in the newsroom. To the contrary, he posited, there were data out there (if they could be winnowed properly) that stood to utterly overhaul the editorial process—for the better—so that the inevitably scattershot enterprise of covering the news of the world without knowing who was following it could become more efficient.

Chartbeat's selling point was that it tracked data in real time. Google's analytics program, a Chartbeat competitor, had all but monopolized the business of showing web editors how their site's content had performed in the past. This was helpful intel to have, for sure, but it empowered an editorial strategy that was still guesswork, backward-looking because it was based on past performance. The shortcoming of Google's service was that it left unanswered the question of what could be done to increase the chances of a story being read at the instant it got posted.

With Chartbeat, no longer would editors have to wait until readers were logged off to learn which content had won them over and which had missed its targets. Chartbeat told editors how many people were on their site at any given second, and which stories they were reading. It offered a digital dashboard that distilled a site's traffic data into three metrics: "Concurrents," "Recirculation," and "Engaged Time." Concurrents measured how many readers (or "heartbeats") were on the client's site, or story, at that moment. Recirculation calculated whether someone landing on a site would stay to read more than one piece of content or flee to another corner of the internet. Most important was Engaged Time: it distilled how worthy of human attention a given piece of content was. To arrive at the figure, Chartbeat wired its computers to pick up on a sophisticated set of cues from the reader— a jiggle of the mouse, a scroll either up or down, a moment of hovering the cursor over an image or a sentence—to determine where he or she had lost interest. Beyond showing how many users opened up a page, it could show how engaged they were once they did.

Chartbeat's algorithms powered programs that could show, with statistical significance, which one of the many conceivable headlines would produce the greatest number of eyeballs for a given story. And its intelligence went far beyond the headline. Chartbeat's data, Haile said, were "a collective map of readers' minds." Journalists were accustomed to entrusting editors to exercise their best judgment on behalf of the multitude of readers; now their profession would no longer require that leap of faith. They could simply click on the Chartbeat button and deploy what Haile was calling "the second-round edit." Haile touted this as *the* key not only to creating higher quality content but also to making it pay the bills.

This was a revolutionary change that made some editors, like Keller at the *Times*, deeply uneasy. Up to a point, he had little hesitation about data-driven changes, like search engine optimization. But Chartbeat could usher in what he feared: editing based solely on popularity. *Times* readers who paid $800 annually for home delivery and full digital packages were buying the paper's editorial judgment about what was important, not Chartbeat's. But even the *Times* published a list of the most emailed stories of the day on its website, and reporters used the list as a measure of what was most important, no matter how many times Keller told them not to.

At the *Post*, some reporters detected changes they were sure stemmed from Chartbeat and Narisetti's traffic board. Stories with little news value but a high human interest quotient were placed at the top of the homepage. Sensational stories, like the time uninvited guests barged into a White House dinner early in the Obama administration, were covered to death. Reporters groused that they would soon be asked to cover the Kardashians, but the changes wrought by Chartbeat were more subtle. The journalists themselves began internalizing its feedback.

Chartbeat's first client was Time.com; its second was the *Wall Street Journal*. And what Chartbeat told them was discouraging. Fully half of all readers who landed on a given web page gave it less than 15 seconds before moving on. "The challenge for people writing important stories," Haile counseled, "is to write them in a not-impenetrable way." Don't bury the lede, for example, but that had long been a trusted axiom; Chartbeat went further, making a case for doing away with anything that could be mistaken for background, context, or introduction.

The reality check didn't stop there. Haile informed publishers whose business models were based on getting readers to share their stories online, like BuzzFeed, "We've found effectively no correlation between social shares and people actually reading" the piece in question. If they weren't reading the article, it was also unlikely they were paying much attention to the ads running next to it.

While businesses in every other industry had long been using the web to monitor the relative success of their products, many legacy media refused to take their orders from market demand. But as their institutions bled cash at a life-threatening rate, the old-timers who might have argued for human judgment over that of a computer saw their standing erode. Their resistance didn't take along to crumble. The premise of Chartbeat was that the customer was always right, hardly an apostasy in the real world. It was similar to BuzzFeed's popularity contest stratagem.

Moreover print journalists craved feedback, a way to keep score. With no ratings, as television had, stories would go into the great beyond and get nothing back except a few letters or online comments from readers and maybe recognition from one's peers—hence the obsession with prizes. So both editors and writers got hooked on the stats. One study published in 2014 found that, overall, readers' clicks exerted more influence over the placement of news stories online than the other way around. This was a sea change. As the new measurability craze swept the sector, virtually every player found their priorities rearranged. At *Times* news meetings, what stories appeared on the website's "Most Emailed" list was obsessively discussed.

Chartbeat soon had retainer contracts as large as a million dollars a year from global companies like the *New York Times* to local papers like the *Oregonian*, which converted to Chartbeat's program wholesale and overhauled the reward system so that editors and reporters would be paid based on their Chartbeat scores.

Especially of note was the case of Gawker, a conglomerate of blogs considered pioneers of online gossip journalism, whose founder, Nick Denton, had anticipated a revolution in measurability and was now determined to profit from it. With Chartbeat's help, Gawker devised what it called the Big Board, a jumbotron version of the *Post*'s display, but with a decidedly personal twist: it rendered, in the form of a constantly updating leaderboard, the site's most popular content. It also displayed the ranking of the staffers themselves, with green "up" and red "down" arrows next to their names, like public commodities. And in a sense they were. The same ranking lived on Gawker's website, for all to see. Under Denton's new framework, the relative value of each and every staffer was a tidily discernible function of how many readers their content brought to the site. Denton used Chartbeat data to come up with a figure, called a CPM, which was the ratio of how much a staffer was getting paid to how many clicks he or she was bringing in, measured out to the penny. When assessing who was worth keeping and who should be cut, he had to look no further than the price tag affixed to every human head.

Haile compared what journalists did with his data to what lecturers do: "You see the eyes, the yawns, the texting in your audience, and you know you need to crack a joke, or go into greater depth on a certain point," he told me. "You mix it up to increase engagement." For some journalists, their Chartbeat score had become their first and last thought each day. It was an addiction, they said, as bad as crack cocaine. One writer called it "sanity-ruining." Another said he was talking to his shrink about his metrics.

Jonah Peretti called Haile an arms dealer, Haile told me glibly, and maybe he was. What Haile did, in effect, was arm every party in the conflict, so that by 2014 the leaders at 40 of the 50 most widely read publishers in America were glued to Haile's dials and diagrams, reshaping their newsrooms to hew ever closer to the machine's feedback to gain an edge over other newsrooms. The newsrooms, meanwhile, moved just as quickly and dispassionately toward that same goal, using the same tool. As I watched everyone line up behind the desk of Ian Fisher, the *Times* editor in charge of the homepage, who was one of the few with access to Chartbeat, I worried that we too had joined the race to the bottom.

Interestingly Haile himself came to have second thoughts about the popularity machine he had created and left Chartbeat in 2016 to launch a company, Scroll, that would devote itself to helping publishers monetize their more substantive stories, the ones Chartbeat had all but incentivized against. A click, after all, if the reader only glanced at a story and then clicked away to something else on another site, wasn't worth much to either the news site or its advertisers. Clicks did not measure engagement, the amount of time readers actually spent consuming an article, a video, or any other type of story. Engagement was the better value proposition. Haile decided he wanted to reeducate advertisers so that engagement, rather than clicks, would become the most important metric.

Narisetti had come to the *Post* to help Brauchli win clicks and engage readers, to navigate the vastly competitive field of digital news. He would do so by recruiting a cadre of digitally experienced editors and bloggers and would make room for them by buying out other journalists. Naturally this created even more resentment among the old guard.

One of his best hires was a 28-year-old Californian, Ezra Klein, who blogged for a boutique policy magazine called the *American Prospect*. Hired by Narisetti in 2009, Klein worked closely with Bell and wrote Wonkblog, which explained the news rather than presenting it. Bell helped power Wonkblog with the best technology, and together they developed a new visual system of explaining complex information and policy details. They would edit the information and present coherent information bullets on individual "cards." Readers loved them. Many people thought Klein had the best coverage of President Obama's complex health overhaul. Klein's fluid writing and original takes quickly made Wonkblog a major attraction on WashingtonPost.com.

Like Nate Silver, who had established his FiveThirtyEight blog before he joined the *Times*, Klein attracted a different audience to the *Post*. But also like Silver, Klein wanted to be his own brand. He was allowed to hire a staff of eight, while the rest of the staffing at the *Post* tightened. As his blog became better known, he also appeared in the *New Yorker* and on CNN. Anyone with an individual brand and proven audience was in high demand as digital news start-ups proliferated, on the left as well as on the right, where Breitbart News was gaining a foothold.

So it wasn't surprising that the *Post* could hold on to Klein for only three years before he and Bell left to create Vox. And they took their audience with them. The *Times* too lost Silver when he left for ESPN and eventually replaced him with a data-driven blog called the Upshot, which also often explained the news the way Klein did.

Thin staffing elsewhere at the *Post* was showing cracks in the editorial system where accuracy was at risk. BlogPOST, an aggregation of news stories trending elsewhere on the web, had a 20-something writer in charge of reglossing stories with a bit of her own reporting and fact-checking. She was processing and publishing as many as seven stories a day, totaling nearly 3,000 words written in great haste. There were bound to be problems with this kind of aggregation, which *Guardian* columnist Ben Goldacre called "flipping news burgers." One story BlogPOST recycled was a false account that Mitt Romney had used Ku Klux Klan slogans, resulting in an embarrassing editor's note and criticism from the *Post*'s ombudsman. This episode triggered a closed-door argument between Narisetti and Brauchli that many reporters could hear. Next the blog failed to credit a news organization for originally publishing a story. This time the young blogger resigned. The ombudsman said the editors, not the young journalist, deserved the blame, for failing to train and oversee the blogger.

While Bell had gloried in the early days of blogging, the work became drudgery for many young journalists, who never got out to cover real news events and spent their lives typing and rehashing news already published on the web. The Awl, a small online magazine that covered the mini-crisis, wrote knowingly, "The whole operation functions smoothly as long as the blogger-journalist doesn't make a mistake, because a mistake draws attention to the inherent cheapness of the product and the ethical dubiety of the entire process. You see, the Post wants to have its cake and other people's cake too, and to do so without damaging its brand as a purveyor of original cake."

Narisetti's team included Haik, another deputy editor whose title— executive producer, news innovations and strategic projects—left reporters and editors unsure where she ranked in the newsroom hierarchy, always a crucial concern at masthead-heavy newspapers. A native digerati, Haik stuck out in the *Post* newsroom. For one, she was young, had two-tone hair (with a scarlet streak), and wore extremely high heels and cool leopard-print dresses. She even wore a dress she had made out of newspapers to one of Weymouth's town hall presentations. She looked perfectly cast for her role as digital innovation czar, and she had the technical chops for the job. She was excited when veteran political reporter Dan Balz decided to give Snapchat a taste of the campaigns he covered.

I first met Balz in the late 1980s when he was strictly a pen-and-notepad guy, in the pre-internet era. He was a superb reporter dedicated to conveying the substance and importance of national politics. When I had coffee with Haik I couldn't help but think what Helen Dewar, a *Post* lifer who had covered the Senate for decades and looked down on anything faddish, would make of Haik or Balz on Snapchat.

Haik earned some measure of respect because she had come from the *Seattle Times*, where she had been the editor of the website. But almost every step forward in digital innovation was followed by a step backward. She developed her own data collector in 2012, measuring how many times the presidential candidates were mentioned on Twitter, to serve as an index of how much buzz they were generating. Called the MentionMachine, it produced data that ran at the end of news articles about the candidates. Haik considered it a big victory when Karen Tumulty, one of the senior political reporters, told her how cool she thought it was. But others thought it cheapened their coverage and was a trivial measurement of candidates.

The pressure to make the *Post* "cooler" for the digital era, to "innovate," increasingly distracted staffers from what had once been their sole focus: the story. Weymouth's team of Brauchli and Narisetti tried to squeeze new ideas, hopefully with dollars attached, out of their newsroom. Periodically they would suspend regular reporting duties for an all-hands-on-deck "hackathon," a brainstorming session they hoped would produce innovation, sessions that had proved fruitful at MIT, which had a "future of news" initiative. Reporters and editors were pressed into duty in the belief that their ideas could be better than those of the pricey consultants who took their fees, then admitted they too were stumped.

By this point the search for a magic bullet to fix a broken business model for news was playing out everywhere, often bringing together news and business executives in the newspaper industry. Many publishers concluded that the hunt was far more urgent than the old concept of the wall between news and business. The truth was that there was no model that would save the failing newspaper industry. Readers preferred to get the news on their computers, phones, and tablets; they no longer wanted their fingers blackened by newsprint. This reality wasn't going to change.

Still there was a human need for well-told, authoritative storytelling. That would never change. Saving newspapers was useless; saving journalism was vital. The riddle, of course, remained how to keep paying for the highest quality news-gathering until digital dimes became digital dollars. Hackathons never discovered a panacea. But there might be lots of little solutions that could add up to a big one.

So the *Post*'s staff was split into innovation teams to dream up new products. One of the better ideas came from Haik and Style-section editor Ned Martel, a feature that would give readers the backstory to how *Post* journalists got and reported their stories. It was a way of personalizing journalism, as bloggers did, and building reporters' profiles. (The *Times* later offered the same idea as a premium product on its website, called Times Insider.) But that idea got beaten out by another hackathon concept, an app that would deliver high school sports scores to readers based on their location, typical of the *Post*'s localized focus and unlikely to find a big digital audience.

For Weymouth and Brauchli the point was not the particular ideas, but getting everyone to think digitally and look out for new revenue streams. Though it was a painful and sometimes clumsy process, the leaders did succeed in improving the website. Don Graham said he was astounded by the creativity inside the *Post*. But this wasn't bringing in enough new money.

Narisetti had succeeded in his primary goal: increasing traffic to WashingtonPost.com. It rose by nearly 30 percent his first two years on the job, ranking second to the *New York Times* among U.S. newspapers' sites. In 2011 the *Post* had a record number of page views. Mobile traffic, which had been negligible, rose by 70 percent. But in the eyes of some of its longest-serving journalists, the improved numbers came at a steep price: the dumbing down of parts of the news report.

There were rumblings that a changing of the guard might be necessary. Narisetti had left, and Brauchli had become an isolated figure, often alone in his office or holed up in business strategy sessions or arguing with Hills about cuts. He often missed the afternoon news meeting, when the editors chose the stories for the front page and homepage. After deliberating, they would take the news agenda to Brauchli for his approval, and sometimes he would tear it up and keep editors late into the evening reshuffling pages and plans. The stain of Salongate was fading, anger over the cuts had turned into resignation, and Brauchli was commanding a bit more affection from his staff for standing up to Hills, a villain in the newsroom because he initiated most of the buyouts.

Another round of buyouts, the *Post*'s fifth since 2004, loomed and was expected to decimate the newsroom ranks. Brauchli wrote a memo to put the best face on it, describing "a limited staff reduction that won't affect the quality, ambition or authority of our journalism." He went on, "We believe this is possible, given the changes in how we work and the great successes we have had building our digital readership lately." But the old do-more-with-less bromide was hardly what the nervous newsroom wanted to hear.

Brauchli and Weymouth had inherited the sour economy, but they also were presiding over a diminished newspaper and depleting it further. Weymouth seemed unable to free herself from Hill's print-centric outlook. With her uncle insisting on holding up the profit margin for shareholders, investing to remain competitive with the *Times* seemed out of the question. Morale sagged when Shadid, an incredibly talented Middle East reporter and winner of two Pulitzers, defected to the *Times* in 2009. Balz, besides Broder the biggest name in politics, considered decamping to Reuters in 2011 and agreed to reconsider only after a much younger *Post* political reporter flew to Iowa to implore him to stay. There were a few additions, like Tumulty, who escaped from the shrinking ambitions of *Time*, and stars like Eugene Robinson and Bob Woodward still burned brightly. But other publishers in Washington, like David Bradley, who purchased the *Atlantic* and expanded it into a digital force, and Politico's owner Allbritton, had scored successes. Commentators weighed in, by turns gloating and rueful, to pronounce the end of the era of the *Post* as a first-tier American newspaper. It had declined, James Fallows wrote in the *Atlantic*, "in talent level, depth and breadth of reporting, international coverage, sophistication, and all the other measures of a nationally ambitious operation." And he was an admirer.

The rest of the newspaper industry still respected the Graham family. The Post Company was also envied because it seemed to have a lifeline through its ownership of Stanley Kaplan, the test-prep company that had grown into an education conglomerate. Arthur Sulzberger Jr. would sometimes muse, "I wish we had a Kaplan." But in 2011 Kaplan's fortunes were reversed by a new slate of regulations initiated by the Obama administration and approved by Congress that impacted the for-profit education sector, where Kaplan was a leader. In the third quarter of the year, Kaplan's revenues tumbled 79 percent, as did its reputation. The lifeline was gone.

The revenue flowing into Kaplan came almost entirely from taxpayers; over 90 percent was in the form of federal grants, like the Pell and Stafford, and funding under the GI Bill for military. The main problem with the for-profit sector, of which Kaplan was one of the largest players, was that students took out large, taxpayer-backed loans and often defaulted on repaying them after they graduated or when they dropped out of the program.

President Obama appointed Robert Shireman, a former head of an industry watchdog group, as deputy undersecretary of education, and when the market closed that day, an index of education company stocks had dropped almost seven points. One of the new regulations he successfully pushed cut federal funding from institutions that saddled their students with debt without leading them to better financial prospects.

As new regulations took effect, the savvy analysts on Wall Street sniffed out a looming disaster for education businesses, and short-sellers began to swarm. Meanwhile operatives working for the Government Accountability Office were conducting an undercover investigation of the for-profit education sector. With hidden cameras affixed to their ball caps, agents posed as prospective students and sat down with recruiters across the country, including two employed by Kaplan, in Florida and California. The footage they recorded could not have been more damning. Not only were Kaplan representatives pushing burdensome loans on unsuspecting students who didn't have the means to repay them; they were using below-the-belt tactics to lure them in.

Recruiters would say anything for a sale. Prospective students considering the massage therapy program at a Kaplan school in California, for example, were promised that with Kaplan degrees, they would land

$100-an-hour jobs, despite the fact that 90 percent of massage therapists in the state earned less than $34 an hour. When students expressed doubts about taking on so much debt to go to school, Kaplan recruiters assured them that *nobody* pays back student loans. One recruiter told undercover agents that he himself wasn't planning to pay back the $85,000 he owed in student loans because, he said, "tomorrow's never promised."

Graham took on the assault and was passionate in his defense of Kaplan. He appeared when evidence was presented to the Senate Committee on Health, Education, Labor, and Pensions to show that these were simply a few bad apples. He fervently believed Kaplan opened the door to higher education for low-income students who otherwise would not have been admitted. These were precisely the people he had protected as a D.C. cop.

But try as he might to defend Kaplan, a caucus of former Kaplan reps had been waiting in the wings and now came forward to corroborate the condemnatory video footage. "They are not outliers," said one former admissions officer, and dozens more testified similarly. Soon Kaplan was facing lawsuits in four different states where whistleblowers filed cases under the False Claims Act.

The Department of Education concluded that fully two-thirds of Kaplan students dropped out before graduating, and nearly one-third defaulted on their student loans within three years. Kaplan was not the only company setting financial traps, but it was one of the largest, and with the fate of the newspaper riding on it, it had the most to lose.

As Congress considered taking legislative action, Graham took up lobbying for his company's cause with a zeal unmatched by anyone else in the industry. He wrote an op-ed for the *Wall Street Journal* imploring lawmakers to refrain from further regulations in order to "avoid disaster for low-income students." He traipsed up and down the marble corridors of Capitol Hill like the lobbyists his own paper sometimes skewered. He went out and hired new lobbyists, including a former aide to President Obama, and marshaled them for the fight of his career.

The other weapon in the Washington Post Company's arsenal was, of course, the *Washington Post*. Though most of the paper's articles on the issue took care to disclose the conflict of interest, the *Post* nevertheless came under criticism for offering scant coverage in the first place (though it did do a thorough investigation, asking "How did we get here?" in 2011). When the paper did run an editorial, it advocated Graham's side. Some staffers proposed bringing in a team of independent reporters to cover the for-profit education area, but nothing ever came of the idea.

In a sense, it hardly mattered what the newspaper did at this juncture. Kaplan had kept the *Washington Post* afloat for years. Now the education business too, that buoy, was severely wounded. Following the sting investigation, the number of new students enrolled in Kaplan colleges plummeted by nearly half, while revenues fell by more than three-quarters. In the span of four months, its stock price dropped by nearly one-fourth. The fall from grace awakened *Post* executives to the necessity of reforming the way Kaplan did business, but onlookers were appalled that it took a congressional investigation and sting operation to effect those changes.

With the Kaplan lifeboat also taking on water, Graham's business was now really sinking. The newspaper was building digital scale but not seeing nearly enough revenue from digital advertising space, which clients were increasingly purchasing programmatically through the tycoons of web real estate, Google and Facebook. The *Post*'s union rep dismissed the company's digital strategy. "We seem to be committed to indiscriminate traffic," he said.

There was no sign that the digital strategy of expanding audience was paying off. After opposing a paywall for many years, Graham and Weymouth decided that it was time to erect one in order to start selling digital subscriptions to readers. But the wall was so porous that few readers ever encountered it or were even aware of it, and even fewer felt moved to pony up for unrestricted access. And unlike the strategy Sulzberger pursued, resisting deep cuts and preserving quality and then asking readers to pay, it was hard to get readers to pay for a diminished product.

Meanwhile the newsroom was rebelling against further cuts. In April 2012 Bradley Graham (no relation to Don), a former national security reporter who had left the *Post* years earlier and was close to Hills, arranged an attempted detente. He invited about a dozen of his former colleagues, including respected members of the old guard like Dana Priest and Carol Leonnig and David Finkel, to a dinner with Hills. Brauchli did not attend. His relationship with Hills was in tatters.

Unhappily the discussion quickly turned contentious. The reporters questioned whether the *Post* was still committed to rigorous journalism, especially its hallmark, investigative reporting. One of the paper's best diggers, Jim Grimaldi, had recently defected to the *Journal*. Hills pronounced that he had little interest in winning awards and put his foot in his mouth when, in talking about the paper's local strategy, he seemed to compare the *Post* to the *Dayton Daily News*, a small paper no one outside of Ohio ever read. And it too was failing.

A crisis point was reached, and Weymouth had to face the hard truth that she had made a poor choice in selecting Brauchli, an outsider, to lead her destabilized newspaper. By October 2012 the rumor mill had caught wind that Brauchli's days were numbered. While Hills made it plain that the headcount would have to shrink, Brauchli staunchly resisted further cuts, which won him the sympathy and support of a newsroom that had at first treated him as the victor in a hostile takeover. But now that he was practically at war with Hills, Weymouth knew she needed a new editor. She was clearheaded when it came to recognizing mistakes and brave about changing course. When she told her uncle she needed to switch horses, his response was "Don't fuck it up twice." Like Downie, Brauchli would be given a cushy job upstairs working with Graham on digital acquisitions. It was the second time in four years he had been shown to a gold-plated exit.

On her second try she would make her best decision, one that would not only steady the paper but also strengthen it for battles with another White House administration blind to the need for a free press. She waited until after the day of Obama's reelection to announce her choice: Marty Baron, the editor of the *Boston Globe*. Baron was reserved and contemplative, known as a leader with flawless news judgment. At the *Globe* he'd resisted draconian cuts proposed by the owners at the New York Times Company while overseeing the creation of a financially viable website in Boston.com. During a bitter strike at the *Globe*, the owners had given him virtually no support. But the reporters in Boston revered him.

Baron was famous for the *Globe*'s hard-won exposé of rampant pedophilia among Boston's Catholic clergy, a courageous undertaking by the investigative team that won a Pulitzer Prize for public service and became the subject of the movie *Spotlight*. The *Post*'s old guard was thrilled with the choice.

Weymouth would barely get the chance to know him. While his arrival had given ballast to her newsroom, the business side was tanking. Just as Baron was settling in that fall, she was reviewing the grim forecast for the coming year. The following years looked no brighter. The downward trajectory seemed irreversible, even with rising web traffic and new digital products that held some promise.

At one of their regular review sessions, she and her uncle discussed a radical notion: if they could no longer guide the *Post* into a secure future, why not think of selling the company? The point of the Graham family owning the *Post*, she had grown up hearing, was doing what was best for the newspaper and serving its customers. Sitting across from Don at a restaurant she said, "The world I see already is one of unending cost cuts, and at some point it's not going to be the *Post* we all know and love." It was wrenching, but he had to agree. Never before had they considered selling the paper, but seven straight years of revenue losses will, as Don would later say repeatedly, "focus the mind." Without the solutions that would enable growth, further decline was inevitable. Already they were doing more with less, especially in pushing new digital initiatives. He had been impressed with the number of new innovations, but they would never fill the hole left by all the print losses. Although Weymouth had returned the *Post* to positive cash flow, cutting was the main route to this success and its problems were secular, not cyclical. She told her uncle she would do whatever he wanted, but she knew that making even deeper cuts would break his heart too. She was already looking haggard: her girl posse was worried about the pressure on her.

There was no getting around the fact that under Graham and Weymouth's leadership, even in an industry facing deadly disruption, the *Post* was doing worse than many of its less distinguished competitors. The family had been good stewards through almost all of their 80-year run as publishers, but now they were done. It would be up to someone else to figure out a fix for the business model. New ownership might also provide new investment. But despite every rational argument in favor of selling, the prospect was still unfathomable. As one *Post* writer put it, "From Eugene Meyer to Philip L. Graham to Katharine Graham to Donald E. Graham to Katharine Weymouth, it was always a question of when power would shift from one generation to the next, not whether it would." Family ownership was a given. Alongside the Sulzbergers, the Grahams were journalism's remaining royalty.

Weymouth thought of her great-grandfather. Perhaps what the *Post* needed now was the very same thing it had needed in 1933, when it had gone bankrupt: a rich new owner who would take the company private while it was under repair. If such a person could be found, the Post Company would not be at the mercy of quarterly earnings and shareholders.

Once the idea of selling was on the table, the Grahams never really looked back. The only other member of the family who was deeply tied to the company's affairs was Don's sister and Katharine's mother, Lally Weymouth, a New Yorker whose pieces on foreign leaders sometimes ran in the editorial section and occasionally on the front page. Her family sinecure paid $300,000, not a lot of money for someone who lived lavishly in New York and Southampton, but enough that journalists at the *Post* complained.

She backed the decision to sell. Even if the paper drew a low price, their fortunes would be secured forever.

In December, Graham told the board of directors. He also told Warren Buffett, still a big shareholder, who approved if they found an owner who was committed to the long-term life of the paper and its editorial independence. Other papers had been bought by local billionaires who either abandoned them after a few years of losses or used them to push their agenda.

To begin a discreet search for the proper white knight, the Grahams tapped Nancy Peretsman of Allen & Co., a top Wall Street banker and a specialist in internet and media deals. Buffett was high on Peretsman, who had been a budding star at Salomon Brothers, the investment bank in which he was a large investor, before she joined forces with Herbert Allen. It was Peretsman who placed the first call to Amazon CEO Jeff Bezos, a casual friend of Graham's for 15 years, to tell him the *Post* was for sale.

He was one of about a dozen people either she or Graham approached. "Don's looking for the right person," she told Bezos. "No Murdoch. No Kochs. No ideologues." And no private equity guys, Graham had told her, because he could not bear to see his family jewel bought only to be hollowed out and flipped.

Starting with Bill Gates in the early 1990s, Graham sought advice from people who were deep in digital technology. The circle expanded to include Steve Case, Ted Leonsis, Steve Jobs, Reid Hoffman, Sheryl Sandberg and Dave Goldberg, and, of course, Zuckerberg. This was how Graham had first come to know Bezos too.

Bezos was surprised by the call. "Why would I even be a candidate to buy the *Post*?" he asked Peretsman. "I don't know anything about the newspaper industry." He seemed cool to the idea. But he'd known about the *Post* since he was a kid and had watched the Watergate hearings on television, lying on the floor of the living room next to his grandfather. The bald but boyish-looking 49-year-old was a notoriously competitive businessman, and people close to him spoke of his peculiar fascination with broken business models. He was intrigued enough about the telephone call to begin looking at some research on the decline of newspapers and wondered whether the *Post*, having been cut to the quick, could ever fully heal. On the other hand, he knew from Amazon's book sales and his success with the Kindle tablet that people were reading more than ever.

Bezos was also notoriously press shy. Most people had no idea what he looked like, and stories about his retail empire almost always contained the line "Amazon declined to comment." But he was a vigorous defender of the First Amendment and had fought efforts to ban controversial books, like Hitler's *Mein Kampf*, from public libraries. Press freedom also aligned with his libertarianism. Bezos wasn't political in a partisan sense. He'd contributed to a few Democratic candidates but also Libertarian Party presidential candidate Gary Johnson and the libertarian Reason Institute. He cared most about issues like gay marriage and had spent millions to help pass an initiative legalizing gay marriage in Washington State. He wasn't the type to interfere with the paper's editorial independence, or at least he didn't seem to be. So he fit Graham's requirement.

Before he could consider the purchase, Bezos said, he would have to answer three essential questions. He called them "gates" he needed to clear. First, was the *Post* still a serious, important institution whose lost luster could be restored? Second, could he be optimistic about the future of the *Post* when the internet had just about destroyed its business? Third, could he *personally* add the value and technical knowledge needed to reverse its downward spiral?

Like Buffett, he invested for the long term. His focus on customer service was maniacal. Besides its giant retail services, Amazon also made billions from offering cloud computing. In both areas Bezos focused on providing a great and frictionless user experience. His strategy was to build a mammoth customer base and huge size. Amazon's profit margin was thin, but Bezos was patient about profits as he built scale. These approaches could help revive the *Post*.

Building Amazon had been an incredible feat. The Everything Store, as it was known, now accounted for almost half of every dollar spent online. Its market capitalization was more than $300 billion, making it one of the most valuable companies in the world. (In 2018 its market valuation would hit a trillion dollars.) More than 90 percent of its value was due to profits expected almost a decade later.

Not everything Bezos invested in succeeded, but the vast majority did. The best known of his passion projects was the space travel company Blue Origin, which expected to send paying customers into suborbital space by 2019. (Bezos himself had nearly died in a helicopter crash in 2003 while scouting a location for the company's launchpad over west Texas.) He also invested in an underground clock that was supposed to continue keeping time for 10,000 years.

Bezos had been the ultimate disrupter, while the *Post* had its ingrained ways that might prove to be intractable. Over the spring and summer he spoke again with Peretsman and then with Graham, but there were long gaps between the calls, so Graham was never sure how serious he was. He had convinced Bezos that newspaper industry knowledge was far less important than knowing the internet, which some argued that Bezos had mastered, or at least monetized, better than anyone else.

He had the head of an engineer and the heart of an adventurer. Ultimately Bezos was convinced that the *Post* would be a terrific premium offering for the Kindle and Prime. Restoring its glory would be a contribution to democracy.

Graham and Bezos agreed to talk further at the annual media summit in Sun Valley they would both be attending, along with most of the rest of the media industry's upper crust. There hadn't been so much as a peep that Graham had decided to sell, nor that Bezos might be his white knight. There could hardly have been a more fraught setting for this sensitive conversation with such a concentration of would-be outbidders.

Among those at the elite gathering were John and Linda Henry of Boston, who had already purchased the Boston Red Sox from the *Times* during Sulzberger's fire sale and who were now contemplating taking the distressed *Boston Globe* off his hands too. Henry asked Graham confidentially whether he thought buying the *Globe* was a sensible move. "Well, it depends on how much you want to pay for it," Graham responded. He didn't think it would be a good investment. Henry confided that his offer would be around $70 million, a pittance of what the *Times* had originally paid. Graham was expecting to get at least $250 million for the *Post*, also a fraction of what it would have fetched a decade earlier. If the lowball figure in Boston got out it could drive down Graham's asking price, so he asked the Henrys to keep their plans quiet. As things turned out, their purchase of the *Globe* became public three days before Bezos's acquisition of the *Post* did, but the price was never an issue for Bezos. (Graham was right that the Henrys would have a rocky financial ride with their acquisition.)

After just two meetings Graham gave Bezos time to review some financial statements. When Graham came back to him with what he thought was a fair selling price Bezos did not blink. With a $25.2 billion personal fortune, the purchase represented 1 percent of his net worth, a rounding error for the world's then-19th-richest man. (At the time, Carlos Slim was number one.) Bezos did not bargain. He did not have his bankers and lawyers do due diligence. He would be buying the *Post* personally, not through Amazon, in part to avoid conflicts of interest. Having decided that his three gates had been cleared, there was nothing left to negotiate.

As the deal was being finalized, it seemed a good omen that the *Post* unearthed its biggest scoop since Watergate. Barton Gellman, well known as a national security expert and one of the big talents who had left the paper in 2010, returned as a freelancer with something huge for Marty Baron. He had a source at the NSA who wanted the world to know about his agency's secret use of widespread domestic spying, aided by most major tech companies, which had been turning over private communications to the government. It was on a scale no one imagined. Gellman's source, who turned out to be Snowden, had decided not to take his stolen documents to the *New York Times*, having seen them hold their earlier NSA story so long. Through filmmaker Laura Poitras, a national security expert, Snowden had also approached the *Guardian*, the British paper that had published Wikileaks. Gellman wanted institutional backing in the U.S., and it made sense to bring the story to his former employer.

Baron had been at the *Post* only a few months when Gellman handed him the kind of story editors dream of. He had come into a cache of classified documents, he told the new executive editor, and would use them to tell an earth-shattering story, but only on the condition that he, Gellman, got final say as to which papers the public saw and which editors would be assigned to him. Baron, like Bezos, did not call in the lawyers. He simply told Gellman, "That will work," and soon he was seeing the astounding reach of the NSA's domestic spying, with trapdoors into Facebook, phone providers, and other places where consumers had no idea their data were being seen by the government. The Snowden NSA stories would affirm for Bezos that he was through his first gate: the *Post* was still an important institution. The run of Snowden scoops, and another big story that forced out the governor of Virginia, made it clear that if reporters were deployed in the right way by the right editor, the paper still had plenty of juice.

A few weeks passed before the deal went public. Graham, the consummate gentleman, phoned Arthur Sulzberger Jr. with the news before he made the announcement. Then he went to the newspaper plant to tell the printers in person, and to thank them. Some had been with the company for decades.

In the late afternoon of August 5, 2013, Graham gathered everyone at the *Post* to make what he called "the most surprising and shocking announcement." In a gray suit and a red power tie, he began his nine-minute address in a steady voice, but it was cracking with emotion by the end. He had never imagined he'd be standing there, in the building he'd first entered as a three-year-old to watch Harry Truman's inaugural parade, to say goodbye. He outlined why he'd decided to sell and why Bezos was the right man to lead the paper into the future.

Family ownership no longer served the *Post*. He and Weymouth were facing questions to which he confessed they "did not have the answers." After seven years of revenue losses, there would have had to be more cutting, and he no longer believed such measures would permit the *Post* to continue to be the paper it once had been. He assured everyone that while it technically could have survived without a sale, "we wanted more for the *Post*. We wanted it to be successful." He reminded everyone that Buffett thought Bezos was the best CEO in America and that he was famous for patiently investing for years in order to solve problems. His voice shook noticeably as he said, "This may be a crucially good day for the *Post*." He thanked many reporters by name as well as his niece, whom he praised for returning the paper to "cash-flow profitability" well before the three-year deadline he had given her. Perhaps because it would have made him even more emotional, he did not invoke his mother. He announced that Bezos intended to keep the management team of Weymouth, Steve Hills, Marty Baron, and editorial page editor Fred Hiatt.

Then Weymouth stood to read a statement from Bezos, who had decided not to appear that day but would meet his new employees in a few weeks. He had written the remarks himself and began reassuringly, "The values of *The Post* do not need changing. The paper's duty will remain to its readers and not to the private interests of its owners." There was the requisite Watergate invocation: "While I hope no one ever threatens to put one of my body parts through a wringer, if they do, thanks to Mrs. Graham's example, I'll be ready." (Attorney General John Mitchell had threatened that if the Watergate coverage continued, Katharine Graham would have her "tit in a wringer." A dentist subsequently sent her a gold charm of a wringer he had fashioned, and Art Buchwald gave her a little breast to go with it.) With the rate of technological change transforming everything in the business, he stressed the need to experiment.

Media analyst John Morton summed up the stunned reaction to news of the sale, saying it was all but unimaginable: "The newspaper is the basic foundation not only of the company but of the family. The only family that would be less likely to sell its principal asset would be the Sulzbergers at the *New York Times*." Indeed, within days Sulzberger sent a note to his staff assuring them that the family had no intention of selling the *Times*.

When Bezos made his entrance in early September for two days of whirlwind meetings, he knew what notes to hit. At a town hall with employees, he spoke at length and without any prepared remarks. The sound system gave him some trouble, but he seemed confident and jovial, sometimes exploding into loud laughter at his own jokes. The presence of 92-year-old Ben Bradlee, Bob Kaiser, Len Downie, and Bob Woodward gave the debut a sense of history and gravitas. Bezos understood that they symbolized the *Post*'s glory, but also had made the paper resistant to change.

"You have to figure out: How can we make the new thing? Because you have to acknowledge that the physical print business is in structural decline," he said. "You can't pretend that that's not the case. You have to accept it and move forward. . . . The death knell for any enterprise is to glorify the past, no matter how good it was, especially for an institution like *The Washington Post*, which has such a hallowed past." Any company that dwelled on its past would become Woolworth's, Bezos often said. All companies should stay "forever young," he added, invoking the Bob Dylan song. He stressed the importance of investigative reporting. Though he did not say the newsroom would be given new resources to grow, he indicated the years of cutting had ended. He wasn't moving from his Washington to theirs, nor would he try to "out-Don Don." He had "to do this as Jeff."

Before the town hall with everyone, Bezos invited Woodward to join him for a one-on-one breakfast in what had once been Don Graham's grand old dining room. The reporter brought with him a list of 14 points, printed out. They represented his suggestions for a distinctly new direction.

Item No. 1 was frank and made clear he was no revanchist: "The Grahams never asked enough of people. Ask for more."

No 3: "Harness the reporting capacity, especially on the White House, CIA, NSA, the Defense establishment."

No. 13 on the surface sounded a bit blasphemous in the internet era: "For reporters our initial customers are our sources." That is, those who provide the information need to have total faith in the incorruptibility of the product. Not only was this a mission that the newsroom would embrace; it was also a smart business principle, showing how great journalism and financial survival were linked. It was a mantra that Bezos, the customer guru, could grasp and was likely to get behind. It opposed the Chartbeat school of thought, which treated the reader, the "user," as the only customer worth serving, to the detriment of quality and civic-mindedness.

No. 5 was more actionable: "Buffett recommendation to Katharine Weymouth." In code, this was a suggestion she be replaced. After Buffett had stepped down from the board in 2011, he made known his professional opinion that for the good of the *Post*, she should step aside, should her family ever sell. It wasn't that either Buffett or Woodward thought she was a bad publisher but that she symbolized the past and therefore would not be the best person to serve the new owner. Bezos decided to give her a chance to prove herself and, for the sake of continuity, promised to keep her on the job for his first year of ownership.

Weymouth seemed to flourish in that year. She offered no resistance when Bezos completely upended her local strategy and decided that, like Amazon, the *Post* needed scale to succeed and had the talent to mount a real challenge to the *Times* with national and international coverage. In fact Weymouth seemed liberated by his grander vision for the newspaper. The *Post* was no longer merely for and about Washington. Bezos's limitless pockets also made life easier for the publisher.

He invited her, Hills, Baron, and Shailesh Prakash, the paper's extremely talented chief technology officer, whom Bezos saw right away was a kindred spirit, out to his 29,000-square-foot estate in the ultra-wealthy enclave of Medina, Washington, where the *Post* contingent camped out in the grand boathouse, with a view of 200 yards of shoreline. For breakfast in the main house, Bezos flipped pancakes, while one of his four kids made a sauce from fresh berries. The pod dubbed themselves the Pancake Group, and Weymouth seemed to fit right in.

Then, on August 18, 2014, Bezos came to Washington, D.C., for what was assumed to be a routine budget meeting. Weymouth's team always prepared assiduously for these sessions, writing up six-page memos that Bezos told them he preferred to the charts Hills had always demanded. After reviewing the budget, Bezos asked to meet privately with Weymouth in her office. He told her that she was being replaced by Fred Ryan, the publisher of Politico, the news site that had stolen the *Post*'s talent and cachet in political journalism. Katharine Graham had known Ryan when he was Ronald Reagan's chief of staff after the president left the White House.

The choice of Ryan, viewed by some as a political has-been who was not the real driving force behind Politico, was surprising and disappointing to some who expected Bezos to appoint a digital visionary to lead the operation. Bezos and Ryan were only casual acquaintances, having been recently introduced by Jean Case, the wife of AOL cofounder Steve Case, after a black-tie gala at which Ryan spoke up for the job.

Ryan was a Reagan man through and through, a White House aide during the administration and the Reagans' chief of staff after they returned to California. He'd been the titular head of the Reagan Presidential Library since it opened and presided at the gala commemoration of Reagan's 100th birthday in 2011. Despite his association with Politico his name was associated with the pre-digital era. After leaving the Reagans, he'd mostly run the broadcasting side of the Allbritton media empire until focusing on Politico. He was a nice, jocular man liked by people from both parties in Washington, an increasing rarity.

What Ryan brought to the publisher's job was deep connections to the Washington establishment, almost as strong as those of the Grahams themselves. Presiding over his new property from Seattle, Bezos had few ties to the other Washington. Ryan knew practically everyone in town, whether through his directorship of the White House Historical Association and Ford's Theater or his service as secretary of the tony Alfalfa Club. Having turned his back on the Grahams' local strategy for the *Post* and expanded its national and global profile, Bezos needed someone to tend the backyard. Ryan was practically born in black tie. And although Bezos hired him to be the face of the *Post* in Obama's Washington, Ryan's Republican pedigree would prove useful when Trump and the Republicans took back the White House.

Bezos was willing to let Weymouth control the timing of the story and say that she had decided to step down. When she sent a note to the staff at 9 a.m. on September 2, she left those details nebulous, saying that after 17 years at the *Post*, seven of them as publisher, it was time for her to "explore other opportunities." She made a special point of saying how proud she was of having shepherded the shift to digital. "We have made the transition to the digital era, and we've done it so successfully that in a time when many media companies seem positioned for retreat, we are positioned for opportunity," she wrote, graciously adding, in classic Graham form, "That's something for all of us to take pride in, and it couldn't have happened without every one of you."

Weymouth was wounded, but she held her cards close. Her mother, who worked in the same office as a senior advertising executive at the *Post*, was less restrained; her anger was palpable. Right after she was let go, Weymouth headed over to the hospital, to the bedside of Cory Haik's daughter, who had been badly burned at a bonfire. Weymouth's own daughter, younger than Haik's, had suffered an accident in which one of her arms had been badly hurt and for which she had undergone surgery and other treatments. The injury had kept Weymouth away from the office for many days. So, despite whatever hurt she was feeling, it was important to her to show support to her friend. "It was way beyond the call," Haik said years later, her voice quavering.

When Ben Bradlee died in October, Woodward emailed Bezos to impress upon him that the funeral would be a significant moment in the life of the paper. "On my way," Bezos promptly emailed back. As the dirges sounded from the Neo-Gothic spires of Washington National Cathedral, Bezos stood shaking hands with dignitaries, including Vice President Joe Biden, Supreme Court Justice Stephen Breyer, and his new competitors, Sulzberger and Baquet. Don Graham was the first speaker, hailing Bradlee as a man even greater than his storied reputation. Weymouth was visibly moved during the service. For her, Don, and most everyone else in attendance, Bradlee's passing was the symbolic coda to the Graham era.

Bezos's promise to Baron and Ryan was that he would "provide the runway" for the *Post* to restore its journalism and he could add the best technology to truly complete its digital transformation. But in no way did he view the purchase as an act of charity. He was in it to make money, not right away but soon. Still, it was a fundamental principle of business, he knew, that you have to spend money to make money. So Baron went on a hiring spree and added 70 people in the first year and a half, to bring the newsroom headcount back to 700. He hired five new political reporters, not only to compete with Politico but also to restore morale by showing they were back at the top of campaign coverage. He did not revive everything that had been cut, however. The old domestic bureaus remained shuttered, but Baron expanded the *Post*'s national reach without them, hiring specialists in key areas, like a new technology reporter in Silicon Valley.

The simple fact of new faces around the office was a shot in the arm for a newsroom whose reporters had spent too long wondering anxiously if they would be the next to go. So was the spike in traffic they saw under Bezos, attributable mainly to the website's new practice of publishing content in the early morning, when audience attention was at its peak. In October 2015, exactly a year after Bezos officially took control, the *Post* actually passed the *Times* in unique monthly users. The victory was by a hair, according to the analytics firm comScore—66.9 million to 65.8 million—but for the *Post* it was an almost 60 percent increase over the previous year. The next month the *Post* widened its lead and even surpassed the traffic behemoth BuzzFeed. The only American news site that attracted a larger audience was CNN.com, with more than 1.4 billion page views.

Bezos took out ads cheekily proclaiming that the *Post* was "the new publication of record." That was overreach, but the *Times* understood the message for what it was, the start of an old-fashioned newspaper war that would end up making both publications stronger and reestablishing their importance. The energy had returned, as blogger Chris Cillizza tweeted, and there was "no more exciting place to work in journalism right now." While others proclaimed the *Post*'s brand was back in action, Baron preferred to think of it as the paper's soul.

Baron also lost some talent, but the defections simply reflected the natural churn in the dynamic digital news world, with new start-ups sprouting up left and right. While Vox poached Klein and Bell, a news site called Mic, aimed at recent college grads, snagged Haik. Another digital editor returned to the Huffington Post. (The *Times*, meanwhile, lost almost every member of the Innovations Committee.)

When Baron traveled to Amazon headquarters in Bellevue, Washington, for one of the first times, Bezos stressed the need to hire the best engineers and to have them embedded right beside the journalists. So new engineers, 35 of them, came on board. This further empowered Prakash, a Graham holdover, newly energized in the Bezos era as chief information officer. He pushed hard to have the newsroom adopt what he called "a product mindset." He believed that content was king, but that it made no sense to have good content without a sleek and fast-loading web design. Baron disliked industry jargon, especially the word "content," which had supplanted "story" or plain "journalism." But in Prakash he had found a perfect partner to mesh journalism with product design.

The presence of the new engineering team changed the job of being a *Post* reporter, with remarkably little backlash in the process. The reporters learned to embed photos and videos in their stories and began using hyperlinks to cite other articles. They got comfortable using a new tool called Bandito, developed by Prakash's team, which allowed them to test various headline options, blurbs, and images to determine which ones would propel the story to social media virality. Bandito even went beyond Chartbeat's headline automator in that after determining which headline package worked best, Bandito applied the insight without needing to get the human editor's approval first.

Baron and Prakash easily forged their partnership because they shared a sense of mission. "One thing I've found is very important is that journalism is cause-operated," asserted Prakash. "Most of us believe if tomorrow *The Washington Post* disappeared it would be bad for society. That cause is important." Bezos agreed.

Metrics by themselves did not constitute a mission, as the uprising against Narisetti had demonstrated. Prakash's Bandito, by contrast, was accepted because he framed it as part of the mission. It got people to read important articles in a news-drenched environment. Prakash also benefited from his timing. By 2015 even the *Times* was incentivizing its reporters with daily metrics reports; keeping score was now a fact of life in newsrooms.

Despite the *Post*'s digital strides, however, its print circulation continued to decline. The roughly 432,000 copies printed most days was half of what the daily circulation was at its peak in 1993. But as long as the paper was quickly expanding its digital readership, the decline in print seemed inevitable to Bezos, who said he thought that one day the print newspaper would become an exotic luxury item, like a horse.

He wanted the *Post* to be attracting the greatest possible number of readers, but he did not believe in the digital mantra that news should be free. He thought people should pay for what they read, but maybe not all of them, and maybe not just yet. Bezos's basic idea for the *Post* was the same one that guided Amazon: get big fast. That was the reason behind abandoning Graham's insistence on being local. On the web, people who read the news wanted national stories from national, or international, outlets.

At the hip South by Southwest tech conference in Austin, Texas, Prakash and Baron previewed another new metrics tool called Loxodo. It was a giant metrics board that allowed journalists to see, in more or less real time, how their versions of stories compared with the same ones done by competitors. If the *Post* stories lagged, the newsroom could quickly figure out why and make adjustments accordingly.

Bezos, Baron, and Prakash decided to go all in with Facebook Instant articles, fast-loading versions of *Post* stories that were published on Facebook. They gave Facebook everything rather than a select number of stories to share for free on the social network, as the *Times* did. (The *Times* thought Facebook's free distribution of everything would erode the paper's cachet and also anger the people paying for it.) The *Post* was also able to sell its new content management system, Arc, to other news organizations because its functionality was so good.

The new app Prakash helped design was extremely attractive, with large photos zooming bigger as readers scrolled down their mobile screens. Besides being more visual—a necessity to attract younger readers, as BuzzFeed had long ago figured out—it contained noticeably more stories that were pure clickbait, which did worry some in the newsroom. "Doctors Were Startled to Find the Cause of This 24-Year-Old's Excruciating Pain," read one such headline. Lots of headlines were straight out of the Matt Stopera frame book at BuzzFeed, with the tease, "This Is What Happened

Next." But no one was complaining about dancing bears anymore. The *Post* needed some clickbait to achieve scale and keep Bezos happy. As long as Baron was being given the resources for great investigative and political reporting, he could stomach the clickbait.

Each time the *Post* beat out the *Times* in the monthly traffic contest, there was jubilation. At the Pulitzers in 2013, the *Times* took home only prizes for its photography, while the *Post* shared the grand prize, Public Service, with the *Guardian* for their Snowden coverage. Soon, Baron would be played by Liev Schreiber, a muscular actor with a strong jaw typically cast in superhero roles, in *Spotlight*. So as Baron went about the duties of editing the presumptive new paper of record, he was followed around by Schreiber, who studied his movements and mannerisms carefully. *Spotlight* would win the Academy Award for Best Picture, and Hollywood would once again make the *Washington Post*'s leader the most well-known editor in America. *Esquire* called him the best editor of his generation, the worthy heir of Ben Bradlee.

PART THREE

CHAPTER NINE

FACEBOOK

L ike Bezos, Mark Zuckerberg had built an online empire by knowing everything about internet users' and customers' desires and serving them constantly, whether in sight or out of view. The reality of incessant corporate surveillance did not even seem all that creepy anymore. By the time Bezos bought the *Washington Post*, web surfers had by and large ceased questioning the fact that the information they encountered was being mediated by warehouses of supercomputers on the West Coast.

On the strength of its superior computer science, Facebook, like Amazon, was filtering and curating the wider world, pulling strings from behind the curtain to get people to stay online and click here, watch there, share this, see if they can believe that, answer these questions to learn who they really are (Facebook's algorithms already knew), then make this or that impulse purchase in hopes of becoming the kind of person they wanted to be (Facebook knew this too).

Horde mentality was baked into these systems. As complex as they were, they effectively highlighted already popular items: accelerated the speed at which stories or shoes or fidget spinners could virally saturate the popular imagination and drowned out other, more worthwhile conversations. The irony was that although the algorithm-powered platforms essentially focused everyone on the same procession of overblown trends and fracases, they did so under the guise of giving each user a personalized experience.

By effortlessly serving up the material its users liked best and shared, Facebook's algorithms relieved readers of the burden of choice. The role that newspaper editors historically served, as curators who chose what the public needed to know on any given day, atrophied. Popularity on Facebook and the micro-measurements of content performance by Chartbeat replaced these functions. What was trending became the most important benchmark of news. Individual pieces became untethered from the bundle of other news offered by the publishers. The stories sank or swam according to the almighty algorithm.

Computer mimicry of sentiment guided editors to material that was or seemed to be responsive, empathetic, adaptive to its audience and could foster a connection with them. Facebook's predictive force represented a monumental advance in the media's ability to offer captivating *experiences*, although those often came at the expense of the informational content. The industry faced a dangerous dilemma: if its artificial intelligence continued to improve, readers might get so used to having their worldview affirmed that they would lose their appetite for ideas that weren't custom-tailored to their predilections.

As its data scientists refined their genius for delivering perfect algorithmic personalization, Facebook exerted ever more influence over each user's experience while managing to make its hand in the conversation increasingly invisible. In 2009 Facebook endowed the News Feed with its first kernel of editorial judgment, mechanizing the task of choosing which posts its users should see, to impose a subtle sense of order upon the babbling chaos of the growing network. The more intelligent News Feed was powered by an algorithm that assessed every post recently shared to a user's network and ranked them more or less according to popularity (based on the number of likes and comments). This ranking determined the order in which the items appeared in the News Feed, which had heretofore arrayed those posts chronologically, so that by scrolling down the page everyone saw everything that anyone in their network had shared, with no particular weight or priority given to any item. Now popular posts got priority, meaning more users saw them.

The ranking system also laid the groundwork for competition: in order to be seen, a publisher's posts had to be popular. As Facebook's algorithm got more intelligent, it became more discriminating over which posts were worthy of a user's time and which weren't. By August 2013, the average user belonged to a network of friends and other outlets that produced about 1,500 posts each day, but typically scrolled and surfed only long enough to see 100, sometimes spending mere seconds glancing at a headline and then moving on. Facebook's algorithm addressed the challenge of making those 100 posts the ones most likely to elicit an "interaction." Merely reading or absorbing the information—and ads—in and next to articles wasn't enough. They had to be shared by others in the user's network and liked or commented on. BuzzFeed made sure its posts were among the top 100.

Originally little thought was given to Facebook's influence on the way people absorbed news. But publishers, from the *Guardian* to the *Times*, which had eschewed giving away any of its prized content to other websites and platforms, suddenly saw social media as the possible panacea for their ruined business model. With the exception of Rupert Murdoch, all of them began giving their stories to Facebook in the hopes of luring a portion of its enormous audience. Advertisers, meanwhile, were coming in droves, responding to Facebook's promise of a mass audience that could be precisely targeted.

Zuckerberg's early backer Peter Thiel was a student of the philosopher René Girard, who came up with the concept of "mimetic desire" and invoked it to explain Facebook's essence. "Man is the creature who does not know what to desire, and who turns to others in order to make up his mind," Girard wrote. "We desire what others desire because we imitate their desires." In other words, monkey see, monkey do. When Girard died in 2015, the *Times*'s obituary noted that his ideas had moved Thiel to make his initial investment in Facebook: "[He] saw Professor Girard's theories being validated in the concept of social media."

"Facebook first spread by word of mouth, and it's about word of mouth, so it's doubly mimetic," Thiel said. "Social media proved to be more important than it looked, because it's about our natures."

The vanguard of new media companies distinguished themselves by taking this premise as their mandate. Unbeholden to the traditional editorial agenda that was determined by current affairs, BuzzFeed and its ilk set out to publish pieces optimized to cater to readers' predilections.

Stories were presented in high-valence terms, crafted and edited to be emotionally resonant, to make readers *feel* things rather than just to inform them. These stories fit right in the feed, matching the tone and topical matter of Facebook at large, as if they came from readers' family or friends. It was a breakthrough in making news personal and connecting with readers on their terms, right there in the streamlined scroll that encapsulated their social lives. Like Amazon's recommendation engine (displaying the products that "customers who bought this item also bought"), BuzzFeed's empire was built on computer processes that, with as little human input as possible, could pull off the illusion of "getting you."

By 2016 Facebook was far larger than any nation-state, the biggest and most centralized congregation of people—friends, readers, consumers, voters—that the world had ever seen. But in the spring of that year, as America hurtled toward a vitriolic presidential election, Zuckerberg was worried. He looked out across the sprawling online universe he had built and saw deep fissures along partisan and ideological lines and the diminishing level of civility in the national discourse. But his aides discouraged him from publicly addressing the increasing polarization or what was a gathering political crisis, both for the United States and Zuckerberg.

When the network welcomed its billionth user, in October 2012, more than half of that population was logging on to the site at least daily. Later, when it hit two billion users, in June 2017, two-thirds were coming daily, and American users spent an average of an hour each day surfing and scrolling through the conversations of their friends and updates from the news outlets they followed. Sixty-two percent of Americans reported social media, especially Facebook, as their main source of news. By and large they did not recall the sources of the news they read or watched on the social network: it came to their attention as a result of Facebook slipping it into their News Feed.

Facebook had begun as a personal, social, and lighthearted way for young people to connect and converse online and had become a defining piece of technology, so broadly adopted that many users had ceased to think of it as an entity of its own. Facebook was all-encompassing. It was the internet for some users who rarely left and where virtually every news organization—prestige, mainstream, fringe, new, and old—posted nearly all of their articles. In just eight years the network had upended the business of publishing and established itself as the internet's effective center of gravity. It transcended international borders and cultural divides and brought internet connectivity to new parts of the globe.

Still, Zuckerberg kept insisting that Facebook was a neutral platform without much responsibility for the quality or accuracy of the content people posted, other than banning pornography, terrorist recruiting materials, and the like. But by 2016 a sizable part of its usership was awakening to the fact that the convenient connectedness of this gated utopia came at a price: all along, almost invisibly, Facebook had been imposing standards and priorities, moderating the conversation through undisclosed contracts with its users, collecting massive amounts of data on them and selling it to advertisers.

People were realizing, though it was too late, that plugging media into a machine that sorted and promoted it based on each piece's ability to elicit clicks, comments, and shares, was not necessarily preferable to the older, slower model of human editorial judgment. Despite the boom in the volume, diversity, and immediacy of information online, people and social structures were no more stable or better informed than they had been in the immediate pre-boom days. For all its merits, the total connectedness that was Zuckerberg's main objective had engendered a more siloed media world, and one that moved at lightning speed.

Many of the young media companies saw their subject matter not simply as current events but as "social news," the kind of stories people *wanted* to hear, and by distilling their outputs according to the constant feedback loop their data provided, they hoped one day to arrive at the perfect recipe for the modern reader. Peretti's lab of amateur behavioral psychologists and data scientists had taken an empirical approach to finding the tone of headline, for example, that garnered the most interactions. And even once they had reached consensus on the phrases and formulations that worked best, the company continued to make its writers brainstorm a plethora of headlines for each story so that through A/B testing, the one most likely to thrive would arise. (The publishers that followed in their footsteps took this practice to an extreme: Vox and Mic, for example, asked their writers to enter some 15 to 20 headline options.)

But even then they were experimenting within Facebook's constraints, which the company's engineers were consistently altering.

Old-guard publishers were slow to pick up on the style and tone they would have to assume on Facebook to cut through the static and the sheer volume of what its users saw on their feeds. Until they got wise, new media outlets like BuzzFeed busily raided the content of their reporting and tuned it to resonant frequency for the Facebook audience. The legacy newspapers like the *Times* and the *Post* did not have all that much content that had natural Facebook appeal, although once they caught on, there was an explosion in lighter and more obviously popular fare, though not as light as BuzzFeed offered. But the BuzzFeed influence was clearly being felt. Both newspapers hired social media editors to generate content with guaranteed Facebook appeal.

Soon everyone was tinkering with the same reductive strategies in a desperate effort to gain an edge over the competition. The older outlets could see that BuzzFeed's popularity was due to the site's attention to affirming and reflecting readers' emotional dispositions. Leading by example, BuzzFeed set the agenda around clickbait gold like Cecil the Lion, whose death in 2015 at the hands of big-game hunters prompted 3.2 million stories, appearing everywhere from the *Times* to the tabloids.

That readers would be better served by newsrooms willing to focus on more substantive, if less clickable, stories was obvious. The Facebook-optimized stories about Cecil and his ilk were mostly everywhere on the internet for free, but that was the point: rather than selling people stories that they would buy, news organizations had resolved to hand out stories that people would grab. The products, in this free model, were the readers. In order to turn a profit, publishers had to attract readers by the millions. Quantity and ubiquity were the objective.

Facebook incontrovertibly established itself as a primary draw for the news media industry in 2013. It did so by luring them to the platform with irresistible traffic incentives, then setting the hook. All it took was a new layer of code that reordered the ranking system to favor posts by publishers over those by a user's friends and family. The effects sent ripples through the industry. By October inbound traffic from Facebook to these media sites had nearly tripled from the previous year. Traffic at BuzzFeed rose nearly 10-fold. That was the proverbial carrot.

The stick came in the form of new strictures that Facebook built into its algorithm to discern which publishers were most worth users' time. One change would privilege "high-quality" content. The algorithm would vet the quality of a post by taking a comprehensive view of the publisher's page on which it appeared. If that page showed a track record of high engagement, meaning shares, comments, and the like, Facebook inferred that it was a reliable hitmaker and thus deserved more attention. But this yardstick for judging the quality of news content had nothing to do with the veracity or depth of stories. Quality, defined by Facebook, was measured strictly by engagement, the number of interactions a reader had with a story. Merely clicking on and reading a story did not indicate high engagement. Commenting on and sharing a story with a user's Facebook friends made it more likely that the user also interacted with the advertising served next to that story.

Pages whose content rated consistently high engagement could then rise in Facebook's rankings over time and ensure that their future posts would be shown to as many of their followers as possible. If the page published a dud, though, Facebook would question whether the publisher was really that "high-quality" after all. This was the consequence of Facebook's new, more holistic way of evaluating the content shared on its network. The sharers now had something to lose. A dud had the long-term effect of diminishing the potential audience of that page's future posts, meaning that in order for a publisher to expand its reach, it was now more imperative than ever to play to its base and post only things with a high likelihood of going viral. For free sites like BuzzFeed, this was crucial. The *Times* too was hungry for audience, but with its more flexible digital subscription plan, instituted in 2011, the number of clicks mattered less than the number of people handing over their credit cards.

The potential for manipulation was huge, but neither Facebook nor Twitter had any incentive to hire squads of human editors to screen material for either quality or veracity. They did not want to be bound by legal regulations and restrictions applied to conventional publishers, news organizations, and broadcasters, or to shoulder the expense of hiring squadrons of editors. But it would not be until well after Donald Trump's election, when it was revealed that Facebook had distributed fake news and false, Russian-manufactured anti-Clinton screeds to millions of its users, that serious backlash coalesced. Under scrutiny and the threat of government regulation, in mid-2018 Zuckerberg apologized to lawmakers in Washington for not being more responsible in monitoring the content on Facebook or protecting users' privacy. What changes Facebook was actually making was less than clear.

Only a few years earlier, in late 2014, Zuckerberg had expressed his goal for News Feed as "build[ing] the perfect personalized newspaper for every person in the world. We're trying to personalize it and show you the stuff that's going to be most interesting to you." Facebook was getting wise to the tricks new-media outlets such as BuzzFeed were pulling in order to maximize their readership. It was important to keep this behavior in check.

So Facebook launched an internal effort to make News Feed, in the words of its creator, Chris Cox, more "fundamentally human." For that to happen, the Facebook engineers would need to bring human subjects into their laboratory for closer examination.

Which is what the company did when it discreetly established a campus in Knoxville, Tennessee, and recruited 30 representatively diverse men and women from the surrounding area to become full-time content assessors on a "Feed Quality Panel." By the time Facebook unveiled the program in February 2016, it included 1,000 panelists nationwide who were paid to rate content and placement on a 1–5 scale under the supervision of Facebook's data scientists. Facebook's interest in improving the News Feed was simple: the company wanted people to stay on its platform for all of their life's needs for as long as possible—and to see the ads in their news feeds.

Facebook had been enabling advertisers to target its users since 2007, continually redrawing the front line of psychological and subliminal influence for commercial purposes. The cascade of advances in user-targeting was initiated in November of that year, when Zuckerberg took the stage to unveil Facebook Ads. "The next hundred years will be different for advertising, and it starts today," the 23-year-old founder said. The model was to sell corporate or other interests a way to embed their message into seemingly organic social situations, "getting into the conversations between people," he said. "Nothing influences people more than a recommendation from a trusted friend. A trusted referral influences people more than the best broadcast message. A trusted referral is the Holy Grail of advertising."

Corporate brands were the first to drink of that grail, and political campaigns followed close behind them. In 2010 opponents of a Florida ballot measure that would have enlarged class sizes at public schools used Facebook's ad technology to target persuadable voters based on background intelligence they could have gotten only through the social network. The campaign targeted Floridians whose profiles identified them, for example, as "math teacher" or affiliated with a PTA, and on top of that, users whose interests included, for instance, "I love my daughter."

All the while Facebook was strengthening its persuasion machine by feeding it information about users' offline lives. Around 2012 the company set out to buy up reams of data from outside firms, the type that collected and sold phone numbers to telemarketers. Its database swelled with records of users' income levels, credit ratings and purchase histories, places of residence, educational attainment, and more. All could easily be matched to each user's already data-rich Facebook profile and activity history. That bundle gave advertisers an unprecedented, 360-degree comprehension of whom to target and how to win them over. This was borderline omniscience, and it was now at the fingertips of not only retailers but also media companies aiming to build audiences, and, of course, politicians.

In the cloisters of Cambridge University, meanwhile, a psychologist named Michal Kosinski was hurtling toward a breakthrough discovery that would make the social landscape quantifiable and greatly enhance Facebook's potential to influence global politics. His work constituted the bedrock of an emerging field known as psychometrics (or psychographics). It was as if, for the first time ever, the sociopolitical genome of America had been mapped. By collating the responses to surveys he'd received from Facebook users and cross-referencing that information with basic details of their profiles on the site, Kosinski was able to build a massive trove. When he ran regressions on the data, he arrived at surprisingly specific correlations that allowed him to extrapolate major insights about a person based on minor indicators. He knew, for instance, that people who "liked" Lady Gaga on Facebook were by and large extroverts; that those who liked "thunderstorms" or "curly fries" were demonstrably intelligent, while "Harley

Davidson" likers were reliably less so. Liking Prada or Sun Tzu meant a person was probably competitive; "scrapbooking" fans tended to be in relationships, while fans of track star Usain Bolt were dependably single. Other interests were correlated with openness, drug use, political party affiliation, or being children of divorce. The database gave him grounds on which to base any number of intelligent predictions about someone about whom he possessed a sliver of seemingly irrelevant information.

"With a mere ten 'likes' as input, his model could appraise a person's character better than an average coworker," Zurich's *Das Magazine* reported. "With seventy, it could 'know' a subject better than a friend; with 150 likes, better than their parents. With 300 likes, Kosinski's machine could predict a subject's behavior better than their partner. With even more likes it could exceed what a person thinks they know about themselves." It was a framework that allowed analysts to know, as if on a deeply personal level, vast numbers of people. Kosinski had provided the basis for understanding populations that transcended demographic labels. Psychographics laid bare a whole system of pressure points, a veritable voodoo doll for anyone intent on earning the public's attention.

How carefully—or not—Facebook safeguarded the intelligence it kept on its users would become an explosive issue following the political calamities of the Brexit vote in Britain and the U.S. election in 2016. In 2018 Facebook finally admitted it had allowed more than 80 million users' data to be collected by Cambridge Analytica, a political consulting firm powered by the Mercers, an ultraconservative U.S. family. Both the firm and the family also worked for the Trump campaign.

Until then, the science behind which content was served and to whom remained opaque. But for years Facebook had been quietly giving the corporate world, especially advertisers, the news media, and now politicians, a switchboard for sentiment manipulation. Informed by Facebook's precise psychographic map of America, they could unleash content that would function like heat-seeking missiles. Those with partisan or ideological passions were served a steady diet of content they were prone to like and share with their network of like-minded Facebook friends.

News became a game of presenting a version of the day's events that would electrify conversation on the social network. As such, it was a field that was now wide open for new players; the barrier to entry had been all but toppled. Targeting was easy. The internet was a remarkably efficient marketplace. Online congregations could spring up wherever there appeared a critical mass of sentiment (around #NeverTrump, say, or in revulsion of the #DeepState). Readers found their Facebook News Feed filling with hot takes and hit pieces as the country grew increasingly polarized. Facebook's crusade to tighten social connections was wildly successful. The company announced that the longtime rule of thumb, that each person was separated from anyone else by at most six degrees, had been shattered. Its internal research revealed that the number had in fact shrunk to 3.57.

The ability to see which types and topics of content were working where and with whom marked a massive leap forward. It lent a welcome degree of predictability to the tiresome task of following the whims of the crowd. What made a story work was not its scope or substance; as Buzz-Feed had all but empirically proven, it was the extent to which the content had the power to make readers *feel* something.

The menu of news changed everywhere. The *Times* was publishing videos of people doing yoga with goats, baby elephants at the vet, Jimmy Kimmel telling jokes, DIY tips for the holidays, and Katherine Hepburn's brownie recipe. They used Facebook's live broadcast tool to welcome the public into an editor's pitch meeting and implored viewers to vote on which videos should be run. The *Washington Post*, meanwhile, had one of its esteemed writers literally eat the newspaper before a live Facebook audience. Its apps were full of headlines surely picked for clickbait potential. I catalogued them each day, though the task quickly became overwhelming. Was it really news when a group of vegans protested outside a local restaurant in Toronto, where the irate restaurant owner responded by brandishing a bloody deer leg? Certainly to vegans, who shared the story in droves. This, in a nutshell, was the Facebook effect on news.

Its unrivaled status as a source of traffic gave Facebook significant bargaining power with the publishers. In May 2015 it debuted a new feature called Instant Publishers, with which publishers would simply hand over copies of their news stories to Facebook, which would host them on its own website and app, so that when users clicked on them, they took no time to load and would bear the sleek, uniform design of Facebook's web pages. The stories would ostensibly get more attention on the network, and Facebook would sell the ads that ran alongside them in return for 30 percent of the proceeds. (If the news organizations sold the ads themselves, the profit was all theirs.)

Naturally BuzzFeed, which helped design the program, was all in. It already used Facebook as its primary distribution platform for news and the vast majority of its other content. Surprisingly, the *New York Times*, which had been so hesitant to give away any of its precious and expensive-to-produce content for free, was also a launch partner. The *Times* decided to give Facebook a limited number of its stories, enough to expose Facebook's massive user base to its high-quality coverage and possibly woo some into buying subscriptions. Various internal studies conducted by the *Times*'s battery of consultants showed that longtime print and digital subscribers, who were paying almost $1,000 a year, were not concerned about other readers getting the articles for free.

Soon the *Washington Post*, like BuzzFeed, was all in, giving Facebook 100 percent of its news report each day. Then came just about everyone else, except for Murdoch's *Wall Street Journal*. A month in, data showed the participating outlets were seeing major boosts in audience for the stories they published as Instant Articles. For BuzzFeed, the made-for-Facebook versions were receiving nearly two and a half times the interactions as their normal links; for the *Times*, they were doing more than nine times better than their average articles.

The period 2012–16 was when this seismic power shift, from individual publishers to Facebook, took hold. It was a quiet revolution in the delivery of news, undercovered by the news media in real time, until it was too late. These years coincided with the increased polarization of the American electorate. Facebook did not cause the political divide in the country, but it fueled the polarization because its algorithms supplied users with ever more thinly sliced news items they would agree with and be moved to share.

On Facebook the fragmentation of the audience into ideological echo chambers continued. All the while, the site's content-serving algorithm bore the increasing burden of matching coverage from various viewpoints to the right users in order to keep everyone happy, or at least engaged, during what was shaping up to be a bitterly divisive 2016 presidential campaign. As the national narrative frayed into contradictory story lines, Facebook gave news providers an ever greater ability to cater to the camp that already bought into their spin. These were the so-called filter bubbles that Eli Pariser had warned about. They weakened democracy by causing the base of common knowledge and truth to wither away, replaced by intensely siloed and refined bands of information designed to appeal to ideological leanings.

All the while, Facebook was increasing the competition among news outlets. The network had already lured them in with new products like Instant Articles and Facebook Live. But suddenly it began weaning them off that honeymoon traffic, forcing them to fight for diminishing numbers of eyeballs. In April 2015 the News Feed algorithm undid the boon to publishers by reverting to the old order of priorities in which a user's friends' posts mattered more than those from the pages he or she followed. But there was a problem.

By 2015 Facebook's individual users were sharing far less on the network than they once had. As reported by the Information, the number of posts shared by individuals was down 21 percent in mid-2015 compared to the year prior. BuzzFeed's technology reporter Alex Kantrowitz pointed out, "With sharing down, content from celebrities, political candidates, and news sites began to fill the void." Fewer organically diverse points of view being aired on the platform meant that, in order for the conversation to maintain its strength, users would gradually find themselves aligning behind the ready-made viewpoints that publishers were piping in. That summer Facebook added new controls to give users more of a say in whose posts they saw first in their News Feed.

In January 2016 Facebook introduced publishers to its new Audience Optimization Tool, which would allow them to dial in the target readership for each item they posted; they could filter readers based on interests, demographics, and geography. In February Facebook added a feature to its algorithm, giving it more power to predict, based on users' past activity, which posts they would want to see from which type of sources. The things it determined as being of interest were displayed at the top of the News Feed. In April they went even further in that direction, enabling the algorithm to base those predictions also on the track record of the source that shared a given post. In other words, publishers' pages were now being evaluated in terms of how high their engagement with readers had been over the long haul.

Each successive adaptation played to politically polarized constituencies. On the right, groups had sorted themselves into coherent ideological camps. Some groups congregated around the ethos of nationalism, while others became de facto clearinghouses for the anti-immigration cause or haters of the liberal bias that was supposedly running rampant in the mainstream media. Some were concerned with the dystopian conspiracies they identified among power players on the left; others preferred to keep the conversation centered on defending the reputation of police agencies unfairly besmirched by unpatriotic protesters. Some were neo-Nazis. As the core identity of each community coalesced, they provided an increasingly powerful apparatus for the distribution of stories spun to substantiate their pet causes. The electorate was segmented into ideological silos of rabid audiences whose collective hunger for content that affirmed their point of view created a strong incentive to cater to it. This was the whole intent behind "traffic farms." They juiced demand, knowing that it would be followed by a surge in the supply.

While the new-media pioneers at BuzzFeed and Upworthy produced LOLs and cultivated trumped-up umbrage over the killing of poor Cecil, a second guard of new-media publishers set out to capture the loyalty of another psychographic swath of America whose disaffection far surpassed mere boredom. The new wave would employ the methods BuzzFeed had pioneered, but used partisan anger as their way of hot-wiring readers' emotional responses.

Stories could go viral by embracing the conspiracy theory of the day. Mike Cernovich and the crowd on 4chan were pandering to these constituencies and becoming massively popular in the process. Most of all, Breitbart News seemed to benefit from the boom of "stigmatized knowledge." Its Facebook following was growing exponentially, and by the middle of 2016 it was getting more reader engagement than the *Times*. By May and June 2016 Breitbart had eclipsed all other political outlets in reader engagement via Facebook and Twitter, with a sizable lead over the second place, left-leaning Huffington Post. It had triple the number of interactions as the sixth-place *Washington Post*, according to NewsWhip, which tracked social media performance. BuzzFeed and the *New York Times* were not even ranked in the top 10.

It was no coincidence that the man who enabled the right's success on the web in 2016 was a friend and sometime partner of Peretti, although the role he would play within the new-media ecosystem pitted him against the liberal and libertarian-leaning BuzzFeed founder. Andrew Breitbart, Peretti's old Huffington Post colleague, liked to explain his mission as mounting a culture war. "The market has forced me to come up with techniques to be noticed," Breitbart would tell Wired in 2010. "And now that I have them, I'm like, wow, this is actually great. This is fun."

Like Peretti, Breitbart had suffered through a childhood that left him feeling like a misfit. In affluent Brentwood he had an attention-deficit disorder so severe that his case was deemed beyond medicating. "Your brain works differently from most people's," a friend told him. "And there is this thing called the Internet that is your brain." He bought a six-pack of beer and a rotisserie chicken that night and set out to explore this new world. Hooking up to the web "was a revelation," he recalled.

"It was just like shooting yourself into outer space, and trying to latch onto anyone else who was out there. I remember finding weather sites and earthquake sites, and being able to monitor earthquakes in real time, and that was weirdly invigorating." The feeling he got on the web was one he likened to a conductor facing his orchestra. "This is the environment I needed in order to become what I needed to become. With the Internet, I have communication with large amounts of people, in perpetuity. Always having a new war, a new battle."

He had worked as a pizza delivery boy and an extra hand at the network E! when, in 1995, he came across a crudely designed website that collated the day's newsworthy and notable clips. The site had just launched and was operating from the modest Hollywood apartment of a show-biz underling named Matt Drudge. Breitbart fell in love with the Drudge Report at first visit. He was smitten by the site's almost whimsical assemblage of clips on everything from the foibles of the Clinton administration to rubberneck-worthy natural disasters and insider rumors about the movie business. "This mixture of news and information was immediately, overwhelmingly sexy," he said. He emailed the 29-year-old Drudge to ask if he could come aboard, got a yes, and hopped to it.

Breitbart was proud to call himself "Matt Drudge's bitch." The Drudge Report was the first prominent example of aggregation, a masterfully curated collection of news and gossip snippets from around the web, with links to each piece where it had originally appeared. Powered by two digital media savants, the Drudge Report gained stature, and the duo managed to build a vast network of connections within the news business without needing to leave their Hollywood digs. From the comfort of their computers, they could cover stories big and small, wherever they arose. Eventually industrious reporters in newsrooms across the country got into the habit of tipping off Drudge and Breitbart anytime they had a big "get." (I did this when I was Washington bureau chief of the *Times*.) Reporters recognized that a mention on the Drudge Report greatly amplified their exposure, thereby advancing their careers.

Toward the end of the 1990s it was Breitbart who increasingly captained the ship, which meant being constantly entreated by pols and the press to highlight their latest stories. From squarely outside the mainstream media's seat of power, Breitbart had effectively established himself as the news cycle's kingmaker. In 1998 the two-man newsroom broke the story of President Clinton's affair with Monica Lewinsky, juicy details of the Oval Office rendezvous, and the explosive fact that *Newsweek* had axed the scoop, all from three time zones away. It was a double whammy: the potential undoing of a Democratic president as well as incontrovertible proof of liberal media complicity, a supposed conspiracy at the highest levels.

In the new millennium Breitbart came to be regarded as the right wing's wunderkind whose digital acumen seemed auspicious. Through Drudge he got to know Arianna Huffington, then a prominent neoconservative pundit, and advised her on the "performance art" of politics. He took a sabbatical from Drudge in 2005 to help launch the Huffington Post, where he worked alongside Peretti, even then a budding rival, who later remembered Breitbart's main asset being an instinct for political provocation. The alliance with his ideological counterparts was short-lived.

He decamped to return to Drudge's lair and began cooking up plans for a venture of his own. This was the very moment Peretti got his idea for a new kind of media company—an irreverent and ill-defined but *contagious* media company—and dared to dream that this creature of his laboratory might someday grow so big and powerful that it would surpass the titans of media, reinvent the business, and redefine news.

Breitbart, meanwhile, fixated on a more violent and direct overthrow of the mainstream media, a coup d'état more than a reformation. His aspirations were colored by the chip on his shoulder, and his approach was adversarial. "The idea," he told *Wired*, "is that I have to screw with media, and I have to screw with the Left, in order to give legitimate stories the ability to reach their natural watermark." It was a lucrative idea. "When the entire media is structured to attack conservatives and Republicans, there is a huge business model to come in and counterbalance that."

He quietly created Breitbart.com in the likeness of the Drudge Report in late 2005, just half a year after HuffPo's launch, when BuzzFeed was still just a twinkle in Peretti's eye. But Breitbart still wasn't sure what he wanted to do with it.

That December Breitbart attended the Liberty Film Festival, where a film called *Reagan's War* was set to debut. The young blogger was casting about for like-minded culture warriors. He saw in the film's director, Stephen K. Bannon, a kindred spirit. As the audience filed out after the Q&A, he approached Bannon. "Brother, we've got to change the culture," he said. "You're one of us." Breitbart liked to say that politics was downstream from culture, and as Joshua Green recounts in *Devil's Bargain*, he and Bannon were in an upstream position at the moment, equipped to assert themselves at the center of a new right-wing media wave. Bannon, a former Wall Street financier, had observed the Huffington Post experiment and remembered the wise words Peretti, whom he called a "genius," imparted to him about the future of media: "You're really not thinking about traffic, you're thinking about community."

Breitbart's project would shift and morph until around 2008, when he decided it would be a news company that went beyond aggregation. From its very origin Breitbart News was, its creator would later intone, "committed to the destruction of the old media guard." It grew out of a triad of websites Breitbart launched and briefly maintained—BigHollywood.com, BigGovernment.com, and BigJournalism.com—which made emotionally resonant content for the large and growing psychographic of people who felt alienated by the "cultural elitism" of mainstream media. "The media class is the wall that we have to climb over in order for our voices to be heard," he would declare.

Breitbart News spoke to a latent social sector and in doing so galvanized a movement that was just getting afoot. It made use of the high-valence dressing typical of BuzzFeed, Upworthy, and other nonpolitical social publishers; indeed it raised the bar several notches. And like BuzzFeed it succeeded by appealing to readers based on their identity, which it defined along psychographic lines. Breitbart News arose out of, and in service to, an amorphous type of antiestablishment thinking, an identity defined principally by what it was *against*.

It would be different things to different people, but at its foundation it was what Bannon would call "the platform for the alt-right." The up-and-coming face of Breitbart, Milo Yiannopoulos, described the alt-right as a lighthearted group of "young rebels" engaged in provocation "because it promises fun, transgression, and a challenge to social norms."

In 2009 Breitbart was still running the site out of his basement in L.A. when he heard from James O'Keefe, a young, wannabe-viral provocateur, whose recent escapade had produced footage so precious and potent that he flew across the country to show it to Breitbart in person. The doctored footage purported to show workers for the community-organizing group ACORN, which promoted voter registration and affordable housing, engaging in nefarious activities. Breitbart knew this was the big break that would put his new website on the map. He put out a call for bloggers and quickly corralled 200 eager hands whom he deployed to swarm the story and catapult it into the consciousness of the mainstream, yielding immediate results. Despite being fake, the heavily doctored stories got wide coverage nonetheless. The faux scandal became a big news story and got ACORN defunded into oblivion after 40 years of operation.

The ACORN case demonstrated Breitbart's intuitive understanding of what fueled fury and how to channel that outrage in a way that was consonant with his own crusade. He termed the ACORN videos "the Abu Ghraib of the Great Society."

That was music to the ears of Bannon, who was still making films. He was so impressed that he set Breitbart up in a modest office space in Santa Monica. From those confines, Breitbart and his young editor Alex Marlow, a recent UCLA graduate, would commandeer the army of free-laboring bloggers who found the honor of being published on the site sufficient compensation for their man-hours.

In May 2011 the site struck back with another giant-killer of a story: Congressman Anthony Weiner had posted a picture of his erection in briefs on Twitter, intending it for a young mistress. Before he deleted the evidence, a Twitter user captured screenshots and forwarded them to Breitbart, who published them. When Weiner claimed he'd been hacked, Breitbart released another photo he'd obtained of the congressman shirtless. It was proof of a separate affair: checkmate. Weiner copped to his disgraceful wayward ways and resigned.

Weinergate, which would come roaring back into the news at the end of the 2016 election, gravely damaging Hillary Clinton's campaign, was proof that Breitbart's ability to generate news was no mere passing fad. He was an emergent force in new media, a dangerously powerful conductor of viral contagions. In ACORN and Weinergate he had produced hits that were perfectly packaged for the media moment in which they arose. They were disasters that invited, even demanded rubbernecking, lurid tidbits that felt, even when the whole country had heard, like illicit gossip. Most important of all, they produced controversies that demanded coverage in the hated mainstream media. It hardly mattered that, in the case of ACORN, the entire scandal was a product manufactured by the Breitbart team. The destruction of the nonprofit was proof to Breitbart that he could contend with BuzzFeed at its own game, he could "make a thing a thing."

BuzzFeed's Matt Stopera had made a name for himself doing the same, as he told me. "You can make a thing a thing," he said, simply by hammering it home. "Like if you just do a ton of Corgi posts," he offered as an example. But why would you? "They're just my favorite dog."

Breitbart's thing-making stunts were designed for ideological ends. He understood the politically instrumental role he was equipped to play. As described in a *New Yorker* profile from 2010, one morning in the wake of a demonstration by black members of Congress, Breitbart was lounging around his L.A. home when he decided to pick a fight with the congressmen. He took to Twitter and launched into a fabricated story of how the Congressional Black Caucus had gathered outside his house and were yelling the "n" word. "OhmyGod, the Dems are screaming the N word outside of my house. I swear. No, really. Trust me. It's true," he tweeted, following it up with "Why are elected Democratic leaders in front of my house in LA standing lock-armed screaming racial epithets & homophobic slurs?" and then again with "Why is Steny Hoyer in Los Angeles sitting on Anthony Weiner's shoulders screaming the N word into my home? Weird." Like the news stories he blasted out, Breitbart's sense of humor lived and died on its shock value. The *New Yorker* quoted him saying that he vacillated between two tonal registers: "righteous indignation and puerile jocularity." In fact there was hardly a distinction between the two, for he operated in both modes simultaneously, often leaving his audience to parse what belonged to which designation. Breitbart and BuzzFeed were both using made-up and exaggerated ploys to attract audiences, not unlike what had made older tabloids, like the *National Enquirer*, so popular. To wit, Stopera's post from 2009, headlined, "Senator Sessions Wants Some Crack," or his 2011 list of "Top 10 Most Badass Anthony Weiner Rants," in which the author, who referred to Weiner as "BuzzFeed Hero," unironically offered the "best, most amazing moments" of "one of the toughest and most outspoken members of the House of Representatives."

Like Peretti, Breitbart recognized that in the new attention economy, entertainment value was essential. "I think Donald Trump—and I don't say this in the negative sense—is for Donald Trump, and right now he's doing an amazing job of promoting his brand. He's utterly entertaining," Breitbart told Joy Behar in an interview way back in 2011. "He's winning, a la, you know, Charlie Sheen, playing the media for what it is. It's obvious." His thoughts are worth quoting in full: "Well, the other candidates are starting to realize what they should have realized, I don't know, 40, 50 years ago when Ed Sullivan got on the air, is that media is everything, and that these guys don't understand that a Donald Trump can go out there, know how to play the media and rise through the ranks when two years ago he was supporting Nancy Pelosi." He went on to boast, "Look, entertainment uber alles. He's very entertaining. You're enjoying it, I'm enjoying it, and I didn't like it when I would hear people on the right doing it. But now that it's become sort of like the center ring at the circus, I'm sitting back and I am enjoying it."

But he would not enjoy it for long. Breitbart, 43 years old, died of heart failure the next year.

Even as late as February 2014, Trump himself seemed unaware of his destiny and a bit oblivious to the pop-cultural precedents that had fallen (were still falling) into place to cue his rise on the American political stage.

The information warfare breaking out in America was so bloody that it could not help but attract the attention of foreign powers, who identified it as an opportunity. Both BuzzFeed's and Breitbart's fabulous successes demonstrated to opportunistic observers, including those as far away as Moscow, that the landscape of public sentiment, long assumed to be mercurial, arcane, or indeterminate, was in fact an outcome that could be predicted based on the inputs one fed into the system. By strategically disseminating content designed to have an emotional effect, the digital companies had altered the state of public opinion on a global scale.

In Russia, technocrats propping up Putin's power were taking advantage of the deepening fissures between American political poles and mobilized a covert campaign to rend it further. Using a tool called Prism, Russian agencies effectively surveilled the social web for grumblings of anti-Moscow sentiment and tried to extinguish it. Other agencies employed loyal supporters of the Kremlin to identify openings in the U.S. election conversation in which they could insert pro-Russian points of view that appeared to come from the Facebook profiles of genuine American patriots.

Though Facebook wouldn't admit it until the spring of 2017, Russian agents were using its ad-placing software to covertly inject bitterly divisive viewpoints into an already well-agitated national conversation. When Facebook did eventually come forward to confess the political ramifications of its platform, it did so in guarded, boilerplate terms, forcing congressional investigators and journalists to dig beneath what appeared to be a cover-up.

Meanwhile in Washington, D.C., Steve Bannon had picked up Andrew Breitbart's mantle and was completing Breitbart News's transformation into the unofficial mouthpiece of the Trump campaign. Long before he would take the helm of the GOP nominee's campaign, Bannon's leadership of the site evinced a happy marriage forming between the two culture warriors. In August 2015, a full year before he officially joined the candidate, he would boast in an email to a former colleague about turning Breitbart into "Trump Central" and ordering up pieces to boost the candidate's support, which he called "Bannon Specials." As Bannon saw it, he already inhabited the role of campaign manager.

As Trump was emerging as the forerunner, Breitbart became his foremost political outlet on Facebook. The 75-person editorial army Bannon employed in Breitbart's D.C. headquarters, an ornately furnished four-bedroom rowhouse he called "the Embassy," located half a block from the Supreme Court, bent over backward to hail the real-estate tycoon as the long-awaited swamp-drainer, Candidate Smith incarnate.

By winning the day on Facebook, Breitbart was establishing itself at the previously unoccupied epicenter of right-wing media. A *Columbia Journalism Review* study of more than a million stories published in the 19 months leading up to the election showed statistically that Bannon's organization came to dominate the conversation among conservatives. But in making the jump from radical fringe to front and center, Breitbart encountered some trouble within its ranks. Its spokesman quit in March 2016, objecting publicly to the site's transformation into "the de facto rapid response arm of the Trump campaign."

"Andrew's life mission has been betrayed," wrote a veteran editor of the site, Ben Shapiro, in his resignation a few days later. "Indeed, Breitbart News, under the chairmanship of Steve Bannon, has put a stake through the heart of Andrew's legacy."

As primary season came to a close, the national conversation took on the quality of horse-race commentary, myopically concerned with lead changes and probabilistic projections, to the detriment of deeper dives. A specialty called data journalism, which Nate Silver had already turned into a popular franchise, was all the rage, and Silver imitators sprouted up across the news landscape, from the *Post*'s Wonkblog to *Times*'s Upshot. Horse-race coverage almost completely supplanted the space formerly given to candidates' policy positions.

A pre-election report from the Shorenstein Center at Harvard concluded that this breathless, substance-free reportage dominated the primary phase, in the opening months of 2016. Week in and week out, Trump received more coverage than all of his Republican opponents combined, and considerably more press attention than Clinton. In the media his trajectory was described in overall positive terms: he was gaining ground and outperforming expectations, while Clinton was failing to meet them. The horse-race coverage reached its pinnacle in the two-week period surrounding Super Tuesday, on March 1, during which time overall media attention focused a mere 5 percent on the "character and policies" of the candidates, the Center reported. All told during this period, Trump received $3 billion worth of free media coverage.

In the meantime, in June, Facebook again adjusted the algorithm in charge of arranging each user's news feed. The new change, engineers announced, would enable the algorithm to go even further. It would give priority to posts by publishers that aligned with Facebook's "core values": to "inform" and "entertain." "Our aim is to deliver the types of stories we've gotten feedback that an individual person most wants to see."

This change removed one crucial limiting factor on the size of the possible audience for any post. It meant that anytime an outlet shared something that showed especially high engagement on Facebook, the platform would now promote the post not only to that outlet's consenting followers but also to their friends. It was an expansion of power for the Facebook algorithm, engineered to allow real-time news coverage and other timely posts to spread virally not just within existing social circles but *between* them.

Facebook had hoped to remain aloof from the culture and political wars that Breitbart feasted on, but in the middle of the 2016 election it was right at the epicenter. The controversy that swept Facebook into politics was a rather obscure section of the News Feed that highlighted trending news stories. The program had launched quietly back in 2014 and aimed to help the site challenge Twitter as the online destination for news. The new Trending section appeared in the top right-hand corner of the Facebook homepage, which collated links to the news stories that were getting the highest engagement among users across its platform. No one had known precisely how the Trending section worked until it came out in the spring of 2016 that all along, Facebook had employed a squad of human editors to cull the most talked-about stories on the network and summarize them for the general public.

The editors' job, as one told the *Times*, was to "massage the algorithm" and to keep the fact they were doing this a secret. That made the work sound perhaps more illicit than it was, but the element of promiscuity lay in the fact that the role crossed the borderline between the people who tended to the platform and the people who filled it with content. The public had always pictured Facebook as a faceless machine manned by IT professionals, people whose roles left no wiggle room for their personal judgment. The Trending editors were not IT people, but were they journalists? Technically, in the sense that what they were preparing were stories for an audience, yes. But they were so much a part of the technological apparatus that they may as well have been unbiased computers, or at least that was what Facebook was claiming.

Facebook recruited the editors mainly out of journalism school and provided them with an elaborate manual containing every detail they would need to do their job. At the beginning of their shift they would each be given a list of some 200 or so items that had been detected by Facebook's machines as talked-about topics. They had no insight into the algorithm they were working alongside; it simply spat out a list. Their task was to determine, by plugging the topic into a specially made database, whether there were any reputable outlets reporting on it. If not, the item was discarded. But if so, they were instructed to mark it as such, and Facebook would give it special priority on the Trending topics list. The editors determined newsworthiness in those cases by consulting the 10 news outlets Facebook considered most trustworthy, the list to which BuzzFeed had just been welcomed. If the topic appeared on the homepage—above the scroll—of five, it got a boost. If it was on eight, that boost was stronger, and if all 10 were reporting the story it got Facebook's maximum boost. The editors would then write up a terse synopsis in journalese and pass it along the pipeline to those who would proof it and post it.

Of the roughly 200 stories editors vetted each day, the number they greenlighted was usually around 15 to 20, maybe 30 if they spent their entire shift in hyperdrive. The goal handed down from upstairs, editors said, was for them all to reach a daily rate of 50 verified stories. The number they produced each day was prominently visible to everyone who worked in the office and was frequently cause for conversation with the bosses. The editors who verified and produced the lowest number of news stories in a given month got last pick when it came time to sign up for the next month's shift slots, meaning they got stuck with overnights on their weekends and the 4 p.m. to midnight shift during the week. Top performers were given "points" that could be spent on Facebook paraphernalia like T-shirts.

It was thankless but undeniably influential work. These "editors" had a hand in determining the snapshot of current affairs for staggering numbers of people. *Time* magazine assigned members of its staff to watch what appeared in the Trending section and dash off quick coverage on the new topics.

Just a couple of weeks after BuzzFeed was named to Facebook's 10 most trusted sources (making it the only new-media organization included), the lid got blown off the Trending program. Gizmodo reported that Facebook's trending editors "routinely suppressed news stories of interest to conservative readers," citing the claim of one former editor who came forward to blow the whistle. To Trump's loyal lieutenants, this made sense, as they were not seeing enough payoff from the viral stories published on Breitbart and other right-wing sites. The aggrieved outlets jumped on the story and skewered Zuckerberg for liberal partisanship and foul play. It didn't matter that the evidence was scant. Real news organizations would not have buckled so easily. That was one of the dangers of Facebook's primacy as a publisher of news.

Senator John Thune, Republican of South Dakota, lodged a formal inquiry, demanding Facebook provide answers to exactly how Trending Topics functioned. "Any attempt by a neutral and inclusive social media platform to censor or manipulate political discussion is an abuse of trust and inconsistent with the values of an open Internet," he said. On the defensive, Zuckerberg responded by proactively inviting a group of conservative leaders, including Glenn Beck and Fox News firebrand Tucker Carlson, to meet with him at headquarters. The young CEO was intent on smoothing things over. When the meeting adjourned, he wrote up a conciliatory summary and posted it on his Facebook page.

"We've built Facebook to be a platform for all ideas," the note read. "Our community's success depends on everyone feeling comfortable sharing anything they want." He needed to restore confidence in Facebook as a hub for political conversation, and he wanted to forestall any thought of congressional regulation. The life or death of his business depended on it. "It doesn't make sense for our mission or our business to suppress political content or prevent anyone from seeing what matters most to them." It wouldn't be enough to assuage the scrutiny, but Facebook had launched an internal investigation to find evidence of wrongdoing.

Conservative observers were going to be watching closely, and not only in light of Facebook's most recent offense. All year they'd seen cause for suspicion that Zuckerberg might be planning to sabotage their candidate from his seat at the switchboard. After Trump introduced his idea for the border wall, Facebook's founder had entertained the idea of publicly condemning the candidate, but his circle of advisors had talked him out of it. It would be best to stay above the fray, they counseled. He'd had to put out another PR fire that spring when one of the Trending editors had leaked a damning glimpse into the company's culture: ahead of the regular all-hands meetings Zuckerberg held, he let employees submit and vote on questions for him to address. The leaked question painted an eerie picture of just how powerful his social network had become: "What responsibility does Facebook have to help prevent President Trump in 2017?" When the leaker shared his screenshot with Gizmodo, the story went viral. The next day, he learned that Facebook had spied on his G-chat messages and caught him. He got a call informing him he'd been fired. "Please shut your laptop and don't reopen it," the company's representative ordered.

A new class of viral-publishing sole proprietors whose carefully cultivated Facebook communities represented their entire livelihoods was watching and waiting. These were the people who occupied the very bleeding edge of the algorithm/platform power struggle. Presently they were lying in wait for Facebook to announce its verdict on the fate of the Trending editors, because the human editors were a detection system for their wild, often made-up rantings.

This hyped material on the social web had not attracted deep coverage in the mainstream press, but a BuzzFeed reporter, Craig Silverman, was paying close attention. What he was most interested in was a fairly new species of online misinformation, explicitly optimized for social media, with all the trappings of a viral BuzzFeed post.

As early as the fall of 2014, Silverman had detected signs of this new scourge on his radar. He was familiar with the varietals of scams and hoaxes that cropped up every so often, and could diagnose spoofs and parodies with the best of them. He knew propaganda when he saw it. This, though, was none of the above. It was more insidious, more menacing for the fact that it presented itself as honest journalism. It assumed the form of a well-sourced article but was beholden to none of the common-law ethics of nonfiction publishing. It may have referred to true events—the Ebola outbreak, for example—but it did so only to enhance the illusion of veracity. It appeared on websites cleverly designed to be mistaken for legitimate news outlets. Its fundamental purpose was not to persuade people or change minds, but to earn their "engagement," using explosive lies masquerading as facts. These stories intended to deceive. He dubbed it "fake news," long before Trump appropriated the term.

Fake news was distinct from the flavors of fiction that preceded it in that it was uniquely a product of its environment. The news business had undergone a fundamental change when its center of gravity shifted to social media. For one thing, it meant that readers increasingly encountered articles from unfamiliar publications, just because their friends shared the link. Stories were items in themselves, unbundled from the newspaper or homepage they once had relied on to reach an audience. The reputation and credibility of the outlet that published it, then, mattered significantly less. This opened the door to new, unestablished brands that in the past readers might have dismissed out of hand. The other precondition Facebook laid for the rise of fake news was that it assembled, all in one place, a potential readership of previously unthinkable scale. For the first time it was possible for a start-up website to turn a profit on the strength of a single hit story. No longer did such a venture have to pursue the long game of earning readers' trust and growing its base of subscribers. By placing ads on its website, the publisher could painlessly monetize the traffic that was certain to flow to its web pages if it dangled the right piece of bait on Facebook.

What defined a fake news site in Silverman's eyes was twofold: first, it traded on the appearance of legitimate journalistic authority; second, it did so for financial gain. Fake news was characterized by the fact that it was in direct competition with real news. And in that head-to-head matchup, it had an inherent advantage. It was clear from the moment Silverman noticed the outbreak of Ebola stories that these hoaxes were many times more viral than the posts that debunked them. "Oh my God," he said to himself, "we're getting our asses kicked." It wasn't helping the problem that Facebook's appointed watchmen were incentivized to let the lies slide; they made commission on clicks and engagement, and hoaxes were reliable hits.

Looking at Facebook through analytical tools like CrowdTangle, Silverman explained, you could plainly see that the most successful posts were often ones that played to bias and emotion. This had always been true. The other fundamental factor that could make or break a publisher's audience, though, was the invisible hand Facebook exercised in the social conversation, and this was becoming only more pronounced as the network elevated winners and buried the laggards in an increasingly competitive field. The only way for a business to be profitable on this network was to be out ahead of the pack of publishers, quickly and unquestioningly adapting to Facebook's constantly evolving calculus. Publishers who relied on Facebook for the bulk of their traffic were thus relegated to "reading Facebook's tea leaves" for ideas to promote. Silverman granted that even BuzzFeed, since its scale was so tied to the platform, could at times seem "slavish" in its pursuit of Facebook popularity.

The internal review of the trending editors had been tense for Facebook, as it faced the possibility of alienating a good half of its American users, losing their confidence forever. Zuckerberg and his executives knew that the editors' process had been airtight and left as little room as possible for human judgment. All they had been trusted to do was check a list of algorithmically predetermined topics against a database of predetermined sources and then briefly write up the matches. Certainly there was no intricate leftist conspiracy at play, but Facebook could not ask that people simply trust them on this. Squeezed from all angles by rising political vitriol and scrutiny, Zuckerberg wished merely to walk away from this near catastrophe with as little added controversy as possible.

Essentially, he buckled under the pressure campaign from the right. With his team of advisors, he decided in August that in order to make the Trending section as uncontroversial as possible, they would have to remove all humans from the process and replace them with an algorithm that replicated their twofold task: first, to verify that the topic was being reported by a significant share of its top 10 trusted outlets, and second, to compose a short, objective summary of the news event in question. Having an intelligent machine handle these tasks met the lowest common denominator of political palatability for Facebook's whole user base. The responsibility for defending the truth would now fall on an algorithm overseen by a unit of engineers based in Seattle.

Before the fired editors' desk chairs could go cold, a cadre of opportunists flooded in to exploit the lowered barrier for inserting themselves (or their links) into an unprecedentedly charged, global conversation. On the very day the editors were fired, a fake story was featured in the Trending sidebar. It claimed that Megyn Kelly, the embattled, iconic Fox News anchor, had been fired by the network "for backing Hillary." The fabrication was the work of EndingTheFed.com, a new entrant in the suddenly thriving industry of opportunistic pro-Trump websites that looked legitimate to the untrained eye. The next one that popped up on the Trending board was a conspiracy theory that alleged the U.S. government's complicity in the 9/11 terror attacks. Then more: that Bush had conspired with Obama to rig the 2008 election. That Siri would jump out of iPhones. That the world would experience six days of darkness.

This was another embarrassment for Facebook, a high-profile drubbing of its technology at the hands of cynical human ingenuity. Zuckerberg finally decided he had to acknowledge that fake news was a problem for Facebook. He did so in early September in a post that ironically celebrated the 10th birthday of News Feed. After lauding how far his company had come, he conceded, "Still, we can help by doing a better job filtering out false information or clickbait."

But the truth was simpler and far scarier. There were no guardrails to safeguard against false alt-right conspiracy theories and Russian bots swamping Facebook. A disaster was in the making.

Silverman was one of the reporters determined not to let Zuckerberg get off that easily. He hunted down hoaxers and sought the input of ex-

pert scientists on whether the challenge Facebook had put to its algorithm was even possible for it to accomplish. Their consensus seemed to
be that, no, artificial intelligence had not yet evolved to that point. Whenever something outrageous tricked Facebook's detectors and began to take
off, Silverman would rush to debunk it, but he knew he was outmatched
and wondered if he was just throwing water on a grease fire. "Here's Why
Facebook's Trending Algorithm Keeps Promoting Fake News," read the
headline of an article he published in late October. The answer boiled
down to this: because its users do. Facebook's failure was its laissez-faire
approach to mediating the more misguided ways of its global population so
that they did not consume the network as a whole. With its hands off, Facebook was effectively enabling these viral pathogens. If its machines did
nothing more than measure the relative volume of voices perpetuating the
story versus those critiquing its veracity, sensationalism was always bound
to drown out rationality.

In November, Silverman cracked open his biggest and most disturbing
case yet. Across the world, in the small Macedonian town of Veles, a legion
of young-adult online marketers had developed a vibrant local industry of
pro-Trump fake news websites with thriving audiences that they had built
on Facebook into lucrative ventures.

Silverman would later visit Veles and meet the internet marketing guru
who had instructed the kids. He told the BuzzFeed reporter that these were
his standout students and that he was proud of them. He had not taught
them explicitly to publish fake news, but rather to do what works. He could
see they'd found content that worked quite well indeed. They were responsible for such gems as the Pope's endorsement of Trump and the line attributed to Mike Pence that Michelle Obama was the "most vulgar first lady
we've ever had." Some of their posts were getting nearly half a million interactions on Facebook, meaning they appeared in the News Feed of millions more users.

They came to the line of work without ideology as much as the intention of making a living. "The beautiful thing about the Macedonians,"
Silverman explained, "is that they are the perfect expression of the social
media publishing economy." Teenagers concocting fake news stories could
make as much as $10,000 a month from the advertising they attracted.

The Macedonians were succeeding because they gauged the desires of
their readership and addressed them directly. They evaluated the market,
saw an outsized demand, and seized the opportunity. Silverman explained
that the national government of the former Yugoslav Republic had for de-

cades undermined and corrupted the local press, leaving Macedonian citizens largely nihilistic when it came to the role of journalism. To them, it was an economic industry to be exploited. They were the people Silverman had described as occupying the "bleeding edge" of social network publishing. That they were beating the market was all the more remarkable in light of the fact that the tools they were using were rudimentary at best. More than a year later federal investigators would uncover Russian operations behind the handiwork of the Macedonian teens, and Silverman broke the news. BuzzFeed had smartly assigned him to this grossly undercovered world of news exploitation, but he was powerless to stop it.

Steve Bannon had ascended to the helm of the Trump campaign in August and was ready for total war. "I wouldn't have come aboard, even for Trump, if I hadn't known they were building this massive Facebook and data engine," Bannon told Bloomberg in October. "Facebook is what propelled Breitbart to a massive audience. We know its power."

The Trump campaign had been harnessing its power all along. Trump's digital director had used Facebook's Custom Audiences tool to round up the Facebook profiles of everyone on the campaign's mailing lists, then used another program, called Lookalike Audiences, to come up with a list of users with similar outlooks and interests. The Mercer-backed company Cambridge Analytica enabled them to take this pool of potential voters and sort them into psychographic silos. They used the data to craft messages tailored exactly to what each person, each outlook, needed to hear to be convinced. They honed those messages even further by using Facebook's A/B testing tool, called Brand Lift. The intricate switchboard Facebook provided for clients allowed them a scary degree of specificity when aiming tailored messages at ideal targets. According to a report in the *Guardian*, the Trump campaign was disseminating more than 50,000 different versions of advertisements each day during the final push. They monitored how people responded to each and methodically elevated the best-performing ads, in the process settling on a posture for their candidate that a significant plurality of Americans, bizarrely, found most electable. Facebook made the process remarkably easy to manage. The man Trump had picked to run social media for his campaign had been his caddie.

One key tool in the campaign's appeal to voters was an ad-placing product Facebook offered, called the Dark Post. An ad could be placed in the News Feed of users with whom the message was supposed to resonate, and it would be invisible to anyone outside of that target audience. It was a way to segment a population without its members noticing they had been segmented, a means of perpetuating a state of informational asymmetry, a tool that could be used to divide and confuse.

It was a crucial component of what the Trump campaign called its "voter suppression operations," of which there were at least three. The goal was to dampen turnout from reliably Democratic voting blocs: idealistic white liberals, young women, and African Americans. To discourage the franchise of African Americans, for example, the Trump campaign blasted out dark posts that reminded them of Clinton's infamous "super-predator" line from 1996, which BuzzFeed's Andrew Kaczynski had proudly resurfaced earlier in the cycle. The soundbite was accompanied by a cartoon Clinton and on-screen text that decontextualized the snippet: "Hillary Thinks African Americans are Super Predators." The Electoral College experts who pored over the results in the wake of Trump's upset victory would conclude that the strategy had worked. In Detroit and Milwaukee, to use just two examples, Clinton's turnout fell short of Obama's by margins that ended up making the critical difference in terms of who carried Michigan and Wisconsin.

While Trump's strategists developed alternate realities and ushered voters along the narrative that best suited their personal preferences, the sector Silverman watched over continued to inject plot twists pulled as if from thin air.

With the election 10 days out, Silverman, one of the few press watchdogs on the story, hectically dashed from pillar to post to thwart new lies as they popped up and engulfed the reading public. The forum boards of 4chan and 8chan, out-of-the-way sites where the alt-right in-crowd gathered to concoct pro-Trump influence campaigns throughout the election season, were abuzz with ideas for last-minute attacks. They were not official political strategists as much as volunteer guerrillas, and as such the voter suppression campaigns they hatched did not need to hew to the facts, as the "super-predator" ad had. BuzzFeed had another good reporter, Joseph Bernstein, who was well-sourced on the alt-right and revealed hacktivists who had created fake ads that were meant to look like they'd been designed by the Clinton campaign so as to mislead the Democrat's supporters into disavowing her candidacy. One, which seemed to originate from Cernovich, lifted Clinton's official branding and applied it to ads that promoted a made-up initiative, #DraftOurDaughters, with photos of young women happily though involuntarily enlisting in the military. Other compatriots blasted out fake Clinton ads advising her supporters to vote by sending a text message to a bogus hotline.

"Forget the press," Trump told the crowd at one of his rallies down the stretch. "Just read the internet." When a claim he had circulated—that a demonstrator at one of his campaign events had "ties to Isis"—was proven untrue, reporters called him on it, but he simply dodged. "What do I know about it?" he shrugged. "All I know is what's on the internet."

What was on the internet was a story from the Denver Guardian, which though it sounded like a news organization was patently not, that an FBI agent investigating Clinton's email server had been murdered. Over half a million people shared the false story on Facebook, catapulting the piece of fiction into the Trending board on News Feed. Referring to this and other malicious misinformation, President Obama, hitting the trail for Clinton the day before his successor would be decided, lamented to an Ann Arbor crowd, "As long as it's on Facebook . . . people start believing it." The consequence: "It creates this dust cloud of nonsense." It also created story after story for Silverman, but most of BuzzFeed's readers were voting for Clinton to begin with, so the real impact of his coverage was unclear. Trump supporters were unlikely to ever see it.

CHAPTER TEN

BUZZFEED III

B en Smith's growing news division was costing an arm and a leg. Despite an injection of another $200 million from Comcast/ NBC Universal in 2016 to pump up its video arm and produce television-style content, Peretti's shiny company was still spending more than it was taking in and the go-go growth years appeared to be ending. Almost every competitor, old and new, was competing for the same 18- to 34-year-old demographic.

The biggest problem was the size and greed of the host, Facebook, which was consuming such a large portion of the advertising pie. Also, what was cool and new in 2008 was beginning to fade in 2016. Smith, meanwhile, had built a large investigative team of more than 20 journalists and, under Janine Gibson, whom he recruited from the *Guardian*, was supporting a big reporting operation in London.

The stories they were breaking, including takeouts on psychiatric hospitals beset by violence, sexual assault at America's largest massage chain, corruption in professional tennis, and Russian assassinations, had impact. Their stories freed prisoners in Chicago and BuzzFeed's coverage of sexual assault and sexual harassment at universities was ahead of its traditional competitors and cost several famous professors and medical researchers their jobs. BuzzFeed was a finalist for many of the top reporting prizes.

The financial support system for the journalism was BuzzFeed Motion Pictures in Hollywood, a mini Paramount for online video, created to churn out short series and one-off clips that would go viral on Facebook. But it too cost millions. The 10-year-old BuzzFeed was, in all, a big and expensive operation.

While the *Times* and the *Post* both had clear missions—breaking news—BuzzFeed was still primarily not a news organization. Peretti was focused almost totally on the studio. Split apart, the two parts of his company, news and entertainment, were not growing in happy coexistence.

Peretti's answer was to split his company in two and separate news from the far more profitable entertainment. That left Smith and his minions in New York worrying that his news division, the loss leader, would be starved of resources. But Peretti promised to come through with a reasonable budget for the 2016 campaign that would make Smith and BuzzFeed players in the election coverage. In fact BuzzFeed would become a major thorn in the side of the leading Republican contender, Donald Trump, whose made-for-reality-TV persona and campaign trail buffoonery seemed tailor-made for BuzzFeed.

After BuzzFeed added serious news in 2012, its editors applied emotional valence to the headlines and presentation of news articles, even serious investigations BuzzFeed launched under Mark Schoofs. The headlines for investigative projects were A/B-tested. For one of its early investigations from Schoofs's group, multiple headlines were tested and two different versions of the story, a long one and a summary, were distributed. This was all to optimize the audience on Facebook. The story, which probed how battered women were being treated as criminals, succeeded in getting millions of clicks.

When Facebook adjusted its News Feed to feature more visual content and fewer text-based posts or links in 2011, BuzzFeed quickly followed suit and prioritized the production of images. That explained the predominance of posts like "The 45 Most Powerful Photos of 2011," "48 Pictures That Perfectly Capture the '90s," and "32 Pictures That Will Make You Say Awwwwwwww." There was also a new publishing hack. When other, less web-savvy outlets published stories that BuzzFeed deemed to contain a juicy bit—a peculiar detail or goofy quote, say—it could simply screenshot that snippet and post it to their Facebook page, where, since it was an image rather than a link, the network would serve it to more users. Sometimes BuzzFeed lifted its photos from other outlets, sharing traffic with a competitor, as long as BuzzFeed got credit for the Facebook interaction.

At the beginning of 2012, BuzzFeed had introduced a new feature that aimed to elicit a more active response from its Facebook followers. The programmers had designed a tool that enabled users who visited Buzz-Feed's Facebook page to choose from buttons beyond the default "Like." The new options were catchier, designed to appeal to the young audience: LOL, OMG, and WTF. The posts BuzzFeed shared would play to these canned reactions. "In a social world, reacting and sharing media is the best way to express yourself and connect with your friends," Peretti said in a press release announcing the new reaction buttons, which quickly became icons of the social media age. At the *Times*, journalists sneered at them and thought they demeaned readers. But Peretti was unapologetic. "By combining BuzzFeed with Facebook Timeline, we allow our readers and their friends to easily express the full range of human emotions."

By the numbers, BuzzFeed had become an established cornerstone of the "perfect newspaper" that Zuckerberg envisioned. At its zenith in 2013, 15 of the 20 most viral Facebook posts by the 200 major sites in the partner network were BuzzFeed posts. Only three had anything resembling news value: "Two Years after She Passed Away, a Woman Gives Her Family an Unforgettable Christmas," "A Lot of People Are Very Upset That an Indian-American Woman Won the Miss America Pageant," and a clip from an interview on Fox News, which BuzzFeed suggested might be "the most embarrassing" the network had ever done. BuzzFeed spent that year and much of the next squarely atop the largest and fastest-growing communications system in history.

In November 2014, just after midterm elections, Smith published an essay in which he forecast that 2016 would be what he called "the Facebook Election," though he did not anticipate the dark tone his phrase would take on. By then, he projected, the social network would have crossed the threshold: it would be the central forum for news media and "the place where American elections are fought and won. The social network may end TV's long dominance of American politics—and open the door to a new kind of populism." This future reality was already in the making.

The evidence was clear. Two years earlier Facebook had run a secret experiment on its users. On Election Day 2012 the site displayed a shiny red, white, and blue VOTE icon atop the News Feed of two million users and measured a significant corresponding increase in turnout among the sample. The results laid bare the fearsome power of Facebook. In 2014 the company ran another experiment: it doctored the nature of the stories that appeared in the News Feed of 689,003 users so that they skewed either more negative or positive than normal, and from there tracked the spread of what it called social contagion. "These results indicate that emotions expressed by others on Facebook influence our own emotions, constituting experimental evidence for massive-scale contagion via social networks," wrote the study's principal investigator.

Smith announced a powerful new partnership between BuzzFeed and Facebook that would give his newsroom (along with ABC News) exclusive access to the social network's proprietary analytics, revealing how American users felt about various politicians, policies, and events. This "sentiment data" would allow BuzzFeed to pore over a deep reservoir of information about the emotional and ideological state of the union, in real time, during the campaign and to inspect on a staggeringly granular level the shifts that occurred. It would allow BuzzFeed to weigh in on topics with intel that would supplement, or supplant, the more conventional opinion-poll data that the networks and newspapers obsessed over. Facebook analyzed users' posts for topical content, then assigned each item a positive, negative, or neutral value. Smith's team would have a grasp on "how Iowans feel about Hillary Clinton" or "which Republican candidate appears to be best liked by women." They could get meaningful data from groups as small as 1,000 people. Smith called it "a powerful new window into the largest political conversation in America."

Perhaps too powerful, thought some critics, who saw the collusion between platform and publisher as potentially destructive. They feared it would give BuzzFeed an unfair advantage, not only in reporting on how voters felt but in keeping that information to themselves and using it, as it did CrowdTangle, to determine what content would perform best with certain audiences. They warned that this might signal the end of the journalistic ideal of objective distance. Despite the flimsy science of "sentiment analysis," BuzzFeed would read Facebook's data as an earnest map of American political sentiment and assume that any clues they gleaned reflected truths about the electorate, when what they were actually observing was likely to be a fold in the fabric of Facebook's own apparatus, a self-fulfilling reflection of its own hand in the conversation. BuzzFeed threatened to amplify and reinforce the unspoken influence that Facebook's supposedly neutral network exerted over public opinion. The old ideal of journalistic distance in news reporting, editing, and presentation could be shattered by this new, clearly emotive model.

Peretti saw this change as a clear example of innovative disruption, but it turned into an unwelcome one. Smith, however, seemed giddy. He was at the helm of an operation that saw itself as unimpeachably in the know, and he relished the chance to gloatingly dismiss the out-of-touch newsmen whose place he was taking. "At some point in the next two years," Smith wrote, "the pollsters and ad makers who steer American presidential campaigns will be stumped: The nightly tracking polls are showing a dramatic swing in the opinions of the electorate, but neither of two typical factors— huge news or a major advertising buy—can explain it. They will, eventually, realize that the viral, mass conversation about politics on Facebook and other platforms has finally emerged as a third force in the core business of politics, mass persuasion."

With Peretti's backing, Smith had hired and trained a first-class team of eight young political reporters, led by a young, 20-something editor, Katherine Miller. Miller, with a solid background from the new, conservative media world, saw Trump as a serious candidate before many of her peers.

Meanwhile the Facebook Election that Smith had so eagerly predicted was turning out not to be the Facebook election he had optimistically envisioned.

BuzzFeed understood the power of Trump's candidacy because it used some of the same brand-building strategies. In many ways Trump was the perfect embodiment of BuzzFeed's reverse-mullet structure: mostly party in the front with business in the back. From his 15 seasons starring in *The Apprentice*, he knew how to throw a party and be the entertaining host. BuzzFeed evinced a similarly jaded view of legacy news organizations and a flair for irreverence whenever things felt overserious. Both the candidate and the website had enhanced their stature by telling stories "you won't believe."

While other news organizations dismissed Trump as a buffoon whose candidacy did not merit serious coverage, BuzzFeed set no such bar. The Huffington Post went so far as to consign coverage of Trump to its entertainment section instead of with its politics coverage. Meanwhile Smith's newsroom would cover Trump's political ascendancy and then, after his election, become a major foil when it acted unilaterally in publishing the uncensored contents of an infamous dossier that contained, among other things, unverified claims about Trump's interactions with Russian prostitutes.

Very early on, in January 2014, BuzzFeed was one of the only news organizations that covered Trump's appearance at the Politics & Eggs forum in Manchester, New Hampshire, an informal but time-honored "screen test" for would-be candidates. The real-estate magnate was toying with a run for New York governor but confronting what felt like the quick-approaching expiration date on his political aspirations. Yet fittingly, at the moment this entertainer's political impact was supposedly hitting an all-time low, BuzzFeed swooped in, as if to resurrect his image.

Having traveled up to New Hampshire for the morning, BuzzFeed's McKay Coppins, one of Smith's political protégés, got his moment with the businessman after his speech to a large but unresponsive crowd. "They didn't ask one question about running for governor," Trump complained to his aides. "They didn't care."

Coppins seemed to be struggling to contain his Schadenfreude. He wrote, "After this morning, Trump can no longer escape the fact that his political 'career'—a long con that the blustery billionaire has perpetrated on the country for 25 years by repeatedly pretending to consider various runs for office, only to bail out after generating hundreds of headlines—finally appears to be on the brink of collapse." His story was cheekily accompanied by a Photoshopped rendering of Trump at a gilded desk in the Oval Office, as if to tempt fate. (Making a thing a thing, it turned out, could backfire.)

By investing attention where the rest of the pack deemed it didn't belong, BuzzFeed turned a 15-minute Q&A opportunity into a 36-hour saga that would provide the basis for a vividly colorful profile, all because Trump was bored and desperate for attention. As Coppins told it, Trump was practically pleading with him for more time. He offered the young reporter a seat on his private plane and a bag of pretzels, put him up at Mar-a-Lago, and personally instructed the waitstaff at his resort to bring Coppins lunch and outfit him with a bathing suit. The profile revealed a distraught Trump, laden with doubts about his fading stardom. It was telling that he seemed troubled by the fact that new-media outlets were more interested in him than old ones. "It used to be the *New York Times*, now it's BuzzFeed," he confessed with what Coppins detected as wistfulness. "The world has changed."

It eluded Trump that this power shift was a precondition for his success. Although not all the pieces were yet in place to make his upset possible, they were starting to align. In the meantime there would be some turbulence. The day after Coppins's piece was published, Trump's handler Sam Nunberg, who had granted the reporter access, resigned, calling the story "an incredible pejorative hit piece" and wishfully declaring the Buzz-Feed writer's "professional reputation . . . null and void." Trump had already blacklisted the site.

In mounting his counterstrike, Trump would call upon a new ally, one who was itching to make use of a well-stocked arsenal. He enlisted Bannon, who had positioned himself to play a big role in politics with funding from Robert Mercer. Mercer wanted to expand Breitbart, and Bannon, seeing his opportunity, wrote up a business plan on his friend's behalf. That summer Mercer ponied up the $10 million and made Bannon a co-owner and director of the company.

In the immediate aftermath of the Coppins piece, Bannon's Breitbart marshalled an impressive multipronged takedown of the BuzzFeed author.

In six distinct stories, all given significant play on the site's homepage, Breit-bart rebutted the smear job. One, for instance, quoted a Mar-a-Lago host-ess who said that during Coppins's stay "he was looking at me like I was yummy." Another quoted Trump calling Coppins a "scumbag" and further alleging that the BuzzFeed writer, a Mormon, had behaved lewdly toward fe-male guests at the resort. In still another takedown, Breitbart reached out to Alaska's former governor and Tea Party figurehead Sarah Palin, who without ever having met Coppins, said, "This nervous geek isn't fit to tie the Don-ald's wingtips." War had been declared between Breitbart and BuzzFeed.

In private conversations early in 2014, soon after the Coppins piece went online, Mercer, who also owned Cambridge Analytica, and Bannon dis-cussed the urgency of finding a candidate to capitalize on the groundswell of national discontent. Charting the rise of the influence of the Mercers on politics, the *New Yorker*'s Jane Mayer detailed how the project was code-named "Candidate Smith," a nod to the archetype made famous by the movie *Mr. Smith Goes to Washington*. But at the time, neither Bannon nor Mercer knew exactly whom to cast for the role of Candidate Smith. Early on, they backed Ted Cruz.

Smith, meanwhile, observed, "What is beginning to dawn on cam-paigns is that persuasion works differently when it relies on sharing. It is a political truism that people are most likely to believe what their friends and neighbors tell them . . . and the social conversation favors things that generations of politicians have been trained to avoid: spontaneity, surprise, authenticity, humor, raw edge, the occasional human stumble." He went on, "A few modern politicians appear to have a real feel for the raw emo-tion and, sometimes, (apparent) spontaneity that people will want to share." Smith's observation was dead on, but in calling his shot he missed the mark. Joe Biden's raw edge might be enough to arouse a stir on the social net-work, he suggested, or maybe this was the year for the "blunt" Elizabeth Warren or the "theatrical" Ted Cruz.

On June 16, 2015, Trump officially declared his candidacy for pres-ident from the gilded lobby of Manhattan's Trump Tower. The next day Coppins's BuzzFeed story was headlined, "Donald Trump, America's Troll, Gets Tricked into Running for President." The subhead was "All The Don-ald wants is for the political world to listen to him again. But is it worth a humiliating 2016 defeat?" Coppins was soon banned from Trump rallies, one of the first political journalists to be blacklisted in what became a very long line of reporters Trump would lambaste as "enemies of the people." By summer the *Washington Post* would be kicked out too. Trump seemed, at first, to be more tolerant of the *Times*, whose coverage and approval he had always craved.

The Breitbart constituency loved the antipress rebukes from Trump, as did a wide swath of the online and self-fashioned culture warriors, and conservative chatboard pontificators and pundits—a sector long marginalized to an insular corner of the web—perked up, thinking Trump might be the antipolitician they had hoped would come along one day. They were, by and large, inclined to antigovernment ideology and liked Trump's trashing of the elite, especially the mainstream media.

Trump had many of the necessary skills for the moment: mastery of Twitter, total comfort on television, the ability to be entertaining, the right message to stir right-wing outrage, and the ability to brazenly lie. He proved to be manna for social media and television.

Before the election there were warnings that the disproportionate coverage of Trump as an entertaining buffoon, with little attention focused on any of his proposed and extremist policy positions, had let him run wild over the U.S. media and build his candidacy on the back of billions' worth of free media attention. At a conference on campaign coverage at Harvard before the election, the *Washington Post*'s Marty Baron bristled and took exception to a Pew study that showed shallow, horse-race coverage that advantaged Trump. When CNN chief Jeff Zucker appeared at a postelection conference, also at Harvard, he was jeered by the audience, which included the campaign managers of Trump's rivals in the GOP primaries. As Zucker defended the network's "balanced" coverage, one attendee shouted that when Trump was slated to appear on the trail, CNN "showed empty podiums!" During that dead airtime, the other candidates were holding events that received no coverage from CNN or anyone. Zucker had allowed Trump to monopolize coverage, his GOP rivals protested.

Katherine Miller, BuzzFeed's political editor, was also at the Harvard conference. With Smith, she'd tailored BuzzFeed's coverage in very different ways from her competitors in the mainstream news media. Miller herself had an unusual profile. She was in her late 20s, a graduate of Vanderbilt University who then interned at the *Washington Times* newspaper, owned by executives from Sun Myung Moon's Unification Church and known for its sharply conservative positions. Later she became "war room director" and the digital managing editor of another conservative publication, the *Washington Free Beacon*. Despite her young age, she was a killer editor, known for fast deployment of investigative teams. Her ties to the right were useful to BuzzFeed, which covered the rise of the alt-right earlier and more thoroughly than almost anyone else.

Smith decided early on to let his reporters call Trump a racist and demagogue in their social media feeds, though Miller avoided those words in BuzzFeed's actual news stories during the GOP primaries. Still, as a youth-focused brand, BuzzFeed was more brazen in the way it described candidates and allowed its reporters a freer writing style. In contrast, it was not until September 2016 that the *Times* used the word "lie" in a front-page headline to describe Trump's false statements about President Obama and the birther movement. The *Post* and the *Wall Street Journal* opted for words like "false" or "falsehood" for Trump's lies. Baron explained in an interview, "I think we should call things false when we know they're false . . . and we have." But using the word "lie" "does suggest that you know [the person] knew it was false" and said it anyway. "Absent evidence of that," Baron added, "don't expect the *Washington Post* to use the L word in reporting about the current administration." While the old guard agonized over shedding traditional journalism diplomatese, BuzzFeed used loaded words as long as they were accurate.

As truths, lies, and all manner of gray areas commingled on Facebook, it was more urgent than ever that BuzzFeed, whose team was perhaps the most fluent in the network's workings, cover its rising influence on politics. The lynchpin of the team was Silverman, the media's foremost expert on the subject of fake news, consistently beating other outlets to the punch.

Silverman's working at BuzzFeed was the ultimate irony. Just months before his hiring, the media watchdog had imparted words of caution to readers in the wake of BuzzFeed's viral hit "The Dress." As a fellow doing research through the Tow Center for Digital Journalism at Columbia University, Silverman had articulated the dangers of viral escapism and the new era of ubiquity in an essay written for the Poynter Institute titled "The Lesson from the Dress Color Debate That Every Journalist Needs to Know."

"We are all at the mercy of our brain and its cognitive processes," Silverman wrote. "Our eyes took in the information in front of us, our brain processed it, and in many cases it gave us the wrong answer. But the fact that it was coming from our brain meant that it seemed like exactly the right answer. People insisted on what they were seeing *because it was what they were actually seeing*." It was a lesson from his recently published report on the state of misinformation and journalists' struggle to combat it. The world of viral publishing was fraught with psychological quagmires of which Silverman thought his peers ought to be wary. He focused on five: the backfire effect, confirmation bias, motivated reasoning, biased assimilation, and group polarization.

Silverman was not merely conveying the cognitive processes at play. He was making a value judgment. "Journalists today have an imperative— and an opportunity," he wrote, "to sift through the mass of content being created and shared in order to separate true from false, and to help the truth to spread."

Before he joined BuzzFeed, Silverman had observed Ben Smith with disinterested curiosity. Smith's project was an experiment in the viability of an operation begun without regard for journalistic ethics (attribution, accountability, etc.) that had gotten a journalistic organ grafted onto it. Silverman watched as Smith stumbled early on, and took him to task when appropriate. Smith, in turn, understood that Silverman was trying to keep him honest. So when Smith wrote to him one day, in the wake of the scandal he'd created by deleting several thousand old posts from BuzzFeed's archives, Silverman was flattered that the site's editor was soliciting his professional advice. Smith wanted Silverman's input on the corrections policy he was drafting. "Oh shit," Silverman remembered thinking to himself, "maybe they're serious."

By that point Silverman had built his credentials as an online media watchdog for more than a decade. He had been living in Montreal in 2004 when he started a blog called Regret the Error, in which he covered the corrections newspapers ran when their reporters or editors slipped up. He rounded up examples of plagiarism and falsified sources, as well as good-faith errors. He found that online, just as in print, misinformation sometimes resulted from journalists making honest mistakes. The difference, though, was that social media accelerated the rate at which those errors both occurred and spread. He ran the blog for 11 years before Poynter acquired it in 2015. Over that time his focus shifted from correction etiquette to the higher-order concern of how journalists verify information in the first place. He researched common pitfalls and best practices and compiled a comprehensive handbook on verification.

Having amassed expertise in an area of rapidly increasing importance, it occurred to Silverman there might be a business opportunity in it. With a partner he established a start-up company called Emergent that would provide outsourced fact-checking and verification to the growing sector of digital publishers incapable of managing that part of the process in-house. Emergent's fact-checking system was simple: Silverman would basically report out the matter in question to find what was true or false.

Facebook became interested and asked how he was doing the checking. Silverman told them it was just himself and one checker. But each case they resolved gave them useful intel about which sources had been trustworthy and which had not. The idea was that over time, their database might be robust enough to allow them to automate the verification process, or at least let the computer handle some share of the burden. In the short term, Emergent's goal was not necessarily to give the fastest true-or-false verdict, but to be sure.

Smith's 2015 offer to join BuzzFeed appealed to Silverman. It would provide a broader journalistic purview for investigating and disclosing how misinformation spread digitally to his new beat: fake news. But before he could dig in, Smith asked him to fill a very different role. BuzzFeed was expanding internationally and needed him to bring the brand to his native Canada. Silverman obliged.

Though he worked from a modest office in Toronto, he found himself exhibiting the BuzzFeed schizophrenia. As the information environment got worse, he possessed the skills to be the company's much-needed digital truth-seeker. But as the editor of BuzzFeed Canada, he was expected to supervise a team of young nonjournalists who churned out viral fluff, pseudoscience, and opiatic diversions for the selfie generation. One of his early hires, a quiz-maker named Sarah Aspler, summed up her purpose at Buzz-Feed: "There's so much *shit* on the internet, it's kind of fun to just be like, What kind of sandwich am I?" She continued, "People want to know what will happen to them, they want to be reaffirmed in their beliefs. People love it when we're accurate, or when we're really inaccurate. If it seems like science, people appreciate that."

Just eight months after Silverman's criticism of Dress-like viral publishing, he found himself in BuzzFeed's New York headquarters with a roundtable of the site's international editors for the purpose of rebounding from a "crappy traffic month" that Luke Lewis, the U.K. editor, blamed on "the Facebook gods." The session centered on easy fixes. Posts that evoked readers' nostalgia for their college years "work every time"; readers liked BuzzFeed's checklists because they lent a sense of control; social justice buzz was reliably popular because readers "think in sharing them they're doing good." When it came to photos, less glitz and gloss gave the impression of something more authentic. Silverman asked the table for advice: "Should we shitty up our images?"

The discussion eventually turned to management advice. The international bureau chiefs wanted new ideas for how to keep the creative output of their staffs steadily high. One suggestion was to have department personnel briefly switch roles, so that news reporters produced buzz and the buzz makers reported the news, as if the skills were fungible. The editor of the Indian bureau, which was focused on creating buzz to quickly increase its national audience, expressed uneasiness that her staffers seemed intimidated whenever she assigned them a story with actual news value. The solution to calming them was simply not to use the word "news" when describing the assignment.

BuzzFeed's staff was not as uniformly liberal as in other news operations. Tim Gionet, who made videos and oversaw BuzzFeed's social media presence, had a bleached-blond mullet and aviators, and his colleagues described him as quirkily jocular, bombastic, and "really fucking good at social media." But a rift was forming between him and the giddy band of viralogists, whom he came to resent as cloyingly politically correct.

He hit his breaking point one day when they chided him for a passing comment about Justin Bieber. "He is totally my spirit animal," Gionet joked, only to be stung by a rebuke from a colleague: "Hey bro, you can't say spirit animal. That's culturally appropriating Native American culture and that's not cool." The pushback only drove Gionet in a more polarized direction. "When I started BuzzFeed, I was making videos about cats and beer pong," he told Business Insider. "By the end of it, it was about feminism and white privilege." He left the company a Trump supporter, wearing a "Make America Great Again" cap and with the candidate's face tattooed on his arm.

A bloc of pro-Trump viralogists began emerging, "doing it in this really dark way." Gionet would find common cause with Milo Yiannopoulos and make a name for himself on the alt-right by cashing in on the cultural capital of BuzzFeed and its tactics of viral influence. He poured his talents into "putting together meme armies" to amplify Trump's message, the process of which he would later detail in a book titled *Meme Magic Secrets Revealed.*

Meanwhile at BuzzFeed, Silverman and Charlie Warzel reported on how Facebook had become a war zone, where the left and right blasted out two differing versions of news. Warzel had started out as the site's technology reporter, hunting for scoops on new products coming out of the industry. Over time his beat took on a watchdog role, as the influence these gigantic companies had on the public and its ability to access and exchange information grew exponentially. Platforms like Facebook had to be held accountable, as did the bad actors who operated on them for ulterior purposes. Warzel made it his business to always be probing the "newest, weirdest parts of the internet," which he said BuzzFeed was uniquely qualified to dig into. "BuzzFeed knows there's a lot of noise, but there's some signal there."

He characterized the conspiracies animating conservative bulletin boards like 4chan and Reddit as being fundamentally "antijournalism," and they became his central focus. Frequenting the rougher, raunchier haunts of the social web, he saw unspeakable, racist things being said, shared, and spreading. What took him aback, though, was that the increasingly deplorable discourse was no longer confined to these insular chatrooms. He was watching their destructive, denigrating ideologies "become talking points in politics." Their memes began to catch on in bigger circles and gain traction: images of journalists were being Photoshopped into gas chambers, and circulated. "It's easy to write off, for example, racist message boards," he told me, "but they presage, for example, Charlottesville."

BuzzFeed was looking into undercovered corners of the web for news and competing on all aspects of the campaign. McKay Coppins and two colleagues, Rosie Gray and Ruby Cramer, were turning out political pieces every bit as good as those in the *New York Times* and *Washington Post*. But throughout the first half of 2016 its newsroom only unevenly grappled with the sobriety of the election.

On the evening of Super Tuesday, Andrew Kaczynski and his three-person team of reporters who made up what BuzzFeed calls the "K-File" were sitting in their corner of the newsroom, each on their two-screen setup, with over-the-ear headphones on, digging into the presidential candidates' pasts to find the most embarrassing moments of their public lives. Kaczynski G-chatted his underlings to assign them micro-investigations. He dished an old radio appearance by John Kasich to one, an Eric Trump interview to another, and an appearance by Donald Trump Jr. to another. Much of the communication among K-File staffers took place over online chat, even though they sat within arm's reach of one another. In case someone did want to address them verbally, they wore one headphone slightly off the ear.

On the desk where they sat was a basketball, an embroidered kitten ball cap, a hard hat with an NRA sticker, a "Make America Great Again" cap, and a piñata of Donald Trump.

At the suggestion of his editor, Kaczynski instructed Chris Massie to dig for old records of police dispatches, wondering if anything on the Trump sons would turn up. Nothing did, but the K-File had been on a roll of late, dredging up plenty of other juicy finds. Kaczynski's latest: "Donald Trump Had No Idea What Overalls Were until 2005." In fact of the last 30 posts Kaczynski had published, 25 revolved around Trump. The revelations included, among other things, that the candidate "isn't into anal," that his wife never poops, and that he once told Howard Stern that if Princess Diana were still alive, he could probably have had sex with her.

"Andrew's team, along with [the *Times*'s] Maggie Haberman, have broken like 50% of the stories this election cycle," Ben Smith beamed to me one day. "It's crazy the extent to which they're driving this." But when pressed which stories Kaczynski's team has broken recently, he went blank except for a gaffe by Ben Carson and the Trump sons' disavowals of David Duke. "It's funny how much political reporting is ephemera," he mused. "In this line of work, you often can't remember your biggest stories one year later." Or one day later.

Super Tuesday would prove to be memorable for BuzzFeed News, as it was the occasion of its first attempt to broadcast coverage of the night's events using Facebook's new live-video streaming tool. The concept for the show that evening was to put Gavon Laessig, the deputy news director and front page editor, in a side office, in front of a whiteboard on which there was a map of states for Laessig to fill in as the results were announced. They had brainstormed several hooks for Laessig's coverage but decided in the end to keep it simple: surround the host with a pantry's worth of junk food and alcohol—Ben & Jerry's ice cream, tubs of peanut butter, marsh-mallows, Oreos, candy, beer, and Southern Comfort—and then film him yukking it up with a procession of other BuzzFeed reporters, some in dog masks, that he would welcome into his makeshift broadcast studio. Two staffers trained their iPhone cameras on the scene—one horizontal, one vertical—broadcasting in real time as Laessig goofed around with col-leagues. He spent a good portion of the evening in a parliamentarian-style wig. He had a drink each time a state was called, and downed shots with his co-correspondents. On Facebook, BuzzFeed promoted the broadcast by urging users, "Watch as Super Tuesday ruins this man's night."

Just as the primary results started to trickle in, the K-File got up from its table and slunk down the corridor into a lounge room, "doing what they always do," their editor, Kyle Blaine, said. They booted up the vintage Nintendo 64 video game console, launched into a spirited round of Super Smash Bros., and let the campaign-inspired trash talk cascade forth. En-gulfing his opponents in fireballs, Kaczynski, whose entire group would be picked off by CNN before the election, enjoined them to "feel the Bern!" Massie, eliminated from the melee first, attributed his loss to "rampant col-lusion" among the other players.

As the livestream passed the two-hour mark, Lisa Tozzi, the editor whom BuzzFeed hired from the *Times* to be its news director, was watching from her standing desk and finally voiced her concern over Laessig's declining state: "I'm worried that we may need to cut down on the alcohol. I'm hearing the drunk voice." She fetched a seltzer from the fridge and delivered it to an obviously intoxicated Laessig. Under the table and out of view of the cameras, the host had positioned a trash bin between his legs. He seemed to be growing disoriented when, having nothing else to say, he declared a win for John Kerry. For one last laugh, a producer handed him a bottle of Coke and a roll of Mentos—the two components of the classic DIY chemistry experiment—and Laessig mixed them in his mouth, producing an explosion that spewed out between his lips and across the meeting room.

Meanwhile Kaczynski was having a laugh at Blaine's expense, tweeting out a colleague's video clip that showed the K-File leader mauling his editor with the piñata. "Kyle getting sodomized by the Trump piñata!" he guffawed.

Around 10 o'clock, as Trump was scoring pivotal wins, they decided to wrap up the livestream. The consensus in the newsroom was that regardless of who won the primaries, the night had been a great success, with plenty of unique viewers, not nearly as big as the livestreams being offered by cable outlets or the big newspaper sites, but certainly distinctive. When Laessig finally emerged from his booth, he was greeted by the cheers of his newsroom colleagues. "Ga-von! Ga-von! Ga-von!" they chanted. Smiling proudly, Laessig declared, "I'm an embarrassment to my profession!"

Laessig's treatment of the night as entertainment echoed the Huffington Post's decision to put its Trump stories in its entertainment vertical. Kaczynski's reporting too treated the race more as a pop-culture spectacle than as an existential referendum on the country's direction. K-File contributed some good scoops, and in February and March their finds had taken center stage when the CNN anchors hosting presidential debates had referred to the BuzzFeed unit's stories. Anderson Cooper had cornered Trump with K-File footage of him supporting the invasion of Iraq in 2002, contrary to his claim throughout the campaign that he opposed it. Then Don Lemon put the screws to Clinton by citing the 1996 clip surfaced by the K-File in which she labeled young men who join gangs "super-predators." The "super-predators" line would figure into Russia's efforts to defeat Clinton and be recycled by various fake Black Lives Matter sites to depress the black vote in battleground states like Michigan.

For the Republican National Convention, held in Cleveland in July 2016, BuzzFeed planned a party that would do their 2012 mermaid bash one better. The rooftop soiree, geared toward similarly banned publishers, was called "Red, White & Blacklisted" and brought together the leading lights of the new-media vanguard; in the words of Gawker's correspondent at the event, "It felt like every single person I follow on Twitter was together in one room." To set the tone, old news clips of the House Un-American Activities Committee sessions were projected on the walls, to the accompaniment of hip-hop mashups and a free-flowing open bar. The self-congratulatory levity got put in check, though, when in walked Rudy Giuliani, surrounded by a troop of bodyguards in bulletproof armor. The former New York City mayor ordered a scotch, neat, and sipped it while puffing on a cigar among the swirl of millennial media types in the 12th-floor lounge. He stuck around for a while, then he and his entourage proceeded toward the exit. That's when BuzzFeed's D.C. bureau chief, John Stanton, approached the onetime presidential candidate with a question. The well-built reporter, whose sleeve tattoos, shaved head, and goatee distinguished him as the member of the Beltway press corps who looked most like an ex-convict, did not get very far before he was tackled to the ground by a security guard near the elevator banks, and Giuliani made his getaway. BuzzFeed's spokesperson would chalk the incident up to a "misunderstanding." Seeing reporters get roughed up or loudly booed became less and less unusual.

When the billionaire businessman and Trump family friend Tom Barrack took the stage, he began his speech with a one-liner that referred to the menu at Trump Tower: "I feel like the anchovy on Ivanka's Caesar salad." As his K-File colleagues played video games, 24-year-old Chris Massie hit pause. His months of scouring the internet for anything that could be considered post-worthy, any little trifle with glancing relevance to the political contest, had prepared him for this moment. "Ivanka's salad is a Greek salad!" he shouted and grabbed his laptop to find the menu on Google. "It was a Greek salad with diced tomatoes, cucumbers, red onions, Mediterranean cured olives, and fucking feta cheese!" he exclaimed, feeling validated, and tweeted out the correction in case anyone cared.

Trump's speech was a joyless tirade, and Kaczynski and the K-File saw little news in it. They hoped for an early night. But before they could shut off their computers, they got pinged by Miller, the politics editor, who was asking them to reach out to a few immigration hardliners (she provided a short list) for comment on what they thought of Trump's speech. Massie saw it first and brought it to Kaczynski's attention. "I don't know any of these people," Massie said.

"You can always just ignore the email," Kaczynski responded.

"It was a G-chat," corrected Massie.

Kaczynski pulled up his inbox to find Miller had written him too. "This is bullshit!" he yelled. "Why the fuck do we have to do this?" It was 11:30 p.m. and Kaczynski had thought he was done. "This is horseshit," he muttered, getting more upset at the fact that Miller hadn't provided the sources' contact information. "I'm not calling anyone."

Blaine chimed in, "This sounds like it was a Ben Smith idea." (It was.)

After a few minutes of huffing and puffing, Kaczynski divvied up the source list, and each member of the K-File made two quick calls before heading home.

Even for BuzzFeed, which had always outperformed its competitors on Facebook, it was imperative to do whatever was necessary to stay in Zuckerberg's good graces. That could be managed easily enough with the fluffy viral fodder that was BuzzFeed's signature. News articles and political items were less exciting to Facebook users. Indeed BuzzFeed might never have entered the news game if Peretti hadn't gotten a strong indication from Facebook that the move would be rewarded. BuzzFeed News remained the company's loss leader, but it was a critical part of Peretti's long-term strategy to build the site's prestige with both advertisers and the online platforms. By doing news, Peretti told me, BuzzFeed was pleasing Facebook and Twitter, both of which depended on news content being shared on their sites but neither of which had the capacity or desire to produce it themselves. If Peretti could demonstrate the vital role BuzzFeed played in their informational ecosystems, they were bound to keep cutting him good deals.

The strategy seemed to be paying off when Facebook made its May 2016 decision to add BuzzFeed to its internal list of the 10 outlets for its moderators to rely upon when it came to policing hoaxes. Being named to the top 10 most-trusted list marked a drastic turnaround for BuzzFeed from the prior year, when a Pew study ranked it dead last among news outlets in terms of readers' trust. Their tenure on the list would be short-lived, however; two weeks later the existence of Facebook's secret group of trending editors was exposed and soon thereafter disbanded, opening the floodgates to fake news.

Right before the election BuzzFeed and Smith got a kick in the gut. On Yom Kippur, the Jewish day of atonement, Smith was home and unreachable. Kaczynski and his two deputies chose the occasion to announce they were leaving BuzzFeed and joining CNN. It was another example of legacy media buying up the trendsetters of the new.

BuzzFeed threw resources into covering Clinton too. Its young audience was not as familiar with her, or as jaded, as older voters, and Smith felt a duty to give them a full portrait. Few covered the Clinton campaign, which assiduously kept reporters from national news organizations at bay, more closely than Ruby Cramer, one of BuzzFeed's top young politics reporters, who had been trailing Clinton since 2013. She traced the unofficial campaign trail through foundation events and book tour stops. In those days Cramer and the *Times*'s Amy Chozick would sometimes carpool with two other reporters who were the only ones assigned to the campaign full time. Cramer was filing typically one or two stories each day and working gradually to plumb the personality behind one of modern America's most visible political personas. "She seemed like such a challenge," Cramer told me. As Clinton's campaign got off the ground and her press pack grew, Cramer got a rare opportunity to spend time with the candidate alone for a profile. "I walked into a pin factory in New Hampshire with her, and the other reporters saw me and they hated me," she said. BuzzFeed's correspondent would have to make the most of that shot, because soon after, when Bernie Sanders won the Iowa primary, the Clinton campaign abruptly cut off access. They deemed the risk of bad press worthwhile only if the interview was going to be on TV.

Cramer had hoped to cover Clinton as her father had covered the 1988 presidential candidates in his classic book *What It Takes*, considered by many the best campaign narrative ever written. Richard Ben Cramer had died in 2013 and so, in a way, had his style of reporting. In-depth pieces about the candidates' biographies, their intellectual influences and the like were now a rarity. And Clinton, for her part, was so inaccessible that such pieces were almost impossible to write. News tidbits, campaign gossip, and the latest polling data were more natural fodder for the fast-paced rhythm of the internet. Though she mostly hewed to the internet's constant demand for new material and the need to compete on a daily basis with all the other political reporters covering Clinton, Cramer succeeded in peeling away from the pack and writing some of the best profile pieces on the candidate, including one on her faith.

Cramer and Chozick both yearned to do deep profiles of Clinton and to show readers what made her tick. But the candidate was so curtained off that the two reporters almost never saw her up close in unguarded situations. Every minute of her campaign was staged and scripted. Their editors, meanwhile, were obsessed with the news of the day: any new developments in the email investigation or reports of clashing campaign aides. Stories about the hacking of the Democratic Party's emails during the convention and then the hacking of Clinton's top aide John Podesta's emails became feeding frenzies, with little digging into Russia's orchestration of the leaks. Being competitive on these stories rather than going deep into the life and character of the candidates was what their editors wanted. The new style of campaign reporting would surely have dismayed Cramer's father.

In 2008, when I directed campaign coverage at the *Times*, *What It Takes* was still an ideal. I assigned a series, "The Long Run," for which *Times* reporters were assigned deep explorations of certain events and turning points in the candidates' lives. We published revelatory pieces about Obama's relationship with his mother and Mitt Romney's years of Mormon service in France as a young man. While the *Times* also ran some excellent pieces in 2016, Chozick was frustrated by how little time she was given to work on these kinds of stories. And when she did leave the pack, as in a story about Clinton's work as a young civil rights activist in the South, Clinton would not talk to her even though the piece was highly flattering.

Cramer faced the same frustrations. With a week to go, she was relieved to have the end in sight. She powered through the final five days on hardly a wink of sleep, with a rising fever and a developing case of bronchitis, jetting from Philadelphia, where Bruce Springsteen was rocking the vote, to Raleigh, North Carolina, for a Lady Gaga benefit concert. The press plane landed in White Plains, New York, at 3 a.m. on the eve of Election Day, and by 4:30 Cramer had checked into her hotel in midtown Manhattan and could go to bed. She slept in the next morning, and when she woke up she checked her email to find a heartfelt note from Peretti, whom she had never met, commending her on three years of hard work. She felt proud and full of hope.

She found her way to the Javits Center around 7 p.m. as the polls were closing and Clinton's party was heating up. She had prewritten the stories that would be expected of her when the election was called, including the main article slated for BuzzFeed's homepage: "She's President," the headline declared triumphantly. It was the same story that everyone in her press pool had drafted. (Indeed, I was at the Javits Center too, to add a bit of scene and color to a 7,000-word piece I had written for the *Guardian* on the election of the first woman president.) But before it could come true, history would revise its course.

Meanwhile, just across town at the BuzzFeed headquarters, the revelry of Smith's newsroom raged on. The evening's festivities featured two themed cocktails, the "Nasty Woman" cosmo and the "Bad Hombre" margarita. The main event would be a live video broadcast, aired via Twitter, that Smith and his editors had spent the past couple of months devising. The idea was to have a panel of BuzzFeed personalities cover not the election returns themselves but the cable TV networks' coverage of those results. In addition to this meta commentary they would analyze and interpret social media data and hope that their forecast ended up being more accurate. There was virtual consensus among every analyst worth listening to that Clinton would carry the vote.

"There's never been anything quite like Donald Trump," Smith told a reporter around 7 p.m. "There will be an immediate global crisis if he's elected."

The panel of BuzzFeed talking heads would mark a departure from the cable TV tradition of rounding up pundits and expert analysts. Instead the roundtable would showcase BuzzFeed's "vibrant pool of generalists"; Tracy Clayton, host of the booze-and–current affairs podcast *Another Round*, would be there, and Eugene Lee Yang of the Try Guys would host alongside two of the site's young politics reporters, merging the entertainment side of BuzzFeed with news, like the cocktail that mixed ad sponsors and ingredients from the popular Tasty videos. The foursome narrated the night's developments between pulls from a flask while a live studio audience cheered them on. Every so often, for a laugh, the hosts would check in with a live video feed of a burning dumpster fire. At regular intervals other BuzzFeed correspondents, like Charlie Warzel, would join the broadcast to lend their two cents.

Meanwhile in Toronto, Silverman was contending with so many last-minute fake news stories he felt like he was playing Whack-a-Mole. Lil Wayne had *not* voted for Trump, that Giuliani account on Twitter was an impostor, as was the CNN account tweeting bogus numbers from Florida, and neither had Ivanka Trump disavowed her father nor had George Soros rigged his voting machines against the Republican candidate.

As the night wore on, Cramer felt tension rising in the Javits Center. "She'll win but win ugly," she thought. But then the jumbotron showed returns from Florida, and they were not looking good. Cramer noticed that all of the Clinton aides who moments before had been standing on the risers now were nowhere to be seen. She G-chatted to one of them, a midlevel aide who'd been helpful in the past. "Do you guys know what's going on?" she typed, and waited nervously for the response, a curt "I don't have anything on that for you."

Back at headquarters, Warzel had joined the on-camera crew for an uproarious discussion of Fox News's preposterous "video chandelier." When he left the stage and went back into the control room, he ran into Smith, who'd just seen the surprise news from Florida. "On the next one, let's pivot on the tone," his editor advised. "No more of the irreverent thing."

At the Javits Center Cramer was in a daze. "I was sick and tired," she told me. "At some point, I asked Katherine [Miller, her editor], 'If this goes down this road, do I have to write something?' I couldn't do it. I was too drained. I couldn't rise to the occasion. I didn't want to do a 'reconstruct' of how she'd lost. I didn't even want to read that story. I didn't want to know."

As the exit polls showed Trump's lead widening, Warzel recalls reading an email that one of his editors sent out to the whole staff. Take a moment to think about your beat, whatever it is, the editor implored. And think about how it is going to change now. The whole newsroom had been blindsided. But they were still a newsroom, and they still fancied themselves the newsroom that more than any other shared the questions and concerns of their readers. The moment of confusion was followed by what Warzel remembers as an unspoken organizational pivot. Their readers needed them, likely more so than ever now that it seemed likely Trump would be president, and they were committed to answering the call. "It was just about adapting," Warzel said, "figuring out a new way to do the thing you do based off of the fact that the paradigm has changed."

Cramer, meanwhile, watched the Clinton team's shell-shock give way to heartbreak as the reality of their defeat became clear. People were sprawled on the ground in tears and huddled in crying circles. She left around 3:30 a.m., just in time to see Trump's happy face grace the monitors on her way out of the convention center as he prepared to deliver his victory speech. She would miss the camaraderie she had known for the past three years. "You feel like you are going down with the ship too," she told me. "It's one organism. You've been surrounded by people on her side, on your side. I felt I was losing something. There was the sense of loss, like when something dies." Most depressing of all, she had to trudge all the way back to the Clinton press hotel in Westchester to finally go to bed. Cramer had given up her apartment in Brooklyn, assuming that if Clinton won, she'd probably be moving to Washington, D.C.

Cramer had wanted to spend years trying to understand Clinton in the same way her father had probed the psyches and aspirations of the presidential candidates in 1988. But even weeks after the election she was plagued by the sense that she'd missed the story. "We're supposed to understand the country," she said, still sounding dejected. After Clinton's concession speech she had left the city to clear her mind.

At BuzzFeed headquarters, the rest of the staff treated itself to some therapy. They would cure the blues the best way they knew how: a double dose of cuteness. Farra Strongwater, the office's head of employee experience and culture, informed the staff that "a small group of puppies" would be visiting the office that afternoon "to cheer us up." The puppies would be available for petting and cuddling on the 16th floor, in a conference room named XOXO.

"If Trump loses," a Macedonian teenager had told Silverman, "I plan to redirect my site to sports." But Trump had won and in doing so ushered in an era in which emergent forces hostile to the very notion of objective journalism had not only a popular mandate but also an ally who now occupied the seat of power. Since it was one of the most ubiquitous and digitally capable members of Facebook's list of trusted sources, this left BuzzFeed to continue to try to cut through the misinformation campaign that was now masterminded by the sitting administration. Smith assigned more reporters to cover Silverman's ever-expanding beat.

It was time for a facelift, the site decided, and unveiled a new slogan: "Reporting to You." In the lobby of its headquarters in New York, a floor-to-ceiling LCD screen welcomed visitors to BuzzFeed. "Reporting to You," it announced in an epilepsy-inducing kaleidoscope of emojis, that then faded as a new one popped up: "But First Let's Take a Selfie." The twin images were a perfect reflection of BuzzFeed and its audience.

In compiling a postmortem report on what had just happened, Silverman found that, for one thing, the truth had been sundered over the preceding 10 months. During that time, his analysis showed, fake news stories had gone from a fringe issue to a calamity that was impossible to ignore. The top 20 fake stories on Facebook significantly outperformed the top 20 real news articles. People found these fake stories engaging. Worse, pure fraudsters were no longer the only problem. A new breed of publisher, trafficking in articles based mostly on actual events but spun or "torqued" and stretched to make partisan points, was rising alongside out-and-out fake news, further muddying the distinction between fact and fabrication.

Tensions between the incoming administration and members of the

press, many of whom still had lingering doubts about the legitimacy of
Trump's electoral victory, mounted during the transition period, as the
president-elect unveiled a cabinet stocked with mavericks and officials bent
on destroying the traditional mandates, like abolishing environmental regulations. Nine days before he would take the oath of office, as the divided
country's wounds continued to bleed, BuzzFeed decided to drop a bomb.
Since September, Smith and his team, along with much of the rest of the
mainstream media outlets, had been briefed on a 35-page document full of
salacious anecdotes and damning allegations of Trump's possibly illicit relationship and entanglement with Russia. In the halls of government, too,
intelligence officials and congressmen had been circulating the so-called
Steele dossier, which had been produced by a former British spy with MI6
named Christopher Steele. He had been retained by Fusion GPS, owned by
my former *Journal* colleague Glenn Simpson, to investigate Trump's business dealings and ties to Russia. Fusion GPS was originally on contract to
the Cruz campaign, then later was hired by a Democratic law firm tied to
the Clinton campaign, which wanted its anti-Trump trove.

By early January, when President Obama and Trump were briefed on
the dossier, American newsrooms had already invested months of man-hours
tracking down the claims it contained, but had little to show for their efforts.
Meanwhile, in secret, elected officials and leaders in the intelligence community had been bandying it about, discussing its contents in private sessions.
The high-level briefings were deemed newsworthy by CNN, which aired a
story but did not publish the dossier. BuzzFeed, meanwhile, had gotten hold
of the dossier, and Smith determined he should not hold out any longer. The
dossier was driving decision-making at the highest levels of government; it
was making news despite being withheld from the public. "Who am I to say
the public isn't ready for this?" Smith thought. Sure, he conceded, in a long
bygone era, when editors played gatekeeper, it might have been appropriate to sit on the dossier, to tell readers, "We have this newsworthy thing but
we don't think you should see it, just trust us." But times had changed, and
with distrust in the media at a high, Smith reasoned, "You have to show your
work." Although parts of the Steele dossier were unverified and wrong, it had
been deemed important enough for Obama and Trump to both be briefed on
it. This outweighed caution or the need to verify the dossier's content, which
the BuzzFeed news story stated had some unverified claims.

Smith called Schoofs, the investigative editor, out of the bathroom and
summoned reporter Ken Bensinger and Nabiha Syed, BuzzFeed's in-house
lawyer, and got Peretti on the phone. Everyone was in favor of publishing.

He brought over two other senior editors, Shani Hilton and Miriam Elder, to consult. They all knew they would take flak for it but would do so gladly as long as they felt confident in the decision. If BuzzFeed truly was serious about its new slogan, "Reporting to You," then they had no right to shelter readers from such explosive information. With everyone on board, Smith hit "Publish," and the 35-page document went public. The mushroom cloud rose on cue.

"This seems preposterous, appalling, opportunistic, and lacking in basic ethics at every level," tweeted media columnist Michael Wolff, whose own account of the Trump administration, *Fire and Fury*, would face similar charges the following year. "Ethics are simple: you shouldn't publish what you don't know to be true."

"It's never been acceptable to publish rumor and innuendo," the *Post*'s Margaret Sullivan agreed.

"Even Donald Trump deserves journalistic fairness," wrote the reporter for *Mother Jones* who had revealed the existence of the dossier back in October.

Trump's own response to BuzzFeed's publication of the Steele dossier was typically fast and furious. "I think it was disgraceful, disgraceful that the intelligence agencies allowed any information that turned out to be so false and fake out. I think it's a disgrace, and I say that, and I say that, and that's something that Nazi Germany would have done and did do," Trump said. "I think it's a disgrace. That information that was false and fake and never happened got released to the public. As far as BuzzFeed, which is a failing pile of garbage, writing it, I think they're going to suffer the consequences."

Meanwhile the newly crowned point-people of the media sector that had catapulted Trump into office immediately came to their leader's defense. Alex Jones, the conspiracy theorist whose talk radio show and spin machine, InfoWars, had long sustained a vicious attack on more mainstream outlets, took BuzzFeed to task. The site's editors, he said, were "completely discrediting themselves." Mike Cernovich piped up with the claim that in publishing the dossier, BuzzFeed had fallen for a troll-authored hoax. Trump piled on with a tweet citing the new father-and-sons outfit One America News Network: "INTELLIGENCE INSIDERS NOW CLAIM THE TRUMP DOSSIER IS 'A COMPLETE FRAUD!'" But by then its unsubstantiated, lurid contents—including the allegation that Trump had paid prostitutes to urinate on the bed the Obamas had slept in during their stay at Moscow's Ritz Carlton Hotel—had established themselves at the very center of the news cycle. And BuzzFeed had spun Trump's insult to its advantage: the site was already selling T-shirts emblazoned with the phrase "failing pile of garbage" and trash cans proudly labeled "BuzzFeed."

Never one to waste attention, Smith undertook a media blitz in defense of his decision, appearing on every outlet from One America to MSNBC.

The Steele dossier had provided Trump with a cudgel to drive a wedge between old media and new. CNN's Zucker was already on record saying he did not consider BuzzFeed or Vice to be real news organizations. In Zucker's view, BuzzFeed had been irresponsible in publishing an unverified intelligence dossier, the equivalent of raw sewage, and had fortified Trump's savage attacks on the news media for trafficking in fake news. CNN, along with the "failing *New York Times*," were the president's most prominent and frequent foils. Now BuzzFeed, the very company Zucker had demeaned, was joined with them in the president's gunsight. While this may have enhanced BuzzFeed's prestige, Zucker worried that it damaged CNN's credibility. The network issued a statement pointedly distancing itself from BuzzFeed, saying, "CNN's decision to publish carefully sourced reporting about the operations of our government is vastly different than BuzzFeed's decision to publish unsubstantiated memos. The Trump team knows this. They are using BuzzFeed's decision to deflect from CNN's reporting, which has been matched by other major news organizations."

One of the CNN anchors, Jake Tapper, usually one of the toughest on President Trump and his aides, denounced BuzzFeed in even tougher language. His CNN colleague, Jim Acosta, had been one of the first newsmen to face personal denunciation by the new president as a fake news purveyor at his first postelection news conference. In Tapper's view, BuzzFeed was only proving Trump's case and had succeeded only in giving Trump cover. "It's irresponsible to put uncorroborated information on the internet. I can understand why president-elect Trump would be upset about that, I would be upset about it too. It's why we did not publish it, and why we did not detail any specifics from it because it was uncorroborated, and it's not what we do. We are in the business of sussing out what is true and what is false," Tapper insisted.

Smith had a few defenders, including the managing editor of the *Columbia Journalism Review,* a top officer at ProPublica, and me. My reasoning was that if the dossier was deemed credible enough for the president and president-elect to be briefed about it, the document was newsworthy and the public deserved to read it.

"It was ironic," Smith told me. "We'd exposed fake news and now it was being thrown in our faces." But he still believed in transparency, and weeks after publishing he told me he thought the punditocracy was turning back his way. But before it could, another shot was fired BuzzFeed's way: it was being sued for publishing the Steele dossier. Facing legal claims that, if successful, threatened to bankrupt the company, BuzzFeed was placing its fate in the hands of its young general counsel, Nabiha Syed. She would have to prove the dossier, or at least a decent portion of it, to be true. Her task was straightforward, from a legal standpoint, but would require a massive investment in top-of-the-line intelligence gathering.

Peter Thiel had bankrolled lawsuits against the media company Gawker that practically bankrupted the once successful gossip news site, which had to be sold to another media company. It appeared that backers of Trump were trying the same legal gambit to take out BuzzFeed. Syed, suddenly on the front line of the site's legal strategy, hired a team of investigators led by the former FBI cybersecurity chief Anthony Ferrante, who had spent his last year or so at the agency running the government's inquiry into Russia's interference in the 2016 election.

Syed, educated at Yale Law and once a junior lawyer at the *Times*, had taken a flyer on BuzzFeed when she became its in-house associate general counsel in 2015. Now she was recognized as a young superstar in the legal profession, a leading light of the First Amendment bar that had long been dominated by older white men like Floyd Abrams, who represented the *Times* in the landmark Pentagon Papers case. After the *Times*, she had joined a small firm specializing in representing media organizations. Some of her Yale classmates expected Syed, who won a prized Marshall Scholarship to study in Oxford after college, to clerk on the Supreme Court as the capstone to her stellar academic career. Instead Syed, whose grandmother was a judge in Pakistan, where the press is controlled by the government, fell in love with the news media and its potential to make positive change. After working at the *Times*, the idea of working for one of the new, all-digital upstarts appealed to her, and she was everything Ben Smith and Jonah Peretti needed. At 28 she was the same age as many of the reporters, and, despite being greeted each day with LOL signs, she loved the work, reviewing stories to avoid libel cases. In the beginning there were not many of them, but as Smith built up his investigative unit, especially in England, where libel protections were nowhere as strong as in the United States, she had more work than at the law firm she came from.

Controversy was nothing new to Syed. In September 2016, right before the election, she had married her Ghanaian boyfriend, Nana Ayensu. They had given themselves little time to recover from their horror over Trump's election before leaving on an African honeymoon. The couple wanted total peace, so they left behind their cell phones and computers. It was only on their return journey from the idyll that they learned of the new president's order banning travel from Muslim countries. When they arrived at JFK after a long flight, Syed and Ayensu were both pulled out of line for questioning. Dirty and exhausted from traveling, Syed was detained for nearly eight hours of questioning about the stamps on her passport, which included trips to Pakistan, a hotbed of Islamic terror. When she was finally let go and rejoined her husband, who had mostly been questioned about her activities, she saw the mobs of protesters who were outside the airport chanting anti-Trump epithets about the unconstitutional ban. Despite her exhaustion, she immediately joined some First Amendment lawyers she knew who were representing airport detainees on an emergency basis. More hours passed until she finally arrived home in Brooklyn. But the politically explosive issue was exactly the kind of legal matter she craved. Soon, with the publication of the Steele dossier, Syed would be at the head of another constitutional storm.

Syed, who would soon win a special award from the prestigious Reporters Committee for Freedom of the Press, believed passionately that BuzzFeed had an absolute legal right to publish the dossier. It was not even a close call. The 1971 Pentagon Papers decision had enshrined the right of the press to publish newsworthy material, without prepublication censorship. Syed was thrilled at the prospect of being in court defending that right.

One of the suits against BuzzFeed was filed in New York by the owners of the Russian Alfa Bank. Steele's dossier had alleged suspicious contacts between the bank and the Trump Organization, the president's family real estate empire. A second was filed earlier in Florida by a Russian internet entrepreneur, Aleksej Gubarev, over claims in the dossier that he and his firms used "botnets and porn traffic" to conduct a variety of cyber operations against Democratic Party leaders. At about the time his suit was filed, BuzzFeed, on Syed's recommendation, had apologized and redacted the information about Gubarev and his companies from the document on its site. But she had lost a bid to have the lawsuit thrown out altogether. Michael Cohen, Trump's embattled personal lawyer, was also involved in one of the lawsuits but dropped it. In April 2018 another of the suits was dropped, a victory for BuzzFeed.

Syed still hoped to go to trial for a case she believed would be her generation's Pentagon Papers. The same issues were at stake as in that storied constitutional battle waged by the *New York Times* and the *Washington Post*. Syed saw herself as a fitting heiress and legal custodian trying to protect their legacy.

Peretti, meanwhile, was enjoying the whole spectacle. After consulting with Syed and Smith, he sprang to his team's defense. In an email to his employees clearly meant to be made public, he wrote, "We stand with Ben on his decision to publish this newsworthy document, which was reported on by multiple news outlets and seen by high level government officials including the president and president-elect." BuzzFeed's founder gleefully continued, "As a result of this decision, we were criticized by the incoming administration. We are not going to respond to these divisive comments, which put us in great company by the way—The New York Times, CNN, and The Washington Post have all been attacked."

In many ways the Steele dossier contretemps showcased the fundamental difference between the new media journalism ethos and the old. Peretti and Smith believed transparency was the new order of the day. The role of arbiter of what was news had devolved from professional journalists to the people, who no longer trusted or wanted editors to decide what they saw or read. With the universal reach of the internet, Peretti and Smith believed, it was important to put the document "out there" to be truth-tested by popular will and shared by millions of people. That was how news, truthful or fake, spread in the age of social media.

Peretti's bigger concerns were far afield of the dossier and the Trump administration. He had moved to Los Angeles to focus on building BuzzFeed's video arm, BuzzFeed Motion Pictures, a full-scale production operation in Hollywood. He had restructured the company, cleaving off the news division, which was prestigious but money-losing, and combining buzz with his expanding video empire.

Setting up the equivalent of a mini Paramount Pictures for video production was an expensive proposition. The success of the studio was vital to support expanding news ambitions. Though NBC-Universal had infused BuzzFeed with $400 million, hiring new staff and expanding operations so rapidly had cost a bundle. For two years in a row, 2016 and 2017, BuzzFeed had missed its revenue targets. Investor Kenneth Lerer pronounced himself unfazed and was determined to get hold of spending in 2018. Peretti saw making and selling video the dominant part of BuzzFeed's output as the way to get back in the black.

Video was the obsession of all digital publishers, including the *New*

York Times and the *Washington Post*. Vice had shifted to video years earlier, and its outsized—ridiculously so, many believed—valuation was largely based on the notion that video content and ads were far more valuable than anything presented in words. Everyone was racing to fill their inventories with video in large part because ad premiums for video were much higher than for print. The huge social platforms, led by Netflix, were also hungry for original programming to stream and willing to pay well for it.

The "pivot to video" became the media industry's catchphrase. Video was one of the few areas where Facebook had not been on the leading edge, and Zuckerberg was angry over lagging behind YouTube. In 2014 the ad industry's bible, *Ad Age*, detailed Facebook's strategy for taking on its main rival. Zuckerberg's first move was mimicry. A popular feature on both BuzzFeed and YouTube was showing how many views a particular video had enjoyed. Viewers liked to watch stories that had high traffic, assuming popular tastes revealed the wisdom of crowds. So Facebook announced that it too would include data on numbers of views for each video. It also gave preference to videos displayed on its own digital player and made it cumbersome to watch YouTube videos on Facebook. YouTube had already established profitable partnerships with content-makers like Vice, giving them a cut of ad revenue. But Facebook resisted doing so until it created partnerships with the *New York Times* and BuzzFeed, which were among the news providers Facebook paid, to the tune of $3 million annually, to provide live video streaming of news, stunts, and other events that drew large audiences to the Facebook app, which had a designated area for video.

Back in 2012 Zuckerberg had lamented his network's inferior status among the news media and reportedly saw his video competitors, especially YouTube, Netflix, and a new social platform, Snapchat, as existential threats. Younger readers, according to all the media prognosticators and data, preferred watching to reading.

Facebook's big video thrust meant BuzzFeed too would pivot. But Peretti had fallen behind, preferring still photography and cascading, vertical slide shows to illustrate BuzzFeed stories. Any changes at Facebook, however, required a prompt repositioning at BuzzFeed to stay in tune.

Every time he feared falling behind, Zuckerberg rewired the News Feed algorithm, weighting it to favor links to certain types of posts and articles, and watched the changes take. Soon those changes rippled through the rest of the media. Twitter's popularity worried him, especially its loyal following among journalists and decision-makers. Still, Facebook drove twice the normal load of traffic to publishers. By mid-2015, shortly after the launch of Instant Articles, Facebook was making Twitter seem like table scraps: it was responsible for 13 times the publisher traffic of its former rival.

Peretti still viewed his nearly thousand-person staff not as a group of writers, editors, and general content producers, but as a technical team devoted to the project of building a perfect machine. Ideally that machine would someday operate automatically, with limited human input, and Buzz-Feed's personnel would be elevated to supervisory roles. This was the vision Peretti laid out to his staff in December 2015, when he introduced the most buzzword-heavy epithet his company would seek to epitomize. Buzz-Feed would become, he said, a "cross-platform, global network."

What that meant was still fuzzy, even, it seemed, for Peretti. It was a renewed commitment to distributed publishing, focusing foremost on making impressions in people's social feeds. Beyond that, the new identity reflected Peretti's aspiration to bolster the feedback loop by which Buzz-Feed collected and acted upon data insights to make content appeal to ever larger numbers of people. He introduced the latest and greatest gadget that BuzzFeed's engineers had developed to aid the process. Called HIVE, the software would allow anyone at BuzzFeed to easily pull insights from the company's entire archives and determine what type of content worked best on which internet platform. It equipped them to derive order from the chaotic pile of data they collected each time they published a piece of content or promoted it on social media. The way Peretti explained it, HIVE made it possible for BuzzFeed's writers to run instantaneous experiments about the predilections of the social web on the enormous data set that was its past work. For example, he told the staff, "You should be able to type in 'pizza' and see all the things BuzzFeed has created on the topic of pizza and how well they did on each platform—so you can adapt them, learn from them, talk to the creator and get advice before you make your pizza content." It would enable BuzzFeed to sync its output across departments, so that when the news team had one of its occasional themed weeks (e.g., Mental Health Week), the viral video personalities who worked in BuzzFeed's Hollywood studio would be able to contribute some comic relief to the conversation.

After unveiling HIVE to his employees, Peretti wanted to step back and explain how the new tool fit into his broader vision for BuzzFeed, which he did by way of analogy: "Self-driving cars are starting to get better than humans at driving. Humans crash a lot more. The reason is that *you* only have your own experience when you drive. If you've never had a ball roll out into the street, or driven on an icy patch, you don't know how to do that." That was the limitation on human expertise: it was necessarily confined to the

lived experience of an individual. It was a limitation that technological uto-
pians like Peretti promised the hive mind would render a thing of the past.
"If you're a Google car," he said, "you have the experience of every other
Google car—any car that drives on an icy patch sends that knowledge and
experience to the hub, and every car gets it and benefits from it."

In the audience Smith, his editor in chief, was laughing. "You do know
we're humans, right?" he chimed in.

"Most of you are humans," Peretti granted. "But if you log on to HIVE,
you're humans that can see and learn from the aggregate." He described the
possibility as if it were a superpower, and in a sense it was. HIVE, and more
broadly the whole stash of new tools like it, had the potential to transform
the media business from one that relied on human expertise, parochial as it
was, into one that could operate just as efficiently by having generalists hook
up to a super-intelligent system that increasingly did their work for them.

"It would be great," Peretti continued, "if we had a very vibrant pool
of generalists so there's a lot of people at BuzzFeed not just creating within
one narrow topical area." In news, however, the danger of this idea was that
it could mean shallow coverage. In a future dominated by data-enhanced
generalists, expertise would be obsolete. Peretti was over the notion that
publishers ought to be bound by any duty beyond that of supplying what
readers demanded. He saw a trend, he told me, of newer brands like Buzz-
Feed being created in collaboration with the consumers who valued relatability more than authority. That was one difference he saw between his
approach and the *Times*'s, for instance. BuzzFeed was more about connection to people than about higher goals, ideals, and "shoulds." This approach,
on the face of it, seemed at odds with journalism's watchdog, First Amendment role of providing the public with vital, truthful information and protecting it against abuses of power.

To lead BuzzFeed Motion Pictures, Peretti had tapped his old friend
and fellow viral whiz Ze Frank. From the early fame of his "Dear Kitten"
native ads, Frank had become a video auteur. By the spring of 2016, when I
visited him there, the studio was bustling with 300 employees spread across
its sprawling campus. Aside from the main office building, the property
boasted a cluster of condos called The Bungalows, a massive studio space
called The Cube, a functional bar that doubled as a set, a building filled with
film studios and editing suites called The Towers, and an expansive roof
deck with a view of the iconic Capitol Records building and the Hollywood
sign. Late in the day, as I toured the premises, a large bearded man stood at
his desk on the fourth floor eating Cheetos with chopsticks.

"The lines are blurred here," Cat Bartosevich, head of publicity for BFMP, told me as she led me around. "There's no church and state. That's Ze's philosophy." The head of branded advertising strategy for the Hollywood operation, Jen White, elaborated on the extent of the blurriness. For entertainment content, she said, BuzzFeed's creators understood they had to operate within parameters that preserved the possibility of doing work with certain brands. In the effort to make content as broadly inoffensive as possible, she liked to think of the myriad multinational corporations with which BuzzFeed might someday do business as people. Before a piece of content was published, it was standard practice for it to be bleached of any lines that could be construed (by any group of people or special interest) as "hatery." Editors of the piece were told to ask, "Is it gonna hurt someone's feelings?" One video in which a BuzzFeed personality taste-tested six different popular brands of nachos, for instance, had to be revised because BuzzFeed was pursuing lucrative branded content contracted with all six of the nacho makers. Since this was entertainment, not news, there were no ethical strictures.

By March 2016 video already accounted for more than half of Buzz-Feed's revenue, and it had been less than three years since the company had hired Frank to launch the venture. The next month it announced that video views had grown 80-fold over the previous year. Not to discredit Frank's ingenuity, Shani Hilton told me, but much of his success was a result of Peretti's well-timed decision. BuzzFeed's pivot to video, she explained, had been precipitated by the advent of a feature on social networking platforms, so when users scrolled through their feeds, the videos they encountered would begin automatically, without their having to click the "play" button. The trend had begun with Vine, the now-defunct network that limited videos to a duration of six seconds. Instagram had caught on, upping Vine's limit to 15 seconds and Instagram's to as long as a whole minute. Facebook, where videos could be any length, had tweaked its News Feed algorithm to favor video posts and incentivized publishers further by instituting a system that counted the number of times it played when scrolled over, and displayed that as the tally of "views." At least until everyone caught on to this counting system, it had the advantage of making every video look more viral than it actually was. Another crucial factor was that as cellular data networks improved, people's monthly smartphone data plans became less constricting, so they could watch more videos before running into overage fees.

In The Towers a cluster of video-makers was putting their heads together to come up with "shorter than short-form" content, in the three- to five-second range. Most of the rest of the space, though, was devoted to the biggest success of BuzzFeed's video venture and indeed the single most viral idea Peretti's company had produced in its first decade. This was the franchise of 30- to 60-second cooking videos BuzzFeed published to a Facebook page it maintained, called Tasty. Launched in mid-2015, Tasty had taken just one month to amass its first million Facebook followers and became, in short order, the most-liked page on the entire social network. Facebook had never seen anything rise this meteorically. After publishing the first video recipe, the Tasty page had attracted so much traffic from users visiting and clicking the "like" button that Facebook's security system assumed the account belonged to some hacker or scam artist and temporarily suspended it.

The short Tasty videos showed only the hands of the food makers, completing their recipes in warp speed. It might have seemed random that the most popular page on the most populous platform in the history of the internet would assume the form of a series of hands making s'more dip and pizza cones. Tasty was also manna for branded advertising and was sponsored by Kraft, Mondelez, and a raft of other food companies.

Tasty's simplicity, using cheap ingredients that any millennial could afford, was its virtue; to make its content more substantive, Frank explained, would be to jeopardize its meteoric growth. "It's food theater," Frank told me, "not a recipe service. It's a magic trick." The frictionlessness of Tasty videos was what made them fundamentally shareable, explained Adam Bianchi, the producer who came up with the format. He had accomplished that effect by taking a hard look at the genre of digital video and paring back every element that added unnecessarily to the complexity.

Bianchi did not have a culinary background; he just really liked food, including junk food. That was true of most of Tasty's producers, but they saw it as an advantage: it aligned them with the lowest common denominator of their viewership and ensured that the recipes they made were not too advanced. Relatability was the watchword, in the kitchen as in the newsroom.

Tasty was the fattest cash cow Frank had yet raised, and it made his boss happy. When Peretti had hired Frank, the direction he had given his friend was "a growth mandate," as opposed to "a content mandate." Frank was gung-ho. He had spent his entire professional life making videos designed to cultivate audiences, and the view-counts on his videos spoke to his track record of success. Exponential growth, he told me, "is a beautiful thing—as close a thing to God as I know."

At 44, Frank had a blond-going-gray crew cut, wide blue eyes, a scruffy beard, and a mustache that was barely visible. He owned two cats and had recently adopted two children, seven-month-old Rose and two-year-old Jonah. Two waving Japanese cats sat on the table in his office alongside a picture of his family and an autographed photo of Danny Glover. On his shelf was the book *Life in Half a Second*.

He was not a journalist in any sense, but he was the epitome of the digital native, having made early videos of himself dancing when YouTube began. He still used that improvisational spirit. Rather than burden his talent with excessive plenary work up front, he urged them to roll tape before they could overthink it. Several short dramas were in production; one, about a group of girl roommates called "You Do You," starred young women who had started at BuzzFeed as web producers. He had chosen them, after all, because their real-life personalities felt different from the hackneyed Hollywood archetypes. He coached them, he told me, to think about their characters as occupying the same "rarefied emotional space" that they did, and then to focus on amplifying that shtick, whatever it was. "They became intense versions of themselves," Frank said. For example, a character named Sarah was a reflection of the actress's own shy inner self. As the series attracted a devout fanbase, BuzzFeed's audience analysts noticed a surprising affinity for Sarah's peculiar disposition. Girls sent her fan mail and fawned over her in the online comments, writing things like "Sarah is beautiful. Sarah is me."

Plot construction, long a significant part of show business, struck Frank as onerous. What made a given movie or show or story great, he thought, was often reducible to its best moments. The best moments in entertainment, he surmised, were the ones that reflected viewers' lived experiences, the ones that resonated. The charm of those moments, as Peretti put it, was their universality: "It's like a thing you think is individual is actually taking place at a network level." Frank likened it to the moment when, as you're reading a good book, it becomes a great book; it happens when the author touches on some idea you've thought of but never voiced. And that, he said, is "when that book becomes a portal to companionship."

Frank proceeded methodically to compile inventories of such moments. His plan was to let the moments, rather than any overarching narrative, determine the course of BuzzFeed's motion pictures, which were shorter than the old newsreels that used to run in movie theaters. When Adele dropped a new album, BuzzFeed would conjure up just the right video to catch the mood of its best song. This snippet approach jibed with the pace of the web and the attenuated attention spans of its devotees.

For new grist, BuzzFeed's video creators would consult with their colleagues in a department they called Facebook Ops, whose job was to analyze what types of videos were blowing up on Facebook, so that BuzzFeed could re-create those wins. One day Facebook Ops noticed that one successful theme on Facebook was men doing ladylike things. They gathered four guys from the talent pool and had them try on lingerie from Victoria's Secret. It was, as predicted, a smash hit. For Halloween the same group modeled sexy costumes, which again drove viewers wild. A little while later *Paper* magazine published an issue with a cover photo of Kim Kardashian nude and drenched by a fountain of Champagne. The image went so viral that people were saying it "broke the internet." On cue, the cross-dressing foursome scrambled to purchase a bottle of cheap Champagne to pop, some baby oil to make their skin shine, a tarp, and another bottle of Champagne to help them muster the courage to go fully nude. The photo shoot cost $20 to produce and catapulted the men to internet stardom. It was the birth of the Try Guys.

When I met Eugene Lee Yang, the Try Guys' de facto frontman, it was immediately clear to me what Peretti had been envisioning when he proposed that BuzzFeed should become a "vibrant pool of generalists." With impeccably manicured eyebrows and sideburns under a backward hat and a button-down tied around his waist, Yang told me his background was in music videos but that he'd found his voice in beauty and "body positivity." He remarked on the strangeness of having suddenly become a celebrity to a conspicuously young audience. But, he clarified, his celebrity was different in nature from the type that Hollywood churned out. He told me that people his age would often approach him on the street and strike up a conversation as if he were their friend or brother. He identified a new trend, which he attributed to social media, of stars becoming more human—less airbrushed and scripted—while everyday humans, using the newly available media avenues, became stars. This, he said, was what people call "the Jennifer Lawrence effect," named after the actress beloved by fans for behaving in a manner that makes them think, "That's what I'd do in that situation!"

Yang was on set in The Cube when I met him, taping a segment that BuzzFeed was producing for its partnership with the cable network Lifetime. The show, called *Mansformation*, explored the world of male makeovers. He was interviewing a hair colorist when I arrived. "When someone changes their hair color, it's the quickest way of changing yourself, your confidence, your being," the stylist was saying. "The happiness just keeps on coming." That, he said, explained the recent stampede of men opting for "mermaid unicorn rainbow-ass hair." Yang had been nodding along enthusiastically. "I love that," he cried. "More on that, please."

Later in the day BuzzFeed's legions of 20-somethings headed up to the rooftop to pool their creative energies and come up with some ideas for new videos. Suggestions included "Makeup through history," "Eyebrows through history," "What does your name taste like?," and a stunt one person suggested in which he would see how long people would let him shake hands before they got creeped out and recoiled. What if we filmed people trying knockoff versions of their favorite cereals, someone proposed. How about "Times you don't want to hear the word 'whoops'?" "Amazing!" a colleague exclaimed. "You could do like ten of those videos with different words!" Struggling to come up with anything better, another member of the group admitted, "I just wanna swim with otters. Can we do a video where I get to swim with otters?" Beer, of course, accompanied the brainstorming.

All of the fun and games produced by the studio was supposed to underwrite the increasingly serious ambition of the news division. The month following my visit to the company's Hollywood branch, the *Financial Times* reported that not everything was as rosy for BuzzFeed as its cheery viralogists would have hoped. Financial documents revealed that the company had significantly underdelivered during the prior year, missing its 2015 revenue projections by a startling 32 percent. In response, Peretti lowered his sights for the 2016 fiscal year, revising his projected revenue from $500 million down to $250 million.

In May a new batch of reports surfaced, citing claims from sources within the company who said BuzzFeed's newsroom was in jeopardy. Amid the pivot to video publishing, anonymous employees explained, and the news team's failure to earn its keep financially (advertisers still weren't sold on the necessity of social news), Smith's unit was "in retrenchment."

The company's elaborate presentation during NewFronts, New York's annual weeklong expo on the upcoming year in digital media, laid bare the road map that they would be following back to profitability. The plan called for doubling down on the signature silliness that was its stock-in-trade. They would do so behind a façade of more lofty and self-congratulatory rhetoric about the media revolution they were effecting, how their series included characters from heretofore excluded groups. BuzzFeed's head of marketing, Frank Cooper, came out to hammer home the point that these series were convenient vehicles for advertisers who wanted to "get inside the story line." As became increasingly evident with each additional young phenom who got trotted onto the stage to make advertisers swoon, Ze Frank was putting his multihyphenated stars up for sale.

After the success of Tasty, BFMP rolled out Nifty, a Facebook channel that served up similarly short and postliterate videos that, rather than food dishes, gave demonstrations on do-it-yourself home improvement projects and crafts. They also introduced Tasty Happy Hour, for mixology, and Tasty Jr., for recipes parents could cook with their children. Plans were in the works for Nifty Kids, Nifty Pets, and Nifty Kitchen.

BuzzFeed knew it was succeeding, Cooper explained, when its content made readers and viewers say, "BuzzFeed gets me." That, he said, is what BuzzFeed wanted to achieve on behalf of its advertising clients. "This is the pathway into pop culture."

BuzzFeed was already leading many of the world's biggest brands down that pathway, but having missed its revenue projections, the company resolved to double down on its native advertising prowess. In the meantime, a contending force was gathering steam and coming down the viral news pike.

As the media industry begrudgingly migrated to Facebook while trying to retain some say in its fate, Peretti and his contemporaries conceived of a way to protect their hard-earned audiences from the threat of Facebook's tweaking its algorithm and wiping them out. The solution was essentially to cultivate a diversified portfolio of Facebook pages, each with a distinct theme and identity, so that the publisher could hedge against the possibility that Facebook would deprioritize its mothership and thereby send its business model into a death spiral.

BuzzFeed's community-specific diversification had begun as a way to corral audiences of particular interests, but it became something of a social experiment in the heterogeneity of the social web. By February 2016 the company had launched and was maintaining a staggering 90 different Facebook pages, each with a different flavor that correlated to a particular psychographic cross section of the online public. By mid-2017 that number had proliferated to become 150. Some pages, like Tasty, were organized around a topical area and functioned like the beat-driven verticals into which most publishers already arranged their websites: there was "Bring Me" (which highlighted eye-popping vacation destinations), "Animals," "Health," "Weddings," and more. But on top of these more obvious delineations, BuzzFeed was cultivating pages defined not by their topical area but by some more intangible facet of the audience each one was designed to attract. "Sweaty," for example, catered to bros of all ages, "Geeky" to geeks, "Obsessed" to pop-culture scenesters and Disney fangirls, "Pero Like" to Spanglish-speaking young women, "Cocoa Butter" predominantly to women of color who took pride in their heritage. The third category of pages BuzzFeed created cohered around an even less tangible ethos or outlook. What distinguished them was mainly tonal. For example, "SOML" (short for "Story of My Life") brought together internet memes and Buzz-Feed listicles that generally spoke to the human condition; "Cheeky," which had a peach emoji as its logo, was for "fuzzy news with bite."

In the news division, with the legal battle bubbling in the background, BuzzFeed had pressing business to attend to when the new administration took the helm. For the Inauguration, Smith had Warzel summon his courage to go to D.C. for a gala organized by the new class of pro-Trump digital publishers to toast their incredible accomplishment. The DeploraBall, as the event was called, was the occasion for them to "celebrate memeing a president into existence."

"We had one million readers a day coming in," announced Jim Hoft, editor of the Gateway Pundit, which he created to "expose the wickedness on the left." "And the reason was because I was telling the truth and the mainstream media was telling the fake fucking news!" His rousing address prompted the crowd to chant, "Real news! Real news! Real news!" Hoft's speech was followed by a procession of fiery remarks by other newly minted heroes of the movement. James O'Keefe, who had posed as a pimp to orchestrate the ACORN sting, took the podium to declare, "One man is more powerful than the *New York Times*. But you guys in this room are one thousand times more powerful than the *New York Times*." Among their ranks, as Warzel pointed out, was one Chuck Johnson, creator of a crowd-funding website called WeSearchr, where users could post "bounties" for mainstream reporters and political adversaries.

Warzel also spoke with Cernovich, whose explanation of the pro-Trump media movement was utterly scary. "We've really created parallel institutions," he told the BuzzFeed correspondent. "Trump supporters didn't think they were being treated fairly or accurately by the media. So many of us weren't sure we could trust the basic facts of what's being reported in the news. And so we created the answer, which is something I call 'reality news.'"

It was fitting that "reality news" had been forged in the crucible of a reality TV star's candidacy, because in both cases the tie to reality was little more than an aesthetic one. "Reality news" had the trappings of investigative reportage—it purported to uncover the uncomfortable truths about government and society—intensified by the high relief in which its surrealist anchors portrayed their stories. It borrowed the new conventions of digital publishing that BuzzFeed had proven effective, but its content, derived from an almost entirely separate set of premises, seemed to describe an altogether different world. It was this aspect of the new vanguard that Warzel captured in labeling this parallel industry the New Media Upside Down.

Unified, the opponents of journalism toasted the dawn of an era in which their counterfactualism would no longer be relegated to the shadows. On the occasion of the new administration's first official press conference, on January 21, Trump's press secretary, Sean Spicer, made inescapably clear on whose side the White House stood. Departing from tradition, Spicer took the podium and wasted no time upbraiding the assembly of correspondents, whom he charged with collectively conspiring to undermine the popular enthusiasm for the new president. After specifically addressing the false claim, made by former BuzzFeeder turned *Time* reporter Zeke Miller, that the bust of Martin Luther King Jr. had been removed from the Oval Office, Spicer took aim at another piece of bad press for Trump, despite the facts being stacked against him. He insisted, apparently at the president's urging, that Trump's inauguration had drawn the largest crowd of any such event in American history. Assertions to the contrary, which already abounded and were strongly supported by photographic evidence and public-transit numbers, were, Spicer said, "deliberately false reporting," admonishing the outlets who published such articles as "shameful and wrong." Delivering the statement as if reading verbatim from the party line, Spicer averred, "This was the largest audience ever to witness an inauguration, period, both in person and around the globe." It was plainly untrue, and the press secretary's straight-faced delivery made the lie downright unnerving to believers in press independence. Spicer refused to take reporters' questions, and the administration showed no signs of backing down.

The next morning, on *Meet the Press*, Trump's pollster-cum-advisor, Kellyanne Conway, went to bat for the demonstrably absurd contention. Pressing Conway, host Chuck Todd asked her to "answer the question of why the president asked the White House press secretary to come out in front of the podium for the first time and utter a falsehood."

"Don't be so overly dramatic about it, Chuck," Conway responded. "You're saying it's a falsehood," she said, but "Sean Spicer, our press secretary, gave alternative facts to that." For many casual observers of the new administration, here was a watershed moment: from Day One, Trump's White House would be intentionally dismissive of, and even hostile to, any reports that shed unbecoming light on it, regardless of their factual content. I promptly bought a T-shirt saying "Alternative Facts Are Lies."

As Silverman saw it, the new presidency was a pressman's quagmire. He had put the treachery of fake news on Americans' radar, and now he was watching as the commander in chief, a principal offender, gutted the term and co-opted it, making real journalists, whom Trump called "the enemies of the people," the purveyors of fake news. Increasingly Silverman's diligent effort to parse fact from fiction felt like a fool's errand. There was a popular meme, a photo of a rural husband calmly mowing his lawn while in the near distance looms a tornado of biblical scale. Silverman sometimes felt like that man.

But what was he going to do? Stop mowing? To throw in the towel would have been unthinkable. So with his trusty second in command, Jane Lytvynenko, Silverman kept his head down and kept ferreting out fabulism. From their northern outpost in Toronto, they would harness the technology of social media surveillance to help keep the conversation as honest as possible. Using tools like CrowdTangle, they watched political pockets on the social network spawn theories—some from thin air, but other, more insidious ones from a mishmash of facts and decontextualized rumors—and bandy them about as they mutated, worming their way into the popular consciousness. They built intelligent lists of bad actors and kept tabs on what each was cooking up. They would surf the expanse of partisan chatter and take deep dives into circles of the New Media Upside Down, where they saw their own reality refracted and distorted as if by a funhouse mirror. They would sit side by side in silence for hours at a time, and then one would let out a surprised chirp. "Oh shit," he or she would say. "I went down this rabbit hole and there's this really weird thing at the bottom."

Like a bomb squad, they braved these fraught areas so that the general, uninitiated public did not have to. In accordance with BuzzFeed's new slogan "Reporting to You," they did their work on their readers' behalf. As a result, much of what they published had a distinctly didactic quality. Their posts bore headlines like "Use This Checklist to Find Out If You're Looking at Fake News" and "6 Easy [as Fuck] Steps to Detect Fake News Like a Pro" and "This Is How You Can Stop Fake News from Spreading on Facebook."

The urgency of their work did not altogether prevent them from enjoying it, but the job also posed certain occupational hazards. Lytvynenko said it had given her nightmares. Her first big BuzzFeed story, for example, was on the German creator of a fake-news site whose anti-immigration fearmongering clickbait doubled as a driver of traffic to his web store, where he sold firearms. "It's all fun and games when it's 'Leonardo DiCaprio Coming to Your Town!'" Lytvynenko said of the fluffier side of fake news. "But when you realize it's enough to mobilize people, it becomes nightmare-inducing." To assuage her fears, she tried to inject a bit of good humor into the work. She had just published the item "If You Get 3/7 on This Quiz, You're Getting Sucker Punched by Fake News," and though I got sucker-punched, she assured me that even Silverman couldn't spot the hoaxes 100 percent of the time. The hoaxers were getting wiser, leaving the truth-tellers to shout over them, which made the whole conversation louder and simultaneously less clear.

"There's a battle for attention going on, for attention to news and politics," she told me. "In that battle, virality often wins, and that really warps the truth." BuzzFeed had to come to terms with the uncomfortable fact that the power source behind its incredible growth was fickle. There was not, in the end, some inherent virtue to the things that went viral. It was a quantitative yardstick, not a qualitative one, and thus subject to the same whims of the often guileless masses whose favor it tabulated. Her concern hearkened back to a perspicacious line from one of Silverman's stories in the lead-up to the election: "Facebook has an optimistic view that in aggregate people will find and share truth, but the data is happening on a massive scale."

More and more Americans were realizing that Facebook was no hyper-connected utopia but a company that made billions selling advertisers the ability to target them ever more accurately and subliminally. And while concerned citizens could bemoan the onslaught of platform-savvy political spin-doctors and salesmen interfering in their news feeds, the constant mixture of real news and corporate messaging was a fact of the fluid new media world.

The year following Trump's election would see a broad effort, involving Facebook employees, legislators, intelligence agents, and journalists, to parse good-faith content (whether served straight-up or spun) from outright propaganda. As the investigation into Russia's interference plumbed deeper, the fact that Facebook had been weaponized became clearer. The social network eventually came forward with evidence that Russians had put up $100,000 for Facebook to target susceptible users with a blast of misinformation from Moscow. And that was just for starters. Most of what Putin's operators had accomplished didn't require that type of over-the-counter transaction; it could be pulled off by applying the same viral science Peretti had helped refine. The Internet Research Agency, based in St.

Petersburg, had been powering an array of Facebook interest groups, strategically using psychographic intel to exacerbate preexisting fissures between
American political groups. A sampling of the groups' posts revealed the
malicious potential of targeting technology. One Russian-made Facebook
group, called Blacktivist, for example, had amassed a following larger than
the authentic Black Lives Matter group it intended to imitate and was, in the
eleventh hour, calling upon its supporters to break with Clinton and vote for
third-party candidate Jill Stein instead.

As the revelations broke on Capitol Hill, Zuckerberg announced in his
earnings call that he would invest in the site's security with a vengeance.
The ensuing months would see him unveil Facebook's attempt to fix its
system, but having established itself as the central forum for information
online, there was no action it could take without the reaction causing collat-
eral damage. His 2018 New Year's resolution, he announced, was to make
News Feed a sanctuary for "meaningful interaction," which meant it would
favor friends' and family's posts over posts by publishers. It was not an
easy decision for Zuckerberg: a month into the new system, data showed
users spending a remarkable 5 percent less time on the site each day. And
the numbers continued to drop. In July news of a disappointing quarter sent
Facebook shares plunging 18 percent. But more damaging revelations piled
up. A *Times* exposé revealed Facebook had hired an opposition research
firm to silence critics.

BuzzFeed, under pressure too, attempted to shore up the sources of
cash flow it could count on. In 2017 the company would push into outright e-commerce with a new shopping vertical that was basically a scrolla-
ble list of coupons and the launch of a new internal unit to invent products
that lent themselves to viral marketing campaigns: a Bluetooth-enabled hot
pot that automatically cooked recipes from Tasty videos; a fidget-spinner
called GlamSpin, with three built-in lip gloss shades; a pumpkin spice–and-
vanilla-scented candle that declared on its label, "This candle smells like
I'm proud to be a basic bitch."

In the spring Smith created a podcast in which he would "host conversations on the intersection of politics, media, and technology—and all of
2017's insanity." Fittingly, he called it *NewsFeed*.

The summer saw BuzzFeed establish a new vertical, for opinion pieces,
to be edited by Tom Gara. Gara hoped it could be a place that showcased
the brilliant diversity of political views that a no-holds-barred election had
brought to the fore. He addressed the dilemma of curating a balanced dis-

cussion when the grounds of political consensus had drastically shrunk: "How do you represent the pro-Trump case in a way that's intellectually honest and that's not a troll? As an observer, it is fascinating how few interesting pro-Trump voices are anywhere right now, and how hard it is to find them. Breitbart made no distinction between news and opinion."

In the fall BuzzFeed debuted a morning news and talk show to air daily at 10 a.m. on Twitter. Called *AM to DM* (a play on the Direct Messages users sent each other on the platform), the broadcast was designed to give viewers half an hour of sweet and savory BuzzFeed signatures, including of course a healthy dose of sponsored content. The editorial department, BuzzFeed News—*not* its advertising department—would be working with corporate partners like Wendy's to craft co-branded segments for which they would charge half a million dollars. The Twitter morning show, like many on the broadcast and cable television networks, was a curious blend of news and entertainment, so those lines between news and advertising were ever fuzzier and less meaningful. People scanning news on their phones, through Snapchat or Instagram, didn't really seem to notice or care.

Once on the leading edge of all these changes and profiting from them, BuzzFeed slid into tight financial straits. After missing their 2016 revenue targets, they missed them again in 2017—this time by around 20 percent—and announced they would be laying off 100 U.S. employees. They would again pivot even further toward the surefire profit drivers—sponsored series and ad products, to name two—and would finally begin selling the white space on their site to advertisers. Peretti gave interviews to reassure his doubters and sound his grievances with Facebook, arguing that Zuckerberg should pay BuzzFeed and other companies whose traffic helped power the social network. He even broached the possibility of an IPO.

BuzzFeed was still dependent on advertising revenue, and the tech giants, Facebook and Google, were eating up those revenues, leaving news, which had never made BuzzFeed a dime, as a drain. Native advertising, once a panacea, was now an area where everyone in the news media was competing for ad dollars. Peretti, once a native purist, announced that BuzzFeed would accept the programmatic ads he once considered clutter.

Peter Lattman saw the numbers. He was the top media advisor to Laurene Powell Jobs, the widow of Apple founder Steve Jobs, whose business, the Emerson Collective, had acquired Atlantic Media. Jobs had considered other media ventures too, and Lattman, who had once directed media coverage for the *New York Times*, knew Peretti fairly well. BuzzFeed's news operation, which Peretti had spun off into a separate division, might be an interesting investment, either as a minority stake or an outright purchase, if Peretti wanted to dump his unprofitable and large, 300-plus employee news operation. Since it was costly and the advertising picture was growing darker and darker, the news division would probably go for a song if Peretti was interested. BuzzFeed, like Vice, had been overvalued on the mistaken belief that the new digital companies would continue to grow exponentially in tandem with their youthful audiences and advertisers.

Peretti even floated the idea of merging BuzzFeed with other ailing new media companies like Vice and Vox. By banding together, he believed, they would be financially stronger and have more leverage over Facebook to share advertising revenue and pay more for content. BuzzFeed, meanwhile, had to make deep staff cuts and it was unclear whether Peretti's merger idea would go anywhere.

Soon Lattman and Smith were meeting in the bar at the hip Nomad Hotel, not far from Lattman's office in the tech heart of Manhattan, Madison Park. The talks were noncommittal. Peretti had come to believe deeply in the mission of BuzzFeed News and liked the prestige it brought his brand. It had up-classed BuzzFeed, and if and when digital advertising bounced back, the company would be poised to benefit. Word of the Lattman-Smith tête-à-tête reached the press, possibly through Ken Lerer, who was connected to almost everyone in the media business. Rumors of a Jobs acquisition spread quickly, but nothing came of them. Whether her interest would flush out other bidders was an unknown. Peretti was looking at other possible mergers, too.

Peretti and Smith were under pressure to find new sources of revenue for news and make BuzzFeed less reliant on advertising. At first BuzzFeed introduced lots of podcasts and built an audio unit. Then podcasts were out, the unit was cut, and video became the priority. For Netflix, BuzzFeed produced a series, "Follow This," that followed their journalists doing their stories on everything from intersex people to black survivalists. The show was something like Vice, with a feminist gloss. Like the old television networks, the big social platforms were hungry for original programming. News shows that personalized and dramatized the hunting and gathering of reporting were popular and everyone was diving in. With staff and investors nervous over missed revenue targets, Smith was thrilled to see the platforms paying well into seven figures for these new streaming video shows.

Opinion was another potential moneymaker, but Gara's experiment with the opinion page would last only a few weeks before touching off a bit of an identity crisis for BuzzFeed. His effort to incorporate pro-Trump voices backfired in the form of a column by Christopher Barron, an LGBT rights activist inside the GOP with Right Turn Strategies, which asserted on a flimsy basis that Roger Stone, the notorious political operative, and his ally Donald Trump had in common "a long history as an ally of the LGBT community." BuzzFeed staffers took to Twitter to denounce the piece and challenge their boss's decision to publish what appeared to them to be a dishonest political fish story. Smith determined his best move would be to appear on the Twitter morning show and candidly answer host Saeed Jones's questions, some of which would be drawn from audience suggestions, including tweets from his staff, who called the piece, among other things, "a disgrace." Smith defended the piece by contextualizing the work of its author: "Chris Barron—love him, hate him—kind of a divisive Twitter figure, but that is who he is and I think that's part of why we thought that he was an interesting voice to hear from." He went on to say that being published by BuzzFeed had no positive effect on the credibility of Barron or his piece.

Jones concluded the interview by commending his boss's transparency, and Smith thanked him for his flattery. Then he took off his earpiece and walked off set to see what else was happening in the newsroom. After a brief commercial break, the show would go on, Smith's interview followed by a recurring BuzzFeed segment, the "Giant Little Story," brought to you by Wendy's Giant Junior Bacon Cheeseburger.

BuzzFeed remained a strange stew of content. But its ambition to be a serious purveyor of news, a worthy competitor to the *Times* and the *Post*, was ever more within reach. Its investigation into a chain of suspicious deaths of Russians in Britain was a finalist for the 2018 Pulitzer Prize in international reporting. Heidi Blake, a talented investigative reporter based in London who would later replace Schoofs as investigations editor, led a team that included a Vice News recruit, Jason Leopold, that linked 14 suspicious deaths to Putin's hand. Despite its lurid red headline, "From Russia with Blood," and somewhat sensationalistic photos of Russian beauties, the investigation was thorough and impressive. It beat out submissions from the *Times* to earn one of three spots as a finalist. The prize itself went to Reuters, a certified member of the old guard. Smith was momentarily disappointed, but there would be a next time. He could taste it.

CHAPTER ELEVEN

VICE III

When he decided to go into the news business full bore in 2013, Shane Smith was, as always, full of bravado, certain that he could sweep away the old guard with the ease with which he made multimillion-dollar advertising deals with well-established American brands.

"Let's fuck news in its naughty ass," he tweeted in typical fashion. Smith's operating theory for why Vice News would succeed was that young people were turned off by TV news, not because they weren't interested in the world but because of how the news was presented. Few mainstream outlets covered the issues that interested them: the antifascist youth movements and student protests across the globe, edgy new art forms, cannabis, new-age health, the world's oppressed, and LGBT culture. Most on-air correspondents were older and white, like their audiences.

Suroosh Alvi, Spike Jonze, and Smith were confident that the lavishly immersive style they used for all of their videos—on subjects from skateboard diplomacy to donkey sex—could be used to knock out CNN. Their pieces would be unanchored and steered by characters who were taking on the establishment. Everyone on camera would be young and relatable.

Like BuzzFeed, Vice prided itself on reflecting the particular political interests of its younger audience and just as BuzzFeed's journalists were out in front on subjects like fake news on Facebook, Vice went deep into the underworld of the alt-right movement earlier than many of its traditional competitors.

Vice was also one of the few media companies that had figured out a surefire business model: taking gobs of other people's money to produce content, both documentaries and ads. It was a content farm, producing an astounding 7,000 different pieces a day. (For comparison, the *New York Times* published 200 to 300 individual pieces a day.) Most of this content was not conventional news but Vice's curious blend of entertaining documentaries full of adventure, danger, and immersive plots.

All this content was distributed on every possible platform so that it could be on all screens all the time. Like BuzzFeed, Vice aimed for massive scale to keep the ad revenue flowing. But Vice added a twist: its content wasn't really free. The company had aggressively grown internationally and charged stiff licensing fees to its foreign partners. So it wasn't just earning vast sums from branded advertising campaigns, but selling and licensing almost everything it created. Smith's sales pitch was simple: Vice alone could speak to the prized youth demographic, 18- to 24-year-olds. (Actually, the *Times* had far more millennial readers.)

On top of the cash Vice pocketed, it took home another fortune slicing and dicing those pieces into versions that were sold to outlets in other countries. Overhead could be kept relatively low. All they needed were 3,000 hip, underpaid 23-year-olds and some editing bays. There were no printing presses or expensive Manhattan offices. They were the media kings of Brooklyn, and with their Emmys, they were also the darlings of HBO, which was riding high with the young audience on the success of *Game of Thrones*. HBO stars who worked with Vice, such as Bill Maher and Fareed Zakaria, gave them cred.

Video was the smart bet. Smith was smug about this, since he had bet heavily on it long before competitors like BuzzFeed. He predicted, wrongly, the death of text-based journalism. (The *Times* would survive, he allowed, on its brand strength.) Virtue, Vice's ad agency, was charging high premiums with a shadow staff of 300 writers, artists, and producers ensconced at a different Brooklyn headquarters just blocks away, churning out branded ads for liquor and other consumer products. The sponsorships for shows and web verticals, modeled on the Creators Project, which had pulled in more than $50 million from Intel, were rolling in. Its text-based digital rivals, even BuzzFeed, struggled to build a brand identity on video. The Huffington Post had flushed away tens of millions on Arianna Huffington's failed idea of doing 24-hour livestreaming news video. She tried to build programming around fresh, diverse faces, but the audience never materialized. The legacy companies, including the *Times* and the *Post*, couldn't produce quality videos at sufficient scale to meet advertiser demand. The *Times*'s T Brand Studio was a success, but not at the level of Virtue.

Suddenly the catchphrase in the news business became "the pivot to video." But Vice had pivoted a decade earlier. Now its second pivot was under way, this one to quality news, for which the company had little in-house expertise and few standards. CNN had more than 30 years of experience in news and established ethics protocols, some earned by learning from its mistakes. In 1998, long before Vice was doing either news or video, CNN was forced to issue a lengthy, painful retraction of a major scoop alleging that in 1970 the U.S. military used lethal sarin nerve gas on the secret "Tailwind" mission in Laos with the intention of killing American defectors. It had spent years reforming and refining its journalism to restore credibility.

The notion that Shane Smith could challenge CNN seemed absurd. The cable giant's wall-to-wall coverage of the first Persian Gulf War and later 9/11 had earned the cable news network a huge audience. By July 2015 CNN was available in 96.3 million U.S. households, more than 82 percent of all U.S. TV households. CNN International could be seen by viewers in more than 212 countries.

Oddly, Vice's effort to destroy CNN was partly playing out under the same corporate umbrella, Time Warner, given the former's connections to HBO. (Eventually, in 2018, they would both move under the ownership of AT&T when it acquired Time Warner in an $85 billion acquisition, one of the biggest media deals ever.) Many media writers were critical of Time Warner as the steward of these important cable holdings, but whatever its weaknesses in corporate governance may have been, they paled next to the sheer chaos that was Vice.

Internally the company was a mess. Despite its rapid growth, Vice had never gelled as a real institution. Employees lacked transparent pathways to developing their careers. As a brand, it was more of an aggregation of shows and products that shared a sensibility rather than a mission. The people who worked there had little or no idea what everyone else working around them was doing. There was almost no training. Smith hated that Vice had a reputation for being cheap and that no one gave him credit for making several hundred of Vice's early employees millionaires, at least on paper, by giving them chunks of stock, like a Silicon Valley start-up. Gawker's Hamilton Nolan frequently reported on the low salaries, bad working conditions, and other flaps inside the company. Many salaries hovered at $28,000 annually, until a vote to unionize pulled most of the news staff closer to $40,000, still low by industry standards. Smith attempted to impose some order by hiring Alyssa Mastromonaco as chief operating officer, but she left for A&E after two years, dashing the hopes of the women she left behind that she would tone down the bro culture and protect them from blatant workplace harassment. Although Smith was successful in hiring first-rate talent from the *Times* and *60 Minutes*, he rarely held on to them for long.

It was no surprise that the staff voted to unionize, especially after they learned of Smith's purchase of a $23 million mansion in Santa Monica. The union's first battle would be for pay raises, but there were other issues. One abiding feature was the draconian nondisclosure and nontraditional workplace agreements staffers were required to sign before joining the company, which demanded, "Individuals employed by Vice must be conscious of Vice's non-traditional environment and comfortable with exposure to and participating in situations that may present themselves during the course of their employment." These situations might include exposure "to highly provocative material, some of it containing extremely explicit sexual and controversial content," as well as shoots on location that involved "unique and unusual situations which may be considered offensive, indecent or unacceptable by others." Employees saw the agreement as barring them from complaining about lewd conduct and sexual come-ons from their supervisors, even if that wasn't stipulated in black and white.

The supervisors were almost all male, and sexual liaisons between bosses and young associate producers were common. (Smith's wife, Tamyka, was once a junior producer at Vice.) There was a huge problem, too, with sexual harassment, incidents that unspooled after work at bars, often following long drinking sessions.

The disorder didn't seem to stop venture capitalists and other big media companies from pouring money into Vice. In January 2017 Smith got another $450 million from TPG and bragged that his company was worth $6 billion, more than three times the value of BuzzFeed, and more than 20 times what Bezos had paid for the *Post*. That same year Smith finally joined the Amazon founder on *Forbes*'s billionaires list. But his company's gaudy valuation was as much a curse as a blessing. If he and the founders were ever going to see the ultimate payday, Vice needed to go public or sell to an even bigger company. At $6 billion, there were not many potential takers. Disney had taken a look at the books and passed, instead acquiring a technology platform called Bamtech in 2017. Like other private equity firms, TPG expected a sale or public offering at some point, and its investment came with strict terms that gave it bigger parts of the company if it missed targets. No one was terribly shocked when the company missed its 2017 target of $805 million, falling $100 million short. The *Wall Street Journal*'s headline was ominous: "Vice Just Had a Big Revenue Miss and Investors

Are Getting Antsy." Assigning value to Smith's empire was a precarious and intangible endeavor.

But Smith kept throwing balls in the air. Happy with the success of the weekly show that aired on cable on Friday nights, HBO's Richard Plepler, a proud news junkie, wanted to launch a nightly news show. Others were dubious that a young audience would tune in to such an old-fashioned format. The demographic wasn't prone to watching "appointment" television, preferring to stream videos and shows online when and where they wanted to. Breaking news was a perishable good, and after a news show was downloaded there was very little reason to ever watch it again. But once he got an idea, Plepler persisted.

The HBO chieftain had many friends who were journalists, and he often invited them to lunch at the corner table he reserved almost every day at the Lamb's Club near Times Square. One of his guests was Josh Tyrangiel, the editor of *Bloomberg Businessweek*. Tyrangiel had jazzed up the magazine after Michael Bloomberg bought the staid title and in 2009 lured him away from Time, Inc., where he was considered a digital wunderkind. With strong investigative covers and design changes, Tyrangiel had made *Businessweek* into a magazine that had people talking about it again. But Tyrangiel was getting restless. Once Bloomberg returned to the company after serving 12 years as mayor of New York, he swiftly reminded everybody that this was his company, scotching the expanded television news initiative that Tyrangiel, whose duties had broadened, was now championing. Plepler thought Tyrangiel might be the right guy to get his nightly news show off the ground. During the next few months he helped plant the same notion with Smith.

Months later Vice announced that Tyrangiel would launch a nightly news show, to air from 7:30 to 8:00 EST on HBO, starting in February 2016. Smith recognized a killer in Tyrangiel and soon after his arrival expanded his responsibilities to include all aspects of Vice News.

That was how Smith liked to work: on impulse. He had no idea, really, what it would take to invent a show that both captured the day's news and showcased long-form, immersive stories. The lead time for producing high-quality daily news stories would be far shorter than the deadlines for the weekly show, and with just four months before the debut date, there was only a loose concept for a show. Smith handed a budget to the slightly panicked Tyrangiel and told him to start hiring.

Tyrangiel needed to move fast. An on-air role at Vice was a dream job for many young journalists, and he weeded through the applicant pool before inviting the final 160 candidates to Williamsburg to vie for 18 correspondent positions. He walked them through their backgrounds and favorite TV shows, then filmed them improvising a report on an unfamiliar subject, evaluating how well they addressed the three prongs of inquiry for Vice's show: "What? So what? And now what?" He introduced them to a production assistant who would play a government official or a powerful business leader in a mock interview.

"Some of the worst [prospects] came from the networks," Tyrangiel told me. "They'd been trained to use their hands." A few, like Michael Moynihan, were experienced journalists and interviewers. Elle Reeve had worked at the *Atlantic* and the *New Republic*, but in fairly junior positions. A few months in, Tyrangiel hired Shawna Thomas from NBC News, a well-regarded professional, to be Washington bureau chief. Josh Hersh, an investigative reporter like his father, Seymour, joined up. (Vice also employed the children of former *60 Minutes* executive producer Jeff Fager and of author and editor Tina Brown.) Soon Tyrangiel had a staff of 20. Some of the new hires were given six-figure salaries, earning the envy of the rank-and-file trustafarians. But most of the on-air talent was very young and had scant experience; only three had ever reported on camera before. What they had was "the look." They were diverse: just about every race and ethnicity and straight, gay, queer, and transgender. They were impossibly hip, with interesting hair.

Smith, as usual, was looking for authenticity, to attract a generation that could smell any hint of fakeness. One of the new faces Tyrangiel chose was Arielle Duhaime-Ross, a recent graduate of NYU, a gender-nonconforming woman from Canada with a degree in zoology and another in journalism who had planned to go to Australia to study poisonous snakes. She was hired to be the environment correspondent, though she had no background in environmental policy. The day I met her she was dressed in a hip blue jacket with matching blue desert boots, her hair closely buzzed. Biracial, she identified as black. She almost missed one of the most important stories on her beat, President Trump's withdrawal from the Paris climate accord, because she had just gotten married and was still on her honeymoon. She rushed back and managed to get a story on the air, one that focused on the implications for the climate, not Trump or the political angle.

Another new hire was the blond and soft-spoken Elle Reeve. She'd interviewed with Tyrangiel at Bloomberg, and he called her to audition. He liked her background. Unlike the Brooklyn sophisticates he was surrounded by, Reeve had grown up in the South and once worked in a Dell computer factory. She wasn't from the Ivy League but had graduated from the University of Missouri–Columbia. "I didn't know how to interact with Harvard people," she recalled, "I kept being taken to these sushi lunches and I didn't know how to use chopsticks."

After her audition she was sure she'd blown it. She'd never done any television. She felt like she was rambling, recounting her unabridged biography, regaling the camera with an awkward story about her childhood neighbor who harassed her family for years. But Tyrangiel hired her, and by June 2016 she would be covering the cultural impact of tech.

As winter turned to spring and spring to summer, the date for the grand debut kept slipping. In order to have the money he needed to launch a good show and to have the loyalty of his staff, Tyrangiel wanted his small kingdom to have a moat, so he banished the previous news chief, Jason Mojica, and most of his original team.

With the delays, Tyrangiel saw his window of opportunity to cover the 2016 election shrink, then shut. It was the only story anyone was thinking about, but Tyrangiel couldn't get a piece of it without a show. The program that did finally air on October 10 looked good, with slick animation and quick transitions between clips of stock footage, paired with a voice-over recapping the day's news. It strung together a few five-minute stories with a marquee piece, an interview by Smith of departed House Majority Leader John Boehner. The two sipped red wine on Boehner's patio as the retired legislator smoked a cigarette and mused about how much happier his post-congressional life was. Smith looked comfortable as a political insider, something that would have undoubtedly horrified his younger self.

It was a perfectly fine 23 minutes, but hardly the revolution Smith had promised. Nor would the revolution arrive in the episodes that aired during the weeks and months that followed. Although it built a respectable audience of 500,000 viewers on HBO, the show drew rare notice besides lukewarm reviews of the debut. Tyrangiel was frustrated that he wasn't breaking through. The young staff wasn't sufficiently sourced at the FBI, Justice Department, or other national security agencies to contribute to the investigation of Trump's ties to Russia. On Election Night, as every other outlet enjoyed Super Bowl–size audiences for the biggest story in easily a decade, Vice flatlined. The next night's show featured the reactions of voters, serviceable but hardly different from what other news organizations were providing. The show lacked urgency. Headlines were rattled off in a distant voice-over. The inexperience of some of the correspondents showed as they tried jumping on competitive stories.

Tyrangiel was under pressure to please two bosses, Smith and Plepler. Plepler preferred that the show focus on serious policy. He had talked to Smith about doing an ambitious documentary on international economics, something he felt the young audience should know about. Smith was hard to read. Neither seemed satisfied with the mix of news on the show. Broadcast television executives knew that daily shows, morning shows, talk shows, and late-night shows took a long time to gestate; they couldn't turn on a dime. But times like these weren't conducive to patience. Reinventing an old medium, the nightly news show, was much harder than the Vice team had predicted.

In Los Angeles, Smith wasn't connected to the nightly HBO show and was increasingly distanced from headquarters in Brooklyn. He began saying, "The brand is no longer me." On Election Night he hosted a party for friends and colleagues with a pizza chef and some vintage wine from his cellar. He was in an ebullient mood. As a newly naturalized U.S. citizen, it was his first time voting in a U.S. election and he was particularly pleased to support California's marijuana legalization ballot measure. He'd been welcomed at the White House by President Obama and expected the cordial relationship to continue with President Clinton. As the men surrounded the pizza oven and got to drinking, the women were watching TV in another room. Suddenly one of them burst out, "Guys, you've got to pay attention." The election wasn't turning out the way it was supposed to. "Suddenly everyone looked like they'd been punched in the face," Smith recalled.

Vice, like everyone else in the news media, was caught by surprise. Though their reporters mostly hadn't used conventional political reporting methods, they had developed contacts in areas sometimes overlooked by their conventional, old-media competitors. Reeve had smartly used her tech-culture beat to cultivate sources on the alt-right, monitoring them on 4chan and other dark corners of the web. She did one story on how some members of the alt-right used the genetic research firm 23andMe to prove the ethnic purity of their whiteness, and interviewed the white nationalist Richard Spencer, whose supporters were known to shout "Sieg Heil" with a Nazi salute. After the election, the sideshow of radical right-wingers moved to center stage, and Vice was well-positioned to cover their story.

Reeve was fascinated by how the alt-right built networks on the internet, much as Silverman and Warzel at BuzzFeed had been. She was periodically trolled, but that was part of reporting these days. When her assistant producer learned that there was going to be a protest in Charlottesville, Virginia, to counter activists who wanted local Confederate statues taken down, Reeve agreed it might be worth covering, and on a secure Slack channel arranged to meet up with a southern white nationalist named Christopher Cantwell. Because it was a political story, she'd be working through Vice's Washington bureau.

Reeve arrived in Charlottesville on Friday afternoon with two cameramen and her producer. The national media were scarce. That night they got great footage of neo-Nazis chanting "Jews will not replace us." A few of the marchers recognized Reeve from previous stories and knew that she had a Jewish boyfriend. "They all recognized me and some heckled me," she said. "What's up, Ell?" one of the marchers shouted. "Say hi to your Jew boyfriend." That night, Cantwell was hit by tear gas, which made for dramatic video footage. Reeve was appalled by the modern-day Ku Klux Klan rally, replete with fiery torches, but she knew it would be a gripping piece, maybe even the opening piece on the Monday show.

On Saturday violence erupted between the whites and members of the far-left Antifa movement. Cantwell and others with him were being told to move. Reeve and a cameraman jumped into the white protesters' van as it raced off, which took guts and resulted in great footage, including an interview with someone from the Daily Stormer, a neo-Nazi website. Reeve kept quiet and made sure the camera was rolling. Though she didn't look it, she had fierce determination.

On Saturday, when a car ran over protesters, killing a civil rights activist, Reeve and her cameraman were close by. The cameraman filmed the car backing up to get away. Reeve managed to keep Cantwell in sight. Her producer asked her to do a standup, talking into the camera, but it was clear to her that the pictures would tell the story; her own commentary would be superfluous. What made the piece powerful was the absence of a professional journalist telling the audience what to think.

Later the Vice crew followed Cantwell to a hotel room where he was hiding out with a small armory of weapons. As Cantwell alternated between bursts of anger and being frightened, the cameraman captured him showing no remorse. It was only then that Reeve did not hold her tongue, telling him, calmly, that she found it chilling that he was justifying someone's death.

In "Charlottesville: Race and Terror," Reeve's almost invisible, nonpropagandistic stance made her documentary all the more powerful. Its choice of images, especially the extensive footage of the torch march of the white nationalists on Friday night, gave the documentary a moral clarity that stood in stark contrast to President Trump's shameful and shocking declaration after a woman was killed that "both sides" were equally to blame for the violence that erupted. "The Viral Vice Documentary Was the Perfect Rebuke to Trump's Charlottesville Remarks," said Slate, in one of many rave reviews. The show went on to win four Emmys.

Vice had 18 hours of footage. It would take forever to transmit to Brooklyn. On Monday they were still chopping and editing the 22-minute piece for HBO. This, of course, would be an unheard-of length for any other nightly news show. Tyrangiel had decided to "shoot the moon" and devote the whole show to Charlottesville. Reeve and her crew watched it in the hotel bar over bad margaritas. Reeve then went to her room and fell asleep in the armchair.

Plepler agreed to put the piece on YouTube too, where people without HBO subscriptions could watch it. Social media lit up with viewers' reactions to the haunting footage. Within three days it had been viewed more than 36 million times. Two weeks later viewership was 50 million. What Vice had captured became the defining image of the violent protests.

With the hit story and her distinctive looks, 35-year-old Reeve became a mini-brand, in demand for panels and interviews about the alt-right and white nationalists. Having Reeve focus on what was an unusual beat for the mainstream political press, allowing her to penetrate 4chan and other chat rooms where extremists hung out, was a shrewd move. This was by far Vice News's biggest moment.

Several other correspondents for the weekly show were helping to secure Vice's reputation as a legitimate news source. Thomas Morton was still appearing on the weekly HBO show and starring in his own Viceland shows. Ben Anderson, a seasoned war correspondent, provided excellent coverage of the Mideast, including the civil war in Syria and continued strife in Iraq. But other stars, like Simon Ostrovsky, whose Ukraine coverage had first put Vice on the news map, had defected to CNN, in a bitter rebuke to Smith.

Vice, in turn, had hired reporters from CNN, including Kaj Larsen, a former Navy SEAL who had undergone simulated torture sessions in training to survive captivity and did a memorable story for Current TV that gave new meaning to immersion journalism: he had himself waterboarded on air to show how terrifying it was. At CNN he felt restrained by the rules of traditional television news, which required him to remain at a journalistic distance from sources and not participate in the events he was covering. He had been reprimanded at CNN, he said, for giving out bags of rice to starving African villagers. Vice was of course not bound by such rules, but Larsen's career there would be implicated when he was embroiled in a company-wide sexual harassment scandal.

Jason Mojica, Tyrangiel's predecessor as head of Vice News, appeared at the annual World Economic Forum Conference in Davos, Switzerland, in the winter of 2016. He had cleaned up nicely. Wearing a crisp suit, a tie, and black horn-rims, and with his short graying hair, the 42-year-old Vice executive looked like a young banker, a full-fledged member of the global financial elite who swarmed Davos. He was there moderating a panel on government secrecy that included Congressman Darrell Issa, a conservative Republican from California and one of Hillary Clinton's chief detractors, as well as government officials from Belgium and Asia. At the end of the stage was the only female on the panel—typical at Davos—an attractive young female hacker. Mojica lit up as he introduced her. Like Larsen, he too would soon be implicated in the sexual harassment scandal. But in 2016 Vice News had arrived, and Mojica was clearly pleased to be representing the company at this pinnacle of the global order.

With Emmys, Peabodys, and DuPont awards under its belt Vice had joined the media elite that it had set out to obliterate when Smith, Alvi, and Jonze launched VBS in 2007. Mojica was the boy wonder who helped get Smith into North Korea and different parts of Africa. He embodied the mantra of "*Jackass* meets *60 Minutes*" and succeeded in doing serious documentaries that appealed to Vice's young, mostly male audience. Many of the awards Vice won were for shows Mojica championed, like the ones on Ukraine and Isis.

If he wasn't entirely Davos Man yet, he was the essence of the Vice Man. When he lived in Chicago, Mojica sang in punk bands, ran a record label, and owned the Jinx Café and a video rental shop called Big Brother. He wrote art reviews. In December 2006 he and two friends traveled to Chad with a camera to explore why Darfur couldn't be saved. The result was the 2008 documentary *Christmas in Darfur*. In 2016 Mojica was still one of the only Vice executives with news chops or journalism credibility. He had worked for respected shows on *Al Jazeera*, done shoots in war zones. But his personal affect was still that of a glib hipster. As a student at George Washington University he'd helped found a group called the Modernist Society, a monthly salon at the bar Bourbon, which he described as "a celebration of multidisciplinary hedonistic individuals." There were speakers, Q&A sessions, and much whiskey sampling. "Tongue-in-cheek pretentiousness" was the guiding principle of the group, Mojica said. He brought that same sensibility to his work for Vice.

Working with Smith, Mojica would hire the fixers for trips to far-flung and dangerous places where the network and cable shows rarely went. He was good at recruiting. With street cred and news cred, he had the pick of the young talent teeming into journalism schools and dying to work for Vice. More than anyone, he had developed Vice's signature style: no voice-of-God narration, fewer montage shots, a more rough-hewn look, and the constant crackle of looming danger that kept the young audience glued to the screen. Most crucially, he was the chief man devoted to the weekly HBO show, making sure every episode was top quality.

The weekly show was a big priority for Smith. He loved the patina that HBO gave to his company, mainly because it enabled him to make even bigger, more lucrative advertising deals. Respectability had its rewards. Smith, to be sure, was still Smith. One cringeworthy moment on camera came when Obama welcomed him into the White House for an interview for an hour-long documentary, *A House Divided*, which was nominated for an Emmy. Smith, in a snug-fitting suit, strode into the president's chambers with a leather folder under his arm, as if trying mightily to act grown-up. His questions, however, sometimes sounded like "Cheech & Chong's Trip to the White House." "Did you know how crazy," he began by asking the president, "the sheer bullgoose lunacy that was gonna happen the minute you came in here?" Smith loved being the show's master of ceremonies and star. Mojica's news unit, with all the personnel and expensive equipment required by the weekly HBO show, was a loss leader. But it helped expand the company's bread and butter, the quick-hit video content and short stories that were tapped out by the drones who crammed into the new, 75,000-square-foot Williamsburg offices in such numbers that Smith and Alvi had to build a larger headquarters nearer the river. As the company matured, almost every aspect of Vice was still in the mold of Shane Smith.

Until Tyrangiel's arrival, Mojica's importance grew. He was the man responsible for Vice News's triumphs and many of its shortcomings, which were still considerable. Pay was still low for the industry, especially compared to places such as CNN. Some of Mojica's documentaries were very good, but everything was done in a mad rush. There was no time for training new employees, some of whom had virtually no experience in news. Hours were long. There was no career management.

Standards of journalistic protocol and safety were not always up to news-industry norms, such as when Ostrovsky and later a Vice team in Turkey were kidnapped. "They had this fixer in Turkey and he was in prison while they dithered in lame efforts to get him out," one Vice producer told me. "They just didn't have any protocol. At CNN, for example, any journalists in conflict zones had a required check-in process, often more than once a day. They had a set list of government officials who were to be called in an emergency." Vice had almost nothing in place, although the company's spokesman emphasized to me that Vice had "never left anyone on the field" and did care about the safety of its journalists. It was a miracle no one died, several producers told me.

The differences were glaring to producers who came to Vice from more seasoned documentary units such as CNN and *Al Jazeera*, where Mojica himself had trained. In 2015 Vice hired Andrea Schmidt from *Al Jazeera* to take on the role of executive producer at Vice Canada. Her arrival coincided with a $100 million investment from Rogers Communications, a big Canadian media company. In announcing the deal, Rogers CEO Guy Laurence declared that by partnering with Smith the Toronto-based company would "build a powerhouse for Canadian digital content focused on 18- to 34-year-olds." The deal, he said, promised "to shake up Canada with exciting, provocative content and we'll export it around the world."

Schmidt was excited to be part of the launch and soon found herself in charge of a number of ambitious series, including one on terror networks to be anchored by Alvi. It was to be in six parts, including one program focused on Pakistan, Alvi's native land. Alvi still enjoyed starring in the Vice documentaries, but he was aging and his millionaire tastes, like Smith's, weren't suited to spending weeks in blighted areas hunting down sources. Therefore his time on the ground would be limited to a few days, and there was extensive preparation to make sure his time in Pakistan was not wasted.

Schmidt became alarmed by some of Vice's procedures. On the day of an interview in Karachi with a couple whose son had been recruited for jihad, Alvi was in transit and nowhere nearby. So, to get Alvi on camera, Schmidt's production team actually re-created the interview. Alvi was brought to the location where the interview was originally shot and repeated into the camera questions similar to what the producers had asked the couple earlier. With a few easy edits, the interview would look like it was conducted by Alvi when in reality he never met the couple.

Doctoring of interviews in this way was not accepted practice at the major news networks. It fooled viewers, who saw an exchange between an interview and a subject that had never actually occurred, one that was staged. In television's early days, when news divisions could afford to use only one camera angle at a time, the practice, known as "reverse questioning," had been fairly common. First the interviewers were filmed asking the questions, then the subjects were filmed repeating their previous answers.

But even then it was considered unethical to film reverse questions without the subject being present.

With the advent of video, the process was streamlined and both parties could be captured in real time. Junior producers often did pre-interviews at shows such as *60 Minutes*, but a real interview would be conducted with the on-air correspondents and the same subjects in a studio or on location together. One network ethical handbook spelled out the rules: "While editing can be used to condense an interview subject's words or a dialogue between the interviewer and the interview subject, such editing must be fair and accurate. For example, if a question and answer are presented together, the answer must have actually followed that specific question. . . . Reverse questions (that is, the practice of re-asking questions with the camera reversed) are no longer acceptable . . . under any circumstances. When it is important for the Correspondent's questions to be on camera, a second camera should be used."

Vice had clearly flouted accepted practice, and now Schmidt, as the supervisor, was caught in a tight spot. Vice has entrusted her with a big job, creating the documentary programming for the Viceland offerings in Canada, pumped up with Rogers's millions, and Alvi was one of her new bosses. But there already had been tension: Schmidt was being yelled at regularly on conference calls to New York; Alvi instructed her "not to push back" at him during what she thought were routine disagreements about editorial and scheduling matters; and she was instructed by a female director of factual content in Canada "to be nicer" to the men in New York. She was willing to put up with this to make good quality documentary journalism. The bogus interview was shoddy journalism, though, and she decided to flag it to management in Canada. In response the head of the studio pulled her into his office, where she was told that the head of content thought she was "a loose cannon" and should be fired. Later Alvi's interview was dropped from the episode; it never aired. Soon after this experience Schmidt quit, but first she took her name off the credits for the entire terror series. Vice was not for her.

Mojica, despite bringing legacy-news experience, wasn't focused on standards either. He had begun an intense affair with one of his junior producers, Martina Veltroni, a young Italian woman who had graduated from NYU and joined his production team. Beautiful and smart, Veltroni functioned like his work wife, according to her coworkers, including taking his verbal abuse. As they traveled the world together, she made sure the right camera people were on the ground and coordinated with Smith and Alvi, who had limited time for on-site shoots. Some of the other people who worked closely with Mojica resented Veltroni's growing importance and privately grumbled when she was promoted over them. Everyone knew she was sleeping with the boss, but that was not at all unusual or even frowned on at Vice.

There was, at least on paper, a human resources office. But employees saw the woman in charge, Nancy Ashbrooke, as the protector and enabler of management. She had come to Vice from Harvey Weinstein's film company. Vice's nontraditional workplace agreement more or less insulated managers from legal complaints about working conditions, including behavior that would be defined as sexual misconduct at most other news organizations. After all, Smith himself had carried on an affair and eventually married one of his employees.

For Veltroni, however, the affair with her boss was not an unalloyed benefit to her career. She was genuinely in love with Mojica, who at one point left his wife, only to return when she became pregnant. Veltroni had to swallow her pain. She tried to avoid listening to office gossip but heard about an incident involving Mojica and another young woman at Vice: on the street after one of the usual drinking fests that took place after work in a nearby Brooklyn bar, Mojica had grabbed and kissed one of the news producers. She said she had to fend him off with her umbrella.

The affair with Veltroni became a company problem. Personally the pair needed to separate, but professionally they were codependent. Ashbrooke, who knew about their affair, helped arrange for Veltroni to be transferred to Vice's burgeoning London office, where her job remained pretty much the same. She still reported to Mojica, who did her annual review and salary adjustments, as he had during the years their romance lasted. Though they were separated by an ocean, they were still attached. Veltroni was working 15-hour days, beginning on London time but not ending until late Brooklyn time. She put up with Mojica's verbal lashings because she wanted to keep her job, but she saw herself turning into an emotional and physical wreck.

As he tried to smooth over his marriage, Mojica faced more setbacks at work. After Tyrangiel banished him, Smith invented new jobs for him, first as head of international news, then as head of documentaries. After surveying the landscape, Tyrangiel fired most of Mojica's original team. Mojica had clearly lost his place in the pecking order of the Vice bro-hood.

That raised the question of what to do with Veltroni, who had moved back to New York. At the NewFronts, the huge party for advertisers where Smith always lined up premier bands and performed his own drunken routines, she was chatting with Eddy Moretti, another member of Smith's original inner circle, when a friend of his from Austria made a pass at her. She rebuffed it, thinking nothing of it; this was part of working at Vice. So Veltroni was surprised when Ashbrooke called her the following week. The man who had flirted with her had told Moretti that she had been trash-talking Tyrangiel behind his back, saying she wanted the new news chief fired. Not only had Tyrangiel been informed of this, but so had Smith. In conversation and emails, Ashbrooke told Veltroni that Tyrangiel had lost all trust in her and could no longer work with her. "You will be apologizing to Josh, Eddy and Shane," Ashbrooke demanded in one email. She noted ominously that it might be difficult for her to remain in news and that if her position was eliminated, they would "discuss severance." She also told Veltroni to consider resigning.

Hurt and scared, Veltroni went to see the only lawyer she knew, who had helped her buy her New York apartment. He referred her to his partner, who specialized in labor law, to whom she told the story of her doomed career at Vice. He advised her she had a clear path to filing a sexual misconduct and wrongful termination lawsuit, and that is exactly what she did.

Veltroni's last day of work was in May 2017, and Vice spent the next months denying the allegations in her lawsuit. The nondisclosure agreement she and all Vice employees signed barred her from presenting her side publicly, even though they were effectively calling her a liar. Then, suddenly, Vice offered a settlement to end the lawsuit and buy her silence. She took it. Hers was one of four sexual misconduct lawsuits Vice settled.

What had changed? The *New York Times* broke the Weinstein scandal and ushered in the Me Too movement, commencing sexual harassment investigations of several companies, including Vice. The probe would end up bringing down not only the Weinsteins, but also Fox's biggest star, Bill O'Reilly, and other media figures. Rumors that a *New York Times* exposé was pending circulated through the Vice building in Williamsburg all fall.

In October 2017, after the Shitty Media Men list began circulating on email among women in the industry, a former Vice producer, Natasha Lennard, tweeted her amazement "that the list isn't yet scarlet with names from @Vice." She later added, "I've never worked for a more disgusting, shameless man than Jason Mojica. He should've been fired, but instead was moved around the company." Lennard told me immediately after her tweet that she hadn't been sexually harassed herself, but knew of plenty of others who had been. She also told me about Mojica's ugly treatment of Martina Veltroni.

When I contacted Mojica, he declined comment on the record about his affair with Veltroni. He did however send me this statement.

> Launching VICE News was one of the most rewarding and most stressful things I've ever done in my life. Looking back on that period of my life, I realize that I often behaved like a raging fucking asshole who was more concerned about the people in our stories than the people in our newsroom. I had a quick temper, and was quite vocal about my displeasure over poor decision-making and other performance issues. This wasn't directed toward any one person, rather it was something that many people were subjected to, and that's something that I regret.

In November the Daily Beast published an exposé about Vice's sexist culture and toleration of harassment. The story focused on the terrible experiences described by a young producer, Phoebe Barghouty, who had also outlined for me her torment at Vice. She said the man who had hired her, Kaj Larsen, the dashing Navy SEAL, had touched her inappropriately in the office and had become so drunk at a work event that she had to drive him, passed out, to his home. On another occasion, he summoned her to his house where she found him taking a shower. She complained to Nancy Ashbrooke, but nothing happened. While Larsen ended up leaving the company for other reasons before the Daily Beast article, it was clear to Barghouty and others that Vice's nontraditional workplace agreement, which all employees signed, provided cover to male bosses who abused younger women and engaged in improper sexual relationships that were firing offenses at other companies.

The *Times* was on Vice's trail too. For many months Emily Steel, who cowrote the O'Reilly stories that cost him his job, had compiled a devastating portrait of Vice's workplace. Because of the *Times*'s high standards it was slow going, however, and Steel's work wasn't published until December 23. She'd gotten scooped by the Daily Beast.

When Tyrangiel fired many of Mojica's old staff, he created an embittered cadre of women who, despite the NDAs they signed, were talking to Steel and to me. Mojica's name kept popping up. The entire Vice staff knew about Veltroni's lawsuit. While some of them had resented her preferential treatment during the height of the affair with Mojica, they now took up her cause, NDAs be damned.

Sexual harassment was an endemic part of Vice's culture. The subject came up in almost every discussion I had over the years with female Vice employees. By the time Steel's article was published, she had interviewed more than 100 Vice employees. Although most spoke on a not-for-attribution basis, a few of the women allowed their names to be used.

Steel's excellent story exposed many cases of misconduct and abuse, including the four settlements. Nonetheless the main reaction inside Vice was relief. As bad as the story was, many employees were expecting far worse. Some on the staff were gleeful that Mojica and others were exposed as serial harassers. Yet there were others who worried that the whole company might go down with the miscreants. "We have this shadow of doom hanging over us," one told me.

How had a culture of sexual harassment festered so long at Vice? Barghouty told me Mojica once, absurdly, explained it to her this way: "The thing about working in this industry is that we have people going into war zones and the only people willing to do that are sociopaths. And you just have to deal with that because that's the only kind of person who can get that story."

Mojica's words were consistent with Smith's long-held attitude. Back when Smith appointed Mastromonaco to try to impose some kind of management structure on Vice, he had sent around a memo that captured, in spirit, what Barghouty heard from Mojica: "We operate on a kind of free-flowing-quasi-hierarchical-non-traditional-management structure that just sort of happened over the years. It's essentially a cult, and thus a nightmare for most status-quo managers."

Personally Smith seemed to have reformed himself in recent years as he expanded the company. While some of the honchos who had big jobs and Vice rings leered at young women as they passed on the stairs, two young women producers told me that Smith usually looked away. He was often secluded in his mansion in California, rarely seen in the office in Williamsburg.

But now the party was over; the "anything goes" culture had caused a full-fledged crisis. One advertising sponsor fled; others expressed concern. Smith worried that Vice's most important partners and investors, like A&E in entertainment and HBO in news, might sever ties if the reaction to negative press was bad enough. In anticipation of trouble, Ashbrooke was pushed out. But it was too late for damage control. (Ashbrook maintained that she had "worked to help companies build respectful workplaces with no tolerance for inappropriate behavior.")

After the Daily Beast story, Mojica and other managers were suspended and Smith predictably appointed a group of female elders to study the culture and recommend changes. Inside Vice the committee was viewed as a belated whitewashing effort, announced just two days after the Beast story broke. The cleanup panel would be chaired by attorney Roberta Kaplan, who had argued against the Defense of Marriage Act before the U.S. Supreme Court, and included Mastromonaco; Gloria Steinem, who joined forces with Viceland for her Emmy-nominated series "Woman"; and Michelle Obama's former chief of staff, Tina Tchen. A new human resources executive was hired to replace Ashbrooke. But it was all too little too late.

The men in charge just didn't get it. Two days after the Daily Beast story broke, Smith and Alvi decided to go ahead with an all-hands meeting at which they appeared, via video from L.A., woefully unprepared. They made no direct mention of the article or the company's sexual harassment problems. Instead they talked about issues such as pay and retention. One producer stood up in the room and shouted, "When the fuck are they going to address sexual harassment? We are all waiting for it, are we not?" The audience erupted in applause. Some employees walked out.

The problem was a broader management issue: the very wealthy Vice founders had lost touch with the young masses in Brooklyn. Once worshipped, they had both become remote figures. They swooped in for shoots for the HBO show, but neither wanted to be in the field for more than a few days. Alvi had married and was redoing his East Village apartment; Smith had recently had a third daughter. They were no longer the guys who in 1994 had joined forces with McInnes and began making their first millions with naked pictures and gross-out antics. That's what they built their brand on. Now, despite the gloss of HBO and Emmys, they were facing the ramifications of how they treated women.

The scandals kept coming, one involving Andrew Creighton, who had joined the company back in 2002 and helped Smith run the business end of things from London. Creighton was a whiz at branding, whether launching topic verticals such as health or announcing Old Blue Last, the company-made beer named for the pub where much early debauchery had occurred. It was now a stop for hip tourists. Smith depended heavily on Creighton for business counsel.

A bearded Englishman who sometimes sported Tom Ford coats and slippers painted with naked women, Creighton reportedly was capable of treating women in the office as though he enjoyed a *droit de seigneur,* as was the original band of Vice bros. In 2016 Creighton secretly paid $135,000 to a former employee who claimed she was fired after rejecting an intimate relationship with him. Steel of the *Times* heard about the settlement and saw some of the legal documents. After Steel's investigation revealed the legal settlement, as well as three others, Vice suspended Creighton. (For his part, in a statement, Creighton denied being involved in the firing of the employee but apologized "for the situation" and pledged to "hold myself and others accountable in constructing a respectful workplace environment.")

Creighton's sidelining couldn't have come at a more inopportune time. Smith, preferring to chill at his mansion in California, wanted to scale back on his day job as CEO and Creighton was supposed to pick up the slack. Then, just as Creighton was suspended, the company's 2017 financial results were leaking out.

The *Wall Street Journal* broke the grim news on February 7, 2018: "Vice, whose $5.7 billion valuation makes it the most valuable new media company in the U.S., missed its 2017 revenue goal of $805 million by more than $100 million, according to people familiar with the matter. . . . Vice has struggled to meet the expectations of its investors, which had bet the company could continue to quickly expand its digital audience and advertising sales while also translating its edgy, youthful brand to television in a financially efficient way. Those investors, which include private-equity firms TPG and TCV, Walt Disney Co., Hearst and 21st Century Fox, are now pushing for the company to turn a profit this year, which would require cost-cutting, the people said. Mr. Smith controls the company through supervoting shares."

The two new-media stars, Vice and BuzzFeed, had both missed their targets, badly. BuzzFeed's valuation was a mere $1.7 billion, and even that figure was far beyond what most business analysts thought it was worth. Vice's had ballooned to $5.7 billion. Rogers Communications, under new management less interested in digital platforms, had already pulled the plug on Viceland Canada, a $100 million write-down that surely rang an alarm for Vice's American stakeholders, both investors and advertisers. Vice lost $100 million in 2017, according to the *Wall Street Journal*, necessitating big staff and other cuts.

In February an advertiser who sponsored one of Vice's verticals told me her company was quietly withdrawing. The reasons were complicated. It wasn't the sexual misconduct per se. "The culture felt a bit like a forced effort to reproduce a Hunter S. Thompson vibe," she said. "It grew even more contrived, and there were no women at the table, which goes beyond misogynistic. We have largely walked away, although in truth, I'm not sure Shane knows it."

A Fox executive told me Rupert Murdoch had grown disenchanted with his investment and was happy to unload his stake, which had grown from an initial $70 million to more than $200 million. Disney would wind up owning it as part of its planned acquisition of 21st Century Fox. James Murdoch remained on Vice's board, but his father was no longer trekking to Brooklyn for cocktails with Smith.

The company did have some encouraging numbers to tout. Its web traffic in the U.S. grew 16 percent, to 78 million monthly unique visitors, in 2017, according to comScore. But some of the web traffic being counted actually belonged to other sites. Its television audiences weren't growing quickly enough, most notably for Viceland, according to Nielsen. The weekly show was still popular, with 1.6 million tuning in, and made a good lead-in for Bill Maher on Friday nights. Plepler thought the Vice nightly show was on track to reach 700,000 viewers, no *Game of Thrones* but respectable for a news show that had to be watched in close to real time.

Tyrangiel's audience for the daily show *Vice News Tonight* grew 19 percent, to 582,000 viewers, across all platforms in 2017, nothing to brag about but not terrible. It had nine Emmy nominations in 2018. Some of its stories were not only gutsy but had real impact. For more than a month, correspondent Antonia Hylton, who joined the nightly HBO program at 22, covered the story of one Guatemalan boy who was separated from his family. She followed the boy, who was only seven, to Texas and Alabama and did reporting in Guatemala too. An audio recording from one of Hylton's pieces between the boy, in detention, and his mother in Guatemala went viral, and Hylton's "reunion" story with the father, which took up almost an entire program, was shattering. Another of Hylton's stories, on an immigrant girl who was refused an abortion, was followed by many other mainstream news outlets. However, the combination that Tyrangiel used to design the show, youth and prestige (Vice being youth, HBO the prestige), did not always harmonize. His young correspondents were full of moral outrage, like much of their generation, and Tyrangiel had to push them to make their stories deeper and more nuanced.

A strength of the show continued to be sending the correspondents into the field for immersive shoots on location. This was the old, expensive way of doing television news, but since Vice didn't have to waste money on sky-high salaries for big-name talent or pay for luxury travel, Tyrangiel could afford it. Giving correspondents time in the field also helped him retain talent, so that Vice could repel raids from CBS, CNN, and elsewhere.

Tyrangiel didn't cover Trump's every tweet and stuck to his strategy of not covering the political story of the day unless Vice could supply a special angle or deeper context. Outrage, he concluded, was in overabundant supply.

On the entertainment side of the company, Vice's relationship with its ad sponsors grew even tighter. One of the shows on Viceland, called *Beerland*, was, unsurprisingly, sponsored by Anheuser-Busch. The show was a quest by host Meg Gill, who ran a subsidiary of AB InBev, to find the country's best craft brewery, which would win the chance to have its product distributed by the transnational beverage giant. There was now little expectation that some Vice-branded programming would be anything other than thinly veiled messages directly from their sponsors.

To win the hearts of Generation Z, whose members hardly watched television at all, Vice would have to dream up new and edgier shows, a taller order now that young people were less tolerant of machismo and ethnic insensitivity, two hallmarks of early Vice. Originality was hard to achieve every time. One new show on Viceland, *It's Suppertime*, promised to teach the audience how to make various dishes. The chef's full collar of neck tattoos aside, it was a premise that seemed generic and more 1950s than cutting edge.

Selling the company in the current media environment was out of the question, unless Smith wanted to conduct a fire sale. Smith had hoped to cash out in 2016, but Disney had walked away. Everyone in new media had shuddered when Mashable, once valued at $250 million and with an expanded news division run by former *New York Times* editor Jim Roberts, was sold to Ziff-Davis for $50 million.

The underlying problem was competition in the branded ad business. New players from old newspapers, such as T Brand Studios, had joined the fray, fighting for leftovers as Facebook and Google, which owned YouTube, devoured the vast majority of digital ad dollars. Licensing content overseas was still profitable for Vice, but no one knew how long that would last.

Smith found himself at a painful juncture. He had built a company of 3,000 employees making thousands of pieces of content a day. It was a digital video factory, keeping its young audience entertained, and sometimes well-informed. Vice operated in more than 40 countries. The company needed to mature, however. Some big gets, like meeting Putin and expanding into Russia, had recently fallen through. Smith, distracted by the scandals and departures, often in California, didn't seem ready to take it to the next level.

Smith had envisioned himself a latter-day Ted Turner, sure to make any top-10 list of digital media gurus. Much earlier than his peers, he had warned against the hegemony of Facebook. Yet Vice was still a prisoner of Google because YouTube still powered so much of Vice's global audience, an audience hard to measure because Smith had licensed his content to so many platforms.

Smith stressed international expansion. Though he didn't say so, the sexual harassment scandals in the U.S. didn't resonate so much overseas. In some parts of Asia, Vice's attitude toward women and its early rebellion against women's lib and political correctness was actually celebrated by young men. At the huge annual Cannes ad festival he announced a major partnership with the Times of India Group to launch a vigorous editorial and ad-producing operation for online, mobile, and broadcast TV. He also struck a deal to build local production operations for mobile and online content across the Middle East and North Africa. Vice opened offices in Singapore and licensed TV shows to Malaysia and Indonesia. These deals carried risk, however. While they assured that his partners paid much of the production, translation, and personnel costs, maintaining the quality and Vice-like brand of the programs was going to be next to impossible. What, for example, were the right components for the bad-boy brand in Malaysia?

Vice's brand was bruised, but Smith knew it couldn't abandon its free-spirited roots. He hadn't entirely shaken off the ghost of Gavin McInnes. And where was Vice's original bad boy? On Election Night 2016, McInnes got wild at a raucous Trump victory party at a bar in New York's Hell's Kitchen. A passionate Trump supporter, McInnes was now a star pundit for Rebel Media, Canada's version of Breitbart. He was also the founder of the Proud Boys, a band of white men united under the banner "I Am a Western Chauvinist and I Refuse to Apologize for Creating the Modern World." He often made incendiary comments about his admiration for the alt-right, though he preferred to self-identify as "alt-lite." The Southern Poverty Law Center designated the Proud Boys as a hate group and some of its members were arrested after a violent scuffle following a talk McInnes gave at a Manhattan Republican Club. Since his expulsion from Vice, he had gotten married and moved to old-line, suburban Westchester County, where he was raising his three kids.

At the beginning of this book project I had met McInnes at a bar in Brooklyn. Still bound by a nondisparagement clause in his separation agreement with Vice, he was careful about what he said, but his bitterness and anger at Smith were still raw. More recently, in August 2017, we sat side by side at an Irish bar across the street from Rebel's studio in Manhattan's garment district. With his man in the White House and his personal brand back in demand, he was a lot jollier. As before, he was nattily dressed in a suit, cutting a very different figure from the drunken, shirtless brawler I had seen in countless videos, such as his recent tirade, "10 Reasons I Hate the Jews." He seemed to have come to terms with his breakup with Vice and had included the story in a ribald and at times even touching memoir, *The Death of Cool*. Abhorrent though his words so often were, the man could write.

Smith was initially reluctant to meet with me because he found out I had talked to McInnes. But two years into my project I finally got word from his assistant that he had an opening for lunch. We met at the same Williamsburg diner where more than a decade earlier Spike Jonze had preached the gospel of video to him, and we had a good talk.

He expressed pride in the empire he built and encouraged me to visit the new Vice offices in Dumbo, where Virtue is housed. He boasted that the branded-ad business still earned Vice north of $350 million. I let him get away with telling me that Disney didn't walk away from making a bid for Vice; he claimed he turned them down. But he was less ebullient than I had expected.

Times had changed. In the pre-Weinstein and pre-fake-news era, Vice might have gone unpunished for its shenanigans, from workplace harassment to shoddy standards. But in the Trump era, the news media were under more scrutiny. As the conduit for report after report of misconduct and alleged corruption, the news media had to adhere to higher standards. Smith had bragged that Vice would replace both CNN and *Time* magazine in the pantheon of respected news organizations. With shows like the one on Charlottesville, he had won praise and standing. But the other lapses prevented Vice from being taken seriously. They were signs that the bad-boy brand, as the *New Yorker* had famously labeled Vice, had not really grown up. On that day in Brooklyn, Smith still wore the gold ring emblazoned with the Vice logo, symbol of the bad boy who made good.

Within months of our meeting he relinquished the CEO title to A&E's former chief Nancy Dubuc, already a Vice board member. It would fall to her to figure out a sustainable business model and the recipe of programming that would make two old platforms, the cable TV channel and the nightly news show, successful in the new-media age.

CHAPTER TWELVE

NEW YORK TIMES III

I t would be an understatement to say that the people working in the *Times* newsroom were stunned at the headline that appeared across the top of the homepage in the wee hours of November 9, "Donald Trump Is Elected President in Stunning Repudiation of the Establishment."

That included one of the authors of the story, Michael Barbaro, a *Times* star political reporter, who had been one of the first to investigate Trump's history of sexual misbehavior. Barbaro, a bulldog, had interviewed dozens of women who had dated Trump or worked for him over the decades. When the story was published the previous May, it caused a mild ruckus, but it was a different Barbaro story, published right after the notorious *Access Hollywood* tape was being played across America, that appeared to be a fatal blow. Barbaro's story contained testimony from two women directly contradicting Trump's claims that he had never inappropriately grabbed or touched women. Unsurprisingly Trump threatened to sue. It seemed impossible that a man who had behaved so heinously could be elected president.

On Election Night Barbaro barely had time to process the shock of Trump's win before he had to go live with his popular podcast, *The Run-Up*, another way the *Times* was showcasing its journalism. His boss, the political editor Carolyn Ryan, had assured everyone at the news meeting earlier in the day that it would probably be an early night, that the election was in the bag for Hillary.

Usually at the *Times* election stories were planned and prewritten in anticipation of either candidate winning, but this time the editors had prepared almost nothing for the unthinkable, a Trump win. Instead, a special section devoted to the election of the first woman president was ready to go. The previous Sunday the editors had downplayed a piece by Nate Cohn saying that there was an actual path to a Trump victory. Baquet had already approved a historic front page for the morning after the election with a banner headline with letters in a huge font: "Madam President."

One of the Washington correspondents, David Sanger, thought a Trump victory was so far-fetched that he spent the early part of the evening at a friend's comedy act in Greenwich Village. When he got back to the *Times* and learned that it looked like Clinton might lose, he raced to a desk and started pounding out an analysis of how the world would react to a President Trump.

For hours on Election Night, the odometer on the *Times*'s homepage, known as "the needle," or sometimes "the hell dial," showed an 85 percent chance of Clinton winning. The needle was one of the most popular features and one that many readers kept clicking on in the weeks leading up to the election for reassurance that Clinton was still in the lead. For months it had leaned with seeming certainty in the Democrat's favor, as its operators fed it more and more poll data indicating a Clinton presidency.

But at around 8:30 p.m. word began to spread from the Peninsula Hotel in Manhattan, where Clinton was watching the returns, that the campaign's models on which predictions of victory were based were off. An hour or so later, the vote count in Florida, perhaps the most crucial state, was mounting for Trump and the hell dial had swung toward him, giving the Republican a 60 percent chance of winning. At 9:47 p.m. Amy Chozick, the main reporter on Clinton, called Ryan from the Javits Center victory headquarters and told her what had been unthinkable only that morning: Hillary was going to lose. At around 10:30, when Florida turned decisively ugly for Clinton, Baquet and Ryan began chucking Clinton stories overboard and ordering up a new batch on Trump. Some of the material from the Hillary special section would later be repurposed for a section on gender, a topic that had been spotlighted for more coverage by the type of committee Mark Thompson championed, led jointly by a news editor and someone from the business side. The committee's goal was to find ways to attract more digital subscriptions.

Earlier in the night, Barbaro had appeared at another event meant to generate new revenue, a live, $250-a-ticket party to watch the election returns with its star campaign team in the Times Center, an auditorium next door to the newsroom. He had also appeared on the *Times*'s Facebook Live video. But given the turn in the vote, he was quickly pressed into duty to write the lede-all, the historic presidential election story the *Times* published every four years that combined all of the main news elements and explained the dynamics of the vote. He was a favorite of Ryan's and a fast and elegant writer.

Writing the lede-all on Election Night used to be a sacred rite, a prized assignment for a reporter. In 2000 Richard Berke, then the chief political correspondent, had been closeted in a small, windowless room in the third-floor newsroom on West 43rd Street banging out the story. There were wild swings that night too: Florida was called for Gore, then Bush, then, at about 2 a.m., it deadlocked, impossible to call. Joe Lelyveld, then the executive editor, ran in and out of Berke's writing chamber, but for the most part, Berke was left alone to compose his masterwork. Lelyveld didn't like his writers to be distracted and insisted that only a few TVs in the newsroom be turned on. He trusted his own decision desk, manned by R. W. "Johnny" Apple, one of the original "Boys on the Bus" from Timothy Crouse's book on the gonzo 1972 campaign, to get the story right. The Florida results began seesawing in the early morning hours, and Lelyveld bellowed "Stop the presses!," the first and only time I have ever heard this shouted in a newsroom. Some copies had already been printed with the premature head-line declaring Bush the winner. Lelyveld ordered these to be retrieved from newsstands and destroyed. (I kept one as a souvenir.) Energy was 100 per-cent focused on the next day's print newspaper.

In 2016 the newsroom had declared itself web-first, and Election Night was a three-ring circus; only a relatively small team was devoted to the print edition. Energy focused on keeping NYTimes.com updated and fortified, and reporters were expected to use all available platforms to promote their work. The Facebook Live video team roamed around the newsroom, in-terviewing reporters about the tumultuous results. Guests from the *Times*'s Election Night party next door were milling on the sidelines.

Barbaro was the Platonic ideal of the new *Times*man, well versed in every media platform, including a new podcast he anchored. In the confu-sion of the night, his byline didn't even appear on the next day's front page under the banner headline "Trump Triumphs" because the overstressed ed-itors had mistakenly substituted the wrong names in a rare Page One mis-take. This was the kind of mistake that would never have happened in the old days when several layers of editors flyspecked the front page. The au-diences for the new *Times* products, like Barbaro's podcast, did not always overlap with the existing readership, so the hope among the business-side leaders was that the new offerings would generate new subscriptions. They had big hopes for Barbaro's podcast, which was already a hit on iTunes.

Barbaro hadn't been Ryan's first choice for the job, but another poli-tics reporter, Nick Confessore, had turned the job down. Barbaro's listeners adored the 37-year-old host; one of them compared his sign-off to Edward Murrow's iconic "Good night and good luck."

By the time Barbaro went live, Trump's victory was known by almost every listener and certainly by every reader before the paper ever arrived at their doors. Many readers had received the news alert on their phones the instant the *Times* called the election. Less than two hours later, Barbaro was ready to explain what had been considered an impossibility earlier in the day. That was the *Times*'s forte: making sense of events.

Instant news was now the expectation, leaving print newspapers to explain and provide context. This was part of the reason newspapers were losing readers while their web versions were gaining them. Except for Sunday, daily print circulation had dipped below 600,000. That the newsroom didn't prioritize the web even further was a financial matter. Despite its decline in circulation and pages, the print paper was still the company's financial rock. Because the daily paper was still responsible for the lion's share of revenue, the company desperately needed the physical newspaper to stay alive. But inside the *Times* it was given less and less attention. The place had innovation fever, led by A. G. Sulzberger and his young cousins, the fifth generation of the Ochs-Sulzberger family.

Online the *Times* had 70 million unique monthly visitors, more than any other daily newspaper, except for occasional months when the *Post* beat it. Yet even with more than one million paying digital subscribers, a number that would swell post-election, only a small portion of the *Times* readers were supporting its online journalism with their wallets, many of them at deeply discounted subscriptions of about $25 a month. With a newsroom budget of more than $250 million, which had ballooned because of the campaign, money was tight. And on Election Night, no one, certainly not Sulzberger or Baquet, could have known that Trump's presidency would turn out to be the paper's financial lifeline.

Barbaro's unexpectedly successful *Run-Up* had made Apple's top-10 list of podcasts and after Election Night it was rebranded and the *Daily* became a smash hit, downloaded more than 100 million times. Its host was a celebrity, recognized, although his show was an audio product, by his trimmed goatee, mop of black hair, and hipster glasses. Sam Dolnick, the fifth-generation Sulzberger who led the newsroom's digital initiatives, was thrilled. "It feels like a franchise," he said. To many young Americans, listening as they walked, biked, or rode the subway to work, Barbaro's podcast was the *New York Times*.

The Election Night show was a tour de force, Barbaro at his brainy best, sometimes tough on his colleagues. If the election, as the headline on his story said, was a repudiation of the establishment, that included the

Times. The night's lineup included three members of the political team: Maggie Haberman, who had covered both Clinton and Trump; Jim Rutenberg, who covered the political press; and Confessore, who covered money and politics. Haberman spoke about the paper's failure to see the rising tide of anger among white voters, while Rutenberg addressed the press's over-reliance on polls. Confessore stressed Trump's skill at running against the establishment, even though he was a New York real estate tycoon supported by billionaires like the Mercer family.

Haberman, despite having live-blogged the election all night while she G-chatted with her sources inside the Trump and Clinton campaigns, sounded calm and alert despite the lateness of the hour and the frantic pace of the night's events. At age 43, she was used to being exhausted and powering through, a scoop machine who was permanently attached to her phone. With three children, she worked out of New York, not Washington, which her admirers believed gave her an edge, especially in understanding Trump, whom she had covered for the New York tabloids. On Barbaro's show, she said that Trump himself hadn't expected to win, revealing that a senior campaign aide had told her earlier in the night, "It doesn't look good."

She hadn't joined the paper until 2015, but she was, in fact, *Times* royalty. Her father, Clyde Haberman, was a veteran New York reporter who had also been a distinguished foreign correspondent. Impressed by the stories she broke when she worked for Politico, I had tried to recruit her when I was managing editor, but she was bound by an ironclad contract. I was gone by the time her contract expired, but Ryan snapped her up, adding her to a team that she filled with lots of other digital newcomers from Politico, a reversal of the usual practice of using *Times* career veterans to cover presidential campaigns. Given the clout of the *Times*, whose coverage Trump resented but whose attention he craved, the president-elect would often speak to her, then turn around and target her with mean tweets, as he did most of the "lame-stream press." She was poised to become the most important reporter covering his White House and would soon land a lucrative contract to appear regularly on CNN as well as a lucrative book deal, on top of her *Times* sinecure. She was also one of the most compelling characters in a documentary, *The Fourth Estate*, that would follow the *Times*'s coverage of Trump's first year in office.

These extras were part of the new *Times* culture. TV appearances and book deals were once frowned on. The *New York Times* was supposed to be the star, not individual journalists. But the rules had loosened and the media culture had changed. When I became executive editor, I worried that the new star system was poisoning the culture of the newsroom and creating a caste system. Lelyveld had been so insistent on keeping the spread between journalists' pay narrow that when I joined his paper in 1997, I had taken a pay cut from my previous position in the *Wall Street Journal*'s Washington bureau. But now, in order to retain its big names, the paper had instituted a "pay for performance" salary structure. Under the new system, star columnist Andrew Ross Sorkin was also paid a large salary by CNBC to co-anchor the morning show *Squawk Box*. At the same time, he ran the *Times*'s DealBook franchise and his column for the business section. When Nate Silver was negotiating a new, richer contract, his lawyer told me his client was "the prettiest girl at the prom." I told him, perhaps echoing the past, "The *Times* is always the prettiest girl." Silver ended up leaving.

With the *Times*'s salary structure still relatively low (few journalists made more than $150,000), it was being outbid for talent by Politico, Buzz-Feed, and others. The extra income was necessary to attract and retain talent. By the time of the Inauguration, more than half a dozen *Times* reporters in the Washington bureau had six-figure contracts with CNN and MSNBC.

Making print journalists into celebrities also helped build audience on social media and made the *Times* sexier to advertisers. Ad director Meredith Kopit Levien loved to bring star journalists to dazzle her clients and motivate her team, something that had once been verboten.

The Run-Up was still broadcasting live when the angry calls started flooding in. Readers were enraged that the *Times* had set such high expectations of a Hillary win. It was hardly alone, of course. Almost every news media outlet, except Fox, had done the same.

Other *Times* loyalists were enraged because they thought the paper's relentless coverage of the email scandal had caused Clinton's unexpected loss. Some editors blamed the glitzy new endeavors, especially a large new group devoted to data journalism. That damn odometer, seemingly hell-bent on a Clinton win, had helped create a toxic conventional wisdom. The data used by the *Times* were an amalgam of various polls, all of which had underweighted the rural white vote. Even Silver, now working at ESPN, had predicted Clinton would win, though by a more modest margin. Still, readers expected more from the *Times*.

Baquet later would concede that it had been a mistake to run the needle so prominently on the homepage and that his reporters hadn't spent enough time in the red states practicing old-fashioned shoe-leather reporting. But with multiple filing deadlines for the website, blogs, and video and time spent tweeting, the political reporters no longer had time to go knocking on voters' doors, as the *Post*'s David Broder and Johnny Apple had done. The reporters traveling with candidates had a tough time getting out of the bubble to talk to voters. The Trump crowds were often so riled up by the candidate's attacks on reporters that leaving the bubble could be, or at least seem, dangerous, especially when Trump pointed out where the "fake news" reporters were standing. NBC's Katy Tur once needed a police escort to protect her from a pro-Trump, antipress mob.

Some readers canceled their subscription the morning after the election, enough to alarm Levien, who had been promoted to chief revenue officer. Within days the *Times* published a highly unusual note from Sulzberger and Baquet, admitting, more or less, that they had let readers down and rededicating the paper to its core mission of fair reporting. "After such an erratic and unpredictable election there are inevitable questions: Did Donald Trump's sheer unconventionality lead us and other news outlets to underestimate his support among American voters?" they wondered. In his book about the news media, David Halberstam had declared the *Times* the ultimate establishment voice. Had the *Times* been blinded by its establishment, coastal, urban bias? "As we reflect on the momentous result, and the months of reporting and polling that preceded it, we aim to rededicate ourselves to the fundamental mission of Times journalism," Sulzberger and Baquet promised. "That is to report America and the world honestly, without fear or favor, striving always to understand and reflect all political perspectives and life experiences in the stories that we bring to you."

The invocation of "without fear or favor," Ochs's famous credo, underscored the importance of the note, which Trump insisted was an apology to him. It wasn't quite that. While Sulzberger and Baquet conceded shortcomings in campaign coverage, their note was, more crucially, a vow to cover the entire country more thoroughly and, notably, "to hold power to account, impartially and unflinchingly."

The paper's campaign coverage would remain a subject of controversy and discord long after the election was decided. Because the editors were so sure Trump would lose, he had not received the microscopic vetting that was directed at Clinton, although the *Times* had published investigations into his real estate empire, his failure to pay and disclose his taxes, the Russia-related lobbying of his campaign manager, Paul Manafort, and other subjects.

Not everyone on the politics team had underestimated Trump. Ashley

Parker, a reporter who traveled with the Trump campaign, was not surprised on Election Night. She recognized something meaningful in the ecstatic crowds who greeted Trump like a demigod during the last weeks of the campaign. Every time he railed about "crooked Hillary" the crowd chanted, ever louder, "Lock her up!" The *Access Hollywood* tape, which Ryan and other editors thought would doom Trump, didn't seem to be resonating between the coasts. FBI director James Comey's reopening of the Clinton email investigation seemed to give Trump's aides a new lease, while Parker's Democratic sources had polls showing Clinton's lead sliding to 3 points. But Parker had trouble getting through to her busy editor, Ryan. She was shut out by the brain trust responsible for planning coverage and was generally undervalued. Not long after the election, she jumped at Marty Baron's offer to join the *Post*'s new White House team and soon was a regular on MSNBC, whose nightly programming was wall-to-wall Trump scandal.

Despite the newspaper's endorsement and coverage showing her to be the prohibitive favorite, Clinton herself greatly mistrusted the *Times*. She believed its news editors were against her, a belief that dated back to the paper's coverage of Whitewater and her commodities trading, a story Baquet had worked on when he was a reporter in the early 1990s. I too had incurred her suspicion, even though I had personal history with her dating back to 1978, before I had even become a journalist. During her 2008 presidential bid, she had become furious over a story that I had assigned about the state of the Clinton marriage. Although it revealed little beyond the fact that Bill and Hillary were rarely in the same city at the same time, she considered it an invasion of privacy. Oddly it was Lelyveld, certainly the *Times* journalist with the least tolerance for tabloid fare, who suggested the story to me. "You should do it," he said, "before others do. And everyone else will. If you wait, you'll just be chasing."

In *What Happened*, her memoir about the campaign, Clinton wrote, "Over the years, going all the way back to the Whitewater inquisition, it's seemed as if many of those in charge of political coverage at the *New York Times* have viewed me with hostility and skepticism." She felt done in by the paper's coverage of her emails and its failure to reveal the FBI's investigation into Russian meddling and ties to the Trump campaign before voters went to the polls.

The charge that there was animus toward her was wrong. The publisher was a fan of hers, and the paper had endorsed her when she ran for the U.S. Senate in 2000, in the primaries in 2008, and again in 2016. When I

directed news coverage, I had a lot of respect for her. I had met her in Little Rock, Arkansas, in 1978, during her husband's first gubernatorial campaign, while I was writing for the political consulting firm that created Bill
Clinton's media. Many years later I covered the Clinton White House as
an investigative reporter for the *Wall Street Journal* and then the *Times*.
Some of my pieces, especially scoops on Democratic fundraising abuses,
she hated. Others, which focused on the overzealousness of special counsel Kenneth Starr in the Whitewater investigation, she liked, as I heard from
two of her confidantes. She was wary of me, but because I had avoided be-
friending Washington politicians anyway, her cool distance never bothered
me. I had plenty of excellent sources close to her. As managing editor, I assigned a full-time reporter to cover her in 2007 because I knew she planned
a presidential bid and had her fundraisers ready to pounce on donors. She
felt the early scrutiny was unfair. I also assigned an investigation of the
Clinton Foundation because I knew it was raising huge sums from overseas donors, which did not seem above board for a charity run by a former
president and first lady who was also a sitting senator. From my experience reporting on them, I had reason to focus on the Clintons' dealings with
money. In 2008 I was told by her press secretary that she felt the *Times* was
tougher on her than on Obama, which was possibly true—but he had fewer
ties to big money.

The *Times* people running the 2016 coverage, including Ryan and Deputy Managing Editor Matt Purdy, were ones I had promoted and worked
closely with. I knew they had no animus toward Clinton. I had recruited
Elisabeth Bumiller, for instance, the current Washington bureau chief, from
the *Times*'s main headquarters in New York to cover the Bush White House.
She was a straight-shooter.

But the paper made some bad judgment calls and blew its Clinton coverage out of proportion. One misstep involved making a deal with Peter
Schweizer, a conservative author whose book, *Clinton Cash*, was bankrolled by Steve Bannon and published in 2015. The *Times* used findings
from his book about the Clinton Foundation's money in a front-page story
about a Canadian uranium mining magnate. This in itself was not unusual,
but the paper had made special arrangements to see Schweizer's manuscript
early and gave him and his book more than the usual mention in the resulting article. The play gave the book immense credibility because of the
agenda-setting role the *Times* still played at the top of the news media food
chain, and once the paper seemed to give the book its stamp of approval, the
rest of the news media followed. *Clinton Cash* fed Trump his talking points

about "crooked Hillary." His campaign aides called the book "Bannon's Bible," and its funding source should have given the *Times* pause.

Just as Jo Becker and Mike McIntire from the investigative team were preparing the story using *Clinton Cash*, another, bigger blow to Clinton was in the works. Michael Schmidt, a new reporter in the Washington bureau who had come from Sports, where he'd broken big stories on athletes and doping, got another anti-Clinton tip, this one about her use of a private email server. Schmidt had the makings of a great Washington reporter. Already, he had developed some good Justice Department and FBI sources too. At first he didn't think much of the tip. He went on a foreign reporting trip and did another assignment before getting back to the email story. But as he proceeded to investigate, he figured out that Clinton had exclusively used private email accounts rather than her government-issued account, ostensibly so that she would be in control of her messages if and when they were subpoenaed.

On March 2, 2015, at the top of the homepage, appeared Schmidt's story, "Hillary Clinton Used Private Email Account at State Dept., Possibly Breaking Rules." Though the headline hedged whether her exclusive use of private rather than government email was an ethical breach, it noted the unusual circumstances. And the story had this deadly paragraph: "The revelation about the private email account echoes longstanding criticisms directed at both the former secretary and her husband, former President Bill Clinton, for a lack of transparency and inclination toward secrecy." This point was repeated over and over again in other stories, creating a narrative that Clinton was "paranoid and hiding something," as one of her campaign advisors, Brian Fallon, put it. It fit perfectly into Trump's "crooked Hillary" rants.

Schmidt, who most recently had covered the FBI and Department of Homeland Security, wasn't experienced in politics. Carolyn Ryan, the Washington bureau chief, rode the story hard. "Ryan is a bloodhound," said a *Times* reporter who had worked with her at the *Boston Globe*. "She'll keep digging until she finds it." Any fresh information about Clinton, even if it came from partisan Republicans on Capitol Hill who were investigating her, subpoenaing documents, and hoping to kill her career, was worth considering.

Clinton herself aggravated the situation by remaining opaque for too long about her reasons for using a private server and was never candid about why she wanted to hide her communications. She was secretive to the point of being paranoid. But the sheer number of stories created the impression that she had committed grave wrongdoing. Some of the stories lacked nuance and unfairly buried exculpatory information, like the fact that few of the emails on the server were marked "classified" and the ones that were did not contain sensitive messages.

From the moment Schmidt's initial story hit, the email issue hung over Clinton like rancid pollution. It tainted the April announcement of her candidacy, which the *Times* didn't even put on the front page, further infuriating her. Baquet defended the peculiar inside play because Clinton herself had announced that she was running on social media, so there was little actual news in the formal event.

"We were basically dead for the rest of 2015," her communications director, Jennifer Palmieri, told me. "Everything was about the email, no matter what issues or events we tried to put out there." There were many front-page and homepage stories, including an interactive graphic focusing on Clinton's shifting explanations of and statements about her email server.

Then came another catastrophic blow.

High on the *Times*'s homepage and the mobile app late on July 23 was the story that haunted Clinton's candidacy through the election: "Criminal Inquiry Sought in Hillary Clinton's Use of Email." A very similar headline ran across three columns on the next morning's front page. Fallon, who had worked at the Justice Department, knew Schmidt and began pushing back. The *Times* reporters had not actually seen the referral letters, Fallon told me.

After the Clinton campaign challenged the story's accuracy, the *Times*'s main Justice source backed off confirming the existence of a criminal probe. Two corrections ended up being appended to the story, one eliminating the word "criminal" and another saying the investigation was not of Clinton personally. But the story, with the original headline, had already been picked up by other news outlets, including NBC News. The *Times*'s public editor, Margaret Sullivan, called the situation "a messy and a regrettable chapter" in a column headlined, "A Clinton Story Fraught with Inaccuracies: How It Happened and What Next?," published on July 27, 2015.

Baquet blamed himself, acknowledging that readers could have felt "whipsawed" by the changing headlines and multiple corrections and that the *Times* should have been more transparent about the changes made to the story in real time. But, as it turned out, the original story was right and the Justice Department had opened a criminal investigation into Clinton's emails.

Clinton Communications Director Palmieri wrote a bitter letter to Baquet and gave it to the *Washington Post*, which published it in full. She went to see Baquet, who was affable and pledged fair coverage, though Clinton still stewed over what she perceived as a journalistic lapse that cost her dearly.

"We did all hyperventilate over her emails," confessed Amy Chozick in her book *Chasing Hillary*. "But Hillary never had a strategy for changing the conversation." Editors defended their work as a diligent follow-up to their original scoop, something the paper had done on many of its most important stories. It was what the *Washington Post* did on Watergate. The problem was that Clinton's emails were not Watergate, though the intense scrutiny of the *Times*'s coverage suggested otherwise. In early 2017 Jonah Peretti's friend Duncan Watts published a comprehensive study of the *Times*'s coverage in the *Columbia Journalism Review*: "In just six days, the *New York Times* ran as many cover stories about Hillary Clinton's emails as they did about all the policy issues combined in the 69 days leading up to the election." Cable and the networks, as they had for decades, followed the *Times*'s lead.

After Trump secured the GOP nomination, Palmieri and Clinton's campaign chairman John Podesta returned for a second conversation with Baquet, this time to plead that the *Times* not feel obliged to run a negative Clinton article for every disclosure on Trump, since the paper had already spent almost two years investigating her and had only begun to scour Trump and his record.

But a trove of Wikileaks documents, hacked by the Russians and damaging to Clinton, triggered a feeding frenzy. Stolen from the computers of Democratic officials, the documents began to leak at the Democratic National Convention, with embarrassing disclosures about the Democratic National Committee's collusion with the Clinton campaign during and after the primaries and the hacked emails of her aides, including Podesta. Clinton's Wall Street speeches, anodyne and unnewsworthy except that she gave them for big fees and insisted on keeping them secret, were included in the hacked Podesta emails released by Wikileaks in September. Chozick admitted in her book that she didn't wrestle enough with the ethics of Podesta's emails being stolen, especially after it became known that Russia was behind the hacking and Putin directly ordered it. *Times* columnist David Leonhardt called the "overhyped" coverage of the hacked emails, including by his own paper, the media's worst mistake in 2016. Baquet defended coverage in an interview published in the *Times* in December 2016, "I get the argument that the standards should be different if the stuff is stolen and that should influence the decision. But in the end, I think that we have an obligation to report what we can about important people and important events. There's just no question that the email exchanges inside the Democratic Party were newsworthy."

There were not clear guidelines. But in 2014, when internal Sony emails were hacked, Baquet and the *Times* decided not to use the stolen material in coverage. Earlier, though, I had opened the door by publishing front-page stories based on stolen documents, relying on contraband first from U.S. Army Private Chelsea Manning and later from NSA contractor Edward Snowden. These documents revealed major stories about failures of the Iraq War and government snooping, which made their publication worth it, I thought. Newsworthiness and the *Times*'s responsibility to inform the public were the right standards to use, but these were all hard calls.

The paper did delve into scandals involving Trump, especially Paul Manafort's financial dealings with shady Ukrainians, for which he was indicted by special counsel Robert Mueller in 2017. But there were so many different controversies swirling around Trump that no single one of them resonated like the email fracas. The *Times* did admirable work investigating Trump's real estate business practices and got hold of one year of his federal income tax filings, which revealed that he benefited enormously from various loopholes and paid very little to the government. David Sanger, one of the strongest veteran reporters in the Washington bureau and an expert on cybersecurity, told me he tried, unsuccessfully, to convince the Clinton campaign to give the *Times* access to Democratic email servers so that he could measure the scope of Russian hacking. The *Times Magazine* did an early probe into the Internet Research Agency, the Russian troll factory responsible for much of the fake anti-Clinton bots on social media.

But writing my own political column for the *Guardian* in 2016, I was frustrated to see the line between investigative reporting and scandalmongering become fuzzy. As a journalist I grew up on the deep stories the *Times* and the *Post* did every election cycle on voters and the issues that were the vital backdrop to every election. They helped explain the rest of the country to me. The coverage of the 1976 election inspired me to spend several years working in Virginia and South Carolina, where I wrote about the changing politics of the South that helped create Jimmy Carter. Political reporters such as Adam Clymer, Robin Toner, and Richard Berke made me want to work for the *Times*. The *New Yorker*'s Jane Mayer, with whom I wrote a book in the 1990s, was a model investigative reporter, often taking months to nail her quarry, including the Koch brothers and the Mercer family. But their reportorial style was going out of fashion, replaced by so-called horse-race reporting that relied on poll data. Scandal-focused investigative reporting was often based on partisan opposition research and opportunistic tip-droppers. It's not that these sources didn't give reporters newsworthy information, but their dominance in 2016 helped tip the coverage out of balance. But the biggest problem of all was the relentless pace of the political news cycle, which required snap decisions and constant, reactive stories.

The imbalances were most glaring when the coverage of Clinton was compared to the coverage of Trump. The *Times* misstated the seriousness of the government's investigation of Russian meddling in the 2016 election and ties to the Trump campaign. Eric Lichtblau, who had won a Pulitzer for the NSA story in 2006, had investigated suspicious communications between the Trump Organization and a bank controlled by a Russian oligarch. As part of his reporting, he found out the FBI had opened an umbrella investigation into Trump's Russia connections. But his story sat unpublished in New York for weeks as Election Day got closer and closer.

Why did the *Times*, which ended up winning a Pulitzer for its coverage of Trump and the Russia investigation and Paul Manafort's sleazy dealings in Ukraine, sit on the story? Lichtblau's original draft, which focused on Russia's Alfa Bank, was a confusing muddle, one editor told me, and although he'd connected the Trump and Russian servers he had not gotten the content of any of the communications between them. Baquet had dismissed the story as "bullshit," so the other editors in New York were wary of it. But Lichtblau pushed on, rewriting draft after draft in growing frustration.

I had hired Lichtblau from the *Los Angeles Times* when I was Washington bureau chief and knew him to be prickly but reliable. He'd drifted in and out of the campaign coverage. After the conventions, along with two other *Times* reporters, he attended two briefings by the opposition research firm Fusion GPS, which had retained the former British spy who produced the Steele dossier.

When Lichtblau went to Alfa Bank's lobbying firm in Washington, D.C., for comment, the Trump Organization disabled the server, and he became even more certain he was onto a big story, but Baquet could not be convinced. The communications could have been anything, or nothing, even random spam. Other reporters Baquet trusted more were being warned off the Russia-Trump story by some of their FBI sources, who, for reasons still unknown, misled the reporters by downplaying it. At one point, the Justice Department asked the *Times* to withhold publication because it was actively investigating Alfa. Then the government gave the paper a green light. By this time it was October. Lichtblau had also learned that Christopher

Steele, author of the infamous dossier, had briefed the FBI on some of his findings about Trump's Russian ties and that the Justice Department had opened its umbrella investigation.

But Lichtblau's editors did not think he had nailed down the story well enough. He pushed again after Senate Democratic leader Harry Reid wrote Comey asking whether the FBI was sitting on evidence about Trump and Russia while hammering Clinton on her emails.

A week before the election, on October 31, the *Times* was scooped by Slate and *Mother Jones*, which published stories on Alfa Bank and Steele's secret findings. Finally, the *Times* published a story that same day. The FBI was still not confirming that it was investigating Russian ties to Trump. The *Times* article, with Lichtblau's byline and that of a colleague, Steven Lee Myers, said the FBI had dismissed the Alfa Bank connection and hadn't found any "conclusive" link between Trump and the Russian government.

Clinton knew about the *Times*'s unpublished story. Campaigning in Cincinnati, she was hoping the paper would push the Russia story onto the front burner of the election and was crestfallen when Palmieri showed her the headline that finally appeared on the 31st: "Investigating Donald Trump, F.B.I. Sees No Clear Link to Russia."

After his surprising win, and as it became clear the Russia-Trump investigation was indeed serious, Lichtblau felt miserable and alienated from his editors, according to his close friend, Jim Risen, who left the paper after the election. Baquet and his editors were annoyed that Lichtblau had never delivered what they considered to be a convincing and publishable story about the Russia probe. As special counsel Robert Mueller began to dig deeper, Baquet joked that he would have to resign if Mueller ended up indicting Alfa or its owners. Liz Spayd, who had replaced Margaret Sullivan as public editor in midcampaign, decided to look into the paper's pre-election coverage and in late 2017 published her conclusion that the *Times* could have published a stronger story before the election on the FBI's investigation. Spayd criticized the initial decision by Baquet to hold off publishing at the FBI's request and proceeding only after getting the government's approval. She accused the editors of being overly timid. Baquet seethed.

Late on January 20, 2017, after he read Spayd's column, Baquet made his feelings plain in an email to Lichtblau. "Eric," he wrote," "read this." Then came the following, lacerating words: "I hope your colleagues rip you a new asshole." He was angry at his whole team, not just Lichtblau, whom he included in another note he fired off to Bumiller and five other reporters he thought had discussed private, internal deliberations over the October 31 story with the public editor. "Gang," he wrote, "that was a really bad public editor's column, among the worst. But I have to admit that the most disturbing thing was that there was information in it that came from very confidential, really difficult conversations we had about whether or not to publish the back channel information. I guess I'm disappointed that this ended up in print. It is hard for a journalist to complain when confidential information goes public. That's what we do for a living, after all. But I'll admit that you may find me less than open, less willing to invite debate, the next time we have a hard decision to make."

It was an unusual rebuke. After the Jayson Blair scandal, when Sulzberger had demanded the creation of this in-house ombudsman, the public editor, to represent readers when the *Times* coverage was called into question, reporters had been encouraged to cooperate with the public editor. Press critics and *Times* people did not consider Spayd, who had been a top editor at the *Post*, to be as good as her predecessor, Margaret Sullivan, but she exhibited guts in taking on the Russia issue. There was surprise and some outrage when the job was entirely eliminated by Sulzberger in May 2017. Some staffers argued that in the age of Twitter, the position was unnecessary—readers would pick up the slack.

It was reasonable for Baquet, one of the least timid editors I ever worked with, to feel unfairly lashed by the public editor. In real time it was hard to evaluate how serious the initial FBI investigations were, and he was hearing conflicting information from his reporters. In late 2018, in a 7,000-word investigation, the *New Yorker* was still asking, "Was there a connection between a Russian bank and the Trump campaign?" But having reporters speak freely to these ombudsmen was important. During Howell Raines's tenure, journalists had been fearful of reprisal if they complained about coverage, such as Jayson Blair's plagiarized articles or Judy Miller's credulous WMD coverage. The public editor's role had been invented, in part, to create a safe backchannel and help the *Times* be more transparent to its readers by explaining how mistakes were sometimes made.

The email from Baquet was the final straw for Lichtblau, who in April 2017 accepted a job at CNN as the Washington editor of a new investigative team. But this too became an ill-starred situation. He was involved in another controversial story, published on the CNN website, claiming that a Trump transition official, Anthony Scaramucci, had met with an executive from a Russian investment fund. Scaramucci claimed the article was false and threatened a lawsuit. CNN retracted the story, and Lichtblau and two colleagues resigned. CNN said that the journalists hadn't taken the proper prepublication editorial steps. But they never made clear what in the story, which appeared to be largely substantiated by later reporting, was wrong. It looked like an example of CNN, which had given Trump so much free coverage by carrying his rallies live, bowing to criticism from his White House. Time Warner, CNN's parent, also needed Trump's approval for its merger with AT&T, which the administration ended up opposing. (A federal court ultimately approved it in mid-2018.)

All of this revealed how complicated campaign coverage had become. Criminal investigations loomed over both presidential candidates, and their partisans eagerly leaked unconfirmed tips to reporters. The investigative reporters who worked on the Clinton email and Trump-Russia stories were shadow-boxing, attempting to apply rigor and ethical standards to their work. The suggestion that the *Times* ran with any scoop tossed its way was patent nonsense. But as fake news flooded the internet, truth became elusive.

After Trump's election, his daily tweetstorms often dominated coverage and made the press overly reactive. Trump's "fake news" rants against the press were strategic, of course, meant to further inflame and polarize. They were a cheap way of trying to undermine the credibility of the *Times*'s reporting as something to be accepted as truth only by liberals in urban, cosmopolitan areas. Rising skepticism about objective facts obviated the possibility of a consensus authority voice. Younger readers resisted the "voice of God" used by network anchors and *Times* writers. *Times* editorials had almost no readership on the web.

There were scores of places to find free news online. The rise of social media had carved everyone up into pools of like-minded communities. To many, it seemed safer to get the news from trusted friends or family than any news site. Facebook's decision in 2017 to reprioritize news from family and friends, not publishers, was a reflection of this reality. Facebook was designed to make people feel good. The news was depressing, and the *Times* was not an institution devoted to making its audience happy and stress-free. But it too began highlighting happy "good news" stories.

Every institution in America, except the military, had lost credibility and respectability since 2008. In the case of news, the overwhelming belief that all sources of news were politically biased fueled the mistrust. A 2016 study by the Pew Foundation, which monitored trust in the news media, found that a fairly astounding 87 percent of Republican conservatives said the news media was biased in favor of one side in covering the news. In a Gallup poll conducted in 2018, Republicans in overwhelming numbers indicated their conviction that "accurate news stories that show a politician or political group in a negative light are always fake news." In still another sad and astonishing poll, this one from July 2018, 91 percent of Republicans said Trump was their most trusted news source; 63 percent named friends and family, and only 11 percent named the news media.

The *Times* was the symbol of the "liberal news media," which Rush Limbaugh had railed against during the Reagan administration, and Spiro Agnew during Nixon's. Their jeremiads seemed quaint now, when nearly three-quarters of people of all political persuasions agreed that the news media was biased. Yet paradoxically an equal number said news organizations kept leaders in check and helped prevent them from doing things they shouldn't do, clearly valuing journalism's watchdog role. Still, only 18 percent of people overall said they had a lot of trust in news organizations. And the popularity of social media notwithstanding, an even smaller percentage trusted family and friends as a source of news. Trust in a piece of news related by "a person like yourself" was at an all-time low. So part of Facebook's operating theory was wrong.

President Trump exploited these trends relentlessly. He and Bannon called the media "the opposition party," often singling out the *Times*. Trump spent many hours each day watching Fox, Breitbart News, and an array of news aggregators even further to the right. Bannon saw tremendous upside in building out Breitbart, perhaps partnering with Sinclair Broadcasting, a company to the right of Fox. But although the right wing's media infrastructure grew quickly, its audiences remained far smaller than those of the broadcast networks, cable, and newspapers such as the *Times* and the *Post*. After Bannon's departure from the White House and then his exit from the company, Breitbart's influence waned.

Given its mostly liberal audience, there was an implicit financial reward for the *Times* in running lots of Trump stories, almost all of them negative: they drove big traffic numbers and, despite the blip of cancellations after the election, inflated subscription orders to 4 million in 2018. But the more anti-Trump the *Times* was perceived to be, the more it was mistrusted for being biased. Ochs's vow to cover the news without fear or favor sounded like an impossible promise in such a polarized environment, where the very definition of "fact" and "truth" was under constant assault.

By the Sunday morning following the election, the *Times* was beginning to benefit from the Trump bump. In tweets the president-elect said the paper was "apologizing for their bad coverage of me," despite the careful wording of the note to readers. Then came, "Wow, the @nytimes is losing thousands of subscribers because of their very poor and highly inaccurate coverage of the 'Trump phenomena.'" Eileen Murphy, the paper's spokeswoman, was told to hit back, although the paper would be judicious in how and when it responded. In an email to media writers she insisted that the paper was gaining print and digital subscriptions at four times the normal rate.

Trump used his Twitter feed as a direct pipeline to voters. In previous elections, presidential candidates had found ways to work around the national news media to speak to people more directly, but no one had ever matched the power of Trump's tweets. On Twitter Trump had called the *Times* "poorly run and managed," a "seriously failing paper" that "allows dishonest reporters to write totally fabricated stories," staffed by "really bad people" and "dopes" who "knowingly write lies" and gave "the most inaccurate coverage constantly." "Failing" was his favorite epithet for the paper: during his first year in office, he tweeted about the *Times*'s supposed failure on 30 occasions. The number of staffers he called out by name to diss was well into the double digits, according to "The 487 People, Places and Things Donald Trump Has Insulted on Twitter."

As was his habit, he singled out some of the paper's female journalists for particularly harsh words, calling Maggie Haberman, whom he actually liked and respected, "a third rate reporter" and op-ed columnist Maureen Dowd "a neurotic dope." He was focusing on the two journalists who understood his psyche and methods better than anyone and had covered him for decades. Unsurprisingly he also gave access to both of them throughout the campaign and the days following the election.

Trump's relationship with the *Times* was far more complex than his tirades on Twitter revealed. He was a man of the New York tabs, the *Daily News* and the *Post*, but he craved the legitimacy and stature that only the *Times* could confer. He knew Sulzberger personally and seemed genuinely awestruck when he was invited for a publisher's lunch with its editorial board and select editors. The *Times* had run hard-hitting investigations of his real estate dealings and bankruptcies, and he had sued one of its reporters for asserting in a book that he inflated his net worth. But none of this seemed to dim his craving for the paper's attention. As waiters served lunch on china and poured the publisher's signature iced tea, Trump repeatedly expressed his respect for the newspaper. As a sign of his esteem, he had brought along his son, Donald Jr.

In his new persona as a right-wing Republican, however, bashing the *Times* and the rest of the "fake news media" was the ultimate crowd-pleaser. At his rallies the candidate whipped the crowds into such antipress fervor that his supporters seemed ready to punch, or worse, any reporter who came near. Haberman regularly received vulgar and anti-Semitic messages, as did other campaign reporters. But away from his rallies and Twitter, the picture was different. Trump called Haberman regularly to exchange political intelligence and to comment for her articles. As the CNN journalist David Gregory noted, he could "not quit Maggie." He privately schmoozed with others. The people they influenced were clearly not going to vote for him, but he recognized that Haberman and other members of the *Times* political team knew a lot more about politics and what was going on inside his campaign than most of his aides and advisors did. Bannon also regularly leaked to the *Times*. After Trump took office, Bannon and other White House aides regularly checked in with Haberman because she knew more than anyone about what was going on in the highly factionalized White House. Everyone talked to her.

On the Sunday night following the election, the *Times*, the *Washington Post*, and ProPublica, which had won Pulitzers for its investigative work, got a boost from the British comedian John Oliver on his HBO show, *Last Week Tonight*. The whole episode, the finale of his third season, was an anti-Trump screed called "Fuck 2016."

"You need to support actual journalism by buying a subscription to outlets like the *Times*, the *Post*, your local newspaper, or donate to groups like ProPublica, a nonprofit group which does great investigative journalism," Oliver said, steering viewers away from fictional websites like "Republigoofs.redneck" and "Democrappy.cuck." Oliver had raked CNN and other news organizations for over-covering Trump during the campaign. With Trump's election, however, times were "not normal," Oliver kept repeating, and good news coverage might be the only thing standing between Trump and authoritarianism.

Almost immediately, donations to ProPublica surged, and the uptick in new *Times* subscriptions was even more dramatic. The "Trump bump" was mostly responsible for its strong financial reports following the election as the paid digital readership began to explode. By the end of the second quarter there were 600,000 new subscriptions, bringing the total number of digital subscribers above two million. In 2017 paid digital subscriptions continued to surge and lifted the *Times*'s revenue picture and stock price in 2018. These new subscriptions helped push revenue up significantly toward CEO Mark Thompson's 2020 goal of $800 million. Jeff Gerth, a formidable investigative reporter who wrote a thoughtful piece in the *Columbia Journalism Review* about the symbiotic relationship between Trump and the *Times*, called them "sparring partners with benefits." He also noted the irony that "an obsessive brand promoter has become the unofficial chief marketing officer of the hometown newspaper he professes to hate."

Besides generating a surge in subscription revenue and helping to lift the stock price to its highest levels since 2008, Trump also prompted healthy changes in the paper's coverage. Baquet fielded the largest team the *Times* had ever put on the White House, seven full-time reporters, subsidized, in part, by an extra $5 million Thompson added to the newsroom budget after the election. Baquet stationed correspondents in the parts of the country that had voted for Trump and that the *Times* had underestimated. He also made the paper's coverage tougher and doubled down on investigative reporting in Washington.

With Trump on the offensive against the "fake news media," editors and reporters in Washington worked around the clock, mindful that if they made a mistake, Trump would jump on it. When a *Post* reporter tweeted about empty seats at a Trump event but was mistakenly looking at a photo taken before the event was under way, the president pounced. And the *Times* ran a big front-page story on an environmental study that was old news, drawing White House ire. Haberman was not the only one sleeping next to her cell phone. The competition between the *Times* and the *Post* made each paper stronger; rather than heated enmity, there was camaraderie between the editors and reporters, working together to cover a hostile, lying president and one of the most secretive administrations in history. Eric Lipton of the *Times* did essential reporting on federal agencies that were rolling back regulations and becoming chummy with business interests. His tough coverage of former EPA administrator Scott Pruitt for gross conflicts of interest won awards and prompted Pruitt's resignation.

Though Baquet said publicly that he didn't want the *Times* to be the opposition party, his news pages were unmistakably anti-Trump, as were the *Post*'s. Some headlines contained raw opinion, as did some of the stories that were labeled as news analysis. And editors worried that reporters such as Lipton were too vocal on social media. His tweets on Trump, like those of another Washington reporter, Glenn Thrush, whom Baquet ultimately ordered off Twitter, were sometimes snarky. Haberman, who was more careful, quit Twitter for a while, calling it unhealthy, but then she came back. In the world of ubiquitous social media, though, monitoring every message was impossible.

The tradition of the news pages was the words carved on former Executive Editor Abe Rosenthal's grave: "He Kept the Paper Straight." Baquet was in a delicate position, in some ways much tougher than in Rosenthal's time, when the paper's reporters turned against the Vietnam War and President Nixon.

Inside the newsroom there was an emerging divide between younger members of the newsroom staff, many of whose jobs were purely digital and did not involve traditional reportorial work, and older journalists who were trained in strict guidelines for fairness. The more "woke" staff thought that urgent times called for urgent measures; the dangers of Trump's presidency obviated the old standards. They saw Twitter, Facebook, and other social media feeds as platforms for free exchange, not to be monitored or censored by editors. They looked to younger, newer editors like the Style section's Choire Sicha and the editor of the *Times Magazine*, Jake Silverstein, for inspiration, rather than to the more distant and older masthead editors like Baquet, Purdy, or Managing Editor Joe Kahn. A symbol of the changing culture was when the old Page One room, with its imposing wooden conference table, was replaced by an open room with glass walls and casual couches. (Younger women on staff complained that the low couches showed too much of their legs when they wore skirts, so they too were abandoned.)

Other changes also reflected a new ethos. During the campaign, after Trump denied having promoted the vile charge that President Obama was not born in the U.S., Baquet overruled more cautious editors and insisted in September that the *Times* use the word "lie" to describe Trump's words in two stories and a headline that read, "Trump Gives Up a Lie but Refuses to Repent." This was brave and right. The paper later published a long catalogue of Trump's lies, a valuable and comprehensive fact-check. Calling Trump's words anything but lies didn't do justice to the wild and serial nature of his blatantly false statements, Baquet decided. In contrast, the editors of the *Washington Post* and *Wall Street Journal* resisted using the harsh word "lie," arguing that it suggested an intent to say something was false and that it was impossible to know Trump's intent without being inside his head.

The most polarizing presidential candidate in U.S. history had changed journalism in other healthy ways. The belief that objectivity required providing equal weight to differing points of view began to erode. The "on the one hand, on the other" style of reporting did damage by creating a false equivalency of arguments, especially when Trump was purposefully undermining the truth.

The effort to include red America in more of its national coverage came with a few missteps. The *Times* drew widespread rebuke for a profile it ran in the wake of Charlottesville that humanized an American neo-Nazi, noting his affection for *Seinfeld* and allowing him to explain that his views were not "edgy." The paper ran an editor's note after critics piled on, regretting that some readers were offended that the man had been normalized. They also took heat from readers when a year into Trump's presidency the editorial pages included more conservative op-ed writers.

It wasn't long after Trump took the oath of office that the paper debuted a refurbished brand identity, built around the sacrosanct notion of capital-T Truth. The paper aired its first television spot in over a decade during the 2017 Oscars, in which the words "The Truth" appeared on-screen amid phrases such as "The Truth is alternative facts are lies," "The Truth is hard," "The Truth is hard to know," "The Truth is more important than ever." Viewers differed over the effectiveness of the "Truth" campaign, but the sobering message was that in the Trump era, journalism itself—even when practiced faultlessly, fearlessly, and without favor—was unavoidably lopsided.

The slogan signaled a determination to hold Trump accountable, and the *Times* published scoop after scoop, often carrying the byline of Michael Schmidt, a vital part of an investigative SWAT team that produced stories at a much faster pace than the paper's regular investigative unit. It was journalism's equivalent of a rapid response team. The *Times* revealed most of the stories showing Trump's attempts to obstruct justice by pressuring Comey to be loyal and drop his probe of Michael Flynn, Trump's first national security advisor. The paper also dropped the bombshell that Comey had made exhaustive notes of his strange meetings with Trump. The depth and intensity of the coverage was masterful. On most days it outshone the *Post*'s. The news report as a whole had never been stronger.

That incredible depth was evident outside of Washington coverage too. In 2017 the *Times* lifted the lid on rampant, endemic sexual harassment in the workplace, beginning with bringing down Fox star Bill O'Reilly and moving on to the film producer Harvey Weinstein. Coverage of the Weinstein scandal, which documented at least eight settlements the producer had reached with different women over three decades, gave tremendous momentum to the burgeoning Me Too social movement and justifiably earned a Pulitzer for Public Service, the highest prize awarded. In the wake of Weinstein's disgraced exit from the movie business, dozens of women similarly victimized by the powerful men in their fields came forward. The women alleged harassment by luminaries at media companies new and old, left, right, and center; at newspapers, magazines, radio stations, websites, literary journals; on morning talk shows, in orchestras and operas, fashion photography and the food business, music, comedy, art, and athletics; in the Senate, the judiciary, the White House, and on Wall Street.

But despite the Trump bump, the financial pressures continued and the newsroom became more acquiescent to moneymaking ventures of all kinds. A senior news editor co-headed an audience committee with a business executive that targeted news coverage areas likely to increase subscriptions. Another promoted content meant to be service journalism that featured traffic-generating subjects like condom reviews. A senior news position was created for someone seeking partnerships to pay for projects.

Soon the *Times* not only had a full-fledged ad agency operating within, as BuzzFeed and Vice did, but it also allowed brands to sponsor specific lines of reporting. In the print newspaper that ethics czar Al Siegal had lorded over, advertisers were not permitted to buy space adjacent to related or specific stories. In digital space there were no such strictures. Vea snacks, for example, a division of the food giant Mondelez, maker of Oreos, directly sponsored and paid for a group of travel writers to cover far-flung, offbeat subcultures, like the gay high school prom scene in Chicago and Grindfest, an annual meet-up of tattooed biohackers in California. The *Times* advertised for journalists to be part of a one-year "residency" program underwritten by Vea to write "image-driven stories focusing on subcultures using tools like Instagram and Snapchat." The resulting stories appeared under the banner "Surfacing" but contained no disclosure to readers that Vea was the sponsor. Vea ads were liberally littered throughout most of the stories. Meanwhile and separately, Vea told its own stories, more directly about food (like the "sweet story of the sweet potato") in sponsored content produced by T Studio; these were also upbeat in tone, much like the "Surfacing" news stories.

Where did advertising end and news begin and where was the line separating financial interests from journalism goals? It was harder and harder to tell.

The *Times* received $12 million from Samsung to run a visual news feature called "The Daily 360," which used a new, 360-degree Samsung camera to produce panoramic pictures that got prominent placement on the Times homepage. Often these big displays took up real estate that could have been filled by real news, causing grumbling among the heads of the news desks.

The march to the digital future, with much closer cooperation between the news and business sides, was unstoppable, however, and thoroughly modernizing the Gray Lady was mostly the vision of A. G. Sulzberger, who, even after he became deputy publisher, kept an office in the newsroom. Baquet told the *Columbia Journalism Review* that the new ways were necessary for the *Times*'s survival. The *Times* strongly disagrees with my view that business considerations have too much of an influence over news coverage.

The story of how A. G. Sulzberger came to be named publisher at age 37 (about the same age his father was when he ascended) also illustrated the dawning of a new era. It was his report that first called for a thinner wall between the news and business sides of the *Times*. Though some colleagues assumed that being the son of the publisher and the author of the "Innovation Report" gave him a leg up, his cousins Sam Dolnick and David Perpich were viable candidates as well. As was tradition, the *Times* complicated the succession race by bringing in an outside consultant and forming special committees to groom the heirs.

With 40 cousins, the branches of the Sulzberger-Ochs family had predictable rivalries, but any tensions simmering within were kept carefully hidden. The family always gathered twice a year, once for meetings at the *Times*, the other for a more relaxed family reunion. They were all, of course, keenly interested in the succession. Sulzberger and Golden had deputized me, when I was managing editor, to carefully groom A.G. and Dolnick, assuming both would migrate from the newsroom to the business side in fairly short order.

Although Perpich was not under my wing, I had worked with him on the digital subscription plan and admired his well-organized presentations and ability to produce good work under extreme pressure. A Harvard Business School grad, he also had lots of outside interests, including music; he had once run a DJ school. His advantage was that he had worked on the business side, where his cousins were unknown, but he was relatively unknown in the newsroom.

Like Perpich, A.G. and Dolnick were expected to apprentice in the newsroom and then move on to the business side, but when it came time to make the jump, neither wanted to move away from the core journalism. Each worried that this reticence might be held against them, but not enough to push them into advertising, circulation, or marketing.

Both were excellent reporters. Dolnick distinguished himself with an investigation into corruption at New Jersey halfway houses run by a crony of Governor Chris Christie, winning a prestigious Polk Award, which thrilled his mother, who had been a member of the family Trust and wanted her son to have a shot at the publisher's job. A.G. was at his happiest as a national correspondent in Kansas City writing colorful features, including a first-person account of his experience as a vegetarian in the epicenter of barbecue. Gawker would regularly poke fun at his pieces, but that was surely the price of bearing the Sulzberger name. He covered a lot of ground, bringing down a corrupt local sheriff when he worked at the *Oregonian* and earning respect from the *Times*'s national editor by traipsing around to every 7-Eleven in Phoenix, following the trail of Jared Lee Loughner, who had shot Representative Gabby Giffords.

I was happy to let them both stay in the newsroom and dutifully promoted them in tandem into jobs where they were in charge of reporters: Dolnick became an editor on the Sports desk and A.G. was named an editor on Metro. They both ascended to masthead jobs after I was fired.

With buzzed hair, dark glasses, and the shadow of a beard, at 36 A.G. appeared younger than he was. His almost daily uniform was a blue Oxford shirt and dark jeans. He was shy, with a self-deprecating sense of humor, often making jokes about his receding hairline. Although his relationship with his father had been strained by his parents' divorce, they had patched things up and sometimes traveled together. It was clear he talked to his father about the paper, as he did to Thompson, whom he shadowed for a few days.

I had regular meals or drinks with A.G. and Dolnick and enjoyed answering A.G.'s questions about how I ran the paper and how dicey editorial decisions were made. He was endlessly curious, a true student of the news report. Once, at breakfast in a downtown restaurant, he practically quoted full paragraphs from a story published that morning by the Chicago bureau chief, Monica Davey. I hadn't even read the story yet.

I admired that he wasn't a creature of the New York high life. In fact he seemed a little ill at ease when he accompanied me to a few outside events, like a black-tie opening at the Met Opera. It impressed me that he loved living in Kansas City. His life away from work seemed to consist mainly of hanging out with friends he met through work or old pals from Brown or Fieldston, the private high school we both had attended. In 2017 he began living with a woman, and they had a daughter the next year. He was serious about investigative reporting, which he had studied in college. Although he'd professed little interest in going into journalism, he took a job at the *Providence Journal* in Rhode Island after a friend and teacher told him he'd regret it for the rest of his life if he didn't give journalism a try. He never looked back.

Dolnick had experience as a foreign correspondent for the Associated

Press in India. He was married with a child and more polished than his cousins. But as the competition wore on, A.G. seemed to gain confidence and stature.

Dolnick and A.G. both held the title of associate editor when the final choice was made. A seven-member committee spent months interviewing the candidates and asked each of them to write two memos before the family Trust and the board approved the committee's recommendation. It surprised no one when, in September 2016, the announcement came that A. G. Sulzberger was becoming deputy publisher, the stepping stone to the big job.

At the end of 2017, right on schedule, Arthur Sulzberger Jr. turned over the publisher's chair to his son in a short, pro forma meeting in the boardroom on the 15th floor. Then father and son appeared together in the newsroom. There was a standing ovation for A.G., though the *Times* press spokesman got into an angry dispute with a media reporter covering the handover, insisting that the applause had been for the father. The reporter saw this as a sad reflection of Arthur Jr.'s insecurity over the degree of loyalty and affection he enjoyed in the newsroom.

The future of the enterprise and whether the *Times* would remain in family hands now rested with A.G. We met for coffee in 2017, and he seemed happy with the paper's progress and undaunted by Trump's constant attacks. He knew I had accepted an assignment for the *Book Review*, for which I had frequently written when I worked at the paper. "I want you to feel you have a place at the *Times*," he said, which touched me.

A.G. quickly made an impact on the institution and its journalists. Anyone not involved in new ventures, anyone not showing innovation, seemed worried that they would find themselves on the next buyout list. Far fewer reporters wanted to become editors. There was a lot of paranoia about being seen as old school. The young deputy publisher, however, was insistent on pushing for near constant innovation. He did worry, he told me, about staff morale since, with deep cuts, especially in the editing system, everyone was working in overdrive on the relentless digital news cycle, which had become even more punishing with the news machine that was Donald Trump.

In August 2017 I entered the newsroom for the first time since I was fired. Metro reporter David Dunlap had invited me to his farewell toast, and I felt ready to see the place again. Immediately I could see why A.G. was worried, even though neither he nor members of his family attended the farewell. There was a brewing backlash, triggered mostly by the departures of beloved figures such as Dunlap, a venerated, veteran reporter who knew more about *Times* history than anyone in the newsroom and wrote stories about the disappearing landscape of old New York. In his departing remarks, Dunlap was nostalgic about his 44 years at the paper. He recalled starting as a clerk for James Reston, one of "Scotty's boys," and answering his phone when the caller was none other than Iphigene Sulzberger, Adolph Ochs's famous daughter, who in another era would have run the paper herself. He was so excited about his first front-page story that day that he gushed to her about it. "Young man," said Mrs. Sulzberger, who died in 1992, "you're on your way."

He talked about the satisfying thud of the print paper hitting his doorstep, and how it still thrilled him. The Sulzbergers and Thompson were often asked how long the print paper would survive; they usually responded, "At least ten more years." Pointedly Dunlap made no mention of anything digital.

I knew to discount all the people who told me "It isn't the same place as when you were here," but a backlash against the cult of novelty was inescapable. Dunlap had led a staff walkout over the firing of many of the paper's copy editors in the months before he retired.

Because they could squeeze a lot of revenue from renting out the floors of the Times Building they still occupied, Thompson had commanded that everyone squeeze into much tighter quarters. He planned to rent out eight floors (in my day the operations had been spread out on more than 20 floors), and many reporters no longer had permanent desks.

As A.G. was taking up his new duties, and was often in the third-floor newsroom, almost all the journalists on the second floor had cleared out their things and were working from home while their desks got crunched together. The office redesign and the buyouts were costly, at nearly $50 million. More painful cutting would probably be required in the future, but during A.G.'s first months as publisher, the stock price hit a high and the number of digital subscriptions soared to more than three million. None other than Trump had brought the *Times* to the cusp of achieving its aggressive 2020 goal for financial security. Given that, with the dominance of Google and Facebook, advertising seemed to be a permanently unstable source of income, the Trump bump offered the possibility of a future in which journalism might be able to survive mainly on the strength of readers' support of digital and print circulation.

The boom in online publishing had eviscerated the old model of advertising and circulation supporting the news. Circulation had brought in a meager 26 percent of revenue at the *Times* at the turn of the millennium; by 2017, on the strength of new digital subscribers and the devoted readers of the hard-copy edition, it had leaped to 64 percent.

These gains were hardly enough to allay the anxious minds at the top of the *Times*, whose drive to diversify the business required growth in every direction at once. In his crusade for innovation, the young Sulzberger would have the aid of CEO Thompson, a man with more objective distance from the heirloom institution and whom a former BBC colleague described (fondly) as the best corporate knife-fighter she had ever known. He was a great marketer for both the *Times* and himself. He touted the success of the *Times*'s digital subscriptions at numerous journalism conferences and in interviews. He was intent on transforming the image of the company from a withering dowager into a digital powerhouse. Thompson had vowed to nearly double digital income by 2020, to more than $800 million, which would require an aggressive annual growth rate of 12.5 percent.

Thompson sometimes grandly described himself as "the conductor of the orchestra." Although some of the journalists resented his $8 million pay package at a time new layoffs were being discussed, at least he seemed to have a strategy for the future. This involved constantly expanding the number of digital subscribers, especially internationally, which could be achievable given that a relatively narrow band of readers (about 12 percent) supplied 90 percent of the digital revenue. Thompson believed there was great potential to expand this group of loyalists internationally, even though other publications, like the *Wall Street Journal*, had failed in similar outreach. The *Times* also offered digital subscriptions at a 50 percent starter discount to almost anyone who was clicking on stories.

He'd also pushed the *Times* into the role of digital innovator by embracing virtual reality and other cutting-edge technology. Money was being generated by *Times*-sponsored events, like the travel show the newsroom had opposed during the Mohonk Group. The event in 2018 did seem to represent everything the newsroom wasn't: glitzy and pushy, as a mariachi band blared and marched to promote Mexico tourism and convention-goers rushed around the Javits Center collecting coupons to win travel prizes. On the tech side, Perpich presided over The Wirecutter, a business the *Times* bought for $30 million that reviewed tech objects and used affiliate links. When a *Times* reader bought something, the paper got part of the payment. There were conferences galore, trips to thrill and educate, and something new every week on NYTimes.com.

New technologies such as virtual reality, which created a lot of buzz in the advertising world, could also be applied to some news stories. Google had produced a million pairs of cardboard VR headsets for the *Times* to tuck into papers and send out to readers for its maiden VR effort, a film on refugees. The experiment had garnered the kind of media attention that Sulzberger loved.

Ken Auletta, a writer who covered major media companies for the *New Yorker*, once wrote, "There is an inherent clash between the culture of business, which wants to maximize profits, and the culture of journalism, which wants to maximize coverage." That clash still abided as a symptom of a healthy newsroom, but Thompson and A.G. agreed that the wall had become too dense a barrier. As head of the BBC, Thompson had been in charge of all entertainment, news, and business, and this was the blended model he preferred.

Conventions of the web, long avoided at the *Times*, were now embraced. The news report became more visual, with more video. The writing style of articles had to be less institutional and more conversational. "Our journalists comfortably use this style on social media, television and radio and it is consistent with the lingua franca of the Internet," an editors' memo stated. Although the editors reassured the troops that they were not engaged in "an arms race for page views," a number of journalists believed all of these changes were dumbing down the paper and that editors were too focused on how many clicks stories got. Unlike the *Post*, the *Times* did not have screens displaying the constantly changing popularity data, although the homepage showed which stories were trending.

Thompson and A.G. had sent a note reassuring the staff that the traditional wall between news and advertising was being preserved, but this did little to calm fears that the business side was dictating changes to the news report, such as padding it with lots of service pieces and a new section on men's fashion, including a Watches section, a subject with no actual news value. The business pages included reviews from The Wirecutter, the company the Times owned, a fact that was not always disclosed in the stories.

The ever-growing T Studio had created 235 native ad campaigns for more than 100 clients, with branches in London and Hong Kong. With a staff of 130, it was bigger than the newsroom of Connecticut's *Hartford Courant*, once a profitable part of the Times Mirror chain. Brand advertising gave some laid-off journalists a new line of work. In 2017 Thompson said he expected T Studio to generate more than $50 million.

Although having what amounted to an ad agency operating inside the *Times* made some employees uncomfortable, it was helping to save jobs. That was the justification offered by Baquet for most of the new initiatives that breached the old divide between business and news.

T Brand Studio billed its output as "Stories that influence the influential," and like mercenary versions of the actual newsroom staff, they would do so on behalf of almost anyone whose checkbook was big enough: Shell, Chevron, Goldman Sachs, Google. While the paper's reporters endeavored earnestly to unearth the improprieties at these corporate behemoths, their colleagues in the ad shop did their best to offset any bad press with warm and fuzzy distractions. As revelations in spring 2018 opened readers' eyes to the potentially dangerous omnipotence and demonstrable malfeasance of Facebook, the social network could simply place an order for some fresh, glowing coverage from T Studio and hope it would obfuscate the erstwhile damage.

Investigations at the *Guardian*, the Intercept, and the *Times* exposed Facebook's failure to protect users from a behind-the-scenes operation to identify and influence impressionable voters. On the strength of stories like the *Times*'s "How Researchers Learned to Use Facebook 'Likes' to Sway Your Thinking," the Cambridge Analytica scandal was inciting mutiny among some Facebook users. But lest it get that far, the flaks at T Brand Studio lent their hands to bail out Facebook's reputation with a branded content package on the company's use of artificial intelligence, highlighting only the most innocuous, confidence-inspiring applications of the controversial technology. Using AI, the piece explained, Facebook could determine that the picture you just liked was of a dog; this intel would help Facebook feed you more photos of that dog in the future. It was an imperfect technology, the ad admitted lightly: Facebook's computers were still occasionally liable to mistake a picture of a curled-up dog for a bagel. But it was a healthy sign of the newspaper's independence that the native ad clients and their money had no influence over news coverage.

The *Times* unveiled other new products to help advertisers, including a new system that would enable them to strategically deploy their messages to the readers it identified as most receptive, using new "perspective targeting." This technology helped the *Times* sort its stories by their topical and emotional content, then infer which readers each piece would resonate with.

In the three years he had been CEO, Thompson had used the "Innovation Report" and its call for more news and business collaboration to increase his clout. Almost immediately after I was gone, Baquet appointed someone from the business side, who had worked on a new cooking app, to the news masthead. He hired someone from NPR's online operation for an extremely senior position who reported jointly to him and Thompson; the new hire's murky job title was head of digital strategy. Senior editors had similarly murky titles containing the words "audience." The advertising department was not supposed to weigh in on what video was made, but often did, according to a former video news editor who was forced out of his job after he resisted. Someone from the T Brand Studio was given a job on the video team, which was technically still part of the newsroom.

Times journalists, including the Washington bureau chief, columnists, and critics, led cruises and expensive tours called Times Journeys. These trips were a common practice among some publications; they were pioneered by *The Nation* magazine. But Times Journeys were more elaborate, advertised in full-page spreads in the newspaper, and pricier. One trip offered the chance to rub shoulders with the paper's publisher. Guests paid $135,000, which included a round-trip flight on a private 757. There were *Times* courses and summer schools taught by its journalists. The paper had resisted such lavish voyages in the past as crass.

The news editors struggled to align with Thompson's ambitious budget targets for 2020 and their response sent everyone into a tizzy. It called for the elimination of "lower value" editing and ending the practice of having many editors touch the same copy to buff it to *Times* standards. It compared the old multi-editing traditions to dogs pissing on the same fire hydrant. (The editors who did this work were called backfielders.)

The new plan also called for the elimination of all 100 copy editors. They were the editors who never got the glory, but they kept opinion from seeping into the news and saved the paper from misspellings, wrong titles, grammatical errors, and more serious mistakes. After their departure in June 2017, readers complained of mangled syntax, typos, and other errors. In the age of "fake news" and rising distrust of news organizations, these readers insisted on the importance of completely accurate journalism. Greg Brock, the editor who dealt with reader complaints, received 500 letters protesting the reduction in copy editors.

Almost everyone empathized with the sentiments expressed by one of the departing copy editors, who wrote in farewell, "I thought we had something special, but it turns out she never really loved me at all. She's trying out a new lipstick each week. . . . Today she's doing a Facebook Live from the Fidget Spinners Convention. Yesterday it was a 360-degree video of a Pokémon Go hunt (sponsored by Samsung). She's even been seen on Snapchat. And the latest desperate move to run with a younger crowd: She's having a few layers removed. . . . A word to the wise: Watch your back—she's not as loyal as she used to be. Now excuse me while I go cease to exist."

The dismissal of the copy editors was accompanied by a new round of buyouts in the summer of 2017. Among the 100 who took them were Dunlap and N. R. Kleinfield on Metro, James Risen in Washington, and some of the paper's most experienced women reporters, including Julia Preston, Deborah Sontag, and Elisabeth Rosenthal. Most startling of all was the departure of senior book critic Michiko Kakutani, a veteran of nearly 40 years who was one of the most feared and respected names in the publishing world. Round after round of buyouts had ravaged the dwindling minority of strict traditionalists in the newsroom, and their kind was now facing extinction. Those who remained were well aware that the surest path to job security was to establish themselves as standalone stars and "innovators."

Baquet issued an edict encouraging a more informal tone in stories, reflecting the looser writing style of the internet. Suddenly the news report was littered with first-person pieces and Q&A's, which took little editing time.

Still, the *Times* maintained its quality and the route back to improved financial health turned out to be its most traditional strength, great reporting.

As he was finishing his run as publisher, Arthur Sulzberger Jr. invited me to a dinner he hosted in Washington after the 100th-year anniversary party for the Pulitzer Prizes. There he recognized me in his speech for helping produce many of the prizes the *Times* had won during my tenure. It was an honor to be in the company of some of the journalists I worshipped, including Neil Sheehan, the reporter who broke the Pentagon Papers and whom I had always wanted to meet but never had. In a brief conversation, Sheehan told me the *Times* was doing a magnificent job trying to inform the public about the possibly criminal cover-ups and lies of the new administration, which reminded him in so many ways of the Nixon White House.

The next day Sulzberger and I bumped into each other at a reception at the *Washington Post*. We were both eager to tour the *Post*'s new newsroom, so when Lois Romano, an old friend, offered to give me a tour, I grabbed Sulzberger to join us. As we walked, chatting amiably with Lois and each other, *Post* journalists looked at us strangely. After all, I was strolling with the man who fired me. But Sulzberger and I were bound together by a lot of fearless journalism we had both helped publish. This was, in the end, far more important than the issues that drove us apart.

CHAPTER THIRTEEN

WASHINGTON POST III

L
ike the *Times*, the *Post* was unprepared for Donald Trump. The tone of its Election Night party struck some of the guests as strange, so retro that it seemed like some vestige of Washington, D.C., circa 1980. As big political names and a few *Post* staffers streamed in, they were greeted by a woman clad in a "napkin dress" from whose slinky bodice they were to pluck off a napkin. This attire was so inappropriate that the soiree became known as "The grab 'em by the napkin" party. It was an odd coda for a campaign marred by sexism, and even odder for the politically correct *Post*.

If the casino-themed party, sponsored by MGM Resorts to celebrate the opening of its newest hotel nearby, felt like something out of the Reagan era, the Election Night party proved to be an unanticipated headache for Ryan, the new publisher who had worked for the Reagans. As *Post* reporters came in and out to update the election results for the guests and TV viewers, some were appalled by the glitzy, sexist display, especially women staffers. On what was expected to be the celebration of the first woman to be elected president, the *Post* was hosting an event more suited to Las Vegas, with blackjack tables and demeaning female costumes. The next day, as Clinton gave her concession speech, 150 male and female staffers signed a letter of protest and delivered it to an unhappy Ryan. The infuriated staffers wrote, "[The] napkin-wearing woman who was being disrobed by guests went beyond inappropriate to offensive to those of us who resent seeing women continually being reduced to and offered as objects of men's sexual desires." It was particularly wrong, they noted, given "the seriousness of election night and the decision that was made about the future direction of our country (not to mention that one of the candidates was a casino-owning mogul who likes to grab women by the crotch)."

Ryan's vice president for events apologized. "Going forward, be assured that even more scrutiny will be placed on the packages offered by our sponsors—before, during, and after each event. You will not encounter anything like this again." The party was an example of one of the "creative" sponsorships that the *Post* and just about every other news organization were seeking to generate revenue, so the *Post* was able to shift some of the blame to the Vegas-based casino company.

Even with a billionaire owner, Ryan and the other business executives were under pressure to find revenue. With Facebook and Google gobbling up the lion's share of digital advertising revenue, sponsorships and live events were fertile ground for generating cash. Bezos's pockets were deep, but not limitless.

In 2016 Ryan celebrated the *Post*'s turning a profit for the first time in years. Digital subscriptions were up, and so were its audience numbers. More crucially to Bezos, the company's technology was the envy of the news profession, and the publisher was beginning to see a nice revenue stream from selling its tech tools, designed in-house, to other newspapers.

The company was on the comeback trail. It wasn't the machine it had been in Bradlee's time, with 1,000 journalists in the newsroom and an average of 832,332 daily subscribers at its height in 1993. Daily print circulation had dropped to under 400,000, but unique monthly visitors to its website were up sharply, from 16.8 million in August 2013, according to comScore, to what the *Post* reported were more than 40 million unique visitors by November 2016. And the formerly shrinking newsroom had added more than 100 people in Bezos's first year as owner, bringing the current number of full-time newsroom employees to about 650.

On Election Night, as Executive Editor Marty Baron scrambled to pull together the best reporting on Trump, his go-to guy was David Fahrenthold, a fast writer who could take feeds from other reporters and cobble together a coherent story. He was an ace investigative reporter who had unearthed some of the most damaging stories about Trump, tracking his charitable contributions (or lack thereof) like a bloodhound. He also had the scoop on the notorious "Grab 'em by the pussy" tape. While many investigative reporters at the *Times* and elsewhere were focused on the Clinton Foundation and Hillary's Goldman Sachs speaking fees and her emails, Fahrenthold wrote story after story on Trump, consistently holding him to account.

Fahrenthold had prepared himself to write in case of a surprise Trump win, but thought this would just be an amusing story for his children one day. Suddenly the joke had become reality. As he sat down to type, he checked whether a Trump victory would be the biggest upset in recent years. National political reporter Dan Balz, a 30-year *Post* veteran, assured him it was. So Fahrenthold began typing the lede for a story that just hours earlier he'd been certain would remain unpublished: "Donald John Trump has been projected as the winner of the presidential election. . . . His win on Tuesday was the biggest surprise of the modern presidential era." At 2:32 a.m., after the Associated Press called the election for Trump, he messaged, "PUB[LISH] TRUMP WINS STORY."

Throughout the campaign, the *Post*'s news pages had become noticeably more partisan. In his popular blog The Fix, Chris Cillizza minced no words about Trump, and on another, called Wonkblog, the liberal leanings of its creator, Ezra Klein, who had left the *Post* in 2014 to start Vox, a popular all-digital site, still predominated. Klein and Vox, like BuzzFeed, rejected staid objectivity and derided the bland "on the one hand, on the other" journalism. The more conversational style and rapid-fire editing of the blogs, plus Trump's serial lying, drove the tone of the *Post*'s coverage in an anti-Trump direction.

Stories about his tweets and taunts predominated. The *Post* sometimes landed in Trump's tweetstorms, and in the summer of 2016, it was the *Post*'s turn to have its press credentials yanked by the Trump campaign, punishment for a story that said, correctly, that the candidate had linked President Obama to the mass shootings in Orlando, Florida. In his tweets, Trump insisted on calling the paper #AmazonWashingtonPost, even though it was owned by Bezos personally, not Amazon.

Trump's Twitter attacks on the *Post* began in 2015, when he became enraged by a fact-checking article that exposed as false his baseless claim to have "predicted Osama bin Laden" in a book he wrote in 2000. The *Post*'s fact-checking system was famous and closely watched. It awarded "Pinocchios," a rating system it used to grade lies and exaggerations. Trump was soon leading the field by far with a record number of long-nosed Pinocchio heads appearing next to his various outrageous and false claims. He hated being called out on his lies and struck back in tweets throughout the campaign, claiming that the *Post* was "losing a fortune," just as he had assailed "the failing New York Times." *Post* readers loved the Pinocchios. Like *Times* readers, they leaned left, although its opinion pages did not. In a Stanford study, *Post* readers were identified as among the most liberal in the country, more so than even *Times* readers.

Trump supporters got their news from right-wing sources, including a site (or subreddit) called /r/The_Donald with 500,000 subscribers. These were internet destinations where the wildest conspiracy theories about Clinton circulated, including charges that she and her campaign chairman were running a child-molestation ring out of a Washington pizza parlor.

Baron was a traditionalist who wanted aggressive coverage of both candidates, including through investigative scrutiny and pieces about their policy proposals. Bezos had come through with the resources Baron needed to restore the *Post*'s political coverage, which had been in a badly depleted state for the 2012 election. Balz was glad he hadn't left the paper for Reuters; he and Karen Tumulty were the seasoned hands. New and younger talent like Robert Costa, Philip Rucker, Matea Gold, and Ashley Parker were recruited for additional political muscle. They were giving heartburn to John Harris, the ex-*Post* journalist who headed Politico, and to the *Times*, where Baron had been a senior editor. Baron's newsroom of under 700 was still a shadow of the *Times*'s 1,350, but Bezos did provide "the runway" he had promised. The campaign trail was the field on which the *Post* could reclaim its glory.

Bezos did a complete about-face, abandoning Graham's local strategy and pushing to be a national and international competitor to the *Times*. His strategy was simple: aggressive growth on both fronts. That strategy had worked brilliantly for Amazon, where he famously focused on growth over profits. He believed the *Post* could reach every English-speaking reader in the world. It could compete with the *Times*, Warren Buffett be damned. Bezos's belief in scale, honed by the success of Amazon, meant that the *Post* became far bolder in expanding its audience, but it came with risks to its credibility, like showcasing even more stories that were glaring examples of clickbait.

On some days the *Post* had as much clickbait as BuzzFeed, promoting stories like this one: "She said she killed her son and hid him in a manure pile. The truth is more sinister, police say." The sensational headlines often sat right underneath investigative exclusives. The print paper, with its older readership, had more sedate headlines on the same stories that were showcased with clickbait banners on the app. The differences were most noticeable on a product designed for the young digerati, "The Post Most," which was chock-full of BuzzFeed-like headlines. Soon online readership doubled.

The new headquarters that symbolized the paper's rebirth under Bezos looked like a Silicon Valley start-up. At the opening celebration in January 2016 Bezos was exultant, proudly showing off the entirely new newsroom design, where technologists sat alongside journalists. Wearing a windowpane suit for the occasion instead of his uniform of open collars and khakis,

Bezos greeted luminaries, including Arthur Sulzberger Jr., and joyfully listened to everyone congratulating him for restoring the *Post* to full strength. "It's wonderful," he kept repeating to the people who crowded around to thank him. "Just wonderful."

Since his acquisition, Bezos's emotional ties to the paper had become much stronger. Standing next to him at the party was *Post* reporter Jason Rezaian, who had been imprisoned in Iran for the past 18 months. Journalism had become a dangerous business, with record numbers of killings and detentions of writers and photographers. Just days earlier, Bezos had flown to Germany on his private plane, rigged out with #FreeJason signs on the seats, to bring the Rezaian family home. He seemed genuinely moved by the experience.

Rezaian's safe return was hardly the only reason for the *Post*'s gratitude. When he became the white knight who rescued it in 2013, Bezos had pumped money and resources into a newsroom that had been cut nearly in half. Under the stewardship of the deceptively low-key Baron, the *Post* had recaptured its excellence and verve, hiring 100 new journalists and 45 engineers and the technologists.

In order to create and promote the franchise players Bezos and Ryan wanted their journalists to be, the *Post* had built two fully equipped video studios and was building out other ones so that reporters could do cable shows remotely and also serve WashingtonPost.com without having to leave the premises. Several *Post* political reporters were regulars on CNN and MSNBC, including Ashley Parker, the former *Times* reporter, who was telegenic and quick on her feet. Costa was picked to replace the late Gwen Ifill on the influential PBS show *Washington Week*, where Balz had long been a panelist and whose producers wanted younger blood. Costa was just 30.

Although his background was in covering business, Baron became fascinated by politics while he was editor of the *Boston Globe*, which produced an investigative biography of Mitt Romney when he was the GOP nominee in 2012. Baron repeated that strategy in 2016, putting together a big team to produce an investigative biography of Trump almost the minute he became the front-runner for the GOP nomination. One of my interviews with Baron was in the early summer of 2016, right before he had scheduled a meeting with the "Trump Revealed" team. My somewhat dour friend was practically jumping out of his seat because he was so excited to hear what his team had unearthed.

For Baron, doing a thorough vetting of Trump, even if Clinton won, was the duty of a newspaper. Like Bradlee, he insisted that his reporters keep following up after they'd had an initial scoop. In the crowded news ecosystem, dominated more and more by social media, a single scoop, no matter how good, might not get the shares and viral boost that now was necessary to get the public's attention. A blockbuster one day could be overtaken the next by someone else's story. The *Globe*'s Spotlight team had been masters of combing large swaths of material for traces of wrongdoing, and then staying on the scent. That's how the investigation of the Catholic Church unfolded, which Baron initiated. The *Post*'s brilliance on Watergate was rooted in Woodward and Bernstein's dogged follow-up. That story had taken months to unwind, and came to fruition because Bradlee and Katharine Graham pushed the duo to keep digging. When the reporters approached her to concede that they might never find the thread that connected the scandal to President Nixon, Mrs. Graham instructed them, "Don't tell me never."

With dwindling reporting staffs, many newspapers couldn't afford to keep reporters on teams for long-range stories. The shortage in accountability journalism was a crisis for the country, according to Paul Steiger, the former managing editor of the *Wall Street Journal*. After retiring from the *Journal*, Steiger had founded ProPublica, which supplied publishable investigations to other news organizations, especially those that could no longer do this work themselves. The *Times* and the *Post* were really the only newspapers left with the full capacity to do the kind of political investigations that required two layers of reporting, a more rapid-fire "run and gun" group and diggers who were cordoned off to work on longer-range targets. At the *Globe*, Baron had resisted the trend to cut investigative muscle and had fought for the funds to keep his Spotlight team at full strength.

The investigative series that produced the Pulitzer for national reporting on the 2016 race was sparked by a chance meeting between Baron and Fahrenthold. The reporter had just published one of his first stories on the Trump Foundation, suggesting that it did not come through with the money for one of Donald Trump's charitable pledges. Baron liked the story, and during a chat by the elevators, he asked Fahrenthold what he was working on next. When Fahrenthold said he wasn't sure, Baron suggested that he keep digging into Trump's foundation to look for a pattern of false donations and misuse of funds. As former business editor of the *Times*, Baron knew quite a bit about Trump, and his gut told him that Trump was the kind of guy who would inflate his generosity. With the editor's blessing, Fahrenthold would spend the year delving into Trump's supposed charitable giving.

The Trump Foundation had caught Fahrenthold's attention during the Iowa caucuses, when Trump appeared before a veterans group in Waterloo and pledged to give $6 million to various veterans' charities, including more than $1 million from his own pocket. In a showy, televised announcement of one gift to a veterans group, Trump posed next to a supersized image of a $100,000 check from the Trump Foundation.

Fahrenthold was curious to know why the contribution came from the Trump Foundation and whether the foundation's money came from Trump personally. So he called Trump's first campaign manager, Corey Lewandowski, to check on the millions Trump had pledged at the staged Waterloo event. He was told it was "fully spent," but Lewandowski refused to supply any records.

What Fahrenthold did next was a textbook example of how to use digital technology and social media in reporting. For Watergate, Woodward and Bernstein had knocked on doors, carefully shielding their steps from other reporters and hiding their inquiries. To check on the foundation's contributions, Fahrenthold took to Trump's favorite medium, Twitter, where he would be maximally visible to the media world. He tweeted out an inquiry asking if any veterans groups had received donations from @realdonaldtrump. He wanted Trump to see him searching, and it worked. Trump phoned him the next night, claiming he'd just given the whole $1 million to a military nonprofit run by a friend. (That meant Lewandowski had lied when he said the money was given away already.) Would Trump have made the donation if he hadn't noticed Fahrenthold fact-checking him? The reporter couldn't resist asking.

"You know, you're a nasty guy," Trump said. This made Fahrenthold's story even better.

Trump again reacted angrily when Fahrenthold's story appeared. The candidate held a press conference to denounce the media for probing his contributions rather than praising him for being a generous man. "I have never received such bad publicity for doing such a good job," he said.

Encouraged by Baron, Fahrenthold broadened his inquiry into Trump's record of charitable giving over the years, and returned to the campaign for more information. Besides the veterans groups, he was told, Trump had given $102 million to other charities over the previous five years. After stalling, the campaign finally gave Fahrenthold a list. "In the beginning," Fahrenthold recalled, "I set out to prove him right." He went through the list of almost 5,000 charities and donations, finding that most of the donations didn't come from Trump personally but from the Trump Foundation. What the hell was the Trump Foundation? he wondered. Contrary to the story the campaign was pushing, Trump was not the benefactor of his foundation; the charitable funds came almost entirely from other wealthy individuals and business associates. The candidate had not given any money to the foundation between 2009 and 2014. In fact, as Fahrenthold discovered, many of the foundation's disbursements came in the form of "in kind" gifts, such as a free round of golf at one of Trump's courses or a subsidized session at one of his hotels' spas. By painlessly giving out these gifts, Trump had credited himself with thousands of dollars in charitable donations.

One itemized gift for $1,136.56 was to a group affiliated with tennis star Serena Williams. When Fahrenthold checked, it wasn't a donation at all; it was Trump's estimate of the cost of a ride he gave her from Florida to a ribbon-cutting event in Virginia and a framed picture of herself with Trump. In another case, the recipient of an $800 gift was listed simply as "Brian." In yet another, his foundation had paid a small sum to the Boy Scouts, in the exact amount, it turned out, as his son's annual dues. (Fahrenthold consulted his Twitter followers on that one.) The Trump Foundation was looking more and more fishy. Fahrenthold spent months calling hundreds of charities to ask if they'd received donations from Trump. Periodically he went on Twitter to ask for information from his followers. He was using digital technology, but it was the same shoe-leather reporting that Woodward and Bernstein had practiced.

At charity auctions, some held at his Palm Beach estate, Mar-a-Lago, Trump had listed as donations money he paid to win a football helmet worn by Tim Tebow and also a six-foot portrait of himself created by a speed painter. His wife, Melania, had bid $20,000 for the picture. The check used to pay for it came from the Trump Foundation. There was another painted portrait bought with $10,000 from the foundation. It is against IRS rules to spend charitable funds on personal purchases. And it would be a stretch to believe any charity wanted to hang massive portraits of the bombastic tycoon.

A stretch, but not impossible. To prove Trump had broken the law, Fahrenthold would need to find where the paintings were. He used digital platforms to get the answer, posting pictures of the portraits on Twitter and asking if anyone had seen them. Most of the replies were dead ends, until someone tweeted back that she was pretty sure she'd seen the smaller portrait at the Doral, a Miami resort owned by Trump. Another follower, who lived nearby, offered to look when he got off work. A fellow journalist, he checked into the place and consulted the cleaning crew, who led him into the Sportsman's Lounge, where Trump's likeness was hanging in all its splendor. Fahrenthold had his proof, using people he had never met to help him on his political scavenger hunt.

There were more stories, and eventually the New York attorney general, a Democrat, opened an investigation into the Trump Foundation and filed a lawsuit. Fahrenthold, meanwhile, ended up not only with the Pulitzer Prize for national reporting but also an MSNBC contract and rafts of paid speaking engagements. David Fahrenthold, a young unknown when the 2016 campaign began, had established himself as a franchise player.

The problem, of course, was that there was always poaching of franchise players. Just as Ben Smith had lost his star political reporters to the *Atlantic* and CNN, Baron lost an asset when Chris Cillizza defected to CNN. Later Adam Entous, another investigative talent, went to the *New Yorker*. Kevin Merida, once Baron's managing editor, accepted a job at ESPN. Baron, in turn, swooped down on Ashley Parker, a second-string political reporter for the *Times* who quickly became a star on Baron's seven-member White House team, the largest in the *Post*'s history. (Two or three was the usual number.) This game of musical chairs was typical of the new-media industry, where few expected or even desired to be lifers like Balz and Woodward or Maureen Dowd and Tom Friedman. Reporters who were well sourced in Trumpworld could more or less write their own ticket.

It was clear to Bezos from the beginning that Baron was a keeper, unlike Weymouth and Hills. Aside from opening his wallet, Bezos did not focus on the journalism. Baron had that covered. Where Bezos could contribute and raise the *Post*'s game was in terms of technology. He was obsessed with improving "the Pipe," the paper's clunky digital delivery system. Articles took way too long to load, seconds more than Facebook and other competitors. Signing up digital subscribers was a confusing and difficult process. He wanted it to be frictionless, like one-click buying from Amazon.

To help the *Post* increase its traffic, it was preloaded onto Amazon's Kindle Fire, bringing its coverage to millions of tablet buyers; then, in late 2015, the paper was offered free for six months to all Prime members. Amazon kept the number of Prime members as secret as Facebook had guarded the secrets of its algorithm, but in a 10-K filing in 2017 it disclosed that the Prime program brought Amazon $6.4 billion in revenue. That works out to about 65 million members whom the *Post* could potentially reach as readers and, ultimately, subscribers. Being tethered to the largest company in the world and owned by the richest man in the world had distinct advantages.

Another effort to expand its national footprint was to offer its content to a network of other newspapers. The *Post* also put its full content on social media platforms, while the *Times* held back some content. It was all-in on Facebook Instant Articles, Facebook Live, Snapchat, and everywhere else it could push out its journalism.

Bezos also pressed for a newly designed app that would be more visual than the original one, optimized for the tablet and mobile. Younger readers seemed to love the new version, and the *Post* began expanding its base of millennial readers after years of worry about its aging newspaper subscribers. Experimentation and serving the customer were the new mantras, and suddenly there were lots of new blogs and newsletters. The paper also aggregated the stories that were most popular on the rest of the web every day.

Before Bezos, the *Post* had installed a paywall and offered digital subscriptions. But because the Grahams had been late and tentative in asking their readers to pay for journalism and had let the paper's quality suffer, Bezos had to start over. Digital revenue from subscriptions began to pick up only in 2016. Bezos took the company private in his acquisition, so it doesn't have to report its financial performance. However, a person on the business side told me that the *Post*'s total circulation and subscription revenue is less than 40 percent of its total revenue, far behind that of the *Times*. Like its New York competitor, though, the *Post* enjoyed a Trump bump after the election, and digital subscriptions reached over 1 million.

Building scale was what Bezos knew, so, from the start, his *Post* was going to use every tool at its disposal to get clicks. Audience traffic exceeded that of the *Times* beginning in October 2015, and by the following July it broke its own record, with 82 million unique users. This was bound to be a compelling story for advertisers. The paper proclaimed itself "the new paper of record," gleefully giving the *Times* a poke in the eye. The competition was good for the *Times*. Dean Baquet and Marty Baron were old friends, and both seemed to enjoy the rivalry. The *Post*'s financial picture by mid-2016 was sunnier too. The company's chief revenue officer wrote to his colleagues, "Overall digital ad sales grew 48% [year over year] through August. (Keep in mind that many of our competitors' digital ad revenues have declined this year.) Within that number, programmatic is up 92%, video is up 82% and brand studio is up 275%. With both a solid nine-figure total for digital ad revenue and better than expected print results, we have dramatically changed our revenue picture in just two years."

The growth in the brand studio stood out. Like the *Times*, the *Post* had a native advertising shop whose work helped subsidize the newsroom. The newsroom, in turn, bore responsibility for helping the unit by increasing readership. As for ad revenue, there was a high road to growing audience and getting clicks and a low road. The low road was clickbait; the high road was breaking big scoops that trended on social media and got picked up by other major news outlets. That was Baron's chosen road. The other lane on the high road was superior technology that was more user-friendly than the competition's. That was Bezos's department.

Of course, Bezos had a day job in Seattle, but improving technology at the *Post* was a priority. He created rapport with the newsroom's chief technologist, Shailesh Prakash, whom Donald Graham had hired from the corporate world, where Prakash had been a star at Sears and Microsoft. With Baron, he took part in twice-monthly phone calls to Bezos.

Within weeks of Bezos's acquisition, Prakash sent technologists to sit with the editors on the news desks and the hub. The message from on high was clear: these technologists were as important as the "text people," equal partners in "the news product." Prakash attended the two daily news meetings at 9:30 and 4:00. Unlike the Brauchli era, when tension abounded between the web and newspaper cultures, this transition went smoothly, even when everyone was still crowded into the old building.

In the course of a two-hour conversation and tour of the spacious new offices, Prakash outlined Bezos's vision for me. Consumers had become spoiled by the excellence of their technology products. The iPhone was Exhibit A. The *Post* needed to be equally excellent in journalism, user experience, and customer interface. The only way to get there was to develop all the technology in-house, as BuzzFeed did, including a content management system. Bezos became the *Post*'s Beta tester. According to Prakash, he liked to go deep into the sausage-making. Even when Prakash and his engineers came up with new product versions that they decided to abandon before taking public, Bezos wanted to be shown the version so he could understand why it had been rejected. At the reborn *Post*, failure was refreshingly destigmatized. It took 10 tries to find one that would work, as one Jeffism went. "There are multiple paths to yes," Prakash repeated. He didn't mind if failure was expensive, as long as it provided clues to success. This meant there could be twice as much experimenting as there had been during the Graham era, when cash had been too tight for risk-taking.

Prakash had a diagnosis for what had failed before Bezos's rescue. Like other legacy newspapers, it had tried to bolt the web operation onto the existing print publishing system without compromising the resources of the newspaper. This was a print-first approach. The plumbing was for the newspaper, and the pipes were often rusty. Prakash felt that for the *Post* to flourish online, the product, design, technology, and journalism would have to be remade as one seamless system, tailored to the needs of digital users. That's what he and his 80 engineers set out to do with a new invention they called Arc.

At the *Times* and the *Post*, an enormous amount of time was spent on the process of converting print stories, data, and visual displays into digital versions. The same copy editors who fly-specked stories for print then coded them for the web. Arc was designed to streamline the production of everything, from copy to video to ads. It had 15 basic publishing functions for digital and print. It was web-first. It took three years to build. Arc was such a supple and well-designed content management system that Bezos decided to sell it to other publications. Among its first customers were university newspapers and a small weekly in Portland, Oregon, *Willamette Week*. Tronc, the renamed Tribune Publishing Co., signed on. Prakash expected Arc sales to become a significant source of revenue within the next few years.

None of these technological innovations created a big splash in the rest of the media, if that's what people were expecting from Bezos. From time to time some of the Prakash team's achievements would get written up in industry trade publications such as Nieman Lab or Digiday, but their impact was mostly felt from within. Ideas were flowing. The customer base was increasing. Data analytics consumed the newsroom. These were the things Bezos cared about.

Engagement was the key, getting readers to click on a story, read it, and stay to read or watch something else on the site. Prakash invented new engagement tools with snazzy names like Loxodo, a predictive analytics platform that used data to predict performance and provided writers and editors with real-time feedback from their audience so they could make changes to keep readers reading. Another homegrown tool, Bandito, allowed editors to test different versions of headlines and "teasers" with small batches of early readers, and then automatically picked the version that brought in the most clicks. It tested images too. This increased audience; it also turned what had solely been the job of editors into a tech-powered popularity contest.

As Bandito took over, clickbait headlines proliferated with come-on phrases such as "This Is What Happened Next" to pique readers' curiosity and get them to click on the article. It was a favorite ploy used by Upworthy, a website that was famous for its artificially enhanced element of suspense. Actual clickbait, like actual fake news, intended to deceive readers. It promised something that wasn't delivered. The *Post* usually stopped short of fooling readers with headlines that bore little relation to the news article. That would have been self-defeating and would have hurt the *Post*'s reputation for quality. What happened at the *Post* was subtler. It had to be, since Facebook, prompted by sites like Upworthy, began cracking down on headlines that were obvious clickbait. Fluffy articles with seductive headlines that would never have run in the old newspaper began appearing on digital *Post* products such as The Post Most, which aggregated the most popular stories trending on the site. (There was also a Most product that aggregated non-*Post* content trending on social media—celebrity gossip and so forth.) Some of these stories got millions of clicks.

"This Is What Happened When I Drove My Mercedes to Pick Up Food Stamps," screamed one 2014 headline. "Pope Francis Saw a Boy with Cerebral Palsy. This Is What Happened Next," came another, and another, "Dunkin' Donuts Just 'Destroyed' Starbucks with This Christmas-y Cup." The paper published games, too, such as Democratic debate bingo. Baron's first managing editor, Kevin Merida, admitted, "I like Doritos." More seriously, he added, "We're in the business of people reading our work. If we were to ignore the information that people are talking about, we would be news snobs."

The *Post* risked cheapening its brand with all the silly stuff and losing traditional readers. It wasn't a question of content: newspapers had long included soft features, humor, games, cooking, gossip, comics. They were a critical part of the mission. It was a matter of quality, style, and positioning. Some stories seemed recycled, and the odd mixture of the evanescent with the serious could be jarring. A story about a California man who killed his urologist because he left the man impotent, for instance, appeared in the *Post* long after it had been published in the *L.A. Times*.

It was a strange stew. The light ingredients seasoned the serious, a formula not that different from Peretti's mullet, except the serious stuff was still in the front. There would always be something for every reader, and thus something for every advertiser to advertise against. The *Post* had become an interactive experience, with buttons that shared the article on Facebook or Twitter, for commenting on each story, and for recommendations based on your past reading habits. The new regime was winning engaged readers, especially younger ones. But for the more traditional audience, especially those who still read the paper in print as well as digitally, it could add up to distracting, annoying clutter.

Occasionally, when I noticed a headline that seemed over the top, I'd email *Post* reporters I knew and ask them if they were comfortable with the presentation of their stories. However, because there were three different *Post* apps, as well as the print papers, they were sometimes unaware of the headline I found objectionable. Reporters wrote their own headlines for the web, but their versions were often changed by social media editors to bump up traffic. They could object, but often they were absorbed with talking to sources or other work when the changes were made. The headlines in the print paper, which were noticeably less spicy, were still written the old-fashioned way, by copy editors.

The *Post* wasn't yet featuring exploding watermelons, but it was doing things it never had done before to juice traffic. The electronic screen that loomed over its editorial hub showing the second-by-second traffic for every story and piece of content—some 500 items a day, twice as many as the *Times*—said it all.

For the journalists, the data increased the pressure to churn out new versions of their stories or call up more new stories. If something didn't get traffic, the story often moved down the page or disappeared. The photo accompanying an article could change instantly. Editors too, along with the reporters, lost track of how different versions of the same story had been published.

Clickbait culture was more pronounced at the *Post* than at the *Times* because its business strategy emphasized scale over subscriptions. A big audience attracted more programmatic advertising. The *Times* aggressively sought digital advertising, but its premium was on building a paying digital readership. Maintaining the highest quality and keeping its news report the deepest and richest was the best business strategy for building those subscriptions. All the A/B data testing at the *Post* had the biggest effect on spot and daily stories, much less on longer-range enterprise journalism that was edited and laid out in advance. But the pace was dizzying for everyone.

The *Post*'s investigative team got new resources to stay competitive with the *Times* on the Trump administration. The *Post* revealed Attorney General Jeff Sessions's undisclosed meetings with Russians, Jared Kushner's setting up secret backchannels, and most of the stories about Michael Flynn, Trump's national security advisor, and his ties to Russia. (Flynn later lost his job and was indicted by Mueller.) The *Post* won a Pulitzer and other prizes for revealing the alleged pedophilia of Alabama Senate candidate Roy Moore and foiling a sting operation in which a conservative group tried to plant a false account about Moore in order to tarnish the newspaper. Although it was overshadowed by the *Times* in coverage of sexual harassment, the *Post* claimed some Me Too scalps, including TV interviewer Charlie Rose.

There was one subject at the *Post* that seemed taboo: Amazon. It had become one of the dominant companies in the world, edging out Walmart in sales and transforming personal technology with Alexa and other products. Franklin Foer, who wrote a book advocating antitrust actions against Amazon and the other huge tech giants (Google, Facebook, and Apple), said the *Post*'s kid-gloves treatment was noteworthy, especially since the company had won hundreds of millions in federal contracts for its Cloud technology. Baron did assign periodic pieces, including one that questioned whether Amazon was too big, but he was not going to go out of his way to bite the hand that fed him. When Trump became president and aimed frequent tweets at Bezos and Amazon, blasting the paper as "the Amazon Washington Post" with false claims about its tax collections and burdens on the U.S. Post Office, the *Post*, along with everyone else, covered them.

The *Times* ran a definitive investigation of the punishing work culture at Amazon, with grizzly anecdotes about employees crying at their desks and burning out because of the unrelenting pressure to fill orders and grow. Bezos attacked the story as anecdotal and unfair on the open website Medium. Baquet responded, defending the piece. Open digital platforms such as Medium now replaced the private conversations and postpublication confrontations that used to take place in editors' offices. The court of public opinion was all that mattered, not private, ongoing relationships between companies and the journalists covering them.

For reporters and editors, the pace was as unrelenting as it was inside Amazon. Before she left for ProPublica, Marilyn Thompson, the investigative reporter and proponent of "slow journalism," found herself editing a slew of stories each day on the national desk. There was so much to edit that she often used one of her days off to work on the longer pieces that probed Washington's underbelly of money and lobbying. With fewer editors and staffers engaged in story production ("the process people"), the responsibility for everything fell on the shoulders of editors who before the social media era had had time to brainstorm with reporters or change a story's architecture and flow. Now they were expected to do and check everything, from writing the myriad headlines for different platforms to inserting hyperlinks referring to other stories—all at a sprinter's pace.

The *Post* was back, filled with investigative and enterprise stories that had been its hallmark since the Bradlee era. Its survival was no longer in question, which had a transformative effect on the institution and restored its morale and confidence. Bezos and Baron forged a cordial working partnership when they met every six months, usually in Seattle with the rest of the Pancake Group. Despite initial worries of some staff, Bezos did not weigh in on coverage, even when he liked something. The era of Donniegrams was over. In 2017 he purchased a $23 million mansion in the swank Kalorama D.C. neighborhood near the Obamas, and it seemed likely Bezos might build a higher profile in the capital. Whether this would bring him into more direct confrontation with President Trump was anyone's guess.

Bezos was traveling in the Middle East on Amazon business on Election Day, and he had little idea what he might be in for once Trump arrived in the White House. During the campaign, he and Trump clashed on Twitter. Trump hit back at Amazon every time he perceived an unfair attack on him from the *Post*. In December 2015 Trump fired off three angry tweets in less than 15 minutes. In the first one, he said, "The @washingtonpost, which loses a fortune, is owned by @JeffBezos for purposes of keeping taxes down at his no profit company." He had attacked Amazon before for supposedly not paying state sales taxes on customers' purchases, but now this became a constant refrain. The next blast from @realDonaldTrump: "The @washingtonpost loses money (a deduction) and gives owner @JeffBezos power to screw public on low taxation of @Amazon! Big tax shelter." Then, a third: "If @amazon ever had to pay fair taxes, its stock would crash and it would crumble like a paper bag. The @washingtonpost scam is saving it!"

What had provoked the initial Trump tweetstorm was a fact-checking article that exposed as false his claim that he had predicted Osama bin Laden's 9/11 attacks in a book he published in 2000. Trump had earned four Pinocchios from the *Post*, and being called out on the lie enraged him.

It was typical of Trump to answer a perceived attack with one of his own, and he thought he had found Bezos's weak spot: Amazon's initial resistance to pay state sales taxes. But by the time he released his fusillade, Amazon was paying sales taxes in every state that levied them, although it didn't at that time collect and pass on the tax from third-party sources, a hefty chunk of its sales. The facts, of course, did not matter to Trump. First, he was highlighting that the *Post* lost money, the only measure of success he used. Second, he was insinuating that the *Post* was a mouthpiece for its new owner. Third, he was suggesting that Bezos was using the *Post* to hide the fact that he was a tax evader, something just as false.

Bezos chose to respond that night with a humorous tweet suggesting he'd like to blast Trump into space on one of the earliest rocket voyages of Blue Origin, his space exploration company: "Finally trashed by @realDonaldTrump. Will still reserve him a seat on the Blue Origin rocket. #sendDonaldtospace."

Trump intensified the fight with Bezos throughout 2016. At a February campaign rally in Texas, he said he respected Bezos for being so rich but accused him of buying the *Post* for "political influence." He added a vague threat that Amazon would have "such problems" if he became president.

In May, after Fahrenthold was getting traction on his Trump Foundation exposés, Trump upped the ante. In a Fox News interview, he called the *Post* a "toy" used by Bezos for political purposes to avoid proper taxation of his company. "Amazon is getting away with murder, tax-wise. He's using the *Washington Post* for power so that the politicians in Washington don't tax Amazon like they should be taxed." In June he revoked the *Post*'s credentials to travel with his campaign, calling its coverage "incredibly inaccurate," only to reverse the decision in September.

When Bezos was asked about Trump's claims at an event in San Francisco a few weeks before the election, he responded, "He's not just going after the media, but threatening retribution to people who scrutinize him. He's also saying he may not give a graceful concession speech if he loses the election. That erodes our democracy around the edges. He's also saying he might lock up his opponent. These aren't appropriate behaviors."

Two days after the election, Bezos tried to bury the hatchet, tweeting, "Congratulations to @realDonaldTrump. I for one give him my most open mind and wish him great success in his service to the country." Trump ended up inviting Bezos to attend a tech summit at the White House in June 2017 to discuss ways to modernize the government's technology. Along with Apple's Tim Cook and Microsoft's CEO Satya Nadella, Bezos was a member of Trump's American Technology Council, sitting with an impassive look on his face just a seat away from the president. But the detente did not last long. Less than a week later, the President tweeted, "The #AmazonWashingtonPost, sometimes referred to as the guardian of Amazon not paying internet taxes (which they should) is FAKE NEWS!" Trump was still bashing Amazon in March 2018, saying the company used the U.S. Postal Service as its "Delivery Boy." A March 28 report that the president was "obsessed" with regulating Amazon caused the company's shares to lose $53 billion in market value that day.

A White House communications advisor told me he thought Trump enjoyed toying with Bezos, but that he had no real intention of following through on his threats. Amazon already supported several internet tax proposals in Congress, anyway, so it was unclear what more the president might demand. But the outside attacks weren't coming only from Trump; the president's close ally, Rupert Murdoch, through Fox News, especially its on-air business hosts and pundits, was constantly upbraiding the four Silicon Valley giants, in part because of their liberalism. Although conservatives like Peter Thiel had made their fortunes there, the dominant ideology and ethos of the place was libertarian-left. Another source of the hostility was the sheer power of the data the four giants had compiled on their users and customers, which advertisers so prized. The data giants were beginning to compete with cable, the base of Fox and Murdoch's power. Stuart Varney, a Fox business host, asked in one of his frequent anti-Amazon tirades, "Why is it that the *Washington Post*, and I don't mean to pick on anybody, but it seems that the *Washington Post* is the most rabid in its opposition to Donald Trump. Now, the *Washington Post* is owned by Jeff Bezos, the guy who built Amazon. Why is he, again, I use that word 'rabid,' in their opposition to Donald Trump? Why the *Washington Post*?"

Amazon has interests before the administration, ranging from its federal contracts to its structure as a global giant. The disclosures about Russian manipulation of Facebook through bots and planting fake news stories in users' feeds heightened Washington's concerns about how the big tech companies used their reams of customer data. There was talk of efforts to regulate this, and hearings were held, but Facebook took most of the heat. Even more threatening to Bezos, there was, for the first time, serious discussion about trying to break up the four tech giants by using the nation's antitrust laws. It was hard to imagine Trump's Justice Department doing this, but no one could predict with any degree of certainty what Trump might do when provoked by perceived enemies. And Bezos, because of the *Post*, was high on Trump's enemies list.

The Amazon chief didn't flinch. In one of his rare public interviews hosted by the Economic Club of Washington, Bezos said, "It's really dangerous to demonize the media," which he called "an essential component of our democracy." Emotion rising in his voice, he added, "It's dangerous to call the media lowlifes. It's dangerous to say they're the 'enemy of the people.' "

The owner, like his editor Baron, was deeply committed to the *Post*'s mission to uphold the First Amendment and hold powerful people and institutions accountable. Perhaps as a symbol of this principle, he had bought an antique clothes wringer, in honor of John Mitchell's famous threat to Kay Graham, which now sat in one of the *Post*'s conference rooms. Though it hadn't yet happened, it seemed all but inevitable that the *Post*'s coverage would one day bring Bezos's commitment to freedom of the press into conflict with Amazon's commercial interests, given the company's size and power as it competed with Apple to become America's first trillion-dollar conglomerate. How the *Post* would pass this test was unknown, but almost everyone, including Bob Woodward, trusted Baron to protect the paper's independence and reputation.

Baron's glassed-in office on the seventh floor was across from the main conference room named for Bradlee. *Post* journalists were heartened when, right after the election, Baron was named editor of the year by the Committee to Protect Journalists. Bezos gave the group $1 million. Baquet, his friend and rival at the *Times*, won the following year.

It was around that time that the *Post* unveiled the slogan "Democracy Dies in Darkness." There was no mistaking it: Bezos had planted a flag declaring he would not allow the new president to trespass on the First Amendment. The slogan had gone through rigorous analytic testing; Ryan had convinced everyone to put the motto on Snapchat and see how the audience responded. In early March it appeared underneath the *Post*'s familiar decades-old logo.

The motto was derided by a few media writers. The *Times*'s Baquet said it "sounds like the next Batman movie." Baron insisted the *Post* was not "at war with President Trump, we're at work."

When Baron stood to accept his Freedom of the Press Award in 2017, he quoted the late *Times* columnist Anthony Lewis, the author of famous books on the First Amendment. "The American press has been given extraordinary freedom by the Supreme Court's interpretation of the First Amendment," Baron said, "In return it owes society courage."

CONCLUSION

The Lipstick Building in midtown Manhattan, so named for its red color and tubular shape, was an unlikely spot for a media uprising. No major news company was headquartered there. The building, codesigned by Philip Johnson, had last seen picketing protesters a decade before, during the financial crisis, because the offices of Wall Street swindler Bernie Madoff were located there.

On this day in May 2018, the street outside was occupied by a group of reporters, editors, and press operators decrying another kind of swindle. They were representatives of a group of regional and local newspapers who had traveled from cities such as Denver and St. Paul and whose newspapers had been acquired and then cut to shreds by a vulture capital fund, Alden Global Capital, which occupied a top floor of the Lipstick Building. None of the Alden suits, who earned millions while wiping out thousands of journalists' jobs, dared to descend to meet their irate employees or respond to their demands that the owners stop cutting costs and cheating readers of important local news.

I had spent time in Denver in 2016 because I had won an award from the Colorado Press Association. The threadbare state of the local press was immediately apparent, especially at the *Denver Post*, a 125-year-old paper that had once been the flagship of the Singleton chain and had won nine Pulitzers. Since Alden had purchased the paper five years earlier, its newsroom had shriveled. When I met the investigations editor, a young woman in her early 20s, she told me in hushed tones that she had no staff to assign projects to, despite a rash of local corruption cases.

Everyone was struggling to do more with less, the mantra of journalism's new class of owners. These included vulture funds like Alden but also local billionaires, like Boston's John Henry, who vowed to keep their newspapers alive, but on the tightest of leashes. In Denver even promising new innovations, like a website devoted to the booming pot trade in Colorado, was on the chopping block. After the opinion editor wrote about the cuts and the harm they were doing to readers, he was censored and forced out. Other editors departed in a show of solidarity.

Those left on the payroll were burning mad; some traveled to New York on their own dime to focus national attention on the harm Alden was doing to the quality of news. But there were only a few reporters on hand to cover the protest. Compared to the latest developments in the Trump-Russia investigation, it was not a big national story.

Yet the decimation of local news was one of the most crushing developments of the internet age, and the few web-only local start-ups that replaced the papers hardly filled the vacuum. Alden Global had shrunk its workforce by 36 percent since it began buying up newspapers in 2009. Nationally, from 2009 to 2015, according to statistics published by the American Society of Newspaper Editors, full-time newspaper jobs plunged from 46,700 to 32,000, largely executed by new owners mandating layoffs, buyouts, and restructuring.

Nick Ferraro, a reporter for the Alden-owned *St. Paul Pioneer Press* in Minnesota, told me he was outraged that the bleeding of local news wasn't garnering more attention. "The readers are the ones who lose," he pointed out. In Dakota County, the populous territory he covered, there had been six reporters covering local government, the police, and the school board when he was hired. While the volume of news hadn't changed, he was the only one left. America's Founders had envisioned a free press to hold power accountable, but Ferraro worried that it was impossible to fulfill his First Amendment obligations with so few resources.

The *Denver Post*'s Chuck Plunkett had just written in his farewell editorial, "Depending on your bogeyman—whether it's Trump Nation or P.C. Elitism—the desire to retreat to echo-chamber news outlets has grown. Local papers look more like advertising supplements filled with content from other sources, and 'serious journalists' are considered something only national brands can afford."

But those national brands couldn't be expected to fill the void or replace the connection between readers and the papers who most directly touched their lives. Though blessed with better owners, they were still under severe pressure to show profits, engage more readers, and, like their local counterparts, do more with less.

Who were those trusted national brands? With a polarized, increasingly skeptical audience, it was almost impossible to say. The *New York Times* seemed to have made the successful and difficult transition from a print newspaper to a digital-first organization that included video, podcasts, stories to engage younger readers, and a wider array of opinion. It had ignited a broad cultural movement for breaking the sexual abuse scandal involving

Hollywood and the media's biggest names. The *Washington Post*, which won a Pulitzer in 2018 for breaking the story about alleged sexual abuse involving the Republican Senate candidate in Alabama, Roy Moore, and also revealed harassment by the TV host Charlie Rose, had added to the movement's impact. Their stories had international impact.

Financial motives were not incidental to the papers' Me Too investigations. Both were looking to expand their subscriptions by appealing to women. The *Post* offered a new, female-centric digital offering called The Lily and launched it with a jargon-filled announcement that was nearly impossible for anyone but a technologist to decipher: "The Washington Post today announces The Lily, an experimental, visually driven product designed for millennial women that will boldly reimagine The Post's award-winning journalism for distributed platforms. The brainchild of The Post's Emerging News Products team, The Lily will emphasize platform-specific storytelling, integrating smart content with striking visuals to inform and entertain. The Lily will appear on Medium, Facebook and Instagram to start."

There was now an array of committees inside the *Times* jointly led by business professionals focused on new products and journalists pushing projects for profit. The newspaper was, in fact, using some data techniques similar to the ones that had become controversial at Facebook. It had begun selling data to advertisers about its readers gleaned from their emotional reactions to each of the articles they read. According to an ad industry newsletter, the *Times* was "now packaging up those emotions as a data point for sale in ad auctioning systems." Based on these new reader data, according to a member of the *Times* ad department, "Our data scientists built a machine learning algorithm, so that now we can look at any piece of content and predict a range or an array of emotions that readers may feel. We are using that now for advertising." A *Times* spokesman denied this was similar to what Facebook was doing because the data the paper shared with advertisers were "aggregated and anonymous."

But at this point, who could or would complain? The *Times*'s rich buffet table of news offerings was constantly expanding and its subscription base fast expanding. Meanwhile, the *New York Daily News*, owned by Tronc, cut its staff by 50 percent. The new products offered opportunities for female journalists to become stars, including a podcast about Isis called *The Caliphate*, hosted by a female correspondent and rising star named Rukmini Callimachi, whose reporting techniques included surfing the Deep Web on her cell phone to connect with sources in the shadowy world of terrorism. Local reporting in New York was one of the few areas of coverage that had become thinner, and, in an irony largely overlooked, the *Times*'s Metro editor had been forced out because of his own indiscretions with female staffers. The *Times* responded to the weakening of the *Daily News* by strengthening the section with a new editor.

At Vice, the Me Too movement had also tarnished founder Shane Smith, whose power and credibility had been clipped by the internal sexual harassment scandal. Although a new female CEO had been appointed to run the company, the Vice brand was still inextricably connected to Smith's persona and bravado. He remained the featured host of the weekly HBO series that had given Vice the patina of mainstream news credibility. It was unclear how long HBO would keep the partnership going. Smith hadn't transformed the cable-news pecking order, as he had brashly promised. Despite the breakthrough success of the Charlottesville documentary, Vice had neither the resources nor the expertise to compete on the biggest news stories, although it was still sending crews to undercovered global hot spots to appeal to its young viewers.

Vice's failure to make much of an impact on the style and content of visual journalism left the cable news shows offered by Fox, CNN, MSNBC, and the networks as the main national TV voices. But cable's daily bill of fare was dominated by panels of arguing experts and partisans who had few journalistic credentials and whose business interests were rarely disclosed to viewers. The cable networks offered journalists from the *Times* and the *Post* six-figure contracts because they added a tone of sobriety—and sometimes real information too—to shows that otherwise often subsisted on anti-Trump rantings. The journalists were wedged between arguing partisans and sometimes the audience couldn't tell them apart. This, too, harmed trust in the news media.

For his part, the president doubled down in his war against the "fake news media" and the journalists he labeled "enemies of the people." He singled out the *Washington Post* and its new owner, and met in the White House with A.G. Sulzberger, who confronted him with much the same argument as Bezos—that the constant attacks on journalists were almost certain to result in violence. Trump's tweets and attacks mainly pumped up his supporters and certainly had no effect on blunting the deservedly tough coverage he received. As they had the previous year, the two newspapers each won Pulitzer Prizes for their Trump coverage in the spring of 2018.

Was the constant bombardment from the White House harming the press? Public trust in the media had begun eroding long before Trump's inauguration and was actually ticking up a bit by 2018. And judging by the bulging numbers of new digital subscribers to the *Times* and the *Post*, the answer was no. But the tone of the coverage and the headlines in both papers had become markedly harsher and more adversarial, in part to appeal to a growing anti-Trump readership. The dispassionate distance that some readers, especially older ones, believed had given the established national brands their authority in the first place.

More than most, BuzzFeed had embraced the crusading tone of the old tabloid press. From the start of the 2016 campaign, it had called out Trump's racism and lies with no pretense of neutrality. In some ways Ben Smith was the news media's answer to tabloid king Rupert Murdoch. He was a serious editor with high news standards who showed how emotional content was eminently shareable, on the left as well as the right.

Along with the *Times*'s Baquet, BuzzFeed's intrepid lawyer Nabiha Syed was honored by the Reporters Committee for Freedom of the Press at a black-tie gala in the ballroom of the Pierre Hotel in May 2018. She told the luminaries present—including David Muir, anchor and managing editor of ABC's *World News Tonight*, and Arthur Sulzberger Jr.—"I fight to make sure that choices, big and small, are not marred by unnecessary fear. I work so reporters can tell the stories, including the stories that confront power, even when they are uncomfortable or inconvenient." In early June she won a key victory in one of the libel cases filed against BuzzFeed by a Russian oligarch.

More than anyone at the Pierre that night, Sulzberger knew the price and reward of doing this work, of standing up to coercive power, of keeping freedom of the press alive. Although he hadn't received proper recognition for it, he had kept quality journalism fortified at what was still arguably the best news organization in the world. During the darkest financial hours, he had kept the lights on. The *Times*, despite a decade of digital disruption that had upended virtually all of its core practices and even its news standards, was still a beacon of truth and fierce protector of facts. In this world, where the news environment was dominated by Facebook, which eschewed the standards that ensured the material on its platform was fair and truthful, the singular importance of the *Times* and Sulzberger's inheritance could not be overstated.

In terms of public trust, Facebook had reached a crisis point. While the journalists at the Lipstick Building were shouting into their bullhorns to decry cuts and the big names gathered at their black-tie award dinner to pay homage to press freedom, Campbell Brown took center stage to try to reassure the public that Facebook was turning a new page.

Brown, a former NBC News anchor turned charter school activist, had been hired by Facebook in 2017 to be the public face of its news partnerships, a tough job as the company faced multiple scandals. First, there were the Russian sites that had invaded the news feed of millions of users. Then came the scandals over massive, unauthorized personal data sharing. Worst of all came disclosures in a *Times* investigation that the company knew about the Russian invasion earlier, but did nothing and secretly hired a Republican firm to attack critics. Zuckerberg denied some of this, but public anger swelled. Facebook's stock tumbled. News organizations also became more vocal about criticizing the company for stealing their ad revenue. Still, Facebook's massive audience was too big to abandon.

Brown was desperately trying to reboot the relationship with news providers and convince the public that Facebook was investing in initiatives that favored trusted news sources over clickbait and sensationalism. In her Tribeca apartment she regularly hosted mixers for Facebook executives and news figures. Lately she'd been touting Facebook's Watch feature and holding out a wallet stuffed with $90 million for publishers to produce original news programming. Zuckerberg had concluded that video and video ads were the key to Facebook's future and feared falling behind Netflix and other streaming services. He desperately needed video content, including news. CNN's Anderson Cooper and others had quickly signed on.

"It's not my role to lobby publishers to be on Facebook if they don't feel like that's the right way to reach their audience, I want to be 100% clear about that," Brown said at one gathering. "But, for the ones who are on Facebook and who see the potential for distribution on Facebook, I want to help them make money. I want to help them find a business model that works so they keep doing what they do best, which is journalism." Meanwhile, of course, Facebook and Google would continue taking the lion's share of digital ad revenue.

BuzzFeed, unsurprisingly, had enlisted right away, although Peretti had become publicly critical of the massive social platform and was trying to reduce his company's dependence on it. But it could never really walk away—the dilemma faced by most news providers.

And there was little sign that Zuckerberg's professed advocacy of quality news was having any effect on popular tastes. In published rankings of what news sources people found most engaging, none of the four companies that were featured in this book appeared at the top. The metrics company, which measured news outlets by likes, comments, reactions, and shares, ranked Fox News in first place in April 2018, with more than 30 million engagements. London's *Daily Mail* rose to fourth from seventh, and a site called Daily Wire, which specialized in conservative news, climbed to eighth with 14 million engagements.

The terrain was still so rocky that no one in the news business could have sure footing. But of all the executives who had faced the ferocious waters of the digital revolution, Arthur Sulzberger Jr. had come closest to crossing to safety. Although the *Post*'s comeback was impressive, the *Times* was in a class by itself, and the Sulzberger family had proved to be admirable and steady over the course of decades. Bezos, on the other hand, was still a newcomer to the news business.

And so, on a balmy evening in early June, I swallowed whatever lingering ill will I had toward the man who had fired me to attend a retirement celebration for him at the Modern, a restaurant adjacent to the Museum of Modern Art.

Sulzberger had hoped that all six of the executive editors during his reign as publisher would attend. Lelyveld, who had recently suffered a stroke, was there with his wife. So were Max Frankel and Howell Raines. But Bill Keller was away on a trip to Russia, so the group photograph of all of us with Sulzberger was missing the man who had led the newsroom during its most financially distressed period, including the most disruptive years of the digital revolution.

The crowd of well-wishers included Senator Chuck Schumer of New York, Tina Brown, Barry Diller, and past *Times* employees like *New York* magazine editor Adam Moss. As for *Times* history, there was James Goodale, the in-house lawyer who had worked on the Pentagon Papers case. When his turn came to speak, Sulzberger Jr. did not use the occasion to make a momentous speech about either the state of journalism or the *Times*'s war with the country's president. Instead Sulzberger emphasized how much fun he had had in the job and stressed that because he was still chairman, he wasn't really going anywhere. He ended by thanking the members of the Ochs-Sulzberger family and joked that when his great-grandfather Adolph Ochs had purchased the newspaper out of near bankruptcy in 1896, they had all taken on the mission of "the failing *New York Times*."

Baquet gave a stirring speech, harking back to the desperate condition the *Times* was in during the financial crisis and how Sulzberger had saved the paper. He almost let a big secret out of the bag: the fact, known by only a few *Times* insiders, that Sulzberger had asked Warren Buffett to bail out the paper before turning to Carlos Slim for the loan that turned out to be its critical lifeline.

Joe Pompeo, a reporter covering the party for *Vanity Fair*, asked Sulzberger the name of that potential investor. Sulzberger turned to A.G. and asked, "Can I tell him?" A.G. said no. Pompeo called me a few days later, and I told him what I had long known but faithfully kept secret until Baquet more or less outed the story.

A.G., the new publisher, still seemed a bit awkward in the role. He told a few anecdotes about his father, but his remarks also barely focused on the momentous developments that were upending the news profession. He had just become a new father and was feeling nervous and sleep-deprived. Willa, like her ancestors, would be fed a rich diet of news, though it was unlikely that the print newspaper would outlast her. But the news, in whatever form its delivery took, would remain a necessary and vital part of her country's social and intellectual fabric. Though no woman had ever been publisher and the profession was still a male-dominated landscape, this sixth-generation Sulzberger would be reared with the values necessary to be both a guardian and a merchant of truth.

NOTES

PROLOGUE

2 *The newspaper industry had shed $1.3 billion*: Evan Horowitz, "Even Fishermen and Coal Miners Are Not Losing Jobs as Fast as the Newspaper Industry," *Boston Globe*, July 3, 2018, https://www.bostonglobe.com/business/2018/07/03/even -fishermen-and-coal-miners-are-faring-better-than-newspaper-employees/snK50 6ritw8UxvD51O336L/story.html.

4 *The* Boston Globe *had closed its foreign news bureaus*: Jim Romenesko, "Globe Closes Foreign Bureaus to Save Jobs in Boston Newsroom," Poynter, January 23, 2007, https://www.poynter.org/news/globe-closes-foreign-bureaus-save-jobs-bos ton-newsroom; Howard Kurtz, "Washington Post Shutters Last U.S. Bureaus," *Washington Post*, November 24, 2009, http://www.washingtonpost.com/wp-dyn /content/article/2009/11/24/AR2009112403014.html.

5 *The* Times *had already and unsuccessfully*: Richard Pérez-Peña, "Times to Stop Charging for Parts of Its Web Site," *New York Times*, September 18, 2007, https:// www.nytimes.com/2007/09/18/business/media/18times.html.

CHAPTER ONE: BUZZFEED I

13 *His younger sister, Chelsea*: Alex Bhattacharji, "Peretti Siblings Share a Sense of Humor, Not Just Genes," *New York Times*, April 1, 2017, https://www.nytimes .com/2017/04/01/fashion/jonah-peretti-chelsea-peretti-get-out-buzzfeed-brook lyn-nine-nine.html.

13 *Their parents divorced*: Jonah Peretti, interviewed by Jill Abramson at BuzzFeed New York, June 17, 2015.

13 *But for Jonah each day*: Jonah Peretti, "Clay," *Falling for Science: Objects in Mind* (Cambridge, Massachusetts: M.I.T. Press, 2008), 62.

14 *His mother's friend*: Jonah Peretti, interviewed by Jill Abramson at BuzzFeed New York, June 17, 2015.

14 *His sister recalls these years*: Chelsea Peretti, interviewed by Jill Abramson, October 8, 2015.

14 *His senior thesis*: Jonah Peretti, "Nativism and Nature: Rethinking Biological Invasion," *Environmental Values* 7, no. 2 (1998): 183–192.

14 *He looked at a couple*: Jonah Peretti, interviewed by Jill Abramson at BuzzFeed New York, June 17, 2015.

14 *As an entry-level teacher*: Felix Salmon, "BuzzFeed's Jonah Peretti Goes Long," *Matter*, June 11, 2014, https://medium.com/matter/buzzfeeds-jonah-peretti-goes -long-e98cf13160e7.

15 *The funky pair*: Peggy Wang, interviewed by Jill Abramson at BuzzFeed New York, September 2015.

15 *One from his first year*: Jonah Peretti, "Capitalism and Schizophrenia: Contemporary Visual Culture and the Acceleration of Identity Formation/Dissolution," *Negations*, 1996.

16 *The 27-year-old Peretti submitted*: Jonah Peretti, "Nike Sweatshop Emails," Shey .net, www.shey.net/niked.html.

17 *Sitting in front of the cameras*: Kathleen Elkins, "How a Fight with Nike Led BuzzFeed's Jonah Peretti to Create a Billion-Dollar Media Empire," CNBC.com, August 3, 2017, https://www.cnbc.com/2017/08/02/how-jonah-peretti-created -buzzfeed-a-billion-dollar-media-empire.html.

17 *One write-up heralded him*: Alexia Tsotsis, "David Karp, Jonah Peretti and Adrian Grenier Are All Ready to Disrupt NYC," TechCrunch, May 7, 2017, https://techcrunch.com/2012/05/07/david-karp-jonah-peretti-and-adrian-grenier -are-all-ready-to-disrupt-nyc/15-6/.

18 *In a 23-point manifesto*: Jonah Peretti, "Notes on Contagious Media," *Structures of Participation in Digital Culture*, edited by Joe Karaganis (New York: Social Science Research Council, 2007), 158–163.

19 *He called his clique*: Jonah Peretti, interviewed by Jill Abramson and John Stillman at BuzzFeed Motion Pictures, Los Angeles, March 14, 2016.

19 *"Digerati Vogues*: Sarah Boxer, "Digerati Vogues, Caught Midcraze," *New York Times*, May 12, 2006, https://www.nytimes.com/2005/05/12/arts/design/digerati -vogues-caught-midcraze.html.

20 *This came with the territory*: Matthew Lynch, "The Jolly, Abrupt, WTF Rise of BuzzFeed," *M Magazine*, n.d., http://mmagazine.tumblr.com/post/45911798703 /the-jolly-abrupt-wtf-rise-of-buzzfeed.

20 *At first Peretti wasn't interested*: Jonah Peretti, interviewed by Jill Abramson at BuzzFeed New York, June 17, 2015.

20 *The antigun campaign*: Kenneth Lerer, interviewed by Jill Abramson, New York, December 2, 2015.

20 *The conversation at dinner revolved*: Jonah Peretti, interviewed by Jill Abramson at BuzzFeed New York, June 17, 2015.

21 *The Oakland-raised son*: Jonah Peretti, interviewed by Jill Abramson at BuzzFeed New York, June 26, 2015.

22 *"I learned from Arianna*: Jonah Peretti, interviewed by Jill Abramson at Buzz-Feed New York, June 17, 2015.

24 *As the official innovator*: Jonah Peretti, interviewed by Jill Abramson at BuzzFeed New York, June 26, 2015.

25 *Just four years after Peretti*: Tim Rutten, "AOL? HuffPo. The Loser? Journalism,"

Los Angeles Times, February 9, 2011, http://articles.latimes.com/2011/feb/09
/opinion/la-oe-rutten-column-huffington-aol-20110209.

25 *Shortly after the Huffington Post's*: Katharine Q. Seelye, "Times Company Announces 500 Job Cuts," *New York Times*, September 21, 2005, https://www.nytimes
.com/2005/09/21/business/media/times-company-announces-500-job-cuts.html.

26 *The* Washington Post *spent millions*: Steven Mufson, "Washington Post Announces Cuts to Employees' Retirement Benefits," *Washington Post*, September
23, 2014, https://www.washingtonpost.com/business/economy/washington-post
-announces-cuts-to-employees-retirement-benefits/2014/09/23/f485981a-436d
-11e4-b437-1a7368204804_story.html?utm_term=.dadf7ca0ef2b.

26 *At the* Post, *Weymouth recalled*: Katharine Weymouth, interviewed by Jill
Abramson, Washington, D.C., July 12, 2016.

26 *The amount of digital data*: Geoff Duncan, "Study: 161 Exabytes of Digital Data
in 2006," Digital Trends, March 6, 2007, https://www.digitaltrends.com/comput
ing/study-161-exabytes-of-digital-data-in-2006/.

26 *A 2008 study commissioned*: Associated Press and the Context-Based Research
Group, "A New Model for News: Studying the Deep Structure of Young-Adult
News Consumption," Social Media Club, June 2008, 37, 43. http://socialmedia
club.pbworks.com/f/apnewmodelfornews.pdf.

26 *A Pew study*: Russell Heimlich, "Can Name the Current Vice President," Pew Research Center, April 23, 2007, http://www.pewresearch.org/fact-tank/2007/04/23
/can-name-the-current-vice-president/.

27 *The balance of objectivity*: "Amendment to No. 9 to Form S-1 Registration Statement, Google, Inc.," Securities and Exchange Commission, Washington, D.C.,
August 18, 2014, A-21, https://www.fbcoverup.com/docs/eclipse/2004-08-18
-Google-Form-S-1-Amendment-No-9-Registration-Statement-SEC-Aug-18
-2004.pdf.

27 *More people consulted the web*: Felicity Barringer, "Pulitzers Focus on Sept. 11,
and The Times Wins 7," *New York Times*, April 9, 2002, https://www.nytimes.com
/2002/04/09/nyregion/pulitzers-focus-on-sept-11-and-the-times-wins-7.html.

28 *"People came to us*: Krishna Bharat, interviewed by Martin Nisenholtz, Digital
Riptide, April 1, 2013, https://www.digitalriptide.org/person/krishna-bharat/.

28 *To Google, it was another step*: "Letter from the Founders," *New York Times*, April
29, 2004, https://www.nytimes.com/2004/04/29/business/letter-from-the-founders
.html.

28 *"There are those who think*: Gabriel Sherman, "The Raging Septuagenarian,"
New York, February 28, 2010, http://nymag.com/nymag/rss/media/64305/index4
.html.

29 *(A full-page ad*: David Streitfeld, "Plot Thickens as 900 Writers Battle Amazon,"
New York Times, August 7, 2014, https://www.nytimes.com/2014/08/08/business
/media/plot-thickens-as-900-writers-battle-amazon.html.

29 *He blamed Arianna Huffington*: Bill Keller, "All the Aggregation That's Fit to Aggregate," *New York Times*, March 10, 2011, https://www.nytimes.com/2011/03/13
/magazine/mag-13lede-t.html.

29 *Huffington struck back:* Arianna Huffington, "Bill Keller Accuses Me of 'Aggregating' an Idea He Had Actually 'Aggregated' from Me," *Huffington Post*, May 25, 2011, https://www.huffingtonpost.com/arianna-huffington/bill-keller-accuses-me-of_b_834289.html.

30 *Twelve months after the Huffington Post:* "The 2006 TIME 100," *Time*, n.d., http://content.time.com/time/specials/packages/completelist/0,29569,1975813,00.html.

30 *"It took just two fingers:* Brett Sokol, "The Drudge Retort," *Miami New Times*, June 28, 2001, https://www.miaminewtimes.com/news/the-drudge-retort-6351876.

30 *"I was just always interested:* Jonah Peretti, interviewed by Jill Abramson at BuzzFeed New York, June 17, 2015.

31 *Years later Lerer would recall:* Kenneth Lerer, interviewed by Jill Abramson, New York, December 2, 2015.

31 *Within 24 hours:* Sarah Phillips, "A Brief History of Facebook," *Guardian*, July 25, 2007, https://www.theguardian.com/technology/2007/jul/25/media.newmedia.

32 *"You had the underpinnings:* Chris Cox, interviewed by Martin Nisenholtz, Digital Riptide, April 1, 2013, https://www.digitalriptide.org/person/chris-cox/.

32 *"iPhone is a revolutionary:* "Apple Reinvents the Phone with iPhone," Apple, Inc. (press release), January 9, 2007, https://www.apple.com/newsroom/2007/01/09Apple-Reinvents-the-Phone-with-iPhone/.

32 *The release date was set:* "Where Would Jesus Queue?," *The Economist*, July 5, 2007, https://www.economist.com/business/2007/07/05/where-would-jesus-queue.

33 *With seed funding:* Tanner Greenring, Scott Lamb, Jack Shepherd, Matt Stopera, and Peggy Wang, interviewed by Jill Abramson and John Stillman, New York, June 26, 2015.

33 *He purchased a few servers:* Ibid.

34 *Function No. 1:* Jonah Peretti, interviewed by Jill Abramson at BuzzFeed New York, June 26, 2015; Alyson Shontell, "Inside BuzzFeed: The Story of How Jonah Peretti Built the Web's Most Beloved New Media Brand," Business Insider, December 11, 2012, https://www.businessinsider.com/buzzfeed-jonah-peretti-interview-2012-12.

35 *"The original editors:* Jonah Peretti, interviewed by Jill Abramson and John Stillman at BuzzFeed Motion Pictures, Los Angeles, March 15, 2016.

35 *Its slogan: "Find:* Jason Del Rey, "BuzzFeed's 2008 Investor Pitch: See Jonah Peretti's Predictions, Right and Wrong," *AdAge*, April 12, 2013, http://adage.com/article/media/buzzfeed-s-2008-investor-pitch-jonah-peretti-s-predictions/240861/.

35 *"BuzzFeed wasn't a content site:* Kenneth Lerer, interviewed by Jill Abramson, New York, December 2, 2015.

36 *Things like "basset hounds running:* Asher Klein, "BuzzFeed Wants You to Look Cool," Chicago Reader, September 28, 2012, https://www.chicagoreader.com/Bleader/archives/2012/09/28/buzzfeed-wants-you-to-look-cool.

37 *One was Peggy Wang:* Peggy Wang, interviewed by Jill Abramson at BuzzFeed New York, September 2015.

37 *She had gotten her college degree*: Madina Papadopoulos, "The Joys of Being Peggy Wang," Tulane University, *New Wave*, June 28, 2017, https://news.tulane .edu/news/joys-being-peggy-wang.

37 *Wang became the site's*: Tanner Greenring, Scott Lamb, Jack Shepherd, Matt Stopera, and Peggy Wang, interviewed by Jill Abramson and John Stillman, New York, June 26, 2015.

37 *He came to BuzzFeed*: "Matt Stopera: Senior Editor at BuzzFeed," How Did You Get That Job?, November 7, 2012, http://howdidyougetthatjob.co/post /35063858612/matt-stopera-senior-editor-buzzfeed.

38 *In college he decided*: Ibid.

38 *He created a website*: Zach Baron, "Where the Wild Things Go Viral," *GQ*, March 4, 2014, https://www.gq.com/story/buzzfeed-beastmaster-profile-march-2014.

38 *Stopera, the baby of the group*: Matt Stopera, interviewed by Jill Abramson and John Stillman, New York, September 2015.

39 *Every so often, Peretti*: Arabelle Sicardi, interviewed by Jill Abramson, New York, July 16, 2015.

39 *Each time a new post*: BuzzFeed International Editorial Meeting, observed by Jill Abramson and John Stillman, New York, October 28, 2015.

39 *When the buzz du jour*: Tanner Greenring, Scott Lamb, Jack Shepherd, Matt Stopera, and Peggy Wang, interviewed by Jill Abramson and John Stillman, New York, June 26, 2015.

39 *His wife had given birth*: Jonah Peretti, interviewed by Jill Abramson at BuzzFeed New York, June 17, 2015.

40 *"BuzzFeed was set up*: Marc Andreessen, telephone interview by Jill Abramson, May 4, 2016.

40 *Peretti's PowerPoint pitch*: Jason Del Rey, "BuzzFeed's 2008 Investor Pitch: See Jonah Peretti's Predictions, Right and Wrong," *AdAge*, April 12, 2013, http:// adage.com/article/media/buzzfeed-s-2008-investor-pitch-jonah-peretti-s-predic tions/240861/.

CHAPTER TWO: VICE I

42 *One of his best friends*: Gavin McInnes, *The Death of Cool: From Teenage Rebellion to the Hangover of Adulthood* (New York: Simon & Schuster, 2013), 47.

42 *At Carleton they had played*: Gavin McInnes, Suroosh Alvi, and Shane Smith, *The Vice Guide to Sex and Drugs and Rock and Roll* (London: Revolver Books, 2006), 2.

42 *"When I was young*: Shane Smith, interviewed by Spike Jonze, "Spike Jonze Spends Saturday with Shane Smith (Part 1/3)," October 2012, https://www.you tube.com/watch?v=GPIPMH_AzAo.

42 *Smith returned to Canada*: Gavin McInnes, Suroosh Alvi, and Shane Smith, *The Vice Guide to Sex and Drugs and Rock and Roll* (London: Revolver Books, 2006), 2–3.

43 *Almost on a whim*: David Sax, "The Vice Guide to Sex, Drugs and Profit," Canadian Business, February 27, 2006, https://www.canadianbusiness.com/business -strategy/the-vice-guide-to-sex-drugs-and-profit/.

44 *"If you're looking at Vice*: Shane Smith, interviewed by Spike Jonze, "Spike Jonze Spends Saturday with Shane Smith (Part 1/3)," October 2012, https://www .youtube.com/watch?v=GPIPMH_AzAo.

44 *When the local Montreal paper*: Alexandra Molotkow, "Giving Offence: Gavin McInnes Co-Founded Vice Magazine: As It Got Big, He Got Ousted," The Walrus, May 1, 2017, https://thewalrus.ca/giving-offence/.

45 *As the founders of* Voice: Jason Tanz, "The Snarky Vice Squad Is Ready to Be Taken Seriously. Seriously," Wired, October 18, 2017, https://www.wired.com /2007/10/ff-vice/.

45 *"When we initially moved*: Pamela Newenham, "Shane Smith: 'How I Went from Serving Pints in the Baggot Inn to Building a $400m Fortune,'" *Irish Times*, October 30, 2013, https://www.irishtimes.com/business/technology/shane-smith -how-i-went-from-serving-pints-in-the-baggot-inn-to-building-a-400m-fortune -1.1577326.

46 *"We realized if we*: "The Engagement Project: The VICE Guide to Engagement," Thinking with Google, June 2013, https://www.thinkwithgoogle.com/marketing -resources/the-vice-guide-to-engagement/.

46 *"It paid to be perceived*: Gavin McInnes, Suroosh Alvi, and Shane Smith, *The Vice Guide to Sex and Drugs and Rock and Roll* (London: Revolver Books, 2006), 11.

46 *McInnes asserted, "This*: Anne Elizabeth Moore, "The Vertically Integrated Rape," *The Baffler*, no. 24, January 2014, https://thebaffler.com/salvos/the-verti cally-integrated-rape-joke.

47 *But before Szalwinski could sell*: Alexandra Molotkow, "Giving Offence: Gavin McInnes Co-Founded Vice Magazine: As It Got Big, He Got Ousted," The Walrus, May 1, 2017, https://thewalrus.ca/giving-offence/.

47 *"Those guys had a real struggle*: Ibid.

47 *Early issues featured writing*: Gavin McInnes, Suroosh Alvi, and Shane Smith, *The Vice Guide to Sex and Drugs and Rock and Roll* (London: Revolver Books, 2006), 8.

48 *By the spring of 2001*: Adam Heimlich, "ViceRising: Why Corporate Media Is Sniffing the Butt of the Magazine World," *New York Press*, October 8, 2002, https://web.archive.org/web/20081010201329/http://nypress.com/15/40/news& columns/feature.cfm.

48 *Music writer Amy Kellner*: Amy Kellner, "Rebel Girls," Vice, November 30, 2000, https://www.vice.com/en_us/article/4wav3w/bratmobile-v7n10.

48 *When Alvi was interviewed*: Dominic Patten, "Vice Squad," *Globe and Mail*, November 11, 2002, https://www.theglobeandmail.com/arts/vice-squad/article414 2684/.

48 *To the founders, staying punk*: Vanessa Grigoriadis, "The Edge of Hip: Vice, the Brand," *New York Times*, September 28, 2003, https://www.nytimes.com/2003/09 /28/style/the-edge-of-hip-vice-the-brand.html.

49 *Vice had already sent*: "Letter to the Editor," *Vice*, 8, no. 8, November 2001.

49 *Alvi had once said*: Dominic Patten, "Vice Squad," *Globe and Mail*, November 11, 2002, https://www.theglobeandmail.com/arts/vice-squad/article4142684/.

49 *They were taking in*: Ryan Bigge, "Hiding in Delight: Transgression, Irony and the Edge of Vice," http://digitalcommons.ryerson.ca/dissertations (2007), *Theses and Dissertations,* Paper 67, 39–40.

49 *Dear Suroosh*: Jenna Schnuer, "Vice," *AdAge*, November 1, 2004, http://adage .com/article/special-report-marketing-50/vice/101078/.

50 *"You guys are going around*: David Itzkoff, "Spike Jonze on the Small Screen," Cineconomy, January 3, 2016, http://www.cineconomy.com/2012/eng/news.php? news=7263.

51 *They wed at her father's vineyard*: Gillian Orr, "The Wedding Day: Sofia Coppola & Spike Jonze," Refinery 29, September 4, 2016, https://www.refinery29.uk/sofia -coppola-spike-jonze-wedding-day; Ethan Smith, "Spike Jonze Unmasked," *New York*, n.d., http://nymag.com/nymetro/movies/features/1267/.

51 *Many viewers couldn't help themselves*: Sandra P. Angulo, "Senator Joe Lieber- man Wants MTV to Cancel 'Jackass,' " *Entertainment*, January 31, 2001, http://ew .com/article/2001/01/31/senator-joe-lieberman-wants-mtv-cancel-jackass/.

53 *With the slogan "Tune In*: Stuart Dredge, "YouTube Was Meant to Be a Video -Dating Website," *Guardian* (UK), March 16, 2016, https://www.theguardian.com /technology/2016/mar/16/youtube-past-video-dating-website.

54 *"This is the next step*: Associated Press, "Google Buys YouTube for $1.65 Bil- lion," NBCNews.com, October 10, 2006, http://www.nbcnews.com/id/15196982 /ns/business-us_business/t/google-buys-youtube-billion/#.W1evqdhKjBU.

54 *The site was attracting*: Reuters, "YouTube Serves Up 100 Million Videos a Day Online," USAToday.com, July 16, 2006, http://usatoday30.usatoday.com/tech /news/2006-07-16-youtube-views_x.htm.

57 *The author David Foster Wallace*: David Foster Wallace, "Deciderization 2007—A Special Report," *The Best American Essays 2007* (Wilmington, Massa- chusetts: Mariner Books, 2007).

57 *"They gave me a pitch*: Robert Levine, "A Guerrilla Video Site Meets MTV," *New York Times*, November 19, 2007, https://www.nytimes.com/2007/11/19/business /media/19vice.html?hp&_r=1.

57 The Vice Guide to Travel: *The Vice Guide to Travel*, VBS.tv, 2006.

58 *"Their default position*: Mercedes La Rosa, "Vice Is Everywhere," *Maison Neuve*, June 8, 2007, https://maisonneuve.org/article/2007/06/8/vice-everywhere/.

59 *The high point for television*: Barbara Boland, "Study: Network News Viewers at All-Time Low; Half under Age 30 Never Watch News," CNSNews.com, January 10, 2014, https://www.cnsnews.com/news/article/barbara-boland/study-network -news-viewers-all-time-low-half-under-age-30-never-watch.

CHAPTER THREE: *NEW YORK TIMES* I

69 *(One outside critic blasted*: Michelle Cottle, "The Gray Lady Wears Prada," *New Republic*, April 17, 2006, https://newrepublic.com/article/62336/the-gray-lady-wears-prada.

70 *To keep his $200 million-plus*: Richard Pérez-Peña, "New York Times Plans to Cut 100 Newsroom Jobs," *New York Times*, February 14, 2008, https://www.nytimes.com/2008/02/14/business/media/14cnd-times.html.

71 *At the* L.A. Times: "Mark Willes: Cereal Killer," Wired, October 16, 1998, https://www.wired.com/1998/10/mark-willes-cereal-killer/.

71 *the paper forged*: David Shaw, "Crossing the Line," *Los Angeles Times*, December 20, 1999, http://articles.latimes.com/1999/dec/20/news/ss-46240.

72 *"Our corporate superiors*: John Carroll, "Last Call at the ASNE Saloon," speech delivered to the American Society of Newspaper Editors convention, Seattle, Washington, April, 2006, https://www.poynter.org/news/last-call-asne-saloon.

75 *Clay Shirky, a journalism professor*: Clay Shirky, "Newspapers and Thinking the Unthinkable," *Shirky* (blog), March 13, 2009, http://www.shirky.com/weblog/2009/03/newspapers-and-thinking-the-unthinkable/.

78 *One devoted reader*: Roberta Smith, "All the News That's Fit to Paint," *New York Times*, January 31, 1997, https://www.nytimes.com/1997/01/31/arts/all-the-news-that-s-fit-to-paint.html.

CHAPTER FOUR: *WASHINGTON POST* I

82 *But the battered state*: Michael Wolff, "*Post* Modern," *Vanity Fair*, September 4, 2009, https://www.vanityfair.com/news/2009/10/wolff200910.

82 *It was more diversified*: James Warren, "Is *The New York Times* vs. *The Washington Post* vs. Trump the Last Great Newspaper War?," *Vanity Fair*, July 30, 2017, https://www.vanityfair.com/news/2017/07/new-york-times-washington-post-donald-trump; Sarah Ellison, "Ghosts in the Newsroom," *Vanity Fair*, March 7, 2012, https://www.vanityfair.com/news/business/2012/04/washington-post-watergate.

83 *The education company*: Frank Aherns, "Post Now an 'Education and Media' Company," *Washington Post*, December 6, 2007, http://www.washingtonpost.com/wp-dyn/content/article/2007/12/05/AR2007120500683.html?noredirect=on.

83 *Katharine and Donald had been tutored*: Amy Argetsinger and Roxanne Roberts, "What Really Happened When Warren Met Katharine," *Washington Post*, September 29, 2008, http://www.washingtonpost.com/wp-dyn/content/article/2008/09/29/AR2008092900068.html.

83 *He believed that local papers*: Mamta Badkar, "Buffett Explains Why He Paid $344 Million for 28 Newspapers, and Thinks the Industry Still Has a Future," Business Insider, March 1, 2013, http://www.businessinsider.com/warren-buffett-buying-newspapers-2013-3; Steven Mutson, "Warren Buffett to Step Down from Washington Post Co. Board," *Washington Post*, January 20, 2011, http://www.washingtonpost.com/wp-dyn/content/article/2011/01/20/AR2011012002972.html.

83 *Priced for a long time*: Max Olson, "Warren Buffett & the Washington Post," *FutureBlind* (blog), December 12, 2006, https://futureblind.com/2006/12/12/warren -buffett-washington-post/.

83 *His ties to the local*: Daniel Okrent, "How Arthur Sulzberger Outwitted Don Graham," Politico, December 15, 2017, https://www.politico.com/magazine/story /2017/12/15/how-arthur-sulzberger-outwitted-don-graham-216105.

83 *Following a year of service*: Leah S. Yared, "From Crimson President to Post Publisher: Donald E. Graham '66," *Harvard Crimson*, May 23, 2016, https://www .thecrimson.com/article/2016/5/23/donald-graham-profile/.

84 *He saw being on the police force*: Jeffrey St. Clair and Alexander Cockburn, "The High Life of Katharine Graham," CounterPunch, July 25, 2001, https://www .counterpunch.org/2001/07/25/the-high-life-of-katharine-graham/."

84 *Downie was such a straight arrow*: Michael Kinsley, "Fess Up, Journalists," *Washington Post*, November 7, 2000, https://www.washingtonpost.com/archive/opin ions/2000/11/07/fess-up-journalists/df5f6468-e678-49b0-a0d9-010a9b566f7a/.

84 *In meetings he'd often say*: Marcus Brauchli, interviewed by Jill Abramson, March 24, 2016.

85 *An early alarm*: Jordan Weissmann, "The Beginning of the End of Print: The Lessons of an Amazing Prescient 1992 WaPo Memo," *Atlantic*, August 21, 2012, https://www.theatlantic.com/business/archive/2012/08/the-beginning-of-the-end -of-print-the-lessons-of-an-amazingly-prescient-1992-wapo-memo/261384/.

85 *There he heard presentations about*: Robert Kaiser memo to Don Graham et al., August 6, 1992, http://recoveringjournalist.typepad.com/files/kaiser-memo.pdf.

86 *Four years later, an eternity*: Jordan Weissmann, "The Beginning of the End of Print: The Lessons of an Amazing Prescient 1992 WaPo Memo," *Atlantic*, August 21, 2012, https://www.theatlantic.com/business/archive/2012/08/the-beginning-of -the-end-of-print-the-lessons-of-an-amazingly-prescient-1992-wapo-memo /261384/.

86 *The next missed opportunity*: Daniel Okrent, "How Arthur Sulzberger Outwitted Don Graham," Politico, December 15, 2017, https://www.politico.com/magazine /story/2017/12/15/how-arthur-sulzberger-outwitted-don-graham-216105.

86 *Steve Coll, a Pulitzer-winning*: Sarah Ellison, "Ghosts in the Newsroom," *Vanity Fair*, March 7, 2012, https://www.vanityfair.com/news/business/2012/04/wash ington-post-watergate.

87 *The* Post *would have to look*: Steven Mufson, "As Jeff Bezos Prepares to Take Over, a Look at Forces That Shaped the Washington Post Sale," *Washington Post*, September 27, 2013, https://www.washingtonpost.com/business/as-jeff-bezos -prepares-to-take-over-a-look-at-forces-that-shaped-the-washington-post-sale /2013/09/27/11c7d01a-2622-11e3-adod-b7c8d2a594b9_story.html.

87 *Coll was ready to present*: Sarah Ellison, "Ghosts in the Newsroom," *Vanity Fair*, March 7, 2012, https://www.vanityfair.com/news/business/2012/04/washington -post-watergate.

88 *Hoping to mend the relationship*: Steve Coll, interviewed by Jill Abramson, New York, August 18, 2015.

88 *Coll's exit in August*: Sarah Ellison, "Ghosts in the Newsroom," *Vanity Fair*, March 7, 2012, https://www.vanityfair.com/news/business/2012/04/washington -post-watergate.

88 *The newsroom was downcast*: Annie Groer, "After Buyouts, the Goodbyes: Washington Post Staffers Gather for a Bittersweet Send-Off," *Huffington Post*, December 6, 2017, https://www.huffingtonpost.com/annie-groer/after-buyouts-the-good bye_b_104571.html.

88 *So the newsroom shrank*: Sarah Ellison, "Ghosts in the Newsroom," *Vanity Fair*, March 7, 2012, https://www.vanityfair.com/news/business/2012/04/washington -post-watergate; Jeremy W. Peters, "A Newspaper, and a Legacy, Reordered," *New York Times*, February 11, 2012, https://www.nytimes.com/2012/02/12/business /media/the-washington-post-recast-for-a-digital-future.html.

89 *The cuts eventually robbed*: Sarah Ellison, "Ghosts in the Newsroom," *Vanity Fair*, March 7, 2012, https://www.vanityfair.com/news/business/2012/04/washing ton-post-watergate; Jeremy W. Peters, "A Newspaper, and a Legacy, Reordered," *New York Times*, February 11, 2012, https://www.nytimes.com/2012/02/12/busi ness/media/the-washington-post-recast-for-a-digital-future.html.

89 *Downie had written a book*: Leonard Downie Jr. and Robert G. Kaiser, *The News about the News: American Journalism in Peril* (New York: Vintage, 2003).

89 *In a 2011 report*: Steven Waldman, "The Information Needs of Communities," FCC Report, June 2011.

89 *The print team didn't trust*: Erik Wemple, "One Mission, Two Newsrooms," *Washington City Paper*, February 15, 2008, https://www.washingtoncitypaper .com/news/article/13034934/one-mission-two-newsrooms.

89 *He also liked that Virginia*: James Warren, "Is *The New York Times* vs. *The Washington Post* vs. Trump the Last Great Newspaper War?," *Vanity Fair*, July 30, 2017, https://www.vanityfair.com/news/2017/07/new-york-times-washington-post -donald-trump.

89 *Its storied history*: Daniel Okrent, "How Arthur Sulzberger Outwitted Don Graham," Politico, December 15, 2017, https://www.politico.com/magazine/story /2017/12/15/how-arthur-sulzberger-outwitted-don-graham-216105.

89 *Classified ads made up*: "Who Killed the Newspaper?," *The Economist*, August 24, 2006, https://www.economist.com/leaders/2006/08/24/who-killed-the-news paper.

90 *A year after he left*: Steve Coll, interviewed by Jill Abramson, New York, August 18, 2015.

90 *So when the* Post's *board advised*: Steven Mufson and Jia Lynn Yang, "The Trials of Kaplan Higher Ed and the Education of the Washington Post Co.," *Washington Post*, April 9, 2011, https://www.washingtonpost.com/business/the-trials -of-kaplan-higher-ed-and-the-education-of-the-washington-post-co/2011/03/20 /AFsGuUAD_story.html?utm_term=.1c31402d4292.

90 *Buffett, the Oracle of Omaha*: Patricia Sullivan, "Test-Prep Pioneer Stanley H. Kaplan Dies at 90," *Washington Post*, August 25, 2009, http://www.washington post.com/wp-dyn/content/article/2009/08/24/AR2009082402105.html.

90 *Graham appointed Don*: Steven Mufson and Jia Lynn Yang, "The Trials of Kaplan Higher Ed and the Education of the Washington Post Co.," *Washington Post*, April 9, 2011, https://www.washingtonpost.com/business/the-trials-of-kaplan-higher -ed-and-the-education-of-the-washington-post-co/2011/03/20/AFsGuUAD_ story.html?utm_term=.1c31402d4292.

90 *Next Grayer found Quest*: "Kaplan, Inc. Completes Acquisition of Quest Education," Kaplan Higher Education Campuses news releases, July 27, 2000, http:// newsroom.kaplan.edu/press-release/kaplan-higher-education-campuses/kaplan -inc-completes-acquisition-quest-education.

90 *The company did not come cheap*: Steven Mufson and Jia Lynn Yang, "The Trials of Kaplan Higher Ed and the Education of the Washington Post Co.," *Washington Post*, April 9, 2011, https://www.washingtonpost.com/business/the-trials -of-kaplan-higher-ed-and-the-education-of-the-washington-post-co/2011/03/20 /AFsGuUAD_story.html?utm_term=.1c31402d4292.

90 *The move kicked off*: Russell Adams and Melissa Kom, "For-Profit Kaplan U. Hears Its Fight Song," *Wall Street Journal*, August 30, 2010, https://www.wsj.com /articles/SB10001424052748703418004575455773289209384.

91 *But George W. Bush packed*: Steven Mufson and Jia Lynn Yang, "The Trials of Kaplan Higher Ed and the Education of the Washington Post Co.," *Washington Post*, April 9, 2011, https://www.washingtonpost.com/business/the-trials-of-ka plan-higher-ed-and-the-education-of-the-washington-post-co/2011/03/20/AFs GuUAD_story.html?utm_term=.1c31402d4292.

91 *As Kaplan mounted*: Libby A. Nelson, "Will Kaplan Survive without WaPo?," Politico, August 5, 2013, https://www.politico.com/story/2013/08/washington-post -sale-kaplan-095208.

91 *The $101 million*: Steven Mufson and Jia Lynn Yang, "The Trials of Kaplan Higher Ed and the Education of the Washington Post Co.," *Washington Post*, April 9, 2011, https://www.washingtonpost.com/business/the-trials-of-kaplan-higher-ed -and-the-education-of-the-washington-post-co/2011/03/20/AFsGuUAD_story.ht ml?utm_term=.1c31402d4292.

91 *In 2006 the Post Company*: Ibid.

91 *"It has been amazing*: Frank Aherns, "Post Now an 'Education and Media' Company," *Washington Post*, December 6, 2007, http://www.washingtonpost.com/wp -dyn/content/article/2007/12/05/AR2007120500683.html?noredirect=on.

91 *Eventually, after taking*: Steven Mufson and Jia Lynn Yang, "The Trials of Kaplan Higher Ed and the Education of the Washington Post Co.," *Washington Post*, April 9, 2011, https://www.washingtonpost.com/business/the-trials-of-kaplan-higher-ed -and-the-education-of-the-washington-post-co/2011/03/20/AFsGuUAD_story.ht ml?utm_term=.1c31402d4292.

91 *His severance package*: Rusty Weiss, "Scandal at the Washington Post: Fraud, Lobbying and Insider Trading," Accuracy in Media, March 8, 2012, https://www .aim.org/special-report/scandal-at-the-washington-post-fraud-lobbying-insider -trading/.

92 *On the editorial side*: Paul Farhi, "On Iraq, Journalists Didn't Fail. They Just Didn't

Succeed," *Washington Post*, March 22, 2013, https://www.washingtonpost.com
/opinions/on-iraq-journalists-didnt-fail-they-just-didnt-succeed/2013/03/22/0ca
6cee6-9186-11e2-9abd-e4c5c9dc5e90_story.html?utm_term=.b01b1e291827.

92 *The* Times *published*: "From the Editors: The Times and Iraq," *New York Times*,
May 26, 2004, https://www.nytimes.com/2004/05/26/world/from-the-editors-the
-times-and-iraq.html.

92 *The* Post *also published*: Howard Kurtz, "The Post on WMDs: An Inside Story,"
Washington Post, August 12, 2004, http://www.washingtonpost.com/wp-dyn/arti
cles/A58127-2004Aug11.html.

92 *On the eve of the war*: "Analysis of Colin Powell's Speech before the U.N.," *Larry
King Live* (transcript), CNN, February 5, 2003, http://transcripts.cnn.com/TRAN
SCRIPTS/0302/05/lkl.00.html.

92 *But they were drowned out*: Howard Kurtz, "The Post on WMDs: An Inside
Story," *Washington Post*, August 12, 2004, http://www.washingtonpost.com/wp
-dyn/articles/A58127-2004Aug11.html.

93 *Thomas Ricks, who covered*: Ibid.

93 *Though Woodward enjoyed*: Andrew Ferguson, "Bob Woodward's Washington,"
Weekly Standard, May 3, 2004, https://www.weeklystandard.com/andrew-fer
guson/bob-woodwards-washington; "Interview: Bob Woodward," PBS *Front-
line* (transcript), December 13, 2006, https://www.pbs.org/wgbh/pages/frontline
/newswar/interviews/woodward.html#1.

93 *Once that had been debunked*: Howard Kurtz, "The Post on WMDs: An Inside
Story," *Washington Post*, August 12, 2004, http://www.washingtonpost.com/wp
-dyn/articles/A58127-2004Aug11.html.

93 *"We were so focused*: Ibid.

93 *In 2005, Lewis "Scooter" Libby*: Zachary Colle, "Libby Was a Driving Force
behind Iraq War; Cheney's Aide Sought to Justify Pre-emptive Strikes to Prevent Threats," SFGATE, October 28, 2005, https://www.sfgate.com/news/article
/Libby-was-a-driving-force-behind-Iraq-war-2598544.php.

93 *Woodward had learned her identity*: Bob Woodward, "Testifying in the CIA Leak
Case," *Washington Post*, November 16, 2005, http://www.washingtonpost.com
/wp-dyn/content/article/2005/11/15/AR2005111501829.html.

93 *When it was later revealed*: David Folkenflik, "Woodward Apologizes for Role in
CIA Leak Case," *All Things Considered*, NPR, November 16, 2005, https://www
.npr.org/templates/story/story.php?storyId=5015605.

94 *When there were government document*: David Glenn, "The (Josh) Marshall
Plan," *Columbia Journalism Review*, September–October 2007, https://archives
.cjr.org/feature/the_josh_marshall_plan.php.

94 *Collaboration instead of competition*: Noam Cohen, "Blogger, Sans Pajamas,
Rakes Muck and a Prize," *New York Times*, February 25, 2008, https://www.ny
times.com/2008/02/25/business/media/25marshall.html.

95 *Their reporters were better sourced*: Gary Younge, "Washington Post Apologises
for Underplaying WMD Scepticism," *Guardian*, August 12, 2004, https://www
.theguardian.com/world/2004/aug/13/pressandpublishing.usa.

95 *During the dawn of digital*: Robert D. McFadden, "Christopher Ma, Washington Post Executive, Dies at 61," *New York Times*, November 24, 2011, https://www.nytimes.com/2011/11/25/business/media/christopher-ma-washington-post-executive-dies-at-61.html.

95 *Ma was hunting*: Steven Mufson, "As Jeff Bezos Prepares to Take Over, a Look at Forces That Shaped the Washington Post Sale," *Washington Post*, September 27, 2013, https://www.washingtonpost.com/business/as-jeff-bezos-prepares-to-take-over-a-look-at-forces-that-shaped-the-washington-post-sale/2013/09/27/11c7d01a-2622-11e3-ad0d-b7c8d2a594b9_story.html.

96 *Graham later told me*: Donald Graham, interviewed by Jill Abramson, Washington, D.C., May 4, 2017.

96 *Zuckerberg, according to a history*: David Kirkpatrick, "Mark Zuckerberg: The Temptation of Facebook's CEO," CNN Money, May 6, 2010, https://money.cnn.com/2010/05/06/technology/facebook_excerpt_full.fortune/index.htm.

96 *Eventually Graham offered $6 million*: Ibid.

96 *According to an account*: Ibid.

96 *They and Zuckerberg went to*: Sarah Ellison, "Ghosts in the Newsroom," *Vanity Fair*, March 7, 2012, https://www.vanityfair.com/news/business/2012/04/washington-post-watergate.

97 *The man persuaded:* David Kirkpatrick, "Mark Zuckerberg: The Temptation of Facebook's CEO," CNN Money, May 6, 2010, https://money.cnn.com/2010/05/06/technology/facebook_excerpt_full.fortune/index.htm.

97 *Graham joined the small Facebook board*: Christopher S. Stewart and Russell Adams, "When Zuckerberg Met Graham: A Facebook Love Story," *Wall Street Journal*, January 5, 2012, https://www.wsj.com/articles/SB10001424052970203686204577116631661990706.

99 *Harris couldn't help*: https://www.vanityfair.com/news/2009/08/wolff200908.

CHAPTER FIVE: BUZZFEED II

103 *On most summer afternoons*: Alyson Shontell, "Inside BuzzFeed: The Story of How Jonah Peretti Built the Web's Most Beloved New Media Brand," Business Insider, December 11, 2012, https://www.businessinsider.com/buzzfeed-jonah-peretti-interview-2012-12.

103 *"Media and content*: Erin Griffith, "Peretti: Human Curation Beats SEO in the Social Web," Pando, September 19, 2012, https://pando.com/2012/09/19/peretti-human-curation-beats-seo-in-the-social-web/.

103 *At HuffPo he had focused*: David Rowan, "How BuzzFeed Mastered Social Sharing to Become a Media Giant for a New Era," Wired, January 2, 2014, https://www.wired.co.uk/article/buzzfeed.

103 *Moving into position*: Kenneth Lerer, interviewed by Jill Abramson, New York, December 2, 2015.

103 *He wrote to his staff*: Jonah Peretti, "BuzzFeed's Strategy," *Cdixon* (blog), July 24, 2012, http://cdixon.org/2012/07/24/buzzfeeds-strategy/.

103 *He would explain this watershed moment*: Jonah Peretti, presentation to the University of Florida, March 2014, https://www.muckrock.com/news/archives/2014/may/12/buzzfeed-founder-quality-religions-dont-just-go-vi/.

104 *This was a welcome departure*: Fred Vogelstein, "The Wired Interview: Facebook's Mark Zuckerberg," Wired, June 29, 2009, https://www.wired.com/2009/06/mark-zuckerberg-speaks/.

105 *"If I had to guess*: John Cassidy, "Me Media," *New Yorker*, May 15, 2006, https://www.newyorker.com/magazine/2006/05/15/me-media.

105 *Five years after its public launch*: Smriti Bhagat et al., "Three and a Half Degrees of Separation," Facebook Research, February 4, 2016, https://research.fb.com/three-and-a-half-degrees-of-separation/.

106 *Some reports cited this number*: Marie Page, "Cracking Facebook's News Feed Algorithm: A New Definition of Edgerank," Digiterati, October 26, 2016, https://thedigiterati.com/cracking-facebooks-news-feed-algorithm-new-definition-edgerank/.

106 *Its prescriptions were based*: Kristoffer Nelson, "Facebook News Feed Algorithm Unlocked: Optimizing for Greater Reach, Engagement," Adweek, September 14, 2017, https://www.adweek.com/digital/kristoffer-nelson-srax-guest-post-facebook-news-feed-algorithm/.

106 *Zuckerberg summarized it*: David Kirkpatrick, *The Facebook Effect: The Inside Story of the Company That Is Connecting the World* (New York: Simon & Schuster, 2010).

106 *In short order it became:* E. Hargittai, "Whose Space? Differences among Users and Non-users of Social Network Sites," *Journal of Computer-Mediated Communication* 13, no. 1 (2008): 276–297; S. Jones and S. Fox, "Generations Online in 2009," Data memo, Pew Internet and American Life Project, from. http://www.pewinternet.org/w/media//Files/Reports/2009/PIP_Generations_2009.pdf.

107 *On February 9, 2009*: Dan Smith, "Facebook Developing Alternative to 'Like' Button for Users to Express Empathy, Mark Zuckerberg Says," ABC, September 15, 2015, http://www.abc.net.au/news/2015-09-16/facebook-gives-thumbs-up-for-like-button-alternative/6779400.

107 *Over one billion likes*: Stephanie Buck, "The History of Facebook's Developer Platform (INFOGRAPHIC)," Mashable, May 24, 2012, https://mashable.com/2012/05/24/facebook-developer-platform-infographic/#nY78UD.XQZqP.

107 *"The Like button*: Matt Stopera, interviewed by Jill Abramson and John Stillman, Buzzfeed New York, September 1, 2015.

108 *It was a sentiment that would infuse*: "Writer, Lists & Quizzes, BuzzFeed, New York, NY," Entertainment Careers (job listing), n.d., https://www.entertainmentcareers.net/buzzfeed/writer-lists-and-quizzes/job/227249/.

108 *"People are looking*: Niklas Wirminghause, "LOL, WIN, OMG: BuzzFeed's Jonah Peretti Justifies His Site's Existence (interview)," Venturevillage, March 3, 2014, https://venturebeat.com/2014/03/03/lol-win-omg-buzzfeed-jonah-peretti-justifies-his-sites-existence-interview/.

108 *In praise of Zuckerberg's*: Matthew Lynch, "The Jolly, Abrupt, WTF Rise of BuzzFeed," *M Magazine*, n.d., http://mmagazine.tumblr.com/post/45911798703 /the-jolly-abrupt-wtf-rise-of-buzzfeed.

109 *Later, when BuzzFeed finally*: Andrew Beaujon, "BuzzFeed Names Isaac Fitzgerald Its First Books Editor," Poynter, November 7, 2013, https://www.poynter.org /news/buzzfeed-names-isaac-fitzgerald-its-first-books-editor.

109 *The success of the venture*: Noah Robischon, "How BuzzFeed's Jonah Peretti Is Building a 100-Year Media Company," Fast Company, February 16, 2016, https:// www.fastcompany.com/3056057/how-buzzfeeds-jonah-peretti-is-building-a-100 -year-media-company.

109 *BuzzFeed had invented*: Andy Serwer, "Inside the Mind of Jonah Peretti," *Fortune*, December 6, 2013, http://fortune.com/2013/12/05/inside-the-mind-of-jonah-peretti/.

110 *He brought in volunteers*: Power to the Pixel, "A Report from the Front Lines of Media Impact Evaluation—John S. Johnson, BuzzFeed and the Harmony Institute," Vimeo (video), October 27, 2014, https://vimeo.com/110129974; Michael Cieply, "Adding Punch to Influence Public Opinion," *New York Times*, July 25, 2010, https://www.nytimes.com/2010/07/26/business/26adco.html.

110 *By 2013 the network boasted*: Andrew Rice, "Does BuzzFeed Know the Secret?," *New York*, April 7, 2013, http://nymag.com/nymag/features/buzzfeed-2013-4 /index4.html; "BuzzFeed Reaches More Than 130 Million Unique Visitors in November," BuzzFeedPress, December 2, 2013, https://www.buzzfeed.com/buzz feedpress/buzzfeed-reaches-more-than-130-million-unique-visitors-in-no?utm_ term=.xnLjMyQOP#.iv3VEbLPo.

110 *To keep them happy*: Charlie Warzel, "BuzzFeed Report to Publishing Partners Demonstrates Power of Social Web," Adweek, August 29, 2012, https://www.ad week.com/digital/buzzfeed-report-publishing-partners-demonstrates-power-so cial-web-143194/.

111 *In the aftermath of the tragedy*: Matt Stopera, "10 Reasons Everyone Should Be Furious about Trayvon Martin's Murder," BuzzFeed, March 22, 2012, https:// www.buzzfeed.com/mjs538/10-reasons-everyone-should-be-furious-about-tray vo?utm_term=.ljpAYDyo6#.mkoBlNqD7.

111 *Another Stopera post*: Matt Stopera, "Florida Representative Frederica Wilson's Emotional Speech about Trayvon Martin's Shooting," BuzzFeed, March 22, 2012, https://www.buzzfeed.com/mjs538/florida-representative-frederica-wilsons-emo tiona?utm_term=.sf646XVkq#.avZpyPEmb.

111 *Additional headlines hawked*: Adrian Carrasquillo, "George Zimmerman Court Case Takes Emotional Turn as Photo of Trayvon Martin's Body Shown to Jury," BuzzFeedNews, June 25, 2013, https://www.buzzfeednews.com/article/adrian carrasquillo/george-zimmerman-court-case-takes-emotional-turn-as-photo-of; Adrian Carrasquillo, "Closing Arguments in George Zimmerman Trial Appeal to Emotion, Justice," BuzzFeedNews, July 12, 2013, https://www.buzzfeednews .com/article/adriancarrasquillo/closing-arguments-in-george-zimmerman-trial -appeal-to-emotio; Adrian Carrasquillo, "George Zimmerman Is Selling a 'Justice

for All' Original Painting on eBay," BuzzFeedNews, December 16, 2013, https://www.buzzfeednews.com/article/adriancarrasquillo/george-zimmerman-is-selling-a-justice-for-all-original-paint; "Jamie Foxx Serenades Trayvon Martin's Parents at Vigil," BuzzFeedNews, February 26, 2013, https://www.buzzfeednews.com/article/nowthisnews/jamie-foxx-serenades-trayvon-martins-parents-at-v-749g; Ryan Broderick, "Bruce Springsteen Dedicated 'American Skin (41 Shots)' to Trayvon Martin," BuzzFeed, July 17, 2013, https://www.buzzfeed.com/ryanhatesthis/bruce-springsteen-dedicated-american-skin-41-shots-to-trayvo?utm_term=.logWYJzeo#.xbYpqkAOy.

111 *He knew that in order*: Jonah Peretti, interviewed by Jill Abramson and John Stillman at BuzzFeed New York, December 14, 2015.

111 *Understanding this, Peretti*: Nic Newman, "Overview and Key Findings of the 2016 Report," Digital News Report, Reuters Institute, n.d., http://www.digitalnewsreport.org/survey/2016/overview-key-findings-2016/.

111 *This was a strategy he proselytized*: Ian Burrell, "BuzzFeed's Jonah Peretti: News Publishers Only Have Themselves to Blame for Losing Out to Google and Facebook," Drum, June 29, 2017, https://www.thedrum.com/opinion/2017/06/29/buzzfeeds-jonah-peretti-news-publishers-only-have-themselves-blame-losing-out.

112 *"The web is ruled*: Jonah Peretti, "Mormons, Mullets, and Maniacs," New York Viral Media Meetup, August 12, 2010, https://www.scribd.com/document/35836865/Jonah-Peretti-Viral-Meetup-Talk.

112 *If he could succeed this way*: Clive Thompson, "Is the Tipping Point Toast?," Fast Company, February 1, 2008, https://www.fastcompany.com/641124/tipping-point-toast.

112 *"The lesson here*: Zach Baron, "Where the Wild Things Go Viral," *GQ*, March 4, 2014, https://www.gq.com/story/buzzfeed-beastmaster-profile-march-2014.

112 *The main idea*: "Does 'Going Viral' Actually Result in More Conversions?," ConversionXL, August 11, 2017, https://conversionxl.com/blog/going-viral-increased-conversions/.

112 *When it came to posting*: Nick Kubinski, "6 Tricks to Be a Social Media Pro," BuzzFeed (video), September 9, 2014, https://www.buzzfeed.com/nickkubinski/6-tricks-to-be-a-social-media-pro?utm_term=.gu2MxPW1G#.eb3Z5PdQo.

112 *They knew that, for whatever reason*: BuzzFeed International Editorial Meeting, observed by Jill Abramson and John Stillman, New York, October 28, 2015.

113 *They reckoned that 92 percent*: Alex Campbell and Kendall Taggart, interviewed by Jill Abramson and John Stillman at BuzzFeed New York, October 2015.

113 *She returned to New York*: Christine Lagorio-Chafkin, "Meet BuzzFeed's Secret Weapon," *Inc.*, September 2, 2014, https://www.inc.com/christine-lagorio/buzzfeed-secret-growth-weapon.html.

113 *The challenge for Nguyen*: Noah Robischon, "What BuzzFeed's Dao Nguyen Knows about Data, Intuition, and the Future of Media," Fast Company, February 17, 2016, https://www.fastcompany.com/3055894/what-buzzfeeds-dao-nguyen-knows-about-data-intuition-and-the-futur.

113 *Nguyen got to work*: Dao Nguyen, interviewed by Jill Abramson and John Stillman at BuzzFeed New York, December 14, 2015.

113 *Her team created*: Mathew Ingram, "BuzzFeed Opens Up Access to Its Viral
Dashboard," Gigaom, September 2, 2010, https://gigaom.com/2010/09/02/buzz
feed-opens-up-access-to-its-viral-dashboard/.

113 *This was called Social Lift*: Dao Nguyen and Ky Harlin, "How BuzzFeed Thinks
about Data Science," BuzzFeed, September 24, 2014, https://www.buzzfeed.com
/daozers/how-buzzfeed-thinks-about-data-science?utm_term=.cuPg946z1#
.uqLpMYjOL.

113 *The dashboard offered more than*: Felix Oberholzer-Gee, "BuzzFeed—The Promise of Native Advertising," Harvard Business School Case 714-512, June 2014
(revised August 2014), 539; Christine Lagorio-Chafkin, "Meet BuzzFeed's Secret Weapon," *Inc.*, September 2, 2014, https://www.inc.com/christine-lagorio
/buzzfeed-secret-growth-weapon.html.

114 *In her first two years*: Christine Lagorio-Chafkin, "Meet BuzzFeed's Secret
Weapon," *Inc.*, September 2, 2014, https://www.inc.com/christine-lagorio/buzz
feed-secret-growth-weapon.html.

114 *"There's the misconception*: Jonah Peretti, interviewed by Jill Abramson and John
Stillman at Buzzfeed New York, December 14, 2015.

114 *"The viral distribution strategy*: Jonah Peretti and BuzzFeed, "Ignition: How to
Make Your Content Go Insanely Viral," SlideShare, December 16, 2010, https://
www.slideshare.net/Ignition/ignition-how-to-make-your-content-go-insanely
-viral-by-jonah-perettibuzzfeed.

114 *While other publishers spent 95 percent*: Angela Haggerty, "Humour, Nostalgia
and Value—BuzzFeed Shares Its Branded Content Lessons," Drum, July 29, 2014,
https://www.thedrum.com/news/2014/07/29/humour-nostalgia-and-value-buzz
feed-shares-its-branded-content-lessons.

114 *He told a Gainesville*: Jonah Peretti, presentation to the University of Florida,
March, 2014, https://www.muckrock.com/news/archives/2014/may/12/buzzfeed
-founder-quality-religions-dont-just-go-vi/.

115 *"Which is better*: Jonah Peretti, "Mormons, Mullets, and Maniacs," presentation accompanying speech delivered to New York Viral Media Meetup, August
12, 2010, https://www.scribd.com/document/35836865/Jonah-Peretti-Viral-Meetup
-Talk.

115 *It was an entrepreneurial philosophy*: Jonah Peretti, "Capitalism and Schizophrenia," *Negations*, January 1, 1996, http://www.datawranglers.com/negations/issues
/96w/96w_peretti.html.

115 *Hence the deluge*: Sara Rubin, "Weird Thoughts You Have in the Shower," BuzzFeed
(video), January 20, 2015, https://www.buzzfeed.com/sararubin/weird-thoughts
-you-have-in-the-shower; Molly Hora, "Why You Should Run a 5K," Buzz-
Feed, September 25, 2012, https://www.buzzfeed.com/mollykateri/14-reasons
-you-should-run-a-5k-421u; Matt Stopera, "40 Things That Will Make You Feel
Old," BuzzFeed, May 11, 2011, https://www.buzzfeed.com/mjs538/40-things-that

-will-make-you-feel-old; MelisBuzzFeed, "20 Ways to Tell Someone Secretly Hates You," BuzzFeed, March 20, 2011, https://www.buzzfeed.com/melismash able/20-ways-to-tell-someone-secretly-hates-you?utm_term=.mfAblQ1pA# .aneak8Bwn; Michael Blackmon, "31 Thoughts You Have When Your Mom Doesn't Answer Your Phone Calls," BuzzFeed, August 30, 2015, https://www .buzzfeed.com/michaelblackmon/mom-pick-up-the-phone-please?utm_term= .yw9zx8ZrO#.vbPB9olyW.

115 *The idea was that by narrowing*: Jen White, interviewed by Jill Abramson and John Stillman at BuzzFeed Motion Pictures, Los Angeles, March 15, 2016.

115 *In this, Stopera was king*: Matt Stopera, interviewed by Jill Abramson and John Stillman at BuzzFeed New York, September 1, 2015.

116 *He dubbed it*: Ibid.

116 *One might suspect aiming low*: Matt Stopera, Dave Stopera, and Lauren Yapal- ater, "24 Pictures That Prove Teenage Girls Are the Future," BuzzFeed, January 25, 2017, https://www.buzzfeed.com/mjs538/teens-r-the-future; Matt Stopera and Brian Galindo, "19 Pictures That Show the Difference between Your Life and Mariah Carey's," BuzzFeed, January 9, 2017, https://www.buzzfeed.com/mjs538 /i-want-to-be-mariah-carey.

116 *Without a trace of ennui*: Matt Stopera, interviewed by Jill Abramson and John Stillman at BuzzFeed New York, September 1, 2015.

116 *Most of them, even*: Dao Nguyen, "What It's Like to Work on BuzzFeed's Tech Team During Record Traffic," BuzzFeed, February 27, 2015, https://www.buzz feed.com/daozers/what-its-like-to-work-on-buzzfeeds-tech-team-during-record -t#.pc6GG2E5O.

116 *This was BuzzFeed's culture*: Jane Martinson, "BuzzFeed's Jonah Peretti: How the Great Entertainer Got Serious," *Guardian*, November 15, 2015, https://www .theguardian.com/media/2015/nov/15/buzzfeed-jonah-peretti-facebook-ads.

116 *Every afternoon they sent out*: Arabelle Sicardi, interviewed by Jill Abramson, New York, July 16, 2015.

116 *Notching 10 posts*: BuzzFeed International Editorial Meeting, observed by Jill Abramson and John Stillman, New York, October 28, 2015.

116 *A few ascended*: Tanner Greenring, Scott Lamb, Jack Shepherd, Matt Stopera, and Peggy Wang, interviewed by Jill Abramson and John Stillman, New York, June 26, 2015.

116 *BuzzFeed had a glossary*: Ibid.

117 *One former staff writer*: Arabelle Sicardi, interviewed by Jill Abramson, New York, July 16, 2015.

117 *Faced with an unbudging*: Ibid.

117 *There were three types of list*: Matt Stopera, interviewed by Jill Abramson and John Stillman at BuzzFeed New York, August 2015.

118 *Among the subjects it claimed*: Tahlia Pritchard, "15 Aussie Moments That Restored Your Faith in Humanity in 2015," BuzzFeed, December 22, 2015, https://www .buzzfeed.com/tahliapritchard/its-just-emotions-taking-me-over; Alan White, "This

Man Eating a Muffin in the Background of a Labour MP's Interview Will Restore Your Faith in Humanity," BuzzFeedNews, May 7, 2015, https://www.buzzfeed.com /alanwhite/literally-me?utm_term=.ugGBZvEVA#.yyGaDEQkY.

118 *As Stopera put it*: Matt Stopera, interviewed by Jill Abramson and John Stillman at BuzzFeed New York, August 2015.

118 *By enumerating the human emotions*: Matt Stopera, interviewed by Jill Abramson and John Stillman at BuzzFeed New York, August 2015.

118 *"Like, '10 ways*: Ibid.

118 *It achieved the ends*: Matt Sitman, "This Is Your Brain on BuzzFeed," Dish, September 2, 2013, http://dish.andrewsullivan.com/2013/09/02/this-is-your-brain-on -buzzfeed-or-the-lists-we-live-by-new-yorker-8-29/.

118 *"If we take the same point*: Susie Mesure, "Jonah Peretti: And at Number One on BuzzFeed's List Is . . . ," *Independent*, October 20, 2013, https://www.independent.co.uk/news/people/profiles/jonah-peretti-and-at-number-one-on-buzzfeeds -list-is-8891785.html.

119 *"Lists are an amazing way*: Jonah Peretti, memo to the BuzzFeed team, published on LinkedIn, September 4, 2013, https://www.linkedin.com/pulse/2013090 4212907-1799428-memo-to-the-buzzfeed-team/.

119 *"You could call that*: Caroline O'Donovan, "The 3 Key Types of BuzzFeed Lists to Learn before You Die," NiemanLab, October 11, 2013, http://www.niemanlab .org/2013/10/the-3-key-types-of-buzzfeed-lists-to-learn-before-you-die/.

119 *Summer Anne Burton:* Caroline O'Donovan, "Are Quizzes the New Lists? What BuzzFeed's Latest Viral Success Means for Publishing," NiemanLab, February 19, 2014, http://www.niemanlab.org/2014/02/are-quizzes-the-new-lists-what-buzz feeds-latest-viral-success-means-for-publishing/.

120 *By answering the eight simple*: Jenn Selby, "Rupert Murdoch Took the 'Which Billionaire Tycoon Are You?' Test . . . and Got Himself," *Independent*, February 13, 2014, https://www.independent.co.uk/news/people/news/rupert-murdoch-got -when-he-took-the-which-billionaire-tycoon-are-you-test-and-got-himself -9126736.html.

120 *This was what they called*: Matt Stopera, interviewed by Jill Abramson and John Stillman at Buzzfeed New York, August 2015.

120 *In 2008 Peretti laid out*: Jason Del Rey, "BuzzFeed's 2008 Investor Pitch: See Jonah Peretti's Predictions, Right and Wrong," *AdAge*, April 12, 2013, http:// adage.com/article/media/buzzfeed-s-2008-investor-pitch-jonah-peretti-s-predic tions/240861/.

120 *To promote the idea of shareability*: Philip Bump, "One Secret to BuzzFeed's Viral Success: Buying Ads," *Atlantic*, April 8, 2013, https://www.theatlantic.com /national/archive/2013/04/one-secret-buzzfeeds-viral-success-buying-ads/316 513/.

121 *He estimated that when*: Felix Oberholzer-Gee, "BuzzFeed—The Promise of Native Advertising," *Harvard Business Review*, June 17, 2014, https://hbr.org/prod uct/buzzfeed-the-promise-of-native-advertising/714512-PDF-ENG.

121 *He pointed to data showing*: Stine Andersen, "Video: BuzzFeed on How to Make Native Advertising Go Viral," Native Advertising Institute, n.d., https://nativead vertisinginstitute.com/blog/make-native-advertising-go-viral/.

121 *In the beginning "there was*: Tanner Greenring, Scott Lamb, Jack Shepherd, Matt Stopera, and Peggy Wang, interviewed by Jill Abramson and John Stillman, New York, June 26, 2015.

121 *"Some editorial content*: Andrew Rice, "Does BuzzFeed Know the Secret?," *New York*, April 7, 2013, http://nymag.com/nymag/features/buzzfeed-2013-4/index4 .html.

121 *Try "10 Date Ideas*: Bud Light—Whatever, USA, "10 Date Ideas That'll Take Your Game to the Next Level," BuzzFeed, July 29, 2014, https://www.buzzfeed .com/budlightwhateverusa/date-ideas-thatll-take-your-game-to-the-next-level.

121 *Here are "20 Tactics*: Bravo, "20 Tactics to Help You Find a Husband," Buzz-Feed, June 6, 2013, https://www.buzzfeed.com/bravo/20-tactics-to-help-you-find -a-husband?utm_term=.yrXgZ8zP1#.qxQxMQEgb.

121 *Consider this recipe*: Walmart, "Holiday Ham Ring," BuzzFeed, December 14, 2016, https://www.buzzfeed.com/walmart/holiday-ham-ring?utm_term=.rqkz6nr B2#.ww5JmR78k.

122 *As BuzzFeed's current president*: Greg Coleman, interviewed by Jill Abramson and John Stillman at BuzzFeed New York, September 25, 2015.

122 *"Dear Kitten" was widely considered*: Rebecca Cullers, " 'Dear Kitten' from Friskies Proves Cats Still Rule the Internet," Adweek, June 12, 2014, https://www .adweek.com/creativity/dear-kitten-friskies-proves-cats-still-rule-internet-158285/.

122 *The sage elder cat's advice*: Dee Robertson, interviewed by Jill Abramson and John Stillman at BuzzFeed Motion Pictures, Los Angeles, March 16, 2016.

123 *When AOL acquired Huffington Post*: "AOL Agrees to Acquire the Huffington Post," Huffington Post, February 7, 2011, https://www.huffingtonpost.com/2011 /02/07/aol-huffington-post_n_819375.html.

123 *"We had this huge hole*: Felix Salmon, "BuzzFeed's Jonah Peretti Goes Long," Matter, June 11, 2014, https://medium.com/matter/buzzfeeds-jonah-peretti-goes -long-e98cf13160e7.

123 *By 2011 revenues were over*: J. K Trotter, "Internal Documents Show Buzz-Feed's Skyrocketing Investment in Editorial," Gawker, August 12, 2015, http:// tktk.gawker.com/internal-documents-show-buzzfeed-s-skyrocketing-investm -1709816353.

123 *But even the king of the listicle*: Felix Salmon, "BuzzFeed's Jonah Peretti Goes Long," Matter, June 11, 2014, https://medium.com/matter/buzzfeeds-jonah-peretti -goes-long-e98cf13160e7.

123 *He had seen success*: Matt Stopera, interviewed by Jill Abramson and John Still-man at BuzzFeed New York, August 2015.

123 *Stopera published "The 45*: Matt Stopera, "The 45 Most Powerful Images of 2011," BuzzFeed, December 2, 2011, https://www.buzzfeed.com/mjs538/the-most -powerful-photos-of-2011.

124 *The post was widely shared:* Megan Garber, "How BuzzFeed Got Its Biggest Traf-

fic Day . . . Ever," NiemanLab, December 5, 2011, http://www.niemanlab.org /2011/12/how-buzzfeed-got-its-biggest-traffic-day-ever/.

124 *"Okay," Peretti thought*: Felix Salmon, "BuzzFeed's Jonah Peretti Goes Long," Matter, June 11, 2014, https://medium.com/matter/buzzfeeds-jonah-peretti-goes -long-e98cf13160e7.

124 *"The reason people are coming*: Tom McGeveran, "The Ben Smith Hire, and Jonah Peretti's Plan to Take BuzzFeed Way beyond Glurge," Politico, December 13, 2011, https://www.politico.com/states/new-york/city-hall/story/2011/12 /the-ben-smith-hire-and-jonah-perettis-plan-to-take-buzzfeed-way-beyond-glurge -000000.

125 *Peretti pointed to Ted Turner*: Ben Popper and Peter Kafka, "BuzzFeed vs. Trump," The Verge, February 7, 2017, https://www.theverge.com/2017/2/7/14531510 /buzzfeed-news-trump-dossier-defamation-lawsuit-jonah-peretti-interview.

125 *Ad execs "respect companies*: Ibid.

125 *At Yale he'd interned*: Ben Smith, interviewed by Jill Abramson, New York, July 13, 2015.

126 *From there he went to the tabloid*: Ben Smith, "Parties' Pols Vie to Catch Bloomy Aye," *New York Daily News*, May 8, 2006, http://www.nydailynews.com/archives /news/parties-pols-vie-catch-bloomy-aye-article-1.648386.

126 *He established a Politicker-esque*: Ben Smith, "Remainders: Vapid," *New York Daily News*, *The Daily Politics* (blog), December 14, 2006, http://archive.li /NgQeE.

126 *Politico's posture as*: Brian Ries, "The Ben Smith Flame War," Daily Beast, September 12, 2010, https://www.thedailybeast.com/the-ben-smith-flame-war.

126 *Operating as a one-man*: Ben Smith, "A Haircut Tip," Politico (blog), November 10, 2009, https://www.politico.com/blogs/ben-smith/2009/11/a-haircut-tip-022732; Ben Smith, "Rudy Calls Billing 'Perfectly Appropriate,'" Politico, November 29, 2007, https://www.politico.com/story/2007/11/rudy-calls-billing-perfectly-appro priate-007104.

126 *He thrived on the speedy*: Dylan Byers, "Can Politico Win Again?," Adweek, September 6, 2011, https://www.adweek.com/digital/can-politico-win-again-134592/.

126 *"I could sit at*: Liz Cox Barrett, "Immediate Returns," *Columbia Journalism Review*, November–December 2011, https://archives.cjr.org/feature/immediate_re turns.php.

126 *Smith began to earn*: Megan Garber, "'A Very Natural Thing for Me': Politico Reporter Ben Smith on His Move to BuzzFeed," NiemanLab, December 12, 2011, http://www.niemanlab.org/2011/12/a-very-natural-thing-for-me-politico-reporter -ben-smith-on-his-move-to-buzzfeed/.

126 *When Peretti got in touch*: Peter Himler, "Is Twitter Influence Portable?," *Forbes*, December 27, 2011, https://www.forbes.com/sites/peterhimler/2011/12/27/is-twitter -influence-portable/#6a21402bfd79; Adam Clark Estes, "The Mystery Team That Recruited Ben Smith to BuzzFeed," *Atlantic*, December 12, 2011, https://www .theatlantic.com/business/archive/2011/12/mystery-team-recruited-ben-smith -buzzfeed/334422/.

127   *"There was a lot of very abstract*: Peter Kafka, "BuzzFeed's Jonah Peretti and Ben Smith Explain How They Turned a 'Great Cat Site' into a Powerful Publisher," Recode, June 12, 2015, https://www.recode.net/2015/6/12/11563480/buzz feeds-jonah-peretti-and-ben-smith-on-the-dress-disappearing-posts.

127   *"I could never do*: Adam Clark Estes, "The Mystery Team That Recruited Ben Smith to BuzzFeed," *Atlantic*, December 12, 2011, https://www.theatlantic.com /business/archive/2011/12/mystery-team-recruited-ben-smith-buzzfeed/334422/.

127   *He took a couple of days*: Ibid.

127   *"I hope I didn't*: Ben Smith email to Jonah Peretti and Kenneth Lerer, October 29, 2011.

128   *On his first day*: Gabriel Sherman, "BuzzFeed: The New Species at Iowa's Media Watering Hole," *New York*, January 2, 2012, http://nymag.com/daily/intelligencer /2012/01/ben-smith-on-buzzfeeds-plan-to-cover-politics.html.

128   *With the other pool reporters*: Ibid.

128   *"I like cat pictures*: David Zax, "WTF, Indeed: Politico's Ben Smith Joins BuzzFeed to Build a 'Social News Organization,'" Fast Company, December 13, 2011, https://www.fastcompany.com/1800780/wtf-indeed-politicos-ben-smith-joins -buzzfeed-build-social-news-organization.

128   *"We're not starting*: Adam Clark Estes, "The Mystery Team That Recruited Ben Smith to BuzzFeed," *Atlantic*, December 12, 2011, https://www.theatlantic.com /business/archive/2011/12/mystery-team-recruited-ben-smith-buzzfeed/334422/.

129   *Miller and Stopera had spent*: Gabriel Sherman, "BuzzFeed: The New Species at Iowa's Media Watering Hole," *New York*, January 2, 2012, http://nymag.com/daily /intelligencer/2012/01/ben-smith-on-buzzfeeds-plan-to-cover-politics.html.

129   *While Stopera composed*: Matt Stopera, "29 Things I Learned from Spending Two Days with Rick Santorum," BuzzFeedNews, January 2, 2012, https://www.buzz feednews.com/article/mjs538/29-things-i-leaned-from-spending-two-days-with-ric.

129   *That day he released a snippet*: Andrew Kaczynski, "Here Is Rick Santorum Dancing the Polka," BuzzFeedNews (video), January 1, 2012, https://www.buzz feednews.com/article/andrewkaczynski/here-is-rick-santorum-dancing-the-polka #.iiiLip3ED.

129   *His excavations laid bare*: Jeff Sonderman, "How BuzzFeed's Andrew Kaczynski Mines the Internet for Video Gold," Poynter, March 20, 2012, https://www.poyn ter.org/news/how-buzzfeeds-andrew-kaczynski-mines-internet-video-gold.

129   *A profile in* New York *magazine*: Jason Zengerie, "Playing with Mud," *New York*, December 11, 2011, http://nymag.com/news/intelligencer/andrew-kaczynski-2011-12/.

129   *Josh Marshall's Talking Points*: Benjy Sarlin, "Meet the 22-Year-Old Who's Driving Romney Crazy," Talking Points Memo, December 13, 2011, https://talking pointsmemo.com/election2012/meet-the-22-year-old-who-s-driving-romney -crazy.

129   *Kaczynski was looking*: Politinerds Radio, "#39: BuzzFeed's Andrew Kaczynski," *Spreaker* (podcast), 35:07, n.d., https://www.spreaker.com/user/thebingedotnet /politinerds-39-buzzfeeds-andrew-kaczynsk.

129 *"I told Ben*: McKay Coppins, Rosie Gray, Andrew Kaczynski, and Ben Smith, interviewed by Jill Abramson and John Stillman, New York, July 13, 2015.

129 *About a week into 2012*: Dino Grandoni, "BuzzFeed Lands $15.5 Million in Financing," *Atlantic*, January 9, 2012, https://www.theatlantic.com/business/archive /2012/01/buzzfeed-lands-155-million-financing/333343/.

129 *The money was needed*: Joe Coscarelli, "BuzzFeed Raises $15.5 Million for Ben Smith Makeover," *New York*, January 9, 2012, http://nymag.com/daily/intelli gencer/2012/01/buzzfeed-raises-155-million-for-makeover.html.

130 *"It's so expensive*: Alexia Tsotsis, "Viral Aggregator BuzzFeed Raises $15.5M to Transform the Way People Get Their News," TechCrunch, January 9, 2012, https://techcrunch.com/2012/01/09/viral-aggregator-buzzfeed-raises-15-5m-to -transform-the-way-people-get-their-news/.

130 *Instead of angling for reporters*: McKay Coppins, Rosie Gray, Andrew Kaczynski, and Ben Smith, interviewed by Jill Abramson and John Stillman, New York, July 13, 2015.

130 *It was a headhunting strategy*: Ben Smith, interviewed by Jill Abramson and John Stillman, New York, July 23, 2015.

130 *One hire was Rosie Gray*: McKay Coppins, Rosie Gray, Andrew Kaczynski, and Ben Smith, interviewed by Jill Abramson and John Stillman, New York, July 13, 2015.

130 *Another was McKay Coppins*: Ibid.

130 *He was best known for*: Michael Hastings, "The Runaway General: The Profile That Brought Down McChrystal," *Rolling Stone*, June 22, 2010, https://www.roll ingstone.com/politics/politics-news/the-runaway-general-the-profile-that-brought -down-mcchrystal-192609/.

130 *Hastings, Smith said, was*: McKay Coppins, Rosie Gray, Andrew Kaczynski, and Ben Smith, interviewed by Jill Abramson and John Stillman, New York, July 13, 2015.

130 *His masterwork*: Ben Smith, "The Book That Defined Modern Campaign Reporting," Politico, December 30, 2010, https://www.politico.com/story/2010/12/the -book-that-defined-modern-campaign-reporting-046906.

130 *Their ranks included*: Max Read, "Weird Internets: A Conversation with 'Online Curiosity Collector' Katie Notopoulos," Gawker, January 25, 2012, http://gawker .com/5877893/weird-internets-a-conversation-with-online-curiosity-collector -katie-notopoulos.

131 *After starting her job*: Matthew Lynch, "The Jolly, Abrupt, WTF Rise of Buzz-Feed," *M Magazine*, n.d., http://mmagazine.tumblr.com/post/45911798703/the -jolly-abrupt-wtf-rise-of-buzzfeed.

131 *"They were undercredentialed:* McKay Coppins, Rosie Gray, Andrew Kaczynski, and Ben Smith, interviewed by Jill Abramson and John Stillman, New York, July 13, 2015.

131 *On the third day of 2012*: Ben Smith, interviewed by Jill Abramson and John Stillman, New York, July 23, 2015.

131 *The* Observer *ran a story*: Adrianne Jeffries, "BuzzFeed Scooped CNN Last

Night," *Observer*, January 4, 2012, http://observer.com/2012/01/buzzfeed-scooped
-cnn-last-night/.

131 *Gray remembers how preposterous*: McKay Coppins, Rosie Gray, Andrew
Kaczynski, and Ben Smith, interviewed by Jill Abramson and John Stillman, New
York, July 13, 2015.

131 *Within a month he had discovered*: Andrew Kaczynski, "The Book on Mitt Romney: Here Is John McCain's Entire Opposition Research File," BuzzFeedNews,
January 17, 2012, https://www.buzzfeednews.com/article/andrewkaczynski/the
-book-on-mitt-romney-here-is-john-mccains-ent.

132 *He also tracked down*: "Q&A with Andrew Kaczynski," C-SPAN (video), 58:03,
August 16, 2012, https://www.c-span.org/video/?307609-1/qa-andrew-kaczynski.

132 *Another video was of Romney*: Jason Zengerie, "Playing with Mud," *New York*, December 11, 2011, http://nymag.com/news/intelligencer/andrew-kaczynski-2011-12/.

132 *Coppins, meanwhile, chased down*: McKay Coppins, Rosie Gray, Andrew
Kaczynski, and Ben Smith, interviewed by Jill Abramson and John Stillman, New
York, July 13, 2015.

132 *Coppins did as he was told*: McKay Coppins, "Exclusive: Marco Rubio's Mormon Roots," BuzzFeedNews, February 23, 2012, https://www.buzzfeednews.com
/article/mckaycoppins/exclusive-marco-rubios-mormon-roots.

132 *Smith's story about the McCain*: Matthew Lynch, "The Jolly, Abrupt, WTF Rise of
BuzzFeed," *M Magazine*, n.d., http://mmagazine.tumblr.com/post/45911798703
/the-jolly-abrupt-wtf-rise-of-buzzfeed.

132 *As Peretti told the* Atlantic: Adam Clark Estes, "The Future of BuzzFeed Looks
Like a Newsier Facebook News Feed," *Atlantic*, January 25, 2012, https://www
.theatlantic.com/business/archive/2012/01/future-buzzfeed-looks-newsier-face
book-news-feed/332628/.

132 *During one leg*: Robin Abcarian, "Michael Hastings: The Importance of Not Following the Rules," *Los Angeles Times*, June 19, 2013, http://www.latimes.com
/local/lanow/la-me-ln-michael-hastings-the-importance-of-not-following-the
-rules-20130619-story.html.

132 *The tense back-and-forth:* "Hillary Clinton Aide Tells Reporter to 'Fuck Off' and
'Have a Good Life,'" BuzzFeedNews, September 24, 2012, https://www.buzz
feednews.com/article/buzzfeedpolitics/hillary-clinton-aide-tells-reporter-to-fuck
-off.

133 *"They didn't even know*: McKay Coppins, Rosie Gray, Andrew Kaczynski, and
Ben Smith, interviewed by Jill Abramson and John Stillman, New York, July 13,
2015.

133 *Hastings, who had covered*: Matt Schudel, "Michael Hastings, Iconoclastic War
Correspondent, Dies at 33," *Washington Post*, June 19, 2013, https://www.washin
gtonpost.com/national/michael-hastings-iconoclastic-war-correspondent-dies-at
-33/2013/06/19/360c8c7c-d8f2-11e2-a9f2-42ee3912ae0e_story.html.

133 *But after 10 years sober*: Associated Press, "BuzzFeed Reporter Michael Hastings' Autopsy Reveals Traces of Drugs," *Guardian*, August 21, 2013, https://

www.theguardian.com/world/2013/aug/21/michael-hastings-buzzfeed-autopsy
-drugs.

133 *"I was caught*: Michael Hastings, *Panic 2012: The Sublime and Terrifying In-side Story of Obama's Final Campaign* (New York: BuzzFeed/Blue Rider Press, 2013).

133 *The challenge Smith issued*: "How BuzzFeed Is Reinventing the Wire Story for the Social Web," MyPRSA, July 27, 2012, http://apps.prsa.org/SearchResults /view/9866/105/How_Buzzfeed_is_reinventing_the_wire_story_for_the#.W1gZZ dhKg1g.

134 *At Politico reporters were trained*: Ben Smith, "Winning the Dawn," Politico (blog), April 1, 2009, https://www.politico.com/blogs/ben-smith/2009/04/winning -the-dawn-017268.

134 *"I feel in general*: Justin Ellis, "How BuzzFeed Wants to Reinvent Wire Stories for Social Media," Nieman Lab, July 26, 2012, http://www.niemanlab.org/2012 /07/how-buzzfeed-wants-to-reinvent-wire-stories-for-social-media/.

134 *BuzzFeed's stated goal*: Ibid.

134 *Headlined "Kim Jong Un*: Jessica Testa, "Kim Jong Un Gets a Promotion," Buzz-Feed, July 18, 2012, https://www.buzzfeed.com/jtes/kim-jong-un-gets-a-promotion ?utm_term=.oeRvErnZ5#.lrA3qJWpN.

134 *From her gyroscopic*: Jessica Testa, "12 Shot Dead at 'Dark Knight Rises' Screen-ing in Colorado," BuzzFeed, July 20, 2012, https://www.buzzfeed.com/jtes/14 -dead-in-shooting-at-colo-screening-of-the-dar?utm_term=.eo5wWnMGk# .ev4DZVEPv.

134 *This method of sourcing*: Marc Tracy, "The Tweeps on the Bus," *New Republic*, August 24, 2012, https://newrepublic.com/article/106490/buzzfeed-influence -campaign-reporting.

135 *In a July 2012 memo*: Jonah Peretti, "The Top 7 Reasons BuzzFeed Is Killing It," memo to BuzzFeed Staff, *Cdixon* (blog), July 24, 2012, http://cdixon.org/2012/07 /24/buzzfeeds-strategy/.

135 *Revenue was on track*: Alyson Shontell, "BuzzFeed Surpasses 30 Million Users and Is on Track to Triple 2011 Revenue," Business Insider, July 24, 2012, https:// www.businessinsider.com/buzzfeed-surpasses-30-million-users-and-is-on-track -to-triple-2011-revenue-2012-7; Marc Tracy, "The Tweeps on the Bus," *New Re-public*, August 24, 2012, https://newrepublic.com/article/106490/buzzfeed-influ ence-campaign-reporting.

135 *Eight months into the job*: "The New York Times and BuzzFeed to Collaborate on Video Coverage of 2012 Conventions," BuzzFeed, June 18, 2012, https://www .buzzfeed.com/buzzfeedpress/the-new-york-times-and-buzzfeed-to-collaborate -on?utm_term=.bg42ZjJGE#.qad3RlLn5.

135 *"The lessons we can learn*: Marc Tracy, "The Tweeps on the Bus," *New Repub-lic*, August 24, 2012, https://newrepublic.com/article/106490/buzzfeed-influence -campaign-reporting.

136 *("We're very pro-animal*: Andrew Gauthier, "BuzzFeed on Local Tampa TV,"

YouTube (video), 2:13, August 30, 2012, https://www.youtube.com/watch?time_continue=133&v=c26gALhsrwA.

136 *Spirits flowed as some*: Erik Maza, "BuzzFeed Hosts Republican National Convention Party," WWD, August 31, 2012, https://wwd.com/business-news/media/buzzfeed-hosts-republican-national-convention-party-6212618/.

136 *As candidates Romney and Obama*: David Carr, "How Obama Tapped into Social Networks' Power," *New York Times*, November 9, 2008, https://www.nytimes.com/2008/11/10/business/media/10carr.html.

136 *In October his campaign*: Justin Ellis, "BuzzFeed Adapts Its Branded Content Approach to Political Advertising, and Obama's In," NiemanLab, October 24, 2012, http://www.niemanlab.org/2012/10/buzzfeed-adapts-its-branded-content-approach-to-political-advertising-and-obamas-in/.

136 *The native advertising team*: Ibid.

136 *One featured a stump speech*: Obama for America, "Jay-Z: 'You Are Starting to See the Power of Our Vote,'" BuzzFeed (video), October 20, 2012, https://www.buzzfeed.com/obamaforamerica/jay-z-on-the-power-of-our-voice-7i6v.

136 *Another lampooned Romney*: Obama for America, "What Mitt Romney's 'Binders Full of Women' Says about His Views," BuzzFeed (video), October, 18, 2012, https://www.buzzfeed.com/obamaforamerica/what-mitt-romneys-binders-full-of-women-s-7i6v?b=1.

137 *A year would pass*: Diane Bartz, "U.S. Says Online Ads Should Be Clearly Marked, Undeceptive," Reuters, December 4, 2013, https://www.reuters.com/article/us-usa-advertising-regulation-idUSBRE9B310420131204?feedType=RSS.

137 *Shortly after Obama was sworn in*: Andrew Sullivan, "Guess Which BuzzFeed Piece Is an Ad," Dish, February 21, 2013, http://dish.andrewsullivan.com/2013/02/21/guess-which-buzzfeed-piece-is-an-ad/.

137 *Smith challenged Sullivan*: Joe Lazauskas, "Why We'll All Stop Worrying and Learn to Love Native Ads," Contently, August 8, 2013, https://contently.com/strategist/2013/08/08/why-well-all-stop-worrying-and-love-native-ads/.

137 *Smith vehemently denied*: Andrew Sullivan, "'Enhanced Advertorial Techniques,'" Dish, January 15, 2013, http://dish.andrewsullivan.com/threads/enhanced-advertorial-techniques/.

137 *Advertisements appeared on*: Jessica Tyner, "BuzzFeed: The Future of Sponsored Content," Pandologic, August 5, 2013, https://www.pandologic.com/publishers/online_media/buzzfeed-the-future-of-sponsored-content/.

137 *When readers seemed to be*: Michelle Castillo, "BuzzFeed Changes Labels on Promoted Content," Adweek, May 30, 2014, https://www.adweek.com/digital/buzzfeed-changes-labels-promoted-content-158060/.

137 *In 2013 BuzzFeed kicked off*: Eddie Scarry, "BuzzFeed Brews: 'It's Like a First Date,'" Adweek, February 6, 2013, https://www.adweek.com/digital/buzzfeed-brews-marco-rubio-ben-smith-john-stanton/.

138 *In September, Peretti*: Jonah Peretti, "Memo to the BuzzFeed Team," LinkedIn, September 4, 2013, https://www.linkedin.com/pulse/20130904212907-1799428-memo-to-the-buzzfeed-team/.

138 *They debuted the two-part*: McKay Coppins, Rosie Gray, Andrew Kaczynski, and
Ben Smith, interviewed by Jill Abramson and John Stillman, New York, July 13,
2015.

138 *In came presidential candidate*: BuzzFeedVideo, "Ted Cruz Auditions for the
Simpsons," YouTube (video), 1:18, June 30, 2015, https://www.youtube.com/watch
?v=_KosRkvX4KE.

138 *He was followed by*: "If Men Were Treated Like Women in the Office with Carly
Fiorina (Presidential Candidate)," YouTube (video), 1:14, July 16, 2015, https://
www.youtube.com/watch?v=Tq5OQafDVxc.

138 *Then it was Governor Bobby Jindal*: BuzzFeedVideo, "Push-Up Contest with
Governor Bobby Jindal," YouTube (video), 3:42, August 4, 2015, https://www
.youtube.com/watch?v=DraW_tu5yno.

138 *Hamilton Nolan of Gawker*: Hamilton Nolan, "BuzzFeed and Bobby Jindal Try to
Out-Whore One Another," Gawker, August 5, 2015, http://gawker.com/buzzfeed
-and-bobby-jindal-try-to-out-whore-one-another-1722246888.

138 *Evidence of Smith's cleanup job*: J. K. Trotter, "Over 4,000 BuzzFeed Posts Have
Completely Disappeared," Gawker, August 12, 2014, http://gawker.com/over-4
-000-buzzfeed-posts-have-completely-disappeared-1619473070.

138 *It was a redaction*: J. K. Trotter, "Don't Ask BuzzFeed Why It Deleted Thousands
of Posts," Gawker, August 14, 2014, http://gawker.com/don-t-ask-buzzfeed-why
-it-deleted-thousands-of-posts-1621830810.

138 *"It's stuff made*: Hadas Gold, "BuzzFeed's Growing Pains," Politico, August 18,
2014, https://www.politico.com/blogs/media/2014/08/buzzfeeds-growing-pains
-194121.

139 *Unlike other newsrooms*: Shani O. Hilton, "The BuzzFeed News Standards and
Ethics Guide," BuzzFeed, January 5, 2018, https://www.buzzfeed.com/shani
/the-buzzfeed-editorial-standards-and-ethics-guide?utm_term=.fdj5J9Xpk#.tbe
65jGzO.

139 *Three posts had gone poof*: Liam Stack, "BuzzFeed Says Posts Were Deleted
Because of Advertising Pressure," *New York Times*, April 19, 2015, https://www
.nytimes.com/2015/04/20/business/media/buzzfeed-says-posts-were-deleted-be
cause-of-advertising-pressure.html.

139 *The posts were critical*: Ravi Somaiya, "BuzzFeed Restores 2 Posts Its Editor
Deleted," *New York Times*, April 10, 2015, https://www.nytimes.com/2015/04/11
/business/media/buzzfeed-restores-2-posts-its-editor-had-deleted.html.

139 *When Smith realized*: Anthony Ha, "BuzzFeed Editor-in-Chief Ben Smith Says
He 'Blew It' by Removing Post Criticizing Dove," TechCrunch, April 10, 2015,
https://techcrunch.com/2015/04/10/buzzfeed-blew-it/.

139 *If your only goal*: Marc Tracy, "The Tweeps on the Bus," *New Republic*, August
24, 2012, https://newrepublic.com/article/106490/buzzfeed-influence-campaign
-reporting.

139 *Smith was following through on*: Ben Smith email to Jonah Peretti and Kenneth
Lerer, October 29, 2011.

139 *BuzzFeed now seemed less like*: Noah Robischon, "How BuzzFeed's Jonah Per-

etti Is Building a 100-Year Media Company," Fast Company, February 16, 2016, https://www.fastcompany.com/3056057/how-buzzfeeds-jonah-peretti-is-building -a-100-year-media-company.

140 *"BuzzFeed has a major role*: Jonah Peretti, "Memo to the BuzzFeed Team," LinkedIn, September 4, 2013, https://www.linkedin.com/pulse/20130904212907 -1799428-memo-to-the-buzzfeed-team/.

140 *Geidner "came along*: Ben Smith, "Marriage Equality," BuzzFeed, June 27, 2015, https://www.buzzfeed.com/bensmith/marriage-equality?utm_term=.qlbq7BLpk# .psm5dYW1p.

140 *Other publishers treated the beat*: Andrew Beaujon, "BuzzFeed Plans to Approach LGBT Coverage with 'Same Kind of Intensity as Politics,'" Poynter, September 27, 2013, https://www.poynter.org/news/buzzfeed-plans-approach-lgbt-coverage-same -kind-intensity-politics.

140 *"We see it as*: Ibid.

140 *It involved what Smith*: Benny Johnson, "13 Young, Secular People Who Also Believe Abortion Is Wrong," Gawker, January 23, 2014, http://gawker.com /buzzfeed-s-support-of-women-s-rights-does-not-include-a-1714932571.

140 *This was house policy*: Shani O. Hilton, "The BuzzFeed News Standards and Ethics Guide," BuzzFeed, January 5, 2018, https://www.buzzfeed.com/shani/the-buzz feed-editorial-standards-and-ethics-guide?utm_term=.fdj5J9Xpk#.tbe65jGzO.

141 *"I want all that*: Matt Stopera, interviewed by Jill Abramson and John Stillman at BuzzFeed New York, November 14, 2015.

141 *Peretti threw more money*: "Lisa Tozzi Joins BuzzFeed as News Director," Buzz-Feed, April 25, 2013, https://www.buzzfeed.com/buzzfeedpress/lisa-tozzi-joins -buzzfeed-as-news-director?utm_term=.koY5lqVL4#.dav8LGRPn.

141 *It was a coup*: Joshua Benton, "In Headline Unimaginable Two Years Ago, BuzzFeed Hires Journalist from New York Times to Take On Breaking News," NiemanLab, April 25, 2013, http://www.niemanlab.org/2013/04/in-headline-un imaginable-two-years-ago-buzzfeed-hires-journalist-from-new-york-times-to -take-on-breaking-news/.

141 *Smith told Tozzi*: McKay Coppins, Rosie Gray, Andrew Kaczynski, and Ben Smith, interviewed by Jill Abramson and John Stillman, New York, July 13, 2015.

141 *He wanted her to lead*: BuzzFeedPress, "BuzzFeed Taps the Guardian's Miriam Elder as Foreign Editor," BuzzFeed, June 10, 2013, https://www.buzzfeed.com /buzzfeedpress/buzzfeed-taps-the-guardians-miriam-elder-as-foreign-editor?utm _term=.ksB4PxmdO#.cvpx52X1v.

141 *Elder received an email*: Miriam Elder, interviewed by Jill Abramson, New York, November 20, 2015.

141 *In a year Smith*: Johana Bhuiyan, "BuzzFeed Hires Pulitzer Winner Mark Schoofs to Head New Investigative Unit," Politico, October 21, 2013, https://www.politico .com/media/story/2013/10/buzzfeed-hires-pulitzer-winner-mark-schoofs-to-head -new-investigative-unit-001235.

142 *In an encouraging sign*: Kendall Taggart and Alex Campbell, "In Texas It's a

Crime to Be Poor," BuzzFeedNews, October 7, 2015, https://www.buzzfeednews
.com/article/kendalltaggart/in-texas-its-a-crime-to-be-poor.

142 *The day after it was published*: Alex Campbell and Kendall Taggart, interviewed
by Jill Abramson and John Stillman at BuzzFeed New York, October, 2015.

142 *Within two years the team*: Benjamin Mullin, "Digital Digging: How BuzzFeed
Built an Investigative Team Inside a Viral Hit Factory," Poynter, February 15, 2016,
https://www.poynter.org/news/digital-digging-how-buzzfeed-built-investigative
-team-inside-viral-hit-factory.

142 *They had relocated*: Lois Weiss, "BuzzFeed Taking the Fifth," *New York Post*,
April 24, 2013, https://nypost.com/2013/04/24/buzzfeed-taking-the-fifth/.

142 *To the web-nurtured*: John Stillman, observations during visit to BuzzFeed New
York for Super Tuesday, March 1, 2016.

143 *Her reporters stalked*: Max Seddon, "Does This Soldier's Instagram Account
Prove Russia Is Covertly Operating in Ukraine?," BuzzFeedNews, July 30, 2014,
https://www.buzzfeednews.com/article/maxseddon/does-this-soldiers-instagram
-account-prove-russia-is-covertl.

143 *"BuzzFeed understands that*: Miriam Elder, interviewed by Jill Abramson, New
York, November 20, 2015.

143 *Upon joining BuzzFeed*: Kate Aurthur interviewed by Jill Abramson and John
Stillman at BuzzFeed Motion Pictures, Los Angeles, March 16, 2016.

143 *Ken Bensinger, another* L.A. Times: Ken Bensinger interviewed by Jill Abramson
and John Stillman at BuzzFeed Motion Pictures, Los Angeles, March 2016.

143 *By February 2014*: Jennifer Saba, "Beyond Cute Cats: How BuzzFeed Is Reinventing Itself," Reuters, February 23, 2014, https://www.reuters.com/article/us
-usa-media-buzzfeed/beyond-cute-cats-how-buzzfeed-is-reinventing-itself-idUS
BREA1M0IQ20140223.

143 *BuzzFeed's journalists "aren't*: Chris Dixon, "BuzzFeed's Strategy," Business Insider, July 24, 2012, https://www.businessinsider.com/buzzfeeds-strategy-2012-10.

144 *Politico reported in 2015*: Lucia Moses, "BuzzFeed's News Is Growing, but Still
a Small Part of Its Traffic," Digiday, May 29, 2015, https://digiday.com/media/17
-percent-buzzfeeds-traffic-goes-news/.

144 *Trying to head off*: Jonah Peretti, "Why BuzzFeed Does News," BuzzFeed, June
18, 2015, https://www.buzzfeed.com/jonah/why-buzzfeed-does-news.

144 *Then he received a gift*: Dao Nguyen, interviewed by Jill Abramson and John
Stillman at BuzzFeed New York, December 14, 2015.

144 *There was little sense of*: Tanner Greenring, Scott Lamb, Jack Shepherd, Matt
Stopera, and Peggy Wang, interviewed by Jill Abramson and John Stillman, New
York, June 26, 2015.

145 *So when BuzzFeed had*: Ben Smith, "The Dress," BuzzFeed, February 27, 2015,
https://www.buzzfeed.com/bensmith/culture-web-culture?utm_term=.ohpvkrq
W2O#.jreamQ67VK.

145 *Before she took off*: Cates Holderness, "What Colors Are This Dress?," BuzzFeed,
February 26, 2015, https://www.buzzfeed.com/catesish/help-am-i-going-insane-its
-definitely-blue?utm_term=.leOJE50Pl9#.heLKwAMP8E.

145 *By the time she got out*: Lucia Moses, "Meet Cates Holderness, the BuzzFeed Employee Behind #TheDress," Digiday, February 27, 2015, https://digiday.com /media/meet-cates-holderness-buzzfeed-employee-behind-thedress/.

145 *Before she had come to New York*: Cates Holderness, interviewed by Jill Abramson, August 18, 2015.

145 *Noting that the dress*: Dao Nguyen, "What It's Like to Work on BuzzFeed's Tech Team During Record Traffic," BuzzFeed, February 27, 2015, https://www.buzz feed.com/daozers/what-its-like-to-work-on-buzzfeeds-tech-team-during-record -t#.pc6GG2E5O.

146 *Their "sys admins"*: Ibid.

146 *The phenomenon itself*: Ben Smith, "The Dress," BuzzFeed, February 27, 2015, https://www.buzzfeed.com/bensmith/culture-web-culture?utm_term=.ohpvkrq W2O#.jreamQ67VK.

146 *He presided over*: Arabelle Sicardi, interviewed by Jill Abramson, New York, July 16, 2015.

CHAPTER SIX: VICE II

147 *It was McInnes to whom*: Thomas Morton, interviewed by Jill Abramson and Elly Brinkly at Vice New York, October 13, 2015.

147 *He'd earned a scholarship*: Ibid.

147 *"I fucking hated those kids*: Ian Frisch, "Working through the Stubble," *Relapse*, Fall, 2014, 68–69.

148 *Morton flipped one open*: Count Chocula, "The VICE Guide to Partying," Vice, November 30, 2004, https://www.vice.com/en_us/article/av759j/the-vice-v11n5.

148 *They called their anniversary bash*: "VICE Magazine: 10 Years of the Worst Parties Ever," Gothamist, October 19, 2004, http://gothamist.com/2004/10/19/vice_ magazine_10_years_of_the_worst_parties_ever.php.

149 *The dictum, Morton recalled*: Thomas Morton, interviewed by Jill Abramson and Elly Brinkly at Vice New York, October 13, 2015.

149 *One colleague bet*: Ibid.

149 *"I was very dandruffy*: Ian Frisch, "Working through the Stubble," *Relapse*, Fall, 2014, 68–69.

149 *Years later, after Morton*: Gwynedd Stuart, "HBO Unleashes Its Vice Squad," Chicago Reader, May 1, 2013, https://www.chicagoreader.com/chicago/vice-on -hbo-with-shane-smith/Content?oid=9490534.

149 *In went a dead rat*: "Gross Jar 2012—Dead Rat," Vice, May 11, 2012, https:// www.vice.com/en_us/article/yv5bgv/gross-jar-2012-part-six-dead-rat.

150 *"We were mostly writing*: Thomas Morton, interviewed by Jill Abramson and Elly Brinkly at Vice New York, October 13, 2015.

150 *In his first three years*: Vanessa Grigoriadis, "The Edge of Hip: Vice, the Brand," *New York Times*, September 28, 2003, https://www.nytimes.com/2003/09/28/style /the-edge-of-hip-vice-the-brand.html.

150 *They even designed an edition*: "Gimix Toys' Dos and Don'ts (from the Pages of *Vice* Magazine)," Millionaire Playboy, n.d., http://millionaireplayboy.com/toys /vice.php.

151 *A watershed moment*: "The Immersionism Issue," Vice, n.d., https://www.vice .com/en_us/topic/the-immersionism-issue.

151 *He had packed an overnight bag*: Thomas Morton, "Hispanic Panic," Vice, November 30, 2005, https://www.vice.com/en_us/article/8gm4kk/hispanic-v12n10.

151 *The following year he joined*: Thomas Morton, "I Joined Three Cults Simultaneously (Vice Magazine, 2007)," Tumblr, October 2006, http://instapaperstories .tumblr.com/post/983262827/cults.

151 *He'd set his sights on*: Thomas Morton, "In the Land of the Juggalos—a Juggalo Is King," Vice, September 30, 2007, https://www.vice.com/en_us/article/4wnjb9 /land-of-juggalos-v14n10.

153 *Cable news, Fox, CNN*: "Leading Cable News Networks in the United States in April 2018, by Number of Primetime Viewers (in 1,000s)," Statista, May 2018, https://www.statista.com/statistics/373814/cable-news-network-viewership-usa/.

153 *The median age of the Fox*: Adam Epstein, "Fox News's Biggest Problem Isn't the Ailes Ouster, It's That Its Average Viewer Is a Dinosaur," Quartz, July 21, 2016, https://qz.com/738346/fox-newss-biggest-problem-isnt-the-ailes-ouster-its-that -its-average-viewer-is-a-dinosaur/.

153 *In the spring of 2006*: Tom Freston, interviewed by Jill Abramson, New York, April 29, 2016.

153 *When Google purchased YouTube*: Andrew Sorkin and Jeremy W. Peters, "Google to Acquire YouTube for $1.65 Billion," *New York Times*, October 9, 2006, https:// www.nytimes.com/2006/10/09/business/09cnd-deal.html.

154 *"We saw that everyone*: Jeff Bercovici, "Tom Freston's $1B Revenge: Ex-Viacom Chief Helps VICE Become the next MTV," *Forbes,* January 3, 2012, https://www .forbes.com/sites/jeffbercovici/2012/01/03/tom-frestons-1-billion-revenge-ex-vi acom-chief-helps-vice-become-the-next-mtv/#b2122c34a553.

154 *Viacom took a 50 percent stake*: Robert Levine, "A Guerrilla Video Site Meets MTV," *New York Times*, November 19, 2007, https://www.nytimes.com/2007/11 /19/business/media/19vice.html.

154 *Unlike Szalwinski, though*: Bloomberg News, "Viacom's Ex-Chief Getting $85 Million," *New York Times*, October 19, 2006, https://www.nytimes.com/2006/10 /19/business/media/19viacom.html.

154 *With Freston gone*: William D. Cohan, "Inside the Viacom 'Brain Drain,'" *Vanity Fair*, April 12, 2016, https://www.vanityfair.com/news/2016/04/inside-the-via com-brain-drain.

155 *One clip featured Morton*: VBS.TV, "Vice with Young Jeezy: The Most Awkward Rap Interview, EVER," Daily Motion (video), n.d., https://www.dailymotion.com /video/x6qfog.

155 *"Great," he remembers*: Ian Frisch, "Working through the Stubble," *Relapse*, Fall 2014, 68–69.

156 *Morton arrived, city-slick*: Thomas Morton, "The Quest for Moonshine," Vice, February 15, 2009, https://www.vice.com/en_us/article/znqzb3/the-quest-for-moon shine.

156 *He was sent to Ghana*: "Fantasy Coffins," *The Vice Guide to Everything*, season 1, episode 1, December 2010.

157 *He shipped out to Mauritania*: Thomas Morton, "The Fat Farms of Mauritania," Vice, May 14, 2013, https://www.vice.com/sv/article/4wqz43/the-fat-farms-of-mauritania.

158 *Vice's fans tuned in*: "Heavy Metal in Baghdad," Vice (video), n.d., https://video .vice.com/en_us/video/heavy-metal-in-baghdad-full-feature/560a7d59d2d2df 3d337a66d2.

158 *They kept coming back*: Thomas Morton, "I Spent an Hour at the Kurdish Front of the Syrian Civil War, and Let Me Just Say, No Thank You," Vice, April 4, 2014, https://www.vice.com/en_us/article/7b7x5y/i-fraught-in-a-war; Thomas Morton, "TOXIC: Garbage Island," Vice, February 17, 2010, http://www.cnn.com/2010 /WORLD/americas/02/16/vbs.toxic.garbage.island/index.html.

159 *"Let's have 14 bottles*: Lizzie Widdicombe, "The Bad-Boy Brand: The Vice Guide to the World," *New Yorker*, April 8, 2013, https://www.newyorker.com/magazine /2013/04/08/the-bad-boy-brand.

159 *Freston recalls that when Vice*: Andrew Goldman, "L.A. VICE: Inside Media Mogul Shane Smith's Santa Monica Estate," *Wall Street Journal*, September 6, 2016, https://www.wsj.com/articles/l-a-vice-inside-media-mogul-shane-smiths -santa-monica-estate-1473165901.

159 *"Readers are leaving newspapers*: Andrew Adam Newman, "The Vice and Virtue of Marketing," *New York Times*, May 27, 2009, https://www.nytimes.com/2009/05 /28/business/media/28adco.html.

160 *"In particular," the company*: Bill Donahue, "Vice Says Marketing Co. Stole 'Vir- tue,'" Law360, June 1, 2015, https://www.law360.com/articles/662168.

160 *"What we have*: Mike Shields, "Vice, BuzzFeed Tread on Madison Avenue's Turf," *Wall Street Journal,* June 22, 2016, https://www.wsj.com/articles/vice-buzz feed-tread-on-madison-avenues-turf-1466568065.

161 *Another, for Absolut*: Medusian23, "'I'm Here' 2010 a Short Film by Spike Jonze FULL," YouTube (video), 31:47, March 30, 2011, https://www.youtube.com /watch?v=6OY1EXZt4ok.

161 *For The North Face*: Aaron Carpenter, interviewed by NewsCred, "Never Stop Exploring: The North Face Goes 'Far Out' with Content Marketing," Newscred, July 5, 2014, https://insights.newscred.com/north-face-content-marketing/.

162 *The idea had come out*: Eliot van Buskirk, "Intel and Vice Launch Creators Proj- ect: Selling Out or Boosting Creativity?," Wired, May 17, 2010, https://www .wired.com/2010/05/intel-and-vice-partner/.

162 *Desperate for a chunk*: "Intel Corporation Advertising Spending in the United States in 2013 and 2014 (in Million U.S. Dollars)," Statista, July 2015, https:// www.statista.com/statistics/308569/intel-advertising-spending-usa/; Reeves Wie- deman, "A Company Built on a Bluff," *New York*, June 10, 2018, http://nymag .com/daily/intelligencer/2018/06/inside-vice-media-shane-smith.html.

162 *The otherwise faceless*: Ashley Rodriguez, "How a Single Deal with a Decidedly Unhip Tech Company Built the Vice Media Behemoth," Quartz, September 8, 2016, https://qz.com/776628/shane-smith-how-a-single-native-advertising-deal -with-intel-intc-built-the-vice-media-behemoth/.

163 *One story touted*: "The Royal Shakespeare Company Uses Real Time Effects to Create a New Version of 'The Tempest,'" *The Creators Project*, December 14, 2016, https://creators.vice.com/en_us/article/bmy9ev/royal-shakespeare-company -uses-real-time-effects-to-create-the-tempest.

163 *Another story, titled "Exploring*: "Exploring Our Relationships to Our Computers: The Evolution of Computer Icons," *The Creators Project*, February 16, 2016, https://creators.vice.com/en_us/article/ypna47/a-look-back-at-the-changing-ico nography.

163 *So soft were the sells*: Julia Kaganskiy, "[#DIGART] Are Brands the New Medicis?" *Creators*, May 11, 2012, http://thecreatorsproject.vice.com/blog/digart-are -brands-the-new-medicis.

163 *As the engine driving 90 percent*: Iris Derouex, "Blows at Vice," Liberation, July 23, 2013, http://www.liberation.fr/ecrans/2013/07/23/coups-de-vice_955122? page=article.

163 *In 2014* AdWeek: Emma Bazilian, "How Shane Smith Built Vice into a $2.5 Billion Empire," Adweek, September 29, 2014, https://www.adweek.com/digital /how-shane-smith-built-vice-25-billion-empire-160379/.

163 *The Creators Project, Smith said*: Andrew Goldman, "L.A. VICE: Inside Media Mogul Shane Smith's Santa Monica Estate," *Wall Street Journal*, September 6, 2016, https://www.wsj.com/articles/l-a-vice-inside-media-mogul-shane-smiths -santa-monica-estate-1473165901.

163 *"We don't have a disconnect:* Andrew Adam Newman, "The Vice and Virtue of Marketing," *New York Times*, May 27, 2009, https://www.nytimes.com/2009/05 /28/business/media/28adco.html.

163 *The* Times *stole* Forbes*'s*: PressRun, "Sebastian Tomich Named Head of Advertising and Marketing Solutions," *New York Times* (press release), November 28, 2017, https://www.nytco.com/sebastian-tomich-named-head-of-advertising-mar keting-solutions/.

163 *But he also said*: Andrew Adam Newman, "The Vice and Virtue of Marketing," *New York Times*, May 27, 2009, https://www.nytimes.com/2009/05/28/business /media/28adco.html.

164 *"We don't do branded*: Miguel Helft, "Vice CEO on Old Media: 'They Can Go to Hell Quite Frankly,'" *Fortune*, October 14, 2013, http://fortune.com/2013/10/14 /vice-ceo-on-old-media-they-can-go-to-hell-quite-frankly/.

164 *So even as he loudly*: Nathan McAlone, "How Vice Convinces the World It's Worth Billions—Even If Its Cable Ratings Are Horrible," Business Insider, September 6, 2016, https://www.businessinsider.com/why-vice-is-worth-billions-2016-9.

164 *When Gawker reporter*: Andy Cush, "Emails: Vice Requires Writers to Get Approval to Write about Brands," Gawker, October 2, 2014, http://gawker.com/this -is-how-your-vice-media-sausage-gets-made-1641615517.

164 *Davis had edited*: Michael Tracey, "It's Time to Start Boycotting the NFL," Vice, September 12, 2014, https://www.vice.com/en_us/article/4w7bbd/its-officially -time-to-start-boycotting-the-nfl-912.

164 *"They constantly edit*: Hamilton Nolan, "Working at Vice Media Is Not as Cool as It Seems," Gawker, May 30, 2014, http://gawker.com/working-at-vice-media-is -not-as-cool-as-it-seems-1579711577.

165 *So it did not come off*: "Introducing 'The Business of Life' (series trailer)," Vice, April 21, 2015, https://news.vice.com/video/introducing-the-business-of-life-series -trailer.

165 *Vice wanted to have it*: Kieran Dahl, "Collectively: The Upworthy of Branded Content, or a Doomed Experiment?," Contently, October 13, 2014, https://con tently.com/strategist/2014/10/13/collectively-the-upworthy-of-branded-content -or-a-doomed-experiment/.

165 *"Today's media is obsessed*: Jason Abbruzzese, "We're Not F*cked, Says New Corporate-Backed Climate Site," Mashable, October 8, 2014, https://mashable .com/2014/10/08/collectively-sponsored-corporations-vice/#06exOQw3UGqN.

166 *The clunkiest case*: Jason Prechtel, "Why Is Vice Using CeaseFire to Sell a Game about Revenge Killing?," Gapers Block, September 19, 2012, http://gap ersblock.com/mechanics/2012/09/19/why-is-vice-using-ceasefire-to-sell-a-game -about-revenge-killing/?utm_source=feedburner&utm_medium=feed&utm_cam paign=Feed%3A+gapersblock%2Fmechanics+%28Gapers+Block%3A+Me chanics%29&utm_content=Google+Reader.

166 *Smith and a very small crew*: "The VICE Guide to North Korea," Top Documentary Films (review), n.d., https://topdocumentaryfilms.com/vice-guide-travel-north -korea/.

167 *"Guess what! I love him*: Associated Press, "Leaving NKorea, Rodman Calls Kims 'Great Leaders,'" Yahoo!, March 1, 2013, https://www.yahoo.com/news /leaving-nkorea-rodman-calls-kims-great-leaders-111905240.html.

167 *Vice's report ran under*: "North Korea Has a Friend in Dennis Rodman and VICE," Vice, February 28, 2013, https://www.vice.com/en_us/article/mvpygv /north-korea-has-a-friend-in-dennis-rodman.

169 *The general supposedly cannibalized*: Shane Smith, "The VICE Guide to Libe- ria," Vice, January 18, 2010, https://www.vice.com/en_us/article/xdg5wz/the-vice -guide-to-liberia-1.

169 *"Your video stirred*: Penelope Chester, "Open Letter to Shane Smith," January 29, 2010, https://penelopemchester.com/2010/01/29/open-letter-to-shane-smith/.

169 *Less than a week after*: Helene Cooper, "On Liberia's Shore, Catching a Wave," *New York Times*, January 22, 2010, https://www.nytimes.com/2010/01/24/travel /24explorer.html.

169 *He was inviting pushback*: "David Carr vs. Some Guys from VICE," from "Page 1 (documentary)," YouTube, November 28, 2011, https://www.youtube.com/watch ?v=iLmkec_4Rfo.

170 *Despite his bluster*: "An Open Letter to Liberia," Vice, February 2, 2010, https:// www.vice.com/en_us/article/mv98vb/10773-revision-5.

172 *The problem was the entire thrust*: Aimen Khalid Butt, "The Vice Approach: Shock First, Explain Later (If Ever)," World Policy, April 16, 2013, https://world policy.org/2013/04/16/the-vice-approach-shock-first-explain-later-if-ever/.

173 *Morton, for one, admitted*: Thomas Morton, interviewed by Jill Abramson and Elly Brinkly at Vice New York, October 13, 2015.

173 *He was sent to the front lines*: Thomas Morton, "I Spent an Hour at the Kurdish Front of the Syrian Civil War, and Let Me Just Say, No Thank You," Vice, April 4, 2014, https://www.vice.com/en_us/article/7b7x5y/i-fraught-in-a-war.

173 *He summoned his inner swashbuckling*: "These Are the Soldiers Pushing Out What's Left of ISIS in Syria," VICE Video, n.d., https://video.vice.com/en_us /video/inside-the-fight-to-push-whats-left-of-isis-out-of-syria/5b15df39f1cdb 34d602428ce.

173 *Morton's nimbleness alone*: Penelope Green, "Nesting, the Vice Media Way," *New York Times*, June 10, 2015, https://www.nytimes.com/2015/06/11/style/nest ing-the-vice-media-way.html.

174 *Vice was generally not prepared*: "Turkey Has Released VICE News Journalist Mohammed Rasool on Bail," Vice, January 5, 2016, https://news.vice.com/article /turkey-has-released-vice-news-journalist-mohammed-rasool-on-bail.

174 *The risks paid off when*: Michael Calderone, "How Vice News Got Unprecedented Access to the Islamic State," *Huffington Post*, August 7, 2014, https://www.huff ingtonpost.com/2014/08/07/vice-islamic-state_n_5656202.html.

175 *The following year's party*: Chris Ip, "The Cult of Vice," *Columbia Journalism Review*, July–August 2015, https://www.cjr.org/analysis/the_cult_of_vice.php.

176 *As he plotted his relocation*: Andrew Goldman, "L.A. VICE: Inside Media Mogul Shane Smith's Santa Monica Estate," *Wall Street Journal*, September 6, 2016, https://www.wsj.com/articles/l-a-vice-inside-media-mogul-shane-smiths-santa -monica-estate-1473165901

177 *As NBC hired Tim Russert*: Hadas Gold, "Reggie Love Joins Vice Sports," Politico, July 9, 2015, https://www.politico.com/blogs/media/2015/07/reggie-love -joins-vice-sports-210237.

177 *Mastromonaco was named*: Emily Steel, "Vice Hires Alyssa Mastromonaco, Former Official in Obama White House, as a Top Executive," *New York Times*, November 16, 2014, https://www.nytimes.com/2014/11/17/business/media/vice-hires-alyssa -mastromonaco-former-official-in-obama-white-house-as-top-executive.html.

177 *The tweet was followed*: Rachel Abrams, "21st Century Fox Buys 5% of Vice Media," *Variety*, August 16, 2013, https://variety.com/2013/biz/news/21st-century -fox-buys-5-of-vice-media-1200579860/.

177 *On Murdoch's heels came*: Sydney Ember, "Vice Gets Cable Channel in Deal with A&E Networks," *New York Times*, November 3, 2015, https://www.nytimes .com/2015/11/04/business/media/vice-is-said-to-near-cable-channel-deal-with-ae -networks.html.

178 *It was Leopold's FOIA request*: Jason Leopold, "How I Got Clinton's Emails," Vice News, November 4, 2016, https://news.vice.com/en_us/article/j5vevy/clinton -email-scandal-foia.

179 *The debut, which aired in April 2013*: Vice, "Killer Kids," HBO (video), https://www.hbo.com/vice/season-01/1-killer-kids.

179 *At the close of its first 10*: "We Were Nominated for an Emmy," Vice, July 18, 2013, https://www.vice.com/en_us/article/jmvyb8/we-were-nominated-for-an-emmy.

180 *The ultimate symbol of Vice's*: Cynthia Littleton, "Shane Smith: 6 Zingers from the Vice Media Chief's NYC Roast," *Variety*, November 18, 2015, https://variety.com/2015/tv/news/shane-smith-vice-media-5-best-lines-roast-1201643961/.

CHAPTER SEVEN: *NEW YORK TIMES* II

182 *After the financial crisis in 2008*: Joe Pompeo, "The U.S. Has Lost More Than 166 Print Newspapers Since 2008," Business Insider, July 6, 2010, https://www.businessinsider.com/the-us-has-lost-more-than-166-print-newspapers-since-2008-2010-7.

182 *Ten thousand newspaper jobs*: Mark Jurkowitz, "The Losses in Legacy," Pew Research Center, March 26, 2014, http://www.journalism.org/2014/03/26/the-losses-in-legacy/.

182 *Print ad sales fell*: Associated Press, "Profit Declines 31% at Gannett," *New York Times*, February 2, 2008, https://www.nytimes.com/2008/02/02/business/media/02gannett.html.

183 *The tabloid* Post: John Koblin, "After 33 Years, Arthur Sulzberger Separates from His Wife, Gail Gregg," *Observer*, May 12, 2008, http://observer.com/2008/05/after-33-years-arthur-sulzberger-separates-from-his-wife-gail-gregg/.

186 *On February 18 the* Times*'s*: Henry Blodget, "New York Times Stock Now Costs Less Than Sunday Paper," Business Insider, February 18, 2009, https://www.businessinsider.com/new-york-times-stock-now-costs-less-than-sunday-paper-2009-2.

187 *The print newspaper was still supplying*: Richard Pérez-Peña, "New York Times Company Posts Loss," *New York Times*, April 17, 2008, https://www.nytimes.com/2008/04/17/business/media/17cnd-times.html.

187 *In a sale-leaseback deal*: Richard Pérez-Peña, "Times Co. Building Deal Raises Cash," *New York Times*, March 9, 2009, https://www.nytimes.com/2009/03/10/business/media/10paper.html.

187 *The company was carrying*: Ibid.

190 *In 2009 Keller was told*: Richard Pérez-Peña, "New York Times Moves to Trim 100 in Newsroom," *New York Times*, October 19, 2009, https://www.nytimes.com/2009/10/20/business/media/20times.html.

193 *On March 28, 2011*: "A Letter to Our Readers about Digital Subscriptions," *New York Times*, March 17, 2011, https://www.nytimes.com/2011/03/18/opinion/l18times.html.

193 *In his blog, BuzzMachine*: Jeff Jarvis, "The Cockeyed Economics of Metering Reading," BuzzMachine, January 17, 2010, https://buzzmachine.com/2010/01/17/the-cockeyed-economics-of-metering-reading/.

193 *Clay Shirky, an adherent*: Decca Aitkenhead, "Clay Shirky: 'Paywall Will Underperform—the Numbers Don't Add Up,'" *Guardian*, July 5, 2010, https://

www.theguardian.com/technology/2010/jul/05/clay-shirky-internet-television
-newspapers.

194 *He saw less of his two*: Emma Gilbey Keller, "A Family Life in News: Emma
Gilbey Keller on Bill Keller's *New York Times* Resignation," *Vanity Fair*, June 3,
2011, https://www.vanityfair.com/news/2011/06/a-family-life-in-news-emma-gil
bey-keller-on-bill-kellers-new-york-times-resignation.

194 *According to* Times *tradition*: Sydney Ember, "New York Times Reinstates Managing Editor Role and Appoints Joseph Kahn," *New York Times*, September 16,
2016, https://www.nytimes.com/2016/09/17/business/media/new-york-times-re
instates-managing-editor-role-appoints-joseph-kahn.html.

197 *He entrusted me to help recruit*: Mike Rogoway, "A. G. Sulzberger, New York
Times' Publisher and Former Oregonian Reporter, Talks Journalism in the Digital
Age," *Oregonian*, February 9, 2018, https://www.oregonlive.com/business/index
.ssf/2018/02/ag_sulzberger_new_york_times_p.html.

199 *When he was fired*: Katharine Q. Seelye, "Los Angeles Paper Ousts Top Editor,"
New York Times, November 8, 2006, https://www.nytimes.com/2006/11/08/busi
ness/media/08paper.html.

200 *He had grown up in New Orleans*: Joe Strupp, "How Baquet Brothers Survived
Setbacks in L.A. and NOLA," Editor & Publisher, December 13, 2006, http://
www.editorandpublisher.com/news/how-baquet-brothers-survived-setbacks-in-l
-a-and-nola/.

200 *He was a first-generation*: Catie Edmonson, "At Columbia College Class Day,
Dean Baquet Urges Graduates Not to Let Ambition Blind Them," *Columbia Spec-
tator*, May 26, 2016, https://www.columbiaspectator.com/news/2016/05/17/co
lumbia-college-class-day-dean-baquet-urges-graduates-not-let-ambition-blind
-them/; Joe Coscarelli, "Everything You Need to Know about Dean Baquet, the
First Black Editor of the New York *Times*," *New York*, May 14, 2014, http://nymag
.com/daily/intelligencer/2014/05/dean-baquet-new-york-times-first-black-execu
tive-editor.html.

202 *In my remarks*: Elaine Woo, "Nan Robertson Dies at 83; Pulitzer-Winning New
York Times Reporter," *Los Angeles Times*, October 15, 2009, http://www.latimes
.com/local/obituaries/la-me-nan-robertson15-2009oct15-story.html.

204 *Its design and perfect synchronicity*: Farhad Manjoo, "A Whole Lot of Bells, Way
Too Many Whistles," Slate, August 15, 2013, http://www.slate.com/articles/tech
nology/technology/2013/08/snow_fall_the_jockey_the_scourge_of_the_new
_york_times_bell_and_whistle.html.

205 *Barboza, who grew up*: Ariel Wittenberg, "New Bedford Native Awarded Two
Pulitzer Prizes," *South Coast Today*, April 17, 2013, http://www.southcoasttoday
.com/article/20130417/NEWS/304170331.

206 *This led him to the family members*: David Barboza, "Billions in Hidden Riches
for Family of Chinese Leader," *New York Times*, October 25, 2012, https://www
.nytimes.com/2012/10/26/business/global/family-of-wen-jiabao-holds-a-hidden
-fortune-in-china.html.

212 *There were several completely wrong*: David Carr, "The Pressure to Be the TV

News Leader Tarnishes a Big Brand," *New York Times*, April 21, 2013, https://www.nytimes.com/2013/04/22/business/media/in-boston-cnn-stumbles-in-rush-to-break-news.html.

217 *The new head of video*: Todd Spangler, "Discovery Hires VR Expert Rebecca Howard, Former New York Times Video GM," *Variety*, November 17, 2016, https://variety.com/2016/digital/exec-shuffle-people-news/rebecca-howard-discovery-new-york-times-1201920639/.

219 *With the recent sale*: Associated Press, "Boston Globe, Once Bought for $1.1 Billion, Sells for $70 Million," NBC News, November 2, 2015, https://www.nbcnews.com/business/boston-globe-once-bought-1-1-billion-sells-70-million-6C10835491.

224 *Wise about the* Times*'s internal:* Charlotte Alter, "Ousted New York Times Editor Says Firing 'Hurt,'" *Time*, May 19, 2014, http://time.com/104518/new-york-times-jill-abramson-wake-forest-commencement/.

CHAPTER EIGHT: *WASHINGTON POST* II

227 *Weymouth didn't have*: Eugene L. Meyer, "Katharine Weymouth," *Bethesda Magazine*, December 23, 2013, http://www.bethesdamagazine.com/Bethesda-Magazine/January-February-2014/Katharine-Weymouth/.

229 *About to be booted*: David Carr, "At Journal, the Words Not Spoken," *New York Times*, April 28, 2008, https://www.nytimes.com/2008/04/28/business/media/28carr.html.

231 *There were almost no digital*: Dylan Byers, "Washington Post President and GM Stephen Hills to Step Down," Politico, September 8, 2015, https://www.politico.com/blogs/media/2015/09/washington-post-president-and-gm-stephen-hills-to-step-down-213406.

232 *Even though he had passed up*: Jeff Bercovici, "Facebook and Don Graham Have Been Very Good to Each Other," *Forbes*, February 2, 2012, https://www.forbes.com/sites/jeffbercovici/2012/02/02/facebook-and-don-graham-have-been-very-good-to-each-other/#6037d29528ba.

232 *The* Post *had several social media*: "Washington Post Social Reader: FAQs," *Washington Post*, n.d., https://www.washingtonpost.com/2010/07/08/gIQAzgKpnK_page.html..

233 *These investigations were what*: Marilyn Thompson, interviewed by Jill Abramson, Cambridge, Massachusetts, May 10, 2016.

238 *"It was the ultimate*: Melissa Bell, interviewed by Jill Abramson, New York, January 26, 2018.

240 *The difference between Weymouth's*: Andy Alexander, "The Post's 'Salon' Plan: A Public Relations Disaster," *Omblog, Washington Post*, July 2, 2009, http://voices.washingtonpost.com/ombudsman-blog/2009/07/wps_salon_plan_a_public_relati.html.

240 *Yet while Weymouth was away*: Michael Calderone and Mike Allen, "WaPo Can-

cels Lobbyist Event," Politico, July 3, 2009, https://www.politico.com/story/2009 /07/wapo-cancels-lobbyist-event-024441.

240 *The* Post *promised "intimate*: Andy Alexander, "The Post's 'Salon' Plan: A Public Relations Disaster," *Omblog, Washington Post*, July 2, 2009, http://voices.washin gtonpost.com/ombudsman-blog/2009/07/wps_salon_plan_a_public_relati.html.

241 *Allen got hold*: Michael Calderone and Mike Allen, "WaPo Cancels Lobbyist Event," Politico, July 3, 2009, https://www.politico.com/story/2009/07/wapo-can cels-lobbyist-event-024441.

241 *She said neither she*: Ibid.

241 *With all their talk of*: Gabriel Sherman, "The Behind the Scenes Feud between 'The Washington Post' and 'The New York Times,'" *New Republic*, October 17, 2009, https://newrepublic.com/article/70382/post-the-behind-the-scenes-feud-be tween-the-washington-post-and-the-new-york-times-ov.

242 *At the* Post, *however*: Sarah Ellison, "Ghosts in the Newsroom," *Vanity Fair*, March 7, 2012, https://www.vanityfair.com/news/business/2012/04/washington-post -watergate.

242 *When asked why the* Times *avoided*: Jay Yarow, "NYT's Bill Keller: We Will Not Fire Journalists Based on Pageviews," Business Insider, October 21, 2009, https:// www.businessinsider.com/nyts-bill-keller-we-dont-judge-journalists-based-on -pageviews-2009-10.

242 *Narisetti, age 45, brought*: Andrew Phelps, "A Post-Mortem with Raju Narisetti: 'I Would Have Actually Tried to Move Faster,'" NiemanLab, January 23, 2012, http://www.niemanlab.org/2012/01/a-post-mortem-with-raju-narisetti-i-would -have-actually-tried-to-move-faster/.

242 *More than 100 editors*: Ken Doctor, "The Newsonomics of WaPo's Reader Dash- board 1.0," NiemanLab, April 7, 2011, http://www.niemanlab.org/2011/04/the -newsonomics-of-wapos-reader-dashboard-1-0/.

243 *There were audible groans*: Jeremy W. Peters, "Some Newspapers, Tracking Readers Online, Shift Coverage," *New York Times*, September 5, 2010, https:// www.nytimes.com/2010/09/06/business/media/06track.html.

243 *Also annoying, Narisetti spoke*: Raju Narisetti, "Ask the Post: Managing Edi- tor Raju Narisetti Takes Your Questions," *Washington Post*, January 25, 2010, http://www.washingtonpost.com/wp-dyn/content/discussion/2010/01/24/DI2010 012401637.html.

243 *The metrics in which Narisetti*: Raju Narisetti, "Mirror, Mirror on the Wall," NiemanLab, n.d., http://www.niemanlab.org/2017/12/mirror-mirror-on-the-wall/.

244 *It was the brainchild*: Tony Haile, interviewed by Jill Abramson and John Still- man, New York, October 14, 2015.

245 *Chartbeat's data, Haile said*: Tony Haile, interviewed by Jill Abramson and John Stillman, New York, October 14, 2015.

245 *But even the* Times *published a list*: Petre, "The Traffic Factories: Metrics at Chartbeat, Gawker Media, and The New York Times," Tow Center for Digital Journalism, May 7, 2015.

245 *Sensational stories*: Helene Cooper and Brian Stelter, "Crashers Met Obama; Secret Service Apologizes," *New York Times*, November 27, 2009, https://www.nytimes.com/2009/11/28/us/politics/28crasher.html.

245 *Fully half of all readers*: Tony Haile, interviewed by Jill Abramson and John Stillman, New York, October 14, 2015.

246 *But as their institutions bled cash*: Petre, "The Traffic Factories: Metrics at Chartbeat, Gawker Media, and The New York Times," https://towcenter.org/research/traffic-factories/.

246 *One study published in 2014*: Angela M. Lee, Seth C. Lewis, and Matthew Powers, "Audience Clicks and News Placement: A Study of Time-Lagged Influence in Online Journalism," *Communication Research* 41, no. 4 (November 20, 2012): 505–530.

246 *Chartbeat soon had retainer*: Petre, "The Traffic Factories: Metrics at Chartbeat, Gawker Media, and The New York Times," https://towcenter.org/research/traffic-factories/; Kathy Zhang, "Metrics Are Everywhere in Media. Here's How They Help," *New York Times*, May 23, 2018, https://www.nytimes.com/2018/05/23/technology/personaltech/metrics-media.html; Aaron Mesh, "With Quotas and Incentive Pay, The Oregonian Is Again Reshaping Its Experience for Readers," *Willamette Week*, March 23, 2014, http://www.wweek.com/portland/blog-31405-with-quotas-and-incentive-pay-the-oregonian-is-again-reshaping-its-experience-for-readers.html.

246 *Especially of note*: Petre, "The Traffic Factories: Metrics at Chartbeat, Gawker Media, and The New York Times," https://towcenter.org/research/traffic-factories/.

247 *Haile compared what journalists*: Tony Haile, interviewed by Jill Abramson and John Stillman, New York, October 14, 2015.

247 *Jonah Peretti called Haile*: Ibid.

247 *Interestingly Haile himself*: "Full Transcript: Scroll CEO Tony Haile on Recode Media," Recode, October 31, 2017, https://www.recode.net/2017/10/31/16579480/transcript-scroll-ceo-tony-haile-chartbeat-advertising-journalism-ad-blocker-recode-media.

247 *Clicks did not measure*: Jack Marshall, "Online Measurement Is a Mess, Says Former Chartbeat CEO Tony Haile," *Wall Street Journal*, November 16, 2016, https://www.wsj.com/articles/online-measurement-is-a-mess-says-former-chartbeat-ceo-tony-haile-1479331309.

247 *Narisetti had come to the* Post: Harry Jaffe, "Post Watch: Meet the Post's 'Mystery Man,'" *Washingtonian*, May 12, 2010, https://www.washingtonian.com/2010/05/12/post-watch-meet-the-posts-mystery-man/.

247 *Naturally this created*: Steven Mufson, "Post Managing Editor," *Washington Post*, January 20, 2012, https://www.washingtonpost.com/business/economy/post-managing-editor/2012/01/20/gIQAlno1EQ_story.html?utm_term=.96a79d16a04a; Pexton, "Is The Post Innovating Too Fast?"

248 *Hired by Narisetti in 2009*: Benjamin Wallace, "Here, Let Ezra Explain," *New York*, February 2, 2014, http://nymag.com/news/features/ezra-klein-2014-2/.

248 *Bell helped power*: Ravi Somaiya, "Top Wonkblog Columnist to Leave Washing-

ton Post," *New York Times*, January 21, 2014, https://www.nytimes.com/2014/01 /22/business/media/ezra-klein-leaving-washington-post.html.

248 *Readers loved them*: Lucia Moses, "The Rapid Rise of Vox Media's Melissa Bell: An Explainer," Digiday, July 6, 2015, https://digiday.com/media/unusual-talents -vox-medias-melissa-bell/.

248 *Many people thought Klein*: Matt Welch, "The Boy in the Bubble," *Columbia Journalism Review*, September–October 2012, https://archives.cjr.org/feature/boy _in_bubble.php.

248 *Klein's fluid writing*: Dylan Byers and Hadas Gold, "Why the Post Passed on Ezra Klein," Politico, January 21, 2014, https://www.politico.com/story/2014/01/ezra -klein-leaves-washington-post-102424.

248 *But also like Silver*: Ibid.

248 *Anyone with an individual brand*: Anson Kaye, "March Madness, GOP Style," *U.S. News*, March 20, 2014, https://www.usnews.com/opinion/blogs/anson-kaye /2014/03/20/attacking-the-liberal-media-has-led-to-conservative-media-madness.

248 *So it wasn't surprising that the* Post: Tom McCarthy, "Washington Post's Ezra Klein Leaving Newspaper to Start 'New Venture,'" *Guardian*, January 21, 2014, https://www.theguardian.com/media/2014/jan/21/washington-posts-ezra-klein -leaving-news-organisation.

248 *The* Times *too lost Silver*: John McDuling, "'The Upshot' Is the New York Times' Replacement for Nate Silver's FiveThirtyEight," Quartz, March 10, 2014, https:// qz.com/185922/the-upshot-is-the-new-york-times-replacement-for-nate-silvers -fivethirtyeight/.

248 *There were bound to be problems*: Trevor Butterworth, "The Latest Sad Fate of an Aggregation Serf," Awl, April 24, 2012, https://www.theawl.com/2012/04/the-lat est-sad-fate-of-an-aggregation-serf/.

248 *One story BlogPOST recycled*: Patrick B. Pexton, "Elizabeth Flock's Resignation: The Post Fails a Young Blogger," *Washington Post*, April 20, 2012, https://www .washingtonpost.com/opinions/elizabeth-flocks-resignation-the-post-fails-a -young-blogger/2012/04/20/gIQAFACXWT_story.html?utm_term=.73965008350f.

248 *This time the young blogger*: Andrew Beaujon, "Washington Post Writer Resigns after Editor's Note about 'Significant Ethical Lapse,'" Poynter, April 26, 2012, https://www.poynter.org/news/washington-post-writer-resigns-after-editors-note -about-significant-ethical-lapse.

248 *The ombudsman said the editors*: Patrick B. Pexton, "Elizabeth Flock's Res-ignation: The Post Fails a Young Blogger," *Washington Post*, April 20, 2012, https://www.washingtonpost.com/opinions/elizabeth-flocks-resignation-the -post-fails-a-young-blogger/2012/04/20/gIQAFACXWT_story.html?utm_ter m=.73965008350f.

249 *The Awl, a small online*: Trevor Butterworth, "The Latest Sad Fate of an Aggre-gation Serf," Awl, April 24, 2012, https://www.theawl.com/2012/04/the-latest-sad -fate-of-an-aggregation-serf/.

249 *Narisetti's team included*: "Cory Haik Named Executive Director for Emerging

News Products," *WashPostPR Blog*, *Washington Post*, July 21, 2015, https://www
.washingtonpost.com/pr/wp/2015/07/21/cory-haik-named-executive-director-for
-emerging-news-products/?utm_term=.afb075bc46b1.

249 *For one, she was young*: "Meet the Post's Mobile Leadership, a Q&A with Cory
Haik and Julia Beizer," *WashPostPR Blog*, *Washington Post*, October 21, 2014,
https://www.washingtonpost.com/pr/wp/2014/10/21/meet-the-posts-mobile-lead
ership-a-qa-with-cory-haik-and-julia-beizer/?utm_term=.19a01fbbcfc6.

249 *She was excited when veteran*: Benjamin Mullin, "Washington Post Campaign Reporter Dan Balz Brings Viewers on the Trail with Snapchat," Poynter, July 17, 2015,
https://www.poynter.org/news/washington-post-campaign-reporter-dan-balz
-brings-viewers-trail-snapchat.

249 *She developed her own data collector*: "@MentionMachine Tracks the 2012 Candidates: Who's Up, Who's Down on Twitter?," *Washington Post*, January 4, 2012,
https://www.washingtonpost.com/blogs/election-2012/post/mentionmachine
-tracks-the-2012-candidates-whos-up-whos-down-on-twitter/2011/12/20/gIQA
PY8r7O_blog.html?utm_term=.69c77f2081ec.

249 *Called the MentionMachine*: Justin Ellis, "Monday Q&A: Washington Post's
Cory Haik on TruthTeller and Prototyping in the Newsroom," NiemanLab, March
18, 2013, http://www.niemanlab.org/2013/03/monday-qa-washington-posts-cory
-haik-on-truthteller-and-prototyping-in-the-newsroom/.

249 *Haik considered it a big victory*: Cory Haik, interviewed by Jill Abramson, New
York, May 5, 2016.

249 *But others thought it cheapened*: Pexton, "Is The Post Innovating Too Fast,"
https://www.washingtonpost.com/opinions/.

249 *The pressure to make the* Post: Ibid.

250 *Periodically they would suspend*: Aleszu Bajak, "Thirteen Cool Ideas from the
Washington Post/Embedly Hackathon," Storybench, July 13, 2015, http://www
.storybench.org/wapo-journalism-hackathon/.

250 *By this point the search*: Francis Cianfrocca, "The Media's Broken Business
Model," Real Clear Markets, May 19, 2009, https://www.realclearmarkets.com/ar
ticles/2009/05/the_medias_broken_business_mod.html; William D. Cohan, "Journalism's Broken Business Model Won't Be Solved by Billionaires," *New Yorker*,
October 19, 2017, https://www.newyorker.com/news/news-desk/journalisms-bro
ken-business-model-wont-be-solved-by-billionaires; Janell Sims, "*Boston Globe*
Editor Says Business Model Is Broken—but Journalism Is Not," Shorenstein Center on Media, Politics and Public Policy, April 8, 2014, https://shorensteincenter
.org/brian-mcgrory/; Arnab Neil Sengupta, "The News Media Industry Is Going
for Broke," *Al Jazeera*, October 7, 2016, https://www.aljazeera.com/indepth/fea
tures/2016/09/news-media-industry-broke-160929090433943.html.

250 *Many publishers concluded that*: Ira Basen, "Breaking Down the Wall," Center
for Journalism Ethics, December 19, 2012, https://ethics.journalism.wisc.edu
/2012/12/19/breaking-down-the-wall/.

251 *Brauchli wrote a memo*: Erik Wemple, "Brauchli to Washington Post Staff: More

with Less!," *Washington Post*, February 8, 2012, https://www.washingtonpost
.com/blogs/erik-wemple/post/brauchli-to-washington-post-staff-more-with-less
/2012/02/08/gIQA9n16yQ_blog.html.

255 *The discussion quickly turned contentious*: https://www.washingtonian.com/2012
/05/10/why-did-washington-post-reporters-meet-with-the-papers-gm/.

260 *In the late afternoon*: https://www.washingtonpost.com/national/washington-post
-to-be-sold-to-jeff-bezos/2013/08/05/ca537c9e-fe0c-11e2-9711-.

264 *When she sent a note*: https://www.washingtonpost.com/business/katherine-wey
mouths-statement/2014/09/02/2ac68dd2-32a5-11e4-8f02-.

266 *they also shared Baron's sense of mission*: https://digiday.com/podcast/digiday
-podcast-shailesh-prakash/.

CHAPTER NINE: FACEBOOK

272 *In 2009 Facebook endowed*: "Facebook Newsfeed Algorithm History," Wallaroo
Media, May 2, 2018, http://wallaroomedia.com/facebook-newsfeed-algorithm
-change-history/#eight.

272 *By August 2013*: Kurt Wagner, "Facebook: Here's How Your News Feed Works,"
Mashable, August 6, 2013, https://mashable.com/2013/08/06/facebook-news-feed
-works/#GbvzcNO54iqI.

273 *With the exception of Rupert Murdoch*: Nicholas Thompson and Fred Vogelstein,
"Inside the Two Years That Shook Facebook—and the World," Wired, February
12, 2018, https://www.wired.com/story/inside-facebook-mark-zuckerberg-2-years
-of-hell/.

273 *Zuckerberg's early backer*: John Lanchester, "You Are the Product," *London Review of Books* 39, no. 16 (August 17, 2017), https://www.lrb.co.uk/v39/n16/john
-lanchester/you-are-the-product.

273 *When Girard died in 2015*: Quentin Hardy, "René Girard, French Theorist of the
Social Sciences, Dies at 91," *New York Times*, November 10, 2015, https://www
.nytimes.com/2015/11/11/arts/international/rene-girard-french-theorist-of-the-so
cial-sciences-dies-at-91.html.

274 *But his aides discouraged him*: Elizabeth Dwoskin, "Facebook Thought It Was
More Powerful Than a Nation-State. Then That Became a Liability," *Washington Post*, January 22, 2018, https://www.washingtonpost.com/business/economy
/inside-facebooks-year-of-reckoning/2018/01/22/cfd7307c-f4c3-11e7-beb6
-c8d48830c54d_story.html?utm_term=.f7d8e787ed34; Max Read, "Does Even
Mark Zuckerberg Know What Facebook Is?," *New York*, October 1, 2017, http://
nymag.com/selectall/2017/10/does-even-mark-zuckerberg-know-what-facebook
-is.html.

274 *When the network welcomed*: John Lanchester, "You Are the Product," *London
Review of Books* 39, no. 16 (August 17, 2017), https://www.lrb.co.uk/v39/n16
/john-lanchester/you-are-the-product.

274 *Sixty-two percent of Americans*: Elisa Shearer and Jeffrey Gottfried, "News Use

across Social Media Platforms 2017," Pew Research Center/Journalism.org, September 7, 2017, http://www.journalism.org/2017/09/07/news-use-across-social-media-platforms-2017/.

275 *Leading by example*: Franklin Foer, "When Silicon Valley Took Over Journalism," *Atlantic*, September 2017, https://www.theatlantic.com/magazine/archive/2017/09/when-silicon-valley-took-over-journalism/534195/.

276 *By October inbound traffic:* Justin Osofsky, "More Ways to Drive Traffic to News and Publishing Sites," Facebook, October 21, 2013, https://www.facebook.com/notes/facebook-media/more-ways-to-drive-traffic-to-news-and-publishing-sites/585971984771628.

276 *One change would privilege*: Varun Kacholia, "News Feed FYI: Showing More High Quality Content," Facebook, August 23, 2013, https://www.facebook.com/business/news/News-Feed-FYI-Showing-More-High-Quality-Content.

277 *Only a few years earlier*: Steven Levy, "Inside the Science That Delivers Your Scary-Smart Facebook and Twitter Feeds," Wired, April 22, 2014, https://www.wired.com/2014/04/perfect-facebook-feed/.

277 *So Facebook launched an internal effort*: Victor Luckerson, "Here's How Facebook's News Feed Actually Works," *Time*, July 9, 2015, http://time.com/collection-post/3950525/facebook-news-feed-algorithm/.

277 *Which is what the company did*: Will Oremus, "Who Controls Your Facebook Feed," Slate, January 3, 2016, http://www.slate.com/articles/technology/cover_story/2016/01/how_facebook_s_news_feed_algorithm_works.html.

277 *By the time Facebook unveiled*: Cheng Zhang, "Using Qualitative Feedback to Show Relevant Stories," Facebook Newsroom, February 1, 2016, https://newsroom.fb.com/news/2016/02/news-feed-fyi-using-qualitative-feedback-to-show-relevant-stories/.

277 *The cascade of advances*: Jonathan Taplin, *Move Fast and Break Things: How Facebook, Google and Amazon Have Cornered Culture and What It Means for All of Us* (Boston: Little, Brown, 2017), 143.

278 *In 2010 opponents of a Florida*: "Case Study: Reaching Voters with Facebook Ads (Vote No on 8)," Facebook, August 16, 2011, https://www.facebook.com/notes/us-politics-on-facebook/case-study-reaching-voters-with-facebook-ads-vote-no-on-8/10150257619200882.

278 *Around 2012 the company set out*: John Lanchester, "You Are the Product," *London Review of Books* 39, no. 16 (August 17, 2017), https://www.lrb.co.uk/v39/n16/john-lanchester/you-are-the-product.

278 *In the cloisters of Cambridge University*: Jane Mayer, "The Reclusive Hedge-Fund Tycoon behind the Trump Presidency," *New Yorker*, March 27, 2017, https://www.newyorker.com/magazine/2017/03/27/the-reclusive-hedge-fund-tycoon-behind-the-trump-presidency.

278 *He knew, for instance*: Michal Kosinski, David Stillwell, and Thore Graepel, "Private Traits and Attributes Are Predictable from Digital Records of Human Behavior," *Proceedings of the National Academy of Sciences* 110, no. 15 (2013): 5802–5805.

279 *"With a mere ten 'likes'*: Hannes Grassegger and Mikael Krogerus, "I Just Showed That the Bomb Was There," *Das Magazin*, December 3, 2016, translated by AntidoteZine.com, January 22, 2017, https://antidotezine.com/2017/01/22/trump-knows-you/.

279 *In 2018 Facebook finally admitted*: Cecilia Kang and Sheera Frenkel, "Facebook Says Cambridge Analytica Harvested Data of Up to 87 Million Users," *New York Times*, April 4, 2018, https://www.nytimes.com/2018/04/04/technology/mark-zuckerberg-testify-congress.html.

280 *The company announced that the longtime*: Smriti Bhagat et al., "Three and a Half Degrees of Separation," Facebook Research, February 4, 2016, https://research.fb.com/three-and-a-half-degrees-of-separation/.

280 *The* Times *was publishing videos*: *New York Times* Facebook page, accessed July 31, 2018, https://www.facebook.com/pg/nytimes/videos/?ref=page_internal.

281 *For BuzzFeed, the made-for-Facebook*: Alex Kantrowitz, "Early Numbers Suggest Facebook Instant Articles Giving BuzzFeed and Other Participating Publishers an Edge," BuzzFeed, June 12, 2015, https://www.buzzfeednews.com/article/alexkantrowitz/early-numbers-are-positive-for-facebooks-instant-articles#.slRzgeOlb.

282 *By 2015 Facebook's individual users:* Amir Efrati, "Facebook Struggles to Stop Decline in 'Original' Sharing," Information, April 7, 2016, https://www.theinformation.com/articles/facebook-struggles-to-stop-decline-in-original-sharing.

282 *BuzzFeed's technology reporter*: Alex Kantrowitz, "How the 2016 Election Blew Up in Facebook's Face," BuzzFeed, November 21, 2016, https://www.buzzfeednews.com/article/alexkantrowitz/2016-election-blew-up-in-facebooks-face.

282 *That summer Facebook added*: Jacob Frantz, "Updated Controls for News Feed," Facebook Newsroom, July 9, 2015, https://newsroom.fb.com/news/2015/07/updated-controls-for-news-feed/.

282 *In January 2016 Facebook*: Peter Roybal, "Introducing Audience Optimization for Publishers," Facebook Media, January 21, 2016, https://media.fb.com/2016/01/21/introducing-audience-optimization/.

282 *In February Facebook added*: Cheng Zhang and Si Chen, "Using Qualitative Feedback to Show Relevant Stories," Facebook Newsroom, February 1, 2016, https://newsroom.fb.com/news/2016/02/news-feed-fyi-using-qualitative-feedback-to-show-relevant-stories/.

282 *In April they went even further*: Moshe Blank and Jie Xu, "More Articles You Want to Spend Time Viewing," Facebook Newsroom, April 21, 2016, https://newsroom.fb.com/news/2016/04/news-feed-fyi-more-articles-you-want-to-spend-time-viewing/.

283 *By May and June 2016*: Grace Duffy, "Who Are the Biggest Politics Publishers on Social?," NewsWhip, June 15, 2016, https://www.newswhip.com/2016/06/biggest-politics-publishers-social/#9tVOGejWIoPSshY6.99.

283 *"The market has forced me*: Noah Shachtman, "How Andrew Breitbart Hacked the Media," Wired, March 11, 2010, https://www.wired.com/2010/03/ff-andrew-brietbart/.

283 *"Your brain works differently*: Rebecca Mead, "Rage Machine," *New Yorker,* May 24, 2010, https://www.newyorker.com/magazine/2010/05/24/rage-machine.

284 *He had worked as a pizza delivery*: Conor Friedersdorf, "Why Breitbart Started Hating the Left," *Atlantic,* April 18, 2011, https://www.theatlantic.com/politics /archive/2011/04/why-breitbart-started-hating-the-left/237459/.

284 *Breitbart was proud*: "Lists: What's Your Source for That?," Reason, October 2007, http://reason.com/archives/2007/10/01/lists-whats-your-source-for-th.

284 *Toward the end of the 1990s*: Noah Shachtman, "How Andrew Breitbart Hacked the Media," Wired, March 11, 2010, https://www.wired.com/2010/03/ff-andrew -brietbart/.

285 *He took a sabbatical*: Alyson Shontell, "The Founder of Breitbart, One of Trump's Favorite Sites, Also Cofounded the Huffington Post—Here's What He Was Like to Work With," Business Insider, June 6, 2017, https://www.businessinsider.com /breitbart-huffington-post-founder-trump-2017-6.

285 *"The idea," he told Wired*: Noah Shachtman, "How Andrew Breitbart Hacked the Media," Wired, March 11, 2010, https://www.wired.com/2010/03/ff-andrew-bri etbart/.

285 *That December Breitbart attended*: Joshua Green, *Devil's Bargain: Steve Bannon, Donald Trump, and the Storming of the Presidency* (New York: Penguin, 2017), 85–87. See also Joshua Green interview with Matthew Boyle, "Exclusive—A Devil's Bargain: How Steve Bannon Met Andrew Breitbart, Then Put Conservatives on Path to Destroy Hillary Clinton Once and For All," Breitbart, July 19, 2017, https://www.breitbart.com/big-government/2017/07/19/exclusive-a-devils -bargain-how-steve-bannon-met-andrew-breitbart-put-conservatives-path-destroy -hillary-clinton-once-for-all/.

286 *From its very origin*: "#WAR—Breitbart 1st Installment," YouTube (video), 1:41, August 6, 2012, https://www.youtube.com/watch?time_continue=1&v=A7Vwc 1jgGSY.

286 *It would be different things*: Sarah Posner, "How Donald Trump's New Campaign Chief Created an Online Haven for White Nationalists," *Mother Jones*, August 22, 2016, https://www.motherjones.com/politics/2016/08/stephen-bannon-donald -trump-alt-right-breitbart-news/.

286 *The up-and-coming face*: Benjamin Wallace-Wells, "Is the Alt-Right for Real?" *New Yorker*, May 5, 2016, https://www.newyorker.com/news/benjamin-wallace -wells/is-the-alt-right-for-real.

286 *He put out a call*: Noah Shachtman, "How Andrew Breitbart Hacked the Media," Wired, March 11, 2010, https://www.wired.com/2010/03/ff-andrew-brietbart/.

287 *He termed the ACORN videos*: Rebecca Mead, "Rage Machine," *New Yorker,* May 24, 2010, https://www.newyorker.com/magazine/2010/05/24/rage-machine.

287 *From those confines*: Ibid.

287 *BuzzFeed's Matt Stopera*: Matt Stopera, interviewed by Jill Abramson and John Stillman, New York, September 1, 2015.

287 *As described in a* New Yorker *profile*: Rebecca Mead, "Rage Machine," *New*

Yorker, May 24, 2010, https://www.newyorker.com/magazine/2010/05/24/rage-machine.

288 *The* New Yorker *quoted him saying*: Ibid.

288 *"I think Donald Trump"*: *Joy Behar Show*, CNN (transcript), April 19, 2011, http://www.cnn.com/TRANSCRIPTS/1104/19/joy.01.html.

289 *Using a tool called Prism*: Adrian Chen, "The Agency," *New York Times Magazine*, June 2, 2015, https://www.nytimes.com/2015/06/07/magazine/the-agency.html.

289 *Long before he would take*: Scott Shane, "Combative, Populist Steve Bannon Found His Man in Donald Trump," *New York Times*, November 27, 2016, https://www.nytimes.com/2016/11/27/us/politics/steve-bannon-white-house.html.

290 *A Columbia Journalism Review study*: Yochai Benkler, Robert Faris, Hal Roberts, and Ethan Zuckerman, "Study: Breitbart-Led Right-Wing Media Ecosystem Altered Broader Media Agenda," *Columbia Journalism Review*, March 3, 2017, https://www.cjr.org/analysis/breitbart-media-trump-harvard-study.php.

290 *Its spokesman quit*: "Bardella: Breitbart Web Site Is a Trump Super Pac," CNN.com (video), August 21, 2016, https://www.cnn.com/videos/tv/2016/08/21/bardella-breitbart-web-site-is-a-trump-super-pac.cnn.

290 *"Andrew's life mission*: Rosie Gray and McKay Coppins, "Michelle Fields, Ben Shapiro Resign from Breitbart," BuzzFeed, March 14, 2016, https://www.buzzfeednews.com/article/rosiegray/michelle-fields-ben-shapiro-resign-from-breitbart.

290 *A pre-election report*: Thomas E. Patterson, "News Coverage of the 2016 Presidential Primaries: Horse Race Reporting Has Consequences," Shorenstein Center on Media, Politics and Public Policy, July 11, 2016, https://shorensteincenter.org/news-coverage-2016-presidential-primaries/.

290 *In the meantime, in June*: Adam Mosseri, "Building a Better News Feed for You," Facebook Newsroom, June 29, 2016, https://newsroom.fb.com/news/2016/06/building-a-better-news-feed-for-you/.

291 *The editors' job, as one told*: Mike Isaac, "Facebook 'Trending' List Skewed by Individual Judgment, Not Institutional Bias," *New York Times*, May 20, 2016, https://www.nytimes.com/2016/05/21/technology/facebook-trending-list-skewed-by-individual-judgment-not-institutional-bias.html.

291 *At the beginning of their shift*: Former Facebook Trending editors, interviewed by John Stillman, New York, August 2017.

292 *Gizmodo reported*: Michael Nunez, "Former Facebook Workers: We Routinely Suppressed Conservative News," Gizmodo, May 9, 2016, https://gizmodo.com/former-facebook-workers-we-routinely-suppressed-conser-1775461006.

293 *Senator John Thune*: Tony Romm, "Senate Committee Presses Facebook on Handling of Conservative News," Politico, May 10, 2016, https://www.politico.com/story/2016/05/john-thune-facebook-conservative-news-trending-223008.

293 *"We've built Facebook*: Mark Zuckerberg's Facebook page, May 18, 2016, https://www.facebook.com/zuck/posts/10102840575485751.

293 *After Trump introduced*: Elizabeth Dwoskin, "Facebook Thought It Was More Powerful Than a Nation-State. Then That Became a Liability," *Washington Post*, January 22, 2018, https://www.washingtonpost.com/business/economy/inside -facebooks-year-of-reckoning/2018/01/22/cfd7307c-f4c3-11e7-beb6-c8d48830c 54d_story.html?utm_term=.f7d8e787ed34.

293 *The leaked question painted*: Michael Nunez, "Facebook Employees Asked Mark Zuckerberg If They Should Try to Stop a Donald Trump Presidency," Gizmodo, April 15, 2016, https://gizmodo.com/facebook-employees-asked-mark-zuckerberg -if-they-should-1771012990.

293 *The next day, he learned that Facebook*: Nicholas Thompson and Fred Vogelstein, "Inside the Two Years That Shook Facebook—and the World," Wired, February 12, 2018, https://www.wired.com/story/inside-facebook-mark-zuckerberg-2 -years-of-hell/.

294 *a BuzzFeed reporter, Craig Silverman*: Craig Silverman, interviewed by John Stillman, Toronto, July 27–28, 2017.

296 *With his team of advisors*: Nicholas Thompson and Fred Vogelstein, "Inside the Two Years That Shook Facebook—and the World," Wired, February 12, 2018, https://www.wired.com/story/inside-facebook-mark-zuckerberg-2-years-of -hell/.

296 *On the very day the editors*: Abby Ohlheiser, "Three Days after Removing Human Editors, Facebook Is Already Trending Fake News," *Washington Post*, August 29, 2016, https://www.washingtonpost.com/news/the-intersect/wp/2016/08/29 /a-fake-headline-about-megyn-kelly-was-trending-on-facebook/?utm_term= .b4df12f85d94.

296 *Then more*: Craig Silverman, "Here's Why Facebook's Trending Algorithm Keeps Promoting Fake News," BuzzFeed, October 26, 2016, https://www.buzzfeednews .com/article/craigsilverman/can-facebook-trending-fight-off-fake-news.

296 *He did so in early September*: Mark Zuckerberg's Facebook profile, September 6, 2016, https://www.facebook.com/zuck/posts/10103087138471551.

297 *"Here's Why Facebook's Trending Algorithm*: Craig Silverman, "Here's Why Facebook's Trending Algorithm Keeps Promoting Fake News," BuzzFeed, October 26, 2016, https://www.buzzfeednews.com/article/craigsilverman/can-face book-trending-fight-off-fake-news.

297 *In November, Silverman cracked open*: Craig Silverman and Lawrence Alexander, "How Teens in the Balkans Are Duping Trump Supporters with Fake News," BuzzFeed, November 3, 2016, https://www.buzzfeednews.com/article/craigsil verman/how-macedonia-became-a-global-hub-for-pro-trump-misinfo.

297 *Silverman would later visit Veles*: Craig Silverman, interviewed by John Stillman, Toronto, July 27–28, 2017.

297 *They came to the line of work*: Ibid.

297 *Silverman explained*: Ibid.

298 *More than a year later*: Craig Silverman, J. Lester Feder, Saska Cvetkovska, and Aubrey Belford, "American Conservatives Played a Secret Role in the Macedonian Fake News Boom Ahead of 2016," BuzzFeed, July 18, 2018, https://www

.buzzfeednews.com/article/craigsilverman/american-conservatives-fake-news
-macedonia-paris-wade-libert.

298 *"I wouldn't have come aboard*: Joshua Green and Sasha Issenberg, "Inside the Trump Bunker, with Days to Go," Bloomberg, October 27, 2016, https://www
.bloomberg.com/news/articles/2016-10-27/inside-the-trump-bunker-with-12
-days-to-go.

298 *The Trump campaign had been harnessing*: Ibid.

298 *According to a report in the* Guardian: Lois Beckett, "Trump Digital Director Says Facebook Helped Win the White House," *Guardian*, October 8, 2017, https://
www.theguardian.com/technology/2017/oct/08/trump-digital-director-brad-par
scale-facebook-advertising.

299 *It was a crucial component*: Joshua Green and Sasha Issenberg, "Inside the Trump Bunker, with Days to Go," Bloomberg, October 27, 2016, https://www.bloomberg
.com/news/articles/2016-10-27/inside-the-trump-bunker-with-12-days-to-go.

299 *The Electoral College experts*: David Plouffe: "What I Got Wrong about the Election," *New York Times*, November 11, 2016, https://www.nytimes.com/2016/11/11
/opinion/what-i-got-wrong-about-the-election.html.

299 *The forum boards of 4chan*: Joseph Bernstein, "Inside 4chan's Election Day Mayhem and Misinformation Playbook," BuzzFeed, November 7, 2016, https://www
.buzzfeednews.com/article/josephbernstein/inside-4chans-election-day-mayhem
-and-misinformation-playboo#.rjDBA5vKZk.

300 *"Forget the press*: Kurt Andersen, "How America Lost Its Mind," *Atlantic*, September 2017, https://www.theatlantic.com/magazine/archive/2017/09/how-america
-lost-its-mind/534231/.

CHAPTER TEN: BUZZFEED III

301 *Despite an injection*: Steven Perlberg and Amol Sharma, "Comcast's NBCUniversal Invests Another $200 Million in BuzzFeed," *Wall Street Journal*, October 20, 2016, https://www.wsj.com/articles/comcasts-nbcuniversal-invests-another-200
-million-in-buzzfeed-1477005136.

302 *At the beginning of 2012*: Alice Suh, "BuzzFeed Adds Emotional Reactions to Facebook Timeline with New Social App," Cision, January 18, 2012, https://
www.prweb.com/releases/2012/1/prweb9117756.htm.

303 *In November 2014*: Ben Smith, "The Facebook Election," BuzzFeedNews, November 9, 2014, https://www.buzzfeednews.com/article/bensmith/the-facebook
-election.

303 *On Election Day 2012*: Maya Kosoff, "A Facebook News Feed Experiment on 1.9 Million Users May Have Increased Voter Turnout in the 2012 Election," Business Insider, https://www.businessinsider.com/facebooks-news-feed-voting-ex
periment-2012-2014-10.

303 *In 2014 the company ran another experiment*: Adam D. I. Kramer, Jamie E. Guillory, and Jeffrey T. Hancock, "Experimental Evidence of Massive-Scale Emotional Contagion through Social Networks," *Proceedings of the National Academy*

of Sciences 111, no. 24 (2014): 8788–8790, http://www.pnas.org/content/111/24/8788.

303 *Smith announced a powerful*: Ben Smith, "The Facebook Election," BuzzFeed-News, November 9, 2014, https://www.buzzfeednews.com/article/bensmith/the-facebook-election.

304 *"At some point*: Ibid.

305 *The Huffington Post went so far*: Arianna Huffington, "A Note on Trump: We Are No Longer Entertained," *Huffington Post*, December 7, 2015, https://www.huffingtonpost.com/arianna-huffington/a-note-on-trump_b_8744476.html.

305 *Meanwhile Smith's newsroom*: Ken Bensinger, Miriam Elder, and Mark Schoofs, "These Reports Allege Trump Has Deep Ties to Russia," BuzzFeedNews, January 10, 2017, https://www.buzzfeednews.com/article/kenbensinger/these-reports-allege-trump-has-deep-ties-to-russia#.bpa5jJbpx.

305 *Very early on*: McKay Coppins, "36 Hours on the Fake Campaign Trail with Donald Trump," BuzzFeed, February 13, 2014, https://www.buzzfeed.com/mckaycoppins/36-hours-on-the-fake-campaign-trail-with-donald-trump?utm_term=.bqmGzbl8V#.xjjgazYKX.

305 *Having traveled up to New Hampshire*: Ibid.

306 *Coppins seemed to be struggling*: Ibid.

306 *The day after Coppins's piece*: Sam Nunberg, email to Brian Stelter, published by *Washington Post*, February 18, 2014, https://www.washingtonpost.com/blogs/erik-wemple/wp/2014/02/18/trump-camp-blasts-buzzfeed-reporter-via-breitbart/?utm_term=.4e1cb35e3548.

306 *That summer Mercer ponied up*: Kyle Swenson, "Rebekah Mercer, the Billionaire Backer of Bannon and Trump, Chooses Sides," *Washington Post*, January 5, 2018, https://www.washingtonpost.com/news/morning-mix/wp/2018/01/05/rebekah-mercer-the-billionaire-backer-of-bannon-and-trump-chooses-sides/?utm_term=.ba7666186440.

307 *One, for instance, quoted*: Matthew Boyle, "Exclusive—Trump: 'Scumbag' BuzzFeed Blogger Ogled Women While He Ate Bison at My Resort," Breitbart, February 18, 2014, https://www.breitbart.com/big-government/2014/02/18/donald-trump-to-mckay-coppins-youre-a-scumbag/.

307 *In still another takedown*: Tony Lee, "Exclusive—Palin Calls for Boycott after BuzzFeed Hit Piece on Trump," Breitbart, February 19, 2014, https://www.breitbart.com/big-journalism/2014/02/19/palin-don-t-give-buzzfeed-blogger-who-isn-t-fit-to-tie-the-donald-s-wingtips-attention-again/.

307 *Charting the rise*: Jane Mayer, "The Reclusive Hedge-Fund Tycoon behind the Trump Presidency," *New Yorker*, March 27, 2017, https://www.newyorker.com/magazine/2017/03/27/the-reclusive-hedge-fund-tycoon-behind-the-trump-presidency; John Hayward, "The Smith Project: What Voters Want," Breitbart, February 3, 2016, https://www.breitbart.com/big-government/2016/02/03/the-smith-project-a-look-at-the-new-american-insurgency/.

307 *Smith, meanwhile, observed*: Ben Smith, "The Facebook Election," BuzzFeed-

News, November 9, 2014, https://www.buzzfeednews.com/article/bensmith/the
-facebook-election.

307 *The next day Coppins's BuzzFeed story*: McKay Coppins, "Donald Trump, America's Troll, Gets Tricked into Running for President," BuzzFeedNews, June 17, 2015, https://www.buzzfeednews.com/article/mckaycoppins/donald-trump-amer icas-troll-gets-tricked-into-running-for-pr.

308 *When CNN chief Jeff Zucker*: Hadas Gold and Gabriel Debenedetti, "Campaign Operatives Blast Jeff Zucker over CNN Coverage at Harvard Event," Politico, December 1, 2016, https://www.politico.com/story/2016/12/jeff-zucker-harvard -heckled-cnn-trump-coverage-232090.

309 *In contrast, it was not until September 2016*: Michael Barbaro, "Donald Trump Clung to 'Birther' Lie for Years, and Still Isn't Apologetic," *New York Times*, September 16, 2016, https://www.nytimes.com/2016/09/17/us/politics/donald-trump -obama-birther.html.

309 *Baron explained in an interview*: Jason Del Rey, "Marty Baron Explains What It Will Take for the Washington Post to Call a Trump Lie a Lie," Re/Code, February 14, 2017, https://www.recode.net/2017/2/14/14613714/marty-baron-washington -post-trump-lie.

309 *As a fellow doing research*: Craig Silverman, "The Lesson from the Dress Color Debate That Every Journalist Needs to Know," Poynter, February 27, 2015, https://www.poynter.org/news/lesson-dress-color-debate-every-journalist-needs -know.

310 *Before he joined BuzzFeed*: Craig Silverman, interviewed by John Stillman at BuzzFeed Toronto, July 27, 2017.

310 *By that point Silverman*: Ibid.

311 *Smith's 2015 offer*: Ibid.

311 *One of his early hires*: Sarah Aspler, interviewed by John Stillman at BuzzFeed Toronto, July 28, 2017.

311 *Just eight months after*: BuzzFeed International Editorial Meeting, observed by Jill Abramson and John Stillman, New York, October 28, 2015.

312 *Tim Gionet, who made videos*: Oliver Darcy, "The Untold Story of Baked Alaska, a Rapper Turned BuzzFeed Personality Turned Alt-Right Troll," Business Insider, April 30, 2017, https://www.businessinsider.com/who-is-baked-alaska-milo-mike -cernovich-alt-right-trump-2017-4.

312 *He hit his breaking point*: Ibid.

312 *Warzel had started out*: Charlie Warzel, interviewed by John Stillman at BuzzFeed New York, August 18, 2017.

313 *On the evening of Super Tuesday*: John Stillman, observations on a visit to BuzzFeed New York for Super Tuesday, March 1, 2016.

313 *Kaczynski's latest*: Andrew Kaczynski, "Donald Trump Had No Idea What Overalls Were until 2005," BuzzFeedNews, March 1, 2016, https://www.buzz feednews.com/article/andrewkaczynski/donald-trump-first-encountered-overalls -in-2005.

314 *"Andrew's team, along*: Ben Smith, interviewed by John Stillman at BuzzFeed New York, March 1, 2016.

314 *Super Tuesday would prove*: John Stillman, observations on a visit to BuzzFeed New York for Super Tuesday, March 1, 2016.

314 *On Facebook, BuzzFeed promoted*: BuzzFeed, "Watch as Super Tuesday Ruins This Man's Night One State at a Time," Facebook (video), March 1, 2016, https:// www.facebook.com/BuzzFeed/videos/watch-as-super-tuesday-ruins/101543 85997975329/.

315 *Then Don Lemon*: Ruby Cramer and Darren Sands, "'Superpredators' Heightens Divide between Clintons and New Generation of Black Activists," BuzzFeedNews, April 13, 2016, https://www.buzzfeednews.com/article/rubycramer /superpredators-heightens-divide-between-clintons-and-new-gen.

318 *She traced the unofficial campaign trail*: Ruby Cramer, interviewed by Jill Abramson, New York, November 20, 2015, and July 18, 2017.

320 *"There's never been anything*: David Uberti, "Trump Comeback Kills Buzz at BuzzFeed's Election-Night Fete," *Columbia Journalism Review*, November 9, 2016, https://www.cjr.org/covering_the_election/buzzfeed_twitter_election_ stream.php.

320 *As the night wore on*: Ruby Cramer, interviewed by Jill Abramson, New York, November 20, 2015, and July 18, 2017.

321 *Back at headquarters*: Charlie Warzel, interviewed by John Stillman at BuzzFeed New York, August 18, 2017.

321 *At the Javits Center*: Ruby Cramer, interviewed by Jill Abramson, New York, November 20, 2015, and July 18, 2017.

321 *As the exit polls showed*: Charlie Warzel, interviewed by John Stillman at Buzz-Feed New York, August 18, 2017.

321 *Cramer, meanwhile, watched*: Ruby Cramer, interviewed by Jill Abramson, New York, November 20, 2015, and July 18, 2017.

322 *At BuzzFeed headquarters*: Farra Strongwater, email to BuzzFeed New York staff, November 9, 2016.

322 *"If Trump loses*: Craig Silverman and Lawrence Alexander, "How Teens in the Balkans Are Duping Trump Supporters with Fake News," BuzzFeed, November 3, 2016, https://www.buzzfeednews.com/article/craigsilverman/how-macedonia -became-a-global-hub-for-pro-trump-misinfo.

323 *"Who am I to say*: Ben Smith, interviewed by Jill Abramson at BuzzFeed New York, August 2017.

324 *"This seems preposterous*: Michael Wolff (@Michael WolffNYC), "1/2 This seems preposterous, appalling, opportunistic, and lacking in basic ethics at every level," Twitter, 4:45 pm, January 10, 2017, https://twitter.com/MichaelWolffNYC /status/818982141866508288?ref_src=twsrc%5Etfw%7Ctwcamp%5Etweetem bed%7Ctwterm%5E818982141866508288&ref_url=https%3A%2F%2Fwww .weeklystandard.com%2Flarry-oconnor%2Fthe-problem-with-buzzfeeds-let-the -readers-decide-standard.

324 *"It's never been acceptable*: Margaret Sullivan, "How BuzzFeed Crossed the

Line in Publishing Salacious 'Dossier' on Trump," *Washington Post*, January 11, 2017, https://www.washingtonpost.com/lifestyle/style/how-buzzfeed-crossed-the -line-in-publishing-salacious-dossier-on-trump/2017/01/11/957b59f6-d801-11e6 -9a36-1d296534b31e_story.html?utm_term=.ca47f551a840.

324 *"Even Donald Trump deserves*: David Corn, "A Veteran Spy Has Given the FBI Information Alleging a Russian Operation to Cultivate Donald Trump," *Mother Jones*, October 31, 2016, https://www.motherjones.com/politics/2016/10/veteran -spy-gave-fbi-info-alleging-russian-operation-cultivate-donald-trump/.

324 *"I think it was disgraceful*: Ayesha Rascoe, "Trump Accuses U.S. Spy Agencies of Nazi Practices over 'Phony' Russia Dossier," Reuters, January 11, 2017, https:// www.reuters.com/article/us-usa-trump-idUSKBN14V18L.

325 *CNN's Zucker was already on record*: Ramin Setoodeh, "How Jeff Zucker Made CNN Great Again," *Variety*, August 2, 2016, https://variety.com/2016/tv/news/jeff -zucker-cnn-fox-news-1201827824/.

325 *The network issued a statement*: "Read CNN's Response to Trump's Accusations of False Reporting," CNN.com, January 11, 2017, https://www.cnn.com/2017/01 /11/politics/cnn-statement-trump-buzzfeed/index.html.

325 *One of the CNN anchors*: Chris Ariens, "CNN's Jake Tapper Calls Out BuzzFeed for Reporting Trump Dossier," Adweek, January 11, 2017, https://www.adweek .com/tvnewser/cnns-jake-tapper-calls-out-buzzfeed-for-reporting-trump-dossier /316792.

325 *Smith had a few defenders*: Vanessa M. Gezari, "BuzzFeed Was Right to Pub- lish Trump-Russia Files," *Columbia Journalism Review*, January 11, 2017, https:// www.cjr.org/criticism/buzzfeed_trump_russia_memos.php.

325 *"It was ironic*: Ben Smith, interviewed by Jill Abramson at BuzzFeed New York, August 16, 2017.

327 *Syed, who would soon win*: Jenn Topper, "5 Things You Should Know about Ris- ing Star Award Winner Nabiha Syed," Reporters Committee for Freedom of the Press, May 10, 2018, https://www.rcfp.org/browse-media-law-resources/news/5 -things-you-should-know-about-rising-star-award-winner-nabiha-syed.

327 *One of the suits against BuzzFeed*: Josh Gerstein, "Russian Bank Owners Sue BuzzFeed over Trump Dossier Publication," Politico, May 26, 2017, https://www .politico.com/blogs/under-the-radar/2017/05/26/trump-dossier-russian-bank -owners-sue-buzzfeed-238876.

327 *Michael Cohen, Trump's embattled*: https://www.wsj.com/articles/michael-cohen -drops-defamation-suits-against-buzzfeed-fusion- gps-over-russia-dossier-152415 2919.

327 *Syed still hoped*: Nabiha Syed, interviewed by Jill Abramson, New York, February 18, 2018.

328 *In an email to his employees*: Kelsey Sutton, "BuzzFeed CEO: 'We Stand with Ben' on Publication of Intel Dossier," Politico, January 11, 2017, https://www.po litico.com/blogs/on-media/2017/01/buzzfeed-ceo-we-stand-with-ben-on-publica tion-of-intel-dossier-233493.

328 *Though NBC-Universal had infused*: Sahil Patel, "NBCUniversal and BuzzFeed

Are Teaming Up for a New Parenting Channel Called Playfull," Digiday, February 6, 2018, https://digiday.com/media/nbcuniversal-and-buzzfeed-are-launching-a-new-parenting-vertical-called-playfull/.

328 *For two years in a row*: Janko Roettgers, "BuzzFeed IPO Dreams Fizzle as Company Said to Miss 2017 Revenue Target," *Variety*, November 16, 2017, https://variety.com/2017/digital/news/buzzfeed-2017-revenue-miss-1202616961/.

329 *By mid-2015, shortly after the launch*: Ibid.

330 *This was the vision*: Jonah Peretti, "A Cross-Platform, Global Network," BuzzFeed, October 23, 2015, https://www.buzzfeed.com/jonah/2015memo?utm_term=.uw9zG7L8R#.rh3BOZLKM.

330 *He introduced the latest and greatest gadget*: Jonah Peretti, presentation to BuzzFeed, observed by Jill Abramson and John Stillman, BuzzFeed New York, December 14, 2015.

330 *After unveiling HIVE*: Ibid.

331 *By the spring of 2016*: Jill Abramson and John Stillman, observations on a visit to BuzzFeed Motion Pictures, Los Angeles, March 14–17, 2016.

332 *"The lines are blurred*: Cat Bartosevich, interviewed by Jill Abramson and John Stillman at BuzzFeed Motion Pictures, Los Angeles, March 14, 2016.

332 *The head of branded advertising strategy*: Jen White, interviewed by Jill Abramson and John Stillman at BuzzFeed Motion Pictures, Los Angeles, March 15, 2016.

332 *The next month it announced*: Erin Griffith, "How Facebook's Video-Traffic Explosion Is Shaking Up the Advertising World," *Fortune*, June 3, 2015, http://fortune.com/2015/06/03/facebook-video-traffic/.

332 *Not to discredit*: Shani Hilton, interviewed by Jill Abramson and John Stillman at BuzzFeed New York, May 6, 2016.

333 *"It's food theater*: Ze Frank, interviewed by Jill Abramson and John Stillman at BuzzFeed Motion Pictures, Los Angeles, March 14, 2016.

333 *The frictionlessness of Tasty videos*: Adam Bianchi, interviewed by Jill Abramson and John Stillman at BuzzFeed Motion Pictures, Los Angeles, March 15, 2016.

333 *When Peretti had hired Frank*: Ze Frank, interviewed by Jill Abramson and John Stillman at BuzzFeed Motion Pictures, Los Angeles, March 14, 2016.

335 *For new grist*: Publishing and curation team, interviewed by John Stillman at BuzzFeed Motion Pictures, Los Angeles, March 16, 2016.

335 *When I met Eugene Lee Yang*: Eugene Lee Yang, interviewed by Jill Abramson and John Stillman at BuzzFeed Motion Pictures, Los Angeles, March 16, 2016.

336 *Later in the day*: Video brainstorm session, observed by John Stillman, BuzzFeed Motion Pictures, Los Angeles, March 16, 2016.

336 *The month following my visit*: Matthew Garrahan and Henry Moore, "BuzzFeed Missed 2015 Revenue Targets and Slashes 2016 Projections," CNBC.com, April 12, 2016, https://www.cnbc.com/2016/04/12/buzzfeed-missed-2015-revenue-targets-and-slashes-2016-projections.html.

336 *In May a new batch*: Dylan Byers, "Can BuzzFeed News Survive the Shift to Video?," CNN.com, May 24, 2016, https://money.cnn.com/2016/05/24/media/buzzfeed-news-video-future/?iid=EL.

336 *The plan called for doubling down*: BuzzFeed NewFronts presentation, New York, May 2, 2016.

338 *For the Inauguration*: Charlie Warzel, "The Right Is Building a New Media 'Upside Down' to Tell Trump's Story," BuzzFeed, January 23, 2017, https://www.buzzfeednews.com/article/charliewarzel/the-right-is-building-a-new-media-upside-down-to-tell-donald.

338 *Warzel also spoke with Cernovich*: Ibid.

339 *Departing from tradition*: "Statement by Press Secretary Sean Spicer," White House, January 21, 2017, https://www.whitehouse.gov/briefings-statements/statement-press-secretary-sean-spicer/.

339 *The next morning, on* Meet the Press: Rachael Revesz, "Donald Trump's Presidential Councellor Kellyanne Conway Says Sean Spicer Gave 'Alternative Facts' at First Press Briefing," *Independent*, January 22, 2017, https://www.independent.co.uk/news/world/americas/kellyanne-conway-sean-spicer-alternative-facts-lies-press-briefing-donald-trump-administration-a7540441.html.

340 *There was a popular meme*: Peter Holley, "The Lawn-Mowing-in-a-Tornado Dad Photo That Inspired a Thousand Memes," *Washington Post*, June 5, 2017, https://www.washingtonpost.com/news/capital-weather-gang/wp/2017/06/05/the-lawn-mowing-in-a-tornado-dad-photo-that-inspired-a-thousand-memes/?utm_term=.ea7a52993b10.

340 *They would sit side by side*: Jane Lytvynenko, interviewed by John Stillman at BuzzFeed Toronto, July 28, 2017.

340 *Their posts bore headlines*: Craig Silverman, "Use This Checklist to Find Out If You're Looking at Fake News," BuzzFeed, December 16, 2016, https://www.buzzfeed.com/craigsilverman/fake-news-checkllist-1?utm_term=.vsb1J2yAD#.bymK6DqMx; Craig Silverman, "6 Easy AF Steps to Detect Fake News Like a Pro," BuzzFeed, December 16, 2016, https://www.buzzfeed.com/craigsilverman/detect-fake-news-like-a-pro-2; Craig Silverman, "This Is How You Can Stop Fake News from Spreading on Facebook," BuzzFeedNews, November 19, 2016, https://www.buzzfeednews.com/article/craigsilverman/heres-how-to-report-fake-news-on-facebook.

341 *Lytvynenko said*: Jane Lytvynenko, interviewed by John Stillman at BuzzFeed Toronto, July 28, 2017.

341 *She had just published*: Jane Lytvynenko, "If You Get 3/7 on This Quiz You're Getting Sucker Punched by Fake News," BuzzFeedNews, July 14, 2017, https://www.buzzfeednews.com/article/janelytvynenko/fake-news-quiz-jul14.

341 *"There's a battle*: Jane Lytvynenko, interviewed by John Stillman at BuzzFeed Toronto, July 28, 2017.

341 *The social network eventually came forward*: Scott Shane and Vindu Goel, "Fake Russian Facebook Accounts Bought $100,000 in Political Ads," *New York Times*, September 6, 2017, https://www.nytimes.com/2017/09/06/technology/facebook-russian-political-ads.html.

342 *One Russian-made Facebook group*: Donie O'Sullivan and Dylan Byers, "Exclusive: Fake Black Activist Accounts Linked to Russian Government," CNN.com,

September 28, 2017, https://money.cnn.com/2017/09/28/media/blacktivist-russia
-facebook-twitter/index.html.

342 *His 2018 New Year's resolution*: Lisa Eadicicco, "Mark Zuckerberg's New Year's
Resolution Is a Huge Deal for Facebook—and the World," *Time*, January 5, 2018,
http://time.com/5089741/mark-zuckerberg-facebook-new-years-resolution-per
sonal-challenge/.

342 *In 2017 the company would push*: BuzzFeedPress, "BuzzFeed Launches a Shop,
Part of Its Growing E-Commerce Strategy—Poynter," BuzzFeed, June 22, 2017,
https://www.buzzfeed.com/buzzfeedpress/buzzfeed-launches-a-shop-part-of-its
-growing-e-commerce?utm_term=.oyWp5Qd3w#.gpzb5e63g.

343 *After missing their 2016 revenue targets*: Janko Roettgers, "BuzzFeed IPO
Dreams Fizzle as Company Said to Miss 2017 Revenue Target," *Variety*, November 16, 2017, https://variety.com/2017/digital/news/buzzfeed-2017-revenue-miss
-1202616961/; Maxwell Tani, "BuzzFeed to Lay Off 100 Staffers in Major Re-
organization," Business Insider, November 29, 2017, https://www.businessinsider
.com/buzzfeed-layoffs-business-uk-2017-11.

343 *He was the top media advisor*: "Emerson Collective to Acquire Majority Ownership of the Atlantic, Forming Partnership with David Bradley," *Atlantic*, July 28,
2017, https://www.theatlantic.com/press-releases/archive/2017/07/emerson-col
lective-to-acquire-majority-ownership-of-the-atlantic-forming-partnership-with
-david-bradley/535230/.

344 *Mashable, which, like BuzzFeed*: Todd Spangler, "Mashable Sold at Fire-Sale
Price of $50 Million to Ziff Davis (Report)," *Variety*, November 16, 2017, https://
variety.com/2017/digital/news/mashable-ziff-davis-pete-cashmore-1202616857/.

344 *Gara's experiment with*: David Uberti, "BuzzFeed Staffers Revolt over Op-Ed
Calling Roger Stone an LGBTQ 'Ally,'" Splinter, October 16, 2017, https://
splinternews.com/buzzfeed-staffers-revolt-over-op-ed-calling-roger-stone
-1819517055.

345 *Heidi Blake, a talented*: Heidi Blake et al., "From Russia with Blood," BuzzFeed,
June 15, 2017, https://www.buzzfeed.com/heidiblake/from-russia-with-blood-14
-suspected-hits-on-british-soil.

CHAPTER ELEVEN: VICE III

346 *It was a content farm*: Rhonda Richford, "Shane Smith Touts Vice's Reach with
'7,000 Pieces of Content a Day,'" *Hollywood Reporter*, June 23, 2016, https://
www.hollywoodreporter.com/news/shane-smith-touts-vices-reach-905907.

348 *In 1998, long before Vice*: "CNN Retracts Tailwind Coverage," CNN.com, July
2, 1998, http://www.cnn.com/US/9807/02/tailwind.johnson/; Robin Pogrebin and
Felicity Barringer, "CNN Retracts Report That U.S. Used Nerve Gas," *New York
Times*, July 3, 1998, https://www.nytimes.com/1998/07/03/us/cnn-retracts-report
-that-us-used-nerve-gas.html.

348 *By July 2015 CNN*: "List of How Many Homes Each Cable Network Is In as of
July 2015," TV by the Numbers, July 21, 2015, https://tvbythenumbers.zap2it

.com/reference/list-of-how-many-homes-each-cable-network-is-in-as-of-july
-2015/.

348 *(Eventually, in 2018*: "AT&T Completes Acquisition of Time Warner Inc.," AT&T Newsroom, June 15, 2018, http://about.att.com/story/att_completes_acquisition_ of_time_warner_inc.html.

348 *Many salaries hovered*: Hamilton Nolan, "Working at Vice Media Is Not as Cool as It Seems," Gawker, May 30, 2014, http://gawker.com/working-at-vice-media-is -not-as-cool-as-it-seems-1579711577.

349 *It was no surprise that the staff*: Reeves Wiedeman, "A Company Built on a Bluff," *New York Magazine*, June 10, 2018, http://nymag.com/daily/intelligencer/2018 /06/inside-vice-media-shane-smith.html.

349 *One abiding feature*: Tracy E. Gilchrist, "Vice Faces More Accusations That It Fostered Toxic Bro Culture," *Advocate*, November 15, 2017, https://www.advocate .com/media/2017/11/15/vice-faces-more-accusations-it-fostered-toxic-bro-culture.

349 *In January 2017 Smith got another*: Lucas Shaw, "Vice Valued at $5.7 Billion with $450 Million TPG Investment," Bloomberg, June 19, 2017, https://www .bloomberg.com/news/articles/2017-06-19/vice-gets-450-million-from-tpg-valu ing-company-at-5-7-billion.

349 *That same year Smith finally joined*: Natalie Robehmed, "Vice Media's Shane Smith Is Now a Billionaire," *Forbes*, June 20, 2017, https://www.forbes.com /sites/natalierobehmed/2017/06/20/vice-medias-shane-smith-is-now-a-billionaire /#2f5a2525611b.

349 *But his company's gaudy valuation*: Reeves Wiedeman, "A Company Built on a Bluff," *New York Magazine*, June 10, 2018, http://nymag.com/daily/intelligencer /2018/06/inside-vice-media-shane-smith.html.

349 *The* Wall Street Journal*'s headline*: Keach Hagey, "Vice Just Had a Big Revenue Miss, and Investors Are Getting Antsy," *Wall Street Journal*, February 7, 2018, https://www.wsj.com/articles/vice-media-confronts-tv-woes-amid-leadership -troubles-1518003121.

350 *The HBO chieftain*: Richard Plepler, interviewed by Jill Abramson, New York, August 3, 2017.

350 *Tyrangiel had jazzed up*: Stephanie Clifford and Davis Carr, "Bloomberg Buys Business Week from McGraw-Hill," *New York Times*, October 13, 2009, https:// www.nytimes.com/2009/10/14/business/media/14bizweek.html.

350 *Months later Vice announced*: Natalie Jarvey, "Vice Taps Former Bloomberg Businessweek Editor to Run Daily HBO Show," *Hollywood Insider*, October 14, 2015, https://www.hollywoodreporter.com/news/vice-hbo-show-taps-bloomberg -832119.

350 *An on-air role at Vice*: Josh Tyrangiel, interviewed by Jill Abramson at Vice New York, February 1, 2017.

351 *One of the new faces*: Arielle Duhaime-Ross, interviewed by Jill Abramson at Vice New York, February 1, 2017.

351 *Unlike the Brooklyn sophisticates*: Elspeth Reeve, interviewed by Jill Abramson and John Stillman at Vice New York, September 28, 2017.

352 *The two sipped red wine*: "VICE Special Report: A House Divided," YouTube (video), August 14, 2017, https://www.youtube.com/watch?v=pdVl3WvgJ50000.

353 *In Los Angeles, Smith*: Jordan Valinsky, "Vice's Shane Smith: 'Expect a Bloodbath' in Media within the Next Year," Digiday, May 20, 2016, https://digiday.com /media/shane-smith-vice-media-interview/.

353 *On Election Night he hosted*: Shane Smith, interviewed by Jill Abramson, Manhattan, August 4, 2017.

353 *She did one story*: Elspeth Reeve, "Alt-Right Trolls Are Getting 23andMe Genetic Tests to 'Prove' Their Whiteness," Vice News, October 9, 2016, https://news.vice .com/en_us/article/vbygqm/alt-right-trolls-are-getting-23andme-genetic-tests-to -prove-their-whiteness.

353 *After the election, the sideshow*: Vice News, "Control Alt Elite: Inside America's Racist 'Alt-Right,'" Vice, December 7, 2016, https://www.vice.com/en_id/article /mgv9nn/control-alt-elite-inside-americas-racist-alt-right.

353 *She was periodically trolled*: Elspeth Reeve, interviewed by Jill Abramson and John Stillman at Vice New York, September 28, 2017.

354 *Reeve arrived in Charlottesville*: Vice News, "Charlottesville: Race and Terror," Vice, August 21, 2017, https://news.vice.com/en_us/article/qvzn8p/vice-news-to night-full-episode-charlottesville-race-and-terror.

354 *Reeve and a cameraman jumped*: Ibid.

354 *The cameraman filmed the car*: Ibid.

355 *Vice had 18 hours*: Elspeth Reeve, interviewed by Jill Abramson and John Stillman at Vice New York, September 28, 2017.

355 *Ben Anderson, a seasoned*: Vice News, "'After ISIS' with Ben Anderson/VICE on HBO," YouTube (video), 1:24, October 11, 2017, https://www.youtube.com /watch?v=5nDSbl3B274.

355 *But other stars, like*: "Simon Ostrovsky Moves to CNN," Cision, February 9, 2017, https://www.cision.com/us/2017/02/simon-ostrovsky-moves-to-cnn/.

355 *Vice, in turn, had hired*: Kaj Larsen, interviewed by Jill Abramson and John Stillman at Vice Los Angeles, March 16, 2016.

356 *Wearing a crisp suit*: Vice News, "VICE News Presents: Privacy and Secrecy in the Digital Age—Davos Open Forum 2016," Vice, January 23, 2016, https://news .vice.com/article/vice-news-presents-privacy-and-secrecy-in-the-digital-age-live -from-the-davos-open-forum-2016.

356 *As a student at George Washington University*: Fritz Hahn, "Socializing with a Hint of Sophistication," *Washington Post*, July 20, 2007, http://www.washington post.com/wp-dyn/content/article/2007/07/19/AR2007071900764.html.

357 *One cringeworthy moment*: Vice, "VICE Special Report: A House Divided," YouTube (video), 1:10:37, August 14, 2017, https://www.youtube.com/watch?v=pd Vl3WvgJ50.

357 *"They had this fixer in Turkey*: Svati Kirsten Narula, "A Turkish Court Jailed Three Vice Journalists for Allegedly Helping ISIL," Quartz, August 31, 2015, https://qz.com/491485/a-vice-news-crew-accused-of-terrorism-goes-to-court-in -turkey/.

358 *Her arrival coincided with*: Todd Spangler, "Vice Media Pacts with Rogers for $100 Million Canadian Studio Venture, TV Channel," *Variety*, October 30, 2014, https://variety.com/2014/digital/news/vice-media-pacts-with-rogers-for-100-million-canadian-studio-venture-1201343254/.

358 *Schmidt became alarmed*: Andrea Schmidt, phone interview with Jill Abramson, February 17, 2018.

359 *But there already had been tension*: Andrea Schmidt, email to Jill Abramson, February 3, 2018.

360 *But employees saw the woman in charge*: Emily Steel, "At Vice, Cutting-Edge Media and Allegations of Old-School Sexual Harassment," *New York Times*, December 23, 2017, https://www.nytimes.com/2017/12/23/business/media/vice-sexual-harassment.html.

360 *Veltroni was working 15-hour days*: Todd Spangler, "Vice Suspends Film Producer Jason Mojica Amid Sexual Harassment Investigation," *Variety*, November 17, 2017, https://variety.com/2017/digital/news/vice-jason-mojica-suspended-sexual-harassment-1202617460/.

361 *So Veltroni was surprised*: Martina Veltroni, phone interview with Jill Abramson, January 24, 2018.

361 *Hurt and scared, Veltroni*: Ibid.

361 *He advised her she had a clear path*: Natalie Jarvey, "Vice Suspends Film Producer Following Sexual Harassment Allegations," *Hollywood Reporter*, November 17, 2017, https://www.hollywoodreporter.com/news/vice-suspends-jason-mojica-sexual-harassment-allegations-1059405.

361 *The* New York Times *broke*: Jodi Kantor and Megan Twohey, "Harvey Weinstein Paid Off Sexual Harassment Accusers for Decades," *New York Times*, October 5, 2017, https://www.nytimes.com/2017/10/05/us/harvey-weinstein-harassment-allegations.html.

361 *In October, 2017, after*: Natasha Lennard (@natashalennard), "It's only by virtue of certain silos of media starting the Shitty Media Men list," Twitter, 10:07 am, October 12, 2017, https://twitter.com/natashalennard/status/918523643122143232.

361 *"I've never worked for a more disgusting*: Brandy Zadronzy, " 'Unsafe and Just Plain Dirty': Women Accuse Vice of 'Toxic' Sexual Harassment Culture," Daily Beast, November 15, 2017, https://www.thedailybeast.com/unsafe-and-just-plain-dirty-women-accuse-vice-of-toxic-sexual-harassment-culture.

361 *Lennard told me immediately*: Natasha Lennard, phone interview with Jill Abramson, October 12, 2017.

362 *In November the Daily Beast*: Brandy Zadronzy, " 'Unsafe and Just Plain Dirty': Women Accuse Vice of 'Toxic' Sexual Harassment Culture," Daily Beast, November 15, 2017, https://www.thedailybeast.com/unsafe-and-just-plain-dirty-women-accuse-vice-of-toxic-sexual-harassment-culture.

363 *Steel's excellent story*: Emily Steel, "At Vice, Cutting-Edge Media and Allegations of Old-School Sexual Harassment," *New York Times*, December 23, 2017, https://www.nytimes.com/2017/12/23/business/media/vice-sexual-harassment.html.

363 *Barghouty told me Mojica*: Phoebe Barghouty, interviewed by Jill Abramson, October 25, 2017.

363 *Back when Smith appointed Mastromonaco*: Hadas Gold, "Alyssa Mastromonaco Joins Vice Media," Politico, November 16, 2014, https://www.politico.com/blogs /media/2014/11/alyssa-mastromonaco-joins-vice-media-198855.

363 *In anticipation of trouble*: Molly Osberg, "Looks Like Embattled HR Exec for Weinstein and Vice Still Has a Job," Splinter, February 12, 2018, https://splin ternews.com/looks-like-embattled-hr-exec-for-weinstein-and-vice-sti-1822932601.

364 *After the Daily Beast story*: Todd Spangler, "Vice Suspends Film Producer Jason Mojica Amid Sexual Harassment Investigation," *Variety*, November 17, 2017, https://variety.com/2017/digital/news/vice-jason-mojica-suspended-sexual-ha rassment-1202617460/.

364 *Two days after the Daily Beast*: Brandy Zadrozny, "Vice Employees 'Furious': 'When the F**k Are They Going to Address Sexual Harassment?'," Daily Beast, November 17, 2017, https://www.thedailybeast.com/vice-employees-furious-when -the-fk-are-they-going-to-address-sexual-harassment.

365 *In 2016 the company secretly paid*: Todd Spangler, "Vice Suspends Two Top Execs in Wake of Sexual Harassment Allegations," *Variety*, January 2, 2018, https://variety.com/2018/digital/news/vice-suspends-sexual-harassment-andrew -creighton-mike-germano-1202650838/.

365 *The* Wall Street Journal *broke*: Keach Hagey, "Vice Just Had a Big Revenue Miss, and Investors Are Getting Antsy," *Wall Street Journal*, February 7, 2018, https:// www.wsj.com/articles/vice-media-confronts-tv-woes-amid-leadership-troubles -1518003121.

365 *BuzzFeed's valuation was*: Lucinda Shen, "BuzzFeed Said to Prepare for a 2018 IPO," *Fortune*, March 29, 2017, http://fortune.com/2017/03/29/buzzfeed-buzz-ipo -snap-nbcuniversal/.

365 *Vice's had ballooned:* Reuters and Nathan McAlone, "Vice Landed a Blockbuster Valuation of $5.7 Billion and $450 Million in Fresh Cash—but Disney Didn't Put in More Money," Business Insider, June 19, 2017, https://www.businessinsider .com/vice-raises-450-million-at-57-billion-valuation-from-tpg-2017-6.

365 *Rogers Communications, under new management:* "Rogers Media Cuts Ties with Vice Canada, Pulls Viceland Channel Off the Air," CTV News, January 22, 2018, https://www.ctvnews.ca/business/rogers-media-cuts-ties-with-vice-canada-pulls -viceland-channel-off-the-air-1.3770212.

366 *For more than a month*: Antonia Hylton, Lindsay Van Dyke, and Jika Gonzalez, "Zero Tolerance: One Immigrant Family's Journey from Separation to Reunification," *Vice News Tonight*, August 1, 2018, https://news.vice.com/en_us/article /8xbmmb/zero-tolerance-one-immigrant-familys-journey-from-separation-to-re unification.

366 *An audio recording*: Antonia Hylton, Lindsay Van Dyke, Jika Gonzalez, and Mimi Dwyer, "Listen to a Distraught Guatemalan Child Call His Mother from a U.S. Immigration Shelter," Vice, June 27, 2018, https://news.vice.com/en_us/article

/a3abjz/listen-to-a-distraught-guatemalan-child-call-his-mother-from-a-us-immi
gration-shelter.

367 *The show was a quest*: Reeves Wiedeman, "A Company Built on a Bluff," *New York Magazine*, June 10, 2018, http://nymag.com/daily/intelligencer/2018/06/in side-vice-media-shane-smith.html.

367 *Smith had hoped to cash out*: Ibid.

367 *Everyone in new media*: Todd Spangler, "Mashable Sold at Fire-Sale Price of $50 Million to Ziff Davis (Report)," *Variety*, November 16, 2017, https://variety.com /2017/digital/news/mashable-ziff-davis-pete-cashmore-1202616857/.

367 *Vice operated in more than 40*: Mark Sweney, "Vice to Launch in More Than 50 New Countries," *Guardian*, June 22, 2016, https://www.theguardian.com/media /2016/jun/22/vice-to-launch-in-more-than-50-new-countries.

368 *At the huge annual Cannes*: Georg Szalai and Rhonda Richford, "Cannes Lions: Viceland to Launch in India, Southeast Asia, Australia, Africa," *Hollywood Reporter*, June 22, 2016, https://www.hollywoodreporter.com/news/cannes-lions -viceland-launch-india-905416.

368 *On Election Night 2016*: Gavin McInnes, interviewed by Jill Abramson, New York, August 4, 2017.

368 *A passionate Trump supporter*: Jonathan Goldsbie and Graeme Gordon, "Gavin McInnes Leaving the Rebel," Canadaland, August 17, 2017, http://www.canada landshow.com/gavin-mcinnes-leaving-rebel/.

368 *He often made incendiary*: Bob Moser, "Why the 'Alt-Lite' Celebrated the Las Vegas Massacre," *New Republic*, October 6, 2017, https://newrepublic.com/article /145192/alt-lite-celebrated-las-vegas-massacre.

369 *As before, he was nattily dressed*: Daniel J. Solomon, "Watch: Vice Co-Founder Makes '10 Things I Hate about Jews' Video," *Forward*, March 15, 2017, https:// forward.com/fast-forward/366077/watch-vice-co-founder-makes-10-things-i -hate-about-jews-video/.

369 *Within months of our meeting*: Nellie Andreeva, "Nancy Dubuc Named CEO of Vice Media, Shane Smith to Be Executive Chairman," Deadline, March 13, 2018, https://deadline.com/2018/03/nancy-dubuc-ceo-vice-media-1202336972/.

CHAPTER TWELVE: *NEW YORK TIMES* III

372 *Barbaro's listeners adored*: Tweet by Lily/PARLOUR TRICKS @lilycato, November 9, 2017, https://twitter.com/lilycato/status/928629484034646017.

373 *Except for Sunday:* Michael Barthel, "Despite Subscription Surges for Largest U.S. Newspapers, Circulation and Revenue Fall for Industry Overall," Pew Research Center, June 1, 2017, http://www.pewresearch.org/fact-tank/2017/06/01 /circulation-and-revenue-fall-for-newspaper-industry/.

373 *Online the* Times *had 70 million*: "Share of Readers of the New York Times in the United States in 2018, by Age," Statista, n.d., https://www.statista.com/statistics /229984/readers-of-the-new-york-times-daily-edition-usa/.

373 *Yet even with more than one million*: Jaclyn Peiser, "New York Times Co. Reports Revenue Growth as Digital Subscriptions Rise," *New York Times*, May 3, 2018, https://www.nytimes.com/2018/05/03/business/media/new-york-times-earnings.html.

373 *Barbaro's unexpectedly successful*: "'The Daily' Exceeds 100 Million Downloads," Nytco.com, October 17, 2017, https://www.nytco.com/the-daily-exceeds -100-million-downloads/.

373 *The Election Night show was a tour de force*: Michael Barbaro, "How Did the Media—How Did We—Get This Wrong?," *New York Times*, November 9, 2016, https://www.nytimes.com/2016/11/09/podcasts/election-analysis-run-up.html.

375 *Under the new system:* "They're Worth How Much? TV Anchors by the Numbers," Daily Beast, August 8, 2012, https://www.thedailybeast.com/theyre-worth -how-much-tv-anchors-by-the-numbers.

375 *Even Silver, now working at ESPN*: Christina Pazzanese, "The Puzzle in Politics and Polling," *Harvard Gazette*, March 30, 2017, https://news.harvard.edu/gazette /story/2017/03/nate-silver-says-conventional-wisdom-not-data-killed-2016-elec tion-forecasts/.

376 *Within days the* Times *published*: "To Our Readers, from the Publisher and Executive Editor," *New York Times*, November 13, 2016, https://www.nytimes.com/2016 /11/13/us/elections/to-our-readers-from-the-publisher-and-executive-editor.html.

376 *The invocation of*: David W. Dunlap, "1896: 'Without Fear or Favor,'" *New York Times*, August 14, 2015, https://www.nytimes.com/2015/09/12/insider/1896-with out-fear-or-favor.html.

379 *On March 2, 2015, at the top*: Michael S. Schmidt, "Hillary Clinton Used Personal Email Account at State Dept., Possibly Breaking Rules," *New York Times*, March 2, 2015, https://www.nytimes.com/2015/03/03/us/politics/hillary-clintons -use-of-private-email-at-state-department-raises-flags.html.

380 *High on the* Times*'s homepage*: Michael S. Schmidt and Matt Apuzzo, "Inquiry Sought in Hillary Clinton's Use of Email," *New York Times*, July 23, 2015, https:// www.nytimes.com/2015/07/24/us/politics/inquiry-is-sought-in-hillary-clinton -email-account.html.

380 *The* Times*'s public editor*: Margaret Sullivan, "A Clinton Story Fraught with Inaccuracies: How It Happened and What Next?," *New York Times*, July 27, 2015, https://publiceditor.blogs.nytimes.com/2015/07/27/a-clinton-story-fraught-with -inaccuracies-how-it-happened-and-what-next/.

380 *Clinton Communications Director Palmieri*: Erik Wemple, "Clinton Campaign Blasts New York Times in Letter to Executive Editor Dean Baquet," *Washington Post*, July 30, 2015, https://www.washingtonpost.com/blogs/erik-wemple/wp /2015/07/30/clinton-campaign-blasts-new-york-times-in-letter-to-executive-edi tor-dean-baquet/.

381 *"We did all hyperventilate*: "Amy Chozick on 'Chasing Hillary,'" *New York Times, Book Review* podcast, May 11, 2018, https://www.nytimes.com/2018/05 /11/books/review/amy-chozick-on-chasing-hillary.html.

381 Times *columnist David Leonhardt*: Eddie Scarry, "New York Times Columnist In-

sists Hillary Clinton Email Coverage 'Media's Worst Mistake in 2016,'" *Washington Examiner*, May 9, 2017, https://www.washingtonexaminer.com/new-york-times-columnist-insists-hillary-clinton-email-coverage-medias-worst-mistake-in-2016.

381 *Baquet defended coverage*: Sydney Ember, "Editors Defend Coverage of Stolen Emails after News of Russian Hacks," *New York Times*, December 15, 2016, https://www.nytimes.com/2016/12/15/business/media/russian-hacking-stolen-emails.html.

382 *The* Times Magazine *did an early probe*: Adrian Chen, "The Agency," *New York Times Magazine*, June 2, 2015, https://www.nytimes.com/2015/06/07/magazine/the-agency.html.

383 *Eric Lichtblau, who had won*: James Risen and Eric Lichtblau, "Bush Lets U.S. Spy on Callers without Courts," *New York Times*, December 16, 2005, https://www.nytimes.com/2005/12/16/politics/bush-lets-us-spy-on-callers-without-courts.html.

383 *Lichtblau's original draft*: Eric Lichtblau and Steven Lee Myers, "Investigating Donald Trump, F.B.I. Sees No Clear Link to Russia," *New York Times*, October 31, 2016, https://www.nytimes.com/2016/11/01/us/politics/fbi-russia-election-donald-trump.html.

384 *A week before the election*: Franklin Foer, "Was a Trump Server Communicating with Russia," Slate, October 31, 2016, http://www.slate.com/articles/news_and_politics/cover_story/2016/10/was_a_server_registered_to_the_trump_organization_communicating_with_russia.html.

384 *Campaigning in Cincinnati*: Eric Lichtblau and Steven Lee Myers, "Investigating Donald Trump, F.B.I. Sees No Clear Link to Russia," *New York Times*, October 31, 2016, https://www.nytimes.com/2016/11/01/us/politics/fbi-russia-election-donald-trump.html.

384 *Liz Spayd, who had replaced*: Liz Spayd, "Trump, Russia, and the News Story That Wasn't," *New York Times*, January 20, 2017, https://www.nytimes.com/2017/01/20/public-editor/trump-russia-fbi-liz-spayd-public-editor.html.

385 *The email from Baquet:* Erik Wemple, "CNN Nabs Eric Lichtblau from the New York Times," *Washington Post*, April 10, 2017, https://www.washingtonpost.com/blogs/erik-wemple/wp/2017/04/10/cnn-nabs-eric-lichtblau-from-the-new-york-times/?utm_term=.a363887dbbd8.

385 *He was involved in another controversial*: Paul Farhi, "The Story behind a Retracted CNN Report on the Trump Campaign and Russia," *Washington Post*, August 17, 2017, https://www.washingtonpost.com/lifestyle/style/the-story-behind-a-retracted-cnn-report-on-the-trump-campaign-and-russia/2017/08/17/afo3cd60-82d6-11e7-ab27-1a21a8e006ab_story.html?utm_term=.ad286b99b622.

386 *A 2016 study*: Amy Mitchell, Jeffrey Gottfried, Michael Barthel, and Elisa Shearer, "7. Party ID and News," Pew Research Center, July 7, 2016, http://www.journalism.org/2016/07/07/party-id-and-news/.

387 *In a Gallup poll*: Erik Wemple, "Study: 42 Percent of Republicans Believe Accurate—but Negative—Stories Qualify as 'Fake News,'" *Washington Post*,

January 16, 2018, https://www.washingtonpost.com/blogs/erik-wemple/wp/2018 /01/16/study-42-percent-of-republicans-believe-accurate-but-negative-stories -qualify-as-fake-news/?utm_term=.f99ba93c1931.

387 *In still another sad and astonishing poll*: Anthony Salvanto, Jennifer De Pinto, Kabir Khanna, and Fred Backus, "Americans Wary of Trump Tariffs' Impact, but Support Plan to Aid Farmers—CBS Poll," CBS News, July 29, 2018, https://www .cbsnews.com/news/americans-wary-of-trump-tariffs-impact-but-support-plan-to -aid-farmers-cbs-poll/?utm_source=newsletter&utm_medium=email&utm_cam paign=newsletter_axiosam&strea m=top-stories.

387 *By the Sunday morning*: Donald J. Trump (@realDonaldTrump), "The @nytimes sent a letter to their subscribers apologizing for their BAD coverage of me," Twitter, 6:43 am, November 13, 2016, https://twitter.com/realDonaldTrump/ status/797812048805695488?ref_src=twsrc%5Etfw%7Ctwcamp%5Etweetem bed%7Ctwterm%5E797812048805695488&ref_url=https%3A%2F%2Fwww .washingtonpost.com%2Fnews%2Fthe-fix%2Fwp%2F2017%2F03%2F29% 2Fno-the-new-york-times-did-not-apologize-because-its-trump-coverage-was-so -wrong%2F.

388 *Then came, "Wow*: Donald J. Trump (@realDonaldTrump), "Wow, the @nytimes is losing thousands of subscribers because of their very poor and highly inaccurate coverage of the 'Trump phenomena [*sic*],'" Twitter, 6:16 am, November 13, 2016, https://twitter.com/realdonaldtrump/status/797805407179866112?lang=en.

388 *On Twitter Trump had called the* Times: Jasmine C. Lee and Kevin Quealy, "The 487 People, Places and Things Donald Trump Has Insulted on Twitter: A Complete List," *New York Times*, July 10, 2018, https://www.nytimes.com/interactive /2016/01/28/upshot/donald-trump-twitter-insults.html.

389 *On the Sunday night*: Ryan Reed, "Watch John Oliver Become Nauseous over Trump, Say 'F—k 2016,'" *Rolling Stone*, November 14, 2016, https://www.roll ingstone.com/tv/tv-news/watch-john-oliver-become-nauseous-over-trump-say-f -k-2016-125250/.

389 *Almost immediately, donations*: Kristen Hare, "New York Times Reports 41,000 New Subscribers Since the Election," Poynter, November 17, 2016, https://www .poynter.org/news/new-york-times-reports-41000-new-subscribers-election.

389 *Jeff Gerth, a formidable*: Jeff Gerth, "For *The New York Times*, Trump Is a Sparring Partner with Benefits," *Columbia Journalism Review*, June 29, 2017, https:// www.cjr.org/special_report/trump_new_york_times.php/.

390 *When a* Post *reporter tweeted*: Zack Johnk, "Trump Wants Washington Post Reporter Fired over Misleading Tweet," *New York Times*, December 10, 2017, https:// www.nytimes.com/2017/12/10/us/politics/trump-dave-weigel.html.

390 *Eric Lipton of the* Times: Eric Lipton, "Trump Rules," series of articles published in *New York Times*, May 20, 2017–February 15, 2018, https://www.nytimes.com /series/trump-rules-regulations.

391 *During the campaign*: Michael Barbaro, "Trump Gives Up a Lie but Refuses to Repent," *New York Times*, September 17, 2016, A1.

392 *The* Times *drew widespread rebuke*: Pete Vernon, "The Media Today: How Not to

Write about a Nazi," *Columbia Journalism Review*, November 27, 2017, https://www.cjr.org/the_media_today/new-york-times-nazi-hovater.php; Richard Fausset, "A Voice of Hate in America's Heartland," *New York Times*, November 25, 2017, https://www.nytimes.com/2017/11/25/us/ohio-hovater-white-nationalist.html.

392 *The paper ran an editor's note*: Marc Lacey, "Readers Accuse Us of Normalizing a Nazi Sympathizer, We Respond," *New York Times*, November 26, 2017, https://www.nytimes.com/2017/11/26/reader-center/readers-accuse-us-of-normalizing-a-nazi-sympathizer-we-respond.html.

393 *The* Times *received $12 million*: "Introducing the Daily 360 from the New York Times," *New York Times*, November 1, 2016, https://www.nytimes.com/2016/11/01/nytnow/the-daily-360-videos.html.

394 *Dolnick distinguished himself*: Sam Dolnick, "As Escapees Stream Out, a Penal Business Thrives," *New York Times*, June 16, 2012, https://www.nytimes.com/2012/06/17/nyregion/in-new-jersey-halfway-houses-escapees-stream-out-as-a-penal-business-thrives.html.

395 *He covered a lot of ground*: Dan Zak, Sarah Ellison, and Ben Terris, " 'He Doesn't Like Bullies': The Story of the 37-Year-Old Who Took Over the New York Times and Is Taking on Trump," *Washington Post*, July 30, 2018, https://www.washingtonpost.com/lifestyle/style/he-doesnt-like-bullies-the-story-of-the-37-year-old-who-took-over-the-ny-times-and-is-taking-on-trump/2018/07/30/61459c96-940c-11e8-a679-b09212fb69c2_story.html?utm_term=.253b6b84ecc3; A. G. Sulzberger and Jennifer Medina, "Shooting Suspect Had Been Known to Use Potent, and Legal, Hallucinogen," *New York Times*, January 17, 2011, https://www.nytimes.com/2011/01/18/us/18salvia.html.

397 *Circulation had brought in a meager*: Derek Thompson, "How to Survive the Media Apocalypse," *Atlantic*, November 29, 2017, https://www.theatlantic.com/business/archive/2017/11/media-apocalypse/546935/.

399 *Ken Auletta, a writer*: Ken Auletta, *Backstory: Inside the Business of News* (New York: Penguin, 2004).

399 *"Our journalists comfortably*: David Leonhardt et al., "Journalism That Stands Apart," Report of the 2020 Group, *New York Times*, January 2017, https://www.nytimes.com/projects/2020-report/.

400 *On the strength of stories*: Keith Collins and Gabriel J. X. Dance, "How Researchers Learned to Use Facebook 'Likes' to Sway Your Thinking," *New York Times*, March 20, 2018, https://www.nytimes.com/2018/03/20/technology/facebook-cambridge-behavior-model.html.

400 *But lest it get that far*: "Artificial Intelligence: How We Help Machines Learn," T Brand Studio, paid post for Facebook, https://paidpost.nytimes.com/facebook/artificial-intelligence-how-we-help-machines-learn.html.

401 *One trip offered*: Paul Farhi, "The New York Times Will Fly You Around the World for $135,000. Is That a Problem?," *Washington Post*, July 5, 2017, https://www.washingtonpost.com/lifestyle/style/the-new-york-times-will-fly-you-around-the-world-for-135000-is-that-a-problem/2017/07/05/9a99d84e-603d-11e7-a4f7-af34fc1d9d39_story.html?utm_term=.9cd9d697a25f.

401 *"I thought we had something special*: The NewsGuild of New York, www.nyguild
.org/front-page-details/the-jilted-copydesk, July 25, 2017.

CHAPTER THIRTEEN: *WASHINGTON POST* III

403 *As big political names*: Michael Calderone, "Washington Post Newsroom Rankled
by 'Offensive' Election Night Party Stunt," Huffington Post, November 14, 2016,
https://www.huffingtonpost.com/entry/washington-post-election-night-party
_us_5829fcfbe4b0c4b63b0dad3f.

403 *If the casino-themed party*: Ibid.

403 *The next day, as Clinton*: Gabrielle Bluestone, "The *Washington Post* Served Nap-
kins Off a Woman's Body at Its Election Party," Jezebel, November 14, 2016,
https://jezebel.com/the-washington-post-served-napkins-off-a-womans-body-at
-1788966492.

404 *In 2016 Ryan celebrated*: Nat Levy, "The Jeff Bezos Effect? Washington Post Is
Profitable and Set to Hire Dozens of Journalists in 2017," GeekWire, December
27, 2016, https://www.geekwire.com/2016/jeff-bezos-effect-washington-post
-profitable-set-hire-dozens-journalists-2017/.

404 *It wasn't the machine*: Jennifer Steinhauer, "A Tailor-Made Publisher Taking Over
Jeff Bezos' Washington Post," *New York Times*, September 22, 2014, https://www
.nytimes.com/2014/09/23/business/media/beltway-insider-takes-helm-at-the
-post.html.

404 *While many investigative reporters*: David A. Fahrenthold, "Trump Recorded
Having Extremely Lewd Conversation about Women in 2005," *Washington Post*,
October 8, 2016, https://www.washingtonpost.com/politics/trump-recorded-hav
ing-extremely-lewd-conversation-about-women-in-2005/2016/10/07/3b9ce776
-8cb4-11e6-bf8a-3d26847eeed4_story.html?utm_term=.1b842821a1a5.

405 *Trump's Twitter attacks*: Glenn Kessler, "Trump's Claim That He 'Predicted
Osama bin Laden,'" *Washington Post*, December 7, 2015, https://www.washing
tonpost.com/news/fact-checker/wp/2015/12/07/trumps-claim-that-he-predicted
-osama-bin-laden/?utm_term=.2f48c96b2f67.

406 *On some days the* Post *had*: Kyle Swenson, "She Said She Killed Her Son and Hid
Him in a Manure Pile. The Truth Is More Sinister, Police Say," *Washington Post*,
March 9, 2018, https://www.washingtonpost.com/news/morning-mix/wp/2018/03
/09/she-said-she-killed-her-son-and-hid-him-in-a-manure-pile-the-truth-is-more
-sinister-police-say/?utm_term=.edf7f33863e2.

406 *At the opening celebration*: Emily Heil, "John Kerry, Jeff Bezos Celebrate Official Opening of New Washington Post Headquarters," *Washington Post*, January
28, 2016, https://www.washingtonpost.com/news/reliable-source/wp/2016/01/28
/john-kerry-jeff-bezos-celebrate-official-opening-of-new-washington-post-head
quarters/?utm_term=.5711131a82ac.

409 *"I have never received*": Jim Newell, "The Media Finally Figured Out How to Rat-
tle Donald Trump," Slate, May 31, 2016, http://www.slate.com/articles/news_and

_politics/politics/2016/05/the_media_finally_figured_out_how_to_rattle_donald
_trump.html.

410 *One itemized gift*: David A. Fahrenthold and Rosalind S. Helderman, "Missing from Trump's List of Charitable Giving: His Own Personal Cash," *Washington Post*, April 10, 2016, https://www.washingtonpost.com/politics/a-portrait -of-trump-the-donor-free-rounds-of-golf-but-no-personal-cash/2016/04/10 /373b9b92-fb40-11e5-9140-e61d062438bb_story.html.

411 *David Fahrenthold, a young*: Pulitzer Prize, "David A. Fahrenthold of *The Washington Post*," 2017 Winner in National Reporting, n.d., http://www.pulitzer.org /winners/david-fahrenthold.

411 *To help the* Post *increase*: Alex Lo, "Amazon Prime Washington Post Promotion: Free 6 Month Digital Subscription," *Hustler Money Blog*, February 19, 2018, http://www.hustlermoneyblog.com/amazon-prime-washington-post-promotion/.

411 *Amazon kept the number*: WashPostPR, "Amazon Prime Members Enjoy Digital Access to the Washington Post for Free," *Washington Post*, September 16, 2015, https://www.washingtonpost.com/pr/wp/2015/09/16/amazon-prime-members -enjoy-digital-access-to-the-washington-post-for-free/?utm_term=.571e0 08cd54b.

412 *Like its New York competitor*: Brian Stelter, "Washington Post Digital Subscriptions Soar Past 1 Million Mark," CNN.com, September 26, 2017, https://money .cnn.com/2017/09/26/media/washington-post-digital-subscriptions/index.html.

412 *Audience traffic exceeded:* Chris Cillizza, "Why the Fight between the Washington Post and New York Times over Traffic Misses the Point," *Washington Post*, December 1, 2015, https://www.washingtonpost.com/news/the-fix/wp/2015/12/01 /why-the-fight-between-the-washington-post-and-new-york-times-over-traffic-is -stupid/?utm_term=.6e4389a16177.

414 *That's what he and his 80 engineers*: WashPostPR, "Nieman Lab: Here's How Arc's Cautious Quest to Become the Go-To Publishing System for News Organizations Is Going," *Washington Post*, February 2, 2018, https://www.washing tonpost.com/pr/wp/2018/02/02/nieman-lab-heres-how-arcs-cautious-quest-to-be come-the-go-to-publishing-system-for-news-organizations-is-going/?utm_ter m=.2cc34763e8bd.

414 *Another homegrown tool*: WashPostPR, "The Washington Post Unveils New Real-Time Content Testing Tool Bandito," *Washington Post*, February 8, 2016, https://www.washingtonpost.com/pr/wp/2016/02/08/the-washington-post-unveils -new-real-time-content-testing-tool-bandito/.

415 *"This Is What Happened*: Darlena Cunha, "This Is What Happened When I Drove My Mercedes to Pick Up Food Stamps," *Washington Post*, July 8, 2014, https://www.washingtonpost.com/posteverything/wp/2014/07/08/this-is-what -happened-when-i-drove-my-mercedes-to-pick-up-food-stamps/?utm_term=.c8f 7753cdbb1; Julie Zauzmer and Sarah Pulliam Bailey, "Pope Francis Saw a Boy with Cerebral Palsy. This Is What Happened Next," *Washington Post*, September 26, 2015, https://www.washingtonpost.com/news/acts-of-faith/wp/2015/09/26

/pope-francis-saw-a-boy-with-cerebral-palsy-this-is-what-happened-next/; Justin Wm. Moyer, "Dunkin' Donuts Just 'Destroyed' Starbucks with This Christmas-y Cup," *Washington Post*, November 12, 2015, https://www.washingtonpost.com /news/morning-mix/wp/2015/11/12/dunkin-donuts-just-destroyed-starbucks-with -this-much-more-christmas-y-holiday-cup/.

415 *Baron's first managing editor*: Ravi Somaiya, "Where Clicks Reign, Audience Is King," *New York Times*, August 16, 2015, https://www.nytimes.com/2015/08/17 /business/where-clicks-reign-audience-is-king.html.

416 *The* Post *revealed Attorney General*: Matt Zapotosky and Sari Horwitz, "Sessions Again Changes His Account of What He Knew about Trump Campaign's Dealings with Russians," *Washington Post*, November 14, 2017, https://www.wash ingtonpost.com/world/national-security/sessions-likely-to-be-questioned-about -trump-campaign-dealings-with-russians-at-house-judiciary-hearing/2017/11/13 /bc20b7fc-c894-11e7-aa96-54417592cf72_story.html?utm_term=.0f93d1223b6f; Ellen Nakashima, Adam Entous, and Greg Miller, "Russian Ambassador Told Moscow That Kushner Wanted Secret Communications Channel with Kremlin," *Washington Post*, May 26, 2017, https://www.washingtonpost.com/world /national-security/russian-ambassador-told-moscow-that-kushner-wanted-secret -communications-channel-with-kremlin/2017/05/26/520a14b4-422d-11e7-9869 -bac8b446820a_story.html?utm_term=.c2cdee363382.

416 *The* Post *won a Pulitzer*: "Washington Post's 2018 Pulitzer Prizes for Roy Moore Investigation, Russia Reporting," *Washington Post*, April 16, 2018, https://www .washingtonpost.com/news/national/wp/2018/04/16/feature/washington-post -wins-pulitzer-prizes-for-roy-moore-investigation-russia-reporting/?utm_ter m=.7b04cb258b66.

417 *The* Times *ran a definitive investigation*: Nick Wingfield and Ravi Somaiya, "Amazon Spars with the Times over Investigative Article," *New York Times*, October 19, 2015, https://www.nytimes.com/2015/10/20/business/amazon-spars-with-the -times-over-investigative-article.html.

418 *In 2017 he purchased*: Mimi Montgomery, "Here Are the Floor Plans for Jeff Bezos's $23 Million DC Home," *Washingtonian*, April 22, 2018, https://www .washingtonian.com/2018/04/22/here-are-the-floor-plans-for-jeff-bezos-23-mil lion-dc-home/.

418 *In December 2015 Trump fired off*: Donald J. Trump (@realDonaldTrump), "The @washingtonpost, which loses a fortune, is owned by @JeffBezos for purposes of keeping taxes down at his no profit company, @amazon," Twitter, 7:08 am, December 7, 2015, https://twitter.com/realdonaldtrump/status/673881733415178240 ?lang=en.

418 *The next blast*: Donald J. Trump (@realDonaldTrump), "The @washingtonpost loses money (a deduction) and gives owner @JeffBezos power to screw public on low taxation of @Amazon! Big tax shelter," Twitter, 7:18 am, December 7, 2015, https://twitter.com/realdonaldtrump/status/673884271954776064?lang=en.

418 *Then, a third*: Donald J. Trump (@realDonaldTrump), "If @amazon ever had to pay fair taxes, its stock would crash and it would crumble like a paper bag. The

@washingtonpost scam is saving it," Twitter, 7:22 am, December 7, 2015, https://twitter.com/realdonaldtrump/status/673885376742825984?lang=en.

418 *Bezos chose to respond*: Jeff Bezos (@JeffBezos), "Finally trashed by @realDonaldTrump. Will still reserve him a seat on the Blue Origin rocket. #sendDonaldtospace," Twitter, 3:30 pm, December 7, 2015, https://twitter.com/jeffbezos/status/674008204838199297?lang=en.

419 *In a Fox News interview*: Reuters, "Amazon 'Getting Away with Murder on Tax,' Says Donald Trump," *Guardian*, May 13, 2016, https://www.theguardian.com/us-news/2016/may/13/amazon-getting-away-with-on-tax-says-donald-trump.

419 *When Bezos was asked*: Olivia Solon, "Jeff Bezos Says Donald Trump's Behavior 'Erodes Democracy,'" *Guardian*, October 20, 2016, https://www.theguardian.com/technology/2016/oct/20/jeff-bezos-donald-trump-criticism-amazon-blue-origin.

419 *Two days after the election*: Deirdre Bosa, "Jeff Bezos Congratulates President-Elect Trump, after Offering to Shoot Him into Space," CNBC.com, November 10, 2016, https://www.cnbc.com/2016/11/10/jeff-bezos-congratulates-president-elect-trump-after-offering-to-shoot-him-into-space.html.

419 *Less than a week later*: Donald J. Trump (@realDonaldTrump), "The #AmazonWashingtonPost, sometimes referred to as the guardian of Amazon not paying internet taxes (which they should) is FAKE NEWS!" Twitter, 6:06 am, June 28, 2017, https://twitter.com/realdonaldtrump/status/880049704620494848?lang=en.

BIBLIOGRAPHY

Anderson, C.W., Emily Bell, and Clay Shirky. "Post-Industrial Journalism: Adapting to the Present." *Geopolitics, History, and International Relations*, vol. 7, no. 2 (2015): 32–123.

Bell, Emily, Taylor Owen, Smitha Khorana, and Jennifer R. Henrichsen, eds. *Journalism after Snowden: The Future of the Free Press in the Surveillance State*. Columbia Journalism Review Books. New York: Columbia University Press, 2017.

Blascovich, Jim, and Jeremy Bailenson. *Infinite Reality: Avatars, Eternal Life, New Worlds, and the Dawn of the Virtual Revolution*. New York: William Morrow and Company, 2011.

Boyd, Gerald M. *My Times in Black and White: Race and Power at the* New York Times. Chicago: Lawrence Hill Books, 2010.

Carr, Nicholas. *The Shallows: What the Internet Is Doing to Our Brains*. New York: W. W. Norton & Company, 2010.

Carroll, John S. "What Will Become of Newspapers?" Speech, Cambridge, MA, April 26, 2006. Shorenstein Center on Media, Politics and Public Policy at the John F. Kennedy School of Government at Harvard University. https://shorensteincenter.org/what-will-become-of-newspapers.

Childress, Diana. *Johannes Gutenberg and the Printing Press*. Minneapolis, MN: Lerner Publishing Group, 2008.

Chozick, Amy. *Chasing Hillary: Ten Years, Two Presidential Campaigns, and One Intact Glass Ceiling*. New York: Harper, an Imprint of HarperCollins Publishers, 2018.

Clinton, Hillary Rodham. *What Happened*. New York: Simon & Schuster, 2017.

Daley, Chris K. *Becoming Breitbart: The Impact of a New Media Revolutionary*. Chris Daley Publishing, 2012.

Downie, Leonard, and Robert G. Kaiser. *The News about the News: American Journalism in Peril*. New York: Alfred A. Knopf, 2002.

Fahrenthold, David A. *Uncovering Trump: The Truth Behind Donald Trump's Charitable Giving.* New York: Diversion Books, 2017.

Foer, Franklin. *World without Mind: The Existential Threat of Big Tech.* New York: The Penguin Press, 2017.

Gelb, Arthur. *City Room.* New York: Putnam, 2003.

Graham, Katharine. *Personal History.* New York: Alfred A. Knopf, 1997.

Greenhouse, Linda. *Just a Journalist: On the Press, Life, and the Spaces Between.* The William E. Massey Sr. Lectures in American Studies. Cambridge, MA: Harvard University Press, 2017.

Halberstam, David. *The Powers That Be.* New York: Alfred A. Knopf, 1979.

Isaacson, Walter. *The Innovators: How a Group of Hackers, Geniuses, and Geeks Created the Digital Revolution.* New York: Simon & Schuster, 2014.

Jones, Alex S. *Losing the News: The Future of the News That Feeds Democracy.* Institutions of American Democracy. New York: Oxford University Press, 2009.

Kakutani, Michiko. *The Death of Truth: Notes on Falsehood in the Age of Trump.* New York: Tim Duggan Books, 2018.

Kemeny, John G. *Man and the Computer.* New York: Scribner, 1972.

Kennedy, Dan. "The Bezos Effect: How Amazon's Founder Is Reinventing *The Washington Post*—and What Lessons It Might Hold for the Beleaguered Newspaper Business." Shorenstein Center on Media, Politics and Public Policy at the John F. Kennedy School of Government at Harvard University, June 8, 2016. https://shorensteincenter.org/bezos-effect-washington-post.

Kennedy, Dan. *The Return of the Moguls: How Jeff Bezos and John Henry Are Remaking Newspapers for the Twenty-first Century.* Lebanon, NH: ForeEdge, an Imprint of University Press of New England, 2018.

Kennedy, Dan. *The Wired City: Reimagining Journalism and Civic Life in the Post-Newspaper Age.* Amherst: University of Massachusetts Press, 2013.

Kindred, Dave. *Morning Miracle: Inside the* Washington Post: *A Great Newspaper Fights for Its Life.* New York: Doubleday, 2010.

Kirkpatrick, David. *The Facebook Effect: The Inside Story of the Company That Is Connecting the World.* New York: Simon & Schuster, 2010.

Kovach, Bill, and Tom Rosenstiel. *The Elements of Journalism: What Newspeople Should Know and the Public Should Expect.* New York: Crown Publishers, 2001.

Liebling, A. J. *The Press.* New York: Ballantine Books, 1961.

Massing, Michael. *Now They Tell Us: The American Press and Iraq*. New York: New York Review Books, 2004.

McInnes, Gavin. *The Death of Cool: From Teenage Rebellion to the Hangover of Adulthood*. New York: Scribner, 2013.

Mnookin, Seth. *Hard News: The Scandals at* The New York Times *and Their Meaning for American Media*. New York: Random House, 2004.

Negroponte, Nicholas. *Being Digital*. New York: Alfred A. Knopf, 1995.

Owen, Taylor. *Disruptive Power: The Crisis of the State in the Digital Age*. Oxford Studies in Digital Politics. New York: Oxford University Press, 2015.

Rich, Frank. *The Greatest Story Ever Sold: The Decline and Fall of Truth from 9/11 to Katrina*. New York: The Penguin Press, 2006.

Shapiro, Michael, and Diane J. Reilly. *Tales from the Great Disruption: The Newspaper That* Almost *Seized the Future*. New York: Columbia University Press, 2011.

Shepard, Richard F. *The Paper's Papers: A Reporter's Journey through the Archives of* The New York Times. New York: Times Books, 1996.

Shirky, Clay. *Here Comes Everybody: The Power of Organizing without Organizations*. New York: The Penguin Press, 2008.

Star, Alexander, Bill Keller, and the *New York Times* Staff. *Open Secrets: WikiLeaks, War and American Diplomacy*. New York: The New York Times Company, 2011.

Stone, Brad. *The Everything Store: Jeff Bezos and the Age of Amazon*. New York: Little, Brown and Company, 2013.

Talese, Gay. *The Kingdom and the Power: Behind the Scenes at* The New York Times*: The Institution That Influences the World*. New York: Random House, 2007.

Taplin, Jonathan. *Move Fast and Break Things: How Facebook, Google, and Amazon Cornered Culture and Undermined Democracy*. New York: Little, Brown and Company, 2017.

Tifft, Susan E., and Alex S. Jones. *The Trust: The Private and Powerful Family Behind* The New York Times. Boston: Little, Brown and Company, 1999.

Zittrain, Jonathan. *The Future of the Internet and How to Stop It*. New Haven: Yale University Press, 2008.

ACKNOWLEDGMENTS

This book, three years in the making, was inspired by my lifelong passion for journalism and my deep admiration of, and gratitude for, thousands of colleagues who devote their working lives digging for the truth. I have always believed that with enough reporting the truth inevitably emerges. Reporters and editors at the *Wall Street Journal*, the *New York Times,* and the *Guardian,* where I have had the privilege to work, have dazzled me with their unshakable bravery and consistent commitment to providing readers with vital, reliable, and hard-to-extract information.

In the fall of 2018, a time of rising public distrust and challenging digital transformation of the news, one of the themes of this book, I gave the T. H. White lecture at Harvard University. At my side was one of journalism's most intrepid investigative reporters, *The New Yorker*'s Jane Mayer. We've been close friends for decades (we met in middle school) and were colleagues at the *Journal,* when we collaborated and coauthored *Strange Justice*, the definitive book on the Clarence Thomas confirmation battle. Jane has been my invaluable sounding board. We know it is crucial to speak out about the value of journalism.

For decades, sometimes while walking dogs or chasing after our children, we've discussed our work and why it is vital to a healthy, functioning democracy. Holding those in power accountable is a difficult mission, but that's exactly the role the Founders of this country gave to a free press. The First Amendment is first for a reason.

I lived through the digital revolution that transformed the news business and believed the subject worthy of a narrative history that was exhaustively reported and compelling to read. This was a massive and daunting project. My first experiences as a reporter were shaped during Watergate, and newspapers were where I spent my career. Though I had led the digital transformation of the *Times*'s newsroom during a very challenging period, it was invaluable for me to have a partner who was a digital native.

John Stillman, my brilliant young friend and assistant, grew up with digital technology and helped me understand the transformation of the news business in a deeper way. He helped shape this book and shared my belief that there was a great story to tell about all four of the companies we followed. As my research, reporting, writing, and editing assistant, he made contributions from beginning to end that made this book possible. John's incisive interviewing and deep research critically illuminated the vast and fast-evolving story of the revolution in media. He drafted portions of this book and provided a sharp eye throughout in editing the manuscript. His perceptive analysis and fluid, vivid prose were crucial in bringing this story to life. I can't thank him enough.

BuzzFeed, Vice, and the *Washington Post* opened their doors to me. At the *Times*, which did not officially cooperate with me, many of my former colleagues were generous in giving me their time and perspectives. Buzz-Feed's leaders, Jonah Peretti and Ben Smith, spent hours answering my questions about the organization they have created. Ashley McCollum was immensely helpful in lining up interviews. At Vice, despite initial trepidation, Alex Detrik and Isabel Evans helped me get to the people who knew the real story, including founders Shane Smith and Suroosh Alvi. At the *Post*, Marty Baron, Fred Ryan, and Shailesh Prakash and many other *Post* journalists, including Dana Priest and Marilyn Thompson, were all extremely generous with their time. Cory Haik and Ned Martel, both no longer with the *Post,* were extremely generous.

At the *Times*, which disputes some of my reporting and conclusions, I owe special thanks to publisher A. G. Sulzberger, who has been a stalwart defender of the press against rising attacks, and to Eileen Murphy, the *Times*'s honest and able communications chief.

At Simon & Schuster, Alice Mayhew was my inspirational editor. She was excited from the moment we (mostly she, naturally) hatched the idea for this book over lunch. She had a perfect ear for tone, for which news organizations were most interesting, and, during the writing process, for anything that was even slightly off-key. Alice knows exactly how to mix up close reporting and anecdotal detail, and when to go big picture to provide analysis and context. She is justifiably known as the best mind and hand for any nonfiction narrative. For my entire career, I have always wanted to write a book for Alice. I was giddy with happiness the day after I turned in a completed draft, when she called to pronounce "It reads!"

Jonathan Karp, President of S&S, has built the most talented team in publishing. He has vast knowledge about the news media and opened doors for me. His enthusiasm for this book pushed me on. Stuart Roberts was always scrupulous and helpful for the past years, dealing with my deadlines, explaining every facet of the publishing process, and watching over every aspect of the manuscript. Thanks also to the rest of the S&S team, especially Richard Rhorer (Associate Publisher); Cary Goldstein (Director of Publicity); Julia Prosser (Deputy Director of Publicity); Stephen Bedford (Director of Marketing); Jessica Chin (Production Editor); Lisa Healy (Production Editor); Jackie Seow (Art Director); Paul Dippolito (Interior Designer); and Amar Deol (Associate Editor).

Suzanne Gluck, my agent at WME, has been my friend, therapist, and forceful advocate. It meant the world to me that she devoted so much time to helping me conceptualize and refine the book, from proposal to the finish line.

Richard Turner, my friend since Harvard days and colleague at the *Journal*, knows more about the media industry than I, and his knowledge and his editing skills were an immense contribution. Elly Brinkley, who preceded John as my assistant, helped me get going. She had been my student at Harvard, where I teach creative writing and two journalism seminars.

My colleagues in the Harvard English Department, especially Darcy Frey, Jorie Graham, and Claire Messud, such terrific writers all, were invaluable sounding boards and friends. My students for the past five years at Harvard, as well as the students I taught much earlier at Princeton and Yale, make me certain that journalism will be in good hands for decades to come.

I'm so grateful to my still-growing family, especially my sister, Jane O'Connor, and my husband, Henry Griggs, who both read and fly-specked many versions of my evolving manuscript. Jane, one of the most successful children's books writers and editors, has been my idol since I arrived on this planet. Henry, the best copy editor and wordsmith I know, has been my rock since we were twenty years old. He and the rest of my family, including children Cornelia Griggs, Will Griggs, and William Woodson, heard far more about news and digital media than anyone should and pulled me up every day, as did Cornelia's husband, Rob Goldstone, and Will's wife, Lindsey Nelson. Eloise, my three-year-old granddaughter, made me laugh at myself constantly. I will forever be in debt to Rob and Cornelia, both ultra-busy surgeons, for bringing "Nana" into their home. Hopefully, along with baby Jonah, we will get the band back together.

My first boss, at the *Times*'s Boston bureau in 1976, was a great mentor. Sandy Burton was the only woman I have ever worked for; there are still scandalously few women occupying the highest ranks of journalism. I was so honored to be the first female Washington Bureau Chief, Managing Editor, and Executive Editor of the *New York Times*, but it's past time that holding these jobs should be such a rarity in our profession.

At this moment of peril, journalists and journalism are more valuable and vital to society than ever. If this book serves to bolster and affirm the work of those currently in the profession; to inspire a new generation to follow their lead; or to inform the larger public about the workings and worth of journalism, it will have achieved its purpose.

INDEX

ABOUT THE AUTHOR

Jill Abramson held senior editorial positions at *The New York Times*, the first woman to serve as Washington bureau chief, managing editor, and executive editor. She spent nine years at *The Wall Street Journal.* She is the coauthor with Jane Mayer of *Strange Justice: The Selling of Clarence Thomas*, a National Book Award finalist. A senior lecturer at Harvard University, she writes a column about U.S. politics for *The Guardian.*